SQL:
The Complete Reference,
Second Edition

About the Authors

James R. Groff is president and CEO of TimesTen, a software company that delivers real-time event processing software to telecom, financial services, and e-business customers. The core of the TimesTen software is a high-performance, memory-optimized, SQL-based DBMS. Prior to joining TimesTen, Groff was the cofounder, with Paul Weinberg, of Network Innovations Corporation, a developer of SQL-based networking software, and coauthor of *Understanding UNIX: A Conceptual Guide* and *SQL: The Complete Reference*. He has also held senior division management and marketing positions at Apple Computer and Hewlett-Packard. Groff holds a B.S. in mathematics from the Massachusetts Institute of Technology and an M.B.A. from Harvard University.

Paul N. Weinberg is president and CEO of A2i, Inc., a software company that develops and markets a system for enterprise-wide product content management and single-source, cross-media catalog publishing. Before that, he was the cofounder, with Jim Groff, of Network Innovations Corporation, an early pioneer in client/server database access that was acquired by Apple Computer, Inc., in 1988, and the coauthor of *Understanding UNIX: A Conceptual Guide* and *SQL: The Complete Reference*. He has also held software development and marketing positions at Bell Laboratories, Hewlett-Packard, and Plexus Computers. In 1981, he collaborated on *The Simple Solution to Rubik's Cube*, the number-one best-selling book of that year with over six million copies sold. He holds a B.S. from the University of Michigan and an M.S. from Stanford University, both in Computer Science.

About the Technical Editor

Greg Guntle has been doing technical editing of computer books for 20 years. He has written several programming books as well.

SQL:
The Complete Reference,
Second Edition

James R. Groff and Paul N. Weinberg

McGraw-Hill/Osborne

New York   Chicago   San Francisco
Lisbon   London   Madrid   Mexico City
Milan   New Delhi   San Juan
Seoul   Singapore   Sydney   Toronto

McGraw-Hill/Osborne
2600 Tenth Street
Berkeley, California 94710
U.S.A.

To arrange bulk purchase discounts for sales promotions, premiums, or fund-raisers, please contact **McGraw-Hill/**Osborne at the above address. For information on translations or book distributors outside the U.S.A., please see the International Contact Information page immediately following the index of this book.

SQL: The Complete Reference, Second Edition

1234567890 DOC DOC 0198765432

Book p/n 0-07-222560-2 and CD p/n 0-07-222561-0
parts of
ISBN 0-07-222559-9

Publisher
  Brandon A. Nordin

Vice President & Associate Publisher
  Scott Rogers

Acquisitions Editor
  Jane Brownlow

Project Editor
  Jennifer Malnick

Acquisitions Coordinator
  Emma Acker, Martin Przybyla

Technical Editor
  Greg Guntle

Copy Editor
  Chrisa Hotchkiss

Proofreader
  Mike McGee

Indexer
  Jack Lewis

Computer Designers
  Kathleen Fay Edwards, Lucie Ericksen, Kelly Stanton-Scott

Illustrators
  Michael Mueller, Lyssa Wald

Series Design
  Peter F. Hancik

This book was composed with Corel VENTURA™ Publisher.

Contents

Part I

An Overview of SQL

Part II

Retrieving Data

Part III

Updating Data

19   SQL APIs

Part VI

SQL Today and Tomorrow

Part VII

Appendixes

Acknowledgments

Special thanks to Matan Arazi for once again doing an exceptional job of assembling the bonus CD-ROM, pulling off another miracle by squeezing three DBMS products onto a single CD, and doing so against impossibly tight deadlines.

Thanks also to the team at Osborne, including Jane Brownlow, Jennifer Malnick, Martin Przybyla, Greg Guntle, and Chrisa Hotchkiss.

Introduction

SQL: *The Complete Reference, Second Edition* provides a comprehensive, in-depth treatment of the SQL language for both technical and nontechnical users, programmers, data processing professionals, and managers who want to understand the impact of SQL in today's computer industry. This book offers a conceptual framework for understanding and using SQL, describes the history of SQL and SQL standards, and explains the role of SQL in various computer industry segments, from enterprise data processing to data warehousing to web site architectures. This new edition contains new chapters specially focused on the role of SQL in application server architectures, and the integration of SQL with XML and other object-based technologies.

This book will show you, step-by-step, how to use SQL features, with many illustrations and realistic examples to clarify SQL concepts. The book also compares SQL products from leading DBMS vendors—describing their advantages benefits and trade-offs—to help you select the right product for your application. The accompanying CD-ROM contains actual trial versions of three of the leading brands of SQL DBMS, plus instructions on how to download a trial version of a fourth version, so you can try them for yourself and gain actual experience in using the major DBMS products from Oracle, Microsoft, and IBM, and the popular open source DBMS MySQL.

In some of the chapters, the subject matter is explored at two different levels—a fundamental description of the topic, and an advanced discussion intended for computer professionals who need to understand some of the internals behind SQL. The more advanced information is covered in sections marked with an asterisk (*). You do not need to read these sections to obtain an understanding of what SQL is and what it does.

How This Book Is Organized

The book is divided into six parts that cover various aspects of the SQL language:

- Part One, "An Overview of SQL," provides an introduction to SQL and a market perspective of its role as a database language. Its four chapters describe the history of SQL, the evolution of SQL standards, and how SQL relates to the relational data model and to earlier database technologies. Part One also contains a quick tour of SQL that briefly illustrates its most important features and provides you with an overview of the entire language early in the book.

- Part Two, "Retrieving Data," describes the features of SQL that allow you to perform database queries. The first chapter in this part describes the basic structure of the SQL language. The next four chapters start with the simplest SQL queries and progressively build to more complex queries, including multitable queries, summary queries, and queries that use subqueries.

- Part Three, "Updating Data," shows how you can use SQL to add new data to a database, delete data from a database, and modify existing database data. It also describes the database integrity issues that arise when data is updated, and how SQL addresses these issues. The last of the three chapters in this part discusses the SQL transaction concept and SQL support for multiuser transaction processing.

- Part Four, "Database Structure," deals with creating and administering a SQL-based database. Its four chapters tell you how to create the tables, views, and indexes that form the structure of a relational database. It also describes the SQL security scheme that prevents unauthorized access to data, and the SQL system catalog that describes the structure of a database. This part also discusses the significant differences between the database structures supported by various SQL-based DBMS products.

- Part Five, "Programming with SQL," describes how application programs use SQL for database access. It discusses the embedded SQL specified by the ANSI standard and used by IBM, Oracle, Ingres, Informix, and many other SQL-based DBMS products. It also describes the dynamic SQL interface that is used to build general-purpose database tables, such as report writers and database browsing programs. Finally, this part describes the popular SQL APIs, including ODBC, the ISO-standard Call-Level Interface, and JDBC, the standard call-level interface for Java, as well as proprietary call-level interfaces such as Oracle's OCI API.

■ Part Six, "SQL Today and Tomorrow," examines the use of SQL in several of today's "hottest" application areas, and the current state of SQL-based DBMS products. Two chapters describe the use of SQL stored procedures and triggers for online transaction processing, and the contrasting use of SQL for data warehousing. Four additional chapters describe SQL-based distributed databases, the influence of object technologies on SQL, and the integration of SQL with XML technologies. Finally, the last chapter explores the future of SQL and some of the most important trends in SQL-based data management.

Conventions Used In This Book

SQL: The Complete Reference, Second Edition describes the SQL features and functions available in the most popular SQL-based DBMS products and those described in the ANSI/ISO SQL standards. Whenever possible, the SQL statement syntax described in this book and used in the examples applies to all dialects of SQL. When the dialects differ, the differences are pointed out in the text, and the examples follow the most common practice. In these cases, you may have to modify the SQL statements in the examples slightly to suit your particular brand of DBMS.

Throughout the book, technical terms appear in *italics* the first time they are used and defined. SQL language elements, including SQL keywords, table, and column names, and sample SQL statements, appear in an UPPERCASE MONOSPACE font. SQL API function names appear in a lowercase monospace font. Program listings also appear in monospace font, and use the normal case conventions for the particular programming language (uppercase for COBOL and FORTRAN, lowercase for C and Java). Note that these conventions are used solely to improve readability; most SQL implementations will accept either uppercase or lowercase statements. Many of the SQL examples include query results, which appear immediately following the SQL statement as they would in an interactive SQL session. In some cases, long query results are truncated after a few rows; this is indicated by a vertical ellipsis (...) following the last row of query results.

Why This Book Is For You

SQL: The Complete Reference, Second Edition is the right book for anyone who wants to understand and learn SQL, including database users, data processing professionals and architects, programmers, students, and managers. It describes—in simple, understandable language liberally illustrated with figures and examples—what SQL is, why it is important, and how you use it. This book is not specific to one particular brand or dialect of SQL. Rather, it describes the standard, central core of the SQL language and then goes on to describe the differences among the most popular SQL products, including Oracle, Microsoft SQL Server, IBM's DB2 Universal Database and Informix, Sybase, and MySQL. It also explains the importance of SQL-based standards, such as ODBC and JDBC, and the ANSI/ISO standards for SQL and SQL-related technologies. This second edition contains new chapters and sections that cover the latest SQL innovations, in the areas of object-relational technologies, XML, and application server architectures.

If you are a new to SQL, this book offers comprehensive, step-by-step treatment of the language, building from simple queries to more advanced concepts. The structure of the book will allow you to quickly start using SQL, but the book will continue to be valuable as you begin to use the more complex features of the language. You can use the SQL software on the companion CD-ROM to try out the examples and build your SQL skills.

If you are a data processing professional, architect, or manager, this book will give you a perspective on the impact that SQL is having across the information technology industry—from personal computers to mainframes to data warehousing to Internet web sites and Internet-based distributed applications. The early chapters describe the history of SQL, its role in the market, and its evolution from earlier database technologies. Later chapters describe the future of SQL and the development of new database technologies, such as distributed databases, object-oriented extensions to SQL, business intelligence databases, and database/XML integration.

If you are a programmer, this book offers a very complete treatment of programming with SQL. Unlike the reference manuals of many DBMS products, it offers a conceptual framework for SQL programming, explaining the why as well as the how of developing a SQL-based application. It contrasts the SQL programming interfaces offered by all of the leading SQL products, including embedded SQL, dynamic SQL, ODBC, JDBC, and proprietary APIs such as the Oracle Call Interface. The description and comparison of programming techniques provides a perspective not found in any other book.

If you are selecting a DBMS product, this book offers a comparison of the SQL features, advantages, and benefits offered by the various DBMS vendors. The differences between the leading DBMS products are explained, not only in technical terms, but also in terms of their impact on applications and their evolving competitive position in the marketplace. The DBMS software on the companion CD-ROM can be used to try out these features in a prototype of your own application.

In short, both technical and nontechnical users can benefit from this book. It is the most comprehensive source of information available about the SQL language, SQL features and benefits, popular SQL-based products, the history of SQL, and the impact of SQL on the future direction of the information technology industry.

The Complete Reference

Part I

An Overview of SQL

The first four chapters of this book provide a perspective and a quick introduction to SQL. Chapter 1 describes what SQL is and explains its major features and benefits. In Chapter 2, a quick tour of SQL shows you many of its capabilities with simple, rapid-fire examples. Chapter 3 offers a market perspective of SQL by tracing its history, describing theSQL standards and the major vendors of SQL-based products, and identifying the reasons for SQL's prominence today. Chapter 4 describes the relational data model upon which SQL is based and compares it to earlier data models.

Chapter 1

Introduction

The SQL language and relational database systems based on it are one of the most important foundation technologies in the computer industry. Over the last two decades, SQL has grown from its first commercial use into a computer product and services market segment worth tens of billions of dollars per year, and SQL stands today as *the* standard computer database language. Literally hundreds of database products now support SQL, running on computer systems from mainframes to personal computers and even handheld devices. An official international SQL standard has been adopted and expanded twice. Virtually every major enterprise software product relies on SQL for its data management, and SQL is at the core of the database products from Microsoft, Oracle, and IBM, the three largest software companies in the world. SQL is also at the heart of open-source database products that are helping to fuel the popularity of Linux and the open-source movement. From its obscure beginnings as an IBM research project, SQL has leaped to prominence as both an important computer technology and a powerful market force.

What, exactly, is SQL? Why is it important? What can it do, and how does it work? If SQL is really a standard, why are there so many different versions and dialects? How do popular SQL products like SQL Server, Oracle, Informix, Sybase, and DB2 compare? How does SQL relate to Microsoft standards, such as ODBC and COM? How does JDBC link SQL to the world of Java and object technology? What role does it play in the emerging "web services" architecture, and the competing web services architectures from the Microsoft and Java-based camps? Does SQL really scale from mainframes to handheld devices? Has it really delivered the performance needed for high-volume transaction processing? How will SQL impact the way you use computers, and how can you get the most out of this important data management tool?

The SQL Language

SQL is a tool for organizing, managing, and retrieving data stored by a computer database. The acronym *SQL* is an abbreviation for *Structured Query Language*. For historical reasons, SQL is usually pronounced "sequel," but the alternate pronunciation "S.Q.L." is also used. As the name implies, SQL is a computer *language* that you use to interact with a database. In fact, SQL works with one specific type of database, called a *relational database*.

Figure 1-1 shows how SQL works. The computer system in the figure has a *database* that stores important information. If the computer system is in a business, the database might store inventory, production, sales, or payroll data. On a personal computer, the database might store data about the checks you have written, lists of people and their phone numbers, or data extracted from a larger computer system. The computer program that controls the database is called a *database management system*, or DBMS.

When you need to retrieve data from a database, you use the SQL language to make the request. The DBMS processes the SQL request, retrieves the requested data, and returns it to you. This process of requesting data from a database and receiving back the results is called a database *query*—hence the name Structured *Query* Language.

Figure 1-1. *Using SQL for database access*

The name Structured Query Language is actually somewhat of a misnomer. First of all, SQL is far more than a query tool, although that was its original purpose, and retrieving data is still one of its most important functions. SQL is used to control all of the functions that a DBMS provides for its users, including:

- **Data definition**. SQL lets a user define the structure and organization of the stored data and relationships among the stored data items.

- **Data retrieval**. SQL allows a user or an application program to retrieve stored data from the database and use it.

- **Data manipulation**. SQL allows a user or an application program to update the database by adding new data, removing old data, and modifying previously stored data.

- **Access control**. SQL can be used to restrict a user's ability to retrieve, add, and modify data, protecting stored data against unauthorized access.

- **Data sharing**. SQL is used to coordinate data sharing by concurrent users, ensuring that they do not interfere with one another.

- **Data integrity**. SQL defines integrity constraints in the database, protecting it from corruption due to inconsistent updates or system failures.

SQL is thus a comprehensive language for controlling and interacting with a database management system.

Second, SQL is not really a complete computer language like COBOL, C, C++, or Java. SQL contains no IF statement for testing conditions, and no GOTO, DO, or FOR statements for program flow control. Instead, SQL is a database *sublanguage*, consisting of about 40 statements specialized for database management tasks. These SQL statements can be *embedded* into another language, such as COBOL or C, to extend that language for use in database access. Alternatively, they can be explicitly sent to a database management system for processing, via a *call-level interface* from a language such as C, C++, or Java, or via messages sent over a computer network.

Finally, SQL is not a particularly structured language, especially when compared to highly structured languages such as C, Pascal, or Java. Instead, SQL statements resemble English sentences, complete with "noise words" that don't add to the meaning of the statement but make it read more naturally. There are quite a few inconsistencies in the SQL language, and there are also some special rules to prevent you from constructing SQL statements that look perfectly legal, but don't make sense.

Despite the inaccuracy of its name, SQL has emerged as *the* standard language for using relational databases. SQL is both a powerful language and one that is relatively easy to learn. The quick tour of SQL in Chapter 2 will give you a good overview of the language and its capabilities.

The Role of SQL

SQL is not itself a database management system, nor is it a stand-alone product. You cannot go into a computer store and "buy SQL." Instead, SQL is an integral part of a database management system, a language and a tool for communicating with the DBMS. Figure 1-2 shows some of the components of a typical DBMS, and how SQL acts as the glue that links them together.

The *database engine* is the heart of the DBMS, responsible for actually structuring, storing, and retrieving the data in the database. It accepts SQL requests from other DBMS components—such as a forms facility, report writer, or interactive query facility—from user-written application programs, and even from other computer systems. As the figure shows, SQL plays many different roles:

- SQL is an *interactive query language*. Users type SQL commands into an interactive SQL program to retrieve data and display it on the screen, providing a convenient, easy-to-use tool for ad hoc database queries.

- SQL is a *database programming language*. Programmers embed SQL commands into their application programs to access the data in a database. Both user-written programs and database utility programs (such as report writers and data entry tools) use this technique for database access.

- SQL is a *database administration language*. The database administrator responsible for managing a minicomputer or mainframe database uses SQL to define the database structure and control access to the stored data.

- SQL is a *client/server language*. Personal computer programs use SQL to communicate over a network with database servers that store shared data. This client/server architecture has become very popular for enterprise-class applications.

- SQL is an *Internet data access language*. Internet web servers that interact with corporate data and Internet applications servers all use SQL as a standard language for accessing corporate databases.

- SQL is a *distributed database language*. Distributed database management systems use SQL to help distribute data across many connected computer systems. The DBMS software on each system uses SQL to communicate with the other systems, sending requests for data access.

- SQL is a *database gateway language*. In a computer network with a mix of different DBMS products, SQL is often used in a *gateway* that allows one brand of DBMS to communicate with another brand.

SQL has thus emerged as a useful, powerful tool for linking people, computer programs, and computer systems to the data stored in a relational database.

Figure 1-2.   *Components of a typical database management system*

SQL Features and Benefits

SQL is both an easy-to-understand language and a comprehensive tool for managing data. Here are some of the major features of SQL and the market forces that have made it successful:

- Vendor independence
- Portability across computer systems
- SQL standards
- IBM endorsement and commitment (DB2)
- Microsoft commitment (SQL Server, ODBC, and ADO)
- Relational foundation
- High-level, English-like structure
- Interactive, ad hoc queries
- Programmatic database access
- Multiple views of data
- Complete database language
- Dynamic data definition
- Client/server architecture
- Enterprise application support
- Extensibility and object technology
- Internet database access
- Java integration (JDBC)
- Industry infrastructure

These are the reasons why SQL has emerged as the standard tool for managing data on personal computers, minicomputers, and mainframes. They are described in the sections that follow.

Vendor Independence

SQL is offered by all of the leading DBMS vendors, and no new database product over the last decade has been highly successful without SQL support. A SQL-based database and the programs that use it can be moved from one DBMS to another vendor's DBMS with minimal conversion effort and little retraining of personnel. Database tools, such as query tools, report writers, and application generators, work with many different brands of SQL databases. The vendor independence thus provided by SQL was one of the most important reasons for its early popularity and remains an important feature today.

Portability Across Computer Systems

SQL-based database products run on computer systems ranging from mainframes and midrange systems to personal computers, workstations, a wide range of specialized server computers, and even handheld devices. They operate on stand-alone computer systems, in departmental local area networks, and in enterprisewide or Internetwide networks. SQL-based applications that begin on single-user or departmental server systems can be moved to larger server systems as they grow. Data from corporate SQL-based databases can be extracted and downloaded into departmental or personal databases. Finally, economical personal computers can be used to prototype a SQL-based database application before moving it to an expensive multiuser system.

SQL Standards

An official standard for SQL was initially published by the American National Standards Institute (ANSI) and the International Standards Organization (ISO) in 1986, and was expanded in 1989 and again in 1992 and 1999. SQL is also a U.S. Federal Information Processing Standard (FIPS), making it a key requirement for large government computer contracts. Over the years, other international, government, and vendor groups have pioneered the standardization of new SQL capabilities, such as call-level interfaces or object-based extensions. Many of these new initiatives have been incorporated into the ANSI/ISO standard over time. The evolving standards serve as an official stamp of approval for SQL and have speeded its market acceptance.

IBM Endorsement and Commitment (DB2)

SQL was originally invented by IBM researchers and has since become a strategic product for IBM based on its flagship DB2 database. SQL support is available on all major IBM product families, from personal computers through midrange systems (AS/400 and UNIX-based servers) to IBM mainframes. IBM's initial work provided a clear signal of IBM's direction for other database and system vendors to follow early in the development of SQL and relational databases. Later, IBM's commitment and broad support speeded the market acceptance of SQL. IBM's SQL reach today extends well beyond its own computer systems business. SQL-based products that IBM has developed or acquired now run across a broad range of hardware, in many cases from competing computer vendors such as Sun or Hewlett-Packard.

Microsoft Commitment (SQL Server, ODBC, and ADO)

Microsoft has long considered database access a key part of its Windows personal computer software architecture. Both desktop and server versions of Windows provide standardized relational database access through Open Database Connectivity (ODBC), a SQL-based call-level API. Leading Windows software applications (spreadsheets, word processors, databases, etc.) from Microsoft and other vendors support ODBC, and all leading SQL databases provide ODBC access. Microsoft has enhanced ODBC support with higher-level, more object-oriented database access layers as part of its Object Linking and Embedding technology (OLE DB), and more recently as part of Active/X (Active/X Data Objects, or ADO). When Microsoft began its effort in the late 1980s to make Windows a viable server operating system, it introduced SQL Server as its own SQL-based offering. SQL Server continues today as a flagship Microsoft product, and a key component of its .NET architecture for web services.

Relational Foundation

SQL is a language for relational databases, and it has become popular along with the relational database model. The tabular, row/column structure of a relational database is intuitive to users, keeping the SQL language simple and easy to understand. The relational model also has a strong theoretical foundation that has guided the evolution and implementation of relational databases. Riding a wave of acceptance brought about by the success of the relational model, SQL has become *the* database language for relational databases.

High-Level, English-Like Structure

SQL statements look like simple English sentences, making SQL easy to learn and understand. This is in part because SQL statements describe the *data* to be retrieved, rather than specifying *how* to find the data. Tables and columns in a SQL database can have long, descriptive names. As a result, most SQL statements "say what they mean" and can be read as clear, natural sentences.

Interactive, Ad Hoc Queries

SQL is an interactive query language that gives users ad hoc access to stored data. Using SQL interactively, a user can get answers even to complex questions in minutes or seconds, in sharp contrast to the days or weeks it would take for a programmer to write a custom report program. Because of SQL's ad hoc query power, data is more accessible and can be used to help an organization make better, more informed decisions. SQL's ad hoc query capability was an important advantage over nonrelational databases early in its evolution and more recently has continued as a key advantage over pure object-based databases.

Programmatic Database Access

SQL is also a database language used by programmers to write applications that access a database. The same SQL statements are used for both interactive and programmatic access, so the database access parts of a program can be tested first with interactive SQL and then embedded into the program. In contrast, traditional databases provided one set of tools for programmatic access and a separate query facility for ad hoc requests, without any synergy between the two modes of access.

Multiple Views of Data

Using SQL, the creator of a database can give different users of the database different *views* of its structure and contents. For example, the database can be constructed so that each user sees data only for his or her department or sales region. In addition, data from several different parts of the database can be combined and presented to the user as a simple row/column table. SQL views can thus be used to enhance the security of a database and tailor it to the particular needs of individual users.

Complete Database Language

SQL was first developed as an ad hoc query language, but its powers now go far beyond data retrieval. SQL provides a complete, consistent language for creating a database, managing its security, updating its contents, retrieving data, and sharing data among many concurrent users. SQL concepts that are learned in one part of the language can be applied to other SQL commands, making users more productive.

Dynamic Data Definition

Using SQL, the structure of a database can be changed and expanded dynamically, even while users are accessing database contents. This is a major advance over static data definition languages, which prevented access to the database while its structure was being changed. SQL thus provides maximum flexibility, allowing a database to adapt to changing requirements while online applications continue uninterrupted.

Client/Server Architecture

SQL is a natural vehicle for implementing applications using a distributed, client/server architecture. In this role, SQL serves as the link between "front-end" computer systems optimized for user interaction and "back-end" systems specialized for database management, allowing each system to do what it does best. SQL also allows personal computers to function as front-ends to network servers or to larger minicomputer and mainframe databases, providing access to corporate data from personal computer applications.

Enterprise Application Support

The largest enterprise applications that support the daily operation of large companies and organizations all use SQL-based databases to store and organize their data. Data about business transactions (orders, sales amounts, customers, inventory levels, payment amounts, etc.) tends to have a structured, records-and-fields format, which converts easily into the row/column format of SQL. By constructing their applications to use enterprise-class SQL databases, major application vendors eliminate the need to develop their own data management software and can benefit from existing tools and programming skills. Because every major enterprise application requires a SQL-based database for its operation, new sales of enterprise applications automatically generate "drag-along" demand for new copies of database software.

Extensibility and Object Technology

The major challenge to SQL's continued dominance as a database standard has come from the emergence of object-based programming, and the introduction of object-based databases as an extension of the broad market trend toward object-based technology. SQL-based database vendors have responded to this challenge by slowly expanding and enhancing SQL to include object features. These "object/relational" databases, which continue to be based on SQL, have emerged as a more popular alternative to "pure object" databases and have perpetuated SQL's dominance through the last decade. The newest wave of object technology, embodied in the XML standard and web services architectures, has once again created a crop of "XML databases" and alternative query languages to challenge SQL. Previous history tends to suggest that XML-based extensions to SQL and the relational model will once again meet this challenge and insure SQL's continuing importance.

Internet Database Access

With the exploding popularity of the Internet and the World Wide Web, and their standards-based foundation, SQL found a new role in the late 1990s as an Internet data access standard. Early in the development of the Web, developers needed a way to retrieve and present database information on web pages and used SQL as a common language for database gateways. More recently, the emergence of three-tiered Internet architectures with distinct thin client, application server and database server layers, has established SQL as the standard link between the application and database tiers. In the future, the role of SQL in the Internet will extend beyond web site architectures to include data management for collaborating applications and distributed objects in a web services architecture.

Java Integration (JDBC)

A major area of SQL development over the last five to ten years has been the integration of SQL with Java. Seeing the need to link the Java language to existing relational databases, Sun Microsystems (the creator of Java) introduced Java Database Connectivity (JDBC), a standard API that allows Java programs to use SQL for database access. JDBC received a further boost when it was adopted as the data access standard within the Java2 Enterprise Edition (J2EE) specification, which defines the operating environment provided by all of the leading Internet application servers. In addition to its role as a programming language from which databases are used, many of the leading database vendors have also announced or implemented Java support *within* their database systems, allowing Java to be used as a language for stored procedures and business logic within the database itself. This trend toward integration between Java and SQL will insure the continued importance of SQL in the new era of Java-based programming.

Industry Infrastructure

Perhaps the most important factor contributing to the growing importance of SQL is the emergence of an entire computer industry infrastructure based on SQL. SQL-based relational database systems are an important part of this infrastructure. Enterprise applications that use SQL and require a SQL-based database are another important part, as are reporting tools, data-entry tools, design tools, programming tools, and a host of other tools that simplify the use of SQL. A large pool of experienced SQL programmers is a critical part of the infrastructure. Another important part is the training and support services that surround SQL and help to create and perpetuate SQL expertise. An entire subindustry has emerged around SQL consulting, optimization, and performance-tuning. All parts of this infrastructure tend to reinforce one another and contribute to the ongoing success of the other parts. Simply stated, to solve data management problems, the easiest, lowest-risk, lowest-cost solution is almost always a solution based on SQL.

Chapter 2

A Quick Tour of SQL

Before diving into the details of SQL, it's a good idea to develop an overall perspective on the language and how it works. This chapter contains a quick tour of SQL that illustrates its major features and functions. The goal of the quick tour is not to make you proficient in writing SQL statements; that is the goal of Part II of this book. Rather, by the time you've finished this chapter, you will have a basic familiarity with the SQL language and an overview of its capabilities.

A Simple Database

The examples in the quick tour are based on a simple relational database for a small distribution company. The database, shown in Figure 2-1, stores the information

ORDERS Table

ORDER_NUM	CUST	PRODUCT	QTY	AMOUNT
112961	2117	2A44L	7	$31,500.00
113012	2111	41003	35	$3,745.00
112989	2101	114	6	$1,458.00
113051	2118	XK47	4	$1,420.00
112968	2102	41004	34	$3,978.00
113036	2107	4100Z	9	$22,500.00
113045	2112	2A44R	10	$45,000.00
112963	2103	41004	28	$3,276.00
113013	2118	41003	1	$652.00
113058	2108	112	10	$1,480.00
112997	2124	41003	1	$652.00
112983	2103	41004	6	$702.00
113024	2114	XK47	20	$7,100.00
113062	2124	114	10	$2,430.00
112979	2114	4100Z	6	$15,000.00
113027	2103	41002	54	$4,104.00
113007	2112	773C	3	$2,925.00
113069	2109	775C	22	$31,350.00
113034	2107	2A45C	8	$632.00
112992	2118	41002	10	$760.00
112975	2111	2A44G	6	$2,100.00
113055	2108	4100X	6	$150.00
113048	2120	779C	2	$3,750.00
112993	2106	2A45C	24	$1,896.00
113065	2106	XK47	6	$2,130.00
113003	2108	779C	3	$5,625.00
113049	2118	XK47	2	$776.00
112987	2103	4100Y	11	$27,500.00
113057	2111	4100X	24	$600.00
113042	2113	2A44R	5	$22,500.00

CUSTOMERS Table

CUST_NUM	COMPANY	CUST_REP	CREDIT_LIMIT
2111	JCP Inc.	103	$50,000.00
2102	First Corp.	101	$65,000.00
2103	Acme Mfg.	105	$50,000.00
2123	Carter & Sons	102	$40,000.00
2107	Ace International	110	$35,000.00
2115	Smithson Corp.	101	$20,000.00
2101	Jones Mfg.	106	$65,000.00
2112	Zetacorp	108	$50,000.00
2121	QMA Assoc.	103	$45,000.00
2114	Orion Corp.	102	$20,000.00
2124	Peter Brothers	107	$40,000.00
2108	Holm & Landis	109	$55,000.00
2117	J.P. Sinclair	106	$35,000.00
2122	Three-Way Lines	105	$30,000.00
2120	Rico Enterprises	102	$50,000.00
2106	Fred Lewis Corp.	102	$65,000.00
2119	Solomon Inc.	109	$25,000.00
2118	Midwest Systems	108	$60,000.00
2113	Ian & Schmidt	104	$20,000.00
2109	Chen Associates	107	$25,000.00
2105	AAA Investments	101	$45,000.00

SALESREPS Table

NAME	REP_OFFICE	QUOTA	SALES
Bill Adams	13	$350,000.00	$367,911.00
Mary Jones	11	$300,000.00	$392,725.00
Sue Smith	21	$350,000.00	$474,050.00
Sam Clark	11	$275,000.00	$299,912.00
Bob Smith	12	$200,000.00	$142,594.00
Dan Roberts	12	$300,000.00	$305,673.00
Tom Snyder	NULL	NULL	$75,985.00
Larry Fitch	21	$350,000.00	$361,865.00
Paul Cruz	12	$275,000.00	$286,775.00
Nancy Angelli	22	$300,000.00	$186,042.00

OFFICES Table

OFFICE	CITY	REGION	TARGET	SALES
22	Denver	Western	$300,000.00	$186,042.00
11	New York	Eastern	$575,000.00	$692,637.00
12	Chicago	Eastern	$800,000.00	$735,042.00
13	Atlanta	Eastern	$350,000.00	$367,911.00
21	Los Angeles	Western	$725,000.00	$835,915.00

Figure 2-1. *A simple relational database*

needed to implement a small order processing application. Specifically, it stores the following information:

- The *customers* who buy the company's products
- The *orders* placed by those customers
- The *salespeople* who sell the products to customers
- The *sales offices* where those salespeople work

This database, like most others, is a model of the "real world." The data stored in the database represents real entities—customers, orders, salespeople, and offices. There is a separate table of data for each different kind of entity. Database requests that you make using the SQL language parallel real-world activities, as customers place, cancel, and change orders, as you hire and fire salespeople, and so on. Let's see how you can use SQL to manipulate data.

Retrieving Data

First, let's list the sales offices, showing the city where each one is located and its year-to-date sales. The SQL statement that retrieves data from the database is called SELECT. This SQL statement retrieves the data you want:

```
SELECT CITY, OFFICE, SALES
   FROM OFFICES

CITY            OFFICE        SALES
------------    -------   ------------
Denver              22    $186,042.00
New York            11    $692,637.00
Chicago             12    $735,042.00
Atlanta             13    $367,911.00
Los Angeles         21    $835,915.00
```

The SELECT statement asks for three pieces of data—the city, the office number, and the amount of sales—for each office. It also specifies that all of this data comes from the OFFICES table, which stores data about sales offices. The results of the query appear, in tabular form, immediately after the request.

The SELECT statement is used for all SQL queries. For example, here is a query that lists the names and year-to-date sales for each salesperson in the database. It also shows the quota (sales target) and the office number where each person works. In this case, the data comes from the next SALESREPS table.

```
SELECT NAME, REP_OFFICE, SALES, QUOTA
  FROM SALESREPS

NAME             REP_OFFICE        SALES          QUOTA
--------------   ----------   ------------   ------------
Bill Adams               13   $367,911.00   $350,000.00
Mary Jones               11   $392,725.00   $300,000.00
Sue Smith                21   $474,050.00   $350,000.00
Sam Clark                11   $299,912.00   $275,000.00
Bob Smith                12   $142,594.00   $200,000.00
Dan Roberts              12   $305,673.00   $300,000.00
Tom Snyder             NULL    $75,985.00          NULL
Larry Fitch              21   $361,865.00   $350,000.00
Paul Cruz                12   $286,775.00   $275,000.00
Nancy Angelli            22   $186,042.00   $300,000.00
```

SQL also lets you ask for calculated results. For example, you can ask SQL to calculate the amount by which each salesperson is over or under quota:

```
SELECT NAME, SALES, QUOTA, (SALES - QUOTA)
  FROM SALESREPS

NAME                 SALES          QUOTA   (SALES-QUOTA)
--------------   ------------   ------------   --------------
Bill Adams       $367,911.00   $350,000.00      $17,911.00
Mary Jones       $392,725.00   $300,000.00      $92,725.00
Sue Smith        $474,050.00   $350,000.00     $124,050.00
Sam Clark        $299,912.00   $275,000.00      $24,912.00
Bob Smith        $142,594.00   $200,000.00     -$57,406.00
Dan Roberts      $305,673.00   $300,000.00       $5,673.00
Tom Snyder        $75,985.00          NULL            NULL
Larry Fitch      $361,865.00   $350,000.00      $11,865.00
Paul Cruz        $286,775.00   $275,000.00      $11,775.00
Nancy Angelli    $186,042.00   $300,000.00    -$113,958.00
```

The requested data (including the calculated difference between sales and quota for each salesperson) once again appears in a row/column table. Perhaps you would like to focus on the salespeople whose sales are less than their quotas. SQL lets you retrieve that kind of selective information very easily, by adding a mathematical comparison to the previous request:

```
SELECT NAME, SALES, QUOTA, (SALES - QUOTA)
  FROM SALESREPS
 WHERE SALES < QUOTA

NAME                    SALES         QUOTA   (SALES-QUOTA)
--------------    ------------   ------------  -------------
Bob Smith          $142,594.00   $200,000.00    -$57,406.00
Nancy Angelli      $186,042.00   $300,000.00   -$113,958.00
```

You can use the same technique to list large orders in the database and find out which customer placed the order, which product was ordered, and in what quantity. You can also ask SQL to sort the orders based on the order amount:

```
SELECT ORDER_NUM, CUST, PRODUCT, QTY, AMOUNT
  FROM ORDERS
 WHERE AMOUNT > 25000.00
 ORDER BY AMOUNT

ORDER_NUM  CUST PRODUCT   QTY     AMOUNT
---------- ----- -------- ---- -----------
   112987  2103 4100Y      11  $27,500.00
   113069  2109 775C       22  $31,350.00
   112961  2117 2A44L       7  $31,500.00
   113045  2112 2A44R      10  $45,000.00
```

Summarizing Data

SQL not only retrieves individual pieces of data from the database, but it can be used to summarize the database contents as well. What's the average size of an order in the database? This request asks SQL to look at all the orders and find the average amount:

```
SELECT AVG(AMOUNT)
  FROM ORDERS

AVG(AMOUNT)
-----------
  $8,256.37
```

You could also ask for the average order size for a particular customer:

```
SELECT AVG(AMOUNT)
  FROM ORDERS
 WHERE CUST = 2103

AVG(AMOUNT)
-----------
  $8,895.50
```

Finally, let's find out the total value of the orders placed by each customer. To do this, you can ask SQL to group the orders together by customer number and then total the orders for each customer:

```
SELECT CUST, SUM(AMOUNT)
  FROM ORDERS
 GROUP BY CUST

CUST   SUM(AMOUNT)
-----  -----------
2101     $1,458.00
2102     $3,978.00
2103    $35,582.00
2106     $4,026.00
2107    $23,132.00
2108     $7,255.00
2109    $31,350.00
2111     $6,445.00
2112    $47,925.00
2113    $22,500.00
2114    $22,100.00
2117    $31,500.00
2118     $3,608.00
2120     $3,750.00
2124     $3,082.00
```

Adding Data to the Database

You can also use SQL to add new data to the database. For example, suppose you just opened a new Western region sales office in Dallas, with target sales of $275,000. Here's the INSERT statement that adds the new office to the database, as office number 23:

```
INSERT INTO OFFICES (CITY, REGION, TARGET, SALES, OFFICE)
    VALUES ('Dallas', 'Western', 275000.00, 0.00, 23)

1 row inserted.
```

Similarly, if Mary Jones (employee number 109) signs up a new customer, Acme Industries, this INSERT statement adds the customer to the database as customer number 2125 with a $25,000 credit limit:

```
INSERT INTO CUSTOMERS (COMPANY, CUST_REP, CUST_NUM, CREDIT_LIMIT)
    VALUES ('Acme Industries', 109, 2125, 25000.00)

1 row inserted.
```

Deleting Data

Just like the SQL INSERT statement adds new data to the database, the SQL DELETE statement removes data from the database. If Acme Industries decides a few days later to switch to a competitor, you can delete Acme's customer information from the database with this statement:

```
DELETE FROM CUSTOMERS
 WHERE COMPANY = 'Acme Industries'

1 row deleted.
```

And if you decide to terminate all salespeople whose sales are less than their quotas, you can remove them from the database with this DELETE statement:

```
DELETE FROM SALESREPS
 WHERE SALES < QUOTA

2 rows deleted.
```

Updating the Database

You can also use SQL to modify data that is already stored in the database. For example, to increase the credit limit for First Corp. to $75,000, you would use the SQL UPDATE statement:

```
UPDATE CUSTOMERS
   SET CREDIT_LIMIT = 75000.00
 WHERE COMPANY = 'First Corp.'

1 row updated.
```

The UPDATE statement can also make many changes in the database at once. For example, this UPDATE statement raises the quota for all salespeople by $15,000:

```
UPDATE SALESREPS
   SET QUOTA = QUOTA + 15000.00

8 rows updated.
```

Protecting Data

An important role of a database is to protect the stored data from access by unauthorized users. For example, suppose your assistant, named Mary, has not been previously authorized to insert data about new customers into the database. This SQL statement grants her that permission:

```
GRANT INSERT
   ON CUSTOMERS
   TO MARY

Privilege granted.
```

Similarly, the following SQL statement gives Mary permission to update data about customers and to retrieve customer data with the SELECT statement:

```
GRANT UPDATE, SELECT
   ON CUSTOMERS
   TO MARY

Privilege granted.
```

If Mary is no longer allowed to add new customers to the database, this REVOKE statement will disallow it:

```
REVOKE INSERT
    ON CUSTOMERS
  FROM MARY

Privilege revoked.
```

Similarly, this REVOKE statement will revoke all of Mary's privileges to access customer data in any way:

```
REVOKE ALL
    ON CUSTOMERS
  FROM MARY

Privilege revoked.
```

Creating a Database

Before you can store data in a database, you must first define the structure of the data. Suppose you want to expand the sample database by adding a table of data about the products your company sells. For each product, the data to be stored includes the following:

- A three-character manufacturer ID code
- A five-character product ID code
- A product description of up to 30 characters
- The price of the product
- The quantity currently on hand

This SQL CREATE TABLE statement defines a new table to store the products' data:

```
CREATE TABLE PRODUCTS
     (MFR_ID CHAR(3),
  PRODUCT_ID CHAR(5),
 DESCRIPTION VARCHAR(20),
       PRICE MONEY,
 QTY_ON_HAND INTEGER)

Table created.
```

Although more cryptic than the previous SQL statement examples, the CREATE TABLE statement is still fairly straightforward. It assigns the name PRODUCTS to the new table and specifies the name and type of data stored in each of its five columns.

Once the table has been created, you can fill it with data. Here's an INSERT statement for a new shipment of 250 size 7 widgets (product ACI-41007), which cost $225.00 apiece:

```
INSERT INTO PRODUCTS (MFR_ID, PRODUCT_ID, DESCRIPTION, PRICE, QTY_ON_HAND)
     VALUES ('ACI', '41007', 'Size 7 Widget', 225.00, 250)

1 row inserted.
```

Finally, if you discover later that you no longer need to store the products' data in the database, you can erase the table (and all of the data it contains) with the DROP TABLE statement:

```
DROP TABLE PRODUCTS

Table dropped.
```

Summary

This quick tour of SQL showed you what SQL can do and illustrated the style of the SQL language, using eight of the most commonly used SQL statements. To summarize:

- Use SQL to *retrieve* data from the database, using the SELECT statement. You can retrieve all or part of the stored data, sort it, and ask SQL to summarize the data, using totals and averages.

- Use SQL to *update* the database, by adding new data with the INSERT statement, deleting data with the DELETE statement, and modifying existing data with the UPDATE statement.

- Use SQL to *control access* to the database, by granting and revoking specific privileges for specific users with the GRANT and REVOKE statements.

- Use SQL to *create* the database by defining the structure of new tables and dropping tables when they are no longer needed, using the CREATE and DROP statements.

Chapter 3

SQL in Perspective

SQL is both a *de facto* and an official standard language for database management. What does it mean for SQL to be a standard? What role does SQL play as a database language? How did SQL become a standard, and what impact is the SQL standard having on personal computers, local area networks, minicomputers, and mainframes? To answer these questions, this chapter traces the history of SQL and describes its current role in the computer market.

SQL and Database Management

One of the major tasks of a computer system is to store and manage data. To handle this task, specialized computer programs known as *database management systems* began to appear in the late 1960s and early 1970s. A database management system, or DBMS, helped computer users to organize and structure their data and allowed the computer system to play a more active role in managing the data. Although database management systems were first developed on large mainframe systems, their popularity quickly spread to minicomputers, and then to personal computers and workstations. Today, many database management systems operate on specialized server computers.

Database management has also played a key role in the explosion of computer networking and the Internet. Early database systems ran on large, monolithic computer systems, where the data, the database management software, and the user or application program accessing the database all operated on the same system. The 1980s and 1990s saw the explosion of a new client/server model for database access, in which a user or an application program running on a personal computer accesses a database on a separate computer system using a network. In the late 1990s, the increasing popularity of the Internet and the World Wide Web intertwined the worlds of networking and data management even further. Now users require little more than a web browser to access and interact with databases, not only within their own organizations, but around the world. Often, these Internet-based architectures involve three or more separate computer systems—one computer that runs the web browser and interacts with the user, connected to a second system that runs an application program or application server, which is in turn connected to a third system that runs the database management system.

Today, database management is very big business. Independent software companies and computer vendors ship billions of dollars worth of database management products every year. The vast majority of enterprise-class computer applications that support the daily operation of large companies and other organizations use databases. These applications include some of the fastest-growing application categories, such as Enterprise Resource Planning (ERP), Customer Relationship Management (CRM), Supply Chain Management (SCM), Sales Force Automation (SFA), and financial applications. Computer manufacturers develop and deliver server computers that are specially configured as database servers; these systems constitute a multibillion-dollar-per-year market of their own. Databases provide the intelligence behind most transaction-oriented web sites, and they are used to capture and to analyze user interactions with web sites. Database management thus touches every segment of the computer market.

Since the late 1980s a specific type of DBMS, called a *relational* database management system (RDBMS), has become so popular that it is *the* standard database form. Relational databases organize data in a simple, tabular form and provide many advantages over earlier types of databases. SQL is specifically a relational database language used to work with relational databases.

A Brief History of SQL

The history of the SQL language is intimately intertwined with the development of relational databases. Table 3-1 shows some of the milestones in its 30-year history. The relational database concept was originally developed by Dr. E.F. "Ted" Codd, an IBM researcher. In June 1970, Dr. Codd published an article entitled "A Relational Model of Data for Large Shared Data Banks" that outlined a mathematical theory of how data could be stored and manipulated using a tabular structure. Relational databases and SQL trace their origins to this article, which appeared in the *Communications of the Association for Computing Machinery.*

Date	Event
1970	Codd defines relational database model
1974	IBM begins System/R project
1974	First article describing the SEQUEL language is published
1978	System/R customer tests are conducted
1979	Oracle introduces first commercial RDBMS
1981	Relational Technology introduces Ingres
1981	IBM announces SQL/DS
1982	ANSI forms SQL standards committee
1983	IBM announces DB2
1986	ANSI SQL1 standard is ratified
1986	Sybase introduces RDBMS for transaction processing
1987	ISO SQL1 standard is ratified

Table 3-1.   *Milestones in SQL Development*

Date	Event
1988	Ashton-Tate and Microsoft announce SQL Server for OS/2
1989	First TPC benchmark (TPC-A) is published
1990	TPC-B benchmark is published
1991	SQL Access Group database access specification is published
1992	Microsoft publishes ODBC specification
1992	ANSI SQL2 standard (SQL-92) is ratified
1992	TPC-C (OLTP) benchmark is published
1993	Specialized SQL data warehousing systems are shipped for the first time
1993	ODBC products are shipped for the first time
1994	Parallel database server technology is shipped commercially
1996	Standard API for OLAP database access and OLAP benchmark is published
1997	IBM DB2 UDB unifies DB2 architecture across IBM and other vendor platforms
1997	Major DBMS vendors announce Java integration strategies
1998	Microsoft SQL Server 7 provides enterprise-level database support for Windows NT
1998	Oracle 8i provides database/Internet integration and moves away from client/server model
1998	Commercial in-memory database products are shipped for the first time
1999	J2EE standardizes JDBC database access from application servers
2000	Oracle introduces application servers with integrated database caching
2000	Microsoft introduces SQL Server 2000, aimed at enterprise applications
2001	XML integration capabilities appear in mainstream RDBMS products
2001	IBM acquires Informix database business
2002	Gartner ranks IBM as #1 database vendor, passing Oracle

Table 3-1.   *Milestones in SQL Development* (continued)

The Early Years

Codd's article triggered a flurry of relational database research, including a major research project within IBM. The goal of the project, called System/R, was to prove the workability of the relational concept and to provide some experience in actually implementing a relational DBMS. Work on System/R began in the mid-1970s at IBM's Santa Teresa laboratories in San Jose, California.

In 1974 and 1975, the first phase of the System/R project produced a minimal prototype of a relational DBMS. In addition to the DBMS itself, the System/R project included work on database query languages. One of these languages was called SEQUEL, an acronym for Structured English Query Language. In 1976 and 1977, the System/R research prototype was rewritten from scratch. The new implementation supported multitable queries and allowed several users to share access to the data.

The System/R implementation was distributed to a number of IBM customer sites for evaluation in 1978 and 1979. These early customer sites provided some actual user experience with System/R and its database language, which, for legal reasons, had been renamed SQL, or Structured Query Language. Despite the name change, the SEQUEL pronunciation remained and continues to this day. In 1979 the System/R research project came to an end, with IBM concluding that relational databases were not only feasible, but could be the basis for a useful commercial product.

Early Relational Products

The System/R project and its SQL database language were well-chronicled in technical journals during the 1970s. Seminars on database technology featured debates on the merits of the new and heretical relational model. By 1976, it was apparent that IBM was becoming enthusiastic about relational database technology and that it was making a major commitment to the SQL language.

The publicity about System/R attracted the attention of a group of engineers in Menlo Park, California, who decided that IBM's research foreshadowed a commercial market for relational databases. In 1977 they formed a company, Relational Software, Inc., to build a relational DBMS based on SQL. The product, named Oracle, shipped in 1979 and became the first commercially available relational DBMS. Oracle beat IBM's first product to market by a full two years and ran on Digital's VAX minicomputers, which were less expensive than IBM mainframes. The company aggressively sold the merits of the new relational style of database management, and eventually renamed itself after its flagship product. Today, Oracle Corporation is the leading vendor of relational database management systems, and a major vendor of enterprise applications based on the Oracle database, with annual sales of many billions of dollars.

Professors at the University of California's Berkeley computer laboratories were also researching relational databases in the mid-1970s. Like the IBM research team, they built a prototype of a relational DBMS and called their system Ingres. The Ingres project included a query language named QUEL that, although more structured than

SQL, was less English-like. Many of today's database experts trace their involvement with relational databases back to the Berkeley Ingres project, including the founders of Sybase and Illustra (now owned by IBM), and many of the object-oriented database startup companies.

In 1980, several professors left Berkeley and founded Relational Technology, Inc., to build a commercial version of Ingres, which was announced in 1981. Ingres and Oracle quickly became arch-rivals, but their rivalry helped to call attention to relational database technology in this early stage. Despite its technical superiority in many areas, Ingres became a clear second-place player in the market, competing against the SQL-based capabilities (and the aggressive marketing and sales strategies) of Oracle. The original QUEL query language was effectively replaced by SQL in 1986, a testimony to the market power of the SQL standard. By the mid-1990s, the Ingres technology had been sold to Computer Associates, a leading mainframe software vendor.

IBM Products

While Oracle and Ingres raced to become commercial products, IBM's System/R project had also turned into an effort to build a commercial product, named SQL/Data System (SQL/DS). IBM announced SQL/DS in 1981 and began shipping the product in 1982. In 1983, IBM announced a version of SQL/DS for VM/CMS, an operating system that was frequently used on IBM mainframes in corporate information center applications.

In 1983, IBM also introduced Database 2 (DB2), another relational DBMS for its mainframe systems. DB2 operated under IBM's MVS operating system, the workhorse operating system used in large mainframe data centers. The first release of DB2 began shipping in 1985, and IBM officials hailed it as a strategic piece of IBM software technology. DB2 has since become IBM's flagship relational DBMS, and with IBM's weight behind it, DB2's SQL language became the *de facto* standard database language. DB2 technology has now migrated across all IBM product lines, from personal computers to network servers to mainframes. In 1997, IBM took the DB2 cross-platform strategy even farther, by announcing DB2 versions for computer systems made by Sun Microsystems, Hewlett-Packard, and other IBM hardware competitors.

IBM made another major stride in its cross-platform strategy in 2001, when it acquired Informix's database business, and especially Informix's installed base on non-IBM UNIX-based servers. According to most industry analysts, IBM is the second-largest vendor of database management software, and some user surveys actually placed it first, slightly ahead of Oracle in market share.

Commercial Acceptance

During the first half of the 1980s, the relational database vendors struggled for commercial acceptance of their products. The relational products had several disadvantages when compared to the traditional database architectures. The performance of relational databases was seriously inferior to that of traditional databases. Except for the IBM products, the relational databases came from small upstart vendors. And, except for the IBM products, the relational databases tended to run on minicomputers rather than on IBM mainframes.

The relational products did have one major advantage, however. Their relational query languages (SQL, QUEL, and others) allowed users to pose ad hoc queries to the database—and get immediate answers—without writing programs. As a result, relational databases began slowly turning up in information center applications as decision-support tools. By May 1985, Oracle proudly claimed to have over 1000 installations. Ingres was installed in a comparable number of sites. DB2 and SQL/DS were also being slowly accepted and counted their combined installations at slightly over 1000 sites.

During the last half of the 1980s, SQL and relational databases were rapidly accepted as the database technology of the future. The performance of the relational database products improved dramatically. Ingres and Oracle, in particular, leapfrogged with each new version claiming superiority over the competitor and two or three times the performance of the previous release. Improvements in the processing power of the underlying computer hardware also helped to boost performance.

Market forces also boosted the popularity of SQL in the late 1980s. IBM stepped up its evangelism of SQL, positioning DB2 as the data management solution for the 1990s. Publication of the ANSI/ISO standard for SQL in 1986 gave SQL official status as a standard. SQL also emerged as a standard on UNIX-based computer systems, whose popularity accelerated in the 1980s. As personal computers became more powerful and were linked in local area networks (LANs), they needed more sophisticated database management. PC database vendors embraced SQL as the solution to these needs, and minicomputer database vendors moved down market to compete in the emerging PC local area network market.

Through the early 1990s, steadily improving SQL implementations and dramatic improvements in processor speeds made SQL a practical solution for transaction processing applications. Finally, SQL became a key part of the client/server architecture that used PCs, local area networks, and network servers to build much lower-cost information processing systems.

SQL's supremacy in the database world has not gone unchallenged. By the early 1990s, object-oriented programming had emerged as the method of choice for applications development, especially for personal computers and their graphical user interfaces. The object model, with its objects, classes, methods, and inheritance, did not provide an ideal fit with the relational model of tables, rows, and columns of data. A new generation of venture capital-backed "object database" companies sprang up, hoping to make relational databases and their vendors obsolete, just as SQL had done to the earlier, nonrelational vendors. However, SQL and the relational model more than withstood the challenge. Total annual revenues for object-oriented databases are measured in the hundreds of millions of dollars, at best, while SQL and relational database systems, tools, and services produce tens of billions of dollars of sales per year.

As SQL grew to address an ever-wider variety of data management tasks, the one-size-fits-all approach showed serious strain. By the late 1990s, database management was no longer a monolithic market. Specialized database systems sprang up to support different market needs. One of the fastest-growing segments was data warehousing, where databases were used to search through huge amounts of data to discover underlying trends and patterns. A second major trend was the incorporation of new data types (such as multimedia data) and object-oriented principles into SQL. A third important segment was mobile databases for portable personal computers that could operate when sometimes connected to, and sometimes disconnected from, a centralized database system. Another important application segment was embedded databases for use within intelligent devices, such as network equipment. In-memory databases emerged as another segment, designed for very high levels of performance.

Despite the emergence of subsegments of the database market, SQL has remained a common denominator across them all. As the computer industry prepares for the next century, SQL's dominance as *the* database standard remains very strong. New challenges continue to emerge—databases rooted in the eXtended Markup Language (XML) are the latest attempt to move outside of the relational model and SQL—but the history of the past 20 years indicates that SQL and the relational model have a powerful ability to embrace and adapt to new data management needs.

SQL Standards

One of the most important developments in the market acceptance of SQL is the emergence of SQL standards. References to "the SQL standard" usually mean the official standard adopted by the American National Standards Institute (ANSI) and the International Standards Organization (ISO). However, there are other important SQL standards, including the *de facto* standard for some parts of the SQL language that have been defined by IBM's DB2 product family, and Oracle's SQL dialect, which has a dominant installed-base market share.

The ANSI/ISO Standards

Work on the official SQL standard began in 1982, when ANSI charged its X3H2 committee with defining a standard relational database language. At first, the committee debated the merits of various proposed database languages. However, as IBM's commitment to SQL increased and SQL emerged as a *de facto* standard in the market, the committee selected SQL as their relational database language and turned their attention to standardizing it.

The resulting ANSI standard for SQL was largely based on DB2 SQL, although it contains some major differences from DB2. After several revisions, the standard was officially adopted as ANSI standard X3.135 in 1986, and as an ISO standard in 1987. The ANSI/ISO standard has since been adopted as a Federal Information Processing Standard (FIPS) by the U.S. government. This standard, slightly revised and expanded in 1989, is usually called the SQL-89 or SQL1 standard.

Many of the ANSI and ISO standards committee members were representatives from database vendors who had existing SQL products, each implementing a slightly different SQL dialect. Like dialects of human languages, the SQL dialects were generally very similar to one another but were incompatible in their details. In many areas, the committee simply sidestepped these differences by omitting some parts of the language from the standard and specifying others as "implementor-defined." These decisions allowed existing SQL implementations to claim broad adherence to the resulting ANSI/ ISO standard but made the standard relatively weak.

To address the holes in the original standard, the ANSI committee continued its work, and drafts for a new, more rigorous SQL2 standard were circulated. Unlike the 1989 standard, the SQL2 drafts specified features considerably beyond those found in current commercial SQL products. Even more far-reaching changes were proposed for a follow-on SQL3 standard. In addition, the draft standards attempted to officially standardize parts of the SQL language where different proprietary standards had long since been set by the various major DBMS brands. As a result, the proposed SQL2 and SQL3 standards were a good deal more controversial than the initial SQL standard. The SQL2 standard weaved its way through the ANSI approval process and was finally approved in October 1992. While the original 1986 standard took less than 100 pages, the SQL2 standard (officially called SQL-92) takes nearly 600 pages.

The SQL2 standards committee acknowledged the large step from SQL1 to SQL2 by explicitly creating three levels of SQL2 standards compliance. The lowest compliance level (Entry-Level) requires only minimal additional capability beyond the SQL-89 standard. The middle compliance level (Intermediate-Level) was created as an achievable major step beyond SQL-89, but one that avoids the most complex and most system-dependent and DBMS brand-dependent issues. The third compliance level (Full) requires a full implementation of all SQL2 capabilities. Throughout the 600 pages of the standard, each description of each feature includes a definition of the specific aspects of that feature that must be supported to achieve Entry, Intermediate, or Full compliance.

Despite the existence of a SQL2 standard for more than ten years, popular commercial SQL products do not, in practice, fully implement the SQL2 specification, and no two commercial SQL products support exactly the same SQL dialect. Moreover, as database vendors introduce new capabilities, they continually expand their SQL dialects and move them slightly further apart. The central core of the SQL language has become fairly standardized, however. Where it could be done without hurting existing customers or features, vendors have brought their products into conformance with the SQL-89 standard, and with the most useful capabilities of the SQL2 standard.

In the meantime, work continues on standards beyond SQL2. The SQL3 effort effectively fragmented into separate standardization efforts and focused on different extensions to SQL. Some of these, such as stored procedure capabilities, are already found in many commercial SQL products and pose the same standardization challenges faced by SQL2. Others, such as proposed object extensions to SQL, are not yet widely available or fully implemented, but have generated a great deal of controversy. With most vendors only recently implementing major SQL2 capabilities, and with the diversity of SQL extensions now available in commercial products, work on SQL3 has taken on less commercial importance.

The "real" SQL standard, of course, is the SQL implemented in products that are broadly accepted by the marketplace. For the most part, programmers and users tend to stick with those parts of the language that are fairly similar across a broad range of products. The innovation of the database vendors continues to drive the invention of new SQL capabilities; some products remain years later only for backward compatibility, and some find commercial success and move into the mainstream.

Other SQL Standards

Although it is the most widely recognized, the ANSI/ISO standard is not the only standard for SQL. X/OPEN, a European vendor group, also adopted SQL as part of its suite of standards for a portable application environment based on UNIX. The X/OPEN standards have played a major role in the European computer market, where portability among computer systems from different vendors is a key concern. Unfortunately, the X/OPEN standard differs from the ANSI/ISO standard in several areas.

IBM also included SQL in the specification of its bold 1990s Systems Application Architecture (SAA) blueprint, promising that all of its SQL products would eventually move to this SAA SQL dialect. Although SAA failed to achieve its promise of unifying the IBM product line, the momentum toward a unified IBM SQL continued. With its mainframe DB2 database as the flagship, IBM introduced DB2 implementations for OS/2, its personal computer operating system, and for its RS/6000 line of UNIX-based workstations and servers.

By 1997, IBM had moved DB2 beyond its own product line and shipped versions of DB2-Universal Database for systems made by rival manufacturers Sun Microsystems, Hewlett-Packard, and Silicon Graphics, and for Windows NT. IBM further shored up its database software position on non-IBM hardware platforms with its 2001 acquisition of the Informix database. With IBM's historical leadership in relational database technology, the SQL dialect supported by DB2 is a very powerful *de facto* standard.

ODBC and the SQL Access Group

An important area of database technology not addressed by official standards is *database interoperability*—the methods by which data can be exchanged among different databases, usually over a network. In 1989, a group of vendors formed the SQL Access Group to address this problem. The resulting SQL Access Group specification for Remote Database Access (RDA) was published in 1991. Unfortunately, the RDA specification was closely tied to the OSI protocols, which were never widely implemented, so it had little impact. Transparent interoperability among different vendors' databases remains an elusive goal.

A second standard from the SQL Access Group had far more market impact. At Microsoft's urging and insistence, the SQL Access Group expanded its focus to include a call-level interface for SQL. Based on a draft from Microsoft, the resulting Call-Level Interface (CLI) specification was published in 1992. Microsoft's own Open Database Connectivity (ODBC) specification, based on the CLI standard, was published the same year. With the market power of Microsoft behind it, and the "open standards" blessing of the SQL Access Group, ODBC has emerged as the *de facto* standard interface for PC access to SQL databases. Apple and Microsoft announced an agreement to support ODBC on Macintosh and Windows in the spring of 1993, giving ODBC industry standard status in both popular graphical user interface environments. ODBC implementations for UNIX-based systems soon followed. In 1995, the ODBC interface effectively became an ANSI/ISO standard, with the publication of the SQL/Call-Level Interface (CLI) standard.

Today, ODBC is in its fourth major revision as a cross-platform database access standard. ODBC support is available for all major DBMS brands. Most packaged application programs that have database access as an important part of their capabilities support ODBC, and they range from multimillion-dollar enterprise-class applications like Enterprise Resource Planning (ERP) and Supply Chain Management (SCM) to PC applications such as spreadsheets, query tools, and reporting programs. Microsoft's focus has moved beyond ODBC to higher-level interfaces (such as OLE/DB) and more recently to Active/X Data Objects (ADO), but these new interfaces are layered on top of ODBC for relational database access, and it remains a key cross-platform database access technology.

SQL and Portability

The existence of published SQL standards has spawned quite a few exaggerated claims about SQL and applications portability. Diagrams such as the one in Figure 3-1 are frequently drawn to show how an application using SQL can work interchangeably with any SQL-based database management system. In fact, the holes in the SQL-89 standard and the current differences between SQL dialects are significant enough that an application must *always* be modified when moved from one SQL database to

Figure 3-1.   *The SQL portability myth*

another. These differences, many of which were eliminated by the SQL2 standard but have not yet been implemented in commercial products, include:

- **Error codes**. The SQL-89 standard does not specify the error codes to be returned when SQL detects an error, and all of the commercial implementations use their own set of error codes. The SQL2 standard specifies standard error codes.

- **Data types**. The SQL-89 standard defines a minimal set of data types, but it omits some of the most popular and useful types, such as variable-length character strings, dates and times, and money data. The SQL2 standard addresses these, but not "new" data types such as graphics and multimedia objects.

- **System tables**. The SQL-89 standard is silent about the system tables that provide information regarding the structure of the database itself. Each vendor has its own structure for these tables, and even IBM's four SQL implementations differ from one another. The tables are standardized in SQL2, but only at the higher levels of compliance, which are not yet provided by most vendors.

- **Interactive SQL**. The standard specifies only the *programmatic* SQL used by an application program, not interactive SQL. For example, the SELECT statement used to query the database in interactive SQL is absent from the SQL-89 standard. Again, the SQL2 standard addressed this issue, but long after all of the major DBMS vendors had well-established interactive SQL capabilities.

- **Programmatic interface**. The original standard specifies an abstract technique for using SQL from within an applications program written in COBOL, C, FORTRAN, and other programming languages. No commercial SQL product uses this technique, and there is considerable variation in the actual programmatic interfaces used. The SQL2 standard specifies an embedded SQL interface for popular programming languages but not a call-level interface. The 1995 SQL/CLI standard finally addressed programmatic SQL access, but not before commercial DBMS products had popularized proprietary interfaces and deeply embedded them in hundreds of thousands of user applications and application packages.

- **Dynamic SQL**. The SQL-89 standard does not include the features required to develop general-purpose database front-ends, such as query tools and report writers. These features, known as *dynamic SQL,* are found in virtually all SQL database systems, but they vary significantly from product to product. SQL2 includes a standard for dynamic SQL. But with hundreds of thousands of existing applications dependent on backward compatibility, DBMS vendors have not implemented it.

- **Semantic differences**. Because the standards specify certain details as implementor-defined, it's possible to run the same query against two different conforming SQL implementations and produce two different sets of query results. These differences occur in the handling of NULL values, column functions, and duplicate row elimination.

- **Collating sequences**. The SQL-89 standard does not address the collating (sorting) sequence of characters stored in the database. The results of a sorted query will be different if the query is run on a personal computer (with ASCII characters) and a mainframe (with EBCDIC characters). The SQL2 standard includes an elaborate specification for how a program or a user can request a specific collating sequence, but it is an advanced-level feature that is not typically supported in commercial products.

- **Database structure**. The SQL-89 standard specifies the SQL language to be used once a particular database has been opened and is ready for processing. The details of database naming and how the initial connection to the database is established vary widely and are not portable. The SQL2 standard creates more uniformity but cannot completely mask these details.

Despite these differences, commercial database tools boasting portability across several different brands of SQL databases began to emerge in the early 1990s. In every case, however, the tools require a special adapter for each supported DBMS, which generates the appropriate SQL dialect, handles data type conversion, translates error codes, and so on. Transparent portability across different DBMS brands based on standard SQL is the major goal of SQL2 and ODBC, and significant progress has been made. Today, virtually all programs that support multiple databases include specific drivers for communicating with each of the major DBMS brands, and usually include an ODBC driver for accessing the others.

SQL and Networking

The dramatic growth of computer networking in the 1990s had a major impact on database management and gave SQL a new prominence. As networks became more common, applications that traditionally ran on a central minicomputer or mainframe moved to local area networks of desktop workstations and servers. In these networks, SQL plays a crucial role as the link between an application running on a desktop workstation with a graphical user interface and the DBMS that manages shared data on a cost-effective server. More recently, the exploding popularity of the Internet and the World Wide Web has reinforced the network role for SQL. In the emerging three-tier Internet architecture, SQL once again provides the link between the application logic (now running in the middle tier, on an application server or web server) and the database residing in the back-end tier. The next few sections discuss the evolution of database network architectures and the role of SQL in each one.

Centralized Architecture

Figure 3-2 shows the traditional database architecture used by DB2, SQL/DS, and the original minicomputer databases such as Oracle and Ingres. In this architecture, the DBMS and the physical data both reside on a central minicomputer or mainframe

Figure 3-2. *Database management in a centralized architecture*

system, along with the application program that accepts input from the user's terminal and displays data on the user's screen. The application program communicates with the DBMS using SQL.

Suppose the user types a query that requires a sequential search of a database, such as a request to find the average order size for all orders. The DBMS receives the query, scans through the database fetching each record of data from the disk, calculates the average, and displays the result on the terminal screen. Both the application processing and the database processing occur on the central computer, so execution of this type of query (and in fact, all kinds of queries) is very efficient.

The disadvantage of the centralized architecture is scalability. As more and more users are added, each of them adds application processing workload to the system. Because the system is shared, each user experiences degraded performance as the system becomes more heavily loaded.

File Server Architecture

The introduction of personal computers and local area networks led to the development of the *file server* architecture, shown in Figure 3-3. In this architecture, an application running on a personal computer can transparently access data located on a file server, which stores shared files. When a PC application requests data from a shared file, the networking software automatically retrieves the requested block of the file from the server. Early PC databases, such as dBASE and later Microsoft's Access, supported this file server approach, with each personal computer running its own copy of the DBMS software.

For typical queries that retrieve only one row or a few rows from the database, this architecture provides excellent performance, because each user has the full power of a personal computer running its own copy of the DBMS. However, consider the query made in the previous example. Because the query requires a sequential scan of the database, the DBMS repeatedly requests blocks of data from the database, which is physically located across the network on the server. Eventually, *every* block of the file will be requested and sent across the network. Obviously, this architecture produces very heavy network traffic and slow performance for queries of this type.

Figure 3-3.   *Database management in a file server architecture*

Client/Server Architecture

Figure 3-4 shows the next stage of network database evolution—the *client/server* database architecture. In this scheme, personal computers are combined in a local area network with a *database server* that stores shared databases. The functions of the DBMS are split into two parts. Database front-ends, such as interactive query tools, report writers, and application

Figure 3-4.   *Database management in a client/server architecture*

programs, run on the personal computer. The back-end database engine that stores and manages the data runs on the server. As the client/server architecture grew in popularity during the 1990s, SQL became the standard database language for communication between the front-end tools and the back-end engine in this architecture.

Consider once more the query requesting the average order size. In the client/server architecture, the query travels across the network to the database server as a SQL request. The database engine on the server processes the request and scans the database, which also resides on the server. When the result is calculated, the database engine sends it back across the network as a single reply to the initial request, and the front-end application displays it on the PC screen.

The client/server architecture reduces the network traffic and splits the database workload. User-intensive functions, such as handling input and displaying data, are concentrated on the user's PC. Data-intensive functions, such as file I/O and query processing, are concentrated in the database server. Most importantly, the SQL language provides a well-defined interface between the front-end and back-end systems, communicating database access requests in an efficient manner.

By the mid-1990s, these advantages made the client/server architecture the most popular scheme for implementing new applications. All of the most popular DBMS products—Oracle, Informix, Sybase, SQL Server, DB2, and many more—offered client/server capability. The database industry grew to include many companies offering tools for building client/server applications. Some of these came from the database companies themselves; others came from independent companies.

Like all architectures, client/server had its disadvantages. The most serious of these was the problem of managing the applications software that was now distributed across hundreds or thousands of desktop PCs instead of running on a central minicomputer or mainframe. To update an application program in a large company, the information systems department had to update thousands of PC systems, one at a time. The situation was even worse if changes to the application program had to be synchronized with changes to other applications, or to the DBMS system itself. In addition, with personal computers on user's desks, users tended to add new personal software of their own or to change the configuration of their systems. Such changes often disrupted existing applications, adding to the support burden. Companies developed strategies to deal with these issues, but by the late 1990s, there was growing concern about the manageability of client/server applications on large, distributed PC networks.

Multitier Architecture

With the emergence of the Internet and especially the World Wide Web, network database architecture took another step in its evolution. At first, the Web was used to access (browse) static documents and evolved outside of the database world. But as the use of web browsers became widespread, it wasn't long before companies thought about using them as a simple way to provide access to corporate databases as well. For example, suppose a company starts using the Web to provide product information to its customers by making product descriptions and graphics available on its web site. A natural next step is to give customers access to current product availability information through the same web browser interface. This requires linking the web server to the database system that stores the (constantly changing) current product inventory levels.

The methods used to link web servers and DBMS systems evolved rapidly in the late 1990s and early 2000s, and have converged on the three-tier network architecture shown in Figure 3-5. The user interface is a web browser running on a PC or some other thin client device in the front tier. It communicates with a web server in the middle tier. When the user request is for something more complex than a simple web page, the web server passes the request to an *application server*, whose role is to handle the business logic required to process the request. Often, the request will involve access to an existing (legacy) application running on a mainframe system or to a corporate database. These systems run in the back tier of the architecture.

As with the client/server architecture, SQL is solidly entrenched as the standard database language for communicating between the application server and back-end databases. All of the packaged application server products provide a SQL-based callable API for database access. As the application server market has converged around the Java2 Enterprise Edition (J2EE) standard, Java DataBase Connectivity (JDBC) has emerged as the standard API for application server access to databases.

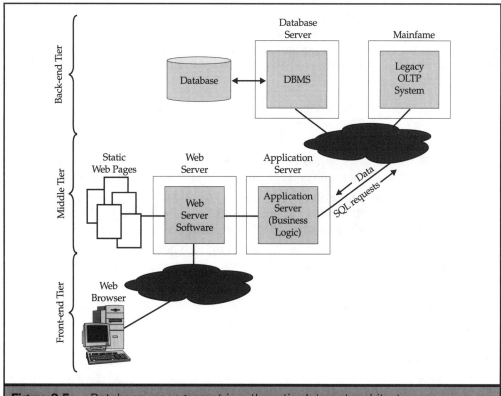

Figure 3-5.   *Database management in a three-tier Internet architecture*

The Proliferation of SQL

As the standard for relational database access, SQL has had a major impact on all parts of the computer market. IBM has adopted SQL as a unifying database technology for its product line. SQL-based databases dominate the market for UNIX-based computer systems. In the PC market, SQL databases on server-oriented Windows operating systems are mounting a serious challenge to the dominance of UNIX as a database processing platform, especially for departmental applications. SQL is accepted as a technology for online transaction processing (OLTP), fully refuting the conventional wisdom of the 1980s that relational databases would never offer performance good enough for transaction processing applications. SQL-based data warehousing and data mining applications are the standard for helping companies to discover customer purchase patterns and offer better products and services. On the Internet, SQL-based databases are the foundation of more personalized products, services, and information services that are a key benefit of electronic commerce.

SQL and IBM's Unified Database Strategy

SQL has played a key role as a common database access language across all of IBM's computer families. Originally, this role was part of IBM's SAA strategy, announced in March 1987. Although IBM's grand goals for SAA were not achieved, the unifying role of SQL has grown even more important over time. The DB2 database system, IBM's flagship SQL-based DBMS, now runs on a broad range of IBM and non-IBM computer systems, including:

- **Mainframes**. DB2 started as the SQL standard-bearer for IBM mainframes running MVS and has now replaced SQL/DS as the relational system for the VM and VSE mainframe operating systems.
- **AS/400**. This SQL implementation runs on IBM's family of midrange business systems, targeted at small- and medium-sized businesses and server applications.
- **Power-architecture servers**. DB2 runs under the UNIX operating system on IBM's family of RISC-based workstations and servers, for engineering and scientific applications, and as IBM's own UNIX database server platform.
- **Other UNIX platforms**. IBM supports DB2 on UNIX-based server platforms from Sun Microsystems and Hewlett-Packard, the two largest UNIX system vendors, and on UNIX-based workstations from Silicon Graphics.
- **Windows**. A PC-LAN server version of DB2 competes with Microsoft SQL Server, Oracle, and others on Windows-based database servers.

SQL on Minicomputers

Minicomputers were one of the most fertile early markets for SQL-based database systems. Oracle and Ingres were both originally marketed on Digital's VAX/VMS minicomputer systems. Both products have since been ported to many other platforms. Sybase, a later database system specialized for online transaction processing, also targeted the VAX as one of its primary platforms.

Through the 1980s, the minicomputer vendors also developed their own proprietary relational databases featuring SQL. Digital considered relational databases so important that it bundled a runtime version of its Rdb/VMS database with every VAX/VMS system. Hewlett-Packard offered Allbase, a database that supported both its HPSQL dialect and a nonrelational interface. Data General's DG/SQL database replaced its older nonrelational databases as DG's strategic data management tool. In addition, many of the minicomputer vendors resold relational databases from the independent database software vendors. These efforts helped to establish SQL as an important technology for midrange computer systems.

By the mid-1990s, the minicomputer vendors' SQL products had largely disappeared, beaten in the marketplace by multiplatform software from Oracle, Informix, Sybase, and others. Accompanying this trend, the importance of proprietary minicomputer operating systems has faded as well, replaced by widespread use of UNIX on midrange systems. Yesterday's minicomputer SQL market has effectively become today's market for UNIX-based database servers based on SQL.

SQL on UNIX-Based Systems

SQL has firmly established itself as the data management solution of choice for UNIX-based computer systems. Originally developed at Bell Laboratories, UNIX became very popular in the 1980s as a vendor-independent, standard operating system. It runs on a wide range of computer systems, from workstations to mainframes, and has become the standard operating system for high-end server systems, including database servers.

In the early 1980s, four major databases were already available for UNIX systems. Two of them, Ingres and Oracle, were UNIX versions of the products that ran on DEC's proprietary minicomputers. The other two, Informix and Unify, were written specifically for UNIX. Neither of them originally offered SQL support, but by 1985, Unify offered a SQL query language, and Informix had been rewritten as Informix-SQL, with full SQL support.

Today, the Oracle, DB2, Informix, and Sybase DBMS products dominate the UNIX-based database market and are available on all of the leading UNIX server platforms. UNIX-based database servers are a mainstream building block for both client/server and three-tier Internet architectures. The constant search for higher SQL database performance has driven some of the most important trends in UNIX system hardware. These include the emergence of symmetric multiprocessing (SMP) as a mainstream server architecture, and the use of RAID (Redundant Array of Independent Disks) technology to boost I/O performance.

SQL on Personal Computers

Databases have been popular on personal computers since the early days of the IBM PC. Ashton-Tate's dBASE product reached an installed base of over one million

MS-DOS-based PCs. Although these early PC databases often presented data in tabular form, they lacked the full power of a relational DBMS and a relational database language such as SQL. The first SQL-based PC databases were versions of popular minicomputer products that barely fit on personal computers. For example, Professional Oracle for the IBM PC, introduced in 1984, required two megabytes of memory—well above the typical 640KB PC configuration of the day.

The real impact of SQL on personal computers began with the announcement of OS/2 by IBM and Microsoft in April 1987. In addition to the standard OS/2 product, IBM announced a proprietary OS/2 Extended Edition (OS/2 EE) with a built-in SQL database and communications support. With the introduction, IBM again signaled its strong commitment to SQL, saying in effect that SQL was so important that it belonged in the computer's operating system.

OS/2 Extended Edition presented Microsoft with a problem. As the developer and distributor of standard OS/2 to other personal computer manufacturers, Microsoft needed an alternative to the Extended Edition. Microsoft responded by licensing the Sybase DBMS, which had been developed for VAX, and began porting it to OS/2. In January 1988, in a surprise move, Microsoft and Ashton-Tate (the PC database leader at the time with its dBASE product) announced that they would jointly sell the resulting OS/2-based product, renamed SQL Server. Microsoft would sell SQL Server with OS/2 to computer manufacturers; Ashton-Tate would sell the product through retail channels to PC users. In September 1989, Lotus Development (the other member of the big three of PC software at the time) added its endorsement of SQL Server by investing in Sybase. Later that year, Ashton-Tate relinquished its exclusive retail distribution rights and sold its investment to Lotus.

SQL Server for OS/2 met with only limited success. But in typical Microsoft fashion, Microsoft continued to invest heavily in SQL Server development and ported it to its Windows NT operating system. For a while, Microsoft and Sybase remained partners, with Sybase focused on the minicomputer and UNIX-based server markets and Microsoft focused on PC LANs and Windows NT. As Windows NT and UNIX systems became more and more competitive as database server operating system platforms, the relationship became less cooperative and more competitive. Eventually, Sybase and Microsoft went their separate ways. The common heritage of Sybase's and Microsoft's SQL products can still be seen in product capabilities and some common SQL extensions (for example, stored procedures), but the product lines have already diverged significantly.

Today, SQL Server is a major database system on Windows-based servers. SQL Server 7, which shipped in late 1998, provided a significant step up in the size and scale of database applications that SQL Server can support. SQL Server 2000, which runs on Windows 2000, provided another major step. SQL Server is slated to continue in a major role as Microsoft rolls out more of its .NET server product family. In addition to SQL Server's impact, the availability of Oracle, and to a lesser extent, Informix, DB2, and other mainstream DBMS products, has helped Windows-based servers to steadily make inroads into UNIX's dominance as a database server platform. While UNIX continues to dominate the largest database server installations, server configurations of the Windows operating system and the Intel architecture systems on which it runs have achieved credibility in the midrange market.

SQL and Transaction Processing

SQL and relational databases originally had very little impact in online transaction processing (OLTP) applications. With their emphasis on queries, relational databases were confined to decision support and low-volume online applications, where their slower performance was not a disadvantage. For OLTP applications, where hundreds of users needed online access to data and subsecond response times, IBM's nonrelational Information Management System (IMS) reigned as the dominant DBMS.

In 1986, a new DBMS vendor, Sybase, introduced a new SQL-based database especially designed for OLTP applications. The Sybase DBMS ran on VAX/VMS minicomputers and Sun workstations, and focused on maximum online performance. Oracle Corporation and Relational Technology followed shortly with announcements that they, too, would offer OLTP versions of their popular Oracle and Ingres database systems. In the UNIX market, Informix announced an OLTP version of its DBMS, named Informix-Turbo.

In 1988, IBM jumped on the relational OLTP bandwagon with DB2 Version 2, with benchmarks showing the new version operating at over 250 transactions per second on large mainframes. IBM claimed that DB2 performance was now suitable for all but the most demanding OLTP applications, and encouraged customers to consider it as a serious alternative to IMS. OLTP benchmarks have now become a standard sales tool for relational databases, despite serious questions about how well the benchmarks actually measure performance in real applications.

The suitability of SQL for OLTP improved dramatically through the 1990s, with advances in relational technology and more powerful computer hardware both leading to ever-higher transaction rates. DBMS vendors started to position their products based on their OLTP performance, and for a few years database advertising focused almost entirely on these performance benchmark wars. A vendor-independent organization, the Transaction Processing Council, jumped into the benchmarking fray with a series of vendor-independent benchmarks (TPC-A, TPC-B, and TPC-C), which only served to intensify the performance focus of the vendors.

By the late 1990s, SQL-based relational databases on high-end UNIX-based database servers evolved well past the 1000-transactions-per-second mark. Client/server systems using SQL databases have become the accepted architecture for implementing OLTP applications. From a position as "unsuitable for OLTP," SQL has grown to be the industry standard foundation for building OLTP applications.

SQL and Workgroup Databases

The dramatic growth of PC LANs through the 1980s and 1990s created a new opportunity for departmental or workgroup database management. The original database systems focused on this market segment ran on IBM's OS/2 operating system. In fact, SQL Server, now a key part of Microsoft's Windows strategy, originally made its debut as an OS/2 database product. In the mid-1990s, Novell also made a concentrated effort to make its NetWare operating system an attractive workgroup database server platform. From the earliest days of PC LANs, NetWare had become established as the dominant network operating system for file and print servers. Through deals with Oracle and others, Novell sought to extend this leadership to workgroup database servers as well.

The arrival of Windows NT on the workgroup computing scene was the catalyst that caused the workgroup database market to really take off. While NetWare offered a clear performance advantage over NT as a workgroup file server, NT had a more robust, general-purpose architecture, more like the minicomputer operating systems. Microsoft successfully positioned NT as a more attractive platform for running workgroup applications (as an application server) and workgroup databases. Microsoft's own SQL Server product was marketed (and often bundled) with NT as a tightly integrated workgroup database platform. Corporate information systems departments were at first very cautious about using relatively new and unproven technology, but the NT/SQL Server combination allowed departments and non-IS executives to undertake smaller-scale, workgroup-level projects on their own, without corporate IS help. This phenomenon, like the grass roots support for personal computers a decade earlier, fueled the early growth of the workgroup database segment.

Today, SQL is well established as a workgroup database standard. Microsoft's SQL Server has been joined by Oracle, Informix, Sybase, DB2, and many other DBMS brands running on the Windows server platforms. Windows-based SQL databases are the second largest segment of the DBMS market and are the fastest growing. From this solid dominance in the workgroup segment, Windows-based server systems are mounting a continued assault on enterprise-class database applications, slowly but surely eating into low-end UNIX-based database deployments.

SQL and Data Warehousing

For several years, the effort to make SQL a viable technology for OLTP applications shifted the focus away from the original relational database strengths of query processing and decision making. Performance benchmarks and competition among the major DBMS brands focused on simple transactions like adding a new order to the database or determining a customer's account balance. Because of the power of the relational database model, the databases that companies used to handle daily business operations could also be used to analyze the growing amounts of data that were being accumulated. A frequent theme of conferences and trade show speeches for IS managers was that a corporation's accumulated data (stored in SQL databases, of course) should be treated as a valuable asset and used to help improve the quality of business decision making.

Although relational databases could, in theory, easily perform both OLTP and decision-making applications, there were some very significant practical problems. OLTP workloads consisted of many short database transactions, and the response time for users was very important. In contrast, decision-support queries could involve sequential scans of large database tables to answer questions like "What is the average order size by sales region?" or "How do inventory trends compare with the same time a year ago?" These queries could take minutes or hours. If a business analyst tried to run one of these queries during a time when business transaction volumes reached their peak, it could cause serious degradation in OLTP performance. Another problem was that the data to answer useful questions about business trends was often spread across many different databases, typically involving different DBMS vendors and different computer platforms.

The desire to take advantage of accumulated business data, and the practical performance problems it caused for OLTP applications, led to the concept of a data warehouse, shown in Figure 3-6. Business data is extracted from OLTP systems, reformatted and validated as necessary, and then placed into a separate database that is dedicated to decision-making queries (the "warehouse"). The data extraction and transformation can be scheduled for off-hours batch processing. Ideally, only new or changed data can be extracted, minimizing the amount of data to be processed in the monthly, weekly, or daily warehouse refresh cycle. With this scheme, the time-consuming business analysis queries use the data warehouse, not the OLTP database, as their source of data.

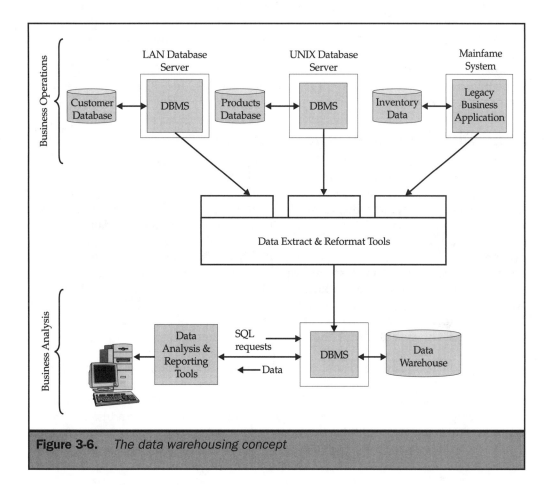

Figure 3-6. *The data warehousing concept*

SQL-based relational databases were a clear choice for the warehouse data store because of their flexible query processing. A series of new companies was formed to build the data extraction, transformation, and database query tools needed by the data warehouse model. In addition, DBMS vendors started to focus on the kinds of database queries that customers tended to run in the data warehouse. These queries tended to be large and complex—such as analyzing tens or hundreds of millions of individual cash-register receipts to look for product purchase patterns. They often involved time-series data—for example, analyzing product sales or market share data over time. They also tended to involve statistical summaries of data—total sales, average order volume, percent growth, and so on—rather than the individual data items themselves.

To address the specialized needs of data warehousing applications (often called *OnLine Analytical Processing* or OLAP), specialized databases began to appear. These databases were optimized for OLAP workloads in several different ways. Their performance was tuned for complex, read-only query access. They supported advanced statistical and other data functions, such as built-in time-series processing. They supported precalculation of database statistical data, so that retrieving averages and totals could be dramatically faster. Some of these specialized databases did not use SQL, but many did (leading to the companion term ROLAP, for *Relational OnLine Analytic Processing*). As with so many segments of the database market, SQL's advantages as a standard proved to be a powerful force. Data warehousing has become a one-billion-dollar-plus segment of the database market, and SQL-based databases are firmly entrenched as the mainstream technology for building data warehouses.

SQL and Distributed Internet Applications

During the late 1990s, the World Wide Web and the web browsing capability that it enabled were the driving force behind the growth of the Internet. With its focus on delivering content in the form of text and graphics, the early uses of the Web had little to do with data management. By the mid-1990s, however, much of the content delivered from corporate web sites had its origins in SQL-based corporate databases. For example, on a commercial web site for a retailer, web pages that contain information about products available for sale, their prices, product availability, special promotions, and the like are typically created on demand, based on data retrieved from a SQL database. The vast majority of the pages displayed by an online auction site or by an online travel site are similarly based on data retrieved from SQL databases, transformed into the Web's HTML page format. In the other direction, data entered by a user into browser page forms is almost always captured into SQL databases that form part of the web site architecture.

By the early 2000s, industry attention had turned to the next phase of the Internet, and the role that Internet technologies can play in connecting computer applications to one another. These distributed applications architectures received widespread trade press coverage under the banner of *web services.* In the long-standing tradition of the computer industry, competing camps emerged, championing different sets of standards and languages for implementing them—a Microsoft-led camp under the .NET framework, and a rival camp focused on Java and J2EE-based application servers. Both architectures embrace a key role for XML, a standard for exchanging structured data like the data that resides in SQL databases.

In response to the industry attention on web services, a flurry of products has been announced that link XML-formatted messages to SQL-based databases. Startup database vendors and some of the object database vendors have announced XML-based database products, arguing that they provide an ideal, native match for the XML-formatted exchange of data over the Internet. The established relational database players have responded with their own XML initiatives, adding XML input/output capabilities, and in some cases, XML data type support, to their products. The interaction between XML and SQL is one of the most active areas in data management today, and the activity in this area will keep SQL in the industry spotlight well into the first decade of the twenty-first century.

Summary

This chapter described the development of SQL and its role as a standard language for relational database management:

- SQL was originally developed by IBM researchers, and IBM's strong support of SQL is a key reason for its success.

- There are official ANSI/ISO SQL standards and several other SQL standards, each slightly different from the ANSI/ISO standards.

- Despite the existence of standards, there are many small variations among commercial SQL dialects; no two SQLs are exactly the same.

- SQL has become the standard database management language across a broad range of computer systems and applications areas, including mainframes, workstations, personal computers, OLTP systems, client/server systems, data warehousing, and the Internet.

The Complete Reference

Chapter 4

Relational Databases

Database management systems organize and structure data so that it can be retrieved and manipulated by users and application programs. The data structures and access techniques provided by a particular DBMS are called its *data model*. A data model determines both the "personality" of a DBMS and the applications for which it is particularly well suited.

SQL is a database language for relational databases that uses the *relational data model*. What exactly is a relational database? How is data stored in a relational database? How do relational databases compare to earlier technologies, such as hierarchical and network databases? What are the advantages and disadvantages of the relational model? This chapter describes the relational data model supported by SQL and compares it to earlier strategies for database organization.

Early Data Models

As database management became popular during the 1970s and 1980s, a handful of popular data models emerged. Each of these early data models had advantages and disadvantages that played key roles in the development of the relational data model. In many ways, the relational data model represented an attempt to streamline and simplify the earlier data models. To understand the role and contribution of SQL and the relational model, it is useful to briefly examine some data models that preceded the development of SQL.

File Management Systems

Before the introduction of database management systems, all data permanently stored on a computer system, such as payroll and accounting records, was stored in individual files. A *file management system*, usually provided by the computer manufacturer as part of the computer's operating system, kept track of the names and locations of the files. The file management system basically had no data model; it knew nothing about the internal contents of files. To the file management system, a file containing a word processing document and a file containing payroll data appeared the same.

Knowledge about the contents of a file—which data it contained and how the data was organized—was embedded in the application programs that used the file, as shown in Figure 4-1. In this payroll application, each of the COBOL programs that processed the employee master file contained a *file description* (FD) that described the layout of the data in the file. If the structure of the data changed—for example, if an additional item of data was to be stored for each employee—every program that accessed the file had to be modified. As the number of files and programs grew over time, more and more of a data-processing department's effort went into maintaining existing applications rather than developing new ones.

The problems of maintaining large file-based systems led in the late 1960s to the development of database management systems. The idea behind these systems was simple:

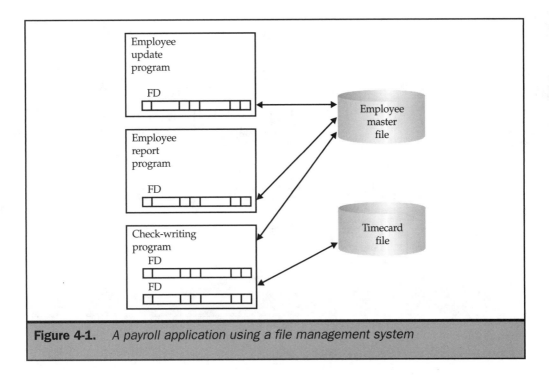

Figure 4-1.   *A payroll application using a file management system*

take the definition of a file's content and structure out of the individual programs, and store it, together with the data, in a database. Using the information in the database, the DBMS that controlled it could take a much more active role in managing both the data and changes to the database structure.

Hierarchical Databases

One of the most important applications for the earliest database management systems was production planning for manufacturing companies. If an automobile manufacturer decided to produce 10,000 units of one car model and 5000 units of another model, it needed to know how many parts to order from its suppliers. To answer the question, the product (a car) had to be decomposed into assemblies (engine, body, chassis), which were decomposed into subassemblies (valves, cylinders, spark plugs), and then into sub-subassemblies, and so on. Handling this list of parts, known as a *bill of materials*, was a job tailor-made for computers.

The bill of materials for a product has a natural hierarchical structure. To store this data, the *hierarchical* data model, illustrated in Figure 4-2, was developed. In this model, each *record* in the database represented a specific part. The records had *parent/child relationships*, linking each part to its subpart, and so on.

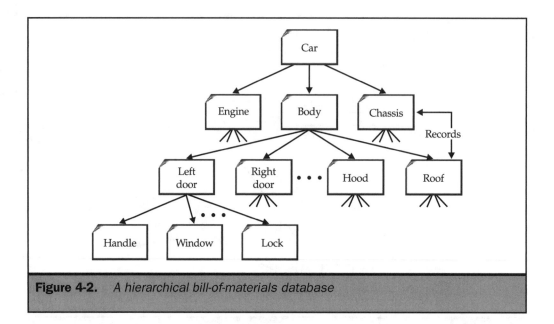

Figure 4-2.   *A hierarchical bill-of-materials database*

To access the data in the database, a program could perform the following tasks:

■ Find a particular part by number (such as the left door)

■ Move "down" to the first child (the door handle)

■ Move "up" to its parent (the body)

■ Move "sideways" to the next child (the right door)

Retrieving the data in a hierarchical database thus required *navigating* through the records, moving up, down, and sideways one record at a time.

One of the most popular hierarchical database management systems was IBM's Information Management System (IMS), first introduced in 1968. The advantages of IMS and its hierarchical model follow.

■ **Simple structure**. The organization of an IMS database was easy to understand. The database hierarchy paralleled that of a company organization chart or a family tree.

■ **Parent/child organization**. An IMS database was excellent for representing parent/child relationships, such as "A is a part of B" or "A is owned by B."

■ **Performance**. IMS stored parent/child relationships as physical pointers from one data record to another, so that movement through the database was rapid. Because the structure was simple, IMS could place parent and child records close to one another on the disk, minimizing disk input/output.

IMS is still a very widely used DBMS on IBM mainframes. Its raw performance makes it the database of choice in high-volume transaction-processing applications such as processing bank ATM transactions, verifying credit card numbers, and tracking the delivery of overnight packages. Although relational database performance has improved dramatically over the last decade, the performance requirements of applications such as these have also increased, so IMS continues to have a role. In addition, the large amount of corporate data stored in IMS databases insures that IMS use will continue long after relational databases have eliminated the performance barrier.

Network Databases

The simple structure of a hierarchical database became a disadvantage when the data had a more complex structure. In an order-processing database, for example, a single order might participate in three *different* parent/child relationships, linking the order to the customer who placed it, the salesperson who took it, and the product ordered, as shown in Figure 4-3. The structure of this type of data simply didn't fit the strict hierarchy of IMS.

To deal with applications such as order processing, a new *network* data model was developed. The network data model extended the hierarchical model by allowing a record to participate in multiple parent/child relationships, as shown in Figure 4-4. These relationships were known as *sets* in the network model. In 1971, the Conference on Data Systems Languages published an official standard for network databases, which became known as the CODASYL model. IBM never developed a network DBMS of its own, choosing instead to extend IMS over the years. But during the 1970s, independent software companies rushed to embrace the network model, creating

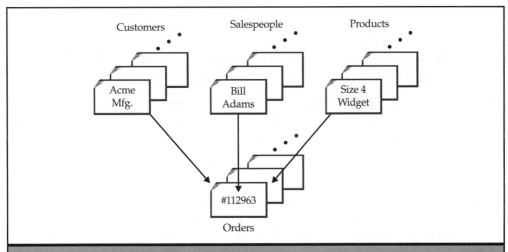

Figure 4-3. *Multiple child/parent relationships*

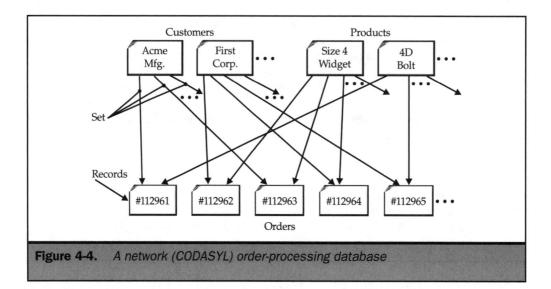

Figure 4-4. *A network (CODASYL) order-processing database*

products such as Cullinet's IDMS, Cincom's Total, and the Adabas DBMS that became very popular.

For a programmer, accessing a network database was very similar to accessing a hierarchical database. An application program could do the following:

- Find a specific parent record by key (such as a customer number)

- Move down to the first child in a particular set (the first order placed by this customer)

- Move sideways from one child to the next in the set (the next order placed by the same customer)

- Move up from a child to its parent in another set (the salesperson who took the order)

Once again, the programmer had to navigate the database record by record, this time specifying which relationship to navigate as well as the direction.

Network databases had several advantages:

- **Flexibility**. Multiple parent/child relationships allowed a network database to represent data that did not have a simple hierarchical structure.

- **Standardization**. The CODASYL standard boosted the popularity of the network model, and minicomputer vendors such as Digital Equipment Corporation and Data General implemented network databases.

- **Performance**. Despite their greater complexity, network databases boasted performance approaching that of hierarchical databases. Sets were represented by pointers to physical data records, and on some systems, the database administrator could specify data clustering based on a set relationship.

Network databases had their disadvantages, too. Like hierarchical databases, they were very rigid. The set relationships and the structure of the records had to be specified in advance. Changing the database structure typically required rebuilding the entire database.

Both hierarchical and network databases were tools for programmers. To answer a question such as "What is the most popular product ordered by Acme Manufacturing?" a programmer had to write a program that navigated its way through the database. The backlog of requests for custom reports often stretched to weeks or months, and by the time the program was written, the information it delivered was often worthless.

The disadvantages of the hierarchical and network models led to intense interest in the new *relational* data model when it was first described by Dr. Codd in 1970. At first the relational model was little more than an academic curiosity. Network databases continued to be important throughout the 1970s and early 1980s, particularly on the minicomputer systems that were surging in popularity. However, by the mid-1980s, the relational model was clearly emerging as the "new wave" in data management. By the early 1990s, network databases were clearly declining in importance, and today they no longer play a major role in the database market.

The Relational Data Model

The relational model proposed by Dr. Codd was an attempt to simplify database structure. It eliminated the explicit parent/child structures from the database, and instead represented all data in the database as simple row/column tables of data values. Figure 4-5 shows a relational version of the network order-processing database in Figure 4-4.

Unfortunately, the practical definition of "What is a relational database?" became much less clear-cut than the precise, mathematical definition in Codd's 1970 paper. Early relational database management systems failed to implement some key parts of Codd's model. As the relational concept grew in popularity, many databases that were called "relational" in fact were not.

In response to the corruption of the term "relational," Dr. Codd wrote an article in 1985 setting forth 12 rules to be followed by any database that called itself "truly relational." Codd's 12 rules have since been accepted as *the* definition of a truly relational DBMS. However, it's easier to start with a more informal definition:

> A relational database is a database where all data visible to the user is organized strictly as tables of data values, and where all database operations work on these tables.

The definition is intended specifically to rule out structures such as the embedded pointers of a hierarchical or network database. A relational DBMS can represent parent/child relationships, but they are represented strictly by the data values contained in the database tables.

PRODUCTS Table

DESCRIPTION	PRICE	QTY_ON_HAND
Size 3 Widget	$107.00	207
Size 4 Widget	$117.00	139
Hinge Pin	$350.00	14
.		
.		
.		

ORDERS Table

ORDER_NUM	COMPANY	PRODUCT	QTY
112963	Acme Mfg.	41004	28
112975	JCP Inc.	2A44G	6
112983	Acme Mfg.	41004	6
113012	JCP Inc.	41003	35
.			
.			
.			

CUSTOMERS Table

COMPANY	CUST_REP	CREDIT_LIMIT
Acme Mfg.	105	$50,000.00
JCP Inc.	103	$50,000.00
.		
.		
.		

Figure 4-5.   *A relational order-processing database*

The Sample Database

Figure 4-6 shows a small relational database for an order-processing application. This sample database is used throughout this book and provides the basis for most of the examples. Appendix A contains a complete description of the database structure and its contents.

The sample database contains five tables. Each table stores information about one particular *kind* of entity:

- The CUSTOMERS table stores data about each customer, such as the company name, credit limit, and the salesperson who calls on the customer.

- The SALESREPS table stores the employee number, name, age, year-to-date sales, and other data about each salesperson.

- The OFFICES table stores data about each of the five sales offices, including the city where the office is located, the sales region to which it belongs, and so on.

- The ORDERS table keeps track of every order placed by a customer, identifying the salesperson who took the order, the product ordered, the quantity and amount of the order, and so on. For simplicity, each order is for only one product.

- The PRODUCTS table stores data about each product available for sale, such as the manufacturer, product number, description, and price.

ORDERS Table

ORDER_NUM	ORDER_DATE	CUST	REP	MFR	PRODUCT	QTY	AMOUNT
112961	17-DEC-89	2117	106	REI	2A44L	7	$31,500.00
113012	11-JAN-90	2111	105	ACI		35	$3,745.00
112989	03-JAN-90	2101				6	$1,458.00
113051	10-FEB-90	2118					
112968	12-OCT-89	2102					
113036	30-JAN-90	2107					
113045	02-FEB-90	2112					
1129	17-DEC-89						

PRODUCTS Table

MFR_ID	PRODUCT_ID	DESCRIPTION	PRICE	QTY_ON_HAND
REI	2A45C	Ratchet Link	$79.00	210
ACI	4100Y	Widget Remover	$2,750.00	25
QSA	XK47	Reducer	$355.00	38
BIC	41672	Plate	$180.00	0
			$1,875.00	9
			$107.00	207
			$117.00	139
			$652.00	3
			$250.00	24
			$134.00	203
			$4,500.00	12
			$148.00	115
			$54.00	223

CUSTOMERS Table

CUST_NUM	COMPANY	CUST_REP	CREDIT_LIMIT
2111	JCP Inc.	103	$50,000.00
2102	First Corp.	101	$65,000.00
2103	Acme Mfg.	105	$50,000.00
2123	Carter & Sons	102	$40,000.00
2107	Ace International	110	$35,000.00
2115	Smithson Corp.	101	$20,000.00
2101	Jones Mfg.	106	$65,000.00
		108	$50,000.00

SALESREPS Table

NAME	AGE	REP_OFFICE	TITLE	HIRE_DATE	MANAGER	QUOTA	SALES
Bill Adams	37	13	Sales Rep	12-FEB-88	104	$350,000.00	$367,911.00
Mary Jones	31	11	Sales Rep	12-OCT-89	106	$300,000.00	$392,725.00
Sue Smith	48	21	Sales Rep	10-DEC-86	108	$350,000.00	$474,050.00
	52	11	VP Sales	14-JUN-88	NULL	$275,000.00	$299,912.00
					106	$200,000.00	$142,594.00
					104	$300,000.00	$305,673.00
					101	NULL	$75,985.00
					106	$350,000.00	$361,865.00
					104	$275,000.00	$286,775.00
					108	$300,000.00	$186,042.00

OFFICES Table

OFFICE	CITY	REGION	MGR	TARGET	SALES
22	Denver	Western	108	$300,000.00	$186,042.00
11	New York	Eastern	106	$575,000.00	$692,637.00
12	Chicago	Eastern	104	$800,000.00	$735,042.00
13	Atlanta	Eastern	105	$350,000.00	$367,911.00
21	Los Angeles	Western	108	$725,000.00	$835,915.00

Figure 4-6. *The sample database*

Tables

The organizing principle in a relational database is the *table,* a rectangular row/column arrangement of data values. Each table in a database has a unique *table name* that identifies its contents. (Actually, each user can choose his or her own table names without worrying about the names chosen by other users, as explained in Chapter 5.)

The row/column structure of a table is shown more clearly in Figure 4-7, which is an enlarged view of the OFFICES table. Each horizontal *row* of the OFFICES table represents a single physical entity—a single sales office. Together the five rows of the table represent all five of the company's sales offices. All of the data in a particular row of the table applies to the office represented by that row.

Each vertical *column* of the OFFICES table represents one item of data that is stored in the database for each office. For example, the CITY column holds the location of each office. The SALES column contains each office's year-to-date sales total. The MGR column shows the employee number of the person who manages the office.

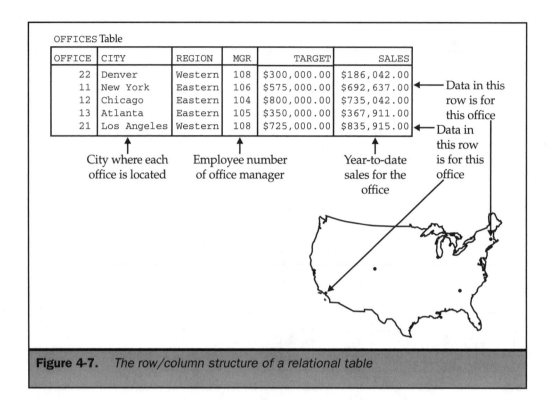

Figure 4-7.   *The row/column structure of a relational table*

Each row of a table contains exactly one data value in each column. In the row representing the New York office, for example, the CITY column contains the value "New York". The SALES column contains the value "$692,637.00", which is the year-to-date sales total for the New York office.

For each column of a table, all of the data values in that column hold the same type of data. For example, all of the CITY column values are words, all of the SALES values are money amounts, and all of the MGR values are integers (representing employee numbers). The set of data values that a column can contain is called the *domain* of the column. The domain of the CITY column is the set of all names of cities. The domain of the SALES column is any money amount. The domain of the REGION column is just two data values, "Eastern" and "Western", because those are the only two sales regions the company has.

Each column in a table has a *column name*, which is usually written as a heading at the top of the column. The columns of a table must all have different names, but there is no prohibition against two columns in two different tables having identical names. In fact, frequently used column names, such as NAME, ADDRESS, QTY, PRICE, and SALES, are often found in many different tables of a production database.

The columns of a table have a left-to-right order, which is defined when the table is first created. A table always has at least one column. The ANSI/ISO SQL standard does not specify a maximum number of columns in a table, but almost all commercial SQL products do impose a limit. Usually the limit is 255 columns per table or more.

Unlike the columns, the rows in a table do *not* have any particular order. In fact, if you use two consecutive database queries to display the contents of a table, there is no guarantee that the rows will be listed in the same order twice. Of course you can ask SQL to sort the rows before displaying them, but the sorted order has nothing to do with the actual arrangement of the rows within the table.

A table can have any number of rows. A table of zero rows is perfectly legal and is called an *empty* table (for obvious reasons). An empty table still has a structure, imposed by its columns; it simply contains no data. The ANSI/ISO standard does not limit the number of rows in a table, and many SQL products will allow a table to grow until it exhausts the available disk space on the computer. Other SQL products impose a maximum limit, but it is always a very generous one—two billion rows or more is common.

Primary Keys

Because the rows of a relational table are unordered, you cannot select a specific row by its position in the table. There is no "first row," "last row," or "thirteenth row" of a table. How, then, can you specify a particular row, such as the row for the Denver sales office?

In a well-designed relational database, every table has some column or combination of columns whose values uniquely identify each row in the table. This column (or columns) is called the *primary key* of the table. Look once again at the OFFICES table in Figure 4-7. At first glance, either the OFFICE column or the CITY column could serve as a primary key for the table. But if the company expands and opens two sales offices in the same city, the CITY column could no longer serve as the primary key. In practice, "ID numbers," such as an office number (OFFICE in the OFFICES table), an employee number (EMPL_NUM in the SALESREPS table), and customer numbers (CUST_NUM in the CUSTOMERS table), are often chosen as primary keys. In the case of the ORDERS table, there is no choice—the only thing that uniquely identifies an order is its order number (ORDER_NUM).

The PRODUCTS table, part of which is shown in Figure 4-8, is an example of a table where the primary key must be a *combination* of columns. The MFR_ID column identifies the manufacturer of each product in the table, and the PRODUCT_ID column specifies the manufacturer's product number. The PRODUCT_ID column might make a good primary key, but there's nothing to prevent two different manufacturers from using the same number for their products. Therefore, a combination of the MFR_ID and PRODUCT_ID columns must be used as the primary key of the PRODUCTS table. Every product in the table is guaranteed to have a unique combination of data values in these two columns.

The primary key has a different unique value for each row in a table, so no two rows of a table with a primary key are exact duplicates of one another. A table where every row is different from all other rows is called a *relation* in mathematical terms. The name "relational database" comes from this term, because relations (tables with distinct rows) are at the heart of a relational database.

PRODUCTS Table

MFR_ID	PRODUCT_ID	DESCRIPTION	PRICE	QTY_ON_HAND
.				
.				
.				
ACI	41003	Size 3 Widget	$107.00	207
ACI	41004	Size 4 Widget	$117.00	139
BIC	41003	Handle	$652.00	3
.				
.				
.				

Primary
key

Figure 4-8. *A table with a composite primary key*

Although primary keys are an essential part of the relational data model, early relational database management systems (System/R, DB2, Oracle, and others) did not provide explicit support for primary keys. Database designers usually ensured that all of the tables in their databases had a primary key, but the DBMS itself did not provide a way to identify the primary key of a table. DB2 Version 2, introduced in April 1988, was the first of IBM's commercial SQL products to support primary keys. The ANSI/ISO standard was subsequently expanded to include a definition of primary key support, and today, most relational database management systems provide it.

Relationships

One of the major differences between the relational model and earlier data models is that explicit pointers, such as the parent/child relationships of a hierarchical database, are banned from relational databases. Yet obviously, these relationships exist in a relational database. For example, in the sample database, each salesperson is assigned to a particular sales office, so there is an obvious relationship between the rows of the OFFICES table and the rows of the SALESREPS table. Doesn't the relational model "lose information" by banning these relationships from the database?

As shown in Figure 4-9, the answer to the question is "no." The figure shows a close-up of a few rows of the OFFICES and SALESREPS tables. Note that the REP_OFFICE column of the SALESREPS table contains the office number of the sales office where each salesperson works. The domain of this column (the set of legal values it may contain) is *precisely* the set of office numbers found in the OFFICE column of the OFFICES table. In fact, you can find the sales office where Mary Jones works by finding the value in Mary's REP_OFFICE column (11) and finding the row of the OFFICES table

AN OVERVIEW OF SQL

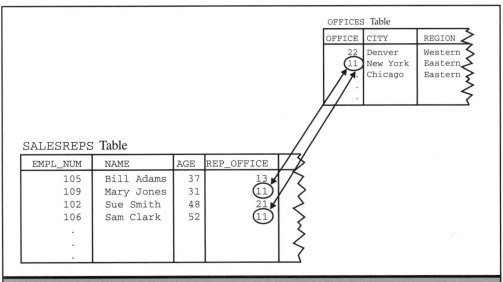

Figure 4-9. *A parent/child relationship in a relational database*

that has a matching value in the OFFICE column (in the row for the New York office). Similarly, to find all the salespeople who work in New York, you could note the OFFICE value for the New York row (11) and then scan down the REP_OFFICE column of the SALESREPS table looking for matching values (in the rows for Mary Jones and Sam Clark).

The parent/child relationship between a sales office and the people who work there isn't lost by the relational model, it's just not represented by an explicit pointer stored in the database. Instead, the relationship is represented by *common data values* stored in the two tables. All relationships in a relational database are represented this way. One of the main goals of the SQL language is to let you retrieve related data from the database by manipulating these relationships in a simple, straightforward way.

Foreign Keys

A column in one table whose value matches the primary key in some other table is called a *foreign key*. In Figure 4-9, the REP_OFFICE column is a foreign key for the OFFICES table. Although REP_OFFICE is a column in the SALESREPS table, the values that this column contains are office numbers. They match values in the OFFICE column, which is the primary key for the OFFICES table. Together, a primary key and a foreign key create a parent/child relationship between the tables that contain them, just like the parent/child relationships in a hierarchical database.

Just like a combination of columns can serve as the primary key of a table, a foreign key can also be a combination of columns. In fact, the foreign key will *always* be a compound (multicolumn) key when it references a table with a compound primary key. Obviously, the number of columns and the data types of the columns in the foreign key and the primary key must be identical to one another.

A table can contain more than one foreign key if it is related to more than one other table. Figure 4-10 shows the three foreign keys in the ORDERS table of the sample database:

- The CUST column is a foreign key for the CUSTOMERS table, relating each order to the customer who placed it.

- The REP column is a foreign key for the SALESREPS table, relating each order to the salesperson who took it.

- The MFR and PRODUCT columns together are a composite foreign key for the PRODUCTS table, relating each order to the product being ordered.

The multiple parent/child relationships created by the three foreign keys in the ORDERS table may seem familiar to you, and they should. They are precisely the same relationships as those in the network database of Figure 4-4. As the example shows, the relational data model has all of the power of the network model to express complex relationships.

Foreign keys are a fundamental part of the relational model because they create relationships among tables in the database. Unfortunately, like with primary keys, foreign key support was missing from early relational database management systems. They

Figure 4-10.   *Multiple parent/child relationships in a relational database*

were added to DB2 Version 2, have since been added to the ANSI/ISO standard, and now appear in many commercial products.

Codd's 12 Rules *

In his 1985 *Computerworld* article, Ted Codd presented 12 rules that a database must obey if it is to be considered truly relational. Codd's 12 rules, shown in the following list, have since become a semiofficial definition of a relational database. The rules come out of Codd's theoretical work on the relational model and actually represent more of an ideal goal than a definition of a relational database.

1. **Information rule**. All information in a relational database is represented explicitly at the logical level and in exactly one way—by values in tables.

2. **Guaranteed access rule**. Each and every datum (atomic value) in a relational database is guaranteed to be logically accessible by resorting to a combination of table name, primary key value, and column name.

3. **Systematic treatment of NULL values**. NULL values (distinct from an empty character string or a string of blank characters and distinct from zero or any other number) are supported in a fully relational DBMS for representing missing information and inapplicable information in a systematic way, independent of the data type.

4. **Dynamic online catalog based on the relational model**. The database description is represented at the logical level in the same way as ordinary data, so that authorized users can apply the same relational language to its interrogation as they apply to the regular data.

5. **Comprehensive data sublanguage rule**. A relational system may support several languages and various modes of terminal use (for example, the fill-in-the-blanks mode). However, there must be at least one language whose statements are expressible, per some well-defined syntax, as character strings, and that is comprehensive in supporting all of the following items:

   ■ Data definition

   ■ View definition

   ■ Data manipulation (interactive and by program)

   ■ Integrity constraints

   ■ Authorization

   ■ Transaction boundaries (begin, commit, and rollback)

6. **View updating rule**. All views that are theoretically updateable are also updateable by the system.

7. **High-level insert, update, and delete**. The capability of handling a base relation or a derived relation as a single operand applies not only to the retrieval of data, but also to the insertion, update, and deletion of data.

8. **Physical data independence**. Application programs and terminal activities remain logically unimpaired whenever any changes are made in either storage representations or access methods.

9. **Logical data independence**. Application programs and terminal activities remain logically unimpaired when information-preserving changes of any kind that theoretically permit unimpairment are made to the base tables.

10. **Integrity independence**. Integrity constraints specific to a particular relational database must be definable in the relational data sublanguage and storable in the catalog, not in the application programs.

11. **Distribution independence**. A relational DBMS has distribution independence.

12. **Nonsubversion rule**. If a relational system has a low-level (single record at a time) language, that low level cannot be used to subvert or bypass the integrity rules and constraints expressed in the higher-level relational language (multiple records at a time).

During the early 1990s, it became popular practice to compile "scorecards" for commercial DBMS products, showing how well they satisfy each of the rules. Unfortunately, the rules are subjective, so the scorecards were usually full of footnotes and qualifications, and they didn't reveal a great deal about the products. Today, the basis of competition for database vendors tends to revolve around performance, features, the availability of development tools, the quality of vendor support, the availability of application programs that support the particular database system, and other issues, rather than conformance to Codd's rules. Nonetheless, they are an important part of the history of the relational model.

Rule 1 is basically the informal definition of a relational database presented at the beginning of this section.

Rule 2 stresses the importance of primary keys for locating data in the database. The table name locates the correct table, the column name finds the correct column, and the primary key value finds the row containing an individual data item of interest. Rule 3 requires support for missing data through NULL values, which are described in Chapter 5.

Rule 4 requires that a relational database be self-describing. In other words, the database must contain certain *system tables* whose columns describe the structure of the database itself. These tables are described in Chapter 16.

Rule 5 mandates using a relational database language, such as SQL, although SQL is not specifically required. The language must be able to support all the central functions of a DBMS—creating a database, retrieving and entering data, implementing database security, and so on.

Rule 6 deals with views, which are *virtual tables* used to give various users of a database different views of its structure. It is one of the most challenging rules to implement in practice, and no commercial product fully satisfies it today. Views and the problems of updating them are described in Chapter 14.

Rule 7 stresses the set-oriented nature of a relational database. It requires that rows be treated as sets in insert, delete, and update operations. The rule is designed to prohibit implementations that support only row-at-a-time, navigational modification of the database.

Rule 8 and Rule 9 insulate the user or application program from the low-level implementation of the database. They specify that specific access or storage techniques used by the DBMS, and even changes to the structure of the tables in the database, should not affect the user's ability to work with the data.

Rule 10 says that the database language should support integrity constraints that restrict the data that can be entered into the database and the database modifications that can be made. This is another rule that is not supported in most commercial DBMS products.

Rule 11 says that the database language must be able to manipulate distributed data located on other computer systems. Distributed data and the challenges of managing it are described in Chapter 23.

Finally, Rule 12 prevents "other paths" into the database that might subvert its relational structure and integrity.

Summary

SQL is based on the relational data model that organizes the data in a database as a collection of tables:

- Each table has a table name that uniquely identifies it.

- Each table has one or more named columns, which are arranged in a specific, left-to-right order.

- Each table has zero or more rows, each containing a single data value in each column. The rows are unordered.

- All data values in a given column have the same data type, and are drawn from a set of legal values called the domain of the column.

Tables are related to one another by the data they contain. The relational data model uses primary keys and foreign keys to represent these relationships among tables:

- A primary key is a column or combination of columns in a table whose value(s) uniquely identify each row of the table. A table has only one primary key.

- A foreign key is a column or combination of columns in a table whose value(s) are a primary key value for some other table. A table can contain more than one foreign key, linking it to one or more other tables.

- A primary key/foreign key combination creates a parent/child relationship between the tables that contain them.

The Complete Reference

Part II

Retrieving Data

Queries are the heart of the SQL language, and many people use SQL as a database query tool. The next five chapters describe SQL queries in depth. Chapter 5 describes the basic SQL language structures that you use to form SQL statements. Chapter 6 discusses simple queries that draw data from a single table of data. Chapter 7 expands the discussion to multitable queries. Queries that summarize data are described in Chapter 8. Finally, Chapter 9 explains the SQL subquery capability that is used to handle complex queries.

The Complete Reference

Chapter 5

SQL Basics

This chapter begins a detailed description of the features of SQL. It describes the basic structure of a SQL statement and the basic elements of the language, such as keywords, data types, and expressions. The way that SQL handles missing data through NULL values is also described. Although these are basic features of SQL, there are some subtle differences in the way they are implemented by various popular SQL products, and in many cases, the SQL products provide significant extensions to the capabilities specified in the ANSI/ISO SQL standard. These differences and extensions are also described in this chapter.

Statements

The main body of the SQL language consists of about 40 statements. The most important and frequently used statements are summarized in Table 5-1. Each statement requests a specific action from the DBMS, such as creating a new table, retrieving data, or inserting new data into the database. All SQL statements have the same basic form, illustrated in Figure 5-1.

Every SQL statement begins with a *verb*, a keyword that describes what the statement does. CREATE, INSERT, DELETE, and COMMIT are typical verbs. The statement continues with one or more *clauses*. A clause may specify the data to be acted on by the statement or provide more detail about what the statement is supposed to do. Every clause also begins with a keyword, such as WHERE, FROM, INTO, and HAVING. Some clauses are

Statement	Description
Data Manipulation	
SELECT	Retrieves data from the database
INSERT	Adds new rows of data to the database
DELETE	Removes rows of data from the database
UPDATE	Modifies existing database data
Data Definition	
CREATE TABLE	Adds a new table to the database
DROP TABLE	Removes a table from the database
ALTER TABLE	Changes the structure of an existing table

Table 5-1.   *Major SQL Statements*

Statement	Description
CREATE VIEW	Adds a new view to the database
DROP VIEW	Removes a view from the database
CREATE INDEX	Builds an index for a column
DROP INDEX	Removes the index for a column
CREATE SCHEMA	Adds a new schema to the database
DROP SCHEMA	Removes a schema from the database
CREATE DOMAIN	Adds a new data value domain
ALTER DOMAIN	Changes a domain definition
DROP DOMAIN	Removes a domain from the database
Access Control	
GRANT	Grants user access privileges
REVOKE	Removes user access privileges
Transaction Control	
COMMIT	Ends the current transaction
ROLLBACK	Aborts the current transaction
SET TRANSACTION	Defines data access characteristics of the current transaction
Programmatic SQL	
DECLARE	Defines a cursor for a query
EXPLAIN	Describes the data access plan for a query
OPEN	Opens a cursor to retrieve query results
FETCH	Retrieves a row of query results
CLOSE	Closes a cursor
PREPARE	Prepares a SQL statement for dynamic execution
EXECUTE	Executes a SQL statement dynamically
DESCRIBE	Describes a prepared query

Table 5-1. *Major SQL Statements* (continued)

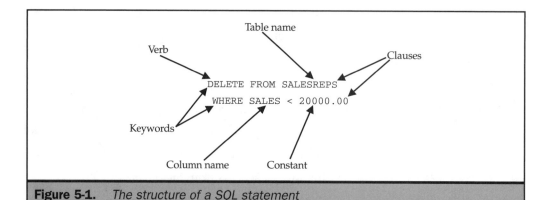

Figure 5-1. *The structure of a SQL statement*

optional; others are required. The specific structure and content vary from one clause to another. Many clauses contain table or column names; some may contain additional keywords, constants, or expressions.

The ANSI/ISO SQL standard specifies the SQL keywords that are used as verbs and in statement clauses. According to the standard, these keywords cannot be used to name database objects, such as tables, columns, and users. Many SQL implementations relax this restriction, but it's generally a good idea to avoid the keywords when you name your tables and columns. Table 5-2 lists the keywords included in the ANSI/ISO SQL2 standard, which roughly tripled the number of keywords reserved by the earlier SQL1 standard.

ABSOLUTE	CROSS	GET	NEXT	SPACE
ACTION	CURRENT	GLOBAL	NO	SQL
ADD	CURRENT_ DATE	GO	NOT	SQLCODE
ALL	CURRENT_ TIME	GOTO	NULL	SQLERROR
ALLOCATE	CURRENT_ TIMESTAMP	GRANT	OCTET_ LENGTH	SQLSTATE
ALTER	CURRENT_ USER	GROUP	OF	SUBSTRING
AND	CURSOR	HAVING	ON	SUM

Table 5-2. *ANSI/ISO SQL2 Keywords*

ANY	DATE	HOUR	ONLY	SYSTEM_ USER
ARE	DAY	IDENTITY	OPEN	TABLE
AS	DEALLOCATE	IMMEDIATE	OPTION	TEMPORARY
ASC	DEC	IN	OR	THEN
ASSERTION	DECIMAL	INDICATOR	ORDER	TIME
AT	DECLARE	INITIALLY	OUTER	TIMESTAMP
AUTHORIZATION	DEFAULT	INNER	OUTPUT	TIMEZONE_ HOUR
AVG	DEFERRABLE	INPUT	OVERLAPS	TIMEZONE_ MINUTE
BEGIN	DEFERRED	INSENSITIVE	PAD	TO
BETWEEN	DELETE	INSERT	PARTIAL	TRAILING
BIT	DESC	INT	POSITION	TRANSACTION
BIT_ LENGTH	DESCRIBE	INTEGER	PRECISION	TRANSLATE
BOTH	DESCRIPTOR	INTERSECT	PREPARE	TRANSLATION
BY	DIAGNOSTICS	INTERVAL	PRESERVE	TRIM
CASCADE	DISCONNECT	INTO	PRIMARY	TRUE
CASCADED	DISTINCT	IS	PRIOR	UNION
CASE	DOMAIN	ISOLATION	PRIVILEGES	UNIQUE
CAST	DOUBLE	JOIN	PROCEDURE	UNKNOWN
CATALOG	DROP	KEY	PUBLIC	UPDATE
CHAR	ELSE	LANGUAGE	READ	UPPER
CHARACTER	END	LAST	REAL	USAGE
CHAR_ LENGTH	END- EXEC	LEADING	REFERENCES	USER
CHARACTER_ LENGTH	ESCAPE	LEFT	RELATIVE	USING
CHECK	EXCEPT	LEVEL	RESTRICT	VALUE

Table 5-2. *ANSI/ISO SQL2 Keywords* (continued)

CLOSE	EXCEPTION	LIKE	REVOKE	VALUES
COALESCE	EXEC	LOCAL	RIGHT	VARCHAR
COLLATE	EXECUTE	LOWER	ROLLBACK	VARYING
COLLATION	EXISTS	MATCH	ROWS	VIEW
COLUMN	EXTERNAL	MAX	SCHEMA	WHEN
COMMIT	EXTRACT	MIN	SCROLL	WHENEVER
CONNECT	FALSE	MINUTE	SECOND	WHERE
CONNECTION	FETCH	MODULE	SECTION	WITH
CONSTRAINT	FIRST	MONTH	SELECT	WORK
CONSTRAINTS	FLOAT	NAMES	SESSION	WRITE
CONTINUE	FOR	NATIONAL	SESSION_ USER	YEAR
CONVERT	FOREIGN	NATURAL	SET	ZONE
CORRESPONDING	FOUND	NCHAR	SIZE	
COUNT	FROM	NULLIF	SMALLINT	
CREATE	FULL	NUMERIC	SOME	

Table 5-2. *ANSI/ISO SQL2 Keywords* (continued)

The SQL2 standard also includes a list of potential keywords that are candidates for future revisions of the standard. These keywords are listed in Table 5-3.

Throughout this book, the acceptable forms of a SQL statement are illustrated by a syntax diagram, such as the one shown in Figure 5-2. A valid SQL statement or clause is constructed by "following the line" through the syntax diagram to the dot that marks the end of the diagram. Keywords in the syntax diagram and in the examples (such as DELETE and FROM in Figure 5-2) are always shown in UPPERCASE, but almost all SQL implementations accept both uppercase and lowercase keywords, and it's often more convenient to actually type them in lowercase.

Variable items in a SQL statement (such as the table name and search condition in Figure 5-2) are shown in *lowercase italics.* It's up to you to specify the appropriate item each time the statement is used. Optional clauses and keywords, such as the WHERE

AFTER	EQUALS	OLD	RETURN	TEST
ALIAS	GENERAL	OPERATION	RETURNS	THERE
ASYNC	IF	OPERATORS	ROLE	TRIGGER
BEFORE	IGNORE	OTHERS	ROUTINE	TYPE
BOOLEAN	LEAVE	PARAMETERS	ROW	UNDER
BREADTH	LESS	PENDANT	SAVEPOINT	VARIABLE
COMPLETION	LIMIT	PREORDER	SEARCH	VIRTUAL
CALL	LOOP	PRIVATE	SENSITIVE	VISIBLE
CYCLE	MODIFY	PROTECTED	SEQUENCE	WAIT
DATA	NEW	RECURSIVE	SIGNAL	WHILE
DEPTH	NONE	REF	SIMILAR	WITHOUT
DICTIONARY	OBJECT	REFERENCING	SQLEXCEPTION	
EACH	OFF	REPLACE	SQLWARNING	
ELSEIF	OID	RESIGNAL	STRUCTURE	

Table 5-3. *ANSI/ISO SQL2 Potential Keywords*

clause in Figure 5-2, are indicated by alternate paths through the syntax diagram. When a choice of optional keywords is offered, the default choice (that is, the behavior of the statement if no keyword is specified) is UNDERLINED.

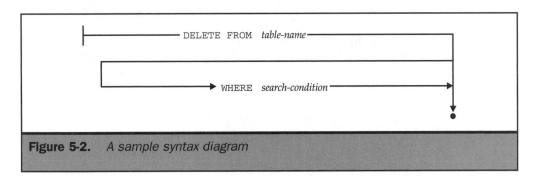

Figure 5-2. *A sample syntax diagram*

Names

The objects in a SQL-based database are identified by assigning them unique names. Names are used in SQL statements to identify the database object on which the statement should act. The most fundamental named objects in a relational database are table names (which identify tables), column names (which identify columns), and user names (which identify users of the database); conventions for naming these objects were specified in the original SQL1 standard. The ANSI/ISO SQL2 standard significantly expanded the list of named entities, to include schemas (collections of tables), constraints (restrictions on the contents of tables and their relationships), domains (sets of legal values that may be assigned to a column), and several other types of objects. Many SQL implementations support additional named objects, such as stored procedures, primary key/foreign key relationships, data entry forms, and data replication schemes.

The original ANSI/ISO standard specified that SQL names must contain 1 to 18 characters, must begin with a letter, and may not contain any spaces or special punctuation characters. The SQL2 standard increased the maximum to 128 characters. In practice, the names supported by SQL-based DBMS products vary significantly. It's common to see tighter restrictions on names that are connected to other software outside of the database (such as user names, which may correspond to login names used by an operating system), and looser restrictions on names that are private to the database. The various products also differ in the special characters they permit in table names. For portability, it's best to keep names relatively short and to avoid the use of special characters.

Table Names

When you specify a table name in a SQL statement, SQL assumes that you are referring to one of your own tables (that is, a table that you created). Usually, you will want to choose table names that are short but descriptive. The table names in the sample database (ORDERS, CUSTOMERS, OFFICES, SALESREPS) are good examples. In a personal or departmental database, the choice of table names is usually up to the database developer or designer.

In a larger, shared-use corporate database, there may be corporate standards for naming tables, to insure that table names do not conflict. In addition, most DBMS brands allow different users to create tables with the same name (that is, both Joe and Sam can create a table named BIRTHDAYS). The DBMS uses the appropriate table, depending on which user is requesting data. With the proper permission, you can also refer to tables owned by other users, by using a *qualified table name*. A qualified table name specifies both the name of the table's owner and the name of the table, separated by a period (.). For example, Joe could access the BIRTHDAYS table owned by Sam by using the qualified table name:

```
SAM.BIRTHDAYS
```

A qualified table name generally can be used in a SQL statement wherever a table name can appear.

The ANSI/ISO SQL2 standard generalizes the notion of a qualified table name even further. It allows you to create a named collection of tables, called a *schema*. You can refer to a table in a specific schema using a qualified table name. For example, the BIRTHDAYS table in the EMPLOYEEINFO schema would be referenced as:

```
EMPLOYEEINFO.BIRTHDAYS
```

Chapter 13 provides more information about schemas, users, and other aspects of SQL database structure.

Column Names

When you specify a column name in a SQL statement, SQL can normally determine from the context which column you intend. However, if the statement involves two columns with the same name from two different tables, you must use a *qualified column name* to unambiguously identify the column you intend. A qualified column name specifies both the name of the table containing the column and the name of the column, separated by a period (.). For example, the column named SALES in the SALESREPS table has the qualified column name:

```
SALESREPS.SALES
```

If the column comes from a table owned by another user, a qualified table name is used in the qualified column name. For example, the BIRTHDATE column in the BIRTHDAYS table owned by the user SAM is specified by the fully qualified column name:

```
SAM.BIRTHDAYS.BIRTH_DATE
```

Qualified column names can generally be used in a SQL statement wherever a simple (unqualified) column name can appear; exceptions are noted in the descriptions of the individual SQL statements.

Data Types

The ANSI/ISO SQL standard specifies the various types of data that can be stored in a SQL-based database and manipulated by the SQL language. The original SQL1 standard specified only a minimal set of data types. The SQL2 standard expanded this list to include variable-length character strings, date and time data, bit strings, and other types. Today's commercial DBMS products can process a rich variety of different kinds of data, and there is considerable diversity in the particular data types supported across different DBMS brands. Typical data types include the following:

- **Integers.** Columns holding this type of data typically store counts, quantities, ages, and so on. Integer columns are also frequently used to contain ID numbers, such as customer, employee, and order numbers.

- **Decimal numbers.** Columns with this data type store numbers that have fractional parts and must be calculated exactly, such as rates and percentages. They are also frequently used to store money amounts.

- **Floating point numbers.** Columns with this data type are used to store scientific numbers that can be calculated approximately, such as weights and distances. Floating point numbers can represent a larger range of values than decimal numbers but can produce round-off errors in computations.

- **Fixed-length character strings.** Columns holding this type of data typically store names of people and companies, addresses, descriptions, and so on.

- **Variable-length character strings.** This data type allows a column to store character strings that vary in length from row to row, up to some maximum length. (The SQL1 standard permitted only fixed-length character strings, which are easier for the DBMS to process but can waste considerable space.)

- **Money amounts.** Many SQL products support a MONEY or CURRENCY type, which is usually stored as a decimal or floating point number. Having a distinct money type allows the DBMS to properly format money amounts when they are displayed.

- **Dates and times.** Support for date/time values is also common in SQL products, although the details can vary considerably from one product to another. Various combinations of dates, times, timestamps, time intervals, and date/time arithmetic are generally supported. The SQL2 standard includes an elaborate specification for DATE, TIME, TIMESTAMP, and INTERVAL data types, including support for time zones and time precision (for example, tenths or hundredths of seconds).

- **Boolean data.** Some SQL products, such as Informix Dynamic Server, support logical (TRUE or FALSE) values as an explicit type, and some permit logical operations (comparison, AND/OR, and so on) on the stored data within SQL statements.

- **Long text.** Several SQL-based databases support columns that store long text strings (typically up to 32,000 or 65,000 characters, and in some cases even larger). This allows the database to store entire documents, product descriptions, technical papers, resumés, and similar unstructured text data. The DBMS usually restricts the use of these columns in interactive queries and searches.

- **Unstructured byte streams.** Several DBMS products allow unstructured, variable-length sequences of bytes to be stored and retrieved. Columns containing this data are used to store compressed video images, executable code, and other types of unstructured data. SQL Server's IMAGE data type, for example, can store a stream of up to 2 billion bytes of data.

■ **Non-Roman characters.** As databases grow to support global applications, DBMS vendors have added support for fixed-length and variable-length strings of 16-bit characters used to represent Kanji and other Asian and Arabic characters. While most modern databases support storing and retrieving such characters (often using the UNICODE convention for representing them), support for searching and sorting on these GRAPHIC and VARGRAPHIC types varies widely.

Table 5-4 lists the data types specified in the ANSI/ISO SQL standard.

Data Type	Description
CHAR (*len*) CHARACTER (*len*)	Fixed-length character strings
VARCHAR (*len*) CHAR VARYING (*len*) CHARACTER VARYING (*len*)	Variable-length character strings*
NCHAR (*len*) NATIONAL CHAR (*len*) NATIONAL CHARACTER (*len*)	Fixed-length national character strings*
NCHAR VARYING (*len*) NATIONAL CHAR VARYING (*len*) NATIONAL CHARACTER VARYING (*len*)	Variable-length national character strings*
INTEGER INT	Integer numbers
SMALLINT	Small integer numbers
BIT (*len*)	Fixed-length bit strings*
BIT VARYING (*len*)	Variable-length bit strings*
NUMERIC (*precision, scale*) DECIMAL (*precision, scale*) DEC (*precision, scale*)	Decimal numbers
FLOAT (*precision*)	Floating point numbers

Table 5-4. *ANSI/ISO SQL Data Types*

Data Type	Description
REAL	Low-precision floating point numbers
DOUBLE PRECISION	High-precision floating point numbers
DATE	Calendar dates*
TIME (*precision*)	Clock times*
TIMESTAMP (*precision*)	Dates and times*
INTERVAL	Time intervals*
*new data type in SQL2	

Table 5-4.   *ANSI/ISO SQL Data Types* (continued)

The differences between the data types offered in various SQL implementations is one of the practical barriers to the portability of SQL-based applications. These differences have come about as a result of innovation as relational databases have evolved to include a broader range of capabilities. This has been the typical pattern:

- A DBMS vendor adds a new data type that provides useful new capabilities for a certain group of users.

- Other DBMS vendors add the same or similar data types, adding their own innovations to differentiate their products from the others.

- Over several years, the popularity of the data type grows, and it becomes a part of the "mainstream" set of data types supported by most SQL implementations.

- The standards bodies become involved to try to standardize the new data type and eliminate arbitrary differences between the vendor implementations. The more well-entrenched the data type has become, the more difficult the set of compromises faced by the standards group. Usually, this results in an addition to the standard that does not exactly match *any* of the current implementations.

- DBMS vendors slowly add support for the new standardized data type as an option to their systems, but because they have a large installed base that is using the older (now "proprietary") version of the data type, they must maintain support for this form of the data type as well.

- Over a very long period of time (typically several major releases of the DBMS product), users migrate to the new, standardized form of the data type, and the DBMS vendor can begin the process of obsoleting the proprietary version.

Date/time data provides an excellent example of this phenomenon and the data type variations it creates. DB2 offered early date/time support, with three different date/time data types:

- **DATE**. Stores a date like June 30, 1991
- **TIME**. Stores a time of day like 12:30 P.M.
- **TIMESTAMP**. A specific instant in history, with a precision down to the nanosecond

Specific dates and times can be specified as string constants, and date arithmetic is supported. Here is an example of a valid query using DB2 dates, assuming that the HIREDATE column contains DATE data:

```
SELECT NAME, HIRE_DATE
  FROM SALESREPS
 WHERE HIRE_DATE >= '05/30/1989' + 15 DAYS
```

SQL Server was introduced with a single date/time data type, called DATETIME, which closely resembles the DB2 TIMESTAMP data type. If HIRE_DATE contained DATETIME data, SQL Server could accept this version of the query (without the date arithmetic):

```
SELECT NAME, HIRE_DATE
  FROM SALESREPS
 WHERE HIRE_DATE >= '06/14/1989'
```

Since no specific time on June 14, 1989, is specified in the query, SQL Server defaults to midnight on that date. The SQL Server query thus *really* means:

```
SELECT NAME, HIRE_DATE
  FROM SALESREPS
 WHERE HIRE_DATE >= '06/14/1989 12:00AM'
```

If a salesperson's hire date were stored in the database as noon on June 14, 1989, the salesperson would not be included in the SQL Server query results but would have been included in the DB2 results (because only the date would be stored). SQL Server also supports date arithmetic through a set of built-in functions. Thus, the DB2-style query can also be specified in this way:

```
SELECT NAME, HIRE_DATE
  FROM SALESREPS
 WHERE HIRE_DATE >= DATEADD(DAY, 15, '05/30/1989')
```

which is considerably different from the DB2 syntax.

Oracle also supports date/time data, with a single data type called DATE. Like SQL Server's DATETIME type, an Oracle DATE is, in fact, a timestamp. Also like SQL Server, the time part of an Oracle DATE value defaults to midnight if no time is explicitly specified. The default Oracle date format is different from the DB2 and SQL Server formats, so the Oracle version of the query becomes:

```
SELECT NAME, HIRE_DATE
  FROM SALESREPS
 WHERE HIRE_DATE >= '14-JUN-89'
```

Oracle also supports limited date arithmetic, so the DB2-style query can also be specified but without the DAYS keyword:

```
SELECT NAME, HIRE_DATE
  FROM SALESREPS
 WHERE HIRE_DATE >= '30-MAY-89' + 15
```

Finally, the ANSI/ISO SQL2 standard added support for date/time data with a set of data types based on, but not identical to, the DB2 types. In addition to the DATE, TIME, and TIMESTAMP data types, the standard specifies an INTERVAL data type, which can be used to store a time interval (for example, a timespan measured in days, or a duration measured in hours, minutes, and seconds). The standard also provides a very elaborate and complex method for dealing with date/time arithmetic, specifying the precision of intervals, adjusting for time zone differences, and so on.

As these examples illustrate, the subtle differences in data types among various SQL products lead to some significant differences in SQL statement syntax. They can even cause the same SQL query to produce slightly different results on different database management systems. The widely praised portability of SQL is thus true but only at a general level. An application can be moved from one SQL database to another, and it can be highly portable if it uses only the most mainstream, basic SQL capabilities. However, the subtle variations in SQL implementations mean that data types and SQL statements must almost always be adjusted somewhat if they are to be moved across DBMS brands. The more complex the application, the more likely it is to become dependent on DBMS-specific features and nuances, and the less portable it will become.

Constants

In some SQL statements a numeric, character, or date data value must be expressed in text form. For example, in this INSERT statement, which adds a salesperson to the database:

```
INSERT INTO SALESREPS (EMPL_NUM, NAME, QUOTA, HIRE_DATE, SALES)
    VALUES (115, 'Dennis Irving', 175000.00, '21-JUN-90', 0.00)
```

the value for each column in the newly inserted row is specified in the VALUES clause. Constant data values are also used in expressions, such as in this SELECT statement:

```
SELECT CITY
  FROM OFFICES
 WHERE TARGET > (1.1 * SALES) + 10000.00
```

The ANSI/ISO SQL standard specifies the format of numeric and string constants, or *literals*, which represent specific data values. These conventions are followed by most SQL implementations.

Numeric Constants

Integer and decimal constants (also called *exact numeric literals*) are written as ordinary decimal numbers in SQL statements, with an optional leading plus or minus sign.

```
21   -375   2000.00   +497500.8778
```

You must not put a comma between the digits of a numeric constant, and not all SQL dialects allow the leading plus sign, so it's best to avoid it. For money data, most SQL implementations simply use integer or decimal constants, although some allow the constant to be specified with a currency symbol:

```
$0.75   $5000.00   $-567.89
```

Floating point constants (also called *approximate numeric literals*) are specified using the *E* notation commonly found in programming languages such as C and FORTRAN. Here are some valid SQL floating point constants:

```
1.5E3   -3.14159E1   2.5E-7   0.783926E21
```

The *E* is read "times ten to the power of," so the first constant becomes "1.5 times ten to the third power," or 1500.

String Constants

The ANSI/ISO standard specifies that SQL constants for character data be enclosed in single quotes ('...'), as in these examples:

```
'Jones, John J.'   'New York'   'Western'
```

If a single quote is to be included in the constant text, it is written within the constant as two consecutive single quote characters. Thus, this constant value:

```
'I can''t'
```

becomes the seven-character string "I can't".

Some SQL implementations, such as SQL Server and Informix, accept string constants enclosed in double quotes (". . ."):

```
"Jones, John J."  "New York"  "Western"
```

Unfortunately, the double quotes can pose portability problems with other SQL products. The SQL2 standard provides the additional capability to specify string constants from a specific national character set (for example, French or German) or from a user-defined character set. The user-defined character set capabilities have typically not been implemented in mainstream SQL products.

Date and Time Constants

In SQL products that support date/time data, constant values for dates, times, and time intervals are specified as string constants. The format of these constants varies from one DBMS to the next. Even more variation is introduced by the differences in the way dates and times are written in different countries.

DB2 supports several different international formats for date, time, and timestamp constants, as shown in Table 5-5. The choice of format is made when the DBMS is installed. DB2 also supports durations specified as special constants, as in this example:

```
HIRE_DATE + 30 DAYS
```

Format Name	Date Format	Date Example	Time Format	Time Example
American	mm/dd/yyyy	5/19/1960	hh:mm am/pm	2:18 PM
European	dd.mm.yyyy	19.5.1960	hh.mm.ss	14.18.08
Japanese	yyyy-mm-dd	1960-5-19	hh:mm:ss	14:18:08
ISO	yyyy-mm-dd	1960-5-19	hh.mm.ss	14.18.08

Table 5-5. *IBM SQL Date and Time Formats*

Format Name	Date Format	Date Example	Time Format	Time Example
TIMESTAMP format	yyyy-mm-dd-hh.mm.ss.nnn nnn			
TIMESTAMP example	1960-05-19-14. 18.08.048632			

Table 5-5. *IBM SQL Date and Time Formats* (continued)

Note that a duration can't be stored in the database, however, because DB2 doesn't have an explicit DURATION data type.

SQL Server also supports date/time data and accepts a variety of different formats for date and time constants. The DBMS automatically accepts all of the alternate formats, and you can intermix them if you like. Here are some examples of legal SQL Server date constants:

```
March 15, 1990   Mar 15 1990   3/15/1990   3-15-90   1990 MAR 15
```

and here are some legal time constants:

```
15:30:25   3:30:25 PM   3:30:25 pm   3 PM
```

Oracle dates and times are also written as string constants, using this format:

```
15-MAR-90
```

You can also use Oracle's built-in TO_DATE() function to convert date constants written in other formats, as in this example:

```
SELECT NAME, AGE
  FROM SALESREPS
 WHERE HIRE_DATE = TO_DATE('JUN 14 1989', 'MON DD YYYY')
```

The SQL2 standard specifies a format for date and time constants, based on the ISO format in Table 5-5, except that time constants are written with colons instead of periods separating the hours, minutes, and seconds.

Symbolic Constants

In addition to user-supplied constants, the SQL language includes special symbolic constants that return data values maintained by the DBMS itself. For example, in some DBMS brands, the symbolic constant CURRENT_DATE yields the value of the current date and can be used in queries such as the following, which lists the salespeople whose hire date is still in the future:

```
SELECT NAME, HIRE_DATE
  FROM SALESREPS
 WHERE HIRE_DATE > CURRENT_DATE
```

The SQL1 standard specified only a single symbolic constant (the USER constant described in Chapter 15), but most SQL products provide many more. Generally, a symbolic constant can appear in a SQL statement anywhere that an ordinary constant of the same data type could appear. The SQL2 standard adopted the most useful symbolic constants from current SQL implementations and provides for CURRENT_DATE, CURRENT_TIME, and CURRENT_TIMESTAMP (note the underscores) as well as USER, SESSION_USER, and SYSTEM_USER.

Some SQL products, including SQL Server, provide access to system values through built-in functions rather than symbolic constants. The SQL Server version of the preceding query is:

```
SELECT NAME, HIRE_DATE
  FROM SALESREPS
 WHERE HIRE_DATE > GETDATE()
```

Built-in functions are described later in this chapter, in the section "Built-In Functions."

Expressions

Expressions are used in the SQL language to calculate values that are retrieved from a database and to calculate values used in searching the database. For example, this query calculates the sales of each office as a percentage of its target:

```
SELECT CITY, TARGET, SALES, (SALES/TARGET) * 100
  FROM OFFICES
```

and this query lists the offices whose sales are more than $50,000 over target:

```
SELECT CITY
  FROM OFFICES
WHERE SALES > TARGET + 50000.00
```

The ANSI/ISO SQL standard specifies four arithmetic operations that can be used in expressions: addition (X + Y), subtraction (X − Y), multiplication (X * Y), and division (X / Y). Parentheses can also be used to form more complicated expressions, like this one:

```
(SALES * 1.05) - (TARGET * .95)
```

Strictly speaking, the parentheses are not required in this query because the ANSI/ISO standard specifies that multiplication and division have a higher precedence than addition and subtraction. However, you should always use parentheses to make your expressions unambiguous because different SQL dialects may use different rules. The parentheses also increase the readability of the statement and make programmatic SQL statements easier to maintain.

The ANSI/ISO standard also specifies automatic data type conversion from integers to decimal numbers, and from decimal numbers to floating point numbers, as required. You can thus mix these data types in a numeric expression. Many SQL implementations support other operators and allow operations on character and date data. DB2, for example, supports a string concatenation operator, written as two consecutive vertical bar characters (| |). If two columns named FIRST_NAME and LAST_NAME contain the values "Jim" and "Jackson", then this DB2 expression:

```
('Mr./Mrs. ' || FIRST_NAME || ' ' || LAST_NAME)
```

produces the string "Mr./Mrs. Jim Jackson". As already mentioned, DB2 also supports addition and subtraction of DATE, TIME, and TIMESTAMP data, for occasions when those operations make sense. This capability has been included in the SQL2 standard.

Built-In Functions

Although the SQL1 standard doesn't specify them, most SQL implementations include a number of useful *built-in functions*. These facilities often provide data type conversion facilities. For example, DB2's built-in MONTH() and YEAR() functions take a DATE or TIMESTAMP value as their input and return an integer that is the month or year portion of the value. This query lists the name and month of hire for each salesperson in the sample database:

```
SELECT NAME, MONTH(HIRE_DATE)
  FROM SALESREPS
```

and this one lists all salespeople hired in 1988:

```
SELECT NAME, MONTH(HIRE_DATE)
  FROM SALESREPS
 WHERE YEAR(HIRE_DATE) = 1988
```

Built-in functions are also often used for data reformatting. Oracle's built-in TO_CHAR() function, for example, takes a DATE data type and a format specification as its arguments and returns a string containing a formatted version of the date. In the results produced by this query:

```
SELECT NAME, TO_CHAR(HIRE_DATE,'DAY MONTH DD, YYYY')
  FROM SALESREPS
```

the hire dates will all have the format "Wednesday June 14, 1989" because of the built-in function.

In general, a built-in function can be specified in a SQL expression anywhere that a constant of the same data type can be specified. The built-in functions supported by popular SQL dialects are too numerous to list here. The IBM SQL dialects include about two dozen built-in functions, Oracle supports a different set of about two dozen built-in functions, and SQL Server has several dozen. The SQL2 standard incorporated the most useful built-in functions from these implementations, in many cases with slightly different syntax. These functions are summarized in Table 5-6.

Function	Returns
BIT_LENGTH (*string*)	The number of bits in a bit string
CAST (*value* AS *data_type*)	The value, converted to the specified data type (e.g., a date converted to a character string)
CHAR_LENGTH (*string*)	The length of a character string
CONVERT (*string* USING *conv*)	A string converted as specified by a named conversion function
CURRENT_DATE	The current date
CURRENT_TIME (*precision*)	The current time, with the specified *precision*

Table 5-6. *Built-In SQL2 Functions*

Function	Returns
CURRENT_TIMESTAMP (*precision*)	The current date and time, with the specified *precision*
EXTRACT (*part* FROM *source*)	The specified part (DAY, HOUR, etc.) from a DATETIME value
LOWER (*string*)	A string converted to all lowercase letters
OCTET_LENGTH (*string*)	The number of 8-bit bytes in a character string
POSITION (*target* IN *source*)	The position where the *target* string appears within the *source* string
SUBSTRING (*source* FROM *n* FOR *len*)	A portion of the *source* string, beginning at the *n*-th character, for a length of *len*
TRANSLATE (*string* USING *trans*)	A string translated as specified by a named translation function
TRIM (BOTH *char* FROM *string*)	A string with both leading and trailing occurrences of *char* trimmed off
TRIM (LEADING *char* FROM *string*)	A string with any leading occurrences of *char* trimmed off
TRIM (TRAILING *char* FROM *string*)	A string with any trailing occurrences of *char* trimmed off
UPPER (*string*)	A string converted to all uppercase letters

Table 5-6. *Built-In SQL2 Functions* (continued)

Missing Data (NULL Values)

Because a database is usually a model of a real-world situation, certain pieces of data are inevitably missing, unknown, or don't apply. In the sample database, for example, the QUOTA column in the SALESREPS table contains the sales goal for each salesperson. However, the newest salesperson has not yet been assigned a quota; this data is missing for that row of the table. You might be tempted to put a zero in the column for this salesperson, but that would not be an accurate reflection of the situation. The salesperson does not have a zero quota; the quota is just "not yet known."

Similarly, the MANAGER column in the SALESREPS table contains the employee number of each salesperson's manager. But Sam Clark, the Vice President of Sales, has no manager in the sales organization. This column does not apply to Sam. Again, you might think about entering a zero, or a 9999 in the column, but neither of these values would really be the employee number of Sam's boss. No data value is applicable to this row.

SQL supports missing, unknown, or inapplicable data explicitly, through the concept of a *null value*. A null value is an *indicator* that tells SQL (and the user) that the data is missing or not applicable. As a convenience, a missing piece of data is often said to have the value NULL. But the NULL value is not a real data value like 0, 473.83, or "Sam Clark." Instead, it's a signal, or a reminder, that the data value is missing or unknown. Figure 5-3 shows the contents of the SALESREPS table. Note that the QUOTA and REP_OFFICE values for Tom Snyder's row and the MANAGER value for Sam Clark's row of the table all contain NULL values.

In many situations, NULL values require special handling by the DBMS. For example, if the user requests the sum of the QUOTA column, how should the DBMS handle the missing data when computing the sum? The answer is given by a set of special rules that govern NULL value handling in various SQL statements and clauses. Because of these rules, some leading database authorities feel strongly that NULL values should not be used. Others, including Dr. Codd, have advocated the use of multiple NULL values, with distinct indicators for "unknown" and "not applicable" data.

Regardless of the academic debates, NULL values are a well-entrenched part of the ANSI/ISO SQL standard and are supported in virtually all commercial SQL products. They also play an important, practical role in production SQL databases. The special rules that apply to NULL values (and the cases where NULL values are handled inconsistently by various SQL products) are pointed out throughout this book.

SALESREPS Table

EMPL_NUM	NAME	AGE	REP_OFFICE	TITLE	HIRE_DATE	MANAGER	QUOTA	SALES
105	Bill Adams	37	13	Sales Rep	12-FEB-88	104	$350,000.00	$367,911.00
109	Mary Jones	31	11	Sales Rep	12-OCT-89	106	$300,000.00	$392,725.00
102	Sue Smith	48	21	Sales Rep	10-DEC-86	108	$350,000.00	$474,050.00
106	Sam Clark	52	11	VP Sales	14-JUN-88	NULL	$275,000.00	$299,912.00
104	Bob Smith	33	12	Sales Mgr	19-MAY-87	106	$200,000.00	$142,594.00
101	Dan Roberts	45	12	Sales Rep	20-OCT-86	104	$300,000.00	$305,673.00
110	Tom Snyder	41	NULL	Sales Rep	13-JAN-90	101	NULL	$75,985.00
108	Larry Fitch	62	21	Sales Mgr	12-OCT-89	106	$350,000.00	$361,865.00
103	Paul Cruz	29	12	Sales Rep	14-NOV-88	108	$275,000.00	$286,775.00
107	Nancy Angelli	49	22	Sales Rep	14-NOV-88	108	$300,000.00	$186,042.00

Value unknown

Value not applicable

Value unknown

Figure 5-3. *NULL values in the SALESREPS table*

Summary

This chapter described the basic elements of the SQL language. The basic structure of SQL can be summarized as follows:

- The SQL language that is in common use includes about 30 statements, each consisting of a verb and one or more clauses. Each statement performs a single, specific function.

- SQL-based databases can store various types of data, including text, integers, decimal numbers, floating point numbers, and usually many more vendor-specific data types.

- SQL statements can include expressions that combine column names, constants, and built-in functions, using arithmetic and other vendor-specific operators.

- Variations in data types, constants, and built-in functions make portability of SQL statements more difficult than it may seem at first.

- NULL values provide a systematic way of handling missing or inapplicable data in the SQL language.

RETRIEVING DATA

The Complete Reference

Chapter 6

Simple Queries

In many ways, queries are the heart of the SQL language. The SELECT statement, which is used to express SQL queries, is the most powerful and complex of the SQL statements. Despite the many options afforded by the SELECT statement, it's possible to start simply and then work up to more complex queries. This chapter discusses the simplest SQL queries—those that retrieve data from a single table in the database.

The SELECT Statement

The SELECT statement retrieves data from a database and returns it to you in the form of query results. You have already seen many examples of the SELECT statement in the quick tour presented in Chapter 2. Here are several more sample queries that retrieve information about sales offices:

List the sales offices with their targets and actual sales.

```
SELECT CITY, TARGET, SALES
   FROM OFFICES

CITY               TARGET         SALES
-----------    ------------   ------------
Denver         $300,000.00    $186,042.00
New York       $575,000.00    $692,637.00
Chicago        $800,000.00    $735,042.00
Atlanta        $350,000.00    $367,911.00
Los Angeles    $725,000.00    $835,915.00
```

List the Eastern region sales offices with their targets and sales.

```
SELECT CITY, TARGET, SALES
   FROM OFFICES
  WHERE REGION = 'Eastern'

CITY               TARGET         SALES
-----------    ------------   ------------
New York       $575,000.00    $692,637.00
Chicago        $800,000.00    $735,042.00
Atlanta        $350,000.00    $367,911.00
```

List Eastern region sales offices whose sales exceed their targets, sorted in alphabetical order by city.

```
SELECT CITY, TARGET, SALES
  FROM OFFICES
 WHERE REGION = 'Eastern'
   AND SALES > TARGET
 ORDER BY CITY

CITY                TARGET          SALES
------------   ------------   ------------
Atlanta        $350,000.00    $367,911.00
New York       $575,000.00    $692,637.00
```

What are the average target and sales for Eastern region offices?

```
SELECT AVG(TARGET), AVG(SALES)
  FROM OFFICES
 WHERE REGION = 'Eastern'

 AVG(TARGET)    AVG(SALES)
------------   ------------
 $575,000.00    $598,530.00
```

For simple queries, the English language request and the SQL SELECT statement are very similar. When the requests become more complex, more features of the SELECT statement must be used to specify the query precisely.

Figure 6-1 shows the full form of the SELECT statement, which consists of six clauses. The SELECT and FROM clauses of the statement are required. The remaining four clauses are optional. You include them in a SELECT statement only when you want to use the functions they provide. The following list summarizes the function of each clause:

- The SELECT clause lists the data items to be retrieved by the SELECT statement. The items may be columns from the database, or columns to be calculated by SQL as it performs the query. The SELECT clause is described in the next section.

- The FROM clause lists the tables that contain the data to be retrieved by the query. Queries that draw their data from a single table are described in this chapter. More complex queries that combine data from two or more tables are discussed in Chapter 7.

- The WHERE clause tells SQL to include only certain rows of data in the query results. A *search condition* is used to specify the desired rows. The basic uses of the WHERE clause are described in the "Row Selection (WHERE Clause)" section later in this chapter. Those that involve subqueries are discussed in Chapter 9.

■ The GROUP BY clause specifies a summary query. Instead of producing one row of query results for each row of data in the database, a summary query groups together similar rows and then produces one summary row of query results for each group. Summary queries are described in Chapter 8.

■ The HAVING clause tells SQL to include only certain groups produced by the GROUP BY clause in the query results. Like the WHERE clause, it uses a search condition to specify the desired groups. The HAVING clause is described in Chapter 8.

■ The ORDER BY clause sorts the query results based on the data in one or more columns. If it is omitted, the query results are not sorted. The ORDER BY clause is described in the "Sorting Query Results (ORDER BY Clause)" section later in this chapter.

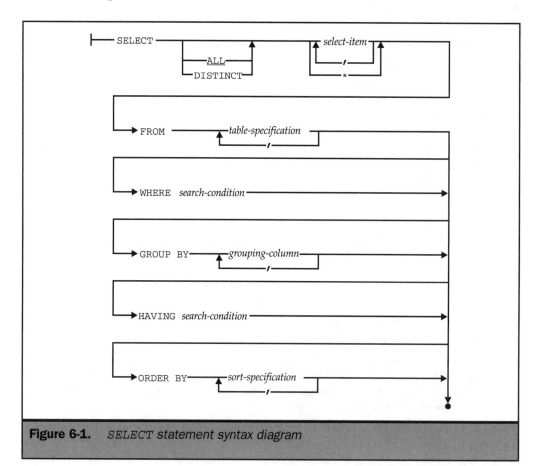

Figure 6-1. *SELECT statement syntax diagram*

The SELECT Clause

The SELECT clause that begins each SELECT statement specifies the data items to be retrieved by the query. The items are usually specified by a *select list*, a list of *select items* separated by commas. Each select item in the list generates a single column of query results, in left-to-right order. A select item can be one of the following:

- A *column name*, identifying a column from the table(s) named in the FROM clause. When a column name appears as a select item, SQL simply takes the value of that column from each row of the database table and places it in the corresponding row of query results.

- A *constant*, specifying that the same constant value is to appear in every row of the query results.

- A *SQL expression*, indicating that SQL must calculate the value to be placed into the query results, in the style specified by the expression.

Each type of select item is described later in this chapter.

The FROM Clause

The FROM clause consists of the keyword FROM, followed by a list of table specifications separated by commas. Each table specification identifies a table containing data to be retrieved by the query. These tables are called the *source tables* of the query (and of the SELECT statement) because they are the source of all of the data in the query results. All of the queries in this chapter have a single source table, and every FROM clause contains a single table name.

Query Results

The result of a SQL query is always a table of data, just like the tables in the database. If you type a SELECT statement using interactive SQL, the DBMS displays the query results in tabular form on your computer screen. If a program sends a query to the DBMS using programmatic SQL, the table of query results is returned to the program. In either case, the query results always have the same tabular, row/column format as the actual tables in the database, as shown in Figure 6-2. Usually the query results will be a table with several columns and several rows. For example, this query produces a table of three columns (because it asks for three items of data) and ten rows (because there are ten salespeople):

List the names, offices, and hire dates of all salespeople.

```
SELECT NAME, REP_OFFICE, HIRE_DATE
  FROM SALESREPS
```

```
NAME            REP_OFFICE HIRE_DATE
-------------- ----------- ----------
Bill Adams              13 12-FEB-88
Mary Jones              11 12-OCT-89
Sue Smith               21 10-DEC-86
Sam Clark               11 14-JUN-88
Bob Smith               12 19-MAY-87
Dan Roberts             12 20-OCT-86
Tom Snyder            NULL 13-JAN-90
Larry Fitch             21 12-OCT-89
Paul Cruz               12 01-MAR-87
Nancy Angelli           22 14-NOV-88
```

In contrast, the following query produces a single row because only one salesperson has the requested employee number. Even though this single row of query results looks less "tabular" than the multirow results, SQL still considers it to be a table of three columns and one row.

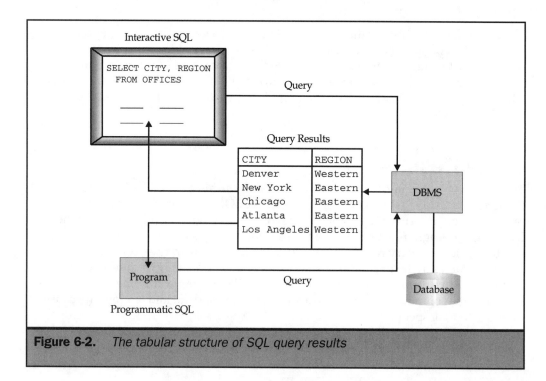

Figure 6-2.   *The tabular structure of SQL query results*

What are the name, quota, and sales of employee number 107?

```
SELECT NAME, QUOTA, SALES
  FROM SALESREPS
 WHERE EMPL_NUM = 107

NAME                  QUOTA        SALES
-------------    ------------  ------------
Nancy Angelli    $300,000.00  $186,042.00
```

In some cases the query results can be a single value, as in the following example:

What are the average sales of our salespeople?

```
SELECT AVG(SALES)
  FROM SALESREPS

 AVG(SALES)
-----------
 $289,353.20
```

These query results are still a table, although it's a very small one consisting of one column and one row.

Finally, it's possible for a query to produce *zero* rows of query results, as in this example:

List the name and hire date of anyone with sales over $500,000.

```
SELECT NAME, HIRE_DATE
  FROM SALESREPS
 WHERE SALES > 500000.00

NAME           HIRE_DATE
-----------  ----------
```

Even in this situation, the query results are still a table. This one is an empty table with two columns and zero rows.

Note that SQL's support for missing data extends to query results as well. If a data item in the database has a NULL value, the NULL value appears in the query results when the data item is retrieved. For example, the SALESREPS table contains NULL values in its QUOTA and MANAGER columns. The next query returns these NULL values in the second and third columns of query results.

List the salespeople, their quotas, and their managers.

```
SELECT NAME, QUOTA, MANAGER
   FROM SALESREPS

NAME                   QUOTA  MANAGER
-------------   ------------  --------
Bill Adams       $350,000.00      104
Mary Jones       $300,000.00      106
Sue Smith        $350,000.00      108
Sam Clark        $275,000.00     NULL
Bob Smith        $200,000.00      106
Dan Roberts      $300,000.00      104
Tom Snyder              NULL      101
Larry Fitch      $350,000.00      106
Paul Cruz        $275,000.00      104
Nancy Angelli    $300,000.00      108
```

The fact that a SQL query always produces a table of data is very important. It means that the query results can be stored back into the database as a table. It means that the results of two similar queries can be combined to form a larger table of query results. Finally, it means that the query results can themselves be the target of further queries. A relational database's tabular structure thus has a very synergistic relationship with the relational query facilities of SQL. Tables can be queried, and queries produce tables.

Simple Queries

The simplest SQL queries request columns of data from a single table in the database. For example, this query requests three columns from the OFFICES table:

List the location, region, and sales of each sales office.

```
SELECT CITY, REGION, SALES
   FROM OFFICES

CITY          REGION          SALES
-----------   --------   ------------
Denver        Western    $186,042.00
New York      Eastern    $692,637.00
Chicago       Eastern    $735,042.00
Atlanta       Eastern    $367,911.00
Los Angeles   Western    $835,915.00
```

The SELECT statement for simple queries like this one includes only the two required clauses. The SELECT clause names the requested columns; the FROM clause names the table that contains them.

Conceptually, SQL processes the query by going through the table named in the FROM clause, one row at a time, as shown in Figure 6-3. For each row, SQL takes the values of the columns requested in the select list and produces a single row of query results. The query results thus contain one row of data for each row in the table.

Calculated Columns

In addition to columns whose values come directly from the database, a SQL query can include *calculated columns* whose values are calculated from the stored data values. To request a calculated column, you specify a SQL expression in the select list. As discussed in Chapter 5, SQL expressions can involve addition, subtraction, multiplication, and division. You can also use parentheses to build more complex expressions. Of course the columns referenced in an arithmetic expression must have a numeric type. If you try to add, subtract, multiply, or divide columns containing text data, SQL will report an error.

This query shows a simple calculated column.

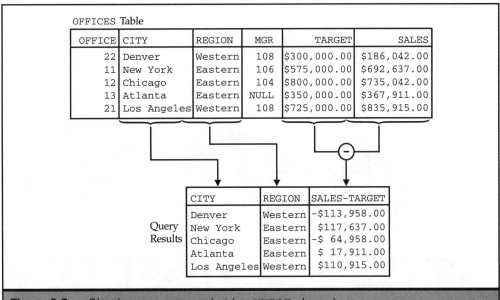

Figure 6-3.   *Simple query processing (no WHERE clause)*

List the city, region, and amount over/under target for each office.

```
SELECT CITY, REGION, (SALES - TARGET)
  FROM OFFICES

CITY            REGION     (SALES-TARGET)
------------    --------   ---------------
Denver          Western       -$113,958.00
New York        Eastern        $117,637.00
Chicago         Eastern        -$64,958.00
Atlanta         Eastern         $17,911.00
Los Angeles     Western        $110,915.00
```

To process the query, SQL goes through the offices, generating one row of query results for each row of the OFFICES table, as shown in Figure 6-4. The first two columns of query results come directly from the OFFICES table. The third column of query results is calculated, row by row, using the data values from the current row of the OFFICES table.

Here are other examples of queries that use calculated columns:

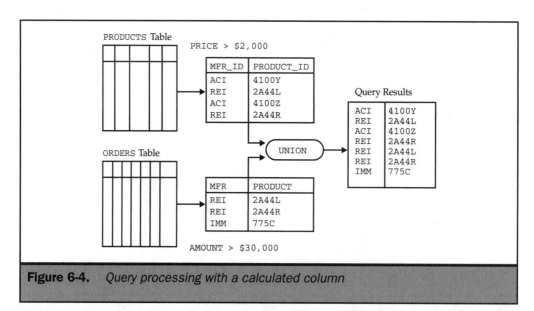

Figure 6-4. *Query processing with a calculated column*

Show the value of the inventory for each product.

```
SELECT MFR_ID, PRODUCT_ID, DESCRIPTION, (QTY_ON_HAND * PRICE)
  FROM PRODUCTS

MFR_ID  PRODUCT_ID  DESCRIPTION      (QTY_ON_HAND*PRICE)
------  ----------  ---------------  -------------------
REI     2A45C       Ratchet Link            $16,590.00
ACI     4100Y       Widget Remover          $68,750.00
QSA     XK47        Reducer                 $13,490.00
BIC     41672       Plate                        $0.00
IMM     779C        900-lb Brace            $16,875.00
ACI     41003       Size 3 Widget           $22,149.00
ACI     41004       Size 4 Widget           $16,263.00
BIC     41003       Handle                   $1,956.00
```

Show me the result if I raised each salesperson's quota by 3 percent of their year-to-date sales.

```
SELECT NAME, QUOTA, (QUOTA + (.03*SALES))
  FROM SALESREPS

NAME                  QUOTA  (QUOTA+(.03*SALES))
--------------  -----------  -------------------
Bill Adams      $350,000.00          $361,037.33
Mary Jones      $300,000.00          $311,781.75
Sue Smith       $350,000.00          $364,221.50
Sam Clark       $275,000.00          $283,997.36
Bob Smith       $200,000.00          $204,277.82
Dan Roberts     $300,000.00          $309,170.19
Tom Snyder             NULL                 NULL
Larry Fitch     $350,000.00          $360,855.95
Paul Cruz       $275,000.00          $283,603.25
Nancy Angelli   $300,000.00          $305,581.26
```

As mentioned in Chapter 5, many SQL products provide additional arithmetic operations, character string operations, and built-in functions that can be used in SQL expressions. These can appear in select list expressions, as in the next DB2 example.

List the name, month, and year of hire for each salesperson.

```
SELECT NAME, MONTH(HIRE_DATE), YEAR(HIRE_DATE)
  FROM SALESREPS
```

SQL constants can also be used by themselves as items in a select list. This can be useful for producing query results that are easier to read and interpret, as in the next example.

List the sales for each city.

```
SELECT CITY, 'has sales of', SALES
  FROM OFFICES
```

```
CITY          HAS SALES OF        SALES
------------  -------------  ------------
Denver        has sales of   $186,042.00
New York      has sales of   $692,637.00
Chicago       has sales of   $735,042.00
Atlanta       has sales of   $367,911.00
Los Angeles   has sales of   $835,915.00
```

The query results appear to consist of a separate "sentence" for each office, but they're really a table of three columns. The first and third columns contain values from the OFFICES table. The second column always contains the same 12-character text string. This distinction is subtle when the query results are displayed on a screen, but it is crucial in programmatic SQL, when the results are being retrieved into a program and used for calculations.

Selecting All Columns (SELECT *)

Sometimes it's convenient to display the contents of all the columns of a table. This can be particularly useful when you first encounter a new database and want to get a quick understanding of its structure and the data it contains. As a convenience, SQL lets you use an asterisk (*) in place of the select list as an abbreviation for "all columns":

Show me all the data in the OFFICES table.

```
SELECT *
  FROM OFFICES
```

```
OFFICE CITY          REGION   MGR       TARGET        SALES
------ ------------  -------  ----  ------------  ------------
    22 Denver        Western  108   $300,000.00   $186,042.00
    11 New York      Eastern  106   $575,000.00   $692,637.00
```

```
12  Chicago       Eastern    104  $800,000.00  $735,042.00
13  Atlanta       Eastern    105  $350,000.00  $367,911.00
21  Los Angeles   Western    108  $725,000.00  $835,915.00
```

The query results contain all six columns of the OFFICES table, in the same left-to-right order as in the table itself.

The ANSI/ISO SQL standard specifies that a SELECT statement can have either an all-column selection or a select list, but not both, as shown in Figure 6-1. However, many SQL implementations treat the asterisk (*) as just another element of the select list. Thus the query:

```
SELECT *, (SALES - TARGET)
   FROM OFFICES
```

is legal in most commercial SQL dialects (for example, in DB2, Oracle, and SQL Server), but it is not permitted by the ANSI/ISO standard.

The all-columns selection is most appropriate when you are using interactive SQL casually. It should be avoided in programmatic SQL, because changes in the database structure can cause a program to fail. For example, suppose the OFFICES table was dropped from the database and then re-created with its columns rearranged and a new seventh column added. SQL automatically takes care of the database-related details of such changes, but it cannot modify your application program for you. If your program expects a SELECT * FROM OFFICES query to return six columns of query results with certain data types, it will almost certainly stop working when the columns are rearranged and a new one is added.

These difficulties can be avoided if you write the program to request the columns it needs by name. For example, the following query produces the same results as SELECT * FROM OFFICES. It is also immune to changes in the database structure, as long as the named columns continue to exist in the OFFICES table:

```
SELECT OFFICE, CITY, REGION, MGR, TARGET, SALES
   FROM OFFICES
```

Duplicate Rows (DISTINCT)

If a query includes the primary key of a table in its select list, then every row of query results will be unique (because the primary key has a different value in each row). If the primary key is not included in the query results, duplicate rows can occur. For example, suppose you made this request:

List the employee numbers of all sales office managers.

```
SELECT MGR
  FROM OFFICES

MGR
----
 108
 106
 104
 105
 108
```

The query results have five rows (one for each office), but two of them are exact duplicates of one another. Why? Because Larry Fitch manages both the Los Angeles and Denver offices, and his employee number (108) appears in both rows of the OFFICES table. These query results are probably not exactly what you had in mind. If there are four different managers, you might have expected only four employee numbers in the query results.

You can eliminate duplicate rows of query results by inserting the keyword DISTINCT in the SELECT statement just before the select list. Here is a version of the previous query that produces the results you want:

List the employee numbers of all sales office managers.

```
SELECT DISTINCT MGR
  FROM OFFICES

MGR
----
 104
 105
 106
 108
```

Conceptually, SQL carries out this query by first generating a full set of query results (five rows) and then eliminating rows that are exact duplicates of one another to form the final query results. The DISTINCT keyword can be specified regardless of the contents of the SELECT list (with certain restrictions for summary queries, as described in Chapter 8).

If the DISTINCT keyword is omitted, SQL does not eliminate duplicate rows. You can also specify the keyword ALL to explicitly indicate that duplicate rows are to be retained, but it is unnecessary since this is the default behavior.

Row Selection (WHERE Clause)

SQL queries that retrieve all rows of a table are useful for database browsing and reports, but for little else. Usually you'll want to select only some of the rows in a table and include only these rows in the query results. The WHERE clause is used to specify the rows you want to retrieve. Here are some examples of simple queries that use the WHERE clause:

Show me the offices where sales exceed target.

```
SELECT CITY, SALES, TARGET
  FROM OFFICES
 WHERE SALES > TARGET

CITY               SALES        TARGET
-----------  ------------  ------------
New York       $692,637.00  $575,000.00
Atlanta        $367,911.00  $350,000.00
Los Angeles    $835,915.00  $725,000.00
```

Show me the name, sales, and quota of employee number 105.

```
SELECT NAME, SALES, QUOTA
  FROM SALESREPS
 WHERE EMPL_NUM = 105

NAME              SALES        QUOTA
-----------  ------------  ------------
Bill Adams     $367,911.00  $350,000.00
```

Show me the employees managed by Bob Smith (employee 104).

```
SELECT NAME, SALES
  FROM SALESREPS
 WHERE MANAGER = 104

NAME              SALES
-----------  ------------
Bill Adams     $367,911.00
Dan Roberts    $305,673.00
Paul Cruz      $286,775.00
```

The WHERE clause consists of the keyword WHERE followed by a search condition that specifies the rows to be retrieved. In the previous query, for example, the search condition is MANAGER = 104. Figure 6-5 shows how the WHERE clause works. Conceptually, SQL goes through each row of the SALESREPS table, one by one, and applies the search condition to the row. When a column name appears in the search condition (such as the MANAGER column in this example), SQL uses the value of the column in the current row. For each row, the search condition can produce one of three results:

- If the search condition is TRUE, the row is included in the query results. For example, the row for Bill Adams has the correct MANAGER value and is included.

- If the search condition is FALSE, the row is excluded from the query results. For example, the row for Sue Smith has the wrong MANAGER value and is excluded.

- If the search condition has a NULL (unknown) value, the row is excluded from the query results. For example, the row for Sam Clark has a NULL value for the MANAGER column and is excluded.

Figure 6-6 shows another way to think about the role of the search condition in the WHERE clause. Basically, the search condition acts as a filter for rows of the table. Rows that satisfy the search condition pass through the filter and become part of the query results. Rows that do not satisfy the search condition are trapped by the filter and excluded from the query results.

Search Conditions

SQL offers a rich set of search conditions that allow you to specify many different kinds of queries efficiently and naturally. Five basic search conditions (called *predicates* in the ANSI/ISO standard) are summarized here and are described in the sections that follow:

Figure 6-5. *Row selection with the WHERE clause*

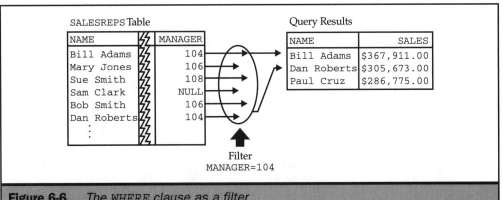

Figure 6-6.   *The WHERE clause as a filter*

■ **Comparison test.** Compares the value of one expression to the value of another expression. Use this test to select offices in the Eastern region, or salespeople whose sales are above their quotas.

■ **Range test.** Tests whether the value of an expression falls within a specified range of values. Use this test to find salespeople whose sales are between $100,000 and $500,000.

■ **Set membership test.** Checks whether the value of an expression matches one of a set of values. Use this test to select offices located in New York, Chicago, or Los Angeles.

■ **Pattern matching test.** Checks whether the value of a column containing string data matches a specified pattern. Use this test to select customers whose names start with the letter *E.*

■ **Null value test.** Checks whether a column has a NULL (unknown) value. Use this test to find the salespeople who have not yet been assigned to a manager.

The Comparison Test (=, <>, <, <=, >, >=)

The most common search condition used in a SQL query is a comparison test. In a comparison test, SQL computes and compares the values of two SQL expressions for each row of data. The expressions can be as simple as a column name or a constant, or they can be more complex arithmetic expressions. SQL offers six different ways of comparing the two expressions, as shown in Figure 6-7.

Next are some examples of typical comparison tests.

Figure 6-7.   *Comparison test syntax diagram*

Find salespeople hired before 1988.

```
SELECT NAME
  FROM SALESREPS
 WHERE HIRE_DATE < '01-JAN-88'

NAME
------------
Sue Smith
Bob Smith
Dan Roberts
Paul Cruz
```

List the offices whose sales fall below 80 percent of target.

```
SELECT CITY, SALES, TARGET
  FROM OFFICES
 WHERE SALES < (.8 * TARGET)

CITY           SALES        TARGET
-------  ------------  ------------
Denver    $186,042.00  $300,000.00
```

List the offices not managed by employee number 108.

```
SELECT CITY, MGR
  FROM OFFICES
 WHERE MGR <> 108
```

```
CITY        MGR
---------   ----
New York    106
Chicago     104
Atlanta     105
```

As shown in Figure 6-7, the inequality comparison test is written as "A < > B" according to the ANSI/ISO SQL specification. Several SQL implementations use alternate notations, such as "A != B" (used by SQL Server) and "AØ=B" (used by DB2 and SQL/DS). In some cases, these are alternative forms; in others, they are the only acceptable form of the inequality test.

When SQL compares the values of the two expressions in the comparison test, three results can occur:

- If the comparison is true, the test yields a TRUE result.
- If the comparison is false, the test yields a FALSE result.
- If either of the two expressions produces a NULL value, the comparison yields a NULL result.

Single-Row Retrieval

The most common comparison test is one that checks whether a column's value is equal to some constant. When the column is a primary key, the test isolates a single row of the table, producing a single row of query results, as in this example:

Retrieve the name and credit limit of customer number 2107.

```
SELECT COMPANY, CREDIT_LIMIT
  FROM CUSTOMERS
 WHERE CUST_NUM = 2107

COMPANY            CREDIT_LIMIT
-----------------  ------------
Ace International  $35,000.00
```

This type of query is the foundation of forms-based database retrieval programs. The user enters a customer number into the form, and the program uses the number to construct and execute a query. It then displays the retrieved data in the form.

Note that the SQL statements for retrieving a specific customer by number, as in this example, and retrieving all customers with a certain characteristic (such as those with credit limits over $25,000) both have exactly the same form. These two types of queries (retrieval by primary key and retrieval based on a search of the data) would be very different operations in a nonrelational database. This uniformity of approach makes SQL much simpler to learn and use than earlier query languages.

NULL **Value Considerations**

The behavior of NULL values in comparison tests can reveal some "obviously true" notions about SQL queries to be, in fact, not necessarily true. For example, it would seem that the results of these two queries would include every row of the SALESREPS table:

List salespeople who are over quota.

```
SELECT NAME
   FROM SALESREPS
  WHERE SALES > QUOTA

NAME
------------
Bill Adams
Mary Jones
Sue Smith
Sam Clark
Dan Roberts
Larry Fitch
Paul Cruz
```

List salespeople who are under or at quota.

```
SELECT NAME
   FROM SALESREPS
  WHERE SALES < = QUOTA

NAME
--------------
Bob Smith
Nancy Angelli
```

However, the queries produce seven and two rows, respectively, for a total of nine rows, while there are ten rows in the SALESREPS table. Tom Snyder's row has a NULL value in the QUOTA column because he has not yet been assigned a quota. This row is not listed by either query; it "vanishes" in the comparison test.

As this example shows, you need to think about NULL value handling when you specify a search condition. In SQL's three-valued logic, a search condition can yield a

TRUE, FALSE, or NULL result. Only rows where the search condition yields a TRUE result are included in the query results.

The Range Test (BETWEEN)

SQL provides a different form of search condition with the range test (BETWEEN) shown in Figure 6-8. The range test checks whether a data value lies between two specified values. It involves three SQL expressions. The first expression defines the value to be tested; the second and third expressions define the low and high ends of the range to be checked. The data types of the three expressions must be comparable.

This example shows a typical range test:

Find orders placed in the last quarter of 1989.

```
SELECT ORDER_NUM, ORDER_DATE, MFR, PRODUCT, AMOUNT
  FROM ORDERS
 WHERE ORDER_DATE BETWEEN '01-OCT-89' AND '31-DEC-89'

ORDER_NUM ORDER_DATE  MFR  PRODUCT     AMOUNT
---------- ----------- ---- -------- -----------
    112961 17-DEC-89   REI  2A44L     $31,500.00
    112968 12-OCT-89   ACI  41004      $3,978.00
    112963 17-DEC-89   ACI  41004      $3,276.00
    112983 27-DEC-89   ACI  41004        $702.00
    112979 12-OCT-89   ACI  4100Z     $15,000.00
    112992 04-NOV-89   ACI  41002        $760.00
    112975 12-OCT-89   REI  2A44G      $2,100.00
    112987 31-DEC-89   ACI  4100Y     $27,500.00
```

Figure 6-8. *Range test (BETWEEN) syntax diagram*

The BETWEEN test includes the endpoints of the range, so orders placed on October 1 or December 31 are included in the query results. Here is another example of a range test:

Find the orders that fall into various amount ranges.

```
SELECT ORDER_NUM, AMOUNT
  FROM ORDERS
WHERE AMOUNT BETWEEN 20000.00 AND 29999.99

ORDER_NUM        AMOUNT
---------- -----------
   113036  $22,500.00
   112987  $27,500.00
   113042  $22,500.00

SELECT ORDER_NUM, AMOUNT
  FROM ORDERS
WHERE AMOUNT BETWEEN 30000.00 AND 39999.99

ORDER_NUM        AMOUNT
---------- -----------
   112961  $31,500.00
   113069  $31,350.00

SELECT ORDER_NUM, AMOUNT
  FROM ORDERS
WHERE AMOUNT BETWEEN 40000.00 AND 49999.99

ORDER_NUM        AMOUNT
---------- -----------
   113045  $45,000.00
```

The negated version of the range test (NOT BETWEEN) checks for values that fall outside the range, as in this example:

List salespeople whose sales are not between 80 percent and 120 percent of quota.

```
SELECT NAME, SALES, QUOTA
  FROM SALESREPS
WHERE SALES NOT BETWEEN (.8 * QUOTA) AND (1.2 * QUOTA)
```

```
NAME                   SALES        QUOTA
--------------      ------------ ------------
Mary Jones          $392,725.00  $300,000.00
Sue Smith           $474,050.00  $350,000.00
Bob Smith           $142,594.00  $200,000.00
Nancy Angelli       $186,042.00  $300,000.00
```

The test expression specified in the BETWEEN test can be any valid SQL expression, but in practice, it's usually just a column name, as in the previous examples.

The ANSI/ISO standard defines relatively complex rules for the handling of NULL values in the BETWEEN test:

- If the test expression produces a NULL value, or if *both* expressions defining the range produce NULL values, then the BETWEEN test returns a NULL result.

- If the expression defining the lower end of the range produces a NULL value, then the BETWEEN test returns FALSE if the test value is greater than the upper bound, and NULL otherwise.

- If the expression defining the upper end of the range produces a NULL value, then the BETWEEN test returns FALSE if the test value is less than the lower bound, and NULL otherwise.

Before relying on this behavior, it's a good idea to experiment with your DBMS.

It's worth noting that the BETWEEN test doesn't really add to the expressive power of SQL, because it can be expressed as two comparison tests. The range test:

```
A BETWEEN B AND C
```

is completely equivalent to:

```
(A >= B) AND (A < = C)
```

However, the BETWEEN test is a simpler way to express a search condition when you're thinking of it in terms of a range of values.

The Set Membership Test (IN)

Another common search condition is the set membership test (IN), shown in Figure 6-9. It tests whether a data value matches one of a list of target values. Here are several queries that use the set membership test:

List the salespeople who work in New York, Atlanta, or Denver.

```
SELECT NAME, QUOTA, SALES
  FROM SALESREPS
 WHERE REP_OFFICE IN (11, 13, 22)
```

NAME	QUOTA	SALES
Bill Adams	$350,000.00	$367,911.00
Mary Jones	$300,000.00	$392,725.00
Sam Clark	$275,000.00	$299,912.00
Nancy Angelli	$300,000.00	$186,042.00

Find all orders placed on a Thursday in January 1990.

```
SELECT ORDER_NUM, ORDER_DATE, AMOUNT
  FROM ORDERS
 WHERE ORDER_DATE IN ('04-JAN-90', '11-JAN-90', '18-JAN-90',
'25-JAN-90')
```

ORDER_NUM	ORDER_DATE	AMOUNT
113012	11-JAN-90	$3,745.00
113003	25-JAN-90	$5,625.00

Find all orders placed with four specific salespeople.

```
SELECT ORDER_NUM, REP, AMOUNT
  FROM ORDERS
 WHERE REP IN (107, 109, 101, 103)
```

ORDER_NUM	REP	AMOUNT
112968	101	$3,978.00

```
113058   109    $1,480.00
112997   107      $652.00
113062   107    $2,430.00
113069   107   $31,350.00
112975   103    $2,100.00
113055   101      $150.00
113003   109    $5,625.00
113057   103      $600.00
113042   101   $22,500.00
```

You can check whether the data value does *not* match any of the target values by using the NOT IN form of the set membership test. The test expression in an IN test can be any SQL expression, but it's usually just a column name, as in the preceding examples. If the test expression produces a NULL value, the IN test returns NULL. All of the items in the list of target values must have the same data type, and that type must be comparable to the data type of the test expression.

Like the BETWEEN test, the IN test doesn't add to the expressive power of SQL, because the search condition:

```
X IN (A, B, C)
```

is completely equivalent to:

```
(X = A) OR (X = B) OR (X = C)
```

However, the IN test offers a much more efficient way of expressing the search condition, especially if the set contains more than a few values. The ANSI/ISO SQL standard doesn't specify a maximum limit to the number of items that can appear in the value list, and most commercial implementations do not state an explicit upper

Figure 6-9.   *Set membership test (IN) syntax diagram*

limit either. For portability reasons, it's generally a good idea to avoid lists with only a single item, such as this one:

```
CITY IN ('New York')
```

and replace them with a simple comparison test:

```
CITY = 'New York'
```

The Pattern Matching Test (LIKE)

You can use a simple comparison test to retrieve rows where the contents of a text column match some particular text. For example, this query retrieves a row of the CUSTOMERS table by name:

Show the credit limit for Smithson Corp.

```
SELECT COMPANY, CREDIT_LIMIT
  FROM CUSTOMERS
 WHERE COMPANY = 'Smithson Corp.'
```

However, you might easily forget whether the company's name was "Smith," "Smithson," or "Smithsonian." You can use SQL's pattern matching test to retrieve the data based on a partial match of the customer's name.

The pattern matching test (LIKE), shown in Figure 6-10, checks to see whether the data value in a column matches a specified *pattern*. The pattern is a string that may include one or more *wildcard* characters. These characters are interpreted in a special way.

Wildcard Characters

The percent sign (%) wildcard character matches any sequence of zero or more characters. Here's a modified version of the previous query that uses the percent sign for pattern matching:

```
SELECT COMPANY, CREDIT_LIMIT
  FROM CUSTOMERS
 WHERE COMPANY LIKE 'Smith% Corp.'
```

Figure 6-10. *Pattern matching test (LIKE) syntax diagram*

The LIKE keyword tells SQL to compare the NAME column to the pattern "Smith%
Corp." Any of the following names would match the pattern:

```
Smith Corp.    Smithson Corp.    Smithsen Corp.    Smithsonian Corp.
```

but these names would not:

```
SmithCorp     Smithson Inc.
```

The underscore (_) wildcard character matches any single character. If you are sure
that the company's name is either "Smithson" or "Smithsen," for example, you can use
this query:

```
SELECT COMPANY, CREDIT_LIMIT
  FROM CUSTOMERS
 WHERE COMPANY LIKE 'Smiths_n Corp.'
```

In this case, any of these names will match the pattern:

```
Smithson Corp.    Smithsen Corp.    Smithsun Corp.
```

but these names will not:

```
Smithsoon Corp.    Smithsn Corp.
```

Wildcard characters can appear anywhere in the pattern string, and several wildcard
characters can be within a single string. This query allows either the "Smithson" or
"Smithsen" spelling and will also accept "Corp.," "Inc.," or any other ending on the
company name:

```
SELECT COMPANY, CREDIT_LIMIT
  FROM CUSTOMERS
 WHERE COMPANY LIKE 'Smiths_n %'
```

You can locate strings that do *not* match a pattern by using the NOT LIKE form of
the pattern matching test. The LIKE test must be applied to a column with a string data
type. If the data value in the column is NULL, the LIKE test returns a NULL result.

If you have used computers through a command-line interface (such as the UNIX
shell), you've probably seen string pattern matching before. Frequently, the asterisk (*)
is used instead of SQL's percent sign (%), and the question mark (?) is used instead of

SQL's underscore (_), but the pattern matching capabilities themselves are similar in most situations where a computer application offers the capability to match selected parts of a word or text.

Escape Characters *

One of the problems with string pattern matching is how to match the wildcard characters themselves as literal characters. To test for the presence of a percent sign character in a column of text data, for example, you can't simply include the percent sign in the pattern because SQL will treat it as a wildcard. With some popular SQL products, you cannot literally match the two wildcard characters. This usually doesn't pose serious problems, because the wildcard characters don't frequently appear in names, product numbers, and other text data of the sort that is usually stored in a database.

The ANSI/ISO SQL standard does specify a way to literally match wildcard characters, using a special *escape character*. When the escape character appears in the pattern, the character immediately following it is treated as a literal character rather than as a wildcard character. (The latter character is said to be *escaped*.) The escaped character can be either of the two wildcard characters, or the escape character itself, which has now taken on a special meaning within the pattern.

The escape character is specified as a one-character constant string in the ESCAPE clause of the search condition, as shown in Figure 6-10. Here is an example using a dollar sign ($) as the escape character:

Find products whose product IDs start with the four letters "A%BC".

```
SELECT ORDER_NUM, PRODUCT
  FROM ORDERS
 WHERE PRODUCT LIKE 'A$%BC%' ESCAPE '$'
```

The first percent sign in the pattern, which follows an escape character, is treated as a literal percent sign; the second functions as a wildcard.

The use of escape characters is very common in pattern matching applications, which is why the ANSI/ISO standard specified it. However, it was not a part of the early SQL implementations and has been slowly adopted. To insure portability, the ESCAPE clause should be avoided.

The Null Value Test (IS NULL)

NULL values create a three-valued logic for SQL search conditions. For any given row, the result of a search condition may be TRUE or FALSE, or it may be NULL because one of the columns used in evaluating the search condition contains a NULL value. Sometimes it's useful to check explicitly for NULL values in a search condition and handle them directly. SQL provides a special NULL value test (IS NULL), shown in Figure 6-11, to handle this task.

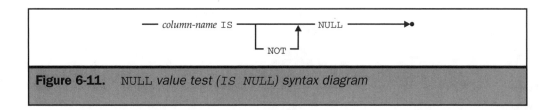

Figure 6-11. NULL *value test (IS NULL) syntax diagram*

This query uses the NULL value test to find the salesperson in the sample database who has not yet been assigned to an office:

Find the salesperson not yet assigned to an office.

```
SELECT NAME
  FROM SALESREPS
 WHERE REP_OFFICE IS NULL

NAME
-----------
Tom Snyder
```

The negated form of the NULL value test (IS NOT NULL) finds rows that do not contain a NULL value:

List the salespeople who have been assigned to an office.

```
SELECT NAME
  FROM SALESREPS
 WHERE REP_OFFICE IS NOT NULL

NAME
--------------
Bill Adams
Mary Jones
Sue Smith
Sam Clark
Bob Smith
Dan Roberts
Larry Fitch
Paul Cruz
Nancy Angelli
```

Unlike the previously described search conditions, the NULL value test cannot yield a NULL result. It is always either TRUE or FALSE.

It may seem strange that you can't just test for a NULL value using a simple comparison search condition, such as this:

```
SELECT NAME
  FROM SALESREPS
 WHERE REP_OFFICE = NULL
```

The NULL keyword can't be used here because it isn't really a value; it's just a signal that the value is unknown. Even if the comparison test:

```
REP_OFFICE = NULL
```

were legal, the rules for handling NULL values in comparisons would cause it to behave differently from what you might expect. When SQL encountered a row where the REP_OFFICE column was NULL, the search condition would test:

```
NULL = NULL
```

Is the result TRUE or FALSE? Because the values on both sides of the equal sign are unknown, SQL can't tell, so the rules of SQL logic say that the search condition itself must yield a NULL result. Because the search condition doesn't produce a true result, the row is excluded from the query results—precisely the opposite of what you wanted to happen! As a result of the way SQL handles NULLs in comparisons, you must explicitly use the NULL value test to check for NULL values.

Compound Search Conditions (AND, OR, and NOT)

The simple search conditions described in the preceding sections return a value of TRUE, FALSE, or NULL when applied to a row of data. Using the rules of logic, you can combine these simple SQL search conditions to form more complex ones, as shown in Figure 6-12. Note that the search conditions combined with AND, OR, and NOT may themselves be compound search conditions.

Figure 6-12. *WHERE clause syntax diagram*

The keyword OR is used to combine two search conditions when one or the other (or both) must be true:

Find salespeople who are under quota or with sales under $300,000.

```
SELECT NAME, QUOTA, SALES
   FROM SALESREPS
 WHERE SALES < QUOTA
    OR SALES < 300000.00
```

```
NAME                   QUOTA         SALES
-------------- ------------ ------------
Sam Clark          $275,000.00  $299,912.00
Bob Smith          $200,000.00  $142,594.00
Tom Snyder                NULL   $75,985.00
Paul Cruz          $275,000.00  $286,775.00
Nancy Angelli      $300,000.00  $186,042.00
```

You can also use the keyword AND to combine two search conditions that must both be true:

Find salespeople who are under quota and with sales under $300,000.

```
SELECT NAME, QUOTA, SALES
   FROM SALESREPS
 WHERE SALES < QUOTA
   AND SALES < 300000.00
```

```
NAME                   QUOTA         SALES
-------------- ------------ ------------
Bob Smith          $200,000.00  $142,594.00
Nancy Angelli      $300,000.00  $186,042.00
```

Finally, you can use the keyword NOT to select rows where a search condition is false:

Find all salespeople who are under quota, but whose sales are not under $150,000.

```
SELECT NAME, QUOTA, SALES
   FROM SALESREPS
 WHERE SALES < QUOTA
   AND NOT SALES < 150000.00
```

```
NAME                 QUOTA        SALES
--------------  ------------  -----------
Nancy Angelli   $300,000.00  $186,042.00
```

Using the logical AND, OR, and NOT keywords and parentheses to group the search criteria, you can build very complex search criteria, such as the one in this query:

Find all salespeople who either: (a) work in Denver, New York, or Chicago; or (b) have no manager and were hired since June 1988; or (c) are over quota, but have sales of $600,000 or less.

```
SELECT NAME
  FROM SALESREPS
 WHERE (REP_OFFICE IN (22, 11, 12))
    OR (MANAGER IS NULL AND HIRE_DATE >= '01-JUN-88')
    OR (SALES > QUOTA AND NOT SALES > 600000.00)
```

Exactly why you might want to see this particular list of names is a mystery, but the example does illustrate a reasonably complex query.

As with simple search conditions, NULL values influence the outcome of compound search conditions, and the results are subtle. In particular, the result of (NULL OR TRUE) is TRUE, not NULL, as you might expect. Tables 6-1, 6-2, and 6-3 specify truth tables for AND, OR, and NOT, respectively, and show the impact of NULL values.

When more than two search conditions are combined with AND, OR, and NOT, the ANSI/ISO standard specifies that NOT has the highest precedence, followed by AND and then OR. To ensure portability, it's always a good idea to use parentheses and remove any possible ambiguity.

AND	TRUE	FALSE	NULL
TRUE	TRUE	FALSE	NULL
FALSE	FALSE	FALSE	FALSE
NULL	NULL	FALSE	NULL

Table 6-1.   *The AND Truth Table*

OR	TRUE	FALSE	NULL
TRUE	TRUE	TRUE	TRUE
FALSE	TRUE	FALSE	NULL
NULL	TRUE	NULL	NULL

Table 6-2.   *The OR Truth Table*

The SQL2 standard adds another logical search condition, the IS test, to the logic provided by AND, OR, and NOT. Figure 6-13 shows the syntax of the IS test, which checks to see whether the logical value of an expression or comparison test is TRUE, FALSE, or UNKNOWN (NULL).

For example, the IS test:

```
((SALES - QUOTA) > 10000.00) IS UNKNOWN
```

can be used to find rows where the comparison cannot be done because either SALES or QUOTA has a NULL value. Similarly, the IS test:

```
((SALES - QUOTA) > 10000.00) IS FALSE
```

will select rows where SALES are not significantly above QUOTA. As this example shows, the IS test doesn't really add to the expressive power of SQL, since the test could just as easily have been written:

```
NOT ((SALES - QUOTA) > 10000.00)
```

For maximum portability, it's a good idea to avoid the tests and write the expressions using only AND, OR, and NOT. It's not always possible to avoid the IS UNKNOWN form of the test.

NOT	TRUE	FALSE	NULL
	FALSE	TRUE	NULL

Table 6-3.   *The Not Truth Table*

Figure 6-13.   *The IS test syntax diagram*

Sorting Query Results (ORDER BY Clause)

Like the rows of a table in the database, the rows of query results are not arranged in any particular order. You can ask SQL to sort the results of a query by including the ORDER BY clause in the SELECT statement. The ORDER BY clause, shown in Figure 6-14, consists of the keywords ORDER BY, followed by a list of sort specifications separated by commas. For example, the results of this query are sorted on two columns, REGION and CITY:

Show the sales for each office, sorted in alphabetical order by region, and within each region by city.

```
SELECT CITY, REGION, SALES
  FROM OFFICES
 ORDER BY REGION, CITY
```

```
CITY          REGION          SALES
------------  --------  ------------
Atlanta       Eastern    $367,911.00
Chicago       Eastern    $735,042.00
New York      Eastern    $692,637.00
Denver        Western    $186,042.00
Los Angeles   Western    $835,915.00
```

Figure 6-14.   *The ORDER BY clause syntax diagram*

The first sort specification (REGION) is the *major* sort key; those that follow (CITY, in this case) are progressively more minor sort keys, used as "tie breakers" when two rows of query results have the same values for the more major keys. Using the ORDER BY clause, you can request sorting in an ascending or descending sequence, and you can sort on any item in the select list of the query.

By default, SQL sorts data in ascending sequence. To request sorting in descending sequence, the keyword DESC is included in the sort specification, as in the next example:

List the offices, sorted in descending order by sales, so that the offices with the largest sales appear first.

```
SELECT CITY, REGION, SALES
  FROM OFFICES
 ORDER BY SALES DESC

CITY           REGION          SALES
------------   --------   ------------
Los Angeles    Western    $835,915.00
Chicago        Eastern    $735,042.00
New York       Eastern    $692,637.00
Atlanta        Eastern    $367,911.00
Denver         Western    $186,042.00
```

As indicated in Figure 6-14, you can also use the keyword ASC to specify an ascending sort, but because that's the default sorting sequence, the keyword is usually omitted.

If the column of query results to be used for sorting is a calculated column, it has no column name to be used in a sort specification. In this case, you must specify a column number instead of a column name, as in this example:

List the offices, sorted in descending order by sales performance, so that the offices with the best performance appear first.

```
SELECT CITY, REGION, (SALES - TARGET)
  FROM OFFICES
 ORDER BY 3 DESC

CITY           REGION     (SALES-TARGET)
------------   --------   ----------------
New York       Eastern      $117,637.00
Los Angeles    Western      $110,915.00
Atlanta        Eastern       $17,911.00
Chicago        Eastern      -$64,958.00
Denver         Western     -$113,958.00
```

These query results are sorted on the third column, which is the calculated difference between the SALES and TARGET for each office. By combining column numbers, column names, ascending sorts, and descending sorts, you can specify quite complex sorting of the query results, as in the following final example:

List the offices, sorted in alphabetical order by region, and within each region in descending order by sales performance.

```
SELECT CITY, REGION, (SALES - TARGET)
  FROM OFFICES
 ORDER BY REGION ASC, 3 DESC

CITY           REGION    (SALES-TARGET)
------------   --------  ---------------
New York       Eastern      $117,637.00
Atlanta        Eastern       $17,911.00
Chicago        Eastern      -$64,958.00
Los Angeles    Western      $110,915.00
Denver         Western     -$113,958.00
```

The SQL2 standard allows you to control the sorting order used by the DBMS for each sort key. This can be important when working with international character sets or to insure portability between ASCII and EBCDIC character set systems. However, this area of the SQL2 specification is quite complex, and in practice, many SQL implementations either ignore sorting sequence issues or use their own proprietary scheme for user control of the sorting sequence.

Rules for Single-Table Query Processing

Single-table queries are generally simple, and it's usually easy to understand the meaning of a query just by reading the SELECT statement. As queries become more complex, however, it's important to have a more precise "definition" of the query results that will be produced by a given SELECT statement. The following steps describe the procedure for generating the results of a SQL query that includes the clauses described in this chapter.

As these steps show, the query results produced by a SELECT statement are specified by applying each of its clauses, one by one. The FROM clause is applied first (selecting the table containing data to be retrieved). The WHERE clause is applied next (selecting specific rows from the table). The SELECT clause is applied next (generating the specific columns of query results and eliminating duplicate rows, if requested). Finally, the ORDER BY clause is applied to sort the query results.

To generate the query results for a SELECT statement, follow these steps:

1. Start with the table named in the FROM clause.

2. If there is a WHERE clause, apply its search condition to each row of the table, retaining those rows for which the search condition is TRUE, and discarding those rows for which it is FALSE or NULL.

3. For each remaining row, calculate the value of each item in the select list to produce a single row of query results. For each column reference, use the value of the column in the current row.

4. If SELECT DISTINCT is specified, eliminate any duplicate rows of query results that were produced.

5. If there is an ORDER BY clause, sort the query results as specified.

The rows generated by this procedure comprise the query results.

These "rules" for SQL query processing will be expanded several times in the next three chapters to include the remaining clauses of the SELECT statement.

Combining Query Results (UNION) *

Occasionally, it's convenient to combine the results of two or more queries into a single table of query results. SQL supports this capability through the UNION feature of the SELECT statement. Figure 6-15 illustrates how to use the UNION operation to satisfy the following request:

List all the products where the price of the product exceeds $2,000 or where more than $30,000 of the product has been ordered in a single order.

The first part of the request can be satisfied with the top query in the figure:

List all the products whose price exceeds $2,000.

```
SELECT MFR_ID, PRODUCT_ID
  FROM PRODUCTS
 WHERE PRICE > 2000.00

MFR_ID  PRODUCT_ID
-------  -----------
ACI      4100Y
REI      2A44L
ACI      4100Z
REI      2A44R
```

Similarly, the second part of the request can be satisfied with the bottom query in the figure:

List all the products where more than $30,000 of the product has been ordered in a single order.

```
SELECT DISTINCT MFR, PRODUCT
  FROM ORDERS
 WHERE AMOUNT > 30000.00

MFR   PRODUCT
----  --------
IMM   775C
REI   2A44L
REI   2A44R
```

As shown in Figure 6-15, the UNION operation produces a single table of query results that combines the rows of the top query results with the rows of the bottom query results. The SELECT statement that specifies the UNION operation looks like this:

List all the products where the price of the product exceeds $2,000 or where more than $30,000 of the product has been ordered in a single order.

```
SELECT MFR_ID, PRODUCT_ID
  FROM PRODUCTS
 WHERE PRICE > 2000.00
 UNION
SELECT DISTINCT MFR, PRODUCT
  FROM ORDERS
 WHERE AMOUNT > 30000.00

ACI    4100Y
ACI    4100Z
IMM    775C
REI    2A44L
REI    2A44R
```

There are severe restrictions on the tables that can be combined by a UNION operation:

■ The two tables must contain the same number of columns.

■ The data type of each column in the first table must be the same as the data type of the corresponding column in the second table.

■ Neither of the two tables can be sorted with the ORDER BY clause. However, the combined query results can be sorted, as described in the following section.

Figure 6-15. *Using UNION to combine query results*

Note that the column names of the two queries combined by UNION do not have to be identical. In the preceding example, the first table of query results has columns named MFR_ID and PRODUCT_ID, while the second table of query results has columns named MFR and PRODUCT. Because the columns in the two tables can have different names, the columns of query results produced by the UNION operation are unnamed.

The ANSI/ISO SQL standard specifies a further restriction on a SELECT statement that participates in a UNION operation. It permits only column names or an all-columns specification (SELECT *) in the select list and prohibits expressions in the select list. Most commercial SQL implementations relax this restriction and permit simple expressions in the select list. However, many SQL implementations do not allow the SELECT statements to include the GROUP BY or HAVING clauses, and some do not allow column functions in the select list (prohibiting summary queries as described in Chapter 8). In fact, some SQL implementations do not support the UNION operation at all.

Unions and Duplicate Rows *

Because the UNION operation combines the rows from two sets of query results, it would tend to produce query results containing duplicate rows. For example, in the query of Figure 6-15, product REI-2A44L sells for $4500.00, so it appears in the top set of query results. There is also an order for $31,500.00 worth of this product in the ORDERS table, so it also appears in the bottom set of query results. By default, the UNION operation *eliminates* duplicate rows as part of its processing. Thus, the combined set of query results contains only *one* row for product REI-2A44L.

If you want to retain duplicate rows in a UNION operation, you can specify the ALL keyword immediately following the word *UNION*. This form of the query produces two duplicate rows for product REI-2A44L:

List all the products where the price of the product exceeds $2,000 or where more than $30,000 of the product has been ordered in a single order.

```
SELECT MFR_ID, PRODUCT_ID
  FROM PRODUCTS
 WHERE PRICE > 2000.00
 UNION ALL
SELECT DISTINCT MFR, PRODUCT
  FROM ORDERS
 WHERE AMOUNT > 30000.00

  ACI    4100Y
  REI    2A44L
  ACI    4100Z
  REI    2A44R
  IMM    775C
  REI    2A44L
  REI    2A44R
```

Note that the default duplicate row handling for the UNION operation and for the simple SELECT statement is exactly opposite. For the SELECT statement, SELECT ALL (duplicates retained) is the default. To eliminate duplicate rows, you must explicitly specify SELECT DISTINCT. For the UNION operation, UNION (duplicates eliminated) is the default. To retain duplicate rows, you must explicitly specify UNION ALL.

Database experts have criticized the handling of duplicate rows in SQL and point to this inconsistency as an example of the problems. The reason for the inconsistency is that the SQL defaults were chosen to produce the correct behavior most of the time:

■ In practice, most simple SELECT statements do not produce duplicate rows, so the default is no duplicate elimination.

■ In practice, most UNION operations would produce unwanted duplicate rows, so the default is duplicate elimination.

Eliminating duplicate rows from query results is a very time-consuming process, especially if the query results contain a large number of rows. If you know, based on the individual queries involved, that a UNION operation cannot produce duplicate rows, you should specifically use the UNION ALL operation because the query will execute much more quickly.

Unions and Sorting *

The ORDER BY clause cannot appear in either of the two SELECT statements combined by a UNION operation. It wouldn't make much sense to sort the two sets of query results anyway, because they are fed directly into the UNION operation and are never visible to the user. However, the *combined* set of query results produced by the UNION operation can be sorted by specifying an ORDER BY clause after the second SELECT statement. Since the columns produced by the UNION operation are not named, the ORDER BY clause must specify the columns by column number.

Here is the same products query as that shown in Figure 6-15, with the query results sorted by manufacturer and product number:

List all the products where the price of the product exceeds $2,000 or where more than $30,000 of the product has been ordered in a single order, sorted by manufacturer and product number.

```
SELECT MFR_ID, PRODUCT_ID
  FROM PRODUCTS
 WHERE PRICE > 2000.00
 UNION
SELECT DISTINCT MFR, PRODUCT
  FROM ORDERS
 WHERE AMOUNT > 30000.00
 ORDER BY 1, 2

 ACI    4100Y
 ACI    4100Z
 IMM    775C
 REI    2A44L
 REI    2A44R
```

Multiple UNIONs*

You can use the UNION operation repeatedly to combine three or more sets of query results, as shown in Figure 6-16. The union of Table B and Table C in the figure produces a single, combined table. This table is then combined with Table A in another UNION operation. The query in the figure is written this way:

```
SELECT *
  FROM A
 UNION (SELECT *
          FROM B
         UNION
        SELECT *
          FROM C)

Bill
Mary
George
Fred
Sue
Julia
Harry
```

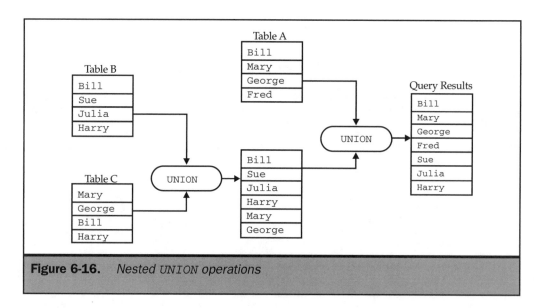

Figure 6-16.   *Nested UNION operations*

The parentheses in the query indicate which UNION operation should be performed first. In fact, if all of the UNIONs in the statement eliminate duplicate rows, or if all of them retain duplicate rows, the order in which they are performed is unimportant. These three expressions are completely equivalent:

```
A UNION (B UNION C)

(A UNION B) UNION C

(A UNION C) UNION B
```

and produce seven rows of query results. Similarly, the following three expressions are completely equivalent and produce twelve rows of query results, because the duplicates are retained:

```
A UNION ALL (B UNION ALL C)

(A UNION ALL B) UNION ALL C

(A UNION ALL C) UNION ALL B
```

However, if the unions involve a mixture of UNION and UNION ALL, the order of evaluation matters. If this expression:

```
A UNION ALL B UNION C
```

is interpreted as:

```
A UNION ALL (B UNION C)
```

then it produces ten rows of query results (six from the inner UNION, plus four rows from Table A). However, if it is interpreted as:

```
(A UNION ALL B) UNION C
```

then it produces only four rows, because the outer UNION eliminates all duplicate rows. For this reason, it's always a good idea to use parentheses in UNIONs of three or more tables to specify the order of evaluation intended.

Summary

This chapter is the first of four chapters about SQL queries. It described the following query features:

- The SELECT statement is used to express a SQL query. Every SELECT statement produces a table of query results containing one or more columns and zero or more rows.

- The FROM clause specifies the table(s) containing the data to be retrieved by a query.

- The SELECT clause specifies the column(s) of data to be included in the query results, which can be columns of data from the database, or calculated columns.

- The WHERE clause selects the rows to be included in the query results by applying a search condition to rows of the database.

- A search condition can select rows by comparing values, by checking a value against a range or set of values, by matching a string pattern, and by checking for NULL values.

- Simple search conditions can be combined with AND, OR, and NOT to form more complex search conditions.

- The ORDER BY clause specifies that the query results should be sorted in ascending or descending order, based on the values of one or more columns.

- The UNION operation can be used within a SELECT statement to combine two or more sets of query results into a single set.

The
Complete
Reference

Chapter 7

Multitable Queries
(Joins)

Many useful queries request data from two or more tables in a database. For example, these requests for data in the sample database draw data from two, three, or four tables:

- List the salespeople and the offices where they work (SALESREPS and OFFICES tables).

- List each order placed last week, showing the order amount, the name of the customer who placed it, and the name of the product ordered (ORDERS, CUSTOMERS, and SALESREPS tables).

- Show all orders taken by salespeople in the Eastern region, showing the product description and salesperson (ORDERS, SALESREPS, OFFICES, and PRODUCTS tables).

SQL allows you to retrieve data that answers these requests through multitable queries that *join* data from two or more tables. These queries and the SQL join facility are described in this chapter.

A Two-Table Query Example

The best way to understand the facilities that SQL provides for multitable queries is to start with a simple request that combines data from two different tables:

"List all orders, showing the order number and amount, and the name and credit limit of the customer who placed it."

The four specific data items requested are clearly stored in two different tables, as shown in Figure 7-1.

- The ORDERS table contains the order number and amount of each order, but doesn't have customer names or credit limits.

- The CUSTOMERS table contains the customer names and balances, but it lacks any information about orders.

There is a link between these two tables, however. In each row of the ORDERS table, the CUST column contains the customer number of the customer who placed the order, which matches the value in the CUST_NUM column in one of the rows in the CUSTOMERS table. Clearly, the SELECT statement that handles the request must somehow use this link between the tables to generate its query results.

Before examining the SELECT statement for the query, it's instructive to think about how you would manually handle the request, using paper and pencil. Figure 7-2 shows what you would probably do:

1. Start by writing down the four column names for the query results. Then move to the ORDERS table, and start with the first order.

2. Look across the row to find the order number (112961) and the order amount ($31,500.00) and copy both values to the first row of query results.

3. Look across the row to find the number of the customer who placed the order (2117), and move to the CUSTOMERS table to find customer number 2117 by searching the CUST_NUM column.

4. Move across the row of the CUSTOMERS table to find the customer's name ("J.P. Sinclair") and credit limit ($35,000.00), and copy them to the query results table.

5. You've generated a row of query results! Move back to the ORDERS table, and go to the next row. Repeat the process, starting with Step 2, until you run out of orders.

Of course this isn't the only way to generate the query results, but regardless of how you do it, two things will be true:

■ Each row of query results draws its data from a specific *pair* of rows, one from the ORDERS table and one from the CUSTOMERS table.

■ The pair of rows are found by matching the contents of *corresponding columns* from the tables.

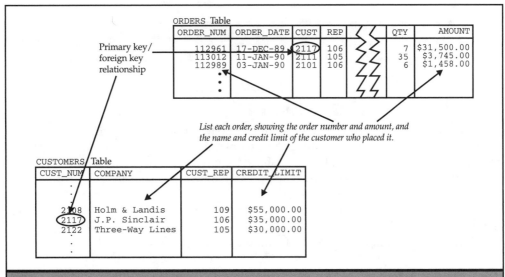

Figure 7-1. *A request that spans two tables*

Figure 7-2. *Manually processing a multitable query*

Simple Joins (Equi-Joins)

The process of forming pairs of rows by matching the contents of related columns is called *joining* the tables. The resulting table (containing data from both of the original tables) is called a *join* between the two tables. (A join based on an exact match between two columns is more precisely called an *equi-join*. Joins can also be based on other kinds of column comparisons, as described later in this chapter.)

Joins are the foundation of multitable query processing in SQL. All of the data in a relational database is stored in its columns as explicit data values, so all possible relationships between tables can be formed by matching the contents of related columns. Joins thus provide a powerful facility for *exercising* the data relationships in a database. In fact, because relational databases do not contain pointers or other mechanisms for relating rows to one another, joins are the *only* mechanism for exercising cross-table data relationships.

Because SQL handles multitable queries by matching columns, it should come as no surprise that the SELECT statement for a multitable query must contain a search condition that specifies the column match. Here is the SELECT statement for the query that was performed manually in Figure 7-2:

List all orders showing order number, amount, customer name, and the customer's credit limit.

```
SELECT ORDER_NUM, AMOUNT, COMPANY, CREDIT_LIMIT
  FROM ORDERS, CUSTOMERS
 WHERE CUST = CUST_NUM
```

```
ORDER_NUM      AMOUNT COMPANY              CREDIT_LIMIT
---------- ----------- -------------------- ------------
    112989  $1,458.00 Jones Mfg.             $65,000.00
    112968  $3,978.00 First Corp.            $65,000.00
    112963  $3,276.00 Acme Mfg.              $50,000.00
    112987 $27,500.00 Acme Mfg.              $50,000.00
    112983    $702.00 Acme Mfg.              $50,000.00
    113027  $4,104.00 Acme Mfg.              $50,000.00
    112993  $1,896.00 Fred Lewis Corp.       $65,000.00
    113065  $2,130.00 Fred Lewis Corp.       $65,000.00
    113036 $22,500.00 Ace International      $35,000.00
    113034    $632.00 Ace International      $35,000.00
    113058  $1,480.00 Holm & Landis          $55,000.00
    113055    $150.00 Holm & Landis          $55,000.00
    113003  $5,625.00 Holm & Landis          $55,000.00
         .
         .
         .
```

This looks just like the queries from the previous chapter, with two new features. First, the FROM clause lists two tables instead of just one. Second, the search condition:

```
CUST = CUST_NUM
```

compares columns from two different tables. We call these two columns the *matching* columns for the two tables. Like all search conditions, this one restricts the rows that appear in the query results. Because this is a two-table query, the search condition restricts the *pairs* of rows that generate the query results. In fact, the search condition specifies the same matching columns you used in the paper-and-pencil query processing. It actually captures the spirit of the manual column matching very well, saying:

"Generate query results only for pairs of rows where the customer number (CUST) in the ORDERS table matches the customer number (CUST_NUM) in the CUSTOMERS table."

Notice that the SELECT statement doesn't say anything about *how* SQL should execute the query. There is no mention of "starting with orders" or "starting with customers." Instead, the query tells SQL *what* the query results should look like and leaves it up to SQL to decide how to generate them.

Parent/Child Queries

The most common multitable queries involve two tables that have a natural parent/ child relationship. The query about orders and customers in the preceding section is an example of such a query. Each order (child) has an associated customer (parent), and each customer (parent) can have many associated orders (children). The pairs of rows that generate the query results are parent/child row combinations.

You may recall from Chapter 4 that foreign keys and primary keys create the parent/child relationship in a SQL database. The table containing the foreign key is the child in the relationship; the table with the primary key is the parent. To exercise the parent/child relationship in a query, you must specify a search condition that compares the foreign key and the primary key. Here is another example of a query that exercises a parent/child relationship, shown in Figure 7-3:

List each salesperson and the city and region where they work.

```
SELECT NAME, CITY, REGION
  FROM SALESREPS, OFFICES
 WHERE REP_OFFICE = OFFICE

NAME             CITY          REGION
--------------   -----------   --------
Mary Jones       New York      Eastern
Sam Clark        New York      Eastern
Bob Smith        Chicago       Eastern
Paul Cruz        Chicago       Eastern
Dan Roberts      Chicago       Eastern
Bill Adams       Atlanta       Eastern
Sue Smith        Los Angeles   Western
Larry Fitch      Los Angeles   Western
Nancy Angelli    Denver        Western
```

The SALESREPS (child) table contains REP_OFFICE, a foreign key for the OFFICES (parent) table. This relationship is used to find the correct OFFICES row for each salesperson, so that the correct city and region can be included in the query results.

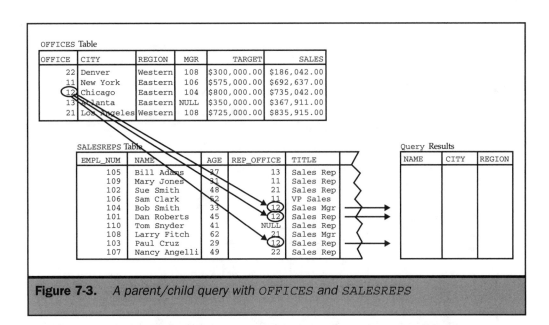

Figure 7-3. *A parent/child query with* OFFICES *and* SALESREPS

Here's another query involving the same two tables, but with the parent and child roles reversed, as shown in Figure 7-4.

List the offices and the names and titles of their managers.

```
SELECT CITY, NAME, TITLE
  FROM OFFICES, SALESREPS
 WHERE MGR = EMPL_NUM
```

```
CITY          NAME          TITLE
------------  ------------  ----------
Chicago       Bob Smith     Sales Mgr
Atlanta       Bill Adams    Sales Rep
New York      Sam Clark     VP Sales
Denver        Larry Fitch   Sales Mgr
Los Angeles   Larry Fitch   Sales Mgr
```

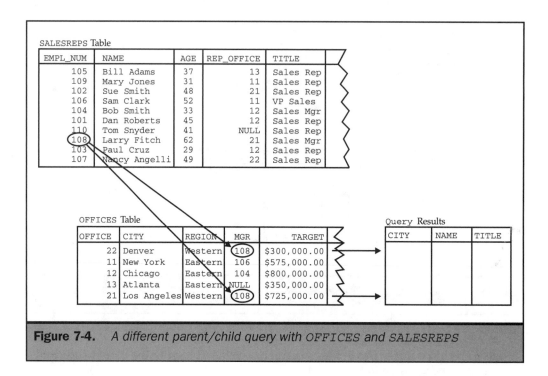

Figure 7-4. *A different parent/child query with OFFICES and SALESREPS*

The OFFICES (child) table contains MGR, a foreign key for the SALESREPS (parent) table. This relationship is used to find the correct SALESREPS row for each salesperson, so that the correct name and title of the manager can be included in the query results.

SQL does not require that the matching columns be included in the results of a multitable query. They are often omitted in practice, as in the two preceding examples. That's because primary keys and foreign keys are often ID numbers (such as the office numbers and employee numbers in the examples), which humans find hard to remember, while the associated names (cities, regions, names, titles) are easier to understand. It's quite common for ID numbers to be used in the WHERE clause to join two tables, and for more descriptive names to be specified in the SELECT clause to generate columns of query results.

Joins with Row Selection Criteria

The search condition that specifies the matching columns in a multitable query can be combined with other search conditions to further restrict the contents of the query results. Suppose you want to rerun the preceding query, showing only offices with large sales targets:

List the offices with a target over $600,000.

```
SELECT CITY, NAME, TITLE
  FROM OFFICES, SALESREPS
 WHERE MGR = EMPL_NUM
   AND TARGET > 600000.00
```

CITY	NAME	TITLE
Chicago	Bob Smith	Sales Mgr
Los Angeles	Larry Fitch	Sales Mgr

With the additional search condition, the rows that appear in the query results are further restricted. The first test (MGR=EMPL_NUM) selects only pairs of OFFICES and SALESREPS rows that have the proper parent/child relationship; the second test further selects only those pairs of rows where the office is above target.

Multiple Matching Columns

The ORDERS table and the PRODUCTS table in the sample database are related by a composite foreign key/primary key pair. The MFR and PRODUCT columns of the ORDERS table together form a foreign key for the PRODUCTS table, matching its MFR_ID and PRODUCT_ID columns, respectively. To join the tables based on this parent/child relationship, you must specify *both* pairs of matching columns, as shown in this example:

List all the orders, showing amounts and product descriptions.

```
SELECT ORDER_NUM, AMOUNT, DESCRIPTION
  FROM ORDERS, PRODUCTS
 WHERE MFR = MFR_ID
   AND PRODUCT = PRODUCT_ID
```

ORDER_NUM	AMOUNT	DESCRIPTION
113027	$4,104.00	Size 2 Widget
112992	$760.00	Size 2 Widget
113012	$3,745.00	Size 3 Widget
112968	$3,978.00	Size 4 Widget
112963	$3,276.00	Size 4 Widget
112983	$702.00	Size 4 Widget
113055	$150.00	Widget Adjuster
113057	$600.00	Widget Adjuster

.
.
.

The search condition in the query tells SQL that the related pairs of rows from the ORDERS and PRODUCTS tables are those where both pairs of matching columns contain the same values. Multicolumn joins involving two tables are less common than single-column joins and are usually found in queries involving compound foreign keys such as this one. There is no SQL restriction on the number of columns that are involved in the matching condition, but joins normally mirror the real-world relationships between entities represented in the database tables, and those relationships are usually embodied in one or just a few columns of the tables.

Queries with Three or More Tables

SQL can combine data from three or more tables using the same basic techniques used for two-table queries. Here is a simple example of a three-table join:

List orders over $25,000, including the name of the salesperson who took the order and the name of the customer who placed it.

```
SELECT ORDER_NUM, AMOUNT, COMPANY, NAME
  FROM ORDERS, CUSTOMERS, SALESREPS
 WHERE CUST = CUST_NUM
   AND REP = EMPL_NUM
   AND AMOUNT > 25000.00
```

ORDER_NUM	AMOUNT	COMPANY	NAME
112987	$27,500.00	Acme Mfg.	Bill Adams
113069	$31,350.00	Chen Associates	Nancy Angelli
113045	$45,000.00	Zetacorp	Larry Fitch
112961	$31,500.00	J.P. Sinclair	Sam Clark

This query uses two foreign keys in the ORDERS table, as shown in Figure 7-5. The CUST column is a foreign key for the CUSTOMERS table, linking each order to the customer who placed it. The REP column is a foreign key for the SALESREPS table, linking each order to the salesperson who took it. Informally speaking, the query links each order to its associated customer and salesperson.

Here is another three-table query that uses a different arrangement of parent/child relationships:

RETRIEVING DATA

List the orders over $25,000, showing the name of the customer who placed the order and the name of the salesperson assigned to that customer.

```
SELECT ORDER_NUM, AMOUNT, COMPANY, NAME
  FROM ORDERS, CUSTOMERS, SALESREPS
 WHERE CUST = CUST_NUM
   AND CUST_REP = EMPL_NUM
   AND AMOUNT > 25000.00
```

```
ORDER_NUM      AMOUNT COMPANY            NAME
---------- ----------- ---------------- ------------
    112987  $27,500.00 Acme Mfg.         Bill Adams
    113069  $31,350.00 Chen Associates   Paul Cruz
    113045  $45,000.00 Zetacorp          Larry Fitch
    112961  $31,500.00 J.P. Sinclair     Sam Clark
```

Figure 7-6 shows the relationships exercised by this query. The first relationship again uses the CUST column from the ORDERS table as a foreign key to the CUSTOMERS table. The second uses the CUST_REP column from the CUSTOMERS table as a foreign key to the SALESREPS table. Informally speaking, this query links each order to its customer, and each customer to their salesperson.

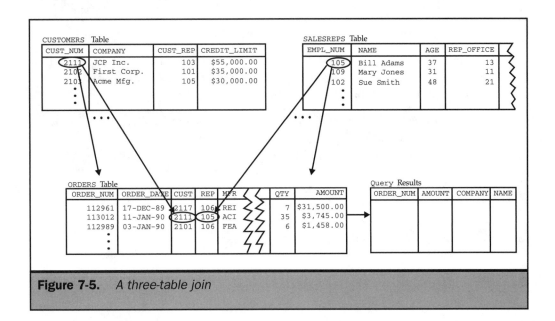

Figure 7-5. *A three-table join*

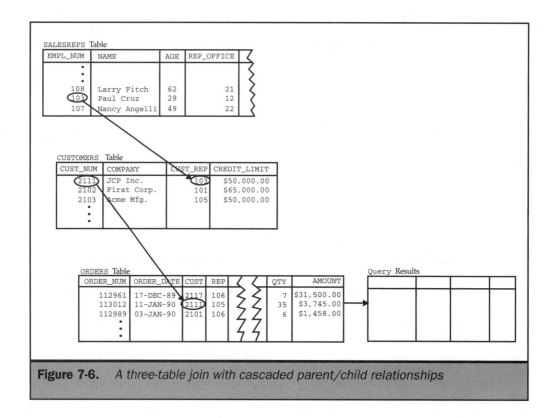

Figure 7-6. *A three-table join with cascaded parent/child relationships*

It's not uncommon to find three-table or even four-table queries used in production SQL applications. Even within the confines of the small, five-table sample database, it's not too hard to find a four-table query that makes sense:

List the orders over $25,000, showing the name of the customer who placed the order, the customer's salesperson, and the office where the salesperson works.

```
SELECT ORDER_NUM, AMOUNT, COMPANY, NAME, CITY
  FROM ORDERS, CUSTOMERS, SALESREPS, OFFICES
 WHERE CUST = CUST_NUM
   AND CUST_REP = EMPL_NUM
   AND REP_OFFICE = OFFICE
   AND AMOUNT > 25000.00
```

```
ORDER_NUM       AMOUNT COMPANY            NAME         CITY
----------  ----------- ----------------  -----------  -----------
   112987   $27,500.00 Acme Mfg.          Bill Adams   Atlanta
   113069   $31,350.00 Chen Associates    Paul Cruz    Chicago
   113045   $45,000.00 Zetacorp           Larry Fitch  Los Angeles
   112961   $31,500.00 J.P. Sinclair      Sam Clark    New York
```

Figure 7-7 shows the parent/child relationships in this query. Logically, it extends the *join* sequence of the previous example one more step, linking an order to its customer, the customer to their salesperson, and the salesperson to their office.

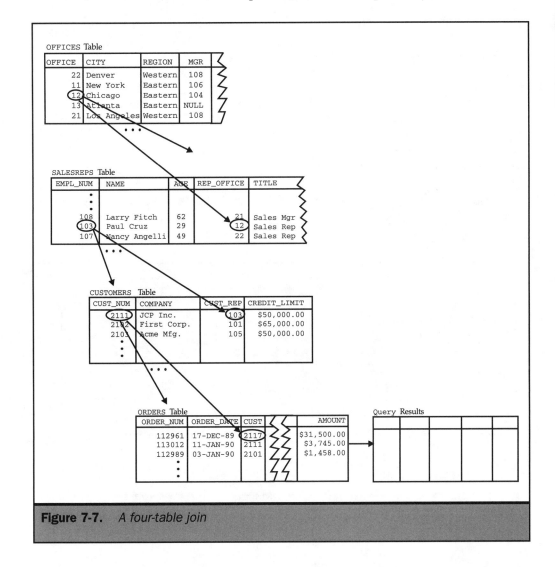

Figure 7-7. *A four-table join*

Other Equi-Joins

The vast majority of multitable queries are based on parent/child relationships, but SQL does not require that the matching columns be related as a foreign key and primary key. Any pair of columns from two tables can serve as matching columns, provided they have comparable data types. The next example demonstrates a query that uses a pair of dates as matching columns.

Find all orders received on days when a new salesperson was hired.

```
SELECT ORDER_NUM, AMOUNT, ORDER_DATE, NAME
  FROM ORDERS, SALESREPS
 WHERE ORDER_DATE = HIRE_DATE

ORDER_NUM       AMOUNT ORDER_DATE  NAME
---------- ----------- ----------- ------------
    112968    $3,978.00 12-OCT-89  Mary Jones
    112979   $15,000.00 12-OCT-89  Mary Jones
    112975    $2,100.00 12-OCT-89  Mary Jones
    112968    $3,978.00 12-OCT-89  Larry Fitch
    112979   $15,000.00 12-OCT-89  Larry Fitch
    112975    $2,100.00 12-OCT-89  Larry Fitch
```

The results of this query come from pairs of rows in the ORDERS and SALESREPS tables where the ORDER_DATE happens to match the HIRE_DATE for the salesperson, as shown in Figure 7-8. Neither of these columns is a foreign key or a primary key,

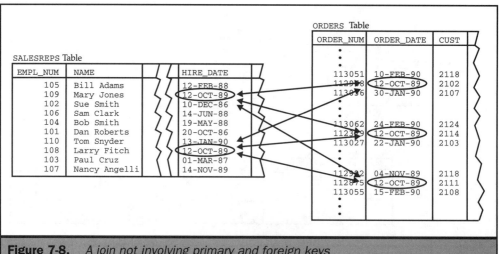

Figure 7-8. *A join not involving primary and foreign keys*

and the relationship between the pairs of rows is admittedly a strange one—the only thing the matched orders and salespeople have in common is that they happen to have the same dates. However, SQL happily joins the tables anyway.

Matching columns like the ones in this example generate a many-to-many relationship between the two tables. Many orders can share a single salesperson's hire date, and more than one salesperson may have been hired on a given order's order date. For example, note that three different orders (112968, 112975, and 112979) were received on October 12, 1989, and two different salespeople (Larry Fitch and Mary Jones) were hired that same day. The three orders and two salespeople produce six rows of query results.

This many-to-many relationship is different from the one-to-many relationship created by primary key/foreign key matching columns. The situation can be summarized as follows:

- Joins that match primary keys to foreign keys always create one-to-many, parent/child relationships.

- Other joins may also generate one-to-many relationships, if the matching column in at least one of the tables has unique values for all rows of the table.

- In general, joins on arbitrary matching columns generate many-to-many relationships.

Note that these three different situations have nothing to do with how you write the SELECT statement that expresses the join. All three types of joins are written the same way—by including a comparison test for the matching column pairs in the WHERE clause. Nonetheless, it's useful to think about joins in this way to understand how to turn an English-language request into the correct SELECT statement.

Non-Equi-Joins

The term *join* applies to any query that combines data from two tables by comparing the values in a pair of columns from the tables. Although joins based on equality between matching columns (equi-joins) are by far the most common joins, SQL also allows you to join tables based on other comparison operators. Here's an example where a greater than (>) comparison test is used as the basis for a join:

List all combinations of salespeople and offices where the salesperson's quota is more than the office's target.

```
SELECT NAME, QUOTA, CITY, TARGET
  FROM SALESREPS, OFFICES
 WHERE QUOTA > TARGET
```

```
NAME                QUOTA CITY           TARGET
-----------    -------------  -------  ------------
Bill Adams     $350,000.00    Denver   $300,000.00
Sue Smith      $350,000.00    Denver   $300,000.00
Larry Fitch    $350,000.00    Denver   $300,000.00
```

As in all two-table queries, each row of the query results comes from a pair of rows, in this case from the SALESREPS and OFFICES tables. The search condition:

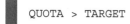

QUOTA > TARGET

selects pairs of rows where the QUOTA column from the SALESREPS row exceeds the TARGET column from the OFFICES row. Note that the pairs of SALESREPS and OFFICES rows selected are related *only* in this way; it is specifically not required that the SALESREPS row represent someone who works in the office represented by the OFFICES row. Admittedly, the example is a bit farfetched, and it illustrates why joins based on inequalities are not very common. However, they can be useful in decision-support applications and other applications that explore more complex interrelationships in the database.

SQL Considerations for Multitable Queries

The multitable queries described thus far have not required any special SQL syntax or language features beyond those described for single-table queries. However, some multitable queries cannot be expressed without the additional SQL language features described in the following sections. Specifically:

■ *Qualified column names* are sometimes needed in multitable queries to eliminate ambiguous column references.

■ *All-column selections* (SELECT *) have a special meaning for multitable queries.

■ *Self-joins* can be used to create a multitable query that relates a table to itself.

■ *Table aliases* can be used in the FROM clause to simplify qualified column names and allow unambiguous column references in self-joins.

Qualified Column Names

The sample database includes several instances where two tables contain columns with the same name. The OFFICES table and the SALESREPS table, for example, both have a column named SALES. The column in the OFFICES table contains year-to-date sales for each office; the one in the SALESREPS table contains year-to-date sales for each salesperson. Normally, there is no confusion between the two columns, because the FROM clause determines which of them is appropriate in any given query, as in these examples:

Show the cities where sales exceed target.

```
SELECT CITY, SALES
  FROM OFFICES
 WHERE SALES > TARGET
```

Show all salespeople with sales over $350,000.

```
SELECT NAME, SALES
  FROM SALESREPS
 WHERE SALES > 350000.00
```

However, here is a query where the duplicate names cause a problem:

Show the name, sales, and office for each salesperson.

```
SELECT NAME, SALES, CITY
  FROM SALESREPS, OFFICES
 WHERE REP_OFFICE = OFFICE
```

```
Error: Ambiguous column name "SALES"
```

Although the English description of the query implies that you want the SALES
column in the SALESREPS table, the SQL query is ambiguous. The DBMS has no way
of knowing whether you want the SALES column from the SALESREPS table or the
one from the OFFICES table, since both are contributing data to the query results. To
eliminate the ambiguity, you must use a qualified column name to identify the column.
Recall from Chapter 5 that a qualified column name specifies the name of a column and
the table containing the column. The qualified names of the two SALES columns in the
sample database are:

```
OFFICES.SALES and SALESREPS.SALES
```

A qualified column name can be used in a SELECT statement anywhere that a
column name is permitted. The table specified in the qualified column name must, of
course, match one of the tables specified in the FROM list. Here is a corrected version
of the previous query that uses a qualified column name:

Show the name, sales, and office for each salesperson.

```
SELECT NAME, SALESREPS.SALES, CITY
  FROM SALESREPS, OFFICES
 WHERE REP_OFFICE = OFFICE
```

```
NAME             SALESREPS.SALES CITY
-------------    --------------- -----------
Mary Jones         $392,725.00 New York
Sam Clark          $299,912.00 New York
Bob Smith          $142,594.00 Chicago
Paul Cruz          $286,775.00 Chicago
Dan Roberts        $305,673.00 Chicago
Bill Adams         $367,911.00 Atlanta
Sue Smith          $474,050.00 Los Angeles
Larry Fitch        $361,865.00 Los Angeles
Nancy Angelli      $186,042.00 Denver
```

Using qualified column names in a multitable query is always a good idea. The disadvantage, of course, is that they make the query text longer. When using interactive SQL, you may want to first try a query with unqualified column names and let SQL find any ambiguous columns. If SQL reports an error, you can edit your query to qualify the ambiguous columns.

All-Column Selections

As discussed in Chapter 6, SELECT * can be used to select all columns of the table named in the FROM clause. In a multitable query, the asterisk selects all columns of *all* tables in the FROM clause. The following query, for example, would produce fifteen columns of query results—the nine columns from the SALESREPS table followed by the six columns from the OFFICES table:

Tell me all about salespeople and the offices where they work.

```
SELECT *
  FROM SALESREPS, OFFICES
 WHERE REP_OFFICE = OFFICE
```

Obviously, the SELECT * form of a query becomes much less practical when there are two, three, or more tables in the FROM clause.

Many SQL dialects treat the asterisk as a special kind of wildcard column name that is expanded into a list of columns. In these dialects, the asterisk can be qualified with a table name, just like a qualified column reference. In the following query, the select item SALESREPS.* is expanded into a list containing only the columns found in the SALESREPS table:

Tell me all about salespeople and the places where they work.

```
SELECT SALESREPS.*, CITY, REGION
  FROM SALESREPS, OFFICES
 WHERE REP_OFFICE = OFFICE
```

The query would produce eleven columns of query results—the nine columns of the SALESREPS table, followed by the two other columns explicitly requested from the OFFICES table. This type of "qualified all-columns" select item is supported in many, but not all brands of SQL-based DBMS. It was not allowed by the SQL1 standard but is part of the ANSI/ISO SQL2 specification.

Self-Joins

Some multitable queries involve a relationship that a table has with itself. For example, suppose you want to list the names of all salespeople and their managers. Each salesperson appears as a row in the SALESREPS table, and the MANAGER column contains the employee number of the salesperson's manager. It would appear that the MANAGER column should be a foreign key for the table that holds data about managers. In fact it is—it's a foreign key for the SALESREPS table itself!

If you tried to express this query like any other two-table query involving a foreign key/primary key match, it would look like this:

```
SELECT NAME, NAME
  FROM SALESREPS, SALESREPS
 WHERE MANAGER = EMPL_NUM
```

This SELECT statement is illegal because of the duplicate reference to the SALESREPS table in the FROM clause. You might also try eliminating the second reference to the SALESREPS table:

```
SELECT NAME, NAME
  FROM SALESREPS
 WHERE MANAGER = EMPL_NUM
```

This query is legal, but it won't do what you want it to do! It's a single-table query, so SQL goes through the SALESREPS table one row at a time, applying the search condition:

```
MANAGER = EMPL_NUM
```

The rows that satisfy this condition are those where the two columns have the same value—that is, rows where a salesperson is their own manager. There are no such rows, so the query would produce no results—not exactly the data that the English-language statement of the query requested.

To understand how SQL solves this problem, imagine there were *two identical copies* of the SALESREPS table, one named EMPS, containing employees, and one named MGRS, containing managers, as shown in Figure 7-9. The MANAGER column of the EMPS table would then be a foreign key for the MGRS table, and the following query would work:

List the names of salespeople and their managers.

```
SELECT EMPS.NAME, MGRS.NAME
  FROM EMPS, MGRS
 WHERE EMPS.MANAGER = MGRS.EMPL_NUM
```

Because the columns in the two tables have identical names, all of the column references are qualified. Otherwise, this looks like an ordinary two-table query.

SQL uses exactly this "imaginary duplicate table" approach to join a table to itself. Instead of actually duplicating the contents of the table, SQL lets you simply refer to it

MGRS (copy of SALESREPS) Table

EMPL_NUM	NAME	AGE	REP_OFFICE
105	Bill Adams	37	13
109	Mary Jones	31	11
102	Sue Smith	48	21
106	Sam Clark	52	11
104	Bob Smith	33	12
101	Dan Roberts	45	12
110	Tom Snyder	41	NULL
108	Larry Fitch	62	21
103	Paul Cruz	29	12
107	Nancy Angelli	49	22

EMPS (copy of SALESREPS) Table

EMPL_NUM	NAME	AGE	REP_OFFICE	TITLE	HIRE_DATE	MANAGER
105	Bill Adams	37	13	Sales Rep	12-JAN-88	104
109	Mary Jones	31	11	Sales Rep	12-OCT-89	106
102	Sue Smith	48	21	Sales Rep	10-DEC-86	108
106	Sam Clark	52	11	VP Sales	14-JUN-88	NULL
104	Bob Smith	33	12	Sales Mgr	19-MAY-87	106
101	Dan Roberts	45	12	Sales Rep	20-OCT-86	104
110	Tom Snyder	41	NULL	Sales Rep	13-JAN-90	101
108	Larry Fitch	62	21	Sales Mgr	12-OCT-89	106
103	Paul Cruz	29	12	Sales Rep	01-MAR-87	104
107	Nancy Angelli	49	22	Sales Rep	14-NOV-88	108

Figure 7-9.   *A self-join of the SALESREPS table*

by a different name, called a *table alias*. Here's the same query, written using the aliases EMPS and MGRS for the SALESREPS table:

List the names of salespeople and their managers.

```
SELECT EMPS.NAME, MGRS.NAME
  FROM SALESREPS EMPS, SALESREPS MGRS
 WHERE EMPS.MANAGER = MGRS.EMPL_NUM
```

```
EMPS.NAME        MGRS.NAME
--------------   ------------
Tom Snyder       Dan Roberts
Bill Adams       Bob Smith
Dan Roberts      Bob Smith
Paul Cruz        Bob Smith
Mary Jones       Sam Clark
Bob Smith        Sam Clark
Larry Fitch      Sam Clark
Sue Smith        Larry Fitch
Nancy Angelli    Larry Fitch
```

The FROM clause assigns a different alias to each of the two "copies" of the SALESREPS table that are involved in the query by specifying the alias name immediately after the actual table name. As the example shows, when a FROM clause contains a table alias, the alias must be used to identify the table in qualified column references. Of course, it's really only necessary to use an alias for one of the two table occurrences in this query. It could just as easily have been written:

```
SELECT SALESREPS.NAME, MGRS.NAME
  FROM SALESREPS, SALESREPS MGRS
 WHERE SALESREPS.MANAGER = MGRS.EMPL_NUM
```

Here the alias MGRS is assigned to one "copy" of the table, while the table's own name is used for the other copy.

Here are some additional examples of self-joins:

List salespeople with a higher quota than their manager.

```
SELECT SALESREPS.NAME, SALESREPS.QUOTA, MGRS.QUOTA
  FROM SALESREPS, SALESREPS MGRS
 WHERE SALESREPS.MANAGER = MGRS.EMPL_NUM
   AND SALESREPS.QUOTA > MGRS.QUOTA
```

```
SALESREPS.NAME    SALESREPS.QUOTA   MGRS.QUOTA
---------------   ---------------   -----------
Bill Adams            $350,000.00   $200,000.00
Dan Roberts           $300,000.00   $200,000.00
Paul Cruz             $275,000.00   $200,000.00
Mary Jones            $300,000.00   $275,000.00
Larry Fitch           $350,000.00   $275,000.00
```

List salespeople who work in different offices than their manager, showing the name and office where each works.

```
SELECT EMPS.NAME, EMP_OFFICE.CITY, MGRS.NAME, MGR_OFFICE.CITY
  FROM SALESREPS EMPS, SALESREPS MGRS,
       OFFICES EMP_OFFICE, OFFICES MGR_OFFICE
 WHERE EMPS.REP_OFFICE = EMP_OFFICE.OFFICE
   AND MGRS.REP_OFFICE = MGR_OFFICE.OFFICE
   AND EMPS.MANAGER = MGRS.EMPL_NUM
   AND EMPS.REP_OFFICE <> MGRS.REP_OFFICE
```

```
EMPS.NAME        EMP_OFFICE.CITY   MGRS.NAME      MGR_OFFICE.CITY
-------------    ---------------   -----------    ----------------
Bob Smith        Chicago           Sam Clark      New York
Bill Adams       Atlanta           Bob Smith      Chicago
Larry Fitch      Los Angeles       Sam Clark      New York
Nancy Angelli    Denver            Larry Fitch    Los Angeles
```

Table Aliases

As described in the previous section, table aliases are required in queries involving self-joins. However, you can use an alias in any query. For example, if a query refers to another user's table, or if the name of a table is very long, the table name can become tedious to type as a column qualifier. This query, which references the BIRTHDAYS table owned by the user named SAM:

List names, quotas, and birthdays of salespeople.

```
SELECT SALESREPS.NAME, QUOTA, SAM.BIRTHDAYS.BIRTH_DATE
  FROM SALESREPS, BIRTHDAYS
 WHERE SALESREPS.NAME = SAM.BIRTHDAYS.NAME
```

becomes easier to read and type when the aliases S and B are used for the two tables:

List names, quotas, and birthdays of salespeople.

```
SELECT S.NAME, S.QUOTA, B.BIRTH_DATE
  FROM SALESREPS S, SAM.BIRTHDAYS B
 WHERE S.NAME = B.NAME
```

Figure 7-10 shows the basic form of the FROM clause for a multitable SELECT statement, complete with table aliases. The clause has two important functions:

- The FROM clause identifies all of the tables that contribute data to the query results. Any columns referenced in the SELECT statement must come from one of the tables named in the FROM clause. (There is an exception for *outer* references contained in a subquery, as described in Chapter 9.)

- The FROM clause specifies the *tag* that is used to identify the table in qualified column references within the SELECT statement. If a table alias is specified, it becomes the table tag; otherwise, the table's name, exactly as it appears in the FROM clause, becomes the tag.

The only requirement for table tags in the FROM clause is that all of the table tags in a given FROM clause must be distinct from each other. The SQL2 specification optionally allows the keyword AS to appear between a table name and table alias. While this makes the FROM clause easier to read, it may not yet be supported in your specific SQL implementation. (Note that the SQL2 specification uses the term *correlation name* to refer to what we have called a *table alias*. The function and meaning of a correlation name are exactly as described here; many SQL products use the term *alias*, and it is more descriptive of the function that a table alias performs. The SQL2 standard specifies a similar technique for designating alternate *column* names, and in that situation the *column alias* name is actually called an *alias* in the standard.)

Figure 7-10.   *The FROM clause syntax diagram*

Multitable Query Performance

As the number of tables in a query grows, the amount of effort required to carry it out increases rapidly. The SQL language itself places no limit on the number of tables joined by a query. Some SQL products do limit the number of tables, with a limit of about eight tables being fairly common. The high processing cost of queries that join many tables imposes an even lower practical limit in many applications.

In online transaction processing (OLTP) applications, it's common for a query to involve only one or two tables. In these applications, response time is critical—the user typically enters one or two items of data and needs a response from the database within a second or two. Here are some typical OLTP queries for the sample database:

- The user enters a customer number into a form, and the DBMS retrieves the customer's credit limit, account balance, and other data (a single-table query).

- A cash register scans a product number from a package and retrieves the product's name and price from the database (a single-table query).

- The user enters a salesperson's name, and the program lists the current orders for that salesperson (a two-table inquiry).

In decision-support applications, by contrast, it's common for a query to involve many different tables and exercise complex relationships in the database. In these applications, the query results are often used to help make expensive decisions, so a query that requires several minutes or even several hours to complete is perfectly acceptable. Here are some typical decision-support queries for the sample database:

- The user enters an office name, and the program lists the 25 largest orders taken by salespeople in that office (a three-table query).

- A report summarizes sales by product type for each salesperson, showing which salespeople are selling which products (a three-table query).

- A manager considers opening a new Seattle sales office and runs a query analyzing the impact on orders, products, customers, and the salespeople who call on them (a four-table query).

The Structure of a Join

For simple joins, it's fairly easy to write the correct SELECT statement based on an English-language request or to look at a SELECT statement and figure out what it does. When many tables are joined or when the search conditions become complex, however, it becomes very difficult just to look at a SELECT statement and figure out what it means. For this reason, it's important to define more carefully and just a bit more formally what a join is, what query results are produced by a given SELECT statement, and just a little bit of the theory of relational database operation that underlies joins.

Table Multiplication

A join is a special case of a more general combination of data from two tables, known as the *Cartesian product* (or just the *product*) of two tables. The product of two tables is another table (the *product table*), which consists of all possible pairs of rows from the two tables. The columns of the product table are all the columns of the first table, followed by all the columns of the second table. Figure 7-11 shows two small sample tables and their product.

If you specify a two-table query without a WHERE clause, SQL produces the product of the two tables as the query result. For example, this query:

Show all possible combinations of salespeople and cities.

```
SELECT NAME, CITY
   FROM SALESREPS, OFFICES
```

would produce the product of the SALESREPS and OFFICES tables, showing all possible salesperson/city pairs. There would be 50 rows of query results (5 offices * 10 salespeople = 50 combinations). Notice that the SELECT statement is exactly the same one you would use to join the two tables, without the WHERE clause that compares the matching columns, as follows:

Show all salespeople and the cities where they work.

```
SELECT NAME, CITY
   FROM SALESREPS, OFFICES
 WHERE REP_OFFICE = OFFICE
```

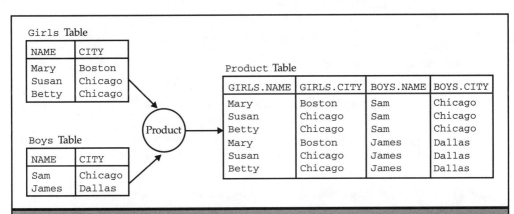

Figure 7-11. *The product of two tables*

These two queries point out an important relationship between joins and products: A join between two tables is just the product of the two tables with some of the rows removed. The removed rows are precisely those that do not meet the matching column condition for the join.

Products are important because they are part of the formal definition of how SQL processes a multitable query, described in the next section.

Rules for Multitable Query Processing

The steps following the code below restate the rules for SQL query processing originally introduced in Figure 6-14 and expands them to include multitable queries. The rules define the meaning of any multitable SELECT statement by specifying a procedure that always generates the correct set of query results. To see how the procedure works, consider this query:

List the company name and all orders for customer number 2103.

```
SELECT COMPANY, ORDER_NUM, AMOUNT
  FROM CUSTOMERS, ORDERS
 WHERE CUST_NUM = CUST
   AND CUST_NUM = 2103
 ORDER BY ORDER_NUM

COMPANY       ORDER_NUM       AMOUNT
----------    ----------    ----------
Acme Mfg.        112963     $3,276.00
Acme Mfg.        112983       $702.00
Acme Mfg.        112987    $27,500.00
Acme Mfg.        113027     $4,104.00
```

To generate the query results for a SELECT statement:

1. If the statement is a UNION of SELECT statements, apply Steps 2 through 5 to each of the statements to generate their individual query results.

2. Form the product of the tables named in the FROM clause. If the FROM clause names a single table, the product is that table.

3. If there is a WHERE clause, apply its search condition to each row of the product table, retaining those rows for which the search condition is TRUE (and discarding those for which it is FALSE or NULL).

4. For each remaining row, calculate the value of each item in the select list to produce a single row of query results. For each column reference, use the value of the column in the current row.

5. If SELECT DISTINCT is specified, eliminate any duplicate rows of query results that were produced.

6. If the statement is a UNION of SELECT statements, merge the query results for the individual statements into a single table of query results. Eliminate duplicate rows unless UNION ALL is specified.

7. If there is an ORDER BY clause, sort the query results as specified.

The rows generated by this procedure comprise the query results.
Following the previous steps:

1. The FROM clause generates all possible combinations of rows from the CUSTOMERS table (21 rows) and the ORDERS table (30 rows), producing a product table of 630 rows.

2. The WHERE clause selects only those rows of the product table where the customer numbers match (CUST_NUM = CUST) and the customer number is the one specified (CUST_NUM = 2103). Only four rows are selected; the other 626 rows are eliminated.

3. The SELECT clause extracts the three requested columns (COMPANY, ORDER_ NUM, and ORD_AMOUNT) from each remaining row of the product table to generate four rows of detailed query results.

4. The ORDER BY clause sorts the four rows on the ORDER_NUM column to generate the final query results.

Obviously no SQL-based DBMS would actually carry out the query this way, but the purpose of the previous definition is not to describe how the query is carried out by a DBMS. Instead, it constitutes a *definition* of how to figure out exactly what a particular multitable query "means"—that is, the set of query results that it should produce.

Outer Joins *

The SQL join operation combines information from two tables by forming *pairs* of related rows from the two tables. The row pairs that make up the joined table are those where the matching columns in each of the two tables have the same value. If one of the rows of a table is unmatched in this process, the join can produce unexpected results, as illustrated by these queries:

List the salespeople and the offices where they work.

```
SELECT NAME, REP_OFFICE
  FROM SALESREPS

NAME            REP_OFFICE
--------------- -----------
Bill Adams              13
Mary Jones              11
Sue Smith               21
```

```
Sam Clark              11
Bob Smith              12
Dan Roberts            12
Tom Snyder           NULL
Larry Fitch            21
Paul Cruz              12
Nancy Angelli          22
```

List the salespeople and the cities where they work.

```
SELECT NAME, CITY
  FROM SALESREPS, OFFICES
 WHERE REP_OFFICE = OFFICE

NAME            CITY
--------------  ------------
Mary Jones      New York
Sam Clark       New York
Bob Smith       Chicago
Paul Cruz       Chicago
Dan Roberts     Chicago
Bill Adams      Atlanta
Sue Smith       Los Angeles
Larry Fitch     Los Angeles
Nancy Angelli   Denver
```

Based on the English-language descriptions of these two queries, you would probably expect them to produce the same number of rows. But the first query includes a row for each of the ten salespeople, while the second query produces only nine. Why? Because Tom Snyder is currently unassigned and has a NULL value in the REP_OFFICE column (which is the matching column for the join). This NULL value doesn't match any of the office numbers in the OFFICES table, so Tom's row in the SALESREPS table is unmatched. As a result, it "vanishes" in the join. The standard SQL join thus has the potential to lose information if the tables being joined contain unmatched rows.

Based on the English-language version of the request, you would probably expect the second query to produce results like these:

List the salespeople and the cities where they work.

```
SELECT NAME, CITY
  FROM SALESREPS, OFFICES
 WHERE REP_OFFICE *= OFFICE
```

```
NAME            CITY
-------------   ------------
Tom Snyder      NULL
Mary Jones      New York
Sam Clark       New York
Bob Smith       Chicago
Paul Cruz       Chicago
Dan Roberts     Chicago
Bill Adams      Atlanta
Sue Smith       Los Angeles
Larry Fitch     Los Angeles
Nancy Angelli   Denver
```

These query results are generated by using a different type of join operation, called an *outer join* (indicated by the "*=" notation in the WHERE clause). The outer join is an extension of the standard join described earlier in this chapter, which is sometimes called an *inner join*. The SQL1 standard specifies only the inner join; it does not include the outer join. The earlier IBM SQL products also support only the inner join. However, the outer join is a well-understood and useful part of the relational database model, and it has been implemented in many non-IBM SQL products, including the flagship database products from Microsoft, Sybase, Oracle, and IBM's Informix. The outer join is also the most natural way to express a certain type of query request, as shown in the remainder of this section.

To understand the outer join well, it's useful to move away from the sample database and consider the two simple tables in Figure 7-12. The GIRLS table lists five girls and the cities where they live; the BOYS table lists five boys and the cities where they live. To find the girl/boy pairs who live in the same city, you could use this query, which forms the inner join of the two tables:

List the girls and boys who live in the same city.

```
SELECT *
  FROM GIRLS, BOYS
 WHERE GIRLS.CITY = BOYS.CITY

GIRLS.NAME    GIRLS.CITY    BOYS.NAME    BOYS.CITY
-----------   -----------   ----------   ----------
Mary          Boston        John         Boston
Mary          Boston        Henry        Boston
Susan         Chicago       Sam          Chicago
Betty         Chicago       Sam          Chicago
```

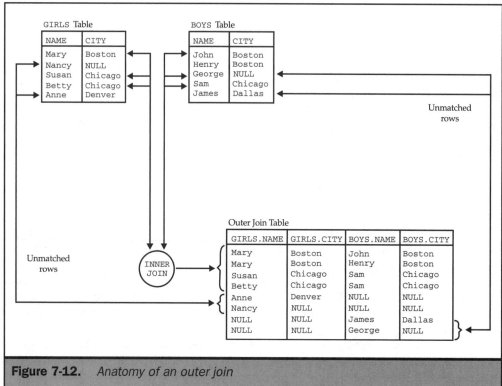

Figure 7-12. *Anatomy of an outer join*

The inner join produces four rows of query results. Notice that two of the girls (Anne and Nancy) and two of the boys (James and George) are not represented in the query results. These rows cannot be paired with any row from the other table, and so they are missing from the inner join results. Two of the unmatched rows (Anne and James) have valid values in their CITY columns, but they don't match any cities in the opposite table. The other two unmatched rows (Nancy and George) have NULL values in their CITY columns, and by the rules of SQL NULL handling, the NULL value doesn't match *any* other value (even another NULL value).

Suppose you wanted to list the girl/boy pairs who share the same cities and include the unmatched girls and boys in the list. The outer join of the GIRLS and BOYS tables produces exactly this result. The following list shows the procedure for constructing the outer join, and the outer join is shown graphically in Figure 7-12.

1. Begin with the inner join of the two tables, using matching columns in the normal way.

2. For each row of the first table that is not matched by any row in the second table, add one row to the query results, using the values of the columns in the first table, and assuming a NULL value for all columns of the second table.

3. For each row of the second table that is not matched by any row in the first table, add one row to the query results, using the values of the columns in the second table, and assuming a NULL value for all columns of the first table.

4. The resulting table is the outer join of the two tables.

Here is the SQL statement that produces the outer join:

List girls and boys in the same city, including any unmatched girls or boys.

```
SELECT *
  FROM GIRLS, BOYS
 WHERE GIRLS.CITY *=* BOYS.CITY

GIRLS.NAME  GIRLS.CITY  BOYS.NAME  BOYS.CITY
----------  ----------  ---------  ----------
Mary        Boston      John       Boston
Mary        Boston      Henry      Boston
Susan       Chicago     Sam        Chicago
Betty       Chicago     Sam        Chicago
Anne        Denver      NULL       NULL
Nancy       NULL        NULL       NULL
NULL        NULL        James      Dallas
NULL        NULL        George     NULL
```

The outer join of the two tables contains eight rows. Four of the rows are identical to those of the inner join between the two tables. Two other rows, for Anne and Nancy, come from the unmatched rows of the GIRLS table. These rows have been NULL-*extended* by matching them to an imaginary row of all NULLs in the BOYS table, and adding them to the query results. The final two rows, for James and George, come from the unmatched rows of the BOYS table. These rows have also been NULL-extended by matching them to an imaginary row of all NULLs in the GIRLS table and then adding them to the query results.

As this example shows, the outer join is an "information-preserving" join. Every row of the BOYS table is represented in the query results (some more than once). Similarly, every row of the GIRLS table is represented in the query results (again, some more than once).

Left and Right Outer Joins *

Technically, the outer join produced by the previous query is called the *full outer join* of the two tables. Both tables are treated symmetrically in the full outer join. Two other well-defined outer joins do not treat the two tables symmetrically.

The *left outer join* between two tables is produced by following Step 1 and Step 2 in the previous numbered list but omitting Step 3. The left outer join thus includes

NULL-extended copies of the unmatched rows from the first (left) table but does not include any unmatched rows from the second (right) table. Here is a left outer join between the GIRLS and BOYS tables:

List girls and boys in the same city and any unmatched girls.

```
SELECT *
  FROM GIRLS, BOYS
 WHERE GIRLS.CITY *= BOYS.CITY
```

GIRLS.NAME	GIRLS.CITY	BOYS.NAME	BOYS.CITY
Mary	Boston	John	Boston
Mary	Boston	Henry	Boston
Susan	Chicago	Sam	Chicago
Betty	Chicago	Sam	Chicago
Anne	Denver	NULL	NULL
Nancy	NULL	NULL	NULL

The query produces six rows of query results, showing the matched girl/boy pairs and the unmatched girls. The unmatched boys are missing from the results.

Similarly, the *right outer join* between two tables is produced by following Step 1 and Step 3 in the previous numbered list but omitting Step 2. The right outer join thus includes NULL-extended copies of the unmatched rows from the second (right) table but does not include the unmatched rows of the first (left) table. Here is a right outer join between the GIRLS and BOYS tables:

List girls and boys in the same city and any unmatched boys.

```
SELECT *
  FROM GIRLS, BOYS
 WHERE GIRLS.CITY =* BOYS.CITY
```

GIRLS.NAME	GIRLS.CITY	BOYS.NAME	BOYS.CITY
Mary	Boston	John	Boston
Mary	Boston	Henry	Boston
Susan	Chicago	Sam	Chicago
Betty	Chicago	Sam	Chicago
NULL	NULL	James	Dallas
NULL	NULL	George	NULL

This query also produces six rows of query results, showing the matched girl/boy pairs and the unmatched boys. This time the unmatched girls are missing from the results.

As noted before, the left and right outer joins do not treat the two joined tables symmetrically. It is often useful to think about one of the tables being the "major" table (the one whose rows are all represented in the query results) and the other table being the "minor" table (the one whose columns contain NULL values in the joined query results). In a left outer join, the left (first-mentioned) table is the major table, and the right (later-named) table is the minor table. The roles are reversed in a right outer join (right table is major, left table is minor).

In practice, the left and right outer joins are more useful than the full outer join, especially when joining data from two tables using a parent/child (primary key/foreign key) relationship. To illustrate, consider once again the sample database. We have already seen one example involving the SALESREPS and OFFICES table. The REP_OFFICE column in the SALESREPS table is a foreign key to the OFFICES table; it tells the office where each salesperson works, and it is allowed to have a NULL value for a new salesperson who has not yet been assigned to an office. Tom Snyder is such a salesperson in the sample database. Any join that exercises this SALESREPS-to-OFFICES relationship and expects to include data for Tom Snyder *must* be an outer join, with the SALESREPS table as the major table. Here is the example used earlier:

List the salespeople and the cities where they work.

```
SELECT NAME, CITY
  FROM SALESREPS, OFFICES
 WHERE REP_OFFICE *= OFFICE

NAME             CITY
--------------   ------------
Tom Snyder       NULL
Mary Jones       New York
Sam Clark        New York
Bob Smith        Chicago
Paul Cruz        Chicago
Dan Roberts      Chicago
Bill Adams       Atlanta
Sue Smith        Los Angeles
Larry Fitch      Los Angeles
Nancy Angelli    Denver
```

Note in this case (a left outer join), the "child" table (SALESREPS, the table with the foreign key) is the major table in the outer join, and the "parent" table (OFFICES) is the minor table. The objective is to retain rows containing NULL foreign key values (like Tom Snyder's) from the child table in the query results, so the child table becomes the major table in the outer join. It doesn't matter whether the query is actually expressed as a left outer join (as it was previously) or as a right outer join like this:

List the salespeople and the cities where they work.

```
SELECT NAME, CITY
  FROM SALESREPS, OFFICES
 WHERE OFFICE =* REP_OFFICE

NAME             CITY
--------------   ------------
Tom Snyder       NULL
Mary Jones       New York
Sam Clark        New York
Bob Smith        Chicago
Paul Cruz        Chicago
Dan Roberts      Chicago
Bill Adams       Atlanta
Sue Smith        Los Angeles
Larry Fitch      Los Angeles
Nancy Angelli    Denver
```

What matters is that the child table is the major table in the outer join.

There are also useful joined queries where the parent is the major table and the child table is the minor table. For example, suppose the company in the sample database opens a new sales office in Dallas, but initially the office has no salespeople assigned to it. If you want to generate a report listing all of the offices and the names of the salespeople who work there, you might want to include a row representing the Dallas office. Here is the outer join query that produces those results:

List the offices and the salespeople who work in each one.

```
SELECT CITY, NAME
  FROM OFFICES, SALESREPS
 WHERE OFFICE *= REP_OFFICE

CITY          NAME
------------  --------------
New York      Mary Jones
New York      Sam Clark
Chicago       Bob Smith
Chicago       Paul Cruz
Chicago       Dan Roberts
Atlanta       Bill Adams
```

```
Los Angeles   Sue Smith
Los Angeles   Larry Fitch
Denver        Nancy Angelli
Dallas        NULL
```

In this case, the parent table (OFFICES) is the major table in the outer join, and the child table (SALESREPS) is the minor table. The objective is to insure that all rows from the OFFICES table are represented in the query results, so it plays the role of major table. The roles of the two tables are precisely reversed from the previous example. Of course, the row for Tom Snyder, which was included in the query results for the earlier example (when SALESREPS was the major table), is missing from this set of query results because SALESREPS is now the minor table.

Outer Join Notation *

Because the outer join was not part of the SQL1 standard and was not implemented in early IBM SQL products, the DBMS vendors who support the outer join have used various notations in their SQL dialects. The "*=*" notation used in the earlier examples of this section is used by SQL Server. This notation indicates an outer join by appending an asterisk (*) to the comparison test in the WHERE clause that defines the join condition. To indicate the full outer join between two tables, TBL1 and TBL2, on columns COL1 and COL2, an asterisk (*) is placed before and after the standard join operator. The resulting full outer join comparison test looks like this:

```
WHERE COL1 *=* COL2
```

To indicate a left outer join of TBL1 to TBL2, only the leading asterisk is specified, giving a comparison test like this:

```
WHERE COL1 *= COL2
```

To indicate a right outer join of TBL1 to TBL2, only the trailing asterisk is specified, giving a comparison test like this:

```
WHERE COL1 =* COL2
```

An outer join can be used with any of the comparison operators using the same notation. For example, a left outer join of TBL1 to TBL2 using a greater than or equal (>=) comparison would produce a comparison test like this:

```
WHERE COL1 *>= COL2
```

RETRIEVING DATA

Oracle also supports the outer join operation but uses a different notation. This notation indicates the outer join in the WHERE clause by including a parenthesized plus sign following the column *whose table is to have the imaginary* NULL *row added* (that is, the minor table in the outer join). The left outer join of TBL1 to TBL2 produces a search condition that looks like this:

```
WHERE COL1 = COL2 (+)
```

and the right outer join of TBL1 to TBL2 produces a search condition that looks like this:

```
WHERE COL1 (+) = COL2
```

Note that the plus sign appears on the *opposite* side of the comparison from where the asterisk appears in the SQL Server notation. Oracle does not support a full outer join, but as indicated earlier, this does not diminish the practical usefulness of the Oracle outer join capability.

Although both of these outer join notations are relatively convenient, they're also somewhat deceiving. Recall that the rules for multitable SQL query processing begin by examining the FROM clause of a query and conceptually building the product of the two (or more) tables. Only after the product table is constructed does the DBMS start eliminating rows that do not meet the WHERE clause search condition. But with the SQL Server or Oracle notation, the FROM clause doesn't tell the DBMS whether to build a product table that is only the inner join or one that includes the NULL-extended rows of an outer join. To determine this, the DBMS must "look ahead" to the WHERE clause. A more serious problem is that a join between two tables may involve more than one pair of matching columns, and it's not clear how the notation should be used when there are two or three matching column pairs.

Other problems with the outer join notation arise when it is extended to three or more tables. It's easy to extend the notion of an outer join to three tables:

```
TBL1 OUTER-JOIN TBL2 OUTER-JOIN TBL3
```

This is a perfectly legitimate set of database operations according to the theory of relational databases. But the result depends upon the order in which the outer join operations are performed. The results of:

```
(TBL1 OUTER-JOIN TBL2) OUTER-JOIN TBL3
```

will in general be different from the results of:

```
TBL1 OUTER-JOIN (TBL2 OUTER-JOIN TBL3)
```

Using either the SQL Server or Oracle notations, it's impossible to specify the evaluation order of the outer joins. Because of this, the results produced by the outer join of three or more tables depend upon the specifics of the DBMS implementation.

Joins and the SQL2 Standard

Outer joins posed a problem for the writers of the SQL2 standard. Because outer joins are the only way to represent some extremely useful queries, it was important that the SQL2 standard include support for outer joins. In addition, outer joins were supported in many commercial SQL products and were becoming a more important part of the SQL language. However, the methods used to represent outer joins varied widely among the different SQL products, as shown in the preceding sections. Furthermore, the methods used to denote outer joins in commercial products all had deficiencies and had been chosen more because of their minor impact on the SQL language than because of their clarity or correctness.

Against this background, the SQL2 standard specified a brand new method for supporting outer joins, which was not based on the established notation of a popular SQL product. The SQL2 specification puts the support for outer joins into the FROM clause, with an elaborate syntax that allows the user to specify exactly how the source tables for a query are to be joined together. The outer join support in the SQL2 standard has two distinct advantages. First, the SQL2 standard can express even the most complex of joins. Second, existing database products can support the SQL2 extensions to SQL1 and retain support for their own proprietary outer join syntax without conflict. IBM's DB2 relational database, for example, has added support for most, but not all, of the new SQL2 join syntax at this writing. It's reasonable to expect that most of the major DBMS brands will follow, and that the SQL2-style join features will become a part of the SQL mainstream over the next several years.

The advantages of the SQL2 expanded join support come at the expense of some significant added complexity for what had previously been one of the simpler parts of the SQL language. In fact, the expanded join support is part of a much larger expansion of query capabilities in SQL2 which add even more capability and complexity. The other expanded features include set operations on query results (union, intersection, and differences of tables) and much richer query expressions that manipulate rows and tables and allow them to be used in subqueries. The expanded join-related capabilities are described in this section. The other expanded capabilities are described in the next chapter, after the discussion of basic subqueries.

Inner Joins in SQL2 *

Figure 7-13 shows a simplified form of the extended SQL2 syntax for the FROM clause. It's easiest to understand all of the options provided by considering each type of join,

Figure 7-13. *Extended FROM clause in the SQL2 standard*

one by one, starting with the basic inner join and then moving to the various forms of outer join. The standard inner join of the GIRLS and BOYS tables can be expressed in SQL1 language:

```
SELECT *
  FROM GIRLS, BOYS
 WHERE GIRLS.CITY = BOYS.CITY
```

This is still an acceptable statement in SQL2. The writers of the SQL2 standard really couldn't have made it illegal without "breaking" all of the millions of multitable SQL queries that had already been written by the early 1990s. But the SQL2 standard specifies an alternative way of expressing the same query:

```
SELECT *
  FROM GIRLS INNER JOIN BOYS
    ON GIRLS.CITY = BOYS.CITY
```

Note that the two tables to be joined are explicitly connected by a JOIN operation, and the search condition that describes the join is now specified in an ON clause within the FROM clause. The search condition following the keyword ON can be any search condition that specifies the criteria used to match rows of the two joined tables. The columns referenced in the search condition must come only from the two joined tables. For example, assume that the BOYS table and the GIRLS table were each extended by adding an AGE column. Here is a join that matches girl/boy pairs in the same city and also requires that the boy and girl in each pair be the same age:

```
SELECT *
  FROM GIRLS INNER JOIN BOYS
    ON (GIRLS.CITY = BOYS.CITY)
   AND (GIRLS.AGE = BOYS.AGE)
```

In these simple two-table joins, the entire contents of the WHERE clause simply moved into the ON clause, and the ON clause doesn't add any functionality to the SQL language. However, recall from earlier in this chapter that in an outer join involving three tables or more, the order in which the joins occur affect the query results. The ON clause provides detailed control over how these multitable joins are processed, as described later in this chapter.

The SQL2 standard permits another variation on the simple inner join query between the GIRLS and BOYS tables. Because the matching columns in the two tables have the same names and are being compared for equality (which is often the case), an alternative form of the ON clause, specifying a list of matching column names, can be used:

```
SELECT *
  FROM GIRLS INNER JOIN BOYS
 USING (CITY, AGE)
```

The USING clause specifies a comma-separated list of the matching column names, which must be identical in both tables. It is completely equivalent to the ON clause that specifies each matching column pair explicitly, but it's a lot more compact and therefore easier to understand. Of course, if the matching columns have different names in the BOYS table and GIRLS table, then an ON clause or a WHERE clause with an equals test must be used. The ON clause must also be used if the join does not involve equality of the matching columns. For example, if you wanted to select girl/boy pairs where the girl was required to be older than the boy, you must use an ON clause to specify the join:

```
SELECT *
  FROM GIRLS INNER JOIN BOYS
    ON (GIRLS.CITY = BOYS.CITY
   AND GIRLS.AGE > BOYS.AGE)
```

There is one final variation on this simple query that illustrates another feature of the SQL2 FROM clause. A join between two tables where the matching columns are *exactly* those specific columns from the two tables that have identical names is called a *natural join*, because usually this is precisely the most "natural" way to join the two tables. The query selecting girl/boy pairs who live in the same city and have the same age can be expressed as a natural join using this SQL2 query:

```
SELECT *
  FROM GIRLS NATURAL INNER JOIN BOYS
```

If the NATURAL keyword is specified, the ON and USING clauses may not be used in the join specification, because the natural join specifically defines the search condition to be used to join the tables—all of the columns with identical column names in both tables are to be matched.

The SQL2 standard assumes that the "default" join between two tables is an inner join. You can omit the keyword INNER from any of the preceding examples, and the resulting query remains a legal SQL2 statement with the same meaning.

Outer Joins in SQL2 *

The SQL2 standard provides complete support for outer joins using the same clauses described in the preceding section for inner joins and additional keywords. For example, the full outer join of the GIRLS and BOYS tables (without the AGE columns) is generated by this query:

```
SELECT *
  FROM GIRLS FULL OUTER JOIN BOYS
    ON GIRLS.CITY = BOYS.CITY
```

As explained earlier in this chapter, the query results will contain a row for each matched girl/boy pair, as well as one row for each unmatched boy, extended with NULL values in the columns from the other, unmatched table. SQL2 allows the same variations for outer joins as for inner joins; the query could also have been written:

```
SELECT *
   FROM GIRLS NATURAL FULL OUTER JOIN BOYS
```

or

```
SELECT *
  FROM GIRLS FULL OUTER JOIN BOYS
 USING (CITY)
```

Just as the keyword INNER is optional in the SQL2 language, the SQL2 standard also allows you to omit the keyword OUTER. The preceding query could also have been written:

```
SELECT *
  FROM GIRLS FULL JOIN BOYS
 USING (CITY)
```

The DBMS can infer from the word FULL that an outer join is required.

By specifying LEFT or RIGHT instead of FULL, the SQL2 language extends quite naturally to left or right outer joins. Here is the left outer join version of the same query:

```
SELECT *
  FROM GIRLS LEFT OUTER JOIN BOYS
 USING (CITY)
```

As described earlier in the chapter, the query results will include matched girl/boy pairs and NULL-extended rows for each unmatched row in the GIRLS table (the "left" table in the join), but the results do not include unmatched rows from the BOYS table. Conversely, the right outer join version of the same query, specified like this:

```
SELECT *
  FROM GIRLS RIGHT OUTER JOIN BOYS
 USING (CITY)
```

includes boy/girl pairs and unmatched rows in the BOYS table (the "right" table in the join) but does not include unmatched rows from the GIRLS table.

Cross Joins and Union Joins in SQL2 *

The SQL2 support for extended joins includes two other methods for combining data from two tables. A *cross join* is another name for the Cartesian product of two tables, as described earlier in this chapter. A *union join* is closely related to the full outer join; its query results are a subset of those generated by the full outer join.

Here is a SQL2 query that generates the complete product of the GIRLS and BOYS tables:

```
SELECT *
  FROM GIRLS CROSS JOIN BOYS
```

By definition, the Cartesian product (also sometimes called the *cross product*, hence the name "CROSS JOIN") contains every possible pair of rows from the two tables. It "multiplies" the two tables, turning tables of, for example, three girls and two boys into a table of six (3×2 = 6) boy/girl pairs. No "matching columns" or "selection criteria" are associated with the cross products, so the ON clause and the USING clause are not allowed. Note that the cross join really doesn't add any new capabilities to the SQL language. Exactly the same query results can be generated with an inner join that specifies no matching columns. So the preceding query could just as well have been written as:

```
SELECT *
  FROM GIRLS, BOYS
```

The use of the keywords CROSS JOIN in the FROM clause simply makes the cross join more explicit. In most databases, the cross join of two tables by itself is of very little practical use. Its usefulness really comes as a building block for more complex query expressions that start with the cross product of two tables and then use SQL2 summary query capabilities (described in the next chapter) or SQL2 set operations to further manipulate the results.

The union join in SQL2 combines some of the features of the UNION operation (described in the previous chapter) with some of the features of the join operations described in this chapter. Recall that the UNION operation effectively combines the rows of two tables, which must have the same number of columns and the same data types for each corresponding column. This query, which uses a simple UNION operation:

```
SELECT *
  FROM GIRLS
UNION ALL
SELECT *
  FROM BOYS
```

when applied to a three-row table of girls and a two-row table of boys yields a five-row table of query results. Each row of query results corresponds precisely to either a row of the GIRLS table or a row of the BOYS table from which it was derived. The query results have two columns, NAME and CITY, because the GIRLS and BOYS tables each have these two columns.

The union join of the GIRLS and BOYS tables is specified by this SQL2 query:

```
SELECT *
  FROM GIRLS
  UNION JOIN BOYS
```

The query results again have five rows, and again each row of results is contributed by exactly one of the rows in the GIRLS table or the BOYS table. But unlike the simple union, these query results have four columns—all of the columns of the first table *plus* all of the columns of the second table. In this aspect, the union join is like all of the other joins. For each row of query results contributed by the GIRLS table, the columns that come from the GIRLS table receive the corresponding data values; the other columns (those that come from the BOYS table) have NULL values. Similarly, for each row of query results contributed by the BOYS table, the columns that come from the BOYS table receive the corresponding data values; the other columns (this time, those that come from the GIRLS table) have NULL values.

Another way of looking at the results of the union join is to compare them to the results of a full outer join of the GIRLS and BOYS tables. The union join results include the NULL-extended rows of data from the GIRLS table *and* the NULL-extended rows of data from the BOYS table, but they do *not* include any of the rows generated by matching columns. Referring back to the definition of an outer join in Figure 7-14, the union join is produced by omitting Step 1 and following Step 2 and Step 3.

Finally, it's useful to examine the relationships between the sets of rows produced by the cross join, the various types of outer joins, and the inner join shown in Figure 7-14. When joining two tables, TBL1 with m rows and TBL2 with n rows, the figure shows that:

- The *cross join* will contain $m \times n$ rows, consisting of all possible row pairs from the two tables.

- TBL1 INNER JOIN TBL2 will contain some number of rows, r, which is less than $m \times n$. The inner join is strictly a subset of the cross join. It is formed by eliminating those rows from the cross join that do not satisfy the matching condition for the inner join.

- The *left outer join* contains all of the rows from the inner join, plus each unmatched row from TBL1, NULL-extended.

- The *right outer join* also contains all of the rows from the inner join, plus each unmatched row from TBL2, NULL-extended.

Figure 7-14.   *Relationships among SQL2 join types*

- The *full outer join* contains all of the rows from the inner join, plus each unmatched row from TBL1, NULL-extended, plus each unmatched row from TBL2, NULL-extended. Roughly speaking, its query results are equal to the left outer join "plus" the right outer join.

- The *union join* contains all of the rows of TBL1, NULL-extended, plus all of the rows of TBL2, NULL-extended. Roughly speaking, its query results are the full outer join "minus" the inner join.×

Multitable Joins in SQL2

An important advantage of the SQL2 notation is that it allows very clear specification of three-table or four-table joins. To build these more complex joins, any of the join expressions shown in Figure 7-13 and described in the preceding sections can be enclosed in parentheses. The resulting join expression can itself be used in another join expression, as if it were a simple table. Just as SQL allows you to combine mathematical operations (+, −, *, and /) with parentheses and build more complex expressions, the SQL2 standard allows you to build more complex join expressions in the same way.

To illustrate multitable joins, assume that a new PARENTS table has been added to the database containing the GIRLS and BOYS example we have been using. The PARENTS table has three columns:

CHILD   Matches the NAME column in the GIRLS or BOYS table

TYPE   Specifies FATHER or MOTHER

PNAME   First name of the parent

A row in the GIRLS or BOYS table can have two matching rows in the PARENTS table, one specifying a MOTHER and one a FATHER, or it can have only one of these rows, or it can have no matching rows if no data on the child's parents is available. The GIRLS, BOYS, and PARENTS tables together provide a rich set of data for some multitable join examples.

For example, suppose you wanted to make a list of all of the girls, along with the names of their mothers and the names of the boys who live in the same city. Here is one query that produces the list:

```
SELECT GIRLS.NAME, PNAME, BOYS.NAME
  FROM ((GIRLS JOIN PARENTS
    ON PARENT.CHILD = NAME)
  JOIN BOYS
    ON (GIRLS.CITY = BOYS.CITY))
 WHERE TYPE = "MOTHER"
```

Because both of these joins are inner joins, any girl who does not have a boy living in the same city or any girl who does not have a mother in the database will not show up in the query results. This may or may not be the desired result. To include those girls without a matching mother in the database, you would change the join between the GIRLS and the PARENTS table to a left outer join, like this:

```
SELECT GIRLS.NAME, PNAME, BOYS.NAME
  FROM ((GIRLS LEFT JOIN PARENTS
    ON PARENT.CHILD = NAME)
  JOIN BOYS
    ON (GIRLS.CITY = BOYS.CITY))
 WHERE (TYPE = "MOTHER") OR (TYPE IS NULL)
```

This query will include all of the girl/boy pairs, regardless of whether the girls have a mother in the database, but it will still omit girls who do not live in a city with any of the boys. To include these girls as well, the second join must also be converted to a left outer join:

```
SELECT GIRLS.NAME, PNAME, BOYS.NAME
  FROM ((GIRLS LEFT JOIN PARENTS
    ON PARENT.CHILD = NAME)
  LEFT JOIN BOYS
    ON (GIRLS.CITY = BOYS.CITY))
WHERE (TYPE = "MOTHER") OR (TYPE IS NULL)
```

Note that the NULL-extension of the GIRLS rows by the outer join with their mothers also creates some additional complication in the WHERE clause. The girls without matching mothers will generate rows with not only a NULL mother's name (PNAME) column but also a NULL value in the TYPE column. The simple selection criterion:

```
WHERE (TYPE = "MOTHER")
```

would generate an "unknown" result for these rows, and they will not be included in the query results. But the entire reason for using the left outer join was to make certain they were included! To solve this problem, the WHERE clause is expanded to also test for, and allow, rows where the parent type is NULL.

As one final example, suppose you want to generate a girl/boy listing again, but this time you want to include the name of the boy's father and the girl's mother in the query results. This query requires a four-table join (BOYS, GIRLS, and two copies of the PARENTS table, one for joining to the boys information to get father names and one for joining to the girls information to obtain mother names). Again the potential for unmatched rows in the joins means there are several possible "right" answers to the query. Suppose, as before, that you want to include all girls and boys in the boy/girl pairing, even if the boy or girl does not have a matching row in the PARENTS table. You need to use outer joins for the (BOYS join PARENTS) and (GIRLS join PARENTS) parts of the query, but an inner join for the (BOYS join GIRLS) part of the query. This SQL2 query yields the desired results:

```
SELECT GIRLS.NAME, MOTHERS.PNAME, BOYS.NAME, FATHERS.PNAME
  FROM ((GIRLS LEFT JOIN PARENTS AS MOTHERS
    ON ((CHILD = GIRLS.NAME) AND (TYPE = "MOTHER")))
  JOIN (BOYS LEFT JOIN PARENTS AS FATHERS
    ON ((CHILD = BOYS.NAME) AND (TYPE = "FATHER"))))
  USING (CITY)
```

This query solves the WHERE-clause test problem in a different way—by moving the test for the TYPE of parent into the ON clause of the join specification. In this position, the test for appropriate TYPE of parent will be performed when the DBMS finds matching columns to construct the join, before the NULL-extended rows are added to the outer join results. Because the PARENTS table is being used twice in the FROM clause, in two different roles, it's necessary to give it two different table aliases so that the correct names can be specified in the select list.

As this example shows, even a four-join query like this one can become quite complex with the SQL2 syntax. However, despite the complexity, the SQL2 query does specify *precisely* the query that the DBMS is to carry out. There is no ambiguity about the order in which the tables are joined, or about which joins are inner or outer joins. Overall, the added capability is well worth the added complexity introduced by the extended SQL2 FROM clause.

Although none of the query examples included in this section had WHERE or ORDER BY clauses, they can be freely used with the extended FROM clause in SQL2. The relationship among the clauses is simple and remains as described earlier in this chapter. The processing specified in the FROM clauses occurs first, including any joins or unions. The join criteria specified in a USING or ON clause are applied as a part of the particular join specification where they appear. When processing of the FROM class is complete, the resulting table is used to apply the selection criteria in the WHERE clause. Thus, the ON clause specifies search criteria that apply to specific joins; the WHERE clause specifies search criteria that apply to the entire table resulting from these joins.

Summary

This chapter described how SQL handles queries that combine data from two or more tables:

- In a multitable query (a *join*), the tables containing the data are named in the FROM clause.

- Each row of query results is a combination of data from a single row in each of the tables, and it is the *only* row that draws its data from that particular combination.

- The most common multitable queries use the parent/child relationships created by primary keys and foreign keys.

- In general, joins can be built by comparing *any* pair(s) of columns from the two joined tables, using either a test for equality or any other comparison test.

- A join can be thought of as the product of two tables from which some of the rows have been removed.

- A table can be joined to itself; self-joins require the use of a table alias.

- Outer joins extend the standard (inner) join by retaining unmatched rows of one or both of the joined tables in the query results, and using NULL values for data from the other table.

- The SQL2 standard provides comprehensive support for inner and outer joins, and for combining the results of joins with other multitable operations such as unions, intersections, and differences.

The
Complete
Reference

Chapter 8

Summary Queries

any requests for information don't require the level of detail provided by the SQL queries described in the last two chapters. For example, each of the following requests asks for a single value or a small number of values that summarize the contents of the database:

- What is the total quota for all salespeople?
- What are the smallest and largest assigned quotas?
- How many salespeople have exceeded their quota?
- What is the size of the average order?
- What is the size of the average order for each sales office?
- How many salespeople are assigned to each sales office?

SQL supports these requests for summary data through column functions and the GROUP BY and HAVING clauses of the SELECT statement, which are described in this chapter.

Column Functions

SQL lets you summarize data from the database through a set of *column functions*. A SQL column function takes an entire column of data as its argument and produces a single data item that summarizes the column. For example, the AVG() column function takes a column of data and computes its average. Here is a query that uses the AVG() column function to compute the average value of two columns from the SALESREPS table:

What are the average quota and average sales of our salespeople?

```
SELECT AVG(QUOTA), AVG(SALES)
  FROM SALESREPS

  AVG(QUOTA)    AVG(SALES)
------------  ------------
 $300,000.00  $289,353.20
```

Figure 8-1 graphically shows how the query results are produced. The first column function in the query takes values in the QUOTA column and computes their average; the second one averages the values in the SALES column. The query produces a single row of query results summarizing the data in the SALESREPS table.

SQL offers six different column functions, as shown in Figure 8-2. The column functions offer different kinds of summary data:

- SUM() computes the total of a column.
- AVG() computes the average value in a column.

- MIN() finds the smallest value in a column.
- MAX() finds the largest value in a column.
- COUNT() counts the number of values in a column.
- COUNT(*) counts rows of query results.

The argument to a column function can be a simple column name, as in the previous example, or it can be a SQL expression, as shown here:

What is the average quota performance of our salespeople?

```
SELECT AVG(100 * (SALES/QUOTA))
  FROM SALESREPS

AVG(100*(SALES/QUOTA))
----------------------
               102.60
```

To process this query, SQL constructs a temporary column containing the value of the expression (100 * (SALES/QUOTA)) for each row of the SALESREPS table and then computes the averages of the temporary column.

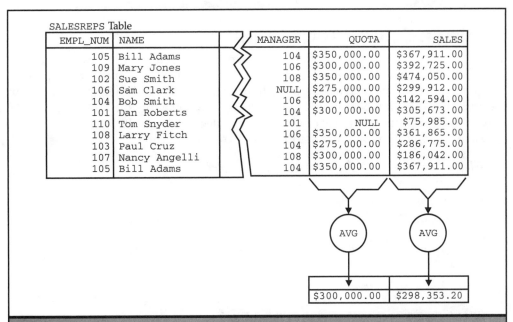

Figure 8-1. *A summary query in operation*

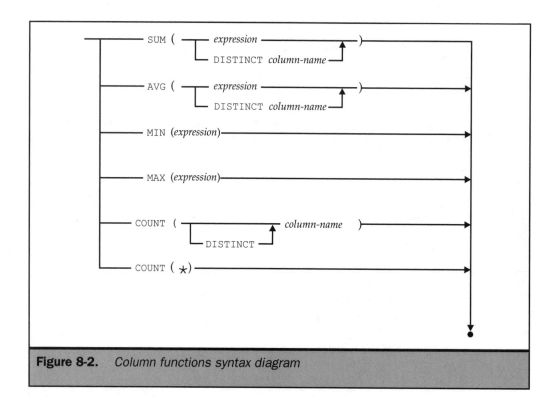

Figure 8-2. *Column functions syntax diagram*

Computing a Column Total (SUM)

The SUM() column function computes the sum of a column of data values. The data in the column must have a numeric type (integer, decimal, floating point, or money). The result of the SUM() function has the same basic data type as the data in the column, but the result may have a higher precision. For example, if you apply the SUM() function to a column of 16-bit integers, it may produce a 32-bit integer as its result.

Here are some examples that use the SUM() column function:

What are the total quotas and sales for all salespeople?

```
SELECT SUM(QUOTA), SUM(SALES)
  FROM SALESREPS

   SUM(QUOTA)      SUM(SALES)
-------------- --------------
 $2,700,000.00  $2,893,532.00
```

What is the total of the orders taken by Bill Adams?

```
SELECT SUM(AMOUNT)
  FROM ORDERS, SALESREPS
 WHERE NAME = 'Bill Adams'
   AND REP = EMPL_NUM

 SUM(AMOUNT)
 ------------
   $39,327.00
```

Computing a Column Average (AVG)

The AVG() column function computes the average of a column of data values. As with the SUM() function, the data in the column must have a numeric type. Because the AVG() function adds the values in the column and then divides by the number of values, its result may have a different data type than that of the values in the column. For example, if you apply the AVG() function to a column of integers, the result will be either a decimal or a floating point number, depending on the brand of DBMS you are using.

Here are some examples of the AVG() column function:

Calculate the average price of products from manufacturer ACI.

```
SELECT AVG(PRICE)
  FROM PRODUCTS
 WHERE MFR_ID = 'ACI'

 AVG(PRICE)
 -----------
    $804.29
```

Calculate the average size of an order placed by Acme Mfg. (customer number 2103).

```
SELECT AVG(AMOUNT)
  FROM ORDERS
 WHERE CUST = 2103

 AVG(AMOUNT)
 ------------
   $8,895.50
```

Finding Extreme Values (MIN and MAX)

The MIN() and MAX() column functions find the smallest and largest values in a column, respectively. The data in the column can contain numeric, string, or date/time information.

The result of the MIN() or MAX() function has exactly the same data type as the data in the column.

Here are some examples that show the use of these column functions:

What are the smallest and largest assigned quotas?

```
SELECT MIN(QUOTA), MAX(QUOTA)
  FROM SALESREPS

  MIN(QUOTA)    MAX(QUOTA)
------------  ------------
 $200,000.00  $350,000.00
```

What is the earliest order date in the database?

```
SELECT MIN(ORDER_DATE)
  FROM ORDERS

MIN(ORDER_DATE)
----------------
04-JAN-89
```

What is the best sales performance of any salesperson?

```
SELECT MAX(100 * (SALES/QUOTA))
  FROM SALESREPS

  MAX(100*(SALES/QUOTA))
----------------------
                135.44
```

When the MIN() and MAX() column functions are applied to numeric data, SQL compares the numbers in algebraic order (large negative numbers are less than small negative numbers, which are less than zero, which is less than all positive numbers). Dates are compared sequentially. (Earlier dates are smaller than later ones.) Durations are compared based on their length. (Shorter durations are smaller than longer ones.)

When using MIN() and MAX() with string data, the comparison of two strings depends on the character set being used. On a personal computer or minicomputer, both of which use the ASCII character set, digits come before the letters in the sorting sequence, and all of the uppercase characters come before all of the lowercase characters. On IBM mainframes, which use the EBCDIC character set, the lowercase characters precede the uppercase characters, and digits come after the letters. Here is a comparison of the ASCII and EBCDIC collating sequences of a list of strings, from smallest to largest:

ASCII	EBCDIC
1234ABC	acme mfg.
5678ABC	zeta corp.
ACME MFG.	Acme Mfg.
Acme Mfg.	ACME MFG.
ZETA CORP.	Zeta Corp.
Zeta Corp.	ZETA CORP.
acme mfg.	1234ABC
zeta corp.	5678ABC

The difference in the collating sequences means that a query with an ORDER BY clause can produce different results on two different systems.

International characters pose additional problems (for example, accented characters in French, German, Spanish, or Italian, or the Cyrillic alphabet letters used in Greek or Russian, or the Kanji symbols used in Japanese). Some brands of DBMS use special international sorting algorithms to sort these characters into their correct position for each language. Others simply sort them according to the numeric value of the code assigned to the character. To address these issues, the SQL2 standard includes elaborate support for national character sets, user-defined character sets, and alternate collating sequences. Unfortunately, support for these SQL2 features varies widely among popular DBMS products. If your application involves international text, you will want to experiment with your particular DBMS to find out how it handles these characters.

Counting Data Values (COUNT)

The COUNT() column function counts the number of data values in a column. The data in the column can be of any type. The COUNT() function always returns an integer, regardless of the data type of the column. Here are some examples of queries that use the COUNT() column function:

How many customers are there?

```
SELECT COUNT(CUST_NUM)
  FROM CUSTOMERS

COUNT(CUST_NUM)
---------------
            21
```

How many salespeople are over quota?

```
SELECT COUNT(NAME)
  FROM SALESREPS
 WHERE SALES > QUOTA

COUNT(NAME)
-----------
          7
```

How many orders for more than $25,000 are on the books?

```
SELECT COUNT(AMOUNT)
  FROM ORDERS
 WHERE AMOUNT > 25000.00

COUNT(AMOUNT)
-------------
            4
```

Note that the COUNT() function ignores the values of the data items in the column; it simply counts how many data items there are. As a result, it doesn't really matter which column you specify as the argument of the COUNT() function. The last example could just as well have been written this way:

```
SELECT COUNT(ORDER_NUM)
  FROM ORDERS
 WHERE AMOUNT > 25000.00

COUNT(ORDER_NUM)
----------------
               4
```

In fact, it's awkward to think of the query as "counting how many order amounts" or "counting how many order numbers"; it's much easier to think about "counting how many orders." For this reason, SQL supports a special COUNT(*) column function, which counts rows rather than data values. Here is the same query, rewritten once again to use the COUNT(*) function:

```
SELECT COUNT(*)
  FROM ORDERS
```

```
WHERE AMOUNT > 25000.00

COUNT(*)
---------
        4
```

If you think of the COUNT(*) function as a "rowcount" function, it makes the query easier to read. In practice, the COUNT(*) function is almost always used instead of the COUNT() function to count rows.

Column Functions in the Select List

Simple queries with a column function in their select list are fairly easy to understand. However, when the select list includes several column functions, or when the argument to a column function is a complex expression, the query can be harder to read and understand. The following steps show the rules for SQL query processing expanded once more to describe how column functions are handled. As before, the rules are intended to provide a precise definition of what a query means, not a description of how the DBMS actually goes about producing the query results.

To generate the query results for a SELECT statement:

1. If the statement is a UNION of SELECT statements, apply Steps 2 through 5 to each of the statements to generate their individual query results.

2. Form the product of the tables named in the FROM clause. If the FROM clause names a single table, the product is that table.

3. If there is a WHERE clause, apply its search condition to each row of the product table, retaining those rows for which the search condition is TRUE (and discarding those for which it is FALSE or NULL).

4. For each remaining row, calculate the value of each item in the select list to produce a single row of query results. For a simple column reference, use the value of the column in the current row. For a column function, use the entire set of rows as its argument.

5. If SELECT DISTINCT is specified, eliminate any duplicate rows of query results that were produced.

6. If the statement is a UNION of SELECT statements, merge the query results for the individual statements into a single table of query results. Eliminate duplicate rows unless UNION ALL is specified.

7. If there is an ORDER BY clause, sort the query results as specified.

The rows generated by this procedure comprise the query results.

One of the best ways to think about summary queries and column functions is to imagine the query processing broken down into two steps. First, you should imagine how the query would work *without* the column functions, producing many rows of detailed query results. Then you should imagine SQL applying the column functions to the detailed query results, producing a single summary row. For example, consider the following complex query:

Find the average order amount, total order amount, average order amount as a percentage of the customer's credit limit, and average order amount as a percentage of the salesperson's quota.

```
SELECT AVG(AMOUNT), SUM(AMOUNT), (100 * AVG(AMOUNT/CREDIT_LIMIT)),
       (100 * AVG(AMOUNT/QUOTA))
  FROM ORDERS, CUSTOMERS, SALESREPS
 WHERE CUST = CUST_NUM
   AND REP = EMPL_NUM

 AVG(AMOUNT)   SUM(AMOUNT)   (100*AVG(AMOUNT/CREDIT_LIMIT))   (100*AVG(AMOUNT/QUOTA))
------------  ------------  -------------------------------  -----------------------
  $8,256.37   $247,691.00                            24.45                      2.51
```

Without the column functions, it would look like this:

```
SELECT AMOUNT, AMOUNT, AMOUNT/CREDIT_LIMIT, AMOUNT/QUOTA
  FROM ORDERS, CUSTOMERS, SALESREPS
 WHERE CUST = CUST_NUM AND
   AND REP = EMPL_NUM
```

and would produce one row of detailed query results for each order. The column functions use the columns of this detailed query results table to generate a single-row table of summary query results.

A column function can appear in the select list anywhere that a column name can appear. It can, for example, be part of an expression that adds or subtracts the values of two column functions. However, the argument of a column function cannot contain another column function, because the resulting expression doesn't make sense. This rule is sometimes summarized as "it's illegal to nest column functions."

It's also illegal to mix column functions and ordinary column names in a select list, again because the resulting query doesn't make sense. For example, consider this query:

```
SELECT NAME, SUM(SALES)
  FROM SALESREPS
```

The first select item asks SQL to generate a ten-row table of detailed query results—one row for each salesperson. The second select item asks SQL to generate a one-row column of summary query results containing the total of the SALES column. The two SELECT items contradict one another, producing an error. For this reason, either all column references in the select list must appear within the argument of a column function (producing a summary query), or the select list must not contain any column functions (producing a detailed query). Actually, the rule is slightly more complex when grouped queries and subqueries are considered. The necessary refinements are described later in the "Group Search Conditions" section.

NULL Values and Column Functions

The SUM(), AVG(), MIN(), MAX(), and COUNT() column functions each take a column of data values as their argument and produce a single data value as a result. What happens if one or more of the data values in the column is a NULL value? The ANSI/ISO SQL standard specifies that NULL values in the column are *ignored* by the column functions.

This query shows how the COUNT() column function ignores any NULL values in a column:

```
SELECT COUNT(*), COUNT(SALES), COUNT(QUOTA)
  FROM SALESREPS

 COUNT(*)   COUNT(SALES)   COUNT(QUOTA)
--------- -------------- --------------
      10             10              9
```

The SALESREPS table contains ten rows, so COUNT(*) returns a count of ten. The SALES column contains ten non-NULL values, so the function COUNT(SALES) also returns a count of ten. The QUOTA column is NULL for the newest salesperson. The COUNT(QUOTA) function ignores this NULL value and returns a count of nine. Because of these anomalies, the COUNT(*) function is almost always used instead of the COUNT() function, unless you specifically want to exclude NULL values in a particular column from the total.

Ignoring NULL values has little impact on the MIN() and MAX() column functions. However, it can cause subtle problems for the SUM() and AVG() column functions, as illustrated by this query:

```
SELECT SUM(SALES), SUM(QUOTA), (SUM(SALES) - SUM(QUOTA)), SUM(SALES-QUOTA)
  FROM SALESREPS

  SUM(SALES)      SUM(QUOTA)    (SUM(SALES)-SUM(QUOTA))    SUM(SALES-QUOTA)
-------------- -------------- ------------------------- ----------------
$2,893,532.00  $2,700,000.00              $193,532.00         $117,547.00
```

You would expect the two expressions:

```
(SUM(SALES) - SUM(QUOTA))   and   SUM(SALES-QUOTA)
```

in the select list to produce identical results, but the example shows that they do not. The salesperson with a NULL value in the QUOTA column is again the reason. The expression:

```
SUM(SALES)
```

totals the sales for all ten salespeople, while the expression:

```
SUM(QUOTA)
```

totals only the nine non-NULL quota values. The expression:

```
SUM(SALES) - SUM(QUOTA)
```

computes the difference of these two amounts. However, the column function:

```
SUM(SALES-QUOTA)
```

has a non-NULL argument value for only nine of the ten salespeople. In the row with a NULL quota value, the subtraction produces a NULL, which is ignored by the SUM() function. Thus, the sales for the salesperson without a quota, which are included in the previous calculation, are excluded from this calculation.

Which is the "correct" answer? Both are! The first expression calculates exactly what it says: "the sum of SALES, less the sum of QUOTA." The second expression also calculates exactly what it says: "the sum of (SALES – QUOTA)." When NULL values occur, however, the two calculations are not quite the same.

The ANSI/ISO standard specifies these precise rules for handling NULL values in column functions:

- If any of the data values in a column are NULL, they are ignored for the purpose of computing the column function's value.

- If every data item in the column is NULL, then the SUM(), AVG(), MIN(), and MAX() column functions return a NULL value; the COUNT() function returns a value of zero.

■ If no data items are in the column (that is, the column is empty), then the SUM(), AVG(), MIN(), and MAX() column functions return a NULL value; the COUNT() function returns a value of zero.

■ The COUNT(*) counts rows and does not depend on the presence or absence of NULL values in a column. If there are no rows, it returns a value of zero.

Although the standard is very clear in this area, commercial SQL products may produce results different from the standard, especially if all of the data values in a column are NULL or when a column function is applied to an empty table. Before assuming the behavior specified by the standard, you should test your particular DBMS.

Duplicate Row Elimination (DISTINCT)

Recall from Chapter 6 that you can specify the DISTINCT keyword at the beginning of the select list to eliminate duplicate rows of query results. You can also ask SQL to eliminate duplicate values from a column before applying a column function to it. To eliminate duplicate values, the keyword DISTINCT is included before the column function argument, immediately after the opening parenthesis.

Here are two queries that illustrate duplicate row elimination for column functions:

How many different titles are held by salespeople?

```
SELECT COUNT(DISTINCT TITLE)
  FROM SALESREPS

 COUNT(DISTINCT TITLE)
 ---------------------
                     3
```

How many sales offices have salespeople who are over quota?

```
SELECT COUNT(DISTINCT REP_OFFICE)
  FROM SALESREPS
 WHERE SALES > QUOTA

 COUNT(DISTINCT REP_OFFICE)
 --------------------------
                          4
```

The SQL1 standard specified that when the DISTINCT keyword is used, the argument to the column function must be a simple column name; it cannot be an expression. The standard allows the DISTINCT keyword for the SUM() and AVG() column functions. The standard does not permit use of the DISTINCT keyword with the MIN() and MAX() column functions because it has no impact on their results, but many SQL implementations allow it anyway. The standard also *requires* the DISTINCT keyword for the COUNT() column function, but many SQL implementations permit the use of the COUNT() function without it. DISTINCT cannot be specified for the COUNT(*) function, because it doesn't deal with a column of data values at all—it simply counts rows. The SQL2 standard relaxed these restrictions, allowing DISTINCT to be applied for any of the column functions and permitting expressions as arguments for any of the functions as well.

In addition, the DISTINCT keyword can be specified only once in a query. If it appears in the argument of one column function, it can't appear in any others. If it is specified before the select list, it can't appear in any column functions. The only exception is that DISTINCT may be specified a second time inside a subquery (contained within the query). Subqueries are described in Chapter 9.

Grouped Queries (GROUP BY Clause)

The summary queries described thus far are like the totals at the bottom of a report. They condense all of the detailed data in the report into a single, summary row of data. Just as subtotals are useful in printed reports, it's often convenient to summarize query results at a "subtotal" level. The GROUP BY clause of the SELECT statement provides this capability.

The function of the GROUP BY clause is most easily understood by example. Consider these two queries:

What is the average order size?

```
SELECT AVG(AMOUNT)
  FROM ORDERS

 AVG(AMOUNT)
------------
   $8,256.37
```

What is the average order size for each salesperson?

```
SELECT REP, AVG(AMOUNT)
  FROM ORDERS
 GROUP BY REP

 REP   AVG(AMOUNT)
----  ------------
 101      $8,876.00
 102      $5,694.00
```

103	$1,350.00
105	$7,865.40
106	$16,479.00
107	$11,477.33
108	$8,376.14
109	$3,552.50
110	$11,566.00

The first query is a simple summary query like the previous examples in this chapter. The second query produces several summary rows—one row for each group, summarizing the orders taken by a single salesperson. Figure 8-3 shows how the second query works. Conceptually, SQL carries out the query as follows:

1. SQL divides the orders into groups of orders, with one group for each salesperson. Within each group, all of the orders have the same value in the REP column.

2. For each group, SQL computes the average value of the AMOUNT column for all of the rows in the group and generates a single, summary row of query results. The row contains the value of the REP column for the group and the calculated average order size.

Figure 8-3. *A grouped query in operation*

RETRIEVING DATA

A query that includes the GROUP BY clause is called a *grouped query* because it groups the data from its source tables and produces a single summary row for each row group. The columns named in the GROUP BY clause are called the *grouping columns* of the query, because they determine how the rows are divided into groups. Here are some additional examples of grouped queries:

What is the range of assigned quotas in each office?

```
SELECT REP_OFFICE, MIN(QUOTA), MAX(QUOTA)
  FROM SALESREPS
 GROUP BY REP_OFFICE

REP_OFFICE    MIN(QUOTA)     MAX(QUOTA)
-----------   ------------   ------------
       NULL          NULL           NULL
         11   $275,000.00    $300,000.00
         12   $200,000.00    $300,000.00
         13   $350,000.00    $350,000.00
         21   $350,000.00    $350,000.00
         22   $300,000.00    $300,000.00
```

How many salespeople are assigned to each office?

```
SELECT REP_OFFICE, COUNT(*)
  FROM SALESREPS
 GROUP BY REP_OFFICE

REP_OFFICE   COUNT(*)
-----------  ---------
       NULL         1
         11         2
         12         3
         13         1
         21         2
         22         1
```

How many different customers are served by each salesperson?

```
SELECT COUNT(DISTINCT CUST_NUM), 'customers for salesrep', CUST_REP
  FROM CUSTOMERS
```

```
GROUP BY CUST_REP

COUNT(DISTINCT CUST_NUM)   CUSTOMERS FOR SALESREP   CUST_REP
------------------------   ----------------------   --------
                       3   customers for salesrep        101
                       4   customers for salesrep        102
                       3   customers for salesrep        103
                       1   customers for salesrep        104
                       2   customers for salesrep        105
                       2   customers for salesrep        106
           .
           .
           .
```

There is an intimate link between the SQL column functions and the GROUP BY clause. Remember that the column functions take a column of data values and produce a single result. When the GROUP BY clause is present, it tells SQL to divide the detailed query results into groups and to apply the column function separately to each group, producing a single result for each group. The following steps show the rules for SQL query processing, expanded once again for grouped queries.

To generate the query results for a SELECT statement:

1. If the statement is a UNION of SELECT statements, apply Steps 2 through 7 to each of the statements to generate their individual query results.

2. Form the product of the tables named in the FROM clause. If the FROM clause names a single table, the product is that table.

3. If there is a WHERE clause, apply its search condition to each row of the product table, retaining those rows for which the search condition is TRUE (and discarding those for which it is FALSE or NULL).

4. If there is a GROUP BY clause, arrange the remaining rows of the product table into row groups, so that the rows in each group have identical values in all of the grouping columns.

5. If there is a HAVING clause, apply its search condition to each row group, retaining those groups for which the search condition is TRUE (and discarding those for which it is FALSE or NULL).

6. For each remaining row (or row group), calculate the value of each item in the select list to produce a single row of query results. For a simple column reference, use the value of the column in the current row (or row group). For a column function, use the current row group as its argument if GROUP BY is specified; otherwise, use the entire set of rows.

7. If SELECT DISTINCT is specified, eliminate any duplicate rows of query results that were produced.

8. If the statement is a UNION of SELECT statements, merge the query results for the individual statements into a single table of query results. Eliminate duplicate rows unless UNION ALL is specified.

9. If there is an ORDER BY clause, sort the query results as specified.

The rows generated by this procedure comprise the query results.

Multiple Grouping Columns

SQL can group query results based on the contents of two or more columns. For example, suppose you want to group the orders by salesperson and by customer. This query groups the data based on both criteria:

Calculate the total orders for each customer of each salesperson.

```
SELECT REP, CUST, SUM(AMOUNT)
  FROM ORDERS
 GROUP BY REP, CUST

 REP   CUST   SUM(AMOUNT)
 ----  -----  ------------
 101   2102     $3,978.00
 101   2108       $150.00
 101   2113    $22,500.00
 102   2106     $4,026.00
 102   2114    $15,000.00
 102   2120     $3,750.00
 103   2111     $2,700.00
 105   2103    $35,582.00
 105   2111     $3,745.00
   .
   .
   .
```

Even with multiple grouping columns, SQL provides only a single level of grouping. The query produces a separate summary row for each salesperson/customer pair. It's impossible to create groups and subgroups with two levels of subtotals in SQL. The best you can do is sort the data so that the rows of query results appear in the appropriate order. In many SQL implementations, the GROUP BY clause will automatically have the side effect of sorting the data, but you can override this sort with an ORDER BY clause, as shown next:

Calculate the total orders for each customer of each salesperson, sorted by customer, and within each customer by salesperson.

```
SELECT CUST, REP, SUM(AMOUNT)
  FROM ORDERS
 GROUP BY CUST, REP
 ORDER BY CUST, REP

 CUST  REP   SUM(AMOUNT)
 ----- ----  -----------
 2101  106      $1,458.00
 2102  101      $3,978.00
 2103  105     $35,582.00
 2106  102      $4,026.00
 2107  110     $23,132.00
 2108  101        $150.00
 2108  109      $7,105.00
 2109  107     $31,350.00
 2111  103      $2,700.00
 2111  105      $3,745.00
   .
   .
   .
```

Note that it's also impossible to get both detailed and summary query results from a single query. To get detailed query results with subtotals or to get multilevel subtotals, you must write an application program using programmatic SQL and compute the subtotals within the program logic. The original developers of SQL Server addressed this limitation of standard SQL by adding an optional COMPUTE clause to the end of the SELECT statement. The COMPUTE clause calculates subtotals and sub-subtotals, as shown in this example:

Calculate the total orders for each customer of each salesperson, sorted by salesperson, and within each salesperson by customer.

```
SELECT REP, CUST, AMOUNT
   FROM ORDERS
  ORDER BY REP, CUST
COMPUTE SUM(AMOUNT) BY REP, CUST
COMPUTE SUM(AMOUNT), AVG(AMOUNT) BY REP
```

```
REP   CUST           AMOUNT
----  -----  --------------
101   2102         $3,978.00
              sum
              --------------
                   $3,978.00


REP   CUST           AMOUNT
----  -----  --------------
101   2108           $150.00
              sum
              --------------
                     $150.00


REP   CUST           AMOUNT
----  -----  --------------
101   2113        $22,500.00
              sum
              --------------
                  $22,500.00
              sum
              --------------
                  $26,628.00
              avg
              --------------
                   $8,876.00


REP   CUST           AMOUNT
----  -----  --------------
102   2106         $2,130.00
102   2106         $1,896.00
              sum
              --------------
                   $4,026.00


REP   CUST           AMOUNT
----  -----  --------------
102   2114        $15,000.00
              sum
              --------------
                  $15,000.00
```

```
REP   CUST         AMOUNT
----  -----  -------------
102   2120       $3,750.00
             sum
             -------------
                 $3,750.00
             sum
             -------------
                $22,776.00
             avg
             -------------
                 $5,694.00
  .
  .
  .
```

The query produces one row of detailed query results for each row of the ORDERS table, sorted by CUST within REP. In addition, it computes the sum of the orders for each customer/salesperson pair (a low-level subtotal) and computes the sum of the orders and average order size for each salesperson (a high-level subtotal). The query results thus contain a mixture of detail rows and summary rows, which include both subtotals and sub-subtotals.

The COMPUTE clause is very nonstandard, and in fact, it is unique to the Transact-SQL dialect used by SQL Server. Furthermore, it violates the basic principles of relational queries because the results of the SELECT statement are not a table, but a strange combination of different types of rows. Nonetheless, as the example shows, it can be very useful.

Restrictions on Grouped Queries

Grouped queries are subject to some rather strict limitations. The grouping columns must be actual columns of the tables named in the FROM clause of the query. You cannot group the rows based on the value of a calculated expression.

There are also restrictions on the items that can appear in the select list of a grouped query. All of the items in the select list must have a single value for each group of rows. Basically, this means that a select item in a grouped query can be:

- A constant
- A column function, which produces a single value summarizing the rows in the group
- A grouping column, which by definition has the same value in every row of the group
- An expression involving combinations of these

In practice, a grouped query will always include *both* a grouping column and a column function in its select list. If no column function appears, the query can be expressed more simply using SELECT DISTINCT, without GROUP BY. Conversely, if you don't include a grouping column in the query results, you won't be able to tell which row of query results came from which group!

Another limitation of grouped queries is that SQL ignores information about primary keys and foreign keys when analyzing the validity of a grouped query. Consider this query:

Calculate the total orders for each salesperson.

```
SELECT EMPL_NUM, NAME, SUM(AMOUNT)
  FROM ORDERS, SALESREPS
 WHERE REP = EMPL_NUM
 GROUP BY EMPL_NUM

Error: "NAME" not a GROUP BY expression
```

Given the nature of the data, the query makes perfectly good sense because grouping on the salesperson's employee number is in effect the same as grouping on the salesperson's name. More precisely, EMPL_NUM, the grouping column, is the primary key of the SALESREPS table, so the NAME column must be single-valued for each group. Nonetheless, SQL reports an error because the NAME column is not explicitly specified as a grouping column. To correct the problem, you simply include the NAME column as a second (redundant) grouping column:

Calculate the total orders for each salesperson.

```
SELECT EMPL_NUM, NAME, SUM(AMOUNT)
  FROM ORDERS, SALESREPS
 WHERE REP = EMPL_NUM
 GROUP BY EMPL_NUM, NAME

EMPL_NUM NAME             SUM(AMOUNT)
-------- -------------- -----------
     101 Dan Roberts      $26,628.00
     102 Sue Smith        $22,776.00
     103 Paul Cruz         $2,700.00
     105 Bill Adams       $39,327.00
     106 Sam Clark        $32,958.00
```

```
107 Nancy Angelli     $34,432.00
108 Larry Fitch       $58,633.00
109 Mary Jones         $7,105.00
110 Tom Snyder        $23,132.00
```

Of course, if the salesperson's employee number is not needed in the query results, you can eliminate it entirely from the select list, giving:

Calculate the total orders for each salesperson.

```
SELECT NAME, SUM(AMOUNT)
  FROM ORDERS, SALESREPS
 WHERE REP = EMPL_NUM
 GROUP BY NAME

NAME            SUM(AMOUNT)
-------------   -----------
Bill Adams       $39,327.00
Dan Roberts      $26,628.00
Larry Fitch      $58,633.00
Mary Jones        $7,105.00
Nancy Angelli    $34,432.00
Paul Cruz         $2,700.00
Sam Clark        $32,958.00
Sue Smith        $22,776.00
Tom Snyder       $23,132.00
```

NULL Values in Grouping Columns

A NULL value poses a special problem when it occurs in a grouping column. If the value of the column is unknown, into which group should the row be placed? In the WHERE clause, when two different NULL values are compared, the result is NULL (not TRUE), that is, the two NULL values are *not* considered to be equal. Applying the same convention to the GROUP BY clause would force SQL to place each row with a NULL grouping column into a separate group by itself.

In practice, this rule proves too unwieldy. Instead, the ANSI/ISO SQL standard considers two NULL values to be equal for purposes of the GROUP BY clause. If two rows have NULLs in the same grouping columns and identical values in all of their non-NULL grouping columns, they are grouped together into the same row group. The

small sample table in Figure 8-4 illustrates the ANSI/ISO handling of NULL values by
the GROUP BY clause, as shown in this query:

```
SELECT HAIR, EYES, COUNT(*)
  FROM PEOPLE
 GROUP BY HAIR, EYES

HAIR    EYES    COUNT(*)
------  ------  ---------
Brown   Blue           1
NULL    Blue           2
NULL    NULL           2
Brown   NULL           3
Brown   Brown          2
Brown   Brown          2
```

Although this behavior of NULLs in grouping columns is clearly specified in the
ANSI/ISO standard, it is not implemented in all SQL dialects. It's a good idea to build
a small test table and check the behavior of your DBMS brand before counting on a
specific behavior.

NAME	HAIR	EYES
Cindy	Brown	Blue
Louise	NULL	Blue
Harry	NULL	Blue
Samantha	NULL	NULL
Joanne	NULL	NULL
George	Brown	NULL
Mary	Brown	NULL
Paula	Brown	NULL
Kevin	Brown	NULL
Joel	Brown	Brown
Susan	Blonde	Blue
Marie	Blonde	Blue

Figure 8-4.   *The PEOPLE table*

Group Search Conditions (HAVING Clause)

Just as the WHERE clause can be used to select and reject the individual rows that participate in a query, the HAVING clause can be used to select and reject row groups. The format of the HAVING clause parallels that of the WHERE clause, consisting of the keyword HAVING followed by a search condition. The HAVING clause thus specifies a search condition for groups.

An example provides the best way to understand the role of the HAVING clause. Consider this query:

What is the average order size for each salesperson whose orders total more than $30,000?

```
SELECT REP, AVG(AMOUNT)
  FROM ORDERS
 GROUP BY REP
HAVING SUM(AMOUNT) > 30000.00

  REP   AVG(AMOUNT)
  ----  -----------
  105    $7,865.40
  106   $16,479.00
  107   $11,477.33
  108    $8,376.14
```

Figure 8-5 shows graphically how SQL carries out the query. The GROUP BY clause first arranges the orders into groups by salesperson. The HAVING clause then eliminates any group where the total of the orders in the group does not exceed $30,000. Finally, the SELECT clause calculates the average order size for each of the remaining groups and generates the query results.

The search conditions you can specify in the HAVING clause are the same ones used in the WHERE clause, as described in Chapters 6 and 9. Here is another example of the use of a group search condition:

For each office with two or more people, compute the total quota and total sales for all salespeople who work in the office.

```
SELECT CITY, SUM(QUOTA), SUM(SALESREPS.SALES)
  FROM OFFICES, SALESREPS
```

```
WHERE OFFICE = REP_OFFICE
 GROUP BY CITY
HAVING COUNT(*) >= 2

CITY            SUM(QUOTA)   SUM(SALESREPS.SALES)
-----------    ------------  --------------------

Chicago        $775,000.00           $735,042.00
Los Angeles    $700,000.00           $835,915.00
New York       $575,000.00           $692,637.00
```

The following steps show the rules for SQL query processing, expanded once again to include group search conditions.

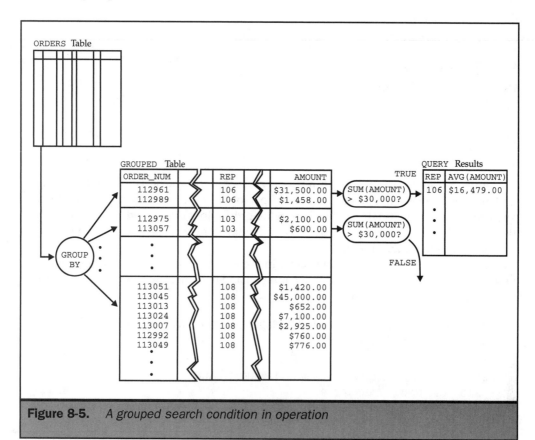

Figure 8-5.   *A grouped search condition in operation*

To generate the query results for a SELECT statement:

1. If the statement is a UNION of SELECT statements, apply Steps 2 through 7 to each of the statements to generate their individual query results.

2. Form the product of the tables named in the FROM clause. If the FROM clause names a single table, the product is that table.

3. If there is a WHERE clause, apply its search condition to each row of the product table, retaining those rows for which the search condition is TRUE (and discarding those for which it is FALSE or NULL).

4. If there is a GROUP BY clause, arrange the remaining rows of the product table into row groups, so that the rows in each group have identical values in all of the grouping columns.

5. If there is a HAVING clause, apply its search condition to each row group, retaining those groups for which the search condition is TRUE (and discarding those for which it is FALSE or NULL).

6. For each remaining row (or row group), calculate the value of each item in the select list to produce a single row of query results. For a simple column reference, use the value of the column in the current row (or row group). For a column function, use the current row group as its argument if GROUP BY is specified; otherwise, use the entire set of rows.

7. If SELECT DISTINCT is specified, eliminate any duplicate rows of query results that were produced.

8. If the statement is a UNION of SELECT statements, merge the query results for the individual statements into a single table of query results. Eliminate duplicate rows unless UNION ALL is specified.

9. If there is an ORDER BY clause, sort the query results as specified.

The rows generated by this procedure comprise the query results.
Following this procedure, SQL handles the query in the previous example as follows:

1. Joins the OFFICES and SALESREPS tables to find the city where each salesperson works.

2. Groups the resulting rows by office.

3. Eliminates groups with two or fewer rows—these represent offices that don't meet the HAVING clause criterion.

4. Calculates the total quota and total sales for each group.

Here is one more example, which uses all of the SELECT statement clauses:

Show the price, quantity on hand, and total quantity on order for each product where the total quantity on order is more than 75 percent of the quantity on hand.

```
SELECT DESCRIPTION, PRICE, QTY_ON_HAND, SUM(QTY)
  FROM PRODUCTS, ORDERS
 WHERE MFR = MFR_ID
   AND PRODUCT = PRODUCT_ID
 GROUP BY MFR_ID, PRODUCT_ID, DESCRIPTION, PRICE, QTY_ON_HAND
HAVING SUM(QTY) > (.75 * QTY_ON_HAND)
 ORDER BY QTY_ON_HAND DESC

DESCRIPTION            PRICE  QTY_ON_HAND  SUM(QTY)
---------------    ----------  ------------  ---------
Reducer              $355.00            38         32
Widget Adjuster       $25.00            37         30
Motor Mount          $243.00            15         16
Right Hinge        $4,500.00            12         15
500-lb Brace       $1,425.00             5         22
```

To process this query, SQL conceptually performs the following steps:

1. Joins the ORDERS and PRODUCTS tables to find the description, price, and quantity on hand for each product ordered.

2. Groups the resulting rows by manufacturer and product ID.

3. Eliminates groups where the quantity ordered (the total of the QTY column for all orders in the group) is less than 75 percent of the quantity on hand.

4. Calculates the total quantity ordered for each group.

5. Generates one summary row of query results for each group.

6. Sorts the query results so that products with the largest quantity on hand appear first.

As described previously, DESCRIPTION, PRICE, and QTY_ON_HAND must be specified as grouping columns in this query solely because they appear in the select list. They actually contribute nothing to the grouping process, because the MFR_ID and PRODUCT_ID completely specify a single row of the PRODUCTS table, automatically making the other three columns single-valued per group.

Restrictions on Group Search Conditions

The HAVING clause is used to include or exclude row groups from the query results, so the search condition it specifies must be one that applies to the group as a whole rather than to individual rows. This means that an item appearing within the search condition in a HAVING clause can be:

- A constant
- A column function, which produces a single value summarizing the rows in the group
- A grouping column, which by definition has the same value in every row of the group
- An expression involving combinations of these

In practice, the search condition in the HAVING clause will always include at least one column function. If it did not, the search condition could be moved to the WHERE clause and applied to individual rows. The easiest way to figure out whether a search condition belongs in the WHERE clause or in the HAVING clause is to remember how the two clauses are applied:

- The WHERE clause is applied to *individual rows,* so the expressions it contains must be computable for individual rows.
- The HAVING clause is applied to *row groups,* so the expressions it contains must be computable for a group of rows.

NULL Values and Group Search Conditions

Like the search condition in the WHERE clause, the HAVING clause search condition can produce one of three results:

- If the search condition is TRUE, the row group is retained, and it contributes a summary row to the query results.
- If the search condition is FALSE, the row group is discarded, and it does not contribute a summary row to the query results.
- If the search condition is NULL, the row group is discarded, and it does not contribute a summary row to the query results.

The anomalies that can occur with NULL values in the search condition are the same as those for the WHERE clause and have been described in Chapter 6.

HAVING Without GROUP BY

The HAVING clause is almost always used in conjunction with the GROUP BY clause, but the syntax of the SELECT statement does not require it. If a HAVING clause appears without a GROUP BY clause, SQL considers the entire set of detailed query results to be a single group. In other words, the column functions in the HAVING clause are applied to one, and only one, group to determine whether the group is included or excluded from the query results, and that group consists of all the rows. The use of a HAVING clause without a corresponding GROUP BY clause is seldom seen in practice.

Summary

This chapter described summary queries, which summarize data from the database:

- Summary queries use SQL column functions to collapse a column of data values into a single value that summarizes the column.

- Column functions can compute the average, sum, minimum, and maximum values of a column, count the number of data values in a column, or count the number of rows of query results.

- A summary query without a GROUP BY clause generates a single row of query results, summarizing all the rows of a table or a joined set of tables.

- A summary query with a GROUP BY clause generates multiple rows of query results, each summarizing the rows in a particular group.

- The HAVING clause acts as a WHERE clause for groups, selecting the row groups that contribute to the summary query results.

Chapter 9

Subqueries and Query Expressions

The SQL subquery feature lets you use the results of one query as part of another query. The ability to use a query within a query was the original reason for the word "structured" in the name Structured Query Language. The subquery feature is less well known than SQL's join feature, but it plays an important role in SQL for three reasons:

- A SQL statement with a subquery is often the most natural way to express a query, because it most closely parallels the English-language description of the query.

- Subqueries make it easier to write SELECT statements, because they let you break a query down into pieces (the query and its subqueries) and then put the pieces back together.

- Some queries cannot be expressed in the SQL language without using a subquery.

The first several sections of this chapter describe subqueries and show how they are used in the WHERE and HAVING clauses of a SQL statement. The later sections of this chapter describe the advanced query expression capabilities that have been added to the SQL2 standard, which substantially expands the power of SQL to perform even the most complex of database operations.

Using Subqueries

A *subquery* is a query within a query. The results of the subquery are used by the DBMS to determine the results of the higher-level query that contains the subquery. In the simplest forms of a subquery, the subquery appears within the WHERE or HAVING clause of another SQL statement. Subqueries provide an efficient, natural way to handle query requests that are themselves expressed in terms of the results of other queries. Here is an example of such a request:

List the offices where the sales target for the office exceeds the sum of the individual salespeople's quotas.

The request asks for a list of offices from the OFFICES table, where the value of the TARGET column meets some condition. It seems reasonable that the SELECT statement that expresses the query should look something like this:

```
SELECT CITY  FROM OFFICES  WHERE TARGET > ???
```

The value "???" needs to be filled in and should be equal to the sum of the quotas of the salespeople assigned to the office in question. How can you specify that value in the query? From Chapter 8, you know that the sum of the quotas for a specific office (say, office number 21) can be obtained with this query:

```
SELECT SUM(QUOTA)
  FROM SALESREPS
 WHERE REP_OFFICE = 21
```

But it would be inefficient to have to type in this query, write down the results, and then type in the previous query with the correct amount. How can you put the results of this query into the earlier query in place of the question marks? It would seem reasonable to start with the first query and replace the "???" with the second query, as follows:

```
SELECT CITY
  FROM OFFICES
 WHERE TARGET > (SELECT SUM(QUOTA)
                   FROM SALESREPS
                  WHERE REP_OFFICE = OFFICE)
```

In fact, this is a correctly formed SQL query. For each office, the *inner* query (the *subquery*) calculates the sum of the quotas for the salespeople working in that office. The *outer* query (the *main* query) compares the office's target to the calculated total and decides whether to add the office to the main query results. Working together, the main query and the subquery express the original request and retrieve the requested data from the database.

SQL subqueries typically appear as part of the WHERE clause or the HAVING clause. In the WHERE clause, they help to select the individual rows that appear in the query results. In the HAVING clause, they help to select the row groups that appear in the query results.

What Is a Subquery?

Figure 9-1 shows the form of a SQL subquery. The subquery is enclosed in parentheses, but otherwise it has the familiar form of a SELECT statement, with a FROM clause and optional WHERE, GROUP BY, and HAVING clauses. The form of these clauses in a subquery is identical to that in a SELECT statement, and they perform their normal functions when used within a subquery. There are, however, a few differences between a subquery and an actual SELECT statement:

- In the most common uses, a subquery must produce a single column of data as its query results. This means that a subquery almost always has a single select item in its SELECT clause.

- The ORDER BY clause cannot be specified in a subquery. The subquery results are used internally by the main query and are never visible to the user, so it makes little sense to sort them anyway.

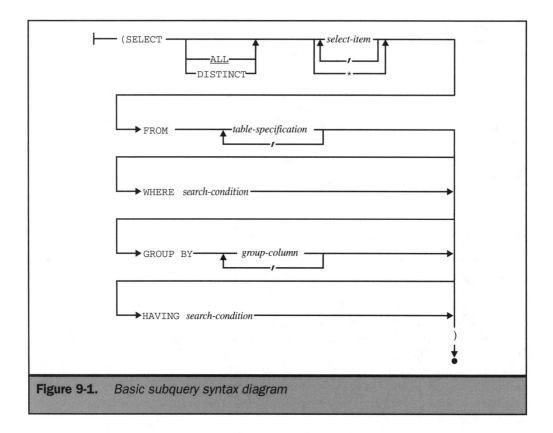

Figure 9-1. *Basic subquery syntax diagram*

- Column names appearing in a subquery may refer to columns of tables in the main query. These outer references are described in detail later in the "Outer References" section.

- In most implementations, a subquery cannot be the UNION of several different SELECT statements; only a single SELECT is allowed. (The SQL2 standard allows much more powerful query expressions and relaxes this restriction, as described later in the section "Advanced Queries in SQL2.")

Subqueries in the WHERE Clause

Subqueries are most frequently used in the WHERE clause of a SQL statement. When a subquery appears in the WHERE clause, it works as part of the row selection process. The very simplest subqueries appear within a search condition and produce a value that is used to test the search condition. Here is an example of a simple subquery:

List the salespeople whose quota is less than 10 percent of the companywide sales target.

```
SELECT NAME
  FROM SALESREPS
 WHERE QUOTA < (.1 * (SELECT SUM(TARGET) FROM OFFICES))

NAME
----------
Bob Smith
```

In this case, the subquery calculates the sum of the sales targets for all of the offices to determine the companywide target, which is multiplied by 10 percent to determine the cutoff sales quota for the query. That value is then used in the search condition to check each row of the SALESREPS table and find the requested names. In this simple case, the subquery produces the same value for every row of the SALESREPS table; the QUOTA value for each salesperson is compared to the same companywide number. In fact, you could carry out this query by first performing the subquery, to calculate the cutoff quota amount ($275,000 in the sample database), and then carry out the main query using this number in a simple WHERE clause:

```
WHERE QUOTA < 275000
```

It's more convenient to use the subquery, but it's not essential. Usually, subqueries are not this simple. For example, consider once again the query from the previous section:

List the offices where the sales target for the office exceeds the sum of the individual salespeople's quotas.

```
SELECT CITY
  FROM OFFICES
 WHERE TARGET > (SELECT SUM(QUOTA)
                   FROM SALESREPS
                  WHERE REP_OFFICE = OFFICE)

CITY
-----------
Chicago
Los Angeles
```

In this (more typical) case, the subquery cannot be calculated once for the entire query. The subquery produces a *different* value for each office, based on the quotas of the salespeople in that particular office. Figure 9-2 shows conceptually how SQL carries out the query. The main query draws its data from the OFFICES table, and the WHERE clause selects which offices will be included in the query results. SQL goes through the rows of the OFFICES table one by one, applying the test stated in the WHERE clause.

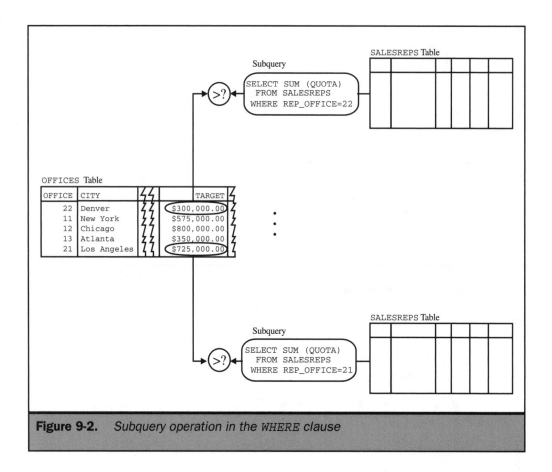

Figure 9-2.   *Subquery operation in the WHERE clause*

The WHERE clause compares the value of the TARGET column in the current row to the value produced by the subquery. To test the TARGET value, SQL carries out the subquery, finding the sum of the quotas for salespeople in the current office. The subquery produces a single number, and the WHERE clause compares the number to the TARGET value, selecting or rejecting the current office based on the comparison. As the figure shows, SQL carries out the subquery repeatedly, once for each row tested by the WHERE clause of the main query.

Outer References

Within the body of a subquery, it's often necessary to refer to the value of a column in the current row of the main query. Consider once again the query from the previous sections:

> *List the offices where the sales target for the office exceeds the sum of the individual salespeople's quotas.*

```
SELECT CITY
  FROM OFFICES
 WHERE TARGET > (SELECT SUM(QUOTA)
                   FROM SALESREPS
                  WHERE REP_OFFICE = OFFICE)
```

The role of the subquery in this SELECT statement is to calculate the total quota for those salespeople who work in a particular office—specifically, the office currently being tested by the WHERE clause of the main query. The subquery does this by scanning the SALESREPS table. But notice that the OFFICE column in the WHERE clause of the subquery doesn't refer to a column of the SALESREPS table; it refers to a column of the OFFICES table, which is a part of the main query. As SQL moves through each row of the OFFICES table, it uses the OFFICE value from the current row when it carries out the subquery.

The OFFICE column in this subquery is an example of an *outer reference*, which is a column name that does not refer to any of the tables named in the FROM clause of the subquery in which the column name appears. Instead, the column name refers to a column of a table specified in the FROM clause of the main query. As the previous example shows, when the DBMS examines the search condition in the subquery, the value of the column in an outer reference is taken from the row currently being tested by the main query.

Subquery Search Conditions

A subquery usually appears as part of a search condition in the WHERE or HAVING clause. Chapter 6 described the simple search conditions that can be used in these clauses. In addition, most SQL products offer these subquery search conditions:

- **Subquery comparison test**. Compares the value of an expression to a single value produced by a subquery. This test resembles the simple comparison test.

- **Subquery set membership test**. Checks whether the value of an expression matches one of the set of values produced by a subquery. This test resembles the simple set membership test.

- **Existence test**. Tests whether a subquery produces any rows of query results.

- **Quantified comparison test**. Compares the value of an expression to each of the set of values produced by a subquery.

The Subquery Comparison Test (=, <>, <, <=, >, >=)

The subquery comparison test is a modified form of the simple comparison test, as shown in Figure 9-3. It compares the value of an expression to the value produced by a subquery and returns a TRUE result if the comparison is true. You use this test to

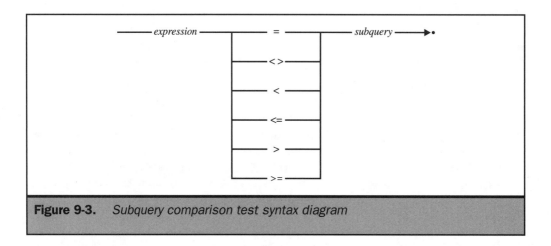

Figure 9-3. *Subquery comparison test syntax diagram*

compare a value from the row being tested to a *single* value produced by a subquery, as in this example:

List the salespeople whose quotas are equal to or higher than the target of the Atlanta sales office.

```
SELECT NAME
  FROM SALESREPS
 WHERE QUOTA >= (SELECT TARGET
                   FROM OFFICES
                  WHERE CITY = 'Atlanta')

NAME
------------
Bill Adams
Sue Smith
Larry Fitch
```

The subquery in the example retrieves the sales target of the Atlanta office. The value is then used to select the salespeople whose quotas are higher than the retrieved target.

The subquery comparison test offers the same six comparison operators (=, <>, <, <=, >, >=) available with the simple comparison test. The subquery specified in this test must produce a single value of the appropriate data type—that is, it must produce a single row of query results containing exactly one column. If the subquery produces multiple rows or multiple columns, the comparison does not make sense, and SQL reports an error condition. If the subquery produces no rows or produces a NULL value, the comparison test returns NULL (unknown).

Here are some additional examples of subquery comparison tests:

List all customers served by Bill Adams.

```
SELECT COMPANY
  FROM CUSTOMERS
 WHERE CUST_REP = (SELECT EMPL_NUM
                     FROM SALESREPS
                    WHERE NAME = 'Bill Adams')

COMPANY
----------------
Acme Mfg.
Three-Way Lines
```

List all products from manufacturer ACI where the quantity on hand is above the quantity on hand of product ACI-41004.

```
SELECT DESCRIPTION, QTY_ON_HAND
  FROM PRODUCTS
 WHERE MFR_ID = 'ACI'
   AND QTY_ON_HAND > (SELECT QTY_ON_HAND
                        FROM PRODUCTS
                       WHERE MFR_ID = 'ACI'
                         AND PRODUCT_ID = '41004')

DESCRIPTION      QTY_ON_HAND
--------------   ------------
Size 3 Widget           207
Size 1 Widget           277
Size 2 Widget           167
```

The subquery comparison test specified by the SQL1 standard and supported by all of the leading DBMS products allows a subquery only on the right side of the comparison operator. This comparison:

A < (subquery)

is allowed, but this comparison:

(subquery) > A

is not permitted. This doesn't limit the power of the comparison test, because the operator in any unequal comparison can always be turned around so that the subquery is put on the right side of the inequality. However, it does mean that you must sometimes turn around the logic of an English-language request to get a form of the request that corresponds to a legal SQL statement.

The SQL2 standard eliminated this restriction and allows the subquery to appear on either side of the comparison operator. In fact, the SQL2 standard goes considerably further and allows a comparison test to be applied to an entire row of values instead of a single value. This and other more advanced query expression features of the SQL2 standard are described in the latter sections of this chapter. However, they are not uniformly supported by the current versions of the major SQL products. For portability, it's best to write subqueries that conform to the SQL1 restrictions, as described previously.

The Set Membership Test (IN)

The subquery set membership test (IN) is a modified form of the simple set membership test, as shown in Figure 9-4. It compares a single data value to a column of data values produced by a subquery and returns a TRUE result if the data value matches one of the values in the column. You use this test when you need to compare a value from the row being tested to a *set* of values produced by a subquery. Here is a simple example:

List the salespeople who work in offices that are over target.

```
SELECT NAME
  FROM SALESREPS
 WHERE REP_OFFICE IN (SELECT OFFICE
                        FROM OFFICES
                       WHERE SALES > TARGET)

NAME
------------
Mary Jones
Sam Clark
Bill Adams
Sue Smith
Larry Fitch
```

The subquery produces a set of office numbers where the sales are above target. (In the sample database, there are three such offices, numbered 11, 13, and 21.) The main

Figure 9-4. *Subquery set membership test (IN) syntax diagram*

query then checks each row of the SALESREPS table to determine whether that particular salesperson works in an office with one of these numbers. Here are some other examples of subqueries that test set membership:

List the salespeople who do not work in offices managed by Larry Fitch (employee 108).

```
SELECT NAME
  FROM SALESREPS
 WHERE REP_OFFICE NOT IN (SELECT OFFICE
                            FROM OFFICES
                           WHERE MGR = 108)

NAME
------------
Bill Adams
Mary Jones
Sam Clark
Bob Smith
Dan Roberts
Paul Cruz
```

List all of the customers who have placed orders for ACI Widgets (manufacturer ACI, product numbers starting with 4100) between January and June 1990.

```
SELECT COMPANY
  FROM CUSTOMERS
 WHERE CUST_NUM IN (SELECT DISTINCT CUST
                      FROM ORDERS
                     WHERE MFR = 'ACI'
                       AND PRODUCT LIKE '4100%'
                       AND ORDER_DATE BETWEEN '01-JAN-90'
                                          AND '30-JUN-90')

COMPANY
------------------
Acme Mfg.
Ace International
Holm & Landis
JCP Inc.
```

In each of these examples, the subquery produces a column of data values, and the WHERE clause of the main query checks to see whether a value from a row of the main query matches one of the values in the column. The subquery form of the IN test thus works exactly like the simple IN test, except that the set of values is produced by a subquery instead of being explicitly listed in the statement.

The Existence Test (EXISTS)

The existence test (EXISTS) checks whether a subquery produces any rows of query results, as shown in Figure 9-5. There is no simple comparison test that resembles the existence test; it is used only with subqueries.

Here is an example of a request that can be expressed naturally using an existence test:

List the products for which an order of $25,000 or more has been received.

The request could easily be rephrased as:

List the products for which there exists at least one order in the ORDERS table (a) that is for the product in question and (b) that has an amount of at least $25,000.

The SELECT statement used to retrieve the requested list of products closely resembles the rephrased request:

```
SELECT DISTINCT DESCRIPTION
  FROM PRODUCTS
 WHERE EXISTS (SELECT ORDER_NUM
                 FROM ORDERS
                WHERE PRODUCT = PRODUCT_ID
                  AND MFR = MFR_ID
                  AND AMOUNT >= 25000.00)

DESCRIPTION
---------------
500-lb Brace
Left Hinge
Right Hinge
Widget Remover
```

Conceptually, SQL processes this query by going through the PRODUCTS table and performing the subquery for each product. The subquery produces a column containing

Figure 9-5. *Existence test (EXISTS) syntax diagram*

the order numbers of any orders for the "current" product that are over $25,000. If there are any such orders (that is, if the column is not empty), the EXISTS test is TRUE. If the subquery produces no rows, the EXISTS test is FALSE. The EXISTS test cannot produce a NULL value.

You can reverse the logic of the EXISTS test using the NOT EXISTS form. In this case, the test is TRUE if the subquery produces no rows, and FALSE otherwise.

Notice that the EXISTS search condition doesn't really *use* the results of the subquery at all. It merely tests to see whether the subquery produces any results. For this reason, SQL relaxes the rule that "subqueries must return a single column of data" and allows you to use the SELECT * form in the subquery of an EXISTS test. The previous subquery could thus have been written:

List the products for which an order of $25,000 or more has been received.

```
SELECT DESCRIPTION
  FROM PRODUCTS
 WHERE EXISTS (SELECT *
                 FROM ORDERS
                WHERE PRODUCT = PRODUCT_ID
                  AND MFR = MFR_ID
                  AND AMOUNT >= 25000.00)
```

In practice, the subquery in an EXISTS test is *always* written using the SELECT * notation.

Here are some additional examples of queries that use EXISTS:

List any customers assigned to Sue Smith who have not placed an order for over $3000.

```
SELECT COMPANY
  FROM CUSTOMERS
 WHERE CUST_REP = (SELECT EMPL_NUM
                     FROM SALESREPS
                    WHERE NAME = 'Sue Smith')
   AND NOT EXISTS (SELECT *
                     FROM ORDERS
                    WHERE CUST = CUST_NUM
                      AND AMOUNT > 3000.00)

COMPANY
----------------
Carter & Sons
Fred Lewis Corp.
```

List the offices where there is a salesperson whose quota represents more than 55 percent of the office's target.

```
SELECT CITY
  FROM OFFICES
 WHERE EXISTS (SELECT *
                 FROM SALESREPS
                WHERE REP_OFFICE = OFFICE
                  AND QUOTA > (.55 * TARGET))

CITY
--------
Denver
Atlanta
```

Note that in each of these examples, the subquery includes an outer reference to a column of the table in the main query. In practice, the subquery in an EXISTS test will always contain an outer reference that links the subquery to the row currently being tested by the main query.

Quantified Tests (ANY and ALL) *

The subquery version of the IN test checks whether a data value is equal to some value in a column of subquery results. SQL provides two quantified tests, ANY and ALL, that extend this notion to other comparison operators, such as greater than (>) and less than (<). Both of these tests compare a data value to the column of data values produced by a subquery, as shown in Figure 9-6.

Figure 9-6.   *Quantified comparison tests (ANY and ALL) syntax diagrams*

The ANY Test *

The ANY test is used in conjunction with one of the six SQL comparison operators
(=, <>, <, <=, >, >=) to compare a single test value to a column of data values produced
by a subquery. To perform the test, SQL uses the specified comparison operator to
compare the test value to *each* data value in the column, one at a time. If *any* of the
individual comparisons yield a TRUE result, the ANY test returns a TRUE result.

Here is an example of a request that can be handled with the ANY test:

List the salespeople who have taken an order that represents more than 10 percent of their quota.

```
SELECT NAME
  FROM SALESREPS
 WHERE (.1 * QUOTA) < ANY (SELECT AMOUNT
                             FROM ORDERS
                            WHERE REP = EMPL_NUM)

NAME
--------------
Sam Clark
Larry Fitch
Nancy Angelli
```

Conceptually, the main query tests each row of the SALESREPS table, one by one.
The subquery finds all of the orders taken by the current salesperson and returns a
column containing the order amounts for those orders. The WHERE clause of the main
query then computes 10 percent of the current salesperson's quota and uses it as a test
value, comparing it to every order amount produced by the subquery. If *any* order
amount exceeds the calculated test value, the ANY test returns TRUE, and the
salesperson is included in the query results. If not, the salesperson is not included in
the query results. The keyword SOME is an alternative for ANY specified by the
ANSI/ISO SQL standard. Either keyword can generally be used, but some DBMS
brands do not support SOME.

The ANY test can sometimes be difficult to understand because it involves an entire
set of comparisons, not just one. It helps if you read the test in a slightly different way
than it appears in the statement. If this ANY test appears:

```
WHERE X < ANY (SELECT Y …)
```

instead of reading the test like this:

```
"where X is less than any select Y…"
```

try reading it like this:

```
"where, for some Y, X is less than Y"
```

When you use this trick, the preceding query becomes:

Select the salespeople where, for some order taken by the salesperson, 10 percent of the salesperson's quota is less than the order amount.

If the subquery in an ANY test produces no rows of query results, or if the query results include NULL values, the operation of the ANY test may vary from one DBMS to another. The ANSI/ISO SQL standard specifies these detailed rules describing the results of the ANY test when the test value is compared to the column of subquery results:

■ If the subquery produces an empty column of query results, the ANY test returns FALSE—there is no value produced by the subquery for which the comparison test holds.

■ If the comparison test is TRUE for at least *one* of the data values in the column, then the ANY search condition returns TRUE—there is indeed some value produced by the subquery for which the comparison test holds.

■ If the comparison test is FALSE for every data value in the column, then the ANY search condition returns FALSE. In this case, you can conclusively state that there is no value produced by the subquery for which the comparison test holds.

■ If the comparison test is not TRUE for any data value in the column, but it is NULL (unknown) for one or more of the data values, then the ANY search condition returns NULL. In this situation, you cannot conclusively state whether there is a value produced by the subquery for which the comparison test holds; there may or may not be, depending on the "actual" (but currently unknown) values for the NULL data.

The ANY comparison operator can be very tricky to use in practice, especially in conjunction with the inequality (<>) comparison operator. Here is an example that shows the problem:

List the names and ages of all the people in the sales force who do not manage an office.

It's tempting to express this query as shown in this example:

```
SELECT NAME, AGE
  FROM SALESREPS
 WHERE EMPL_NUM <> ANY (SELECT MGR
                          FROM OFFICES)
```

The subquery:

```
SELECT MGR
  FROM OFFICES
```

obviously produces the employee numbers of the managers, and therefore the query seems to be saying:

Find each salesperson who is not the manager of any office.

But that's not what the query says! What it does say is this:

Find each salesperson who, for some office, is not the manager of that office.

Of course for any given salesperson, it's possible to find some office where that salesperson is not the manager. The query results would include all the salespeople and therefore fail to answer the question that was posed! The correct query is:

```
SELECT NAME, AGE
  FROM SALESREPS
 WHERE NOT (EMPL_NUM = ANY (SELECT MGR
                              FROM OFFICES))

NAME            AGE
--------------  ----
Mary Jones       31
Sue Smith        48
Dan Roberts      45
Tom Snyder       41
Paul Cruz        29
Nancy Angelli    49
```

You can always turn a query with an ANY test into a query with an EXISTS test by moving the comparison inside the search condition of the subquery. This is usually a very good idea because it eliminates errors like the one just described. Here is an alternative form of the query, using the EXISTS test:

```
SELECT NAME, AGE
  FROM SALESREPS
 WHERE NOT EXISTS (SELECT *
                     FROM OFFICES
                    WHERE EMPL_NUM = MGR)
```

```
NAME            AGE
--------------  ----
Mary Jones       31
Sue Smith        48
Dan Roberts      45
Tom Snyder       41
Paul Cruz        29
Nancy Angelli    49
```

The ALL Test *

Like the ANY test, the ALL test is used in conjunction with one of the six SQL comparison operators (=, <>, <, <=, >, >=) to compare a single test value to a column of data values produced by a subquery. To perform the test, SQL uses the specified comparison operator to compare the test value to each data value in the column, one at a time. If all of the individual comparisons yield a TRUE result, the ALL test returns a TRUE result.

Here is an example of a request that can be handled with the ALL test:

List the offices and their targets where all of the salespeople have sales that exceed 50 percent of the office's target.

```
SELECT CITY, TARGET
  FROM OFFICES
 WHERE (.50 * TARGET) < ALL (SELECT SALES
                               FROM SALESREPS
                              WHERE REP_OFFICE = OFFICE)
```

```
CITY           TARGET
------------   ------------
Denver         $300,000.00
New York       $575,000.00
Atlanta        $350,000.00
```

Conceptually, the main query tests each row of the OFFICES table, one by one. The subquery finds all of the salespeople who work in the current office and returns a column containing the sales for each salesperson. The WHERE clause of the main query then computes 50 percent of the office's target and uses it as a test value, comparing it to every sales value produced by the subquery. If all of the sales values exceed the calculated test value, the ALL test returns TRUE, and the office is included in the query results. If not, the office is not included in the query results.

Like the ANY test, the ALL test can be difficult to understand because it involves an entire set of comparisons, not just one. Again, it helps if you read the test in a slightly different way than it appears in the statement. If this ALL test appears:

```
WHERE X < ALL (SELECT Y …)
```

instead of reading it like this:

```
"where X is less than all select Y…"
```

try reading the test like this:

```
"where, for all Y, X is less than Y"
```

When you use this trick, the preceding query becomes:

Select the offices where, for all salespeople who work in the office, 50 percent of the office's target is less than the salesperson's sales.

If the subquery in an ALL test produces no rows of query results, or if the query results include NULL values, the operation of the ALL test may vary from one DBMS to another. The ANSI/ISO SQL standard specifies these detailed rules describing the results of the ALL test when the test value is compared to the column of subquery results:

- If the subquery produces an empty column of query results, the ALL test returns TRUE. The comparison test does hold for every value produced by the subquery; there just aren't any values.

- If the comparison test is TRUE for every data value in the column, then the ALL search condition returns TRUE. Again, the comparison test holds true for every value produced by the subquery.

- If the comparison test is FALSE for any data value in the column, then the ALL search condition returns FALSE. In this case, you can conclusively state that the comparison test does not hold true for every data value produced by the query.

- If the comparison test is not FALSE for any data value in the column, but it is NULL for one or more of the data values, then the ALL search condition returns NULL. In this situation, you cannot conclusively state whether there is a value produced by the subquery for which the comparison test does not hold true; there may or may not be, depending on the "actual" (but currently unknown) values for the NULL data.

The subtle errors that can occur when the ANY test is combined with the inequality (<>) comparison operator also occur with the ALL test. As with the ANY test, the ALL test can always be converted into an equivalent EXISTS test by moving the comparison inside the subquery.

Subqueries and Joins

You may have noticed as you read through this chapter that many of the queries that were written using subqueries could also have been written as multitable queries, or joins. This is often the case, and SQL allows you to write the query either way. This example illustrates the point:

List the names and ages of salespeople who work in offices in the Western region.

```
SELECT NAME, AGE
  FROM SALESREPS
 WHERE REP_OFFICE IN (SELECT OFFICE
                        FROM OFFICES
                       WHERE REGION = 'Western')

NAME            AGE
-------------- ----
Sue Smith        48
Larry Fitch      62
Nancy Angelli    49
```

This form of the query closely parallels the stated request. The subquery yields a list of offices in the Western region, and the main query finds the salespeople who work in one of the offices in the list. Here is an alternative form of the query, using a two-table join:

List the names and ages of salespeople who work in offices in the Western region.

```
SELECT NAME, AGE
  FROM SALESREPS, OFFICES
 WHERE REP_OFFICE = OFFICE
   AND REGION = 'Western'

NAME            AGE
-------------- ----
Sue Smith        48
Larry Fitch      62
Nancy Angelli    49
```

This form of the query joins the SALESREPS table to the OFFICES table to find the region where each salesperson works, and then eliminates those who do not work in the Western region.

Either of the two queries will find the correct salespeople, and neither one is right or wrong. Many people will find the first form (with the subquery) more natural, because the English request doesn't ask for any information about offices, and because it seems a little strange to join the SALESREPS and OFFICES tables to answer the request. Of course if the request is changed to ask for some information from the OFFICES table:

List the names and ages of the salespeople who work in offices in the Western region and the cities where they work.

the subquery form will no longer work, and the two-table query must be used. Conversely, many queries with subqueries *cannot* be translated into an equivalent join. Here is a simple example:

List the names and ages of salespeople who have above average quotas.

```
SELECT NAME, AGE
  FROM SALESREPS
 WHERE QUOTA > (SELECT AVG(QUOTA)
                  FROM SALESREPS)

NAME            AGE
------------    ----
Bill Adams       37
Sue Smith        48
Larry Fitch      62
```

In this case, the inner query is a summary query and the outer query is not, so there is no way the two queries can be combined into a single join.

Nested Subqueries

All of the queries described thus far in this chapter have been two-level queries, involving a main query and a subquery. Just as you can use a subquery inside a main query, you can use a subquery inside another subquery. Here is an example of a request that is naturally represented as a three-level query, with a main query, a subquery, and a sub-subquery:

List the customers whose salespeople are assigned to offices in the Eastern sales region.

```
SELECT COMPANY
  FROM CUSTOMERS
 WHERE CUST_REP IN (SELECT EMPL_NUM
```

```
                            FROM SALESREPS
                           WHERE REP_OFFICE IN (SELECT OFFICE
                                                  FROM OFFICES
                                                 WHERE REGION = 'Eastern'))


COMPANY
----------------
First Corp.
Smithson Corp.
AAA Investments
JCP Inc.
Chen Associates
QMA Assoc.
Ian & Schmidt
Acme Mfg.
      .
      .
      .
```

In this example, the innermost subquery:

```
SELECT OFFICE
  FROM OFFICES
 WHERE REGION = 'Eastern'
```

produces a column containing the office numbers of the offices in the Eastern region. The next subquery:

```
SELECT EMPL_NUM
  FROM SALESREPS
 WHERE REP_OFFICE IN (subquery)
```

produces a column containing the employee numbers of the salespeople who work in one of the selected offices. Finally, the outermost query:

```
SELECT COMPANY
  FROM CUSTOMERS
 WHERE CUST_REP IN (subquery)
```

finds the customers whose salespeople have one of the selected employee numbers.

The same technique used in this three-level query can be used to build queries with four or more levels. The ANSI/ISO SQL standard does not specify a maximum number of nesting levels, but in practice, a query becomes much more time-consuming as the number of levels increases. The query also becomes more difficult to read, understand, and maintain when it involves more than one or two levels of subqueries. Many SQL implementations restrict the number of subquery levels to a relatively small number.

Correlated Subqueries *

In concept, SQL performs a subquery over and over again—once for each row of the main query. For many subqueries, however, the subquery produces the *same* results for every row or row group. Here is an example:

List the sales offices whose sales are below the average target.

```
SELECT CITY
  FROM OFFICES
 WHERE SALES < (SELECT AVG(TARGET)
                  FROM OFFICES)

CITY
--------
Denver
Atlanta
```

In this query, it would be silly to perform the subquery five times (once for each office). The average target doesn't change with each office; it's completely independent of the office currently being tested. As a result, SQL can handle the query by first performing the subquery, yielding the average target ($550,000), and then converting the main query into:

```
SELECT CITY
  FROM OFFICES
 WHERE SALES < 550000.00
```

Commercial SQL implementations automatically detect this situation and use this shortcut whenever possible to reduce the amount of processing required by a subquery. However, the shortcut cannot be used if the subquery contains an outer reference, as in this example:

List all of the offices whose targets exceed the sum of the quotas of the salespeople who work in them:

```
SELECT CITY
  FROM OFFICES
```

```
WHERE TARGET > (SELECT SUM(QUOTA)
                    FROM SALESREPS
                    WHERE REP_OFFICE = OFFICE)

CITY
-----------
Chicago
Los Angeles
```

For each row of the OFFICES table to be tested by the WHERE clause of the main query, the OFFICE column (which appears in the subquery as an outer reference) has a different value. Thus, SQL has no choice but to carry out this subquery five times—once for each row in the OFFICES table. A subquery containing an outer reference is called a *correlated subquery* because its results are correlated with each individual row of the main query. For the same reason, an outer reference is sometimes called a *correlated reference.*

A subquery can contain an outer reference to a table in the FROM clause of any query that contains the subquery, no matter how deeply the subqueries are nested. A column name in a fourth-level subquery, for example, may refer to one of the tables named in the FROM clause of the main query, or to a table named in the FROM clause of the second-level subquery or the third-level subquery that contains it. Regardless of the level of nesting, an outer reference always takes on the value of the column in the current row of the table being tested.

Because a subquery can contain outer references, there is even more potential for ambiguous column names in a subquery than in a main query. When an unqualified column name appears within a subquery, SQL must determine whether it refers to a table in the subquery's own FROM clause, or to a FROM clause in a query containing the subquery. To minimize the possibility of confusion, SQL always interprets a column reference in a subquery using the nearest FROM clause possible. To illustrate this point, in this example, the same table is used in the query and in the subquery:

List the salespeople who are over 40 and who manage a salesperson over quota.

```
SELECT NAME
  FROM SALESREPS
 WHERE AGE > 40
   AND EMPL_NUM IN (SELECT MANAGER
                        FROM SALESREPS
                        WHERE SALES > QUOTA)
```

```
NAME
------------
Sam Clark
Larry Fitch
```

The MANAGER, QUOTA, and SALES columns in the subquery are references to the SALESREPS table in the subquery's own FROM clause; SQL does not interpret them as outer references, and the subquery is not a correlated subquery. SQL can perform the subquery first in this case, finding the salespeople who are over quota and generating a list of the employee numbers of their managers. SQL can then turn its attention to the main query, selecting managers whose employee numbers appear in the generated list.

If you want to use an outer reference within a subquery like the one in the previous example, you must use a table alias to force the outer reference. This request, which adds one more qualifying condition to the previous one, shows how:

List the managers who are over 40 and who manage a salesperson who is over quota and who does not work in the same sales office as the manager.

```
SELECT NAME
  FROM SALESREPS MGRS
 WHERE AGE > 40
   AND MGRS.EMPL_NUM IN (SELECT MANAGER
                           FROM SALESREPS EMPS
                          WHERE EMPS.QUOTA > EMPS.SALES
                            AND EMPS.REP_OFFICE <> MGRS.REP_OFFICE)

NAME
------------
Sam Clark
Larry Fitch
```

The copy of the SALESREPS table used in the main query now has the tag MGRS, and the copy in the subquery has the tag EMPS. The subquery contains one additional search condition, requiring that the employee's office number does not match that of the manager. The qualified column name MGRS.OFFICE in the subquery is an outer reference, and this subquery is a correlated subquery.

Subqueries in the HAVING Clause *

Although subqueries are most often found in the WHERE clause, they can also be used in the HAVING clause of a query. When a subquery appears in the HAVING clause, it works as part of the row group selection performed by the HAVING clause. Consider this query with a subquery:

List the salespeople whose average order size for products manufactured by ACI is higher than overall average order size.

```
SELECT NAME, AVG(AMOUNT)
  FROM SALESREPS, ORDERS
 WHERE EMPL_NUM = REP
   AND MFR = 'ACI'
 GROUP BY NAME
HAVING AVG(AMOUNT) > (SELECT AVG(AMOUNT)
                          FROM ORDERS)


NAME           AVG(AMOUNT)
-----------    ------------
Sue Smith       $15,000.00
Tom Snyder      $22,500.00
```

Figure 9-7 shows conceptually how this query works. The subquery calculates the overall average order size. It is a simple subquery and contains no outer references, so SQL can calculate the average once and then use it repeatedly in the HAVING clause. The main query goes through the ORDERS table, finding all orders for ACI products, and groups them by salesperson. The HAVING clause then checks each row group to see whether the average order size in that group is bigger than the average for all orders, calculated earlier. If so, the row group is retained; if not, the row group is discarded. Finally, the SELECT clause produces one summary row for each group, showing the name of the salesperson and the average order size for each.

You can also use a correlated subquery in the HAVING clause. Because the subquery is evaluated once for each row *group,* however, all outer references in the correlated subquery must be single-valued for each row group. Effectively, this means that the outer reference must either be a reference to a grouping column of the outer query or be contained within a column function. In the latter case, the value of the column function for the row group being tested is calculated as part of the subquery processing.

If the previous request is changed slightly, the subquery in the HAVING clause becomes a correlated subquery:

List the salespeople whose average order size for products manufactured by ACI is at least as big as that salesperson's overall average order size.

```
SELECT NAME, AVG(AMOUNT)
  FROM SALESREPS, ORDERS
```

```
WHERE EMPL_NUM = REP
  AND MFR = 'ACI'
GROUP BY NAME, EMPL_NUM
HAVING AVG(AMOUNT) >= (SELECT AVG(AMOUNT)
                         FROM ORDERS
                        WHERE REP = EMPL_NUM)


NAME            AVG(AMOUNT)
-----------    ------------
Bill Adams        $7,865.40
Sue Smith        $15,000.00
Tom Snyder       $22,500.00
```

In this new example, the subquery must produce the overall average order size for the salesperson whose row group is currently being tested by the HAVING clause. The

Figure 9-7.   *Subquery operation in the HAVING clause*

subquery selects orders for that particular salesperson, using the outer reference EMPL_NUM. The outer reference is legal because EMPL_NUM has the same value in all rows of a group produced by the main query.

Subquery Summary

This chapter has described subqueries, which allow you to use the results of one query to help define another query. Before moving on to the advanced query facilities of the SQL2 specification, let's summarize subqueries:

- A subquery is a "query within a query." Subqueries appear within one of the subquery search conditions in the WHERE or HAVING clause.

- When a subquery appears in the WHERE clause, the results of the subquery are used to select the individual rows that contribute data to the query results.

- When a subquery appears in the HAVING clause, the results of the subquery are used to select the row groups that contribute data to the query results.

- Subqueries can be nested within other subqueries.

- The subquery form of the comparison test uses one of the simple comparison operators to compare a test value to the single value returned by a subquery.

- The subquery form of the set membership test (IN) matches a test value to the set of values returned by a subquery.

- The existence test (EXISTS) checks whether a subquery returns any values.

- The quantified tests (ANY and ALL) use one of the simple comparison operators to compare a test value to all of the values returned by a subquery, checking to see whether the comparison holds for some or all of the values.

- A subquery may include an outer reference to a table in any of the queries that contain it, linking the subquery to the current row of that query.

Figure 9-8 shows the final version of the rules for SQL query processing, extended to include subqueries. It provides a complete definition of the query results produced by a SELECT statement.

Advanced Queries in SQL2 *

The SQL queries described thus far in Chapters 6–9 are the mainstream capabilities provided by most SQL implementations. The combination of features they represent— column selection in the SELECT clause, row selection criteria in the WHERE clause, multitable joins in the FROM clause, summary queries in the GROUP BY and HAVING clauses, and subqueries for more complex requests—give the user a powerful set of data retrieval and data analysis capabilities. However, database experts have pointed out many limitations of these mainstream query capabilities, including these:

■ **No decision making within queries**. Suppose you wanted to generate a two-column report from the sample database showing the name of each sales office and either its annual sales target or its year-to-date sales, whichever is larger. With standard SQL query features, this is hard to do. Or suppose you had a database that kept track of sales by quarter (four columns of data for each office) and wanted to write a program that displayed offices and their sales for

---

To generate the query results for a SELECT statement:

1. If the statement is a UNION of SELECT statements, apply Steps 2 through 7 to each of the statements to generate their individual query results.

2. Form the product of the tables named in the FROM clause. If the FROM clause names a single table, the product is that table.

3. If there is a WHERE clause, apply its search condition to each row of the product table, retaining those rows for which the search condition is TRUE (and discarding those for which it is FALSE or NULL). If the HAVING clause contains a subquery, the subquery is performed for each row as it is tested.

4. If there is a GROUP BY clause, arrange the remaining rows of the product table into row groups, so that the rows in each group have identical values in all of the grouping columns.

5. If there is a HAVING clause, apply its search condition to each row group, retaining those groups for which the search condition is TRUE (and discarding those for which it is FALSE or NULL). If the HAVING clause contains a subquery, the subquery is performed for each row group as it is tested.

6. For each remaining row (or row group), calculate the value of each item in the select list to produce a single row of query results. For a simple column reference, use the value of the column in the current row (or row group). For a column function, use the current row group as its argument if GROUP BY is specified; otherwise, use the entire set of rows.

7. If SELECT DISTINCT is specified, eliminate any duplicate rows of query results that were produced.

8. If the statement is a UNION of SELECT statements, merge the query results for the individual statements into a single table of query results. Eliminate duplicate rows unless UNION ALL is specified.

9. If there is an ORDER BY clause, sort the query results as specified.

The rows generated by this procedure comprise the query results.

Figure 9-8.   *SQL query processing rules (final version)* a specific (user-supplied) quarter. Again, this program is more difficult to write using standard SQL queries. You must include four separate SQL queries (one for each quarter), and the program logic must select which query to run, based on user input. This simple case isn't too difficult, but in a more general case, the program could become much more complex.

■ **Limited use of subqueries**. The simplest example of this limitation is the SQL1 restriction that a subquery can appear only on the right side of a comparison test in a WHERE clause. The database request "list the offices where the sum of the salesperson's quotas is greater than the office target" is most directly expressed as this query:

```
SELECT OFFICE
  FROM OFFICES
 WHERE (SELECT SUM(QUOTA)
          FROM SALESREPS
         WHERE REP_OFFICE = OFFICE) > TARGET
```

But this isn't a legal SQL1 statement. Instead, you must turn the inequality around:

```
SELECT OFFICE
  FROM OFFICES
 WHERE TARGET > (SELECT SUM(QUOTA)
                   FROM SALESREPS
                  WHERE REP_OFFICE = OFFICE)
```

In this simple example, it isn't hard to turn the logic around, but the restriction is a nuisance at best, and it does prevent you from comparing the results of two subqueries, for example.

■ **Limited-row expressions**. Suppose you wanted to list the suppliers, item numbers, and prices for a set of products that are substitutes for one another. Conceptually, these are a set of products whose identification (a manufacturer-ID/product-ID pair) matches one of a set of values, and it would be natural to write the query using a set membership test as:

```
SELECT MFR_ID, PRODUCT_ID, PRICE
  FROM PRODUCTS
 WHERE (MFR_ID, PRODUCT_ID) IN (('ACI',41003),('BIC',41089), …)
```

The SQL1 standard doesn't permit this kind of set membership test. Instead, you must construct the query as a long set of individual comparisons, connected by ANDs and ORs.

the sample database) and HIRE_DATE (a date in the sample database) into character strings for the returned query results:

```
SELECT NAME, CAST REP_OFFICE AS VARCHAR, HIRE_DATE AS VARCHAR
  FROM SALESREPS
```

The CAST expression can generally appear anywhere that a scalar-valued expression can appear within a SQL statement. In this example, it's used in the WHERE clause to convert a character string customer number into an integer, so that it can be compared with the data in the database:

```
SELECT PRODUCT, QTY, AMOUNT
  FROM ORDERS
 WHERE CUST = CAST '2107' AS INTEGER
```

Instead of specifying a data type in the CAST expression, you can specify a SQL2 domain. Domains are specific collections of legal data values that can be defined in the database under the SQL2 standard. They are fully described in Chapter 11 because of the role they play in SQL data integrity. Note that you can also generate a NULL value of the appropriate data type for use in SQL expressions using the CAST expression.

The most common uses for the CAST expression are:

- To convert data from within a database table where the column is defined with the wrong data type. For example, when a column is defined as a character string, but you know it actually contains numbers (that is, strings of digits) or dates (strings that can be interpreted as a month/day/year).

- To convert data from data types supported by the DBMS that are not supported by a host programming language. For example, most host programming languages do not have explicit date and time data types and require that date/time values be converted into character strings for handling by a program.

- To eliminate differences between data types in two different tables. For example, if an order date is stored in one table as DATE data, but a product availability date is stored in a different table as a character string, you can still compare the columns from the two tables by CASTing one of the columns into the data type of the other. Similarly, if you want to combine data from two different tables with a UNION operation, their columns must have identical data types. You can achieve this by CASTing the columns of one of the tables.

The CASE Expression (SQL2)

The SQL2 CASE expression provides for limited decision making within SQL expressions. Its basic structure, shown in Figure 9-10, is similar to the IF...THEN...ELSE statement found in many programming languages. When the DBMS encounters a CASE expression, it evaluates the first search condition, and if it is TRUE, then the value of the CASE expression

Figure 9-10. *SQL2 CASE expression syntax diagram*

is the value of the first result expression. If the result of the first search condition is not
TRUE, the DBMS proceeds to the second search condition and checks whether it is TRUE. If
so, the value of the CASE expression is the value of the second result expression, and so on.

Here is a simple example of the use of the CASE expression. Suppose you want to
do an A/B/C analysis of the customers from the sample database according to their
credit limits. The *A* customers are the ones with credit limits over $60,000, the *B* customers
are those with limits over $30,000 and the *C* customers are the others. Using SQL1, you
would have to retrieve customer names and credit limits from the database and then
rely on an application program to look at the credit limit values and assign an *A*, *B*, or
C rating. Using a SQL2 CASE expression, you can have the DBMS do the work for you:

```
SELECT COMPANY, CASE WHEN CREDIT_LIMIT > 60000 THEN 'A'
                     WHEN CREDIT_LIMIT > 30000 THEN 'B'
                     ELSE 'C'
  FROM CUSTOMERS
```

For each row of query results, the DBMS evaluates the CASE expression by first
comparing the credit limit to $60,000, and if the comparison is TRUE, returns an A in the
second column of query results. If that comparison fails, the comparison to $30,000 is
made and returns a B if this second comparison is TRUE. Otherwise, the third column
of query results will return a C.

This is a very simple example of a CASE expression. The results of the CASE
expression are all literals here, but in general, they can be any SQL expression. Similarly,
there is no requirement that the tests in each WHEN clause are similar, as they are here.
The CASE expression can also appear in other clauses of a query. Here is an example of a
query where it's useful in the WHERE clause. Suppose you want to find the total of the
salesperson's sales, by office. If a salesperson is not yet assigned to an office, that person
should be included in the total for his or her manager's office. Here is a query that
generates the appropriate office groupings:

```
SELECT CITY, SUM(SALES)
  FROM OFFICES, SALESREPS
 WHERE OFFICE =
```

```
CASE WHEN (REP_OFFICE IS NOT NULL) THEN REP_OFFICE
     ELSE (SELECT REP_OFFICE
             FROM SALESREPS AS MGRS
             WHERE MGRS.EMPL_NUM = MANAGER)
```

The SQL2 standard provides a shorthand version of the CASE expression for the common situation where you want to compare a test value of some kind to a sequence of data values (usually literals). This version of the CASE syntax is shown in Figure 9-11. Instead of repeating a search condition of the form:

test_value = value1

in each WHEN clause, it lets you specify the *test_value* calculation once. For example, suppose you wanted to generate a list of all of the offices, showing the names of their managers and the cities and states where they are located. The sample database doesn't include state names, so the query must generate this information itself. Here is a query, with a CASE expression in the SELECT list, that does the job:

```
SELECT NAME, CITY, CASE OFFICE WHEN 11 THEN 'New York'
                               WHEN 12 THEN 'Illinois'
                               WHEN 13 THEN 'Georgia'
                               WHEN 21 THEN 'California'
                               WHEN 22 THEN 'Colorado'
  FROM OFFICES, SALESREPS
WHERE MGR = EMPL_NUM
```

The COALESCE Expression (SQL2)

One of the most common uses for the decision-making capability of the CASE expression is for handling NULL values within the database. For example, it's frequently desirable to have a NULL value from the database represented by some literal value (such as the word "missing") or by some default value when using SQL to generate a report. Here is a report that lists the salespeople and their quotas. If a salesperson has not yet been assigned a quota, assume that the salesperson's actual year-to-date sales should be listed

Figure 9-11.   *SQL2 CASE expression alternative syntax*

instead. If for some reason the actual year-to-date sales are also NULL (unknown), then a zero amount should be listed. The CASE statement generates the desired IF...THEN... ELSE logic:

```
SELECT NAME, CASE WHEN (QUOTA IS NOT NULL) THEN QUOTA
                  WHEN (SALES IS NOT NULL) THEN SALES
                  ELSE 0.00
  FROM SALESREPS
```

This type of NULL-handling logic is needed frequently, so the SQL2 standard includes a specialized form of the CASE expression, the COALESCE expression, to handle it. The syntax for the COALESCE expression is shown in Figure 9-12. The processing rules for the COALESCE expression are very straightforward. The DBMS examines the first value in the list. If its value is not NULL, it becomes the value of the COALESCE expression. If the first value is NULL, the DBMS moves to the second value and checks to see whether it is NULL. If not, it becomes the value of the expression. Otherwise, the DBMS moves to the third value, and so on. Here is the same example just given, expressed with the COALESCE expression instead of a CASE expression:

```
SELECT NAME, COALESCE (QUOTA, SALES, 0.00)
  FROM SALESREPS
```

As you can see by comparing the two queries, the simplicity of the COALESCE syntax makes it easier to see, at a glance, the meaning of the query. However, the operation of the two queries is identical. The COALESCE expression adds simplicity, but no new capability, to the SQL2 language.

The NULLIF Expression (SQL2)

Just as the COALESCE expression is used to eliminate NULL values when they are not desired for processing, sometimes you may need to create NULL values. In many data processing applications (especially older ones that were developed before relational databases were popular), missing data is not represented by NULL values. Instead, some special code value that is otherwise invalid is used to indicate that the data is missing.

For example, suppose that in the sample database, the situation where a salesperson had not yet been assigned a manager was indicated by a zero (0) value in the MANAGER

Figure 9-12.   *SQL2 COALESCE expression syntax diagram*

column instead of a NULL value. In some circumstances, you will want to detect this situation within a SQL query and substitute the NULL value for the zero "code." The NULLIF expression, shown in Figure 9-13, is used for this purpose. When the DBMS encounters a NULLIF expression, it examines the first value (usually a column name) and compares it to the second value (usually the code value used to indicate missing data). If the two values are equal, the expression generates a NULL value. Otherwise, the expression generates the first value.

Here is a query that handles the case where missing office numbers are represented by a zero:

```
SELECT CITY, SUM(SALES)
  FROM OFFICES, SALESREPS
 WHERE OFFICE = (NULLIF REP_OFFICE, 0)
 GROUP BY CITY
```

Together, the CASE, COALESCE, and NULLIF expressions provide a solid decision-making logic capability for use within SQL statements. They fall far short of the complete logical flow constructs provided by most programming languages (looping, branching, and so on) but do provide for much greater flexibility in query expressions. The net result is that more processing work can be done by the DBMS and reflected in query results, leaving less work to be done by the human user or the application program.

Row-Valued Expressions (SQL2)

Although columns and the scalar data values they contain are the atomic building blocks of a relational database, the structuring of columns into rows that represent real-world entities, such as individual offices or customers or orders, is one of the most important features of the relational model. The SQL1 standard, and most mainstream commercial database products, certainly reflect this row/column structure, but they provide very limited capability to actually manipulate rows and groups of rows. Basically, SQL1 operations allow you to insert a row into a table, or to retrieve, update, or delete groups of rows from a database (using the SELECT, UPDATE, or DELETE statements).

The SQL2 standard goes well beyond these capabilities, allowing you to generally use rows in SQL expressions in much the same way that you can use scalar values. It provides a syntax for constructing rows of data. It allows row-valued subqueries. And it defines row-valued meanings for the SQL comparison operators and other SQL structures.

Figure 9-13. *SQL2 NULLIF expression syntax diagram*

The Row-Value Constructor (SQL2)

SQL2 allows you to specify a row of data values by using a *row-value constructor* expression, whose syntax is shown in Figure 9-14. In its most common form, the row constructor is a comma-separated list of literal values, or expressions. For example, here is a row-value constructor for a row of data whose structure matches the OFFICES table in the sample database:

```
(23, 'San Diego', 'Western', NULL, DEFAULT, 0.00)
```

The result of this expression is a single row of data with six columns. The NULL keyword in the fourth column position indicates that the fourth column in the constructed row should contain a NULL (unknown) value. The DEFAULT keyword in the fifth column position indicates that the fifth column in the constructed row should contain the default value for the column. This keyword may appear in a row-value constructor only in certain situations—for example, when the row-value constructor appears in an INSERT statement to add a new row to a table.

When a row constructor is used in the WHERE clause of a SQL statement, column names can also appear as individual data items within the row constructor, or as part of an expression within the row constructor. For example, consider this query:

List the order number, quantity, and amount of all orders for ACI-41002 widgets.

```
SELECT ORDER_NUM, QTY, AMOUNT
  FROM ORDERS
 WHERE (MFR, PRODUCT) = ('ACI', '41002')
```

Under the normal rules of SQL query processing, the WHERE clause is applied to each row of the ORDERS table, one by one. The first row-value constructor in the

Figure 9-14. *SQL2 row-value constructor syntax diagram*

WHERE clause (to the left of the equal sign) generates a two-column row, containing the manufacturer code and the product number for the current order being considered. The second row-value constructor (to the right of the equal sign) generates a two-column row, containing the (literal) manufacturer code ACI and product number 41002. The equal sign is now comparing two *rows* of values, not two scalar values. The SQL2 standard defines this type of row-valued comparison for equality, which is processed by comparing, pairwise, each of the columns in the two rows. The result of the comparison is TRUE only if all of the pairwise column comparisons are TRUE. Of course, it's possible to write the query without the row-value constructors, like this:

List the order number, quantity, and amount of all orders for ACI-41002 widgets.

```
SELECT ORDER_NUM, QTY, AMOUNT
  FROM ORDERS
 WHERE (MFR = 'ACI') AND (PRODUCT = '41002')
```

and in this simple example, the meaning of the query is probably equally clear with either form. However, row-value constructors can be very useful in simplifying the appearance of more complex queries, and they become even more useful when combined with row-valued subqueries.

Row-Valued Subqueries (SQL2)

As described throughout the earlier parts of this chapter, the SQL1 standard provides a subquery capability for expressing more complex database queries. The subquery takes the same form as a SQL query (that is, a SELECT statement), but a SQL1 subquery must be scalar-valued—that is, it must produce a *single* data value as its query results. The value generated by the subquery is then used as part of an expression within the main SQL statement that contains the subquery. This use of subqueries is supported by the major enterprise-class relational database systems today.

The SQL2 standard dramatically expands the subquery facility, including support for *row-valued subqueries*. A row-valued subquery returns not just a single data item, but a row of data items, which can be used in SQL2 expressions and compared to other rows. For example, suppose you wanted to show the order numbers and dates for all of the orders placed against the highest-priced product in the sample database. A logical way to start building the appropriate SQL query is to find an expression that will give you the identity (manufacturer ID and product ID) of the high-priced product in question. Here is a query that finds the right product:

Find the manufacturer ID and product ID of the product with the highest unit price.

```
SELECT MFR_ID, PRODUCT_ID
  FROM PRODUCTS
 WHERE PRICE = (SELECT MAX(PRICE)
                  FROM PRODUCTS)
```

Ignoring the possibility of a tie for the most expensive product for a moment, this query will generate a single row of query results, consisting of two columns. Using SQL2's row-valued subquery capability, you can embed this entire query as a subquery within a SELECT statement to retrieve the order information:

List the order numbers and dates of all orders placed for the highest-priced product.

```
SELECT ORDER_NUM, ORDER_DATE
  FROM ORDERS
 WHERE (MFR, PRODUCT) = (SELECT MFR_ID, PRODUCT_ID
                           FROM PRODUCTS
                          WHERE PRICE = (SELECT MAX(PRICE)
                                           FROM PRODUCTS))
```

The top-level WHERE clause in this query contains a row-valued comparison. On the left side of the equal sign is a row-value constructor consisting of two column names. Each time the WHERE clause is examined to carry out the top-level query, the value of this row-valued expression is a manufacturer-ID/product-ID pair from a row of the ORDERS table. On the right side of the equal sign is the subquery that generates the identity of the product with the highest dollar value. The result of this subquery is again a row value, with two colu

mns, whose data types match those of the row-valued expression on the left side of the equal sign.

It's possible to express this query without the row-valued subquery, but the resulting query will be much less straightforward:

List the order numbers and dates of all orders placed for the highest-priced product.

```
SELECT ORDER_NUM, ORDER_DATE
  FROM ORDERS
 WHERE (MFR = (SELECT MFR_ID
                 FROM PRODUCTS
                WHERE PRICE = (SELECT MAX(PRICE)
                                 FROM PRODUCTS)))
   AND (PRODUCT = (SELECT PRODUCT_ID
                     FROM PRODUCTS
                    WHERE PRICE = (SELECT MAX(PRICE)
                                     FROM PRODUCTS)))
```

Instead of a single row-valued comparison in the WHERE clause, the resulting query has two separate scalar-valued comparisons, one for the manufacturer ID and one for the product ID. Because the comparison must be split, the lower-level subquery to find the maximum price must be repeated twice as well. Overall, the form of the query using the row-valued expression is a more direct translation of the English-language request, and it's easier to read and understand.

Row-Valued Comparisons (SQL2)

The most common use of row-valued expressions in the WHERE or HAVING clause is within a test for equality, as illustrated by the last few examples. A constructed row (often consisting of column values from a candidate row of query results) is compared to another constructed row (perhaps a row of subquery results or a row of literal values), and if the rows are equal, the candidate row is included in the query results. The SQL2 standard also provides for row-valued forms of the inequality comparison tests and the range test. When comparing two rows for inequality, SQL2 uses the same rules that it would use if the columns were being used to sort the rows. It compares the contents of the first column in the two rows, and if they are unequal, uses them to order the rows. If they are equal, the comparison moves to the second column, and then the third, and so on. Here are the resulting comparisons for some three-column constructed rows derived from the ORDERS table:

('ACI','41002',54) < ('REI','2A44R',5)—based on first column
('ACI','41002',54) < ('ACI','41003',35)—based on second column
('ACI','41002',10) < ('ACI','41002',54)—based on third column

Table-Valued Expressions (SQL2)

In addition to its extended capabilities for expressions involving simple scalar data values and row values, the SQL2 standard dramatically extends the SQL capabilities for table processing. It provides a mechanism for constructing a table of data values in place within a SQL statement. It allows table-valued subqueries and extends the SQL1 subquery tests to handle them. It also allows subqueries to appear in many more places within a SQL statement—for example, a subquery can appear in the FROM clause of a SELECT statement as of its source tables. Finally, it provides expanded capabilities for combining tables, including the UNION, INTERSECTION, and DIFFERENCE operations.

The Table-Value Constructor (SQL2)

SQL2 allows you to specify a table of data values within a SQL statement by using a *table-value constructor* expression, whose syntax is shown in Figure 9-15. In its simplest form, the table-value constructor is a comma-separated list of row-value constructors, each of which contains a comma-separated set of literals that form individual column values. For example, the SQL2 INSERT statement uses a table-value constructor as the source of the data to be inserted into a database. While the SQL1 INSERT statement (described in Chapter 10) allows you to insert only a single row of data, the next SQL2 INSERT statement inserts three rows into the OFFICES table.

Figure 9-15. *SQL2 table-value constructor syntax diagram*

Add three offices to the OFFICES table.

```
INSERT INTO OFFICES (OFFICE,CITY,REGION,MGR,SALES)
    VALUES (23, 'San Diego', 'Western', 108, 0.00),
           (24, 'Seattle', 'Western', 104, 0.00),
           (14, 'Boston', 'Eastern, NULL, 0.00)
```

Note that the individual rows in the table-value constructor are not restricted to contain only literal values. The source of a data value can be a scalar-valued subquery, or an entire row can be the result of a row-valued subquery. Although it doesn't make much sense in the sample database, this is a legal SQL2 INSERT statement that illustrates these capabilities:

Add three offices to the OFFICES table.

```
INSERT INTO OFFICES (OFFICE,CITY,REGION,MGR,SALES)
    VALUES (23, 'San Diego', 'Western', 108, 0.00),
           (24, 'Seattle', 'Western', (SELECT MANAGER
                                         FROM SALESREPS
                                         WHERE EMPL_NUM = 105),
0.00),
           (SELECT 'BOSTON', 'EASTERN', REGION, MGR, 0.00
              FROM OFFICES
             WHERE OFFICE = 12)
```

Like the preceding example, the VALUES clause in this INSERT statement generates a three-row table to be inserted. The first row is specified with literal values. In the second row, the fourth column is specified as a scalar-valued subquery that retrieves the manager of employee number 105. In the third row, the entire row is generated by a row-valued subquery. In this case, three of the column values in the subquery's SELECT clause are actually literal values, but the third and fourth columns are produced by the subquery, which retrieves the manager and region for the New York office (number 12).

Table-Valued Subqueries (SQL2)

Just as SQL2 expands the use of scalar subqueries into row-valued subqueries, it also extends the SQL subquery facility to support *table-valued subqueries*—that is, subqueries that return a full table of results. One useful role for table-valued subqueries is within the WHERE or HAVING clause, where it is combined with extended forms of the subquery tests. For example, suppose you wanted to list the descriptions and prices of all products with orders exceeding $20,000 in the sample database. Perhaps the most straightforward way to express this request is in this SQL2 statement that uses a table-valued subquery:

List the description and price of all products with individual orders over $20,000.

```
SELECT DESCRIPTION, PRICE
  FROM PRODUCTS
 WHERE (MFR_ID, PRODUCT_ID) IN (SELECT MFR, PRODUCT
                                  FROM ORDERS
                                 WHERE AMOUNT > 20000.00)
```

The top-level query is a straightforward statement of the English-language request—it asks for the description and price of those products whose identification (as in previous examples, a manufacturer-ID/product-ID pair) matches some set of products. This is expressed as a subquery set membership test in the WHERE clause. The subquery generates a two-column table of subquery results, which are the identifications of the products that meet the stated order size criterion.

It's certainly possible to express this query in other ways. From the discussion in Chapter 7, you probably recognize that it can be stated as a join of the PRODUCTS and ORDERS tables with a compound search condition:

List the description and price of all products with individual orders over $20,000.

```
SELECT DESCRIPTION, PRICE
  FROM PRODUCTS, ORDERS
 WHERE (MFR_ID = MFR)
   AND (PRODUCT_ID = PRODUCT)
   AND (AMOUNT > 20000.00)
```

This is an equally valid statement of the query, but it's a lot further removed from the English-language request, and therefore more difficult to understand for most people. As queries become more complex, the ability to use table-valued subqueries becomes even more useful to simplify and clarify SQL requests.

The SQL2 Query Specification

The SQL2 standard formalizes the definition of what we have loosely been calling a SELECT statement or a query in the last three chapters into a basic building block called a *query specification*. For a complete understanding of the SQL2 table expression capabilities in the next section, it's useful to understand this formal definition. The form of a SQL2 query specification is shown in Figure 9-16. Its components should be familiar from the earlier chapters:

- A *select list* specifies the columns of query results. Each column is specified by an expression that tells the DBMS how to calculate its value. The column can be assigned an optional alias with the AS clause.

- The keywords ALL or UNIQUE control duplicate row elimination in the query results.

- The FROM clause specifies the tables that contribute to the query results.

- The WHERE clause describes how the DBMS should determine which rows are included in the query results and which should be discarded.

- The GROUP BY and HAVING clauses together control the grouping of individual query results rows in a grouped query, and the selection of row groups for inclusion or exclusion in the final results.

The query specification is the basic query building block in the SQL2 standard. Conceptually, it describes the process of combining data from the tables in the FROM clause into a row/column table of query results. The value of the query specification is a *table* of data. In the simplest case, a SQL2 query consists of a simple query specification. In a slightly more complex case, a query specification is used to describe a subquery, which appears within another (higher-level) query specification. Finally, query specifications can be combined using table-valued operations to form general-purpose query expressions, as described in the next section.

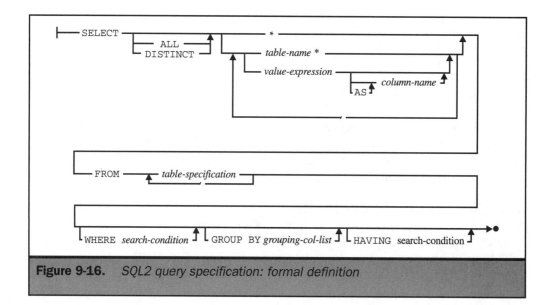

Figure 9-16. *SQL2 query specification: formal definition*

Query Expressions (SQL2)

The SQL2 standard defines a *query expression* as the full, general-purpose way that you can specify a table of query results in the SQL2 language. The basic building blocks you can use to create a query expression are the following:

- A query specification, as described in the preceding section (SELECT...FROM...). Its value is a table of query results.

- A table-value constructor, as previously described (VALUES ...). Its value is a table of constructed values.

- An explicit table reference (TABLE *tblname*). Its value is the contents of the named table.

Using these building blocks, SQL2 lets you combine their table values using the following operations:

- **JOIN**. SQL2 provides explicit support for full cross-product joins (cross joins), natural joins, inner joins, and all types of outer joins (left, right, and full), as described in Chapter 7. A JOIN operation takes two tables as its input and produces a table of combined query results according to the join specification.

- **UNION**. The SQL2 UNION operation provides explicit support for merging the rows of two compatible tables (that is, two tables having the same number of columns and with corresponding columns having the same data types). The UNION operation takes two tables as its input and produces a single merged table of query results.

- **DIFFERENCE**. The SQL2 EXCEPT operation takes two tables as its input and produces as its output a table containing the rows that appear in the first table but that do not appear in another table—that is, the rows that are missing from the second table. Conceptually, the EXCEPT operation is like table subtraction. The rows of the second table are taken away from the rows of the first table, and the answer is the remaining rows of the first table.

- **INTERSECT**. The SQL2 INTERSECT operation takes two tables as its input and produces as its output a table containing the rows that appear in both input tables.

SQL2 UNION, INTERSECT, and DIFFERENCE Operations

The SQL2 UNION, INTERSECT, and DIFFERENCE operations provide set operations for combining two input tables to form an output table. All three of the operations require that the two input tables be *union-compatible*—they must have the same number of columns, and the corresponding columns of each table must have identical data types. Here are some simple examples of SQL2 query expressions involving UNION, INTERSECT, and DIFFERENCE operations based on the sample database:

Show all products for which there is an order over $30,000 or more than $30,000 worth of inventory on hand.

```
(SELECT MFR, PRODUCT
   FROM ORDERS
  WHERE AMOUNT > 30000.00)
  UNION
(SELECT MFR_ID, PRODUCT_ID
   FROM PRODUCTS
  WHERE (PRICE * QTY_ON_HAND) > 30000)
```

Show all products for which there is an order over $30,000 and more than $30,000 worth of inventory on hand.

```
(SELECT MFR, PRODUCT
   FROM ORDERS
  WHERE AMOUNT > 30000.00)
INTERSECT
(SELECT MFR_ID, PRODUCT_ID
   FROM PRODUCTS
  WHERE (PRICE * QTY_ON_HAND) > 30000)
```

Show all products for which there is an order over $30,000 except for those products that sell for under $1000.

```
(SELECT MFR, PRODUCT
   FROM ORDERS
  WHERE AMOUNT > 30000.00)
 EXCEPT
(SELECT MFR_ID, PRODUCT_ID
   FROM PRODUCTS
  WHERE PRICE < 100.00)
```

By default, the UNION, INTERSECT, and EXCEPT operations eliminate duplicate rows during their processing. This is usually the desired result, as it is in these examples, but occasionally, you may need to suppress the elimination of duplicate rows. You can do this by specifying the UNION ALL, INTERSECT ALL, or EXCEPT ALL forms of the operations.

Note each of these examples produces a two-column table of query results. The results come from two different source tables within the database—the ORDERS table and the PRODUCTS table. However, the columns selected from these tables have the same corresponding data types, so they can be combined using these operations. In the sample database, the corresponding columns have different names in the two tables. (The manufacturer-ID column is named MFR in the ORDERS table but named MFR_ID in the PRODUCTS table.)

However, corresponding columns such as these will often have the same name in each of the tables being combined. As a convenience, SQL2 lets you specify the corresponding columns in a CORRESPONDING clause attached to the UNION, INTERSECT, or EXCEPT operation. Here is the preceding UNION example, changed for the situation where the ORDERS and PRODUCTS tables have parallel column names for manufacturer ID and product ID:

Show all products for which there is an order over $30,000 or more than $30,000 worth of inventory on hand.

```
(SELECT *
   FROM ORDERS
  WHERE AMOUNT > 30000.00)
  UNION CORRESPONDING BY (MFR, PRODUCT)
(SELECT *
   FROM PRODUCTS
  WHERE (PRICE * QTY_ON_HAND) > 30000)
```

In a case like this one where *all* of the corresponding (that is, identically named) columns from the two tables participate in the UNION operation, SQL2 even allows you to leave off the explicit list of column names:

Show all products for which there is an order over $30,000 or more than $30,000 worth of inventory on hand.

```
(SELECT *
   FROM ORDERS
  WHERE AMOUNT > 30000.00)
  UNION CORRESPONDING
(SELECT *
   FROM PRODUCTS
  WHERE (PRICE * QTY_ON_HAND) > 30000)
```

Finally, it's worth noting that the column alias capability of the query specification can be used to rename or assign names to the columns from the individual query results that are being combined with the UNION operation. If we eliminate the assumption that the PRODUCTS and ORDERS tables use the same column names, it's still possible to use the CORRESPONDING form of the UNION operation in this query simply by renaming the columns in one of the tables:

Show all products for which there is an order over $30,000 or more than $30,000 worth of inventory on hand.

```
(SELECT *
   FROM ORDERS
  WHERE AMOUNT > 30000.00)
```

RETRIEVING DATA

```
     UNION CORRESPONDING
(SELECT MFR_ID AS MFR, PRODUCT_ID AS PRODUCT
   FROM PRODUCTS
   WHERE (PRICE * QTY_ON_HAND) > 30000)
```

In this simple example, there is not much advantage in this construct, but in the more general case where the individual queries involve calculated columns or are grouped queries, the CORRESPONDING clause and column aliases can help to clarify the meaning of the query.

Query Expressions in the FROM Clause

SQL2 query expressions provide a much more powerful and flexible method for generating and combining tables of query results than the simple subquery and UNION operations provided by the SQL1 standard. To make query expressions even more useful and more general-purpose, the SQL2 standard allows them to appear almost anywhere that a table reference could appear in a SQL1 query. In particular, a query expression can appear in place of a table name in the FROM clause. Here is a simple example of a SQL2 query for the sample database that uses this feature:

Show the names and total outstanding orders of all customers with credit limits over $50,000.

```
SELECT COMPANY, TOT_ORDERS
   FROM CUSTOMER, (SELECT CUST, SUM(AMOUNT) AS TOT_ORDERS
                    FROM ORDERS
                    GROUP BY CUST),
   WHERE (CREDIT_LIMIT > 50000.00)
     AND (CUST_NUM = CUST)
```

The second "table name" in the FROM clause of the main query is not a table name at all, but a full-blown query expression. In fact, the expression could have been much more complex, involving UNION or JOIN operations. When a query expression appears in the FROM clause, as it does here, the DBMS conceptually carries it out *first*, before any other processing of the query, and creates a temporary table of the query results generated by the query expression. In this case, this temporary table consists of two columns, listing each customer number and the total of orders for that customer number. This temporary table then acts as one of the source tables for the main query. In this example, its contents are joined to the CUSTOMER table to obtain the company name and generate the answer to the main question.

There are many other ways in which this query could be written. The entire query could be written as one top-level grouped query that joins the CUSTOMER and ORDERS table. The join operation could be made explicit with a SQL2 JOIN operator, and then the results of the join could be grouped in the top-level query. As this example shows, one of the benefits of the SQL2 query expression capabilities is that they typically provide several different ways to obtain the same query results.

The general philosophy behind the SQL2 capabilities in this area is that the SQL language should provide the flexibility to express a query in the most natural form. The underlying DBMS must be able to take the query, however expressed, break it down into its fundamentals, and then determine the most efficient way to carry out the query. This internal query execution plan may be quite different than the apparent plan called for by the actual SQL statement, but as long as it produces the same query results, the net effect is to shift the optimization workload from the human user or programmer to the DBMS.

SQL Queries: A Final Summary

This concludes the discussion of the SQL queries and the SELECT statement that began in Chapter 6. As described in Chapters 6–9, the clauses of the SELECT statement provide a powerful, flexible set of capabilities for retrieving data from the database. Each clause plays a specific role in data retrieval:

- The FROM clause specifies the source tables that contribute data to the query results. Every column name in the body of the SELECT statement must unambiguously identify a column from one of these tables, or it must be an outer reference to a column from a source table of an outer query.

- The WHERE clause, if present, selects individual combinations of rows from the source tables to participate in the query results. Subqueries in the WHERE clause are evaluated for each individual row.

- The GROUP BY clause, if present, groups the individual rows selected by the WHERE clause into row groups.

- The HAVING clause, if present, selects row groups to participate in the query results. Subqueries in the HAVING clause are evaluated for each row group.

- The SELECT clause determines which data values actually appear as columns in the final query results.

- The DISTINCT keyword, if present, eliminates duplicate rows of query results.

- The UNION operator, if present, merges the query results produced by individual SELECT statements into a single set of query results.

- The ORDER BY clause, if present, sorts the final query results based on one or more columns.

- The SQL2 query expression capabilities add row-valued and table-valued expressions and INTERSECT and EXCEPT operations to the SQL1 capabilities. The fundamental flow of query processing is not changed, but the capability to express queries within queries is greatly enhanced.

The
Complete
Reference

Part III

Updating Data

SQL is not only a query language, it's a complete language for retrieving and modifying data in a database. Chapters 10–12 focus on database updates. Chapter 10 describes SQL statements that add data to a database, remove data from a database, and modify existing database data. Chapter 11 describes how SQL maintains the integrity of stored data when the data is modified. Chapter 12 describes the SQL transaction-processing features that support concurrent database updates by many different users.

The
Complete
Reference

Chapter 10

Database Updates

S QL is a complete data manipulation language that is used not only for database queries, but also to modify and update data in the database. Compared to the complexity of the SELECT statement, which supports SQL queries, the SQL statements that modify database contents are extremely simple. However, database updates pose some challenges for a DBMS beyond those presented by database queries. The DBMS must protect the integrity of stored data during changes, ensuring that only valid data is introduced into the database, and that the database remains self-consistent, even in the event of system failures. The DBMS must also coordinate simultaneous updates by multiple users, ensuring that the users and their changes do not interfere with one another.

This chapter describes the three SQL statements that are used to modify the contents of a database:

- **INSERT**. Adds new rows of data to a table
- **DELETE**. Removes rows of data from a table
- **UPDATE**. Modifies existing data in the database

In Chapter 11, SQL facilities for maintaining data integrity are described. Chapter 12 covers SQL support for multiuser concurrency.

Adding Data to the Database

A new row of data is typically added to a relational database when a new entity represented by the row appears in the outside world. For example, in the sample database:

- When you hire a new salesperson, a new row must be added to the SALESREPS table to store the salesperson's data.
- When a salesperson signs a new customer, a new row must be added to the CUSTOMERS table, representing the new customer.
- When a customer places an order, a new row must be added to the ORDERS table to contain the order data.

In each case, the new row is added to maintain the database as an accurate model of the real world. The smallest unit of data that can be added to a relational database is a single row. In general, a SQL-based DBMS provides three ways to add new rows of data to a database:

- **Single-row INSERT**. A *single-row* INSERT statement adds a single new row of data to a table. It is commonly used in daily applications—for example, data entry programs.

- **Multi-row INSERT**. A *multirow* INSERT statement extracts rows of data from another part of the database and adds them to a table. It is commonly used in end-of-month or end-of-year processing when old rows of a table are moved to an inactive table.

- **Bulk load**. A *bulk load* utility adds data to a table from a file that is outside of the database. It is commonly used to initially load the database or to incorporate data downloaded from another computer system or collected from many sites.

The Single-Row INSERT Statement

The single-row INSERT statement, shown in Figure 10-1, adds a new row to a table. The INTO clause specifies the table that receives the new row (the *target* table), and the VALUES clause specifies the data values that the new row will contain. The column list indicates which data value goes into which column of the new row.

Figure 10-1. *Single-row INSERT statement syntax diagram*

UPDATING DATA

Suppose you just hired a new salesperson, Henry Jacobsen, with the following personal data:

Name:	Henry Jacobsen
Age:	36
Employee Number:	111
Title:	Sales Manager
Office:	Atlanta (office number 13)
Hire Date:	July 25, 1990
Quota:	Not yet assigned
Year-to-Date Sales:	$0.00

Here is the INSERT statement that adds Mr. Jacobsen to the sample database:

Add Henry Jacobsen as a new salesperson.

```
INSERT INTO SALESREPS (NAME, AGE, EMPL_NUM, SALES, TITLE,
                       HIRE_DATE, REP_OFFICE)
   VALUES ('Henry Jacobsen', 36, 111, 0.00, 'Sales Mgr',
                       '25-JUL-90', 13)

1 row inserted.
```

Figure 10-2 graphically illustrates how SQL carries out this INSERT statement. Conceptually, the INSERT statement builds a single row of data that matches the column structure of the table, fills it with the data from the VALUES clause, and then adds the new row to the table. The rows of a table are unordered, so there is no notion of inserting the row at the top, at the bottom, or between two rows of the table. After the INSERT statement, the new row is simply a part of the table. A subsequent query against the SALESREPS table will include the new row, but it may appear anywhere among the rows of query results.

Suppose Mr. Jacobsen now receives his first order, from InterCorp, a new customer who is assigned customer number 2126. The order is for 20 ACI-41004 widgets, for a total price of $2340, and has been assigned order number 113069. Here are the INSERT statements that add the new customer and the order to the database:

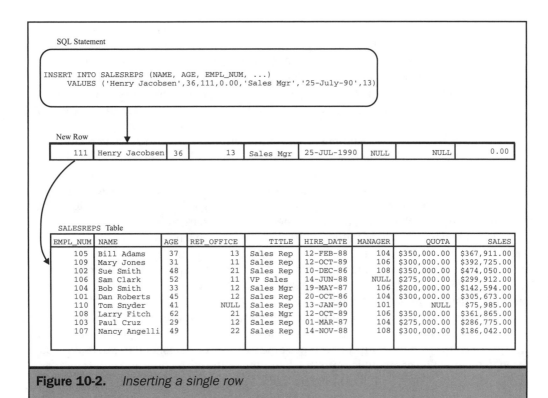

Figure 10-2. *Inserting a single row*

Insert a new customer and order for Mr. Jacobsen.

```
INSERT INTO CUSTOMERS (COMPANY, CUST_NUM, CREDIT_LIMIT, CUST_REP)
     VALUES ('InterCorp', 2126, 15000.00, 111)
```

1 row inserted.

```
INSERT INTO ORDERS (AMOUNT, MFR, PRODUCT, QTY, ORDER_DATE,
                    ORDER_NUM, CUST, REP)
     VALUES (2340.00, 'ACI', '41004', 20, CURRENT_DATE, 113069,
                    2126, 111)
```

1 row inserted.

UPDATING DATA

As this example shows, the INSERT statement can become lengthy if there are many columns of data, but its format is still very straightforward. The second INSERT statement uses the system constant CURRENT_DATE in its VALUES clause, causing the current date to be inserted as the order date. This system constant is specified in the SQL2 standard and is supported by many of the popular SQL products. Other brands of DBMS provide other system constants or built-in functions to obtain the current date and time.

You can use the INSERT statement with interactive SQL to add rows to a table that grows very rarely, such as the OFFICES table. In practice, however, data about a new customer, order, or salesperson is almost always added to a database through a forms-oriented data entry program. When the data entry is complete, the application program inserts the new row of data using programmatic SQL. Regardless of whether interactive or programmatic SQL is used, however, the INSERT statement is the same.

The table name specified in the INSERT statement is normally an unqualified table name, specifying a table that you own. To insert data into a table owned by another user, you can specify a qualified table name. Of course, you must also have permission to insert data into the table, or the INSERT statement will fail. The SQL security scheme and permissions are described in Chapter 15.

The purpose of the column list in the INSERT statement is to match the data values in the VALUES clause with the columns that are to receive them. The list of values and the list of columns must both contain the same number of items, and the data type of each value must be compatible with the data type of the corresponding column, or an error will occur. The ANSI/ISO standard mandates unqualified column names in the column list, but many implementations allow qualified names. Of course, there can be no ambiguity in the column names anyway, because they must all reference columns of the target table.

Inserting NULL Values

When SQL inserts a new row of data into a table, it automatically assigns a NULL value to any column whose name is missing from the column list in the INSERT statement. In this INSERT statement, which added Mr. Jacobsen to the SALESREPS table, the QUOTA and MANAGER columns were omitted:

```
INSERT INTO SALESREPS (NAME, AGE, EMPL_NUM, SALES, TITLE,
                       HIRE_DATE, REP_OFFICE)
     VALUES ('Henry Jacobsen', 36, 111, 0.00, 'Sales Mgr',
                       '25-JUL-90', 13)
```

As a result, the newly added row has a NULL value in the QUOTA and MANAGER columns, as shown in Figure 10-2. You can make the assignment of a NULL value more explicit by including these columns in the column list and specifying the keyword NULL in the values list. This INSERT statement has exactly the same effect as the previous one:

```
INSERT INTO SALESREPS (NAME, AGE, EMPL_NUM, SALES, QUOTA, TITLE,
                       MANAGER, HIRE_DATE, REP_OFFICE)
    VALUES ('Henry Jacobsen', 36, 111, 0.00, NULL, 'Sales Mgr',
                       NULL, '25-JUL-90', 13)
```

Inserting All Columns

As a convenience, SQL allows you to omit the column list from the INSERT statement. When the column list is omitted, SQL automatically generates a column list consisting of all columns of the table, in left-to-right sequence. This is the same column sequence generated by SQL when you use a SELECT * query. Using this shortcut, the previous INSERT statement could be rewritten equivalently as:

```
INSERT INTO SALESREPS
    VALUES (111, 'Henry Jacobsen', 36, 13, 'Sales Mgr',
            '25-JUL-90', NULL, NULL, 0.00)
```

When you omit the column list, the NULL keyword *must* be used in the values list to explicitly assign NULL values to columns, as shown in the example. In addition, the sequence of data values must correspond exactly to the sequence of columns in the table.

Omitting the column list is convenient in interactive SQL because it reduces the length of the INSERT statement you must type. For programmatic SQL, the column list should always be specified because it makes the program easier to read and understand. In addition, table structures often change over time to include new columns or drop columns that are no longer used. A program that contains an INSERT statement without an explicit column list may work correctly for months or years, and then suddenly begin producing errors if the number of columns or data types of columns is changed by a database administrator.

The Multirow INSERT Statement

The second form of the INSERT statement, shown in Figure 10-3, adds multiple rows of data to its target table. In this form of the INSERT statement, the data values for the new rows are not explicitly specified within the statement text. Instead, the source of new rows is a database query, specified in the statement.

Figure 10-3.   *Multirow INSERT statement syntax diagram*

Adding rows whose values come from within the database itself may seem strange at first, but it's very useful in some special situations. For example, suppose you want to copy the order number, date, and amount of all orders placed before January 1, 1990, from the ORDERS table into another table, called OLDORDERS. The multirow INSERT statement provides a concise, efficient way to copy the data:

Copy old orders into the OLDORDERS table.

```
INSERT INTO OLDORDERS (ORDER_NUM, ORDER_DATE, AMOUNT)
    SELECT ORDER_NUM, ORDER_DATE, AMOUNT
      FROM ORDERS
     WHERE ORDER_DATE < '01-JAN-90'

9 rows inserted.
```

This INSERT statement looks complicated, but it's really very simple. The statement identifies the table to receive the new rows (OLDORDERS) and the columns to receive the data, just like the single-row INSERT statement. The remainder of the statement is a query that retrieves data from the ORDERS table. Figure 10-4 graphically illustrates the

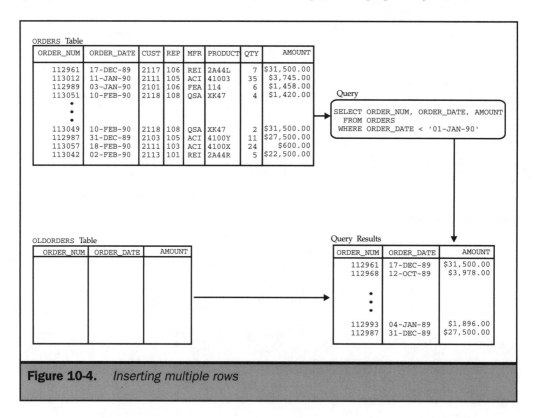

Figure 10-4. *Inserting multiple rows*

operation of this INSERT statement. Conceptually, SQL first performs the query against the ORDERS table and then inserts the query results, row by row, into the OLDORDERS table.

Here's another situation where you could use the multirow INSERT statement. Suppose you want to analyze customer buying patterns by looking at which customers and salespeople are responsible for big orders—those over $15,000. The queries that you will be running will combine data from the CUSTOMERS, SALESREPS, and ORDERS tables. These three-table queries will execute fairly quickly on the small sample database, but in a real corporate database with many thousands of rows, they would take a long time. Rather than running many long, three-table queries, you could create a new table named BIGORDERS to contain the required data, defined as follows:

Column	Information
AMOUNT	Order amount (from ORDERS)
COMPANY	Customer name (from CUSTOMERS)
NAME	Salesperson name (from SALESREPS)
PERF	Amount over/under quota (calculated from SALESREPS)
MFR	Manufacturer ID (from ORDERS)
PRODUCT	Product ID (from ORDERS)
QTY	Quantity ordered (from ORDERS)

Once you have created the BIGORDERS table, this multirow INSERT statement can be used to populate it:

Load data into the BIGORDERS table for analysis.

```
INSERT INTO BIGORDERS (AMOUNT, COMPANY, NAME, PERF, PRODUCT, MFR, QTY)
    SELECT AMOUNT, COMPANY, NAME, (SALES - QUOTA), PRODUCT, MFR, QTY
      FROM ORDERS, CUSTOMERS, SALESREPS
     WHERE CUST = CUST_NUM
       AND REP = EMPL_NUM
       AND AMOUNT > 15000.00

6 rows inserted.
```

In a large database, this INSERT statement may take a while to execute because it involves a three-table query. When the statement is complete, the data in the BIGORDERS table will duplicate information in other tables. In addition, the BIGORDERS table won't be automatically kept up to date when new orders are added to the database, so its data may quickly become outdated. Each of these factors seems like a disadvantage. However, the subsequent data analysis queries against the BIGORDERS table can be expressed very simply—they become single-table queries.

Furthermore, each of those queries will run much faster than if it were a three-table join. Consequently, this is probably a good strategy for performing the analysis, especially if the three original tables are large. In this situation, it's likely that the BIGORDERS table will be used as a temporary table for doing the analysis. It will be created and populated with data, representing a snapshot of the order status in time, the analysis programs will be run, and then the table will be emptied or dropped.

The SQL1 standard specifies several logical restrictions on the query that appears within the multirow INSERT statement:

- The query cannot contain an ORDER BY clause. It's useless to sort the query results anyway, because they're being inserted into a table that is, like all tables, unordered.

- The query results must contain the same number of columns as the column list in the INSERT statement (or the entire target table, if the column list is omitted), and the data types must be compatible, column by column.

- The query cannot be the UNION of several different SELECT statements. Only a single SELECT statement may be specified.

- The target table of the INSERT statement cannot appear in the FROM clause of the query or any subqueries that it contains. This prohibits inserting part of a table into itself.

The first two restrictions are structural, but the latter two were included in the standard simply to avoid complexity. As a result, these restrictions were relaxed in the SQL2 standard. The standard now allows UNION and JOIN operations and expressions in the query, basically allowing the results of a general database query to be retrieved and then inserted into a table with the INSERT statement. It also allows various forms of self-insertion, where the source table for the data to be inserted and the destination table are the same.

Bulk Load Utilities

Data to be inserted into a database is often downloaded from another computer system or collected from other sites and stored in a sequential file. To load the data into a table, you could write a program with a loop that reads each record of the file and uses the single-row INSERT statement to add the row to the table. However, the overhead of having the DBMS repeatedly execute single-row INSERT statements may be quite high. If inserting a single row takes half a second under a typical system load, that is probably acceptable performance for an interactive program. But that performance quickly becomes unacceptable when applied to the task of bulk loading 50,000 rows of data. In this case, loading the data would require over six hours.

For this reason, most commercial DBMS products include a bulk load feature that loads data from a file into a table at high speed. The ANSI/ISO SQL standard does not address this function, and it is usually provided as a stand-alone utility program rather than as part of the SQL language. Each vendor's utility provides a slightly different set of features, functions, and commands.

When SQL is used from within an application program, another technique is frequently provided for more efficiently inserting a large amount of data into a database. The standard programmatic INSERT statement inserts a single row of data, just like the interactive single-row INSERT statements in the preceding examples. But many commercial DBMS products allow data from two or more rows (often up to hundreds of rows) to be supplied as part of a single bulk INSERT statement. All of the supplied data must be for new rows of the single table that is the target of the INSERT statement, and named in the INTO clause.

Executing a bulk INSERT statement for 100 rows of data has exactly the same effect as executing 100 individual single-row INSERT statements. However, it is usually much more efficient, because it involves only one call to the DBMS. Efficiency gains from 20 percent to 30 percent and up to 300 percent or more times over single-row INSERT statements are common, depending on the DBMS brand and the particular kind of data being inserted.

Deleting Data from the Database

A row of data is typically deleted from a database when the entity represented by the row disappears from the outside world. For example, in the sample database:

- When a customer cancels an order, the corresponding row of the ORDERS table must be deleted.

- When a salesperson leaves the company, the corresponding row of the SALESREPS table must be deleted.

- When a sales office is closed, the corresponding row of the OFFICES table must be deleted. If the salespeople in the office are terminated, their rows should be deleted from the SALESREPS table as well. If they are reassigned, their REP_OFFICE columns must be updated.

In each case, the row is deleted to maintain the database as an accurate model of the real world. The smallest unit of data that can be deleted from a relational database is a single row.

The DELETE Statement

The DELETE statement, shown in Figure 10-5, removes selected rows of data from a single table. The FROM clause specifies the target table containing the rows. The WHERE clause specifies which rows of the table are to be deleted.

Suppose Henry Jacobsen, the new salesperson hired earlier in this chapter, has just decided to leave the company. The DELETE statement that removes his row from the SALESREPS table is shown next.

Figure 10-5. *DELETE statement syntax diagram*

Remove Henry Jacobsen from the database.

```
DELETE FROM SALESREPS
 WHERE NAME = 'Henry Jacobsen'

1 row deleted.
```

The WHERE clause in this example identifies a single row of the SALESREPS table, which SQL removes from the table. The WHERE clause should have a familiar appearance—it's exactly the same WHERE clause that you would specify in a SELECT statement to *retrieve* the same row from the table. The search conditions that can be specified in the WHERE clause of the DELETE statement are the same ones available in the WHERE clause of the SELECT statement, as described in Chapters 6 and 9.

Recall that search conditions in the WHERE clause of a SELECT statement can specify a single row or an entire set of rows, depending on the specific search condition. The same is true of the WHERE clause in a DELETE statement. Suppose, for example, that Mr. Jacobsen's customer, InterCorp (customer number 2126) has called to cancel all its orders. Here is the DELETE statement that removes the orders from the ORDERS table:

Remove all orders for InterCorp (customer number 2126).

```
DELETE FROM ORDERS
 WHERE CUST = 2126

2 rows deleted.
```

In this case, the WHERE clause selects several rows of the ORDERS table, and SQL removes all of the selected rows from the table. Conceptually, SQL applies the WHERE clause to each row of the ORDERS table, deleting those where the search condition yields a TRUE result and retaining those where the search condition yields a FALSE or NULL result.

Because this type of DELETE statement searches through a table for the rows to be deleted, it is sometimes called a *searched* DELETE statement. This term is used to contrast it with another form of the DELETE statement, called the *positioned* DELETE statement, which always deletes a single row. The positioned DELETE statement applies only to programmatic SQL and is described in Chapter 17.

Here are some additional examples of searched DELETE statements:

Delete all orders placed before November 15, 1989.

```
DELETE FROM ORDERS
 WHERE ORDER_DATE < '15-NOV-89'

5 rows deleted.
```

Delete all rows for customers served by Bill Adams, Mary Jones, or Dan Roberts (employee numbers 105, 109, and 101).

```
DELETE FROM CUSTOMERS
 WHERE CUST_REP IN (105, 109, 101)

7 rows deleted.
```

Delete all salespeople hired before July 1988 who have not yet been assigned a quota.

```
DELETE FROM SALESREPS
 WHERE HIRE_DATE < '01-JUL-88'
   AND QUOTA IS NULL

0 rows deleted.
```

Deleting All Rows

The WHERE clause in a DELETE statement is optional, but it is almost always present. If the WHERE clause is omitted from a DELETE statement, *all* rows of the target table are deleted, as in this example:

Delete all orders.

```
DELETE FROM ORDERS

30 rows deleted.
```

Although this DELETE statement produces an empty table, it does not erase the ORDERS table from the database. The definition of the ORDERS table and its columns is still stored in the database. The table still exists, and new rows can still be inserted into the ORDERS table with the INSERT statement. To erase the definition of the table from the database, the DROP TABLE statement (described in Chapter 13) must be used.

Because of the potential damage from such a DELETE statement, be careful to always specify a search condition, and be sure that it actually selects the rows you want. When using interactive SQL, it's a good idea first to use the WHERE clause in a SELECT statement to display the selected rows. Make sure they are the ones you want to delete, and only then use the WHERE clause in a DELETE statement.

DELETE with Subquery *

DELETE statements with simple search conditions, such as those in the previous examples, select rows for deletion based solely on the contents of the rows themselves. Sometimes the selection of rows must be made based on data from other tables. For example, suppose you want to delete all orders taken by Sue Smith. Without knowing her employee number, you can't find the orders by consulting the ORDERS table alone. To find the orders, you could use a two-table query:

Find the orders taken by Sue Smith.

```
SELECT ORDER_NUM, AMOUNT
  FROM ORDERS, SALESREPS
 WHERE REP = EMPL_NUM
   AND NAME = 'Sue Smith'

ORDER_NUM      AMOUNT
----------  -----------
   112979   $15,000.00
   113065    $2,130.00
   112993    $1,896.00
   113048    $3,750.00
```

But you can't use a join in a DELETE statement. The parallel DELETE statement is illegal:

```
DELETE FROM ORDERS, SALESREPS
  WHERE REP = EMPL_NUM
    AND NAME = 'Sue Smith'

Error: More than one table specified in FROM clause
```

The way to handle the request is with one of the subquery search conditions. Here is a valid form of the DELETE statement that handles the request:

Delete the orders taken by Sue Smith.

```
DELETE FROM ORDERS
 WHERE REP = (SELECT EMPL_NUM
                FROM SALESREPS
               WHERE NAME = 'Sue Smith')

4 rows deleted.
```

The subquery finds the employee number for Sue Smith, and the WHERE clause then selects the orders with a matching value. As this example shows, subqueries can play an important role in the DELETE statement because they let you delete rows based on information in other tables. Here are two more examples of DELETE statements that use subquery search conditions:

Delete customers served by salespeople whose sales are less than 80 percent of quota.

```
DELETE FROM CUSTOMERS
 WHERE CUST_REP IN (SELECT EMPL_NUM
                      FROM SALESREPS
                     WHERE SALES < (.8 * QUOTA))

2 rows deleted.
```

Delete any salesperson whose current orders total less than 2 percent of their quota.

```
DELETE FROM SALESREPS
 WHERE (.02 * QUOTA) > (SELECT SUM(AMOUNT)
                          FROM ORDERS
                         WHERE REP = EMPL_NUM)

1 row deleted.
```

Subqueries in the WHERE clause can be nested just as they can be in the WHERE clause of the SELECT statement. They can also contain outer references to the target table of the DELETE statement. In this respect, the FROM clause of the DELETE statement functions like the FROM clause of the SELECT statement. Here is an example of a deletion request that requires a subquery with an outer reference:

Delete customers who have not ordered since November 10, 1989.

```
DELETE FROM CUSTOMERS
  WHERE NOT EXISTS (SELECT *
                      FROM ORDERS
                     WHERE CUST = CUST_NUM
                       AND ORDER_DATE < '10-NOV-89')

16 rows deleted.
```

Conceptually, this DELETE statement operates by going through the CUSTOMERS table, row by row, and checking the search condition. For each customer, the subquery selects any orders placed by that customer before the cutoff date. The reference to the CUST_NUM column in the subquery is an outer reference to the customer number in the row of the CUSTOMERS table currently being checked by the DELETE statement. The subquery in this example is a correlated subquery, as described in Chapter 9.

Outer references will often be found in subqueries of a DELETE statement, because they implement the join between the table(s) in the subquery and the target table of the DELETE statement. In the SQL1 standard, a restriction on the use of subqueries in a DELETE statement prevents the target table from appearing in the FROM clause of a subquery or any of its subqueries at any level of nesting. This prevents the subqueries from referencing the target table (some of whose rows may already have been deleted), except for outer references to the row currently being tested by the DELETE statement's search condition.

The SQL2 standard eliminates this restriction by specifying that the DELETE statement should treat such a subquery as applying to the entire target table, before any rows have been deleted. This places more overhead on the DBMS (which must handle the subquery processing and row deletion more carefully), but the behavior of the statement is well defined by the standard.

Modifying Data in the Database

Typically, the values of data items stored in a database are modified when corresponding changes occur in the outside world. For example, in the sample database:

- When a customer calls to change the quantity on an order, the QTY column in the appropriate row of the ORDERS table must be modified.

- When a manager moves from one office to another, the MGR column in the OFFICES table and the REP_OFFICE column in the SALESREPS table must be changed to reflect the new assignment.

- When sales quotas are raised by 5 percent in the New York sales office, the QUOTA column of the appropriate rows in the SALESREPS table must be modified.

In each case, data values in the database are updated to maintain the database as an accurate model of the real world. The smallest unit of data that can be modified in a database is a single column of a single row.

The UPDATE Statement

The UPDATE statement, shown in Figure 10-6, modifies the values of one or more columns in selected rows of a single table. The target table to be updated is named in the statement, and you must have the required permission to update the table as well as each of the individual columns that will be modified. The WHERE clause selects the rows of the table to be modified. The SET clause specifies which columns are to be updated and calculates the new values for them.

Here is a simple UPDATE statement that changes the credit limit and salesperson for a customer:

Raise the credit limit for Acme Manufacturing to $60,000 and reassign them to Mary Jones (employee number 109).

```
UPDATE CUSTOMERS
   SET CREDIT_LIMIT = 60000.00, CUST_REP = 109
 WHERE COMPANY = 'Acme Mfg.'

1 row updated.
```

Figure 10-6. *UPDATE statement syntax diagram*

In this example, the WHERE clause identifies a single row of the CUSTOMERS table, and the SET clause assigns new values to two of the columns in that row. The WHERE clause is exactly the same one you would use in a DELETE or SELECT statement to identify the row. In fact, the search conditions that can appear in the WHERE clause of an UPDATE statement are exactly the same as those available in the SELECT and DELETE statements.

Like the DELETE statement, the UPDATE statement can update several rows at once with the proper search condition, as in this example:

Transfer all salespeople from the Chicago office (number 12) to the New York office (number 11), and lower their quotas by 10 percent.

```
UPDATE SALESREPS
   SET REP_OFFICE = 11, QUOTA = .9 * QUOTA
 WHERE REP_OFFICE = 12

3 rows updated.
```

In this case, the WHERE clause selects several rows of the SALESREPS table, and the value of the REP_OFFICE and QUOTA columns are modified in all of them. Conceptually, SQL processes the UPDATE statement by going through the SALESREPS table row by row, updating those rows for which the search condition yields a TRUE result and skipping over those for which the search condition yields a FALSE or NULL result.

Because it searches the table, this form of the UPDATE statement is sometimes called a *searched* UPDATE statement. This term distinguishes it from a different form of the UPDATE statement, called a *positioned* UPDATE statement, which always updates a single row. The positioned UPDATE statement applies only to programmatic SQL and is described in Chapter 17.

Here are some additional examples of searched UPDATE statements:

Reassign all customers served by employee numbers 105, 106, or 107 to employee number 102.

```
UPDATE CUSTOMERS
   SET CUST_REP = 102
 WHERE CUST_REP IN (105, 106, 107)

5 rows updated.
```

Assign a quota of $100,000 to any salesperson who currently has no quota.

```
UPDATE SALESREPS
   SET QUOTA = 100000.00
```

```
WHERE QUOTA IS NULL

1 row updated.
```

The SET clause in the UPDATE statement is a list of assignments separated by commas. Each assignment identifies a target column to be updated and specifies how to calculate the new value for the target column. Each target column should appear only once in the list; there should not be two assignments for the same target column. The ANSI/ISO specification mandates unqualified names for the target columns, but some SQL implementations allow qualified column names. There can be no ambiguity in the column names anyway, because they must refer to columns of the target table.

The expression in each assignment can be any valid SQL expression that yields a value of the appropriate data type for the target column. The expression must be computable based on the values of the row currently being updated in the target table. In most DBMS implementations, the expression may not include any column functions or subqueries.

If an expression in the assignment list references one of the columns of the target table, the value used to calculate the expression is the value of that column in the current row before any updates are applied. The same is true of column references that occur in the WHERE clause. For example, consider this (somewhat contrived) UPDATE statement:

```
UPDATE OFFICES
   SET QUOTA = 400000.00, SALES = QUOTA
 WHERE QUOTA < 400000.00
```

Before the update, Bill Adams had a QUOTA value of $350,000 and a SALES value of $367,911. After the update, his row has a SALES value of $350,000, not $400,000. The order of the assignments in the SET clause is thus immaterial; the assignments can be specified in any order.

Updating All Rows

The WHERE clause in the UPDATE statement is optional. If the WHERE clause is omitted, then all rows of the target table are updated, as in this example:

Raise all quotas by 5 percent.

```
UPDATE SALESREPS
   SET QUOTA = 1.05 * QUOTA

10 rows updated.
```

Unlike the DELETE statement, in which the WHERE clause is almost never omitted, the UPDATE statement without a WHERE clause performs a useful function. It basically performs a bulk update of the entire table, as demonstrated in the preceding example.

UPDATE with Subquery *

As with the DELETE statement, subqueries can play an important role in the UPDATE statement because they let you select rows to update based on information contained in other tables. Here are several examples of UPDATE statements that use subqueries:

Raise by $5000 the credit limit of any customer who has placed an order for more than $25,000.

```
UPDATE CUSTOMERS
   SET CREDIT_LIMIT = CREDIT_LIMIT + 5000.00
 WHERE CUST_NUM IN (SELECT DISTINCT CUST
                      FROM ORDERS
                     WHERE AMOUNT > 25000.00)

4 rows updated.
```

Reassign all customers served by salespeople whose sales are less than 80 percent of their quota.

```
UPDATE CUSTOMERS
   SET CUST_REP = 105
 WHERE CUST_REP IN (SELECT EMPL_NUM
                      FROM SALESREPS
                     WHERE SALES < (.8 * QUOTA))

2 rows updated.
```

Have all salespeople who serve over three customers report directly to Sam Clark (employee number 106).

```
UPDATE SALESREPS
   SET MANAGER = 106
 WHERE 3 < (SELECT COUNT(*)
              FROM CUSTOMERS
             WHERE CUST_REP = EMPL_NUM)

1 row updated.
```

As in the DELETE statement, subqueries in the WHERE clause of the UPDATE statement can be nested to any level and can contain outer references to the target table of the UPDATE statement. The column EMPL_NUM in the subquery of the preceding example is such an outer reference; it refers to the EMPL_NUM column in the row of the SALESREPS table currently being checked by the UPDATE statement. The subquery in this example is a correlated subquery, as described in Chapter 9.

Outer references will often be found in subqueries of an UPDATE statement, because they implement the join between the table(s) in the subquery and the target table of the UPDATE statement. The same SQL1 restriction applies as for the DELETE statement: the target table cannot appear in the FROM clause of any subquery at any level of nesting. This prevents the subqueries from referencing the target table (some of whose rows may have already been updated). Any references to the target table in the subqueries are thus outer references to the row of the target table currently being tested by the UPDATE statement's WHERE clause. The SQL2 standard again removed this restriction and specifies that a reference to the target table in a subquery is evaluated as if none of the target table had been updated.

Summary

This chapter described the SQL statements that are used to modify the contents of a database:

- The single-row INSERT statement adds one row of data to a table. The values for the new row are specified in the statement as constants.

- The multirow INSERT statement adds zero or more rows to a table. The values for the new rows come from a query, specified as part of the INSERT statement.

- The DELETE statement deletes zero or more rows of data from a table. The rows to be deleted are specified by a search condition.

- The UPDATE statement modifies the values of one or more columns in zero or more rows of a table. The rows to be updated are specified by a search condition. The columns to be updated, and the expressions that calculate their new values, are specified in the UPDATE statement.

- Unlike the SELECT statement, which can operate on multiple tables, the INSERT, DELETE, and UPDATE statements work on only a single table at a time.

- The search condition used in the DELETE and UPDATE statements has the same form as the search condition for the SELECT statement.

UPDATING DATA

The
Complete
Reference

Chapter 11

Data Integrity

The term *data integrity* refers to the correctness and completeness of the data in a database. When the contents of a database are modified with the INSERT, DELETE, or UPDATE statements, the integrity of the stored data can be lost in many different ways. For example:

- Invalid data may be added to the database, such as an order that specifies a nonexistent product.

- Existing data may be modified to an incorrect value, such as reassigning a salesperson to a nonexistent office.

- Changes to the database may be lost due to a system error or power failure.

- Changes may be partially applied, such as adding an order for a product without adjusting the quantity available for sale.

One of the important roles of a relational DBMS is to preserve the integrity of its stored data to the greatest extent possible. This chapter describes the SQL language features that assist the DBMS in this task.

What Is Data Integrity?

To preserve the consistency and correctness of its stored data, a relational DBMS typically imposes one or more *data integrity constraints*. These constraints restrict the data values that can be inserted into the database or created by a database update. Several different types of data integrity constraints are commonly found in relational databases, including:

- **Required data**. Some columns in a database must contain a valid data value in every row; they are not allowed to contain missing or NULL values. In the sample database, every order must have an associated customer who placed the order. Therefore, the CUST column in the ORDERS table is a *required column*. The DBMS can be asked to prevent NULL values in this column.

- **Validity checking**. Every column in a database has a *domain*, a set of data values that are legal for that column. The sample database uses order numbers that begin at 100,001, so the domain of the ORDER_NUM column is positive integers greater than 100,000. Similarly, employee numbers in the EMPL_NUM column must fall within the numeric range of 101 to 999. The DBMS can be asked to prevent other data values in these columns.

- **Entity integrity**. The primary key of a table must contain a unique value in each row, which is different from the values in all other rows. For example, each row of the PRODUCTS table has a unique set of values in its MFR_ID and PRODUCT_ID columns, which uniquely identifies the product represented by that row. Duplicate values are illegal, because they wouldn't allow the database to distinguish one product from another. The DBMS can be asked to enforce this unique values constraint.

■ **Referential integrity**. A foreign key in a relational database links each row in the child table containing the foreign key to the row of the parent table containing the matching primary key value. In the sample database, the value in the REP_ OFFICE column of each SALESREPS row links the salesperson represented by that row to the office where he or she works. The REP_OFFICE column *must* contain a valid value from the OFFICE column of the OFFICES table, or the salesperson will be assigned to an invalid office. The DBMS can be asked to enforce this foreign key/primary key constraint.

■ **Other data relationships**. The real-world situation modeled by a database will often have additional constraints that govern the legal data values that may appear in the database. For example, in the sample database, the sales vice president may want to ensure that the quota target for each office does not exceed the total of the quota targets for the salespeople in that office. The DBMS can be asked to check modifications to the office and salesperson quota targets to make sure that their values are constrained in this way.

■ **Business rules**. Updates to a database may be constrained by business rules governing the real-world transactions that are represented by the updates. For example, the company using the sample database may have a business rule that forbids accepting an order for which there is an inadequate product inventory. The DBMS can be asked to check each new row added to the ORDERS table to make sure that the value in its QTY column does not violate this business rule.

■ **Consistency**. Many real-world transactions cause multiple updates to a database. For example, accepting a customer order may involve adding a row to the ORDERS table, increasing the SALES column in the SALESREPS table for the person who took the order, and increasing the SALES column in the OFFICES table for the office where that salesperson is assigned. The INSERT and both UPDATEs must *all* take place in order for the database to remain in a consistent, correct state. The DBMS can be asked to enforce this type of consistency rule or to support applications that implement such rules.

The ANSI/ISO SQL standard specifies some of the simpler data integrity constraints. For example, the required data constraint is supported by the ANSI/ISO standard and implemented in a uniform way across almost all commercial SQL products. More complex constraints, such as business rules constraints, are not specified by the ANSI/ISO standard, and there is a wide variation in the techniques and SQL syntax used to support them. The SQL features that support the first five integrity constraints are described in this chapter. The SQL transaction mechanism, which supports the consistency constraint, is described in Chapter 12.

Required Data

The simplest data integrity constraint requires that a column contain a non-NULL value. The ANSI/ISO standard and most commercial SQL products support this constraint by allowing you to declare that a column is NOT NULL when the table containing the column is first created. The NOT NULL constraint is specified as part of the CREATE TABLE statement, described in Chapter 13.

When a column is declared NOT NULL, the DBMS enforces the constraint by ensuring the following:

- Every INSERT statement that adds a new row or rows to the table must specify a non-NULL data value for the column. An attempt to insert a row containing a NULL value (either explicitly or implicitly) results in an error.

- Every UPDATE statement that updates the column must assign it a non-NULL data value. Again, an attempt to update the column to a NULL value results in an error.

One disadvantage of the NOT NULL constraint is that it must usually be specified when a table is first created. Typically, you cannot go back to a previously created table and disallow NULL values for a column. Usually, this disadvantage is not serious because it's obvious when the table is first created which columns should allow NULLs and which should not. There is also a potential logical problem with adding the NOT NULL constraint to an existing table. If one or more rows of that table already contain NULL values, then what should the DBMS do with those rows? They represent valid real-world objects, but they now violate the (new) required data constraint.

The inability to add a NOT NULL constraint to an existing table is also partly a result of the way most DBMS brands implement NULL values internally. Usually a DBMS reserves an extra byte in every stored row of data for each column that permits NULL values. The extra byte serves as a null indicator for the column and is set to some specified value to indicate a NULL value. When a column is defined as NOT NULL, the indicator byte is not present, saving disk storage space. Dynamically adding and removing NOT NULL constraints would thus require on-the-fly reconfiguration of the stored rows on the disk, which is not practical in a large database.

Simple Validity Checking

The SQL1 standard provides limited support for restricting the legal values that can appear in a column. When a table is created, each column in the table is assigned a data type, and the DBMS ensures that only data of the specified type is introduced into the column. For example, the EMPL_NUM column in the SALESREPS table is defined as an INTEGER, and the DBMS will produce an error if an INSERT or UPDATE statement tries to store a character string or a decimal number in the column.

However, the SQL1 standard and many commercial SQL products do not provide a way to restrict a column to certain specific data values. The DBMS will happily insert a SALESREPS row with an employee number of 12345, even though employee numbers in the sample database have three digits by convention. A hire date of December 25 would also be accepted, even though the company is closed on Christmas day.

Some commercial SQL implementations provide extended features to check for legal data values. In DB2, for example, each table in the database can be assigned a corresponding *validation procedure,* a user-written program to check for valid data values. DB2 invokes the validation procedure each time a SQL statement tries to change or insert a row of the table, and gives the validation procedure the proposed column values for the row. The validation procedure checks the data and indicates by its return value whether the data is acceptable. The validation procedure is a conventional program (written in S/370 assembler or PL/I, for example), so it can perform whatever data value checks are required, including range checks and internal consistency checks within the row. However, the validation procedure *cannot* access the database, so it cannot be used to check for unique values or foreign key/primary key relationships.

SQL Server also provides a data validation capability by allowing you to create a *rule* that determines what data values can legally be entered into a particular column. SQL Server checks the rule each time an INSERT or UPDATE statement is attempted for the table that contains the column. Unlike DB2's validation procedures, SQL Server rules are written in the Transact-SQL dialect that is used by SQL Server. For example, here is a Transact-SQL statement that establishes a rule for the QUOTA column in the SALESREPS table:

```
CREATE RULE QUOTA_LIMIT
    AS @VALUE BETWEEN 0.00 AND 500000.00
```

This rule prevents you from inserting or updating a quota to a negative value or to a value greater than $500,000. As shown in the example, SQL Server allows you to assign the rule a name (QUOTA_LIMIT, in this example). Like DB2 validation procedures, however, SQL Server rules may not reference columns or other database objects.

The SQL2 standard provides extended support for validity checking through two different features—column check constraints and domains. Both give the database creator a way to tell the DBMS how to determine whether a data value is valid. The check-constraint feature specifies the data validity test for a single column. The domain feature lets you specify the validity test once, and then reuse it in the definition of many different columns whose legal data values are the same.

Column Check Constraints (SQL2)

A SQL2 *check constraint* is a search condition, like the search condition in a WHERE clause, that produces a true/false value. When a check constraint is specified for a column, the DBMS automatically checks the value of that column each time a new row is inserted or a row is updated to ensure that the search condition is true. If not, the INSERT or UPDATE statement fails. A column check constraint is specified as part of the column definition within the CREATE TABLE statement, described in Chapter 13.

Consider this excerpt from a CREATE TABLE statement, modified from the definition of the demo database to include three check constraints:

```
CREATE TABLE SALESREPS
    (EMPL_NUM INTEGER NOT NULL
            CHECK (EMPL_NUM BETWEEN 101 AND 199),
        AGE INTEGER
            CHECK (AGE >= 21),
        .
        .
        .
      QUOTA MONEY
            CHECK (MONEY >= 0.0)
        .
        .
        .
```

The first constraint (on the EMPL_NUM column) requires that valid employee numbers be three-digit numbers between 101 and 199. The second constraint (on the AGE column) similarly prevents hiring of minors. The third constraint (on the QUOTA column) prevents a salesperson from having a quota target less than $0.00.

All three of these column check constraints are very simple examples of the capability specified by the SQL2 standard. In general, the parentheses following the keyword CHECK can contain any valid search condition that makes sense in the context of a column definition. With this flexibility, a check constraint can compare values from two different columns of the table, or even compare a proposed data value against other values from the database. These capabilities are more fully described in the "Advanced Constraint Capabilities" section later in this chapter.

Domains (SQL2)

A SQL2 *domain* generalizes the check-constraint concept and allows you to easily apply the same check constraint to many different columns within a database. A domain is a collection of legal data values. You specify a domain and assign it a domain name using the SQL2 CREATE DOMAIN statement, described in Chapter 13. As with the check-constraint definition, a search condition is used to define the range of legal data values. For example, here is a SQL2 CREATE DOMAIN statement to create the domain VALID_EMPLOYEE_ID, which includes all legal employee numbers:

```
CREATE DOMAIN VALID_EMPLOYEE_ID INTEGER
  CHECK (VALUE BETWEEN 101 AND 199)
```

After the VALID_EMPLOYEE_ID domain has been defined, it may be used to define columns in database tables instead of a data type. Using this capability, the example CREATE TABLE statement for the SALESREPS table would appear as:

```
CREATE TABLE SALESREPS
    (EMPL_NUM VALID_EMPLOYEE_ID,
         AGE INTEGER
             CHECK (AGE >= 21),
             .
             .
             .
       QUOTA MONEY
             CHECK (MONEY >= 0.0)
             .
             .
             .
```

The advantage of using the domain is that if other columns in other tables also contain employee numbers, the domain name can be used repeatedly, simplifying the table definitions. The OFFICES table contains such a column:

```
CREATE TABLE OFFICES
    (OFFICE INTEGER NOT NULL,
       CITY VARCHAR(15) NOT NULL,
     REGION VARCHAR(10) NOT NULL,
        MGR VALID_EMPLOYEE_ID,
     TARGET MONEY,
      SALES MONEY NOT NULL
           .
           .
           .
```

Another advantage of domains is that the definition of valid data (such as valid employee numbers, in this example) is stored in one central place within the database. If the definition changes later (for example, if the company grows and employee numbers in the range 200–299 must be allowed), it is much easier to change one domain definition than to change many column constraints scattered throughout the database. In a large enterprise database, there may literally be hundreds of defined domains, and the benefits of SQL2 domains for change management can be very substantial.

Entity Integrity

A table's primary key must have a unique value for each row of the table, or the database will lose its integrity as a model of the outside world. For example, if two rows of the SALESREPS table both had value 106 in their EMPL_NUM column, it would be impossible to tell which row really represented the real-world entity associated with that key value—Bill Adams, who is employee number 106. For this reason, the requirement that primary keys have unique values is called the *entity integrity* constraint.

Support for primary keys was not found in the first commercial SQL databases but it is now very common. It was added to DB2 in 1988 and was added to the original ANSI/ISO SQL standard in an intermediate update, before the full SQL2 standard appeared. You specify the primary key as part of the CREATE TABLE statement, described in Chapter 13. The sample database definition in Appendix A includes primary key definitions for all of its tables, following the ANSI/ISO standard syntax.

When a primary key is specified for a table, the DBMS automatically checks the uniqueness of the primary key value for every INSERT and UPDATE statement performed on the table. An attempt to insert a row with a duplicate primary key value or to update a row so that its primary key would be a duplicate will fail with an error message.

Other Uniqueness Constraints

It is sometimes appropriate to require a column that is not the primary key of a table to contain a unique value in every row. For example, suppose you wanted to restrict the data in the SALESREPS table so that no two salespeople could have exactly the same name in the table. You could achieve this goal by imposing a *uniqueness* constraint on the NAME column. The DBMS enforces a uniqueness constraint in the same way that it enforces the primary key constraint. Any attempt to insert or update a row in the table that violates the uniqueness constraint will fail.

The ANSI/ISO SQL standard uses the CREATE TABLE statement to specify uniqueness constraints for columns or combinations of columns. However, uniqueness constraints were implemented in DB2 long before the publication of the ANSI/ISO standard, and DB2 made them a part of its CREATE INDEX statement. This statement is one of the SQL database administration statements that deals with physical storage of the database on the disk. Normally, the SQL user doesn't have to worry about these statements at all; they are used only by the database administrator.

Many commercial SQL products followed the original DB2 practice rather than the ANSI/ISO standard for uniqueness constraints and required the use of a CREATE INDEX statement. Subsequent versions of DB2 added a uniqueness constraint to the CREATE TABLE statement. Most of the other commercial vendors have followed the same path, and now support the ANSI/ISO syntax for the uniqueness constraint.

Uniqueness and NULL Values

NULL values pose a problem when they occur in the primary key of a table or in a column that is specified in a uniqueness constraint. Suppose you tried to insert a row with a primary key that was NULL (or partially NULL, if the primary key is composed of more than one column). Because of the NULL value, the DBMS cannot conclusively decide whether the primary key duplicates one that is already in the table. The answer must be "maybe," depending on the "real" value of the missing (NULL) data.

For this reason, the SQL standard requires that every column that is part of a primary key must be declared NOT NULL. The same restriction applies for every column that is named in a uniqueness constraint. Together, these restrictions ensure that columns that are supposed to contain unique data values in each row of a table actually do contain unique values.

Referential Integrity

Chapter 4 discussed primary keys, foreign keys, and the parent/child relationships that they create between tables. Figure 11-1 shows the SALESREPS and OFFICES tables and illustrates once again how foreign keys and primary keys work. The OFFICE column is the primary key for the OFFICES table, and it uniquely identifies each row. The REP_OFFICE column, in the SALESREPS table, is a foreign key for the OFFICES table. It identifies the office where each salesperson is assigned.

The REP_OFFICE and OFFICE columns create a parent/child relationship between the OFFICES and SALESREPS rows. Each OFFICES (parent) row has zero or more

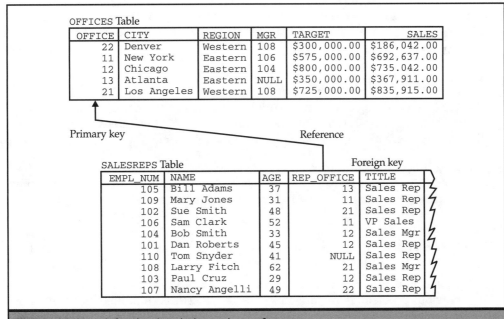

Figure 11-1. *A foreign key/primary key reference*

SALESREPS (child) rows with matching office numbers. Similarly, each SALESREPS (child) row has exactly one OFFICES (parent) row with a matching office number.

Suppose you tried to insert a new row into the SALESREPS table that contained an invalid office number, as in this example:

```
INSERT INTO SALESREPS (EMPL_NUM, NAME, REP_OFFICE, AGE,
                       HIRE_DATE, SALES)
    VALUES (115, 'George Smith', 31, 37, '01-APR-90', 0.00)
```

On the surface, there's nothing wrong with this INSERT statement. In fact, many SQL implementations will successfully add the row. The database will show that George Smith works in office number 31, even though no office number 31 is listed in the OFFICES table. The newly inserted row clearly breaks the parent/child relationship between the OFFICES and SALESREPS tables. In fact, the office number in the INSERT statement is probably an error—the user may have intended office number 11, 21, or 13.

It seems clear that every legal value in the REP_OFFICE column should be forced to match some value that appears in the OFFICE column. This rule is known as a *referential integrity* constraint. It ensures the integrity of the parent/child relationships created by foreign keys and primary keys.

Referential integrity has been a key part of the relational model since it was first proposed by Codd. However, referential integrity constraints were not included in IBM's prototype System/R DBMS, nor in early releases of DB2 or SQL/DS. IBM added referential integrity support to DB2 in 1989, and referential integrity was added to the SQL1 standard after its initial release. Most DBMS vendors today support referential integrity constraints.

Referential Integrity Problems

Four types of database updates can corrupt the referential integrity of the parent/child relationships in a database. Using the OFFICES and SALESREPS tables in Figure 11-1 as illustrations, these four update situations are the following:

- **Inserting a new child row**. When an INSERT statement adds a new row to the child (SALESREPS) table, its foreign key (REP_OFFICE) value *must* match one of the primary key (OFFICE) values in the parent table (OFFICES). If the foreign key value does not match any primary key, inserting the row will corrupt the database, because there will be a child without a parent (an *orphan*). Note that inserting a row in the parent table never poses a problem; it simply becomes a parent without any children.

- **Updating the foreign key in a child row**. This is a different form of the previous problem. If the foreign key (REP_OFFICE) is modified by an UPDATE statement, the new value must match a primary key (OFFICE) value in the parent (OFFICES) table. Otherwise, the updated row will be an orphan.

- **Deleting a parent row**. If a row of the parent table (OFFICES) that has one or more children (in the SALESREPS table) is deleted, the child rows will become orphans. The foreign key (REP_OFFICE) values in these rows will no longer match any primary key (OFFICE) value in the parent table. Note that deleting a row from the child table never poses a problem; the parent of this row simply has one less child after the deletion.

- **Updating the primary key in a parent row**. This is a different form of the previous problem. If the primary key (OFFICE) of a row in the parent table (OFFICES) is modified, all of the current children of that row become orphans because their foreign keys no longer match a primary key value.

The referential integrity features of the ANSI/ISO SQL standard handle each of these four situations. The first problem (INSERT into the child table) is handled by checking the values of the foreign key columns before the INSERT statement is permitted. If they don't match a primary key value, the INSERT statement is rejected with an error message. In Figure 11-1, this means that before a new salesperson can be added to the SALESREPS table, the office to which the salesperson is assigned must already be in the OFFICES table. As you can see, this restriction makes sense in the sample database.

The second problem (UPDATE of the child table) is similarly handled by checking the updated foreign key value. If there is no matching primary key value, the UPDATE statement is rejected with an error message. In Figure 11-1, this means that before a salesperson can be reassigned to a different office, that office must already be in the OFFICES table. Again, this restriction makes sense in the sample database.

The third problem (DELETE of a parent row) is more complex. For example, suppose you closed the Los Angeles office and wanted to delete the corresponding row from the OFFICES table in Figure 11-1. What should happen to the two child rows in the SALESREPS table that represent the salespeople assigned to the Los Angeles office? Depending on the situation, you might want to:

- Prevent the office from being deleted until the salespeople are reassigned.

- Automatically delete the two salespeople from the SALESREPS table as well.

- Set the REP_OFFICE column for the two salespeople to NULL, indicating that their office assignment is unknown.

- Set the REP_OFFICE column for the two salespeople to some default value, such as the office number for the headquarters office in New York, indicating that the salespeople are automatically reassigned to that office.

The fourth problem (UPDATE of the primary key in the parent table) has similar complexity. For example, suppose for some reason you wanted to change the number of the Los Angeles office from 21 to 23. As with the previous example, the question is what should happen to the two child rows in the SALESREPS table that represent salespeople from the Los Angeles office. Again, there are four logical possibilities:

■ Prevent the office number from being changed until the salespeople are reassigned. In this case, you should first add a new row to the OFFICES table with the new office number for Los Angeles, then update the SALESREPS table, and finally delete the old OFFICES row for Los Angeles.

■ Automatically update the office number for the two salespeople in the SALESREPS table, so that their rows are still linked to the Los Angeles row in the OFFICES table, via its new office number.

■ Set the REP_OFFICE column for the two salespeople to NULL, indicating that their office assignment is unknown.

■ Set the REP_OFFICE column for the two salespeople to some default value, such as the office number for the headquarters office in New York, indicating that the salespeople are automatically reassigned to that office.

Although some of these alternatives may seem more logical than others in this particular example, it's relatively easy to come up with examples where any one of the four possibilities is the right thing to do, if you want the database to accurately model the real-world situation. The SQL1 standard provided only the first possibility for the preceding examples—it prohibited the modification of a primary key value that was in use and prohibited the deletion of a row containing such a primary key. DB2, however, permitted other options through its concept of *delete rules*. The SQL2 standard has expanded these delete rules into *delete and update rules* that cover both deleting of parent rows and updating of primary keys.

Delete and Update Rules *

For each parent/child relationship created by a foreign key in a database, the SQL2 standard allows you to specify an associated delete rule and an associated update rule. The delete rule tells the DBMS what to do when a user tries to delete a row of the parent table. These four delete rules can be specified:

■ **RESTRICT delete rule.** The RESTRICT delete rule prevents you from deleting a row from the parent table if the row has any children. A DELETE statement that attempts to delete such a parent row is rejected with an error message. Deletions from the parent table are thus restricted to rows without any children. Applied to Figure 11-1, this rule can be summarized as "You can't delete an office if any salespeople are assigned to it."

■ **CASCADE delete rule.** The CASCADE delete rule tells the DBMS that when a parent row is deleted, all of its child rows should *also* automatically be deleted from the child table. For Figure 11-1, this rule can be summarized as "Deleting an office automatically deletes all the salespeople assigned to that office."

■ **SET NULL delete rule.** The SET NULL delete rule tells the DBMS that when a parent row is deleted, the foreign key values in all of its child rows should automatically be set to NULL. Deletions from the parent table thus cause a "set to NULL" update on selected columns of the child table. For the tables in Figure 11-1, this rule can be summarized as "If an office is deleted, indicate that the current office assignment of its salespeople is unknown."

■ **SET DEFAULT delete rule.** The SET DEFAULT delete rule tells the DBMS that when a parent row is deleted, the foreign key values in all of its child rows should automatically be set to the default value for that particular column. Deletions from the parent table thus cause a "set to DEFAULT" update on selected columns of the child table. For the tables in Figure 11-1, this rule can be summarized as "If an office is deleted, indicate that the current office assignment of its salespeople is the default office specified in the definition of the SALESREPS table."

There are some slight differences between the SQL2 and DB2 implementations of the delete rules. The current DB2 implementation does not support the SET DEFAULT rule; it is specified only by the SQL2 standard. The SQL2 standard actually calls the previously described RESTRICT rule, NO ACTION. The SQL2 naming is somewhat confusing. It means "If you try to delete a parent row that still has children, the DBMS will take no action on the row." The DBMS will, however, generate an error code. Intuitively, the DB2 name for the rule, *restrict*, seems a better description of the situation—the DBMS will restrict the DELETE operation from taking place and generate an error code.

Recent releases of DB2 support both a RESTRICT and a NO ACTION delete rule. The difference between them is the timing of the enforcement of the rule. The RESTRICT rule is enforced before any other constraints; the NO ACTION rule is enforced after other referential constraints. Under almost all circumstances, the two rules operate identically.

Just as the delete rule tells the DBMS what to do when a user tries to delete a row of the parent table, the update rule tells the DBMS what to do when a user tries to update the value of one of the primary key columns in the parent table. Again, there are four possibilities, paralleling those available for delete rules:

■ **RESTRICT update rule.** The RESTRICT update rule prevents you from updating the primary key of a row in the parent table if that row has any children. An UPDATE statement that attempts to modify the primary key of such a parent row is rejected with an error message. Changes to primary keys in the parent table are thus restricted to rows without any children. Applied to Figure 11-1, this rule can be summarized as "You can't change an office number if salespeople are assigned to the office."

■ **CASCADE update rule.** The CASCADE update rule tells the DBMS that when a primary key value is changed in a parent row, the corresponding foreign key value in all of its child rows should *also* automatically be changed in the child table, to match the new primary key. For Figure 11-1, this rule can be summarized as "Changing an office number automatically changes the office number for all the salespeople assigned to that office."

- **SET NULL update rule.** The SET NULL update rule tells the DBMS that when a primary key value in a parent row is updated, the foreign key values in all of its child rows should automatically be set to NULL. Primary key changes in the parent table thus cause a "set to NULL" update on selected columns of the child table. For the tables in Figure 11-1, this rule can be summarized as "If an office number is changed, indicate that the current office assignment of its salespeople is unknown."

- **SET DEFAULT update rule.** The SET DEFAULT update rule tells the DBMS that when a primary key value in a parent row is updated, the foreign key values in all of its child rows should automatically be set to the default value for that particular column. Primary key changes in the parent table thus cause a "set to DEFAULT" update on selected columns of the child table. For the tables in Figure 11-1, this rule can be summarized as "If an office number is changed, automatically change the office assignment of its salespeople to the default office specified in the definition of the SALESREPS table."

The same differences between DB2 and the SQL2 standard described for the delete rules apply to the update rules. The SET DEFAULT update rule is present only in the standard, not in the current DB2 implementation. The RESTRICT update rule is a DB2 naming convention; the SQL2 standard again calls this update rule NO ACTION.

You can specify two different rules as the delete rule and the update rule for a parent/child relationship, although in most cases, the two rules will be the same. If you do not specify a rule, the RESTRICT rule is the default, because it has the least potential for accidental destruction or modification of data. Each of the rules is appropriate in different situations. Usually, the real-world behavior modeled by the database will indicate which rule is appropriate. In the sample database, the ORDERS table contains three foreign key/primary key relationships, as shown in Figure 11-2. These three relationships link each order to:

- The product that was ordered
- The customer who placed the order
- The salesperson who took the order

For each of these relationships, different rules seem appropriate:

- The relationship between an order and the product that is ordered should probably use the RESTRICT rule for delete and update. It shouldn't be possible to delete product information from the database if there are still current orders for that product, or to change the product number.

- The relationship between an order and the customer who placed it should probably use the CASCADE rule for delete and update. You probably will delete a customer row from the database only if the customer is inactive or ends the customer's relationship with the company. In this case, when you delete the customer, any current orders for that customer should also be deleted. Similarly, changes in a customer number should automatically propagate to orders for that customer.

■ The relationship between an order and the salesperson who took it should probably use the SET NULL rule. If the salesperson leaves the company, any orders taken by that salesperson become the responsibility of an unknown salesperson until they are reassigned. Alternatively, the SET DEFAULT rule could be used to automatically assign these orders to the sales vice president. This relationship should probably use the CASCADE update rule, so that employee number changes automatically propagate to the ORDERS table.

Cascaded Deletes and Updates *

The RESTRICT rule for deletes and updates is a single-level rule—it affects only the parent table in a relationship. The CASCADE rule, on the other hand, can be a multilevel rule, as shown in Figure 11-3.

Assume for this discussion that the OFFICES/SALESREPS and SALESREPS/ ORDERS relationships shown in the figure both have CASCADE rules. What happens when you delete Los Angeles from the OFFICES table? The CASCADE rule for the OFFICES/SALESREPS relationship tells the DBMS to automatically delete all of the

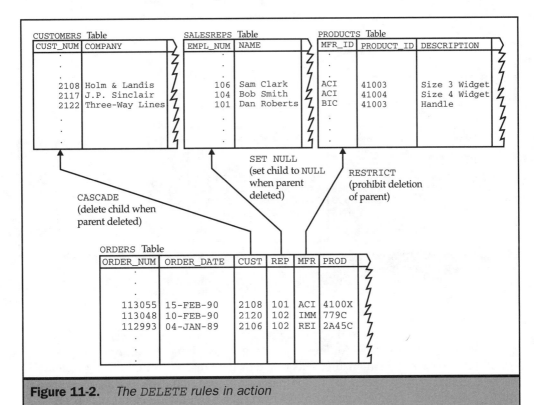

Figure 11-2. *The DELETE rules in action*

UPDATING DATA

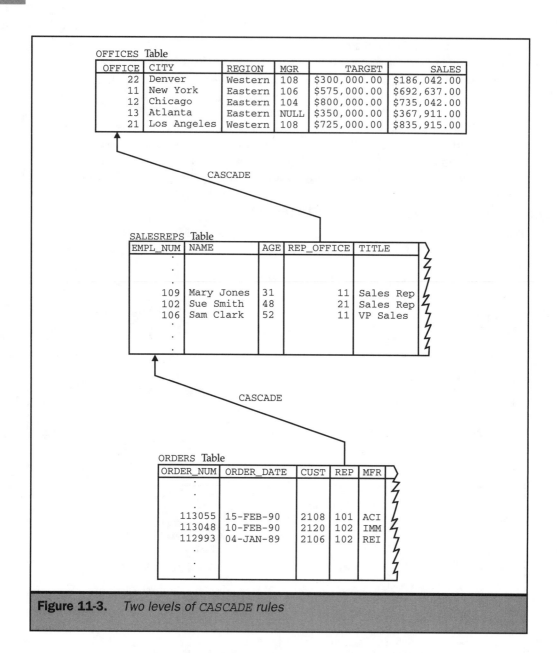

Figure 11-3.   *Two levels of CASCADE rules*

SALESREPS rows that refer to the Los Angeles office (office number 21) as well. But deleting the SALESREPS row for Sue Smith brings into play the CASCADE rule for the SALESREPS/ORDERS relationship. This rule tells the DBMS to automatically delete all of the ORDERS rows that refer to Sue (employee number 102). Deleting an office thus causes cascaded deletion of salespeople, which causes cascaded deletion of orders.

As the example shows, CASCADE delete rules must be specified with care because they can cause widespread automatic deletion of data if they're used incorrectly. Cascaded update rules can cause similar multilevel updates if the foreign key in the child table is also its primary key. In practice, this is not very common, so cascaded updates typically have less far-reaching effects than cascaded deletes.

The SET NULL and SET DEFAULT update and delete rules are both two-level rules; their impact stops with the child table. Figure 11-4 shows the OFFICES, SALESREPS,

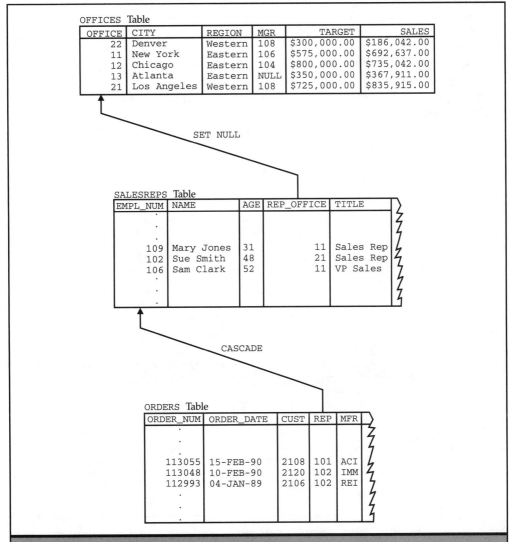

OFFICES Table

OFFICE	CITY	REGION	MGR	TARGET	SALES
22	Denver	Western	108	$300,000.00	$186,042.00
11	New York	Eastern	106	$575,000.00	$692,637.00
12	Chicago	Eastern	104	$800,000.00	$735,042.00
13	Atlanta	Eastern	NULL	$350,000.00	$367,911.00
21	Los Angeles	Western	108	$725,000.00	$835,915.00

SET NULL

SALESREPS Table

EMPL_NUM	NAME	AGE	REP_OFFICE	TITLE	
109	Mary Jones	31	11	Sales Rep	
102	Sue Smith	48	21	Sales Rep	
106	Sam Clark	52	11	VP Sales	

CASCADE

ORDERS Table

ORDER_NUM	ORDER_DATE	CUST	REP	MFR	
113055	15-FEB-90	2108	101	ACI	
113048	10-FEB-90	2120	102	IMM	
112993	04-JAN-89	2106	102	REI	

Figure 11-4. *A combination of DELETE rules*

and ORDERS tables again, with a SET NULL delete rule for the OFFICES/SALESREPS relationship. This time, when the Los Angeles office is deleted, the SET NULL delete rule tells the DBMS to set the REP_OFFICE column to NULL in the SALESREPS rows that refer to office number 21. The rows remain in the SALESREPS table, however, and the impact of the delete operation extends only to the child table.

Referential Cycles *

In the sample database, the SALESREPS table contains the REP_OFFICE column, a foreign key for the OFFICES table. The OFFICES table contains the MGR column, a foreign key for the SALESREPS table. As shown in Figure 11-5, these two relationships form a *referential cycle*. Any given row of the SALESREPS table refers to a row of the OFFICES table, which refers to a row of the SALESREPS table, and so on. This cycle includes only two tables, but it's also possible to construct cycles of three or more tables.

Regardless of the number of tables that they involve, referential cycles pose special problems for referential integrity constraints. For example, suppose that NULL values were not allowed in the primary or foreign keys of the two tables in Figure 11-5. (This

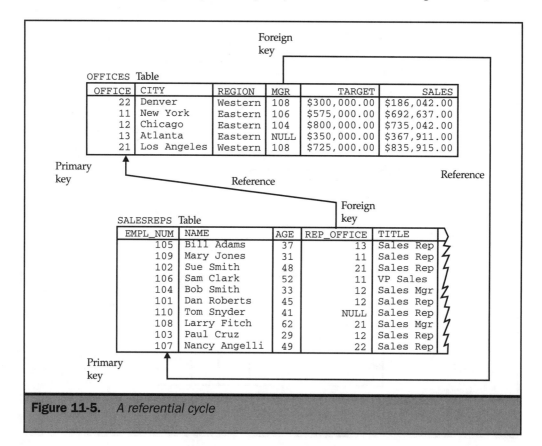

Figure 11-5. *A referential cycle*

is not, in fact, the way the sample database is actually defined, for reasons that will become obvious in a moment.) Consider this database update request and the INSERT statements that attempt to implement it:

You have just hired a new salesperson, Ben Adams (employee number 115), who is the manager of a new sales office in Detroit (office number 14).

```
INSERT INTO SALESREPS (EMPL_NUM, NAME, REP_OFFICE,
                       HIRE_DATE, SALES)
     VALUES (115,'Ben Adams', 14, '01-APR-90', 0.00)

INSERT INTO OFFICES (OFFICE, CITY, REGION, MGR, TARGET, SALES)
     VALUES (14,'Detroit', 'Eastern', 115, 0.00, 0.00)
```

Unfortunately, the first INSERT statement (for Ben Adams) will fail. Why? Because the new row refers to office number 14, which is not yet in the database! Of course, reversing the order of the INSERT statements doesn't help:

```
INSERT INTO OFFICES (OFFICE, CITY, REGION, MGR, TARGET, SALES)
     VALUES (14,'Detroit', 'Eastern', 115, 0.00, 0.00)

INSERT INTO SALESREPS (EMPL_NUM, NAME, REP_OFFICE,
                       HIRE_DATE, SALES)
     VALUES (115,'Ben Adams', 14, '01-APR-90', 0.00)
```

The first INSERT statement (for Detroit this time) will still fail, because the new row refers to employee number 115 as the office manager, and Ben Adams is not yet in the database! To prevent this insertion deadlock, at least one of the foreign keys in a referential cycle *must* permit NULL values. In the actual definition of the sample database, the MGR column does not permit NULLs, but the REP_OFFICE does. The two-row insertion can then be accomplished with two INSERTs and an UPDATE, as shown here:

```
INSERT INTO SALESREPS (EMPL_NUM, NAME, REP_OFFICE,
                       HIRE_DATE, SALES)
     VALUES (115,'Ben Adams', NULL, '01-APR-90', 0.00)

INSERT INTO OFFICES (OFFICE, CITY, REGION, MGR, TARGET, SALES)
     VALUES (14,'Detroit', 'Eastern', 115, 0.00, 0.00)

UPDATE SALESREPS
   SET REP_OFFICE = 14
 WHERE EMPL_NUM = 115
```

As the example shows, there are times when it would be convenient if the referential integrity constraint were not checked until after a series of interrelated updates are performed. Unfortunately, this type of complex deferred checking is not provided by most current SQL implementations. Some deferred checking capabilities are specified by the SQL2 standard, as described later in the "Deferred Constraint Checking" section.

Referential cycles also restrict the delete and update rules that can be specified for the relationships that form the cycle. Consider the three tables in the referential cycle shown in Figure 11-6. The PETS table shows three pets and the boys they like, the GIRLS table shows three girls and the pets they like, and the BOYS table shows four boys and the girls they like, forming a referential cycle. All three of the relationships in the cycle specify the RESTRICT delete rule. Note that George's row is the *only* row you can delete from the three tables. Every other row is the parent in some relationship and is therefore protected from deletion by the RESTRICT rule. Because of this anomaly, you should not specify the RESTRICT rule for all of the relationships in a referential cycle.

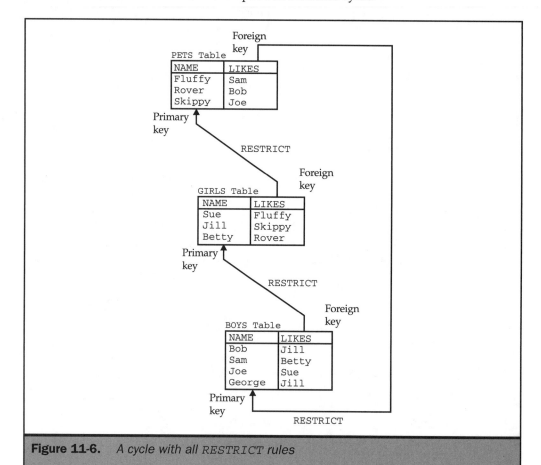

Figure 11-6. *A cycle with all RESTRICT rules*

The CASCADE rule presents a similar problem, as shown in Figure 11-7. This figure contains exactly the same data as in Figure 11-6, but all three delete rules have been changed to CASCADE. Suppose you try to delete Bob from the BOYS table. The delete rules force the DBMS to delete Rover (who likes Bob) from the PETS table, which forces you to delete Betty (who likes Rover) from the GIRLS table, which forces you to delete Sam (who likes Betty), and so on, until all of the rows in all three tables have been deleted. For these small tables this might be practical, but for a production database with thousands of rows, it would quickly become impossible to keep track of the cascaded deletions and retain the integrity of the database. For this reason, DB2 enforces a rule that prevents referential cycles of two or more tables where all of the delete rules are CASCADE. At least one relationship in the cycle *must* have a RESTRICT or SET NULL delete rule to break the cycle of cascaded deletions.

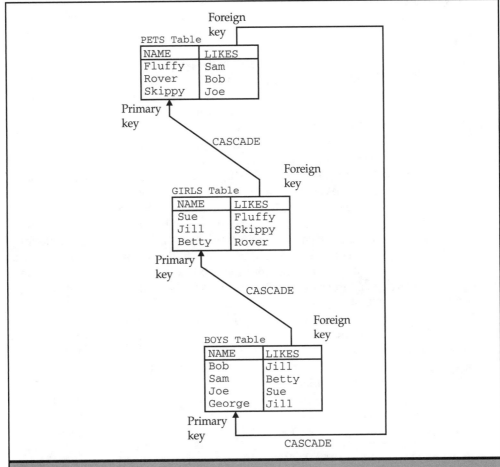

Figure 11-7. *An illegal cycle with all CASCADE rules*

UPDATING DATA

Foreign Keys and NULL Values *

Unlike primary keys, foreign keys in a relational database are allowed to contain NULL values. In the sample database, the foreign key REP_OFFICE in the SALESREPS table permits NULL values. In fact, this column does contain a NULL value in Tom Snyder's row, because Tom has not yet been assigned to an office. But the NULL value poses an interesting question about the referential integrity constraint created by the primary key/foreign key relationship. Does the NULL value match one of the primary key values, or doesn't it? The answer is "maybe"—it depends on the real value of the missing or unknown data.

The ANSI/ISO SQL1 standard automatically assumes that a foreign key that contains a NULL value satisfies the referential integrity constraint. In other words, it gives the row the benefit of the doubt and allows it to be part of the child table, even though its foreign key value doesn't match any row in the parent table. Interestingly, the referential integrity constraint is assumed to be satisfied if *any part* of the foreign key has a NULL value. This can produce unexpected and unintuitive behavior for compound foreign keys, such as the one that links the ORDERS table to the PRODUCTS table.

Suppose for a moment that the ORDERS table in the sample database permitted NULL values for the PRODUCT column, and that the PRODUCTS/ORDERS relationship had a SET NULL delete rule. (This is not the actual structure of the sample database, for the reasons illustrated by this example.) An order for a product with a manufacturer ID (MFR) of ABC and a NULL product ID (PRODUCT) can be successfully inserted into the ORDERS table because of the NULL value in the PRODUCT column. DB2 and the ANSI/ISO standard assume that the row meets the referential integrity constraint for ORDERS and PRODUCTS, even though no product in the PRODUCTS table has a manufacturer ID of ABC.

The SET NULL delete rule can produce a similar effect. Deleting a row from the PRODUCTS table will cause the foreign key value in all of its child rows in the ORDERS table to be set to NULL. Actually, only those columns of the foreign key that accept NULL values are set to NULL. If there were a single row in the PRODUCTS table for manufacturer DEF, deleting that row would cause its child rows in the ORDERS table to have their PRODUCT column set to NULL, but their MFR column would continue to have the value DEF. As a result, the rows would have an MFR value that did not match any row in the PRODUCTS table.

To avoid creating this situation, you should be very careful with NULL values in compound foreign keys. An application that enters or updates data in the table that contains the foreign key should usually enforce an "all NULLs or no NULLs" rule on the columns of the foreign key. Foreign keys that are partially NULL and partially non-NULL can easily create problems.

The SQL2 standard addresses this problem by giving the database administrator more control over the handling of NULL values in foreign keys for integrity constraints. The integrity constraint in the CREATE TABLE statement provides two options:

■ **MATCH FULL option**. The MATCH FULL option requires that foreign keys in a child table fully match a primary key in the parent table. With this option, no part of the foreign key can contain a NULL value, so the issue of NULL value handling in delete and update rules does not arise.

■ **MATCH PARTIAL option.** The MATCH PARTIAL option allows NULL values in parts of a foreign key, so long as the non-NULL values match the corresponding parts of some primary key in the parent table. With this option, NULL value handling in delete and update rules proceeds as previously described.

Advanced Constraint Capabilities (SQL2)

Primary key and foreign key constraints, uniqueness constraints, and restrictions on missing (NULL) values all provide data integrity checking for very specific structures and situations within a database. The SQL2 standard goes beyond these capabilities to include a much more general capability for specifying and enforcing data integrity constraints. The complete scheme includes four types of constraints:

■ **Column constraints**. Specified as part of a column definition when a table is created. Conceptually, they restrict the legal values that may appear in the column. Column constraints appear in the individual column definitions within the CREATE TABLE statement.

■ **Domains**. A specialized form of column constraints. They provide a limited capability to define new data types within a database. In effect, a domain is one of the predefined database data types plus some additional constraints, which are specified as part of the domain definition. Once a domain is defined and named, the domain name can be used in place of a data type to define new columns. The columns inherit the constraints of the domain. Domains are defined outside of the table and column definitions of the database, using the CREATE DOMAIN statement.

■ **Table constraints**. Specified as part of the table definition when a table is created. Conceptually, they restrict the legal values that may appear in rows of the table. Table constraints are specified in the CREATE TABLE statement that defines a table. Usually, they appear as a group after the column definitions, but the SQL2 standard allows them to be interspersed with the column definitions.

■ **Assertions**. The most general type of SQL2 constraint. Like domains, they are specified outside of the table and column structure of the database. Conceptually, an assertion specifies a relationship among data values that crosses multiple tables within the database.

Each of the four different types of constraints has its own conceptual purpose, and each appears in a different part of the SQL2 statement syntax. However, the distinctions between them are somewhat arbitrary. Any column constraint that appears for an individual column definition can just as easily be specified as a table constraint. Similarly, any table constraint can be specified as an assertion. In practice, it's probably best to specify each database constraint where it seems to most naturally fit, given the real-world situation that the database is trying to model. Constraints that apply globally to the entire situation (business processes, interrelationships among customers and products, and so on) should appear as assertions. Constraints that apply to a specific type of entity (a customer or an order) should appear as table constraints or column constraints within the appropriate table that describes that type of entity. When the same constraint applies to many different columns in the database that all refer to the same type of entity, then a domain is appropriate.

Assertions

Examples of the first three types of constraints have previously appeared in earlier sections of this chapter. An *assertion* is specified using the SQL2 CREATE ASSERTION statement. Here is an assertion that might be useful in the demo database:

Ensure that an office's quota target does not exceed the sum of the quotas for its salespeople.

```
CREATE ASSERTION quota_valid
  CHECK ((OFFICES.QUOTA <= SUM(SALESREPS.QUOTA)) AND
         (SALESREPS.REP_OFFICE = OFFICES.OFFICE))
```

Because it is an object in the database (like a table or a column), the assertion must be given a name (in this case, it's `quota_valid`). The name is used in error messages produced by the DBMS when the assertion is violated. The assertion causing an error may be obvious in a small demo database, but in a large database that might contain dozens or hundreds of assertions, it's critical to know which of the assertions was violated.

Here is another example of an assertion that might be useful in the sample database:

Ensure that the total of the orders for any customer does not exceed their credit limit:

```
CREATE ASSERTION credit_orders
  CHECK (CUSTOMER.CREDIT_LIMIT <=
         SELECT SUM(ORDERS.AMOUNT)
           FROM ORDERS
          WHERE ORDERS.CUST = CUSTOMER.CUST_NUM)
```

As these examples show, a SQL2 assertion is defined by a search condition, which is enclosed in parentheses and follows the keyword CHECK. Every time an attempt is made to modify the contents of the database, through an INSERT or UPDATE or DELETE statement, the search condition is checked against the (proposed) modified database contents. If the search condition remains TRUE, the modification is allowed. If the search condition would become untrue, the DBMS does not carry out the proposed modification, and an error code is returned, indicating an assertion violation.

In theory, assertions could cause a very large amount of database processing overhead as they are checked for each statement that might modify the database. In practice, the DBMS will analyze the assertion and determine which tables and columns it involves. Only changes that involve those particular tables or columns will actually trigger the search condition. Nonetheless, assertions should be defined with great care to ensure that they impose a reasonable amount of overhead for the benefit they provide.

SQL2 Constraint Types

The types of constraints that can be specified in SQL2, and the role played by each, can be summarized as follows:

- **NOT NULL constraint.** The NOT NULL constraint can appear only as a column constraint. It prevents the column from being assigned a NULL value.

- **PRIMARY KEY constraint.** A PRIMARY KEY constraint can appear as a column constraint or a table constraint. If the primary key consists of a single column, the column constraint may be more convenient. If it consists of multiple columns, it should be specified as a table constraint.

- **UNIQUE constraint.** A UNIQUE constraint can appear as a column constraint or a table constraint. If the unique values restriction is being enforced only for a single column, the column constraint is the easiest way to specify it. If the unique values restriction applies to a set of two or more columns (that is, the *combination* of values for those columns must be unique for all rows in the table), then the table constraint form should be used.

- **Referential (FOREIGN KEY) constraint.** A referential (FOREIGN KEY) constraint can appear as a column constraint or a table constraint. If the foreign key consists of a single column, the column constraint may be more convenient. If it consists of multiple columns, it should be specified as a table constraint. If a table has many foreign key relationships to other tables, it may be most convenient to gather *all* of its foreign key constraints together at one place in the table definition, rather than having them scattered throughout the column definitions.

- **CHECK constraint.** A CHECK constraint can appear as a column constraint or a table constraint. It is also the *only* kind of constraint that forms part of the definition of a domain or an assertion. The check constraint is specified as a search condition, like the search condition that appears in the WHERE clause of a database query. The constraint is satisfied if the search condition has a TRUE value.

Each individual constraint within a database (no matter what its type) may be assigned a *constraint name* to uniquely identify it from the other constraints. It's probably not necessary to assign constraint names in a simple database where each constraint is clearly associated with a single table, column, or domain, and where there is little potential for confusion. In a more complex database involving multiple constraints on a single table or column, it can be very useful to be able to identify the individual constraints by name (especially when errors start to occur!). Note that the check constraint in an assertion *must* have a constraint name; this name effectively becomes the name of the assertion containing the constraint.

Deferred Constraint Checking

In their simplest form, the various constraints that are specified within a database are checked every time an attempt is made to change the database contents—that is, during the execution of every attempted INSERT, UPDATE, or DELETE statement. For database systems claiming only Intermediate-Level or Entry-Level conformance to the SQL2 standard, this is the only mode of operation allowed for database constraints. The Full-Level SQL2 standard specifies an additional capability for *deferred* constraint checking.

When constraint checking is deferred, the constraints are not checked for each individual SQL statement. Instead, constraint checking is held in abeyance until the end of a SQL transaction. (Transaction processing and the associated SQL statements are described in detail in Chapter 12.) When the completion of the transaction is signaled by the SQL COMMIT statement, the DBMS checks the deferred constraints. If all of the constraints are satisfied, then the COMMIT statement can proceed, and the transaction can complete normally. At this point, any changes made to the database during the transaction become permanent. If, however, one or more of the constraints would be violated by the proposed transaction, then the COMMIT statement fails, and the transaction is *rolled back*—that is, all of the proposed changes to the database are reversed, and the database goes back to its state before the transaction began.

Deferred constraint checking can be very important when several updates to a database must all be made at once to keep the database in a consistent state. For example, suppose the demo database contained this assertion:

Ensure that an office's quota target is exactly equal to the sum of the quotas for its salespeople.

```
CREATE ASSERTION quota_totals
  CHECK ((OFFICES.QUOTA = SUM(SALESREPS.QUOTA)) AND
         (SALESREPS.REP_OFFICE = OFFICES.OFFICE))
```

Without the deferred constraint checking, this constraint would effectively prevent you from ever adding a salesperson to the database. Why? Because to keep the office quota and the salespersons' quotas in the right relationship, you must both add a new salesperson row with the appropriate quota (using an INSERT statement) and increase the quota for the appropriate office by the same amount (using an UPDATE statement). If you try to perform the INSERT statement on the SALESREPS table first, the OFFICES table will not yet have been updated, the assertion will not be TRUE, and the statement will fail.

Similarly, if you try to perform the UPDATE statement on the OFFICES table first, the SALESREPS table will not yet have been updated, the assertion will not be TRUE, and the statement will fail. The only solution to this dilemma is to defer constraint checking until both statements have completed, and then check to make sure that both operations, taken together, have left the database in a valid state.

The SQL2 deferred constraint mechanism provides for this capability, and much more. Each individual constraint (of all types) within the database can be identified as either DEFERRABLE or NOT DEFERRABLE when it is first created or defined:

■ **DEFERRABLE constraint**. A DEFERRABLE constraint is one whose checking can be deferred to the end of a transaction. The assertion in the previous example is one that should be deferrable. When updating quotas or adding new salespeople to the database, you certainly want to be able to defer constraint checking, as the example showed.

■ **NOT DEFERRABLE constraint.** A NOT DEFERRABLE constraint is one whose checking cannot be deferred. A primary key constraint, a uniqueness constraint, and many column check constraints would usually fall into this category. These data integrity checks typically don't depend on other database interactions. They can and should be checked after *every* SQL statement that tries to modify the database.

Because it provides the most stringent integrity checking, NOT DEFERRABLE is the default. You must explicitly declare a constraint to be DEFERRABLE if you want to defer its operation. Note also that these constraint attributes define only the *deferability* of a constraint—that is, whether or not its operation can be deferred. The constraint definition may also specify the initial state of the constraint:

■ **INITIALLY IMMEDIATE constraint**. An INITIALLY IMMEDIATE constraint is one that starts out as an immediate constraint; that is, it will be checked immediately for each SQL statement.

■ **INITIALLY DEFERRED constraint.** An INITIALLY DEFERRED constraint is one that starts out as a deferred constraint; that is, its checking will be deferred until the end of a transaction. Of course, this option cannot be specified if the constraint is defined as NOT DEFERRABLE.

The constraint is put into the specified initial state when it is first created. It is also reset into this initial state at the beginning of each transaction. Because it provides the most stringent integrity checking, INITIALLY IMMEDIATE is the default. You must explicitly declare a constraint to be INITIALLY DEFERRED if you want it to automatically start out each transaction in a deferred state.

SQL2 adds one more mechanism to control the immediate or deferred processing of constraints. You can dynamically change the processing of a constraint during database operation using the SET CONSTRAINTS statement. For example, suppose the sample database contains this assertion:

```
CREATE ASSERTION quota_totals
  CHECK ((OFFICES.QUOTA = SUM(SALESREPS.QUOTA)) AND
         (SALESREPS.REP_OFFICE = OFFICES.OFFICE))
      DEFERRABLE INITIALLY IMMEDIATE
```

The initially immediate checking causes the constraint to be processed, statement by statement, for all normal database processing. For the special transaction that adds a new salesperson to the database, however, you will need to temporarily defer constraint processing. This sequence of statements accomplishes the goal:

```
SET CONSTRAINTS quota_totals DEFERRED

    INSERT INTO SALESREPS (EMPL_NUM, NAME, REP_OFFICE, HIRE_DATE,
              QUOTA, SALES)
        VALUES (:num, :name, :office_num, :date, :amount, 0)

        UPDATE OFFICES SET TARGET = TARGET + :amount
         WHERE (OFFICE = :office_num)

    COMMIT
```

After the COMMIT statement ends the transaction, the quota_totals constraint is reset back into IMMEDIATE mode because of the INITIALLY IMMEDIATE specification. If there were more work to be done after the UPDATE statement before the end of the transaction, you could manually set the constraint back into IMMEDIATE mode using this statement:

```
SET CONSTRAINTS quota_totals IMMEDIATE
```

You can set the same mode for several different constraints by including the constraint names in a comma-separated list:

```
SET CONSTRAINTS quota_totals, rep_totals IMMEDIATE
```

Finally, you can set the processing mode for all constraints with a single statement:

```
SET CONSTRAINTS ALL DEFERRED
```

The SQL2 capabilities for deferred constraint checking form a very comprehensive facility for managing the integrity of a database. As with many SQL2 capabilities, individual pieces of the SQL2 capability were taken from existing SQL implementations, and individual pieces have found their way into other implementations since the publication of the standard. IBM's DB2, for example, includes deferred constraint checking capability and supports SQL2-style deferability options. Its SET CONSTRAINTS statement, however, differs from the SQL2 standard. It operates on individual tables in the database, turning on and off the deferral of constraint checking associated with the table contents.

Business Rules

Many of the data integrity issues in the real world have to do with the rules and procedures of an organization. For example, the company that is modeled by the sample database might have rules like these:

- No customer is allowed to place orders that would exceed the customer's credit limit.

- The sales vice president must be notified whenever any customer is assigned a credit limit higher than $50,000.

- Orders may remain on the books for only six months; orders older than six months must be canceled and reentered.

In addition, there are often accounting rules that must be followed to maintain the integrity of totals, counts, and other amounts stored in a database. For the sample database, these rules probably make sense:

- Whenever a new order is taken, the SALES column for the salesperson who took the order and for the office where that salesperson works should be increased by the order amount. Deleting an order or changing the order amount should also cause the SALES columns to be adjusted.

- Whenever a new order is taken, the QTY_ON_HAND column for the product being ordered should be decreased by the quantity of products ordered. Deleting an order, changing the quantity, or changing the product ordered should also cause corresponding adjustments to the QTY_ON_HAND column.

These rules fall outside the realm of the SQL language as defined by the SQL1 standard and as implemented by many SQL-based DBMS products today. The DBMS takes responsibility for storing and organizing data and ensuring its basic integrity, but enforcing the business rules is the responsibility of the application programs that access the database.

Placing the burden of enforcing business rules on the application programs that access the database has several disadvantages:

- **Duplication of effort**. If six different programs deal with various updates to the ORDERS table, each of them must include code that enforces the rules relating to ORDERS updates.

- **Lack of consistency**. If several programs written by different programmers handle updates to a table, they will probably enforce the rules somewhat differently.

- **Maintenance problems**. If the business rules change, the programmers must identify every program that enforces the rules, then locate the code and modify it correctly.

- **Complexity**. There are often many rules to remember. Even in the small sample database, a program that handles order changes must worry about enforcing credit limits, adjusting sales totals for salespeople and offices, and adjusting the quantities on hand. A program that handles simple updates can become complex very quickly.

The requirement that application programs enforce business rules is not unique to SQL. Application programs have had that responsibility since the earliest days of COBOL programs and file systems. However, there has been a steady trend over the years to put more "understanding" of the data and more responsibility for its integrity into the database itself. In 1986, the Sybase DBMS introduced the concept of a *trigger* as a step toward including business rules in a relational database. The concept proved to be very popular, so support for triggers began to appear in many SQL DBMS products in the early 1990s, including those of the mainstream enterprise DBMS vendors. Triggers and the enforcement of business rules that they provide have been especially useful in enterprise database environments. When hundreds of application programs are being developed or modified every year by dozens of application programmers, the ability to centralize the definition and administration of business rules can be very useful.

What Is a Trigger?

The concept of a trigger is relatively straightforward. For any event that causes a change in the contents of a table, a user can specify an associated action that the DBMS should carry out. The three events that can trigger an action are attempts to INSERT, DELETE, or UPDATE rows of the table. The action triggered by an event is specified by a sequence of SQL statements.

To understand how a trigger works, let's examine a concrete example. When a new order is added to the ORDERS table, these two changes to the database should also take place:

- The SALES column for the salesperson who took the order should be increased by the amount of the order.

- The QTY_ON_HAND amount for the product being ordered should be decreased by the quantity ordered.

This Transact-SQL statement defines a SQL Server trigger, named NEWORDER, that causes these database updates to happen automatically:

```
CREATE TRIGGER NEWORDER
    ON ORDERS
    FOR INSERT
```

```
AS UPDATE SALESREPS
      SET SALES = SALES + INSERTED.AMOUNT
    FROM SALESREPS, INSERTED
   WHERE SALESREPS.EMPL_NUM = INSERTED.REP
  UPDATE PRODUCTS
      SET QTY_ON_HAND = QTY_ON_HAND - INSERTED.QTY
    FROM PRODUCTS, INSERTED
   WHERE PRODUCTS.MFR_ID = INSERTED.MFR
     AND PRODUCTS.PRODUCT_ID = INSERTED.PRODUCT
```

The first part of the trigger definition tells SQL Server that the trigger is to be invoked whenever an INSERT statement is attempted on the ORDERS table. The remainder of the definition (after the keyword AS) defines the action of the trigger. In this case, the action is a sequence of two UPDATE statements, one for the SALESREPS table and one for the PRODUCTS table. The row being inserted is referred to using the pseudo-table name inserted within the UPDATE statements. As the example shows, SQL Server extends the SQL language substantially to support triggers. Other extensions not shown here include IF/THEN/ELSE tests, looping, procedure calls, and even PRINT statements that display user messages.

The trigger capability, while popular in many DBMS products, is not a part of the ANSI/ISO SQL2 standard. As with other SQL features whose popularity has preceded standardization, this has led to a considerable divergence in trigger support across various DBMS brands. Some of the differences between brands are merely differences in syntax. Others reflect real differences in the underlying capability.

DB2's trigger support provides an instructive example of the differences. Here is the same trigger definition shown previously for SQL Server, this time using the DB2 syntax:

```
CREATE TRIGGER NEWORDER
        AFTER INSERT ON ORDERS
  REFERENCING NEW AS NEW_ORD
     FOR EACH ROW MODE DB2SQL
        BEGIN ATOMIC
        UPDATE SALESREPS
          SET SALES = SALES + NEW_ORD.AMOUNT
        WHERE SALESREPS.EMPL_NUM = NEW_ORD.REP;
        UPDATE PRODUCTS
          SET QTY_ON_HAND = QTY_ON_HAND - NEW_ORD.QTY
        WHERE PRODUCTS.MFR_ID = NEW_ORD.MFR
          AND PRODUCTS.PRODUCT_ID = NEW_ORD.PRODUCT;
        END
```

The beginning of the trigger definition includes the same elements as the SQL Server definition, but rearranges them. It explicitly tells DB2 that the trigger is to be invoked *after* a new order is inserted into the database. DB2 also allows you to specify that the trigger is to be carried out *before* a triggering action is applied to the database contents. This doesn't make sense in this example, because the triggering event is an INSERT operation, but it does make sense for UPDATE or DELETE operations.

The DB2 REFERENCING clause specifies a *table alias* (NEW_ORD) that will be used to refer to the row being inserted throughout the remainder of the trigger definition. It serves the same function as the INSERTED keyword in the SQL Server trigger. The statement references the new values in the inserted row because this is an INSERT operation trigger. For a DELETE operation trigger, the old values would be referenced. For an UPDATE operation trigger, DB2 gives you the ability to refer to both the old (pre-UPDATE) values and new (post-UPDATE) values.

BEGIN ATOMIC and END serve as brackets around the sequence of SQL statements that define the triggered action. The two searched UPDATE statements in the body of the trigger definition are straightforward modifications of their SQL Server counterparts. They follow the standard SQL syntax for searched UPDATE statements, using the table alias specified by the REFERENCING clause to identify the particular row of the SALESREPS table and the PRODUCTS table to be updated. The row being inserted is referred to using the pseudo-table name inserted within the UPDATE statements.

Here is another example of a trigger definition, this time using Informix Universal Server:

```
CREATE TRIGGER NEWORDER
        INSERT ON ORDERS
        AFTER (EXECUTE PROCEDURE NEW_ORDER)
```

This trigger again specifies an action that is to take place after a new order is inserted. In this case, the multiple SQL statements that form the triggered action can't be specified directly in the trigger definition. Instead, the triggered statements are placed into an Informix stored procedure, named NEW_ORDER, and the trigger causes the stored procedure to be executed. As this and the preceding examples show, although the core concepts of a trigger mechanism are very consistent across databases, the specifics vary a great deal. Triggers are certainly among the least portable aspects of SQL databases today.

Triggers and Referential Integrity

Triggers provide an alternative way to implement the referential integrity constraints provided by foreign keys and primary keys. In fact, advocates of the trigger feature point out that the trigger mechanism is more flexible than the strict referential integrity provided by the ANSI/ISO standard. For example, here is a trigger that enforces referential integrity for the OFFICES/SALESREPS relationship and displays a message when an attempted update fails:

```
CREATE TRIGGER REP_UPDATE
   ON SALESREPS
  FOR INSERT, UPDATE
   AS IF ((SELECT COUNT(*)
             FROM OFFICES, INSERTED
            WHERE OFFICES.OFFICE = INSERTED.REP_OFFICE) = 0)
       BEGIN
          PRINT "Invalid office number specified."
          ROLLBACK TRANSACTION
       END
```

Triggers can also be used to provide extended forms of referential integrity. For example, DB2 initially provided cascaded deletes through its CASCADE delete rule but did not support cascaded updates if a primary key value is changed. This limitation need not apply to triggers, however. The following SQL Server trigger cascades any update of the OFFICE column in the OFFICES table down into the REP_OFFICE column of the SALESREPS table:

```
CREATE TRIGGER CHANGE_REP_OFFICE
   ON OFFICES
  FOR UPDATE
   AS IF UPDATE (OFFICE)
       BEGIN
          UPDATE SALESREPS
             SET SALESREPS.REP_OFFICE = INSERTED.OFFICE
            FROM SALESREPS, INSERTED, DELETED
           WHERE SALESREPS.REP_OFFICE = DELETED.OFFICE
       END
```

As in the previous SQL Server example, the references DELETED.OFFICE and INSERTED.OFFICE in the trigger refer, respectively, to the values of the OFFICE column before and after the UPDATE statement. The trigger definition must be able to differentiate between these before and after values to perform the appropriate search and update actions specified by the trigger.

Trigger Advantages and Disadvantages

Over the last several years, the trigger mechanisms in many commercial DBMS products have expanded significantly. In many commercial implementations, the distinctions between triggers and stored procedures (described in Chapter 20) have blurred, so the action triggered by a single database change may be defined by hundreds of lines of stored procedure programming. The role of triggers has thus evolved beyond the enforcement of data integrity into a programming capability within the database.

A complete discussion of triggers is beyond the scope of this book, but even these simple examples show the power of the trigger mechanism. The major advantage of triggers is that business rules can be stored in the database and enforced consistently with each update to the database. This can dramatically reduce the complexity of application programs that access the database. Triggers also have some disadvantages, including these:

- **Database complexity**. When the rules are moved into the database, setting up the database becomes a more complex task. Users who could reasonably be expected to create small ad hoc applications with SQL will find that the programming logic of triggers makes the task much more difficult.

- **Hidden rules**. With the rules hidden away inside the database, programs that appear to perform straightforward database updates may, in fact, generate an enormous amount of database activity. The programmer no longer has total control over what happens to the database. Instead, a program-initiated database action may cause other, hidden actions.

- **Hidden performance implications**. With triggers stored inside the database, the consequences of executing a SQL statement are no longer completely visible to the programmer. In particular, an apparently simple SQL statement could, in concept, trigger a process that involves a sequential scan of a very large database table, which would take a long time to complete. These performance implications of any given SQL statement are invisible to the programmer.

Triggers and the SQL Standard

Triggers were one of the most widely praised and publicized features of Sybase SQL Server when it was first introduced, and they have since found their way into many commercial SQL products. Although the SQL2 standard provided an opportunity to standardize the DBMS implementation of triggers, the standards committee included check constraints instead. As the trigger and check-constraint examples in the preceding sections show, check constraints can be effectively used to limit the data that can be added to a table or modified in a table. However, unlike triggers, they lack the ability to cause an independent action in the database, such as adding a row or changing a data item in another table.

The extra capability provided by triggers has led several industry experts to advocate that they be included in a future SQL3 standard. Other experts have argued that triggers are a pollution of the data management function of a database, and that the functions performed by triggers belong in fourth generation languages (4GLs) and other database tools, rather than in the DBMS itself. While the debate continues, DBMS products have experimented with new trigger capabilities that extend beyond the database itself. These extended trigger capabilities allow modifications to data in a database to automatically cause actions such as sending mail, alerting a user, or launching another program to perform a task. This makes triggers even more useful and will add to the debate over including them in future official SQL standards. Regardless of the official stance, triggers have become a more and more important part of the SQL language in enterprise applications over the last several years.

Summary

The SQL language provides a number of features that help to protect the integrity of data stored in a relational database:

- Required columns can be specified when a table is created, and the DBMS will prevent NULL values in these columns.

- Data validation is limited to data type checking in standard SQL, but many DBMS products offer other data validation features.

- Entity integrity constraints ensure that the primary key uniquely identifies each entity represented in the database.

- Referential integrity constraints ensure that relationships among entities in the database are preserved during database updates.

- The SQL2 standard and newer implementations provide extensive referential integrity support, including delete and update rules that tell the DBMS how to handle the deletion and modification of rows that are referenced by other rows.

- Business rules can be enforced by the DBMS through the trigger mechanism popularized by Sybase and SQL Server. Triggers allow the DBMS to take complex actions in response to events such as attempted INSERT, DELETE, or UPDATE statements. Check constraints provide a more limited way to include business rules in the definition of a database and have the DBMS enforce them.

UPDATING DATA

Chapter 12

Transaction Processing

D atabase updates are usually triggered by real-world events, such as the receipt of a new order from a customer. In fact, receiving a new order would generate not just one, but this series of *four* updates to the sample database:

- Add the new order to the ORDERS table.
- Update the sales total for the salesperson who took the order.
- Update the sales total for the salesperson's office.
- Update the quantity-on-hand total for the ordered product.

To leave the database in a self-consistent state, all four updates must occur as a unit. If a system failure or another error creates a situation where some of the updates are processed and others are not, the integrity of the database will be lost. Similarly, if another user calculates totals or ratios partway through the sequence of updates, the calculations will be incorrect. The sequence of updates must thus be an all-or-nothing proposition in the database. SQL provides precisely this capability through its transaction-processing features, which are described in this chapter.

What Is a Transaction?

A *transaction* is a sequence of one or more SQL statements that together form a logical unit of work. The SQL statements that form the transaction are typically closely related and perform interdependent actions. Each statement in the transaction performs some part of a task, but all of them are required to complete the task. Grouping the statements as a single transaction tells the DBMS that the entire statement sequence should be executed *atomically*—all of the statements must be completed for the database to be in a consistent state.

Here are some examples of typical transactions for the sample database, along with the SQL statement sequence that comprises each transaction:

- **Add-an-order**. To accept a customer's order, the order-entry program should (a) query the PRODUCTS table to ensure that the product is in stock, (b) insert the order into the ORDERS table, (c) update the PRODUCTS table, subtracting the quantity ordered from the quantity-on-hand of the product, (d) update the SALESREPS table, adding the order amount to the total sales of the salesperson who took the order, and (e) update the OFFICES table, adding the order amount to the total sales of the office where the salesperson works.

- **Cancel-an-order**. To cancel a customer's order, the program should (a) delete the order from the ORDERS table, (b) update the PRODUCTS table, adjusting the quantity-on-hand total for the product, (c) update the SALESREPS table, subtracting the order amount from the salesperson's total sales, and (d) update the OFFICES table, subtracting the order amount from the office's total sales.

■ **Reassign-a-customer**. When a customer is reassigned from one salesperson to another, the program should (a) update the CUSTOMERS table to reflect the change, (b) update the ORDERS table to show the new salesperson for all orders placed by the customer, (c) update the SALESREPS table, reducing the quota for the salesperson losing the customer, and (d) update the SALESREPS table, raising the quota for the salesperson gaining the customer.

In each of these cases, a sequence of four or five actions, where each action consists of a separate SQL statement, is required to handle the single logical transaction.

The transaction concept is critical for programs that update a database because it ensures the integrity of the database. A SQL-based DBMS makes this commitment about the statements in a transaction:

The statements in a transaction will be executed as an atomic unit of work in the database. Either all of the statements will be executed successfully, or none of the statements will be executed.

The DBMS is responsible for keeping this commitment even if the application program aborts or a hardware failure occurs in the middle of the transaction, as shown in Figure 12-1. In each case, the DBMS must make sure that when failure recovery is complete, the database never reflects a partial transaction.

COMMIT and ROLLBACK

SQL supports database transactions through two SQL transaction-processing statements, shown in Figure 12-2:

■ **COMMIT**. The COMMIT statement signals the successful end of a transaction. It tells the DBMS that the transaction is now complete; all of the statements that comprise the transaction have been executed, and the database is self-consistent.

■ **ROLLBACK**. The ROLLBACK statement signals the unsuccessful end of a transaction. It tells the DBMS that the user does not want to complete the transaction; instead, the DBMS should back out any changes made to the database during the transaction. In effect, the DBMS restores the database to its state before the transaction began.

The COMMIT and ROLLBACK statements are executable SQL statements, just like SELECT, INSERT, and UPDATE. Here is an example of a successful update transaction that changes the quantity and amount of an order and adjusts the totals for the product, salesperson, and office associated with the order. A change like this would typically be handled by a forms-based change order program, which would use programmatic SQL to execute the statements shown here.

UPDATING DATA

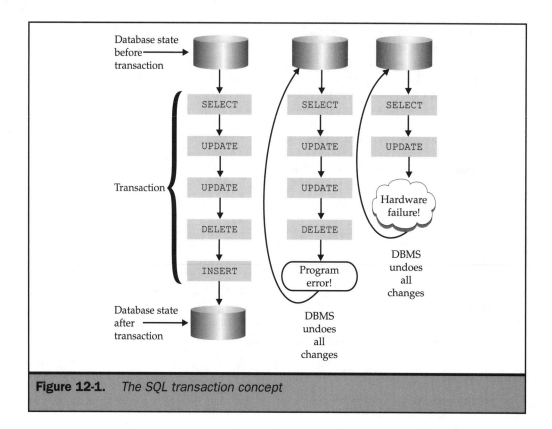

Figure 12-1. *The SQL transaction concept*

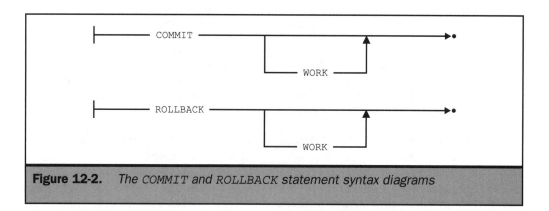

Figure 12-2. *The COMMIT and ROLLBACK statement syntax diagrams*

*Change the quantity on order number 113051 from 4 to 10, which raises its amount from
$1458 to $3550. The order is for QSA-XK47 reducers and was placed with Larry Fitch
(employee number 108) who works in Los Angeles (office number 21).*

```
UPDATE ORDERS
   SET QTY = 10, AMOUNT = 3550.00
 WHERE ORDER_NR = 113051

UPDATE SALESREPS
   SET SALES = SALES - 1458.00 + 3550.00
 WHERE EMPL_NUM = 108

UPDATE OFFICES
   SET SALES = SALES - 1458.00 + 3550.00
 WHERE OFFICE = 21

UPDATE PRODUCTS
   SET QTY_ON_HAND = QTY_ON_HAND + 4 - 10
 WHERE MFR_ID = 'QSA'
   AND PRODUCT_ID = 'XK47'
```

. . . confirm the change one last time with the customer . . .

```
COMMIT WORK
```

Here is the same transaction, but this time assume that the user makes an error
entering the product number. To correct the error, the transaction is rolled back, so that
it can be reentered correctly:

*Change the quantity on order number 113051 from 4 to 10, which raises its amount from
$1458 to $3550. The order is for QAS-XK47 reducers and was placed with Larry Fitch
(employee number 108), who works in Los Angeles (office number 21).*

```
UPDATE ORDERS
   SET QTY = 10, AMOUNT = 3550.00
 WHERE ORDER_NR = 113051

UPDATE SALESREPS
   SET SALES = SALES - 1458.00 + 3550.00
 WHERE EMPL_NUM = 108
```

UPDATING DATA

```
UPDATE OFFICES
   SET SALES = SALES - 1458.00 + 3550.00
 WHERE OFFICE = 21

UPDATE PRODUCTS
   SET QTY_ON_HAND = QTY_ON_HAND + 4 - 10
 WHERE MFR_ID = 'QAS'
   AND PRODUCT_ID = 'XK47'
```

. . . oops! the manufacturer is "QSA," not "QAS" . . .

```
ROLLBACK WORK
```

The ANSI/ISO Transaction Model

The ANSI/ISO SQL standard defines a SQL *transaction model* and the roles of the COMMIT and ROLLBACK statements. Most, but not all, commercial SQL products use this transaction model, which is based on the transaction support in the early releases of DB2. The standard specifies that a SQL transaction automatically begins with the first SQL statement executed by a user or a program. The transaction continues through subsequent SQL statements until it ends in one of four ways:

- **COMMIT**. A COMMIT statement ends the transaction successfully, making its database changes permanent. A new transaction begins immediately after the COMMIT statement.

- **ROLLBACK**. A ROLLBACK statement aborts the transaction, backing out its database changes. A new transaction begins immediately after the ROLLBACK statement.

- **Successful program termination**. For programmatic SQL, successful program termination also ends the transaction successfully, just as if a COMMIT statement had been executed. Because the program is finished, there is no new transaction to begin.

- **Abnormal program termination**. For programmatic SQL, abnormal program termination also aborts the transaction, just as if a ROLLBACK statement had been executed. Because the program is finished, there is no new transaction to begin.

Figure 12-3 shows typical transactions that illustrate these four conditions. Note that the user or program is always in a transaction under the ANSI/ISO transaction model. No explicit action is required to begin a transaction; it begins automatically with the first SQL statement or immediately after the preceding transaction ends.

Recall that the ANSI/ISO SQL standard is primarily focused on a *programmatic* SQL language for use in application programs. Transactions play an important role in programmatic SQL, because even a simple application program often needs to carry out

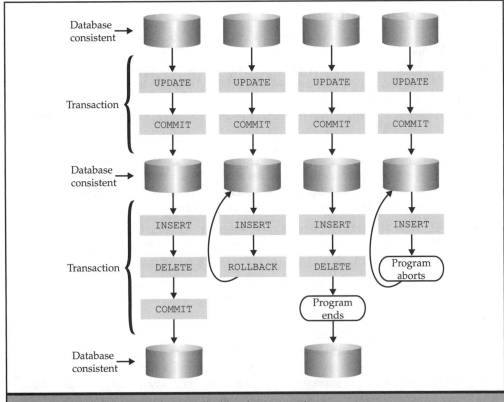

Figure 12-3. *Committed and rolled back transactions*

a sequence of two or three SQL statements to accomplish its task. Because users can change their minds and other conditions can occur (such as being out of stock on a product that a customer wants to order), an application program must be able to proceed partway through a transaction and then choose to abort or continue. The COMMIT and ROLLBACK statements provide precisely this capability.

The COMMIT and ROLLBACK statements can also be used in interactive SQL, but in practice, they are rarely seen in this context. Interactive SQL is generally used for database queries; updates are less common, and multistatement updates are almost never performed by typing the statements into an interactive SQL facility. As a result, transactions are typically a minor concern in interactive SQL. In fact, many interactive SQL products default to an autocommit mode, where a COMMIT statement is automatically executed after each SQL statement typed by the user. This effectively makes each interactive SQL statement its own transaction.

Other Transaction Models

A few commercial SQL products depart from the ANSI/ISO transaction model to provide additional transaction-processing capability for their users. The Sybase DBMS, which is designed for online transaction-processing applications, is one example. SQL Server, which was derived from the Sybase product, also uses the Sybase transaction model.

The Transact-SQL dialect used by Sybase includes four transaction-processing statements:

- **BEGIN TRANSACTION**. The BEGIN TRANSACTION statement signals the beginning of a transaction. Unlike the ANSI/ISO transaction model, which implicitly begins a new transaction when the previous one ends, Sybase requires an explicit statement to start a transaction.

- **COMMIT TRANSACTION**. Signals the successful end of a transaction. As in the ANSI/ISO model, all changes made to the database during the transaction become permanent. However, a new transaction is not automatically started.

- **SAVE TRANSACTION**. Establishes a *savepoint* in the middle of a transaction. Sybase saves the state of the database at the current point in the transaction and assigns the saved state a savepoint name, specified in the statement.

- **ROLLBACK TRANSACTION**. Has two roles. If a savepoint is named in the ROLLBACK statement, Sybase backs out the database changes made since the savepoint, effectively rolling the transaction back to the point where the SAVE TRANSACTION statement was executed. If no savepoint is named, the ROLLBACK statement backs out all database changes made since the BEGIN TRANSACTION statement.

The Sybase savepoint mechanism is especially useful in complex transactions involving many statements, as shown in Figure 12-4. The application program in the figure periodically saves its status as the transaction progresses, establishing two named savepoints. If problems develop later during the transaction, the application program does not have to abort the entire transaction. Instead, it can roll the transaction back to any of its savepoints and proceed from there. All of the statements executed before the savepoint remain in effect; those executed since the savepoint are backed out by the rollback operation.

Note that the entire transaction is still the logical unit of work for Sybase, as it is for the ANSI/ISO model. If a system or hardware failure occurs in the middle of a transaction, for example, the entire transaction is backed out of the database. Thus, savepoints are a convenience for the application program, but not a fundamental change to the ANSI/ISO transaction model.

The explicit use of a BEGIN TRANSACTION statement is, however, a significant departure from the ANSI/ISO model. SQL statements that are executed outside a transaction (that is, statements that do not appear between a BEGIN/COMMIT or a

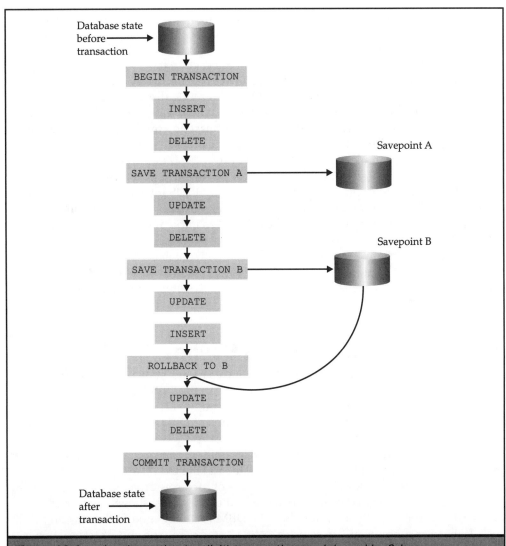

Figure 12-4. *An alternative (explicit) transaction model used by Sybase*

BEGIN/ROLLBACK statement pair) are effectively handled in autocommit mode. Each statement is committed as it is executed; there is no way to roll back the statement once it has succeeded.

Some DBMS brands that use a Sybase-style transaction model prohibit statements that alter the structure of a database or its security from occurring within a transaction (such as CREATE TABLE, ALTER TABLE, and DROP TABLE, discussed in Chapter 13, and GRANT and REVOKE, discussed in Chapter 15). These statements must be executed outside a transaction. This restriction makes the transaction model easier to implement, because it ensures that the structure of the database cannot change during a transaction.

In contrast, in a complete implementation of the ANSI/ISO-style transaction model, the structure of a database can change significantly during a transaction. (Tables can be dropped, created, and populated, for example.) The DBMS must be able to undo all of these alterations if the user later decides to roll back the transaction, including the structural changes. In practice, this can be difficult to implement, and many popular DBMS products introduce simplifying restrictions. A common restriction is that database structure changes cannot be intermixed with database access operations within a transaction. Another common restriction is that a transaction that alters the database structure may contain one and only one SQL statement (such as a CREATE TABLE or a DROP TABLE statement).

Transactions: Behind the Scenes *

The all-or-nothing commitment that a DBMS makes for the statements in a transaction seems almost like magic to a new SQL user. How can the DBMS possibly back out the changes made to a database, especially if a system failure occurs during the middle of a transaction? The actual techniques used by brands of DBMS vary, but almost all of them are based on a *transaction log*, as shown in Figure 12-5.

Here is how the transaction log works, in simplified, conceptual form. When a user executes a SQL statement that modifies the database, the DBMS automatically writes a record in the transaction log showing two copies of each row affected by the statement. One copy shows the row *before* the change, and the other copy shows the row *after* the change. Only after the log is written does the DBMS actually modify the row on the disk. If the user subsequently executes a COMMIT statement, the end-of-transaction is noted in the transaction log. If the user executes a ROLLBACK statement, the DBMS examines the log to find the "before" images of the rows that have been modified since the transaction began. Using these images, the DBMS restores the rows to their earlier state, effectively backing out all changes to the database that were made during the transaction.

If a system failure occurs, the system operator typically recovers the database by running a special recovery utility supplied with the DBMS. The recovery utility examines the end of the transaction log, looking for transactions that were not committed before

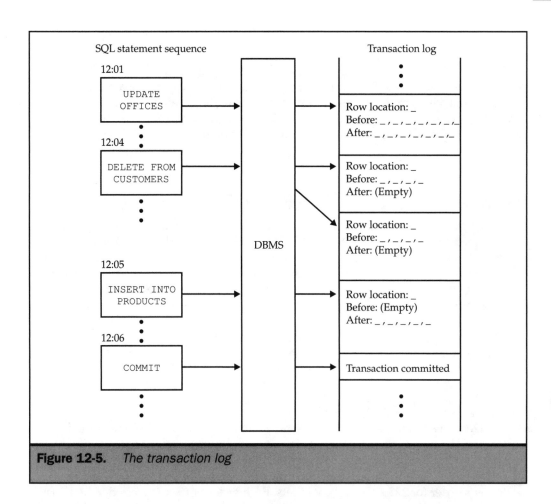

Figure 12-5.   *The transaction log*

the failure. The utility rolls back each of these incomplete transactions, so that only committed transactions are reflected in the database; transactions in process at the time of the failure have been rolled back.

The use of a transaction log obviously imposes an overhead on updates to the database. In practice, the mainstream commercial DBMS products use much more sophisticated logging techniques than the simple scheme described here to minimize this overhead. In addition, the transaction log is usually stored on a fast disk drive, different from the one that stores the database, to minimize disk access contention.

Some personal computer DBMS brands allow you to disable transaction logging to increase the performance of the DBMS.

Specialized databases, such as in-memory databases or cached database copies, may also use this log-free architecture. This may also be an acceptable alternative in specialized production databases, for example, where the database contents are replicated on a duplicate computer system. In most common production databases, however, a logging scheme and its overhead are an integral part of the database operation.

Transactions and Multiuser Processing

When two or more users concurrently access a database, transaction processing takes on a new dimension. Now the DBMS must not only recover properly from system failures or errors, but it must also ensure that the users' actions do not interfere with one another. Ideally, each user should be able to access the database as if he or she had exclusive access to it, without worrying about the actions of other users. The SQL transaction model allows a SQL-based DBMS to insulate users from one another in this way.

The best way to understand how SQL handles concurrent transactions is to look at the problems that result if transactions are not handled properly. Although they can show up in many different ways, four fundamental problems can occur. The next four sections give a simple example of each problem.

The Lost Update Problem

Figure 12-6 shows a simple application where two users accept telephone orders from customers. The order-entry program checks the PRODUCTS file for adequate inventory before accepting the customer's order. In the figure, Joe starts entering an order for 100 ACI-41004 widgets from his customer. At the same time, Mary starts entering her customer's order for 125 ACI-41004 widgets. Each order-entry program does a query on the PRODUCTS file, and each finds that 139 widgets are in stock—more than enough to cover the customer's request. Joe asks his customer to confirm the order, and his copy of the order-entry program updates the PRODUCTS file to show (139 – 100) = 39 widgets remaining for sale and inserts a new order for 100 widgets into the ORDERS table. A few seconds later, Mary asks her customer to confirm the order. Her copy of the order-entry program updates the PRODUCTS file to show (139 – 125) = 14 widgets remaining in stock and inserts a new order for 125 widgets into the ORDERS table.

The handling of the two orders has obviously left the database in an inconsistent state. The first of the two updates to the PRODUCTS file has been lost! Both customers' orders have been accepted, but not enough widgets are in inventory to satisfy both orders. Further, the database shows that there are still 14 widgets remaining for sale. This example illustrates the lost update problem that can occur whenever two programs read the same data from the database, use the data as the basis for a calculation, and then try to update the data.

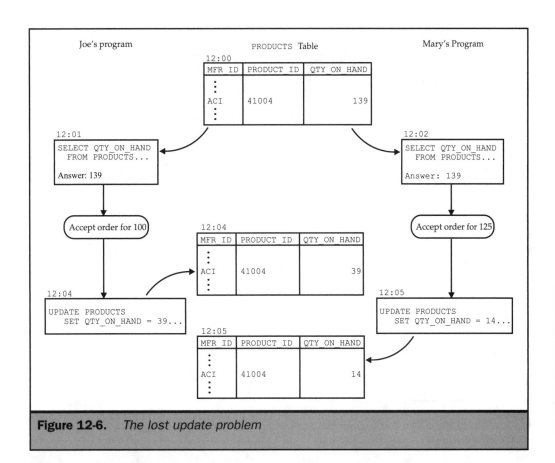

Figure 12-6. *The lost update problem*

The Uncommitted Data Problem

Figure 12-7 shows the same order-processing application as Figure 12-6. Joe again begins taking an order for 100 ACI-41004 widgets from his customer. This time, Joe's copy of the order-processing program queries the PRODUCTS table, finds 139 widgets available, and updates the PRODUCTS table to show 39 widgets remaining after the customer's order. Then Joe begins to discuss with the customer the relative merits of the ACI-41004 and ACI-41005 widgets.

In the meantime, Mary's customer tries to order 125 ACI-41004 widgets. Mary's copy of the order-processing program queries the PRODUCTS table, finds only 39 widgets available, and refuses the order. It also generates a notice telling the purchasing manager to buy more ACI-41004 widgets, which are in great demand. Now Joe's customer decides not to order the size 4 widgets after all, and Joe's order-entry program does a ROLLBACK to abort its transaction.

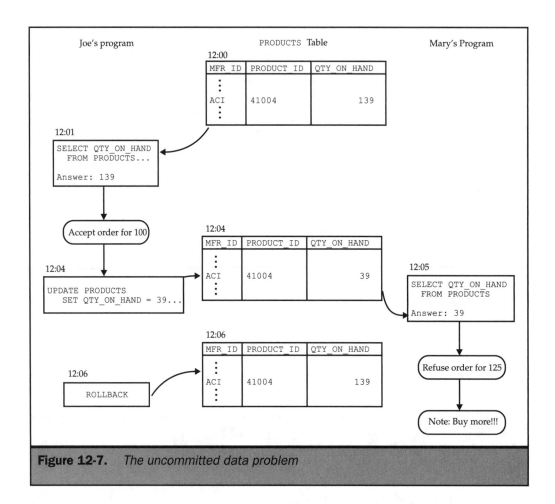

Figure 12-7. *The uncommitted data problem*

Because Mary's order-processing program was allowed to see the uncommitted update of Joe's program, the order from Mary's customer was refused, and the purchasing manager will order more widgets, even though 139 of them are still in stock. The situation would have been even worse if Mary's customer had decided to settle for the 39 available widgets. In this case, Mary's program would have updated the PRODUCTS table to show zero units available. But when the ROLLBACK of Joe's transaction occurred, the DBMS would have set the available inventory back to 139 widgets, even though 39 of them are committed to Mary's customer.

The problem in this example is that Mary's program has been allowed to see the uncommitted updates from Joe's program and has acted on them, producing the erroneous results. The SQL2 standard refers to this as problem *P1*, also known as the *dirty read* problem. In the parlance of the standard, the data that Mary's program has seen is dirty because it has not been committed by Joe's program.

The Inconsistent Data Problem

Figure 12-8 shows the order-processing application once more. Again, Joe begins taking an order for 100 ACI-41004 widgets from his customer. A short time later, Mary also begins talking to her customer about the same widgets, and her program does a single-row query to find out how many are available. This time Mary's customer inquires about the ACI-41005 widgets as an alternative, and Mary's program does a single-row query on that row.

Meanwhile, Joe's customer decides to order the widgets, so his program updates that row of the database and does a COMMIT to finalize the order in the database. After considering the ACI-41005 widgets as an alternative, Mary's customer decides to order the ACI-41004 widgets that Mary originally proposed. Her program does a new single-row query to get the information for the ACI-41004 widgets again. But instead of finding the 139 widgets that were in stock just a moment ago, the new query shows only 39 in stock.

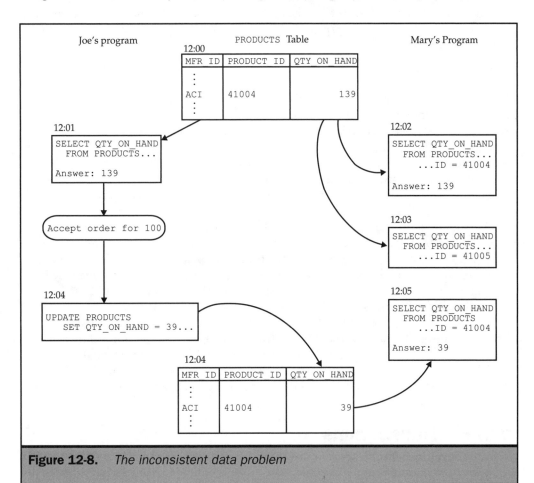

Figure 12-8. *The inconsistent data problem*

In this example, unlike the preceding two, the status of the database has remained an accurate model of the real-world situation. There *are* only 39 ACI-41004 widgets left because Joe's customer has purchased 100 of them. There is no problem with Mary having seen uncommitted data from Joe's program—the order was complete and committed to the database. However, from the point of view of Mary's program, the database did not remain consistent during her transaction. At the beginning of the transaction, a row contained certain data, and later in the same transaction, it contained different data, so external events have interfered with her consistent view of the database. This inconsistency can cause problems even if Mary's program never tries to update the database based on the results of the first query.

For example, if the program is accumulating totals or calculating statistics, it cannot be sure that the statistics reflect a stable, consistent view of the data. The problem in this case is that Mary's program has been allowed to see committed updates from Joe's program that affect rows that it has already examined. The SQL2 standard refers to this problem as *P2*, also known as the *nonrepeatable read* problem. The name comes from the fact that Mary's program can't repeat the same read access to the database and obtain the same results.

The Phantom Insert Problem

Figure 12-9 shows an order-processing application once more. This time, the sales manager runs a report program that scans the ORDERS table, printing a list of the orders from customers of Bill Adams and computing their total. In the meantime, a customer calls Bill to place an additional order for $5000. The order is inserted into the database, and the transaction is committed. A short time later, the sales manager's program (still operating within its initial transaction) again scans the ORDERS table, running the very same query. This time, there is an additional order, and the total is $5000 higher than for the first query.

Like the previous example, the problem here is inconsistent data. The database remains an accurate model of the real-world situation, and its integrity is intact, but the same query executed twice during the same transaction yielded two different results. In the previous example, the query was a single-row query, and the inconsistency in the data was caused by a committed UPDATE statement. A committed DELETE statement could cause the same kind of problem.

In the example of Figure 12-9, the problem is caused by a committed INSERT statement. The additional row did not participate in the first query, but it shows up as a phantom row, out of nowhere in the second query. Like the inconsistent data problem, the consequences of the phantom insert problem can be inconsistent and incorrect calculations. The SQL2 standard refers to this as *P3*, and also uses the name *phantom* to describe it.

Concurrent Transactions

As the three multiuser update examples show, when users share access to a database and one or more users is updating data, there is a potential for database corruption.

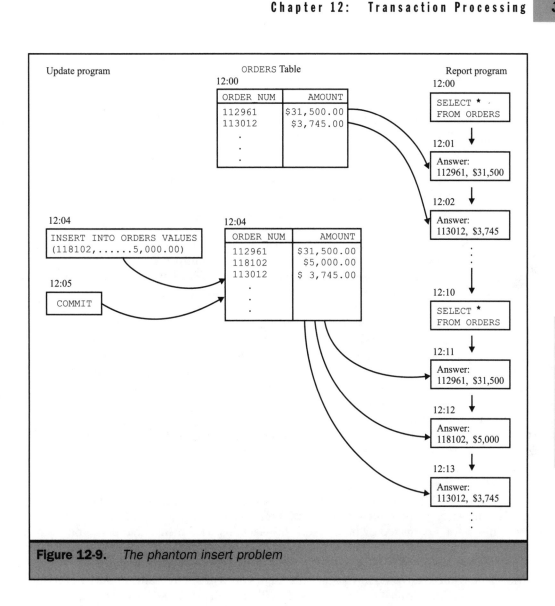

Figure 12-9. *The phantom insert problem*

SQL uses its transaction mechanism to eliminate this source of database corruption. In addition to the all-or-nothing commitment for the statements in a transaction, a SQL-based DBMS makes this commitment about transactions:

During a transaction, the user will see a completely consistent view of the database. The user will never see the uncommitted changes of other users, and even committed changes made by others will not affect data seen by the user in mid-transaction.

Transactions are thus the key to both recovery and concurrency control in a SQL database. The previous commitment can be restated explicitly in terms of concurrent transaction execution:

If two transactions, A and B, are executing concurrently, the DBMS ensures that the results will be the same as they would be if either (a) Transaction A were executed first, followed by Transaction B, or (b) Transaction B were executed first, followed by Transaction A.

This concept is known as the *serializability* of transactions. Effectively, it means that each database user can access the database as if no other users were concurrently accessing the database. In practice, dozens or hundreds of transactions may be concurrently executing within a large production database. The serializability concept can be directly extended to cover this situation. Serializability guarantees that, if some number, *N*, concurrent transactions are executing, the DBMS must ensure that its results are the same as if they had been executed in some sequence, one at a time. The concept does not specify *which* sequence of transactions must be used, only that the results must match the results of *some* sequence.

The fact that a DBMS insulates you from the actions of other concurrent users doesn't mean, however, that you can forget all about the other users. In fact, the situation is quite the opposite. Because other users want to concurrently update the database, you should keep your transactions as short and simple as possible, to maximize the amount of parallel processing that can occur.

Suppose, for example, that you run a program that performs a sequence of three large queries. Since the program doesn't update the database, it might seem that it doesn't need to worry about transactions. It certainly seems unnecessary to use COMMIT statements. But in fact, the program should use a COMMIT statement after each query. Why? Recall that SQL automatically begins a transaction with the first SQL statement in a program. Without a COMMIT statement, the transaction continues until the program ends. Further, SQL guarantees that the data retrieved during a transaction will be self-consistent, unaffected by other users' transactions. This means that once your program retrieves a row from the database, no other user can modify the row until your transaction ends, because you might try to retrieve the row again later in your transaction, and the DBMS must guarantee that you will see the same data. Thus, as your program performs its three queries, it will prevent other users from updating larger and larger portions of the database.

The moral of this example is simple: you must always worry about transactions when writing programs for a production SQL database. Transactions should always be as short as possible "COMMIT early and COMMIT often" is good advice when you are using programmatic SQL.

In practice, implementing a strict multiuser transaction model can impose a substantial overhead on the operation of a database with dozens, hundreds, or thousands of concurrent users. In addition, the specifics of the application may not require the absolute isolation among the user programs that the SQL transaction model implies. For example, maybe the application designer knows that an order inquiry program has been designed so that it will *never* attempt to read and then reread a row of the database during a single transaction. In this case, the inconsistent data problem can't occur because of the program structure. Alternatively, maybe the application designer knows that all of a program's access to particular tables of a database is read-only. If the programmer can convey information like this to the DBMS, some of the overhead of SQL transactions can be eliminated.

The SQL1 standard did not address this database performance issue, and most of the major DBMS brands implemented proprietary schemes for enhancing the performance of SQL transactions. The SQL2 standard specified a new SET TRANSACTION statement whose function is to specify the level of SQL transaction-model support that an application needs. You don't need to use the SET TRANSACTION statement for casual use of SQL or for relatively simple or low-volume SQL transaction processing. To fully understand its operation, it's useful to understand the locking and other techniques used by commercial DBMS products to implement multiuser SQL transactions. The remainder of this chapter discusses locking, the performance-optimizing capabilities of SQL2, and the various DBMS brands that depend on it.

Locking *

Most major DBMS products use sophisticated locking techniques to handle concurrent SQL transactions for many simultaneous users. However, the basic concepts behind locking and transactions are very simple. Figure 12-10 shows a simple locking scheme and how it handles contention between two concurrent transactions.

As Transaction A in the figure accesses the database, the DBMS automatically locks each piece of the database that the transaction retrieves or modifies. Transaction B proceeds in parallel, and the DBMS also locks the pieces of the database that it accesses. If Transaction B tries to access part of the database that has been locked by Transaction A, the DBMS blocks Transaction B, causing it to wait for the data to be unlocked. The DBMS releases the locks held by Transaction A only when it ends in a COMMIT or ROLLBACK operation. The DBMS then unblocks Transaction B, allowing it to proceed. Transaction B can now lock that piece of the database on its own behalf, protecting it from the effects of other transactions.

As the figure shows, the locking technique temporarily gives a transaction exclusive access to a piece of a database, preventing other transactions from modifying the locked data. Locking thus solves all of the concurrent transaction problems. It prevents lost updates, uncommitted data, and inconsistent data from corrupting the database. However, locking introduces a new problem—it may cause a transaction to wait for a very long time while the pieces of the database that it wants to access are locked by other transactions.

Locking Levels

Locking can be implemented at various levels of the database. In its most basic form, the DBMS could lock the entire database for each transaction. This locking strategy

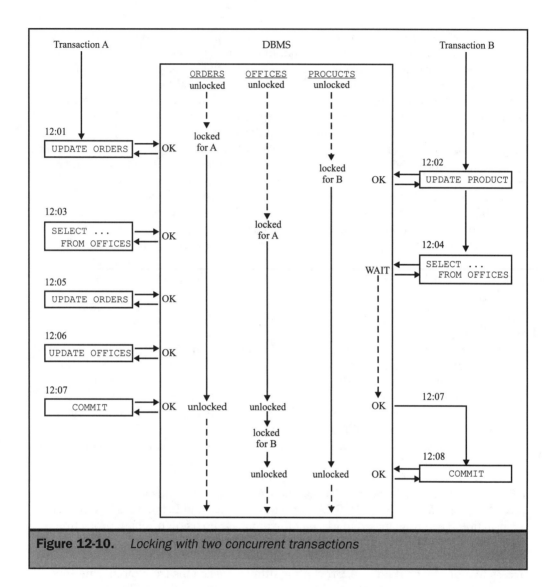

Figure 12-10. *Locking with two concurrent transactions*

would be simple to implement, but it would allow processing of only one transaction at a time. If the transaction included any think time at all (such as time to discuss an order with a customer), all other access to the database would be blocked during that time, leading to unacceptably slow performance. However, database-level locking may be appropriate for certain types of transactions, such as those that modify the structure of the database or for complex queries that must sequentially scan many large tables. In these cases, it may be more efficient to rapidly do a single locking operation, quickly execute the database operation, and then quickly unlock the database than to individually lock dozens of tables.

An enhanced form of locking is *table-level* locking. In this scheme, the DBMS locks only the tables accessed by a transaction. Other transactions can concurrently access other tables. This technique permits more parallel processing, but can still lead to unacceptably slow performance in applications such as order entry, where many users must share access to the same table or tables.

Many DBMS products implement locking at the *page level.* In this scheme, the DBMS locks individual blocks of data (pages) from the disk as they are accessed by a transaction. Other transactions are prevented from accessing the locked pages but may access (and lock for themselves) other pages of data. Page sizes of 2KB, 4KB, and 16KB are commonly used. Since a large table will be spread out over hundreds or thousands of pages, two transactions trying to access two different rows of a table will usually be accessing two different pages, allowing the two transactions to proceed in parallel.

Over the last several years, most of the major commercial DBMS systems have moved beyond page-level locking to *row-level* locks. Row-level locking allows two concurrent transactions that access two different rows of a table to proceed in parallel, even if the two rows fall in the same disk block. While this may seem a remote possibility, it can be a real problem with small tables containing small records, such as the OFFICES table in the sample database.

Row-level locking provides a high degree of parallel transaction execution. Unfortunately, keeping track of locks on variable-length pieces of the database (in other words, rows) rather than fixed-size pages is a much more complex task, so increased parallelism comes at the cost of more sophisticated locking logic and increased overhead. In fact, for certain transactions or applications, the overhead of row-level locking might be greater than the performance gains of permitting more parallel operation within the database.

Some DBMS products address this situation by automatically promoting many individual row-level locks into a page-level or table-level lock when the number of row-level locks for a given transaction rises above a certain limit. As this example shows, it's not always the case that a more granular (smaller) level of lock implementation is better; the best scheme heavily depends on the specific transactions and the SQL operations that they contain.

It's theoretically possible to move beyond row-level locking to locking at the individual data item level. In theory, this would provide even more parallelism than row-level locks, because it would allow concurrent access to the same row by two different transactions, provided they were accessing different sets of columns. The overhead in managing item-level locking, however, has thus far outweighed its potential advantages. No commercial SQL DBMS uses item-level locking. In fact, locking is an area of considerable research in database technology, and the locking schemes used in commercial DBMS products are much more sophisticated than the fundamental scheme described here. The most straightforward of these advanced locking schemes, using shared and exclusive locks, is described in the next section.

UPDATING DATA

Shared and Exclusive Locks

To increase concurrent access to a database, most commercial DBMS products use a locking scheme with more than one type of lock. A scheme using shared and exclusive locks is quite common:

- ■ **Shared lock**. Used by the DBMS when a transaction wants to read data from the database. Another concurrent transaction can also acquire a shared lock on the same data, allowing the other transaction to also read the data.

- ■ **Exclusive lock**. Used by the DBMS when a transaction wants to update data in the database. When a transaction has an exclusive lock on some data, other transactions cannot acquire any type of lock (shared or exclusive) on the data.

Figure 12-11 shows the rules for this locking scheme and the permitted combinations of locks that can be held by two concurrent transactions. Note that a transaction can acquire an exclusive lock only if no other transaction currently has a shared or an exclusive lock on the data. If a transaction tries to acquire a lock not permitted by the rules in Figure 12-11, it is blocked until other transactions unlock the data that it requires.

Figure 12-12 shows the same transactions shown in Figure 12-10, this time using shared and exclusive locks. If you compare the two figures, you can see how the new locking scheme improves concurrent access to the database. Mature and complex DBMS products, such as DB2, have more than two types of locks and use different locking techniques at different levels of the database. Despite the increased complexity, the goal of the locking scheme remains the same: to prevent unwanted interference between transactions while providing the greatest possible concurrent access to the database, all with minimal locking overhead.

Deadlocks *

Unfortunately, the use of any locking scheme to support concurrent SQL transactions leads to a problem called a *deadlock*. Figure 12-13 illustrates a deadlock situation.

		Transaction B		
		Unlocked	Shared lock	Exclusive lock
Transaction A	Unlocked	OK	OK	OK
	Shared lock	OK	OK	NO
	Exclusive lock	OK	NO	NO

Figure 12-11. *Rules for shared and exclusive locks*

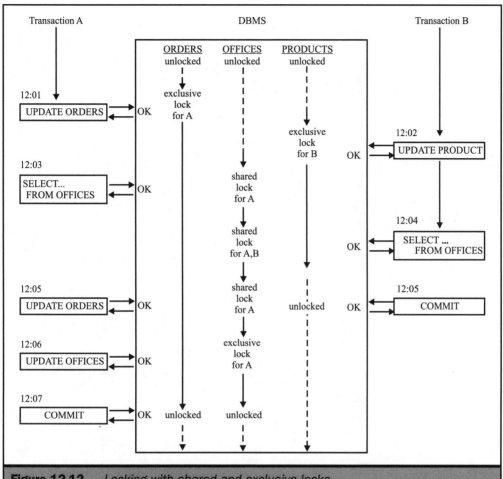

Figure 12-12.   *Locking with shared and exclusive locks*

Program A updates the ORDERS table, thereby locking part of it. Meanwhile, Program B updates the PRODUCTS table, locking part of it. Now Program A tries to update the PRODUCTS table and Program B tries to update the ORDERS table, in each case trying to update a part of the table that has been previously locked by the other program (the same row or the same page, depending on the type of locking implemented). Without outside intervention, each program will wait forever for the other program to commit its transaction and unlock the data. The situation in the figure is a simple deadlock between two programs, but more complex situations can occur where three, four, or

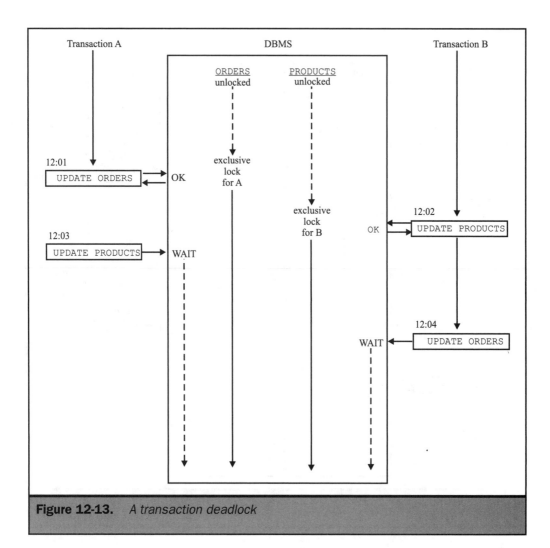

Figure 12-13.   *A transaction deadlock*

more programs are in a cycle of locks, each waiting for data that is locked by one of the other programs.

To deal with deadlocks, a DBMS typically includes logic that periodically (for example, once every five seconds) checks the locks held by various transactions. When it detects a deadlock, the DBMS arbitrarily chooses one of the transactions as the deadlock loser and rolls back the transaction. This frees the locks held by the losing transaction, allowing the deadlock winner to proceed. The losing program receives an error code informing it that it has lost a deadlock and that its current transaction has been rolled back.

This scheme for breaking deadlocks means that any SQL statement can potentially return a deadlock loser error code, even if nothing is wrong with the statement per se. Thus, even though COMMIT and ROLLBACK are the SQL transaction-processing statements, it's possible for other SQL statements—an INSERT statement, for example, or even a SELECT statement—to be a deadlock loser. The transaction attempting the statement is rolled back through no fault of its own, but because of other concurrent activity in the database. This may seem unfair, but in practice, it's much better than the other two alternatives—eternal deadlock or database corruption. If a deadlock loser error occurs in interactive SQL, the user can simply retype the SQL statement(s). In programmatic SQL, the application program must be prepared to handle the deadlock loser error code. Typically, the program will respond by either alerting the user or automatically retrying the transaction.

The probability of deadlocks can be dramatically reduced by carefully planning database updates. All programs that update multiple tables during a transaction should, whenever possible, update the tables in the same sequence. This allows the locks to flow smoothly across the tables, minimizing the possibility of deadlocks. In addition, some of the advanced locking features described in later sections of this chapter can be used to further reduce the number of deadlocks that occur.

Advanced Locking Techniques *

Many commercial database products offer advanced locking facilities that go well beyond those provided by standard SQL transactions. These include:

- **Explicit locking**. A program can explicitly lock an entire table or some other part of the database if it will be repeatedly accessed by the program.

- **Isolation levels**. You can tell the DBMS that a specific program will not reretrieve data during a transaction, allowing the DBMS to release locks before the transaction ends.

- **Locking parameters**. The database administrator can manually adjust the size of the lockable piece of the database and other locking parameters to tune locking performance.

These facilities tend to be nonstandard and product-specific. However, several of them, particularly those initially introduced in mainframe versions of DB2 years ago, have been implemented in several commercial SQL products and have achieved the status of common, if not standard, features. In fact, the isolation-level capabilities introduced in DB2 have found their way into the SQL2 standard.

UPDATING DATA

Explicit Locking *

If a transaction repeatedly accesses a table, the overhead of acquiring small locks on many parts of the table can be very substantial. A bulk update program that walks through every row of a table, for example, will lock the entire table, piece by piece, as it proceeds. For this type of transaction, the program should explicitly lock the entire table, process the updates, and then unlock the table. Locking the entire table has three advantages:

- It eliminates the overhead of row-by-row (or page-by-page) locking.

- It eliminates the possibility that another transaction will lock part of the table, forcing the bulk update transaction to wait.

- It eliminates the possibility that another transaction will lock part of the table and deadlock the bulk update transaction, forcing it to be restarted.

Of course, locking the table has the disadvantage that all other transactions attempting to access the table must wait while the update is in process. However, because the bulk update transaction can proceed much more quickly, the overall throughput of the DBMS can be increased by explicitly locking the table.

In the IBM databases, the LOCK TABLE statement, shown in Figure 12-14, is used to explicitly lock an entire table. It offers two locking modes:

- **EXCLUSIVE** mode acquires an exclusive lock on the entire table. No other transaction can access any part of the table for any purpose while the lock is held. This is the mode you would request for a bulk update transaction.

- **SHARE** mode acquires a shared lock on the entire table. Other transactions can read parts of the table (that is, they can also acquire shared locks), but they cannot update any part of it. Of course, if the transaction issuing the LOCK TABLE statement now updates part of the table, it will still incur the overhead of acquiring exclusive locks on the parts of the table that it updates. This is the mode you would request if you wanted a snapshot of a table, accurate at a particular point in time.

Oracle also supports a DB2-style LOCK TABLE statement. The same effect can be achieved in Ingres with a different statement. Several other database management systems do not support explicit locking at all, choosing instead to optimize their implicit locking techniques.

Isolation Levels *

Under the strict definition of a SQL transaction, no action by a concurrently executing transaction is allowed to impact the data visible during the course of your transaction. If your program performs a database query during a transaction, proceeds with other work, and later performs the same database query a second time, the SQL transaction mechanism guarantees that the data returned by the two queries will be identical (unless *your* transaction acted to change the data). This ability to reliably reretrieve a

Figure 12-14.   *The LOCK TABLE statement syntax diagram*

row during a transaction is the highest level of isolation that your program can have from other programs and users. The level of isolation is called the *isolation level* of your transaction.

This absolute isolation of your transaction from all other concurrently executing transactions is very costly in terms of database locking and loss of database concurrency. As your program reads each row of query results, the DBMS must lock the row (with a shared lock) to prevent concurrent transactions from modifying the row. These locks must be held until the end of your transaction, just in case your program performs the query again. In many cases, the DBMS can significantly reduce its locking overhead if it knows in advance how a program will access a database during a transaction.

To gain this efficiency, the major IBM mainframe databases added support for the concept of a user-specified isolation level that gives the user control over the trade-off between isolation and processing efficiency. The SQL2 specification formalized the IBM isolation-level concept and expanded it to include four isolation levels, shown in Figure 12-15. The isolation levels are linked directly to the fundamental multiuser update problems discussed earlier in this chapter. As the level of isolation decreases (moving down the rows of the table), the DBMS insulates the user from fewer of the multiuser update problems.

The SERIALIZABLE isolation level is the highest level provided. At this level, the DBMS guarantees that the effects of concurrently executing transactions are exactly the same as if they executed in sequence. This is the default isolation level specified in the ANSI/ISO SQL standard, because it is the way SQL databases are supposed to work. If your program needs to perform the same multirow query twice during a transaction and be guaranteed that the results will be identical regardless of other activity in the database, then it should use the SERIALIZABLE isolation level.

The REPEATABLE READ isolation level is the second highest level. At this level, your transaction is not allowed to see either committed or uncommitted updates from other transactions, so the lost update, uncommitted data, and modified data problems cannot occur. However, a row inserted into the database by another concurrent transaction may become visible during your transaction. As a result, a multirow query run early in your transaction may yield different results than the same query run later in the same transaction (the phantom insert problem). If your program does not depend on the capability to repeat a multirow query during a single transaction, you can safely use the REPEATABLE READ isolation level to improve DBMS performance without sacrificing

Multiuser Update Problem				
Isolation Level	Lost Update	Uncommitted Data	Inconsistent Data	Phantom Insert
SERIALIZABLE	Prevented by DBMS	Prevented by DBMS	Prevented by DBMS	Prevented by DBMS
REPEATABLE READ	Prevented by DBMS	Prevented by DBMS	Prevented by DBMS	Can occur
READ COMMITTED	Prevented by DBMS	Prevented by DBMS	Can occur	Can occur
READ UNCOMMITTED	Prevented by DBMS	Can occur	Can occur	Can occur

Figure 12-15. *Isolation levels and multiuser updates*

data integrity. This is one of the isolation levels supported in the IBM mainframe database products.

The READ COMMITTED isolation level is the third highest level. In this mode, your transaction is not allowed to see uncommitted updates from other transactions, so the lost update and the uncommitted data problems cannot occur. However, updates that are committed by other concurrently executing transactions may become visible during the course of your transaction. Your program could, for example, perform a single-row SELECT statement twice during the course of a transaction and find that the data in the row had been modified by another user. If your program does not depend on the capability to reread a single row of data during a transaction, and it is not accumulating totals or doing other calculations that rely on a self-consistent set of data, it can safely use the READ COMMITTED isolation level. Note that if your program attempts to update a row that has already been updated by another user, your transaction will automatically be rolled back, to prevent the lost update problem from occurring.

The READ UNCOMMITTED isolation level is the lowest level specified in the SQL standard. In this mode, your transaction may be impacted by committed or uncommitted updates from other transactions, so the uncommitted data, modified data, and phantom insert problems can occur. The DBMS still prevents the lost update problem. Generally, the READ UNCOMMITTED level is appropriate only for certain ad hoc query applications where the user can tolerate the fact that the query results may contain dirty data. (Some DBMS brands call this isolation mode a dirty read capability because of this possibility.)

If it is important that query results contain only information that has, in fact, been committed to the database, your program should not use this mode.

The SQL2 standard specifies a SET TRANSACTION statement, shown in Figure 12-16, which is used to set the isolation level of the current transaction. The SET TRANSACTION statement also allows you to specify whether the transaction is READ ONLY (that is, it will only query the database) or READ WRITE (it may query or update the database). The DBMS can use this information, along with the isolation level, to optimize its database processing. The default isolation level is SERIALIZABLE. If the READ UNCOMMITTED isolation level is specified, then READ ONLY is assumed, and you may not specify a READ WRITE transaction. Otherwise, a READ WRITE transaction is the default. These defaults provide for the maximum safety of transactions, at the expense of database performance, but they prevent inexperienced SQL programmers from inadvertently suffering one of the multiuser transaction-processing problems.

Note that the SET TRANSACTION statement specified in the SQL2 standard is an executable SQL statement. It's possible, in fact sometimes very desirable, to have one transaction of a program execute in one mode and have the next transaction execute in a different mode. However, you can't switch isolation levels or read/write modes in the middle of a transaction. The standard effectively requires that the SET TRANSACTION statement be the first statement of a transaction. This means it must be executed as the first statement after a COMMIT or ROLLBACK, or as the first statement of a program, before any other statements affecting the content or structure of a database.

As noted earlier in the "Advanced Locking Techniques" section, many of the commercial DBMS products implemented their own locking and performance-enhancement schemes long before the publication of the SQL2 standard, and these locking strategies affect the heart of the internal database architecture and logic. It's not surprising that the adoption of the SQL2 standard in this area has been relatively slow compared to some other areas where implementation was much easier. For example, the IBM mainframe databases (DB2 and SQL/DS) historically offered a choice of two isolation levels—REPEATABLE READ or READ COMMITTED (called CURSOR STABILITY mode in IBM terminology). In the IBM implementations, the choice is made during the program development process, in the BIND step described in Chapter 17.

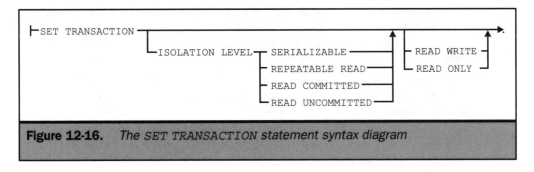

Figure 12-16. *The SET TRANSACTION statement syntax diagram*

UPDATING DATA

Although the modes are not strictly part of the SQL language, the choice of mode strongly impacts how the application performs and how it can use retrieved data.

The Ingres DBMS offers a capability similar to the isolation modes of the IBM databases but provides it in a different form. Using the SET LOCKMODE statement, an application program can tell Ingres which type of locking to use when handling a database query. The options are the following:

- **No locking**. Similar to the IBM CURSOR STABILITY mode just described
- **Shared locking**. Similar to the IBM REPEATABLE READ mode just described
- **Exclusive locking**. Provides exclusive access to the table during the query and offers a capability like the IBM LOCK TABLE statement

The Ingres default is shared locking, which parallels the repeatable read default in the IBM scheme. Note, however, that the Ingres locking modes are set by an executable SQL statement. Unlike the IBM modes, which must be chosen at compile time, the Ingres modes can be chosen when the program executes and can even be changed from one query to the next.

Locking Parameters *

A mature DBMS such as DB2, SQL/DS, Oracle, Informix, Sybase, or SQL Server employs much more complex locking techniques than those described here. The database administrator can improve the performance of these systems by manually setting the locking parameters. Typical parameters that can be tuned include these:

- **Lock size**. Some DBMS products offer a choice of table-level, page-level, row-level, and other lock sizes. Depending on the specific application, a different size lock may be appropriate.

- **Number of locks**. A DBMS typically allows each transaction to have some finite number of locks. The database administrator can often set this limit, raising it to permit more complex transactions or lowering it to encourage earlier lock escalation.

- **Lock escalation**. A DBMS will often automatically escalate locks, replacing many small locks with a single larger lock (for example, replacing many page-level locks with a table-level lock). The database administrator may have some control over this escalation process.

- **Lock timeout**. Even when a transaction is not deadlocked with another transaction, it may wait a very long time for the other transaction to release its locks. Some DBMS brands implement a *timeout* feature, where a SQL statement fails with a SQL error code if it cannot obtain the locks it needs within a certain period of time. The timeout period can usually be set by the database administrator.

Versioning *

The locking techniques described in the preceding sections are the most widely used techniques for supporting concurrent multiuser transaction processing in relational DBMS products. Locking is sometimes called a pessimistic approach to concurrency, because by locking parts of the database, the DBMS is implicitly assuming that concurrent transactions will probably interfere with one another. In recent years, a different approach to concurrency, called *versioning*, has been implemented in some DBMS products and has been increasing in popularity. Versioning is sometimes called an optimistic approach to concurrency because in this approach, the DBMS implicitly assumes that concurrent transactions will not interfere with one another.

With a locking (pessimistic) architecture, the DBMS internally maintains one and only one copy of the data for each row in the database. As multiple users access the database, the locking scheme arbitrates the access to this row of data among the users (more precisely, among their concurrent transactions). In contrast, with a versioning (optimistic) architecture, the DBMS will create two or more copies of the data for a row in the database when a user attempts to update the row. One copy of the row will contain the old data for the row, before the update; the other copy of the row will contain the new data for the row, after the update. The DBMS internally keeps track of which transactions should see which version of the row, depending on their isolation levels.

Versioning in Operation *

Figure 12-17 shows a simple versioning architecture in action. Transaction A starts the action, reading a row of the PRODUCTS table, and finding 139 units of ACI-41004 size 4 widgets available. Transaction B comes along next and updates the same row, reducing the quantity available to 39 units. In response, the DBMS internally creates a new copy of the row. From this point on, if Transaction B rereads the contents of the row, the contents will come from this new copy, since it reflects Transaction B's updated quantity on hand (39 units). Next, Transaction C comes along and tries to read the same row. Because Transaction B's update has not yet been committed, the DBMS gives Transaction C the data from the old copy of the row, showing 139 units available. The same thing happens a few seconds later for Transaction D; it will also see 139 units available. Now Transaction B performs a COMMIT operation, making its update of the row permanent. A short time later, Transaction E attempts to read the row. With Transaction B's update now committed, the DBMS will give Transaction E the data from the new copy, showing 100 units. Finally, Transactions C, D, and E end their database activity with a COMMIT operation.

The activity shown in Figure 12-17 meets the serializability requirement for proper DBMS operation. The sequential transaction series A-C-D-B-E would produce the same results shown in the Figure. (In fact, the series A-D-C-B-E would also produce these results.) Furthermore, the versioning implementation delivers the correct operation without causing any of the transactions to wait. This is not true of the typical locking implementation, as shown in Figure 12-18.

Figure 12-17. Concurrent transactions in a versioning architecture

In Figure 12-18, Transaction A again starts the action, finding 139 units of ACI-41004 widgets available. Internally, the DBMS places a shared lock on the row. Transaction B next tries to update the row, reducing quantity on hand to 39 units. If Transaction A is operating at a strict isolation level (such as REPEATABLE READ), Transaction B will be held at this point, because it cannot acquire the required exclusive lock. If Transaction A is operating at a less strict isolation level, the DBMS can allow Transaction B to proceed, giving it an exclusive lock on the row and actually updating the data. The internal row in the database (recall that there is only a single copy of the row in this locking architecture) now shows 39 units available. When Transaction C comes along, it must wait for Transaction B to release

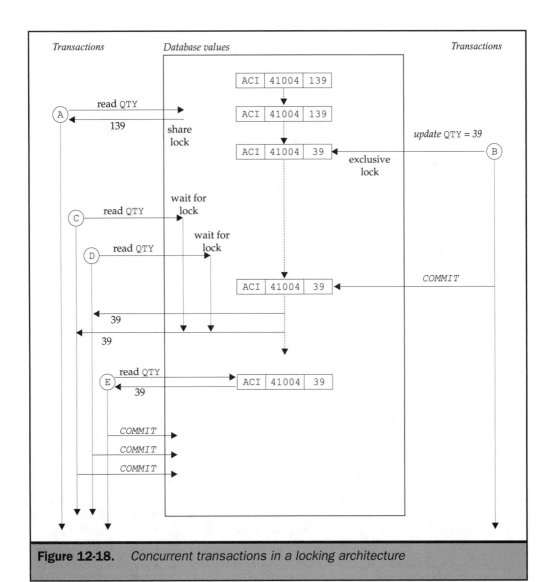

Figure 12-18. *Concurrent transactions in a locking architecture*

its lock unless Transaction C is operating at a very low (READ UNCOMMITTED) isolation level. The same is true of Transaction D. Only after Transaction B has committed its changes can Transactions C and D proceed.

Comparing the operations in Figures 12-17 and 12-18, two differences are worth noting. First, and more fundamentally, the versioning approach in Figure 12-17 allows more concurrent transactions to proceed in parallel. The locking approach in Figure 12-18 will, under most circumstances, cause two or more transactions to wait for others to complete and free their locks. The second, and more subtle, difference is that the effective order of serial transaction execution is different between the two figures. As noted, in Figure 12-17, the transaction sequence A-C-D-B-E produces the results. In Figure 12-18, the sequence A-B-C-D-E produces the results. Note that neither is correct; the serializability principle states only that the results produced by the DBMS must match *some* sequence of serial transactions.

The example in Figure 12-17 includes only one updating transaction, so only two copies of the updated row are required (before and after the update). The versioning architecture is easily extended to support more concurrent updates. For each attempt to update the row, the DBMS can create another new row, reflecting the update. With this multiversioned approach, the task of keeping track of which transactions should see which version of the row obviously becomes more complex. In practice, the decision about which version of the row should be visible to each concurrent transaction depends not only on the sequence of database operations, but also on the isolation levels requested by each of the transactions.

Versioning does not completely eliminate the possibility of deadlocks within the database. The two transactions in Figure 12-13, with their interleaved attempts to update two different tables, each in a different order, will still produce problems, even for a versioning scheme. However, for workloads with a mix of database READ operations and database UPDATE operations, versioning can significantly reduce the locking and lock timeouts or deadlocks associated with shared locks.

Versioning Advantages and Disadvantages *

The advantage of a versioning architecture is that, under the right circumstances, it can significantly increase the number of concurrent transactions that can execute in parallel. Concurrent execution is becoming more and more important in large DBMS installations, especially those that support web sites that may have thousands or tens of thousands of concurrent users. Versioning is also becoming more useful as the number of processors on typical DBMS server computer systems increases. Servers containing 16 or more processors are becoming increasingly common, and large DBMS servers may support 64 or more processors in a symmetric multiprocessing (SMP) configuration. These servers can actually execute many database-access applications in parallel by spreading the workload out over many processors.

The disadvantage of a versioning architecture is the internal DBMS overhead that it creates. One obvious overhead is the added memory requirement of storing two or more copies of rows that are being updated. In practice, a more serious overhead is the memory management required to allocate memory for each temporary copy of a row as it is needed (potentially thousands of times per second), and then releasing the memory to be reused when the older copies of the row are no longer needed. An additional overhead is keeping track of which transactions should see which copies of which rows.

Implicitly, a versioning architecture is based on the underlying assumption that most concurrent transactions will tend not to interfere with one another. If this assumption proves accurate (i.e., if concurrently executing transactions mostly access and update different rows, or if the transaction workload is dominated by READ operations rather than UPDATEs), then the added overhead of the versioning scheme will be more than offset by a significant boost in the amount of parallel work that can be performed. If the assumption proves inaccurate (i.e., if concurrently executing transactions tend to access and update the same rows), then the overhead of the versioning technique will tend to become very high, swamping the concurrency gains.

Summary

This chapter described the transaction mechanism provided by the SQL language:

■ A transaction is a logical unit of work in a SQL-based database. It consists of a sequence of SQL statements that are effectively executed as a single unit by the DBMS.

■ The COMMIT statement signals successful completion of a transaction, making all of its database modifications permanent.

■ The ROLLBACK statement asks the DBMS to abort a transaction, backing out all of its database modifications.

■ Transactions are the key to recovering a database after a system failure; only transactions that were committed at the time of failure remain in the recovered database.

■ Transactions are the key to concurrent access in a multiuser database. A user or program is guaranteed that its transaction will not be interfered with by other concurrent transactions.

■ Occasionally, a conflict with another concurrently executing transaction may cause the DBMS to roll back a transaction through no fault of its own. An application program that uses SQL must be prepared to deal with this situation if it occurs.

■ The subtleties of transaction management, and their impact on DBMS performance, are one of the more complex areas of using and operating a large production database. This is also an area where major DBMS brands diverge in their capabilities and tuning options.

■ Many DBMS brands use locking techniques to handle concurrent transactions. For these products, adjustments to the locking parameters and explicit locking statements allow you to tune transaction-processing performance.

■ An alternative versioning technique for handling concurrent transactions is gaining in popularity. For DBMS products that use versioning, adjustments to the depth of the versioning scheme and to the transaction mix itself are the keys to performance tuning.

The Complete Reference

Part IV

Database Structure

An important role of SQL is to define the structure and organization of a database. Chapters 13–16 describe the SQL features that support this role. Chapter 13 describes how to create a database and its tables. Chapter 14 describes views, an important SQL feature that lets users see alternate organizations of database data. The SQL security features that protect stored data are described in Chapter 15. Finally, Chapter 16 discusses the system catalog, a collection of system tables that describe the structure of a database.

The Complete Reference

Chapter 13

Creating a Database

Many SQL users don't have to worry about creating a database; they use interactive or programmatic SQL to access a database of corporate information or to access some other database that has been created by someone else. In a typical corporate database, for example, the database administrator may give you permission to retrieve and perhaps to update the stored data. However, the administrator will not allow you to create new databases or to modify the structure of the existing tables.

As you grow more comfortable with SQL, you will probably want to start creating your own private tables to store personal data such as engineering test results or sales forecasts. If you are using a multiuser database, you may want to create tables or even entire databases that will be shared with other users. If you are using a personal computer database, you will certainly want to create your own tables and databases to support your personal applications.

This chapter describes the SQL language features that let you create databases and tables and define their structure.

The Data Definition Language

The `SELECT`, `INSERT`, `DELETE`, `UPDATE`, `COMMIT`, and `ROLLBACK` statements described in Parts II and III of this book are all concerned with manipulating the data in a database. These statements collectively are called the SQL *Data Manipulation Language,* or DML. The DML statements can modify the data stored in a database, but they cannot change its structure. None of these statements creates or deletes tables or columns, for example.

Changes to the structure of a database are handled by a different set of SQL statements, usually called the SQL *Data Definition Language,* or DDL. Using DDL statements, you can:

- Define and create a new table
- Remove a table that's no longer needed
- Change the definition of an existing table
- Define a virtual table (or view) of data
- Establish security controls for a database
- Build an index to make table access faster
- Control the physical storage of data by the DBMS

For the most part, the DDL statements insulate you from the low-level details of how data is physically stored in the database. They manipulate abstract database objects, such as tables and columns. However, the DDL cannot avoid physical storage issues entirely, and by necessity, the DDL statements and clauses that control physical storage vary from one DBMS to another.

The core of the Data Definition Language is based on three SQL verbs:

- **CREATE**. Defines and creates a database object
- **DROP**. Removes an existing database object
- **ALTER**. Changes the definition of a database object

In all major SQL-based DBMS products, these three DDL verbs can be used while the DBMS is running. The database structure is thus dynamic. The DBMS can be creating, dropping, or changing the definition of the tables in the database, for example, while it is simultaneously providing access to the database for its users. This is a major advantage of SQL and relational databases over earlier systems, where the DBMS had to be stopped before you could change the structure of the database. It means that a relational database can grow and change easily over time. Production use of a database can continue while new tables and applications are added.

Although the DDL and DML are two distinct parts of the SQL language, in most SQL-based DBMS products, the split is only a conceptual one. Usually, the DDL and DML statements are submitted to the DBMS in exactly the same way, and they can be freely intermixed in both interactive SQL sessions and programmatic SQL applications. If a program or user needs a table to store its temporary results, it can create the table, populate it, manipulate the data, and then delete the table. Again, this is a major advantage over earlier data models, in which the structure of the database was fixed when the database was created.

Although virtually all commercial SQL products support the DDL as an integral part of the SQL language, the SQL1 standard did not require it. In fact, the SQL1 standard implies a strong separation between the DML and the DDL, allowing vendors to achieve compliance with the DML part of the standard through a SQL layer on top of a non-SQL underlying database. The SQL2 standard still differentiates between different types of SQL statements. (It calls the DDL statements SQL-schema statements and the DML statements SQL-data statements and SQL-transaction statements.) However, it brings the standard into alignment with the actual implementation of popular SQL products by requiring that DDL statements be executed interactively and by a program.

The SQL2 standard specifies only the parts of the DDL that are relatively independent of physical storage structures, operating system dependencies, and other DBMS brand-specific capabilities. In practice, all DBMS brands include significant extensions to the standard DDL to deal with these issues and other enhanced database capabilities. The differences between the ANSI/ISO standard and the DDL as implemented in popular SQL products are described for each SQL statement through the remainder of this chapter.

Creating a Database

In a large mainframe or enterprise-level network DBMS installation, the corporate database administrator is solely responsible for creating new databases. On smaller workgroup DBMS installations, individual users may be allowed to create their own personal databases, but it's much more common for databases to be created centrally and then accessed by individual users. If you are using a personal computer DBMS, you are probably both the database administrator and the user, and you will have to create the database(s) that you use personally.

The SQL1 standard specified the SQL language used to describe a database structure, but it did not specify how databases are created, because each DBMS brand had taken a slightly different approach. Those differences persist in present-day mainstream DBMS products. The techniques used by these SQL products illustrate the differences:

- IBM's DB2 has a simple default database structure. A DB2 database is associated with a running copy of the DB2 server software, and users access the database by connecting to the DB2 server. A DB2 "database" is thus effectively defined by an installation of the DB2 software on a particular computer system.

- Oracle, by default, creates a database as part of the Oracle software installation process, like DB2. For the most part, user tables are always placed in this single, systemwide database, which is named by an Oracle configuration file and associated with this particular copy of the Oracle server software. More recent versions of Oracle have been extended with a CREATE DATABASE statement for defining database names.

- Microsoft SQL Server and Sybase include a CREATE DATABASE statement as part of their Data Definition Language. A companion DROP DATABASE statement destroys previously created databases. These statements can be used with interactive or programmatic SQL. The names of these databases are tracked in a special master database that is associated with a single installation of SQL Server. Database names must be unique within this SQL Server installation. Options to the CREATE DATABASE statement specify the physical I/O device on which the database is to be located.

- Informix Universal Server supports CREATE DATABASE and DROP DATABASE SQL statements as well. An option to the CREATE DATABASE statement allows the database to be created in a specific *dbspace*, which is a named area of disk storage controlled by the Informix software. Another option controls the type of database logging to be performed for the new database, with trade-offs between performance and data integrity during system failures.

The SQL2 standard specifically avoids a specification of the term *database* because it is so overloaded with contradictory meanings from DBMS products. SQL2 uses the term *catalog* to describe a named collection of tables that is called a database by most popular DBMS brands. (Additional information about the database structure specified by the SQL2 standard is provided later in the section "Database Structure and the ANSI/ ISO Standard.") The standard does not specify how a catalog is created or destroyed, and specifically says that creation or destruction is implementation dependent. It also indicates how many catalogs there are, and whether individual SQL statements that can access data from different catalogs are implementation defined. In practice, as shown by the preceding examples, many of the major DBMS vendors have moved toward the use of a CREATE DATABASE/DROP DATABASE statement pair.

Table Definitions

The most important structure in a relational database is the table. In a multiuser production database, the major tables are typically created once by the database administrator and then used day after day. As you use the database, you will often find it convenient to define your own tables to store personal data or data extracted from other tables. These tables may be temporary, lasting for only a single interactive SQL session, or more permanent, lasting weeks or months. In a personal computer database, the table structure is even more fluid. Because you are both the user and the database administrator, you can create and destroy tables to suit your own needs, without worrying about other users.

Creating a Table (CREATE TABLE)

The CREATE TABLE statement, shown in Figure 13-1, defines a new table in the database and prepares it to accept data. The various clauses of the statement specify the elements of the table definition. The syntax diagram for the statement appears complex because there are so many parts of the definition to be specified and so many options for each element. In addition, some of the options are available in some DBMS brands or in the SQL2 standard, but not in other brands. In practice, creating a new table is relatively straightforward.

When you execute a CREATE TABLE statement, you become the owner of the newly created table, which is given the name specified in the statement. The table name must be a legal SQL name, and it must not conflict with the name of one of your existing tables. The newly created table is empty, but the DBMS prepares it to accept data added with the INSERT statement.

Column Definitions

The columns of the newly created table are defined in the body of the CREATE TABLE statement. The column definitions appear in a comma-separated list enclosed in parentheses. The order of the column definitions determines the left-to-right order of the columns in the table. In the CREATE TABLE statements supported by the major DBMS brands, each column definition specifies the following:

- **Column name**. Used to refer to the column in SQL statements. Every column in the table must have a unique name, but the names may duplicate those of columns in other tables.

- **Data type**. Identifies the kind of data that the column stores. Data types were discussed in Chapter 5. Some data types, such as VARCHAR and DECIMAL, require additional information, such as the length or number of decimal places in the data. This additional information is enclosed in parentheses following the keyword that specifies the data type.

DATABASE STRUCTURE

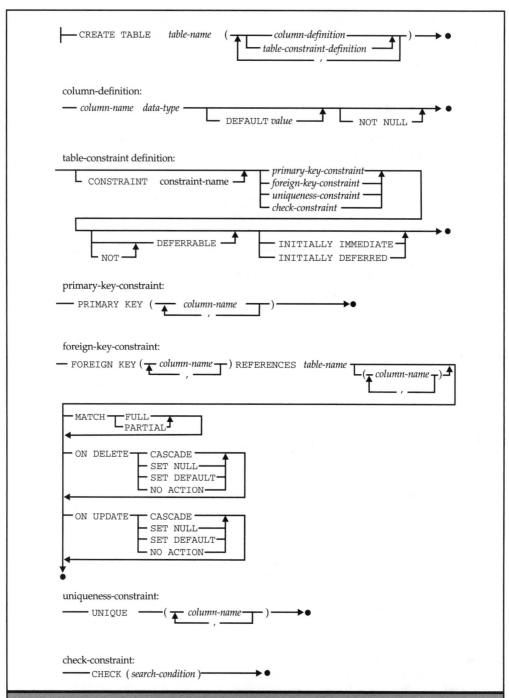

Figure 13-1. *Basic CREATE TABLE syntax diagram*

■ **Required data**. Determines whether the column contains *required data*, and prevents NULL values from appearing in the column; otherwise, NULL values are allowed.

■ **Default value**. Uses an optional *default value* for the column when an INSERT statement for the table does not specify a value for the column.

The SQL2 standard allows several additional parts of a column definition, which can be used to require that the column contains unique values, to specify that the column is a primary key or a foreign key or to restrict the data values that the column may contain. These are single-column versions of capabilities provided by other clauses in the CREATE TABLE statement and are described as part of that statement in the following sections.

Here are some simple CREATE TABLE statements for the tables in the sample database:

Define the OFFICES table and its columns.

```
CREATE TABLE OFFICES
     (OFFICE INTEGER NOT NULL,
        CITY VARCHAR(15) NOT NULL,
      REGION VARCHAR(10) NOT NULL,
         MGR INTEGER,
      TARGET MONEY,
       SALES MONEY NOT NULL)
```

Define the ORDERS table and its columns.

```
CREATE TABLE ORDERS
   (ORDER_NUM INTEGER NOT NULL,
    ORDER_DATE DATE NOT NULL,
         CUST INTEGER NOT NULL,
          REP INTEGER,
          MFR CHAR(3) NOT NULL,
      PRODUCT CHAR(5) NOT NULL,
          QTY INTEGER NOT NULL,
       AMOUNT MONEY NOT NULL)
```

The CREATE TABLE statement for a given table can vary slightly from one DBMS brand to another, because each DBMS supports its own set of data types and uses its own keywords to identify them in the column definitions. In addition, the SQL2 standard allows you to specify a *domain* instead of a data type within a column definition. (Domains were described in Chapter 11.) A domain is a specific collection of valid data values, which is defined within the database and assigned a name. The domain definition is based on one of the DBMS' supported data types but performs additional data-value checking that restricts the legal values. For example, if this domain definition appeared in a SQL2-compliant database:

```
CREATE DOMAIN VALID_OFICE_ID INTEGER
  CHECK (VALUE BETWEEN 11 AND 99)
```

then the OFFICES table definition could be modified to:

Define the OFFICES table and its columns.

```
CREATE TABLE OFFICES
    (OFFICE VALID_OFFICE_ID NOT NULL,
       CITY VARCHAR(15) NOT NULL,
     REGION VARCHAR(10) NOT NULL,
        MGR INTEGER,
     TARGET MONEY,
      SALES MONEY NOT NULL)
```

and the DBMS would automatically check any newly inserted rows to insure that their office numbers fall in the designated range. Domains are particularly effective when the same legal data values restrictions apply to many different columns within the database. In the sample database, office numbers appear in the OFFICES and the SALESREPS table, and the VALID_OFFICE_ID domain would be used to define the columns in both of these tables. In a real-world database, there may be dozens or hundreds of such columns whose data is drawn from the same domain.

Missing and Default Values

The definition of each column within a table tells the DBMS whether the data for the column is allowed to be missing—that is, whether the column is allowed to have a NULL value. In most of the major DBMS brands and in the SQL standard, the default is to allow missing data for a column. If the column must contain a legal data value for every row of a table, then its definition must include the NOT NULL clause. The Sybase DBMS products and Microsoft SQL Server use the opposite convention, assuming that NULL values are not allowed unless the column is explicitly declared NULL or the default nullability mode defined for the database is set to allow NULLs by default.

The SQL2 standard and many of the major SQL DBMS products support default values for columns. If a column has a default value, it is specified within the column definition. For example, here is a CREATE TABLE statement for the OFFICES table that specifies default values:

Define the OFFICES table with default values (ANSI/ISO syntax).

```
CREATE TABLE OFFICES
    (OFFICE INTEGER NOT NULL,
       CITY VARCHAR(15) NOT NULL,
     REGION VARCHAR(10) NOT NULL DEFAULT 'Eastern',
        MGR INTEGER DEFAULT 106,
     TARGET MONEY DEFAULT NULL,
      SALES MONEY NOT NULL DEFAULT 0.00)
```

With this table definition, only the office number and the city need to be specified when you insert a new office. The region defaults to Eastern, the office manager to Sam Clark (employee number 106), the sales to zero, and the target to NULL. Note that the target would default to NULL even without the DEFAULT NULL specification.

Primary and Foreign Key Definitions

In addition to defining the columns of a table, the CREATE TABLE statement identifies the table's primary key and the table's relationships to other tables in the database. The PRIMARY KEY and FOREIGN KEY clauses handle these functions. These clauses have been supported by the IBM SQL databases for some time and have been added to the ANSI/ISO specification. Most major SQL products support them.

The PRIMARY KEY clause specifies the column or columns that form the primary key for the table. Recall from Chapter 4 that this column (or column combination) serves as a unique identifier for each row of the table. The DBMS automatically requires that the primary key value be unique in every row of the table. In addition, the column definition for every column in the primary key must specify that the column is NOT NULL.

The FOREIGN KEY clause specifies a foreign key in the table and the relationship that it creates to another (parent) table in the database. The clause specifies:

- The column or columns that form the foreign key, all of which are columns of the table being created.

- The table that is referenced by the foreign key. This is the parent table in the relationship; the table being defined is the child.

- An optional name for the relationship. The name is not used in any SQL data manipulation statements, but it may appear in error messages and is required if you want to be able to drop the foreign key later.

- How the DBMS should treat a NULL value in one or more columns of the foreign key, when matching it against rows of the parent table.

- An optional delete rule for the relationship (CASCADE, SET NULL, SET DEFAULT, or NO ACTION as described in Chapter 11), which determines the action to take when a parent row is deleted.

■ An optional update rule for the relationship as described in Chapter 11, which determines the action to take when part of the primary key in a parent row is updated.

■ An optional check constraint, which restricts the data in the table so that its rows meet a specified search condition.

Here is an expanded CREATE TABLE statement for the ORDERS table, which includes a definition of its primary key and the three foreign keys that it contains:

Define the ORDERS table with its primary and foreign keys.

```
CREATE TABLE ORDERS
  (ORDER_NUM INTEGER NOT NULL,
  ORDER_DATE DATE NOT NULL,
        CUST INTEGER NOT NULL,
         REP INTEGER,
         MFR CHAR(3) NOT NULL,
     PRODUCT CHAR(5) NOT NULL,
         QTY INTEGER NOT NULL,
      AMOUNT MONEY NOT NULL,
  PRIMARY KEY (ORDER_NUM),
  CONSTRAINT PLACEDBY
  FOREIGN KEY (CUST)
   REFERENCES CUSTOMERS
    ON DELETE CASCADE,
  CONSTRAINT TAKENBY
  FOREIGN KEY (REP)
   REFERENCES SALESREPS
    ON DELETE SET NULL,
  CONSTRAINT ISFOR
  FOREIGN KEY (MFR, PRODUCT)
   REFERENCES PRODUCTS
    ON DELETE RESTRICT)
```

Figure 13-2 shows the three relationships created by this statement and the names it assigns to them. In general, it's a good idea to assign a relationship name, because it helps to clarify the relationship created by the foreign key. For example, each order was placed by the customer whose number appears in the CUST column of the ORDERS table. The relationship created by this column has been given the name PLACEDBY.

When the DBMS processes the CREATE TABLE statement, it checks each foreign key definition against the definition of the table that it references. The DBMS makes sure that the foreign key and the primary key of the referenced table agree in the number of columns they contain and their data types. The referenced table must already be defined in the database for this checking to succeed.

Note that the FOREIGN KEY clause also specifies the delete and update rules that are to be enforced for the parent/child table relationship that it creates. Delete and

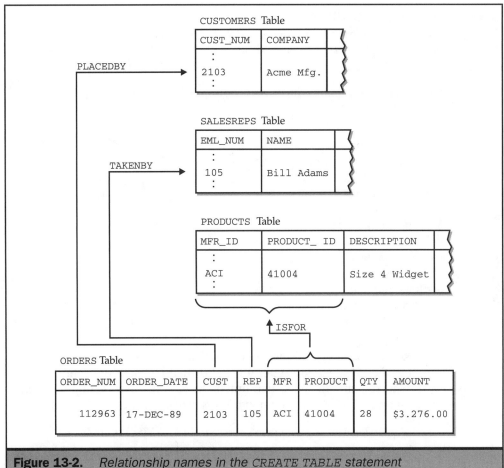

Figure 13-2. *Relationship names in the CREATE TABLE statement*

update rules, and the actions that can trigger them, are described in Chapter 11. The DBMS enforces the default rules (NO ACTION) if no rule is explicitly specified.

If you want to create two or more tables from a referential cycle (like the OFFICES and SALESREPS tables in the sample database), you cannot include the foreign key definition in the first CREATE TABLE statement because the referenced table does not yet exist. The DBMS will reject the attempted CREATE TABLE statement with an error saying that the table definition refers to an undefined table. Instead, you must create the first table without its foreign key definition and add the foreign key later using the ALTER TABLE statement. (The SQL2 standard and several of the major DBMS products offer a different solution to this problem with the CREATE SCHEMA statement, which creates an entire set of tables at once. This statement and the other database objects that are included within a SQL2 schema are described later in the "SQL2 Schemas" section.)

Uniqueness Constraints

The SQL2 standard specifies that uniqueness constraints are also defined in the CREATE TABLE statement, using the UNIQUE clause shown in Figure 13-1. Here is a CREATE TABLE statement for the OFFICES table, modified to require unique CITY values:

Define the OFFICES table with a uniqueness constraint.

```
CREATE TABLE OFFICES
     (OFFICE INTEGER NOT NULL,
         CITY VARCHAR(15) NOT NULL,
       REGION VARCHAR(10) NOT NULL,
         MGR INTEGER,
       TARGET MONEY,
        SALES MONEY NOT NULL,
  PRIMARY KEY (OFFICE),
   CONSTRAINT HASMGR
 FOREIGN KEY (MGR)
   REFERENCES SALESREPS
    ON DELETE SET NULL,
       UNIQUE (CITY))
```

If a primary key, foreign key, uniqueness constraint, or check constraint involves a single column, the ANSI/ISO standard permits a shorthand form of the definition. The primary key, foreign key, uniqueness constraint, or check constraint is simply added to the end of the column definition, as shown in this example:

Define the OFFICES table with a uniqueness constraint (ANSI/ISO syntax).

```
CREATE TABLE OFFICES
     (OFFICE INTEGER NOT NULL PRIMARY KEY,
         CITY VARCHAR(15) NOT NULL UNIQUE,
       REGION VARCHAR(10) NOT NULL,
  MGR INTEGER REFERENCES SALESREPS,
       TARGET MONEY,
        SALES MONEY NOT NULL)
```

Several of the major DBMS brands, including SQL Server, Informix, Sybase, and DB2, support this shorthand.

Check Constraints

Another SQL2 data integrity feature, the check constraint (described in Chapter 11) is also specified in the CREATE TABLE statement. A check constraint specifies a check condition (identical in form to a search condition in a SQL query) that is checked every time an attempt is made to modify the contents of the table (with an INSERT, UPDATE, or DELETE statement). If the check condition remains TRUE after the modification, it is allowed; otherwise, the DBMS disallows the attempt to modify the data and returns an error. The following is a CREATE TABLE statement for the OFFICES table, with a very simple check condition to make sure the TARGET for the office is greater than $0.00.

Define the OFFICES table with a uniqueness constraint.

```
CREATE TABLE OFFICES
     (OFFICE INTEGER NOT NULL,
        CITY VARCHAR(15) NOT NULL,
      REGION VARCHAR(10) NOT NULL,
         MGR INTEGER,
      TARGET MONEY,
       SALES MONEY NOT NULL,
 PRIMARY KEY (OFFICE),
  CONSTRAINT HASMGR
 FOREIGN KEY (MGR)
  REFERENCES SALESREPS
   ON DELETE SET NULL,
       CHECK (TARGET >= 0.00))
```

You can optionally specify a name for the check constraint, which will be used by the DBMS when it reports an error if the constraint is violated. Here is a slightly more complex check constraint for the SALESREPS table to enforce the rule "Salespeople whose hire date is later than January 1, 1988, shall not be assigned quotas higher than $300,000." The CREATE TABLE statement names this constraint QUOTA_CAP:

```
CREATE TABLE SALESREPS
   (EMPL_NUM INTEGER NOT NULL,
        NAME VARCHAR (15) NOT NULL,
        .
        .
        .
  CONSTRAINT WORKSIN
 FOREIGN KEY (REP_OFFICE)
  REFERENCES OFFICES
   ON DELETE SET NULL
  CONSTRAINT QUOTA_CAP CHECK ((HIRE_DATE < "01-JAN-88") OR
                             (QUOTA <= 300000)))
```

This check constraint capability is supported by many of the major DBMS brands.

DATABASE STRUCTURE

Physical Storage Definition *

The CREATE TABLE statement typically includes one or more optional clauses that specify physical storage characteristics for a table. Generally, these clauses are used only by the database administrator to optimize the performance of a production database. By their nature, these clauses are very specific to a particular DBMS. Although they are of little practical interest to most SQL users, the different physical storage structures provided by various DBMS products illustrate their different intended applications and levels of sophistication.

Most of the personal computer databases provide very simple physical storage mechanisms. Many personal computer database products store an entire database within a single Windows file, or use a separate Windows file for each database table. They may also require that the entire table or database be stored on a single physical disk volume.

Multiuser databases typically provide more sophisticated physical storage schemes to support improved database performance. For example, Ingres allows the database administrator to define multiple named *locations*, which are physical directories where database data can be stored. The locations can be spread across multiple disk volumes to take advantage of parallel disk input/output operations. You can optionally specify one or more locations for a table in the Ingres CREATE TABLE statement:

```
CREATE TABLE OFFICES (table-definition)
   WITH LOCATION = (AREA1, AREA2, AREA3)
```

By specifying multiple locations, you can spread a table's contents across several disk volumes for greater parallel access to the table.

Sybase offers a similar approach, allowing the database administrator to specify multiple named *logical database devices* that are used to store data. The correspondence between Sybase's logical devices and the actual physical disk drives of the computer system is handled by a Sybase utility program, and not within the SQL language. The Sybase CREATE DATABASE statement can then specify that a database should be stored on one or more database devices:

```
CREATE DATABASE OPDATA
    ON DBFILE1, DBFILE2, DBFILE3
```

Within a given database device, Sybase then allows the database administrator to define logical *segments,* using one of the Sybase system-provided stored procedures. Finally, a Sybase CREATE TABLE statement can specify the segment where a table's data is to be stored:

```
CREATE TABLE OFFICES (table-definition)
    ON SEGMENT SEG1A
```

DB2 offers a similarly comprehensive scheme for managing physical storage, based on the concepts of *tablespaces* and *nodegroups*. A tablespace is a logical-level storage container, whereas nodegroups are defined more specifically in terms of physical storage. When you create a DB2 table, you can optionally assign it to a specific tablespace:

```
CREATE TABLE OFFICES (table-definition)
    IN ADMINDB.OPSPACE
```

Unlike Sybase, DB2 puts most of the management of these storage entities within the SQL language itself, through the CREATE TABLESPACE and CREATE NODEGROUP statements. A consequence is that these statements include operating system–dependent specifications of filenames and directories, which vary from one supported DB2 operating system to another. Other clauses specify the DB2 buffer pool to be used, the overhead and transfer rate of the storage medium, and other characteristics closely related to the physical storage medium. DB2 uses this information in its performance optimization algorithms.

Removing a Table (DROP TABLE)

Over time, the structure of a database grows and changes. New tables are created to represent new entities, and some old tables are no longer needed. You can remove an unneeded table from the database with the DROP TABLE statement, shown in Figure 13-3.

The table name in the statement identifies the table to be dropped. Normally, you will be dropping one of your own tables and will use an unqualified table name. With proper permission, you can also drop a table owned by another user by specifying a qualified table name. Here are some examples of the DROP TABLE statement:

The CUSTOMERS table has been replaced by two new tables, CUST_INFO and ACCOUNT_INFO, and is no longer needed.

```
DROP TABLE CUSTOMERS
```

Sam gives you permission to drop his table, named BIRTHDAYS.

```
DROP TABLE SAM.BIRTHDAYS
```

When the DROP TABLE statement removes a table from the database, its definition and all of its contents are lost. There is no way to recover the data, and you would have

Figure 13-3. *DROP TABLE statement syntax diagram*

to use a new CREATE TABLE statement to recreate the table definition. Because of its serious consequences, you should use the DROP TABLE statement with care.

The SQL2 standard requires that a DROP TABLE statement include either CASCADE or RESTRICT, which specifies the impact of dropping a table on other database objects (such as views, described in Chapter 14) that depend on the table. If CASCADE is specified, the DROP TABLE statement fails if other database objects reference the table. Most commercial DBMS products accept the DROP TABLE statement with no option specified.

Changing a Table Definition (ALTER TABLE)

After a table has been in use for some time, users often discover that they want to store additional information about the entities represented in the table. In the sample database, for example, you might want to:

■ Add the name and phone number of a key contact person to each row of the CUSTOMERS table, as you begin to use it for contacting customers

■ Add a minimum inventory-level column to the PRODUCTS table, so the database can automatically alert you when stock of a particular product is low

■ Make the REGION column in the OFFICES table a foreign key for a newly created REGIONS table, whose primary key is the region name

■ Drop the foreign key definition linking the CUST column in the ORDERS table to the CUSTOMERS table, replacing it with two foreign key definitions linking the CUST column to the newly created CUST_INFO and ACCOUNT_INFO tables

Each of these changes, and some others, can be handled with the ALTER TABLE statement, shown in Figure 13-4. As with the DROP TABLE statement, you will normally use the ALTER TABLE statement on one of your own tables. With proper permission, however, you can specify a qualified table name and alter the definition of another user's table. As shown in the figure, the ALTER TABLE statement can:

■ Add a column definition to a table

■ Drop a column from a table

■ Change the default value for a column

■ Add or drop a primary key for a table

■ Add or drop a new foreign key for a table

■ Add or drop a uniqueness constraint for a table

■ Add or drop a check constraint for a table

The clauses in Figure 13-4 are specified in the SQL standard. Many DBMS brands lack support for some of these clauses or offer clauses unique to the DBMS, which alters other table characteristics. The SQL2 standard restricts each ALTER TABLE statement to a single table change. To add a column and define a new foreign key, for

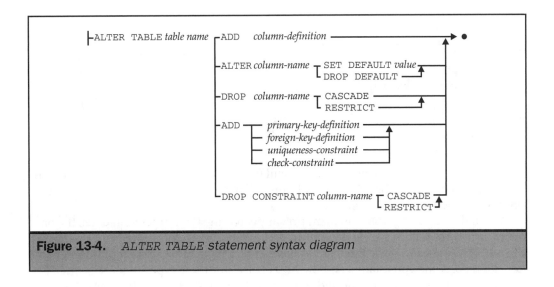

Figure 13-4.   *ALTER TABLE statement syntax diagram*

example, requires two separate ALTER TABLE statements. Several DBMS brands relax this restriction and allow multiple action clauses in a single ALTER TABLE statement.

Adding a Column

The most common use of the ALTER TABLE statement is to add a column to an existing table. The column definition clause in the ALTER TABLE statement is just like the one in the CREATE TABLE statement, and it works the same way. The new column is added to the end of the column definitions for the table, and it appears as the rightmost column in subsequent queries. The DBMS normally assumes a NULL value for a newly added column in all existing rows of the table. If the column is declared to be NOT NULL with a default value, the DBMS instead assumes the default value.

Note that you cannot simply declare the new column NOT NULL, because the DBMS would assume NULL values for the column in the existing rows, immediately violating the constraint! (When you add a new column, the DBMS doesn't actually go through all of the existing rows of the table adding a NULL or default value. Instead, it detects the fact that an existing row is too short for the new table definition when the row is retrieved, and extends it with a NULL or default value before displaying it or passing it to your program.)

Some sample ALTER TABLE statements that add new columns are:

Add a contact name and phone number to the CUSTOMERS table.

```
ALTER TABLE CUSTOMERS
  ADD CONTACT_NAME VARCHAR(30)
```

DATABASE STRUCTURE

```
ALTER TABLE CUSTOMERS
   ADD CONTACT_PHONE CHAR(10)
```

Add a minimum inventory-level column to the PRODUCTS table.

```
ALTER TABLE PRODUCTS
   ADD MIN_QTY INTEGER NOT NULL WITH DEFAULT 0
```

In the first example, the new columns will have NULL values for existing customers. In the second example, the MIN_QTY column will have the value zero (0) for existing products, which is appropriate.

When the ALTER TABLE statement first appeared in SQL implementations, the only major structures within a table were the column definitions, and it was very clear what the ADD clause meant. Since then, tables have grown to include primary and foreign key definitions and constraints, and the ADD clauses for these types of objects specify which type of object is being added. For consistency with these other ADD/DROP clauses, the SQL2 standard includes the optional keyword COLUMN after the keyword ADD. With this addition, the preceding example becomes:

Add a minimum inventory-level column to the PRODUCTS table.

```
ALTER TABLE PRODUCTS
   ADD COLUMN MIN_QTY INTEGER NOT NULL WITH DEFAULT 0
```

Dropping a Column

The ALTER TABLE statement can be used to drop one or more columns from an existing table when they are no longer needed. Here is an example that drops the HIRE_DATE column from the SALESREPS table:

Drop a column from the SALESREPS table.

```
ALTER TABLE SALESREPS
 DROP HIRE_DATE
```

The SQL2 standard forces you to issue a separate ALTER TABLE statement if you want to drop several columns, but several of the major DBMS brands allow you to drop multiple columns with a single statement.

Note that dropping a column can pose the same kinds of data-integrity issues that were described in Chapter 11 for database update operations. For example, if you drop a column that is a primary key in some relationship, the foreign key columns that refer to the dropped column become invalid. A similar problem can arise if you drop a column that is referenced in a check constraint—the column that provides the data value for checking the constraint is now gone. A similar problem is created in views that are defined based on the dropped column.

The SQL2 standard deals with these issues the same way it handled the potential data-integrity problems posed by DELETE and UPDATE statements—with a *drop rule* (actually called a *drop behavior* in the standard) that operates just like the delete rules and update rules. You can specify one of two drop rules:

- **RESTRICT**. If any other objects in the database (foreign keys, constraints, and so on) depend on the column to be dropped, the ALTER TABLE statement fails with an error and the column is not dropped.

- **CASCADE**. Any other objects in the database (foreign keys, constraints, and so on) that depend on the column are *also* dropped as a cascaded effect of the ALTER TABLE statement.

The CASCADE effect can cause quite dramatic changes in the database; therefore, use it with care. It's usually a better idea to use the RESTRICT mode (explicitly drop the dependent foreign keys and constraints, using the appropriate ALTER or DROP statements) before dropping the column.

Changing Primary and Foreign Keys

The other common use for the ALTER TABLE statement is to change or add primary key and foreign key definitions for a table. Since primary key and foreign key support is being provided in new releases of several SQL-based database systems, this form of the ALTER TABLE statement is particularly useful. It can be used to inform the DBMS about intertable relationships that already exist in a database, but which have not been explicitly specified before.

Unlike column definitions, primary key and foreign key definitions can be added *and* dropped from a table with the ALTER TABLE statement. The clauses that add primary key and foreign key definitions are exactly the same as those in the CREATE TABLE statement, and they work the same way. The clauses that drop a primary key or foreign key are straightforward, as shown in the following examples. Note that you can drop a foreign key only if the relationship that it creates was originally assigned a name. If the relationship was unnamed, there is no way to specify it in the ALTER TABLE statement. In this case, you cannot drop the foreign key unless you drop and re-create the table, using the procedure described for dropping a column.

Here is an example that adds a foreign key definition to an existing table:

Make the REGION column in the OFFICES table a foreign key for the newly created REGIONS table, whose primary key is the region name.

```
   ALTER TABLE OFFICES
ADD CONSTRAINT INREGION
   FOREIGN KEY (REGION)
     REFERENCES REGIONS
```

Here is an example of an ALTER TABLE statement that modifies a primary key. Note that the foreign key corresponding to the original primary key must be dropped because it is no longer a foreign key for the altered table:

Change the primary key of the OFFICES table.

```
ALTER TABLE SALESREPS
        DROP CONSTRAINT WORKSIN
FOREIGN KEY (REP_OFFICE)
  REFERENCES OFFICES


ALTER TABLE OFFICES
        DROP PRIMARY KEY (CITY)
```

Constraint Definitions

The tables in a database define its basic structure, and in most early commercial SQL products, the table definitions were the only specification of database structure. With the advent of primary key/foreign key support in DB2 and in the SQL2 standard, the definition of database structure was expanded to include the *relationships* among the tables in a database. More recently, through the SQL2 standard and the evolution of commercial products, the definition of database structure has expanded to include a new area—database constraints that restrict the data that can be entered into the database. The types of constraints, and the role that they play in maintaining database integrity, are described in Chapter 11.

Four types of database constraints (uniqueness constraints, primary and foreign key constraints, and check constraints) are closely associated with a single database table. They are specified as part of the CREATE TABLE statement and can be modified or dropped using the ALTER TABLE statement. The other two types of database integrity constraints, assertions and domains, are created as stand-alone objects within a database, independent of any individual table definition.

Assertions

An *assertion* is a database constraint that restricts the contents of the database as a whole. Like a check constraint, an assertion is specified as a search condition. But unlike a check constraint, the search condition in an assertion can restrict the contents of multiple tables and the data relationships among them. For that reason, an assertion is specified as part of the overall database definition, via a SQL2 CREATE ASSERTION statement. Suppose you wanted to restrict the contents of the sample database so that the total orders for any given customer may not exceed that customer's credit limit. You can implement that restriction with the statement:

```
CREATE ASSERTION CREDLIMIT
        CHECK ((CUSTOMERS.CUST_NUM = ORDERS.CUST) AND
               (SUM (AMOUNT) <= CREDIT_LIMIT))
```

With the assertion named CREDLIMIT as part of the database definition, the DBMS is required to check that the assertion remains true each time a SQL statement attempts to modify the CUSTOMER or ORDERS tables. If you later determine that the assertion is no longer needed, you can drop it using the DROP ASSERTION statement:

```
DROP ASSERTION CREDLIMIT
```

There is no SQL2 ALTER ASSERTION statement. To change an assertion definition, you must drop the old definition and then specify the new one with a new CREATE ASSERTION statement.

Domains

The SQL2 standard implements the formal concept of a domain as a part of a database definition. As described in Chapter 11, a domain is a named collection of data values that effectively functions as an additional data type, for use in database definitions. A domain is created with a CREATE DOMAIN statement. Once created, the domain can be referenced as if it were a data type within a column definition. Here is a CREATE DOMAIN statement to define a domain named VALID_EMPL_IDS, which consists of valid employee identification numbers in the sample database. These numbers are three-digit integers in the range 101 to 999, inclusive:

```
CREATE DOMAIN VALID_EMPL_IDS INTEGER
  CHECK (VALUE BETWEEN 101 AND 199)
```

If a domain is no longer needed, you can drop it using one of the forms of the SQL2 DROP DOMAIN statement:

```
DROP DOMAIN VALID_EMPL_IDS CASCADE
```

```
DROP DOMAIN VALID_EMPL_IDS RESTRICT
```

The CASCADE and RESTRICT drop rules operate just as they do for dropped columns. If CASCADE is specified, any column defined in terms of the dropped domain will also be automatically dropped from the database. If RESTRICT is specified, the attempt to drop the domain will fail if any column definitions are based on it. You must first drop or alter the column definitions so that they no longer depend on the domain before dropping it. This provides an extra margin of safety against accidentally dropping columns (and more importantly, the data that they contain).

Aliases and Synonyms (CREATE/DROP ALIAS)

Production databases are often organized like the copy of the sample database shown in Figure 13-5, with all of their major tables collected together and owned by the database administrator. The database administrator gives other users permission to access the tables, using the SQL security scheme described in Chapter 15. Recall, however, that you must use qualified table names to refer to another user's tables. In practice, this means that *every* query against the major tables in Figure 13-5 must use qualified table names, which makes queries like the following one long and tedious to type:

List the name, sales, office, and office sales for everyone.

```
SELECT NAME, OP_ADMIN.SALESREPS.SALES, OFFICE,
OP_ADMIN.OFFICES.SALES
  FROM OP_ADMIN.SALESREPS, OP_ADMIN.OFFICES
```

To address this problem, many SQL DBMS products provide an *alias* or *synonym* capability. A synonym is a name that you define that stands for the name of some other table. In DB2, you create an alias using the CREATE ALIAS statement. (Older versions of DB2 actually used a CREATE SYNONYM statement, and Oracle still uses this form of the statement, but it has the same effect as the CREATE ALIAS statement.) If you were

Figure 13-5. *Typical organization of a production database*

the user named George in Figure 13-5, for example, you might use this pair of CREATE ALIAS statements:

Create synonyms for two tables owned by another user.

```
CREATE ALIAS REPS
   FOR OP_ADMIN.SALESREPS

CREATE ALIAS OFFICES
   FOR OP_ADMIN.OFFICES
```

Once you have defined a synonym or alias, you can use it just like a table name in SQL queries. The previous query thus becomes:

```
SELECT NAME, REPS.SALES, OFFICE, OFFICES.SALES
   FROM REPS, OFFICES
```

The use of aliases doesn't change the meaning of the query, and you must still have permission to access the other users' tables. Nonetheless, synonyms simplify the SQL statements you use and make it appear as if the tables were your own. If you decide later that you no longer want to use the synonyms, they can be removed with the DROP ALIAS statement:

Drop the synonyms created earlier.

```
DROP ALIAS REPS

DROP ALIAS OFFICES
```

Synonyms or aliases are supported by DB2, Oracle, and Informix. They are not specified by the ANSI/ISO SQL standard.

Indexes (CREATE/DROP INDEX)

One of the physical storage structures that is provided by most SQL-based database management systems is an *index*, which is a structure that provides rapid access to the rows of a table based on the values of one or more columns. Figure 13-6 shows the PRODUCTS table and two indexes that have been created for it. One of the indexes

Figure 13-6. *Two indexes on the* PRODUCTS *table*

provides access based on the DESCRIPTION column. The other provides access based on the primary key of the table, which is a combination of the MFR_ID and PRODUCT_ID columns.

The DBMS uses the index as you might use the index of a book. The index stores data values and pointers to the rows where those data values occur. In the index the data values are arranged in ascending or descending order, so that the DBMS can quickly search the index to find a particular value. It can then follow the pointer to locate the row containing the value.

The presence or absence of an index is completely transparent to the SQL user who accesses a table. For example, consider this SELECT statement:

Find the quantity and price for size 4 widgets.

```
SELECT QTY_ON_HAND, PRICE
  FROM PRODUCTS
 WHERE DESCRIPTION = 'Size 4 Widget'
```

The statement doesn't say whether there is an index on the DESCRIPTION column, and the DBMS will carry out the query in either case.

If there were no index for the DESCRIPTION column, the DBMS would be forced to process the query by sequentially scanning the PRODUCTS table, row by row, examining the DESCRIPTION column in each row. To make sure it had found all of the rows that satisfied the search condition, it would have to examine *every* row in the table. For a large table with thousands or millions of rows, the scan of the table could take minutes or hours.

With an index for the DESCRIPTION column, the DBMS can locate the requested data with much less effort. It searches the index to find the requested value ("Size 4 widget") and then follows the pointer to find the requested row(s) of the table. The index search is very rapid because the index is sorted and its rows are very small. Moving from the index to the row(s) is also very rapid because the index tells the DBMS where on the disk the row(s) are located.

As this example shows, the advantage of having an index is that it greatly speeds the execution of SQL statements with search conditions that refer to the indexed column(s). One disadvantage of having an index is that it consumes additional disk space. Another disadvantage is that the index must be updated every time a row is added to the table and every time the indexed column is updated in an existing row. This imposes additional overhead on INSERT and UPDATE statements for the table.

In general, it's a good idea to create an index for columns that are used frequently in search conditions. Indexing is also more appropriate when queries against a table are more frequent than inserts and updates. Most DBMS products *always* establish an index for the primary key of a table, because they anticipate that access to the table will most frequently be via the primary key.

Most DBMS products also automatically establish an index for any column (or column combination) defined with a uniqueness constraint. The DBMS must check the value of such a column in any new row to be inserted, or in any update to an existing row, to make certain that the value does not duplicate a value already contained in the table. Without an index on the column(s), the DBMS would have to sequentially search through every row of the table to check the constraint. With an index, the DBMS can simply use the index to find a row (if it exists) with the value in question, which is a much faster operation than a sequential search.

In the sample database, these columns are good candidates for additional indexes:

- The COMPANY column in the CUSTOMERS table should be indexed if customer data is often retrieved by company name.

- The NAME column in the SALESREPS table should be indexed if data about salespeople is often retrieved by salesperson name.

DATABASE STRUCTURE

- The REP column in the ORDERS table should be indexed if orders are frequently retrieved based on the salesperson who took them.

- The CUST column in the ORDERS table should similarly be indexed if orders are frequently retrieved based on the customer who placed them.

- The MFR and PRODUCT columns, together, in the ORDERS table should be indexed if orders are frequently retrieved based on the product ordered.

The SQL2 standard doesn't talk about indexes or how to create them. It treats database indexes as an implementation detail, which is outside of the core, standardized SQL language. However, the use of indexes is essential to achieve adequate performance in any sizeable enterprise-class database.

In practice, most popular DBMS brands (including Oracle, Microsoft SQL Server, Informix, Sybase, and DB2) support indexes through some form of the CREATE INDEX statement, shown in Figure 13-7. The statement assigns a name to the index and specifies the table for which the index is created. The statement also specifies the column(s) to be indexed and whether they should be indexed in ascending or descending order. The DB2 version of the CREATE INDEX statement, shown in Figure 13-7, is the most straightforward. Its only option is the keyword UNIQUE, which is used to specify that the combination of columns being indexed must contain a unique value for every row of the table.

The following is an example of a CREATE INDEX statement that builds an index for the ORDERS table based on the MFR and PRODUCT columns and that requires combinations of columns to have a unique value.

Create an index for the ORDERS table.

```
CREATE UNIQUE INDEX ORD_PROD_IDX
    ON ORDERS (MFR, PRODUCT)
```

Figure 13-7. *Basic CREATE INDEX statement syntax diagram*

In most major DBMS products, the CREATE INDEX statement includes additional DBMS-specific clauses that specify the disk location for the index and for performance-tuning parameters. Typical performance parameters include the size of the index pages, the percentage of free space that the index should allow for new rows, the type of index to be created, whether it should be clustered (an arrangement that places the physical data rows on the disk medium in the same sequence as the index), and so on. These options make the CREATE INDEX statement quite DBMS-specific in actual use.

Some DBMS products support two or more different types of indexes, which are optimized for different types of database access. For example, a *B-tree* index uses a tree structure of index entries and index blocks (groups of index entries) to organize the data values that it contains into ascending or descending order. This type of index provides efficient searching for a single value or for a range of values, such as the search required for an inequality comparison operator or a range test (BETWEEN) operation.

A different type of index, a hash index, uses a randomizing technique to place all of the possible data values into a moderate number of buckets within the index. For example, if there are 10,000,000 possible data values, an index with 500 hash buckets might be appropriate. Since a given data value is always placed into the same bucket, the DBMS can search for that value simply by locating the appropriate bucket and searching within it. With 500 buckets, the number of items to be searched is reduced, on average, by a factor of 500. This makes hash indexes very fast when searching for an exact match of a data value. But the assignment of values to buckets does not preserve the order of data values, so a hash index cannot be used for inequality or range searches.

Other types of indexes are appropriate for other specific DBMS situations. For example, a variation of the B-tree index, known as a *T-tree* index, is optimized for in-memory databases. A *bit-map* index is useful when there is a relatively small number of possible data values. When a DBMS supports multiple index types, the CREATE INDEX statement not only defines and creates the index, but defines its type as well.

If you create an index for a table and later decide that it is not needed, the DROP INDEX statement removes the index from the database. The statement removes the index created in the previous example:

Drop the index created earlier.

```
DROP INDEX ORD_PROD_IDX
```

Managing Other Database Objects

The CREATE, DROP, and ALTER verbs form the cornerstone of the SQL Data Definition Language. Statements based on these verbs are used in all SQL implementations to manipulate tables, indexes, and views (described in Chapter 14). Most of the popular SQL-based DBMS products also use these verbs to form additional DDL statements that create, destroy, and modify other database objects unique to that particular brand of DBMS.

DATABASE STRUCTURE

The Sybase DBMS, for example, pioneered the use of triggers and stored procedures, which are treated as objects within a SQL database, along with its tables, assertions, indexes, and other structures. Sybase added the CREATE TRIGGER and CREATE PROCEDURE statements to its SQL dialect to define these new database structures, and the corresponding DROP statements to delete them when no longer needed. As these features became popular, other DBMS products added the capabilities, along with their own variants of the CREATE TRIGGER and CREATE PROCEDURE statements.

The common conventions across DBMS brands is (a) the use of the CREATE/DROP/ALTER verbs, (b) the next word in the statement is the type of object being managed, and (c) the third word is the name of the object, which must obey SQL naming conventions. Beyond the first three words, the statements become very DBMS-specific and nonstandard. Nonetheless, this commonality gives a uniform feel to the various SQL dialects. At the very least, it tells you where to look in the reference manual for a description of a new capability. If you encounter a new SQL-based DBMS and know that it supports an object known as a BLOB, the odds are that it uses CREATE BLOB, DROP BLOB, and ALTER BLOB statements. Table 13-1 shows how some of the popular SQL products use the CREATE, DROP, and ALTER verbs in their expanded DDL. The SQL2 standard adopts this same convention to deal with the creation, destruction, and modification of all objects in a SQL2 database.

SQL DDL Statements	Managed Object
Supported by almost all DBMS brands	
CREATE/DROP/ALTER TABLE	Table
CREATE/DROP/ALTER VIEW	View
CREATE/DROP/ALTER	INDEX
Supported by DB2	
CREATE/DROP ALIAS	Alias for a table or view
CREATE/DROP/ALTER BUFFERPOOL	Collection of I/O buffers used by DB2
CREATE/DROP DISTINCT TYPE	Distinct user-defined data type
CREATE/DROP FUNCTION	User-defined function
CREATE/DROP/ALTER NODEGROUP	Group of database partitions or nodes
DROP PACKAGE	DB2 program access module
CREATE/DROP PROCEDURE	User-defined DB2 stored procedure
CREATE/DROP SCHEMA	Database schema

Table 13-1. *DDL Statements in Popular SQL-Based Products*

SQL DDL Statements	Managed Object
CREATE/DROP/ALTER TABLESPACE	Tablespace (storage area for DB2 data)
CREATE/DROP TRIGGER	Database trigger
Supported by Informix	
CREATE/DROP CAST	Cast for converting data types
CREATE/DROP DATABASE	Named Informix database
CREATE/DROP DISTINCT TYPE	Distinct user-defined data type
CREATE/DROP FUNCTION	User-defined function
CREATE/DROP OPAQUE TYPE	User-defined opaque data type
CREATE/DROP OPCLASS	User-defined disk storage access method
CREATE/DROP PROCEDURE	User-defined Informix stored procedure
CREATE/DROP ROLE	User role within the database
CREATE/DROP ROUTINE	User-defined Informix stored procedure
CREATE/DROP ROW TYPE	Named row type (object extension)
CREATE SCHEMA	Database schema
CREATE/DROP SYNONYM	Synonym (alias) for table or view
CREATE/DROP TRIGGER	Database trigger
Supported by Microsoft SQL Server	
CREATE/DROP/ALTER DATABASE	Database
CREATE/DROP DEFAULT	Default column value
CREATE/DROP/ALTER PROCEDURE	SQL Server stored procedure
CREATE/DROP RULE	Column integrity rule
CREATE SCHEMA	Database schema
CREATE/DROP/ALTER TRIGGER	Stored trigger
Supported by Oracle	
CREATE/DROP CLUSTER	Cluster of tables for performance tuning
CREATE DATABASE	Named Oracle database
CREATE/DROP DATABASE LINK	Network link for remote table access

Table 13-1.   *DDL Statements in Popular SQL-Based Products* (continued)

SQL DDL Statements	Managed Object
CREATE/DROP DIRECTORY	O/S directory for large object storage
CREATE/DROP/ALTER FUNCTION	User-defined function
CREATE/DROP LIBRARY	External functions callable from PL/SQL
CREATE/DROP/ALTER PACKAGE	Group of sharable PL/SQL procedures
CREATE/DROP/ALTER PROCEDURE	User-defined Oracle stored procedure
CREATE/DROP/ALTER PROFILE	Limits on database resource usage
CREATE/DROP/ALTER ROLE	User role within the database
CREATE/DROP/ALTER ROLLBACK SEGMENT	Storage area for database recovery
CREATE SCHEMA	Database schema
CREATE/DROP/ALTER SEQUENCE	User-defined value sequence
CREATE/DROP/ALTER SNAPSHOT	Table of read-only query results
CREATE/DROP SYNONYM	Synonym (alias) for table or view
CREATE/DROP/ALTER TABLESPACE	Tablespace (storage area for Oracle data)
CREATE/DROP/ALTER TRIGGER	Database trigger
CREATE/DROP TYPE	User-defined abstract data type
CREATE/DROP TYPE BODY	Methods for an abstract data type
CREATE/DROP/ALTER USER	Oracle user-id
Supported by Sybase	
CREATE/DROP/ALTER DATABASE	Database
CREATE/DROP DEFAULT	Default column value
CREATE EXISTING TABLE	Local copy of existing remote table
CREATE/DROP PROCEDURE	Sybase stored procedure
CREATE/DROP/ALTER ROLE	User role within the database
CREATE/DROP RULE	Column integrity rule
CREATE SCHEMA	Database schema
CREATE/DROP TRIGGER	Stored trigger

Table 13-1.   *DDL Statements in Popular SQL-Based Products* (continued)

SQL DDL Statements	Managed Object
Specified by the ANSI/ISO SQL standard	
CREATE/DROP ASSERTION	Schemawide check constraint
CREATE/DROP CHARACTER SET	Extended character set
CREATE/DROP COLLATION	Sorting sequence for character set
CREATE/DROP/ALTER DOMAIN	Specification of valid data values
CREATE/DROP SCHEMA	Database schema
CREATE/DROP TRANSLATION	Conversion between character sets

Table 13-1. *DDL Statements in Popular SQL-Based Products* (continued)

Database Structure

The SQL1 standard specified a simple structure for the contents of a database, shown in Figure 13-8. Each user of the database has a collection of tables that are owned by that user. Virtually all major DBMS products support this scheme, although some (particularly those focused on special-purpose or embedded applications or personal computer usage) do not support the concept of table ownership. In these systems, all of the tables in a database are part of one large collection.

Although different brands of SQL-based database management systems provide the same structure within a single database, there is wide variation in how they organize and

Figure 13-8. *SQL1 organization of a database*

structure the various databases on a particular computer system. Some brands assume a single systemwide database that stores all of the data on that system. Other DBMS brands support multiple databases on a single computer, with each database identified by name. Still other DBMS brands support multiple databases within the context of the computer's directory system.

These variations don't change the way you use SQL to access the data within a database. However, they do affect the way you organize your data—for example, do you mix order processing and accounting data in one database, or do you divide it into two databases? They also affect the way you initially gain access to the database—for example, if there are multiple databases, you need to tell the DBMS which one you want to use. To illustrate how various DBMS brands deal with these issues, suppose the sample database were expanded to support a payroll and an accounting application, in addition to the order-processing tasks it now supports.

Single-Database Architecture

Figure 13-9 shows a single-database architecture where the DBMS supports one systemwide database. Mainframe and minicomputer databases (such as the mainframe version of DB2 and Oracle) have historically tended to use this approach. Order processing, accounting, and payroll data are all stored in tables within the database. The major tables for each application are gathered together and owned by a single user, who is probably the person in charge of that application on this computer.

An advantage of this architecture is that the tables in the various applications can easily reference one another. The TIMECARDS table of the payroll application, for example, can contain a foreign key that references the OFFICES table, and the applications can use that

Figure 13-9. *A single-database architecture*

relationship to calculate commissions. With proper permission, users can run queries that combine data from the various applications.

A disadvantage of this architecture is that the database will grow huge over time as more and more applications are added to it. A DB2 or Oracle database with several hundred tables is common. The problems of managing a database of that size—performing backups, recovering data, analyzing performance, and so on—usually require a full-time database administrator.

In the single-database architecture, gaining access to the database is very simple—there's only one database, so no choices need to be made. For example, the programmatic SQL statement that connects you to an Oracle database is CONNECT, and users tend to speak in terms of connecting to Oracle, rather than connecting to a specific database. (In fact, in this architecture, the database is usually associated with a single running copy of the DBMS software, so in a very real sense, the user is connecting to the DBMS.)

Oracle and DB2 installations frequently do run two separate databases, one for production work and one for testing. Fundamentally, however, all production data is collected into a single database.

Multidatabase Architecture

Figure 13-10 shows a multidatabase architecture where each database is assigned a unique name. Sybase, Microsoft SQL Server, Ingres, and many others use this scheme. As shown in the figure, each of the databases in this architecture is usually dedicated to a particular application. When you add a new application, you will probably create a new database.

The main advantage of the multidatabase architecture over the single-database architecture is that it divides the data management tasks into smaller, more manageable pieces. Each person responsible for an application can now be the database administrator of his or her own database, with less worry about overall coordination. When it's time to add a new application, it can be developed in its own database, without disturbing the existing databases. Users and programmers are also more likely to remember the overall structure of their own databases.

The main disadvantage of the multidatabase architecture is that the individual databases may become islands of information, unconnected to one another. Typically, a table in one database cannot contain a foreign key reference to a table in a different database. Often, the DBMS does not support queries across database boundaries, making it impossible to relate data from two applications. If cross-database queries are supported, they may impose substantial overhead or require the purchase of additional distributed DBMS software from the DBMS vendor.

If a DBMS uses a multidatabase architecture and supports queries across databases, it must extend the SQL table and column naming conventions. A qualified table name must specify not only the owner of the table, but also which database contains the

DATABASE STRUCTURE

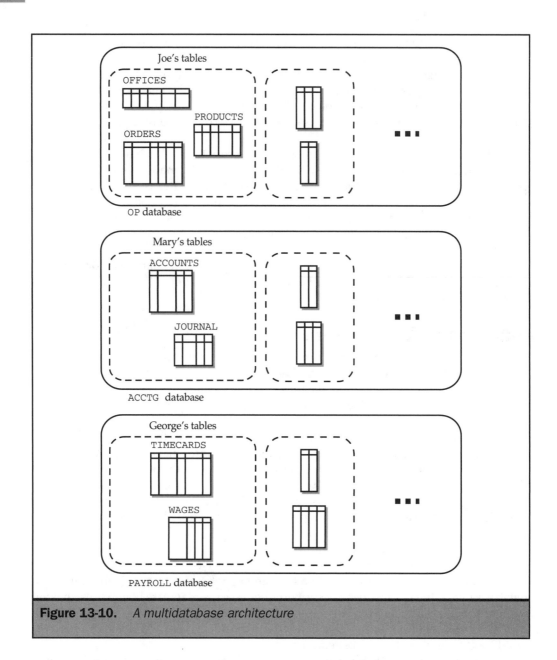

Figure 13-10.   *A multidatabase architecture*

table. Typically, the DBMS extends the dot notation for table names by prefixing the database name to the owner name, separated by a period (.). For example, in a Sybase or SQL Server database, this table reference:

```
OP.JOE.OFFICES
```

refers to the OFFICES table owned by the user JOE in the order-processing database named OP, and the following query joins the SALESREPS table in the payroll database with that OFFICES table:

```
SELECT OP.JOE.OFFICES.CITY, PAYROLL.GEORGE.SALESREPS.NAME
  FROM OP.JOE.OFFICES, PAYROLL.GEORGE.SALESREPS
 WHERE OP.JOE.OFFICES.MGR = PAYROLL.GEORGE.SALESREPS.EMPL_NUM
```

Fortunately, such cross-database queries are the exception rather than the rule, and default database and user names can normally be used.

With a multidatabase architecture, gaining access to a database becomes slightly more complex because you must tell the DBMS which database you want to use. The DBMS' interactive SQL program will often display a list of available databases or ask you to enter the database name along with your user name and password to gain access. For programmatic access, the DBMS generally extends the embedded SQL language with a statement that connects the program to a particular database. The Ingres form for connecting to the database named OP is:

```
CONNECT 'OP'
```

For Sybase and Microsoft SQL Server, the parallel statement is:

```
USE 'OP'
```

Multilocation Architecture

Figure 13-11 shows a multilocation architecture that supports multiple databases and uses the computer system's directory structure to organize them. Several of the earlier minicomputer databases (including Rdb/VMS and Informix) used this scheme for supporting multiple databases. As with the multidatabase architecture, each application is typically assigned to its own database. As Figure 13-11 shows, each database has a name, but it's possible for two different databases in two different directories to have the same name.

The major advantage of the multilocation architecture is flexibility. It is especially appropriate in applications such as engineering and design, where many sophisticated users of the computer system may all want to use several databases to structure their own information. The disadvantages of the multilocation architecture are the same as those of the multidatabase architecture. In addition, the DBMS typically doesn't know about all of the databases that have been created, which may be spread throughout the system's directory structure. There is no master database that keeps track of all the databases, which makes centralized database administration very difficult.

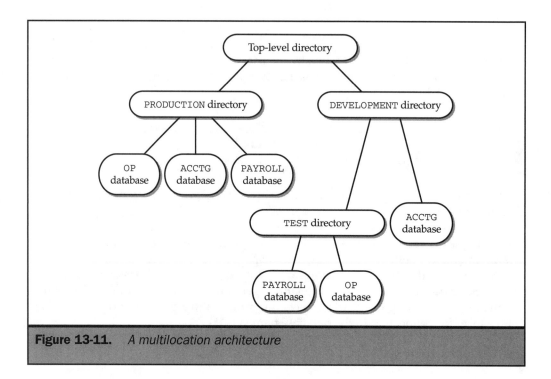

Figure 13-11.   *A multilocation architecture*

The multilocation architecture makes gaining access to a database more complex once again, because both the name of the database and its location in the directory hierarchy must be specified. The VAX SQL syntax for gaining access to an Rdb/VMS database is the DECLARE DATABASE statement. For example, this DECLARE DATABASE statement establishes a connection to the database named OP in the VAX/VMS directory named SYS$ROOT:[DEVELOPMENT.TEST]:

```
DECLARE DATABASE
        FILENAME 'SYS$ROOT:[DEVELOPMENT.TEST]OP'
```

If the database is in the user's current directory (which is often the case), the statement simplifies to:

```
DECLARE DATABASE
        FILENAME 'OP'
```

Some of the DBMS brands that use this scheme allow you to have access to several databases concurrently, even if they don't support queries across database boundaries. Again, the most common technique used to distinguish among the multiple databases is with a superqualified table name. Since two databases in two different directories can have the same name, it's also necessary to introduce a *database alias* to eliminate ambiguity. These VAX SQL statements open two different Rdb/VMS databases that happen to have the same name:

```
DECLARE DATABASE OP1
        FILENAME 'SYS$ROOT:[PRODUCTION\]OP'
DECLARE DATABASE OP2
        FILENAME 'SYS$ROOT:[DEVELOPMENT.TEST]OP'
```

The statements assign the aliases OP1 and OP2 to the two databases, and these aliases are used to qualify table names in subsequent VAX SQL statements.

As this discussion shows, there can be a tremendous variety in the way various DBMS brands organize their databases and provide access to them. This area of SQL is one of the most nonstandard, and yet it is often the first one that a user encounters when trying to access a database for the first time. The inconsistencies also make it impossible to transparently move programs developed for one DBMS to another, although the conversion process is usually tedious rather than complex.

Databases on Multiple Servers

With the rise of database servers and local area networks, the notion of database location embodied in the multilocation architecture is naturally extended to the notion of a physical database server. In practice, most DBMS products today appear to be converging on a multidatabase architecture, implemented within a physical server. At the highest level, a database is associated with a named server on the network. Within the server, there can be multiple named databases. The mapping of server names to physical server locations is handled by the networking software. The mapping of database names to physical files or file systems on a server is handled by the DBMS software.

Database Structure and the ANSI/ISO Standard

The ANSI/ISO SQL1 standard made a very strong distinction between the SQL Data Manipulation Language and Data Definition Language, defining them effectively as two separate languages. The standard did not require that the DDL statements be accepted by the DBMS during its normal operation. One of the advantages of this separation of the DML and DDL was that the standard permitted a static database structure like that used by older hierarchical and network DBMS products, as shown in Figure 13-12.

The database structure specified by the SQL1 standard was fairly straightforward. Collections of tables were defined in a *database schema,* associated with a specific user. In Figure 13-12, the simple database has two schemas. One schema is associated with (the common terminology is *owned by*) a user named Joe, and the other is owned by Mary. Joe's schema contains two tables, named PEOPLE and PLACES. Mary's schema also contains two tables, named THINGS and PLACES. Although the database contains two tables named PLACES, it's possible to tell them apart because they have different owners.

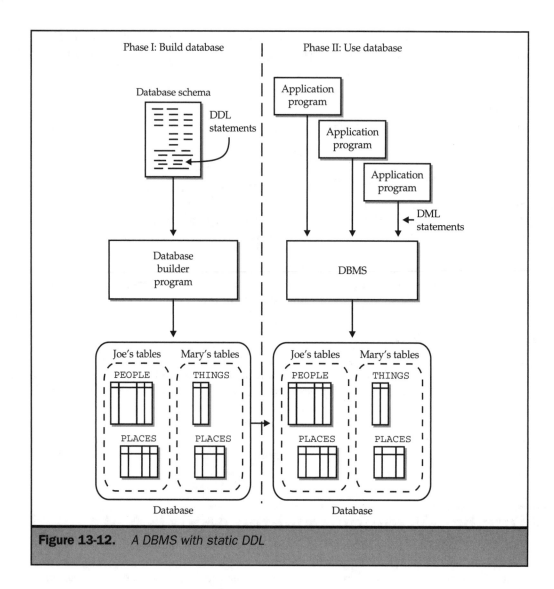

Figure 13-12. *A DBMS with static DDL*

The SQL2 standard significantly extended the SQL1 notion of database definition and database schemas. As previously noted, the SQL2 standard requires that data definition statements be executable by an interactive SQL user or by a SQL program. With this capability, changes to the database structure can be made at any time, not just when the database is created. In addition, the SQL1 concepts of schemas and users (officially called *authorization-ids* in the standard) is significantly expanded. Figure 13-13 shows the high-level database structure specified by the SQL2 standard.

The highest-level database structure described by the SQL2 standard is the *SQL-environment*. This is a conceptual collection of the database entities associated with a

Figure 13-13. *SQL2 database structure*

DBMS implementation that conforms to the SQL2 standard. The standard doesn't specify how a SQL-environment is created; that depends on the particular DBMS implementation. The standard defines these components of a SQL-environment:

■ **DBMS software** that conforms to the SQL2 standard.

■ **Named users** (called *authorization-ids* in the standard) who have the privileges to perform specific actions on the data and structures within the database.

■ **Program modules** that are used to access the database. The SQL2 standard specifies the actual execution of SQL statements in terms of a module language, which in practice is not used by most major commercial SQL products. No matter how the SQL programs are actually created, however, the standard says that, conceptually, the SQL-environment includes the program's database access code.

■ **Catalogs** that describe the structure of the database. SQL1-style database schemas are contained within these catalogs.

■ **Database data**, which is managed by the DBMS software, accessed by the users through the programs, and whose structure is described in the catalogs. Although the standard conceptually describes the data as outside of the catalog structure, it's common to think of data as being contained in a table that is in a schema, which is in a catalog.

SQL2 Catalogs

Within a SQL-environment, the database structure is defined by one or more named *catalogs*. The word "catalog" in this case is used in the same way that it has historically been used on mainframe systems—to describe a collection of objects (usually files). On minicomputer and personal computer systems, the concept is roughly analogous to a directory. In the case of a SQL2 database, the catalog is a collection of named database schemas. The catalog also contains a set of system tables (confusingly, often called the system catalog) that describe the structure of the database. The catalog is thus a self-describing entity within the database. This characteristic of SQL2 catalogs (which is provided by all major SQL products) is described in detail in Chapter 16.

The SQL2 standard describes the role of the catalog and specifies that a SQL-environment may contain one or more (actually zero or more) catalogs, each of which must have a distinct name. It explicitly says that the mechanism for creating and destroying catalogs is implementation-defined. The standard also says that the extent to which a DBMS allows access across catalogs is implementation defined. Specifically, whether a single SQL statement can access data from multiple catalogs, whether a single SQL transaction can span multiple catalogs, or even whether a single user session with the DBMS can cross catalog boundaries are all implementation-defined characteristics.

The standard says that when a user or program first establishes contact with a SQL-environment, one of its catalogs is identified as the default catalog for the session. (Again, the way in which this catalog is selected is implementation-defined.) During the course of a session, the default catalog can be changed with the SET CATALOG statement.

SQL2 Schemas

The SQL2 *schema* is the key high-level container for objects in a SQL2 database structure. A schema is a named entity within the database and includes the definitions for the following:

- **Tables**. Along with their associated structures (columns, primary and foreign keys, table constraints, and so on), tables remain the basic building blocks of a database in a SQL2 schema.

- **Views**. These are virtual tables, derived from the actual tables defined in the schema, as described in Chapter 14.

- **Domains**. Function like extended data types for defining columns within the tables of the schema, as described in Chapter 11.

- **Assertions**. These database integrity constraints restrict the data relationships across tables within the schema, as described earlier in the section "Assertions."

- **Privileges**. Database privileges control the capabilities that are given to various users to access and update data in the database and to modify the database structure. The SQL security scheme created by these privileges is described in Chapter 14.

■ **Character sets**. Databases support international languages and manage the representation of non-Roman characters in those languages (for example, the diacritical accent marks used by many European languages or the 2-byte representations of the word-symbols used in many Asian languages) through character sets defined by the schema.

■ **Collations**. Work hand-in-hand with character sets, defining the sorting sequence for a character set.

■ **Translations**. Control how text data is converted from one character set to another and how comparisons are made of text data from different character sets.

A schema is created with the CREATE SCHEMA statement, shown in Figure 13-14. Here is a simple SQL2 schema definition for the simple two-table schema for the user JOE shown in Figure 13-12:

```
CREATE SCHEMA JSCHEMA AUTHORIZATION JOE
  CREATE TABLE PEOPLE
        (NAME VARCHAR(30),
          AGE INTEGER)
  CREATE TABLE PLACES
        (CITY VARCHAR(30),
        STATE VARCHAR(30))
        GRANT ALL PRIVILEGES
            ON PEOPLE
            TO PUBLIC
        GRANT SELECT
            ON PLACES
            TO MARY
```

The schema defines the two tables and gives certain other users permission to access them. It doesn't define any additional structures, such as views or assertions. Note that the CREATE TABLE statements within the CREATE SCHEMA statement are legitimate SQL statements in their own right. If you type them into an interactive SQL program, the DBMS will create the specified tables in the current *default schema* for your interactive SQL session, according to the standard.

Note that in SQL2, the schema structure is related to, but independent of, the user-id structure. A given user can be the owner of several different named schemas. For backward compatibility with the SQL1 standard, however, the SQL2 standard allows you to create a schema with:

■ Both a schema name and a user-id (as in the last example).

■ Only a schema name. In this case, the user who executes the CREATE SCHEMA statement automatically becomes the owner of the schema.

- Only a user-id. In this case, the schema name becomes the user-id. This conforms to the SQL1 standard, and to the practice of many commercial DBMS products where there was conceptually one schema per user.

A SQL2 schema that is no longer needed can be dropped using the DROP SCHEMA statement, shown in Figure 13-15. The statement requires that you specify one of the drop rules previously described for dropping columns—either CASCADE or RESTRICT. If you specify CASCADE, then all of the structures within the schema definition (tables, views, assertions, and so on) are automatically dropped. If you specify RESTRICT, the statement will not succeed if any of these structures are remaining within the schema. Effectively, the RESTRICT rule forces you to first drop the individual tables, views, and other structures within the schema before dropping the schema itself. This is a protection against accidentally dropping a schema that contains data or database definitions of value. No ALTER SCHEMA table is specified by the SQL2 standard. Instead, you can individually alter the definitions of the structures within a schema, using statements like ALTER TABLE.

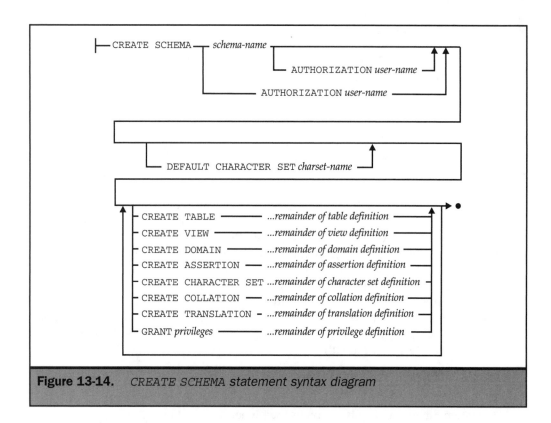

Figure 13-14.   *CREATE SCHEMA statement syntax diagram*

Figure 13-15. *DROP SCHEMA statement syntax diagram*

At any time while a user or program is accessing a SQL2 database, one of its schemas is identified as the default schema. Any DDL statements that you execute to create, drop, or alter schema structures implicitly apply to this schema. In addition, all tables named in SQL2 data manipulation statements are assumed to be tables defined within this default schema. The schema name implicitly qualifies the names of all tables used in the SQL statements. As noted in Chapter 5, you can use a qualified table name to refer to tables from other schemas. According to the SQL2 standard, the name used to qualify the table name is the schema name. For example, if the sample database were created as part of a schema named SALES, the qualified table name for the OFFICES table would be:

    SALES.OFFICES

If a SQL2 schema is created with just a user-id as the schema name, then the table qualification scheme becomes exactly the simple one described in Chapter 5. The schema name is the user name, and the qualified table name specifies this name before the dot.

The SQL2 CREATE SCHEMA statement has one other nonobvious advantage. You may recall from the earlier discussion of the CREATE TABLE statement that you could not easily create a referential cycle (two or more tables that refer to one another using foreign key/primary key relationships). Instead, one of the tables had to be created first without its foreign key definition, and then the foreign key definition had to be added (with the ALTER TABLE statement) after the other table(s) had been created. The CREATE SCHEMA statement avoids this problem, since the DBMS does not check the referential integrity constraints specified by the schema until *all* of the tables it defines have been created. In practice, the CREATE SCHEMA statement is generally used to create a new set of interrelated tables for the first time. Subsequently, individual tables are added, dropped, or modified using the CREATE/DROP/ALTER TABLE capabilities.

Many of the major DBMS brands have moved to adopt some form of the CREATE SCHEMA statement, although there are significant variations across the brands. Oracle's CREATE SCHEMA statement allows you to create tables, views, and privileges, but not the other SQL2 structures, and it requires that the schema name and the user name be one and the same. Informix Universal Server follows a similar pattern, requiring a user-id as the schema name and extending the objects within the schema to include indexes, triggers, and synonyms. Sybase provides similar capabilities. In each case, the offered capabilities conform to the SQL2 Entry level implementation requirements.

Summary

This chapter described the SQL Data Definition Language features that define and change the structure of a database:

- The CREATE TABLE statement creates a table and defines its columns, primary key, and foreign keys.

- The DROP TABLE statement removes a previously created table from the database.

- The ALTER TABLE statement can be used to add a column to an existing table and to change primary key and foreign key definitions.

- The CREATE INDEX and DROP INDEX statements define indexes, which speed database queries but add overhead to database updates.

- Most DBMS brands support other CREATE, DROP, and ALTER statements used with DBMS-specific objects.

- The SQL2 standard specifies a database schema containing a collection of tables, and the database schema is manipulated with CREATE SCHEMA and DROP SCHEMA statements.

- Various DBMS brands use very different approaches to organizing the one or more databases that they manage, and these differences affect the way you design your databases and gain access to them.

Chapter 14

Views

The tables of a database define the structure and organization of its data. However, SQL also lets you look at the stored data in other ways by defining alternative views of the data. A *view* is a SQL query that is permanently stored in the database and assigned a name. The results of the stored query are visible through the view, and SQL lets you access these query results as if they were, in fact, a real table in the database.

Views are an important part of SQL for several reasons:

■ Views let you tailor the appearance of a database so that different users see it from different perspectives.

■ Views let you restrict access to data, allowing different users to see only certain rows or certain columns of a table.

■ Views simplify database access by presenting the structure of the stored data in the way that is most natural for each user.

This chapter describes how to create views and how to use views to simplify processing and enhance the security of a database.

What Is a View?

A *view* is a virtual table in the database whose contents are defined by a query, as shown in Figure 14-1. To the database user, the view appears just like a real table, with a set of named columns and rows of data. But unlike a real table, a view does not exist in the database as a stored set of data values. Instead, the rows and columns of data visible through the view are the query results produced by the query that defines the view. SQL creates the illusion of the view by giving the view a name like a table name and storing the definition of the view in the database.

The view shown in Figure 14-1 is typical. It has been given the name REPDATA and is defined by this two-table query:

```
SELECT NAME, CITY, REGION, QUOTA, SALESREPS.SALES
  FROM SALESREPS, OFFICES
 WHERE REP_OFFICE = OFFICE
```

The data in the view comes from the SALESREPS and OFFICES tables. These tables are called the *source tables* for the view because they are the source of the data that is visible through the view. This view contains one row of information for each salesperson, extended with the name of the city and region where the salesperson works. As shown in the figure, the view appears as a table, and its contents look just like the query results that you would obtain if you actually ran the query.

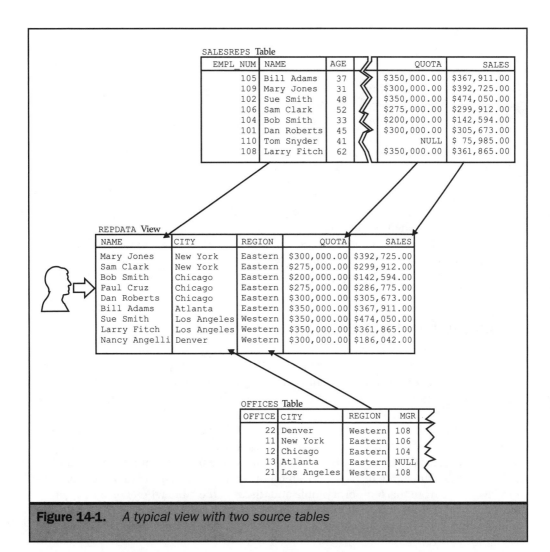

Figure 14-1. *A typical view with two source tables*

Once a view is defined, you can use it in a SELECT statement, just like a real table, as in this query:

List the salespeople who are over quota, showing the name, city, and region for each salesperson.

```
SELECT NAME, CITY, REGION
  FROM REPDATA
 WHERE SALES > QUOTA
```

```
NAME          CITY          REGION
-----------   -----------   --------
Mary Jones    New York      Eastern
Sam Clark     New York      Eastern
Dan Roberts   Chicago       Eastern
Paul Cruz     Chicago       Eastern
Bill Adams    Atlanta       Eastern
Sue Smith     Los Angeles   Western
Larry Fitch   Los Angeles   Western
```

The name of the view, REPDATA, appears in the FROM clause just like a table name, and the columns of the view are referenced in the SELECT statement just like the columns of a real table. For some views, you can also use the INSERT, DELETE, and UPDATE statements to modify the data visible through the view, as if it were a real table. Thus, for all practical purposes, the view can be used in SQL statements as if it *were* a real table.

How the DBMS Handles Views

When the DBMS encounters a reference to a view in a SQL statement, it finds the definition of the view stored in the database. Then the DBMS translates the request that references the view into an equivalent request against the source tables of the view and carries out the equivalent request. In this way, the DBMS maintains the illusion of the view while maintaining the integrity of the source tables.

For simple views, the DBMS may construct each row of the view on the fly, drawing the data for the row from the source table(s). For more complex views, the DBMS must actually *materialize* the view; that is, the DBMS must actually carry out the query that defines the view and store its results in a temporary table. The DBMS fills your requests for view access from this temporary table and discards the table when it is no longer needed. Regardless of how the DBMS actually handles a particular view, the result is the same for the user—the view can be referenced in SQL statements exactly as if it were a real table in the database.

Advantages of Views

Views provide a variety of benefits and can be useful in many different types of databases. In a personal computer database, views are usually a convenience, defined to simplify database requests. In a production database installation, views play a central role in defining the structure of the database for its users and enforcing its security. Views provide these major benefits:

- **Security**. Each user can be given permission to access the database only through a small set of views that contain the specific data the user is authorized to see, thus restricting the user's access to stored data.

■ **Query simplicity**. A view can draw data from several different tables and present it as a single table, turning multitable queries into single-table queries against the view.

■ **Structural simplicity**. Views can give a user a personalized view of the database structure, presenting the database as a set of virtual tables that make sense for that user.

■ **Insulation from change**. A view can present a consistent, unchanged image of the structure of the database, even if the underlying source tables are split, restructured, or renamed.

■ **Data integrity**. If data is accessed and entered through a view, the DBMS can automatically check the data to ensure that it meets specified integrity constraints.

Disadvantages of Views

While views provide substantial advantages, there are also two major disadvantages to using a view instead of a real table:

■ **Performance**. Views create the appearance of a table, but the DBMS must still translate queries against the view into queries against the underlying source tables. If the view is defined by a complex multitable query, then even a simple query against the view becomes a complicated join, and it may take a long time to complete.

■ **Update restrictions**. When a user tries to update rows of a view, the DBMS must translate the request into an update on rows of the underlying source tables. This is possible for simple views, but more complex views cannot be updated; they are read-only.

These disadvantages mean that you cannot indiscriminately define views and use them instead of the source tables. Instead, you must in each case consider the advantages provided by using a view and weigh them against the disadvantages.

Creating a View (CREATE VIEW)

The CREATE VIEW statement, shown in Figure 14-2, is used to create a view. The statement assigns a name to the view and specifies the query that defines the view. To create the view successfully, you must have permission to access all of the tables referenced in the query.

The CREATE VIEW statement can optionally assign a name to each column in the newly created view. If a list of column names is specified, it must have the same number of items as the number of columns produced by the query. Note that only the column names are specified; the data type, length, and other characteristics of each column are

Figure 14-2. The CREATE VIEW statement syntax diagram

derived from the definition of the columns in the source tables. If the list of column names is omitted from the CREATE VIEW statement, each column in the view takes the name of the corresponding column in the query. The list of column names must be specified if the query includes calculated columns or if it produces two columns with identical names.

Although all views are created in the same way, in practice, different types of views are typically used for different purposes. The next few sections examine these types of views and give examples of the CREATE VIEW statement.

Horizontal Views

A common use of views is to restrict a user's access to only selected rows of a table. For example, in the sample database, you may want to let a sales manager see only the SALESREPS rows for salespeople in the manager's own region. To accomplish this, you can define two views, as follows:

Create a view showing Eastern region salespeople.

```
CREATE VIEW EASTREPS AS
    SELECT *
      FROM SALESREPS
     WHERE REP_OFFICE IN (11, 12, 13)
```

Create a view showing Western region salespeople.

```
CREATE VIEW WESTREPS AS
    SELECT *
      FROM SALESREPS
     WHERE REP_OFFICE IN (21, 22)
```

Now you can give each sales manager permission to access either the EASTREPS or the WESTREPS view, denying them permission to access the other view and the

SALESREPS table itself. This effectively gives the sales manager a customized view of the SALESREPS table, showing only salespeople in the appropriate region.

A view like EASTREPS or WESTREPS is often called a *horizontal view.* As shown in Figure 14-3, a horizontal view slices the source table horizontally to create the view. All of the columns of the source table participate in the view, but only some of its rows are visible through the view. Horizontal views are appropriate when the source table contains data that relates to various organizations or users. They provide a private table for each user, composed only of the rows needed by that user.

Here are some more examples of horizontal views:

Define a view containing only Eastern region offices.

```
CREATE VIEW EASTOFFICES AS
     SELECT *
       FROM OFFICES
      WHERE REGION = 'Eastern'
```

Figure 14-3. *Two horizontal views of the SALESREPS table*

Define a view for Sue Smith (employee number 102) containing only orders placed by customers assigned to her.

```
CREATE VIEW SUEORDERS AS
     SELECT *
       FROM ORDERS
      WHERE CUST IN (SELECT CUST_NUM
                       FROM CUSTOMERS
                      WHERE CUST_REP = 102)
```

Define a view showing only those customers who have more than $30,000 worth of orders currently on the books.

```
CREATE VIEW BIGCUSTOMERS AS
     SELECT *
       FROM CUSTOMERS
      WHERE 30000.00 < (SELECT SUM(AMOUNT)
                          FROM ORDERS
                         WHERE CUST = CUST_NUM)
```

In each of these examples, the view is derived from a single source table. The view is defined by a SELECT * query and therefore has exactly the same columns as the source table. The WHERE clause determines which rows of the source table are visible in the view.

Vertical Views

Another common use of views is to restrict a user's access to only certain columns of a table. For example, in the sample database, the order-processing department may need access to the employee number, name, and office assignment of each salesperson, because this information may be needed to process an order correctly. However, there is no need for the order-processing staff to see the salesperson's year-to-date sales or quota. This selective view of the SALESREPS table can be constructed with the following view:

Create a view showing selected salesperson information.

```
CREATE VIEW REPINFO AS
     SELECT EMPL_NUM, NAME, REP_OFFICE
       FROM SALESREPS
```

By giving the order-processing staff access to this view and denying access to the SALESREPS table itself, access to sensitive sales and quota data is effectively restricted.

A view like the REPINFO view is often called a *vertical view*. As shown in Figure 14-4, a vertical view slices the source table vertically to create the view. Vertical views are commonly found where the data stored in a table is used by various users or groups of users. They provide a private table for each user, composed only of the columns needed by that user.

Here are some more examples of vertical views:

Define a view of the OFFICES table for the order-processing staff that includes the office's city, office number, and region.

```
CREATE VIEW OFFICEINFO AS
    SELECT OFFICE, CITY, REGION
        FROM OFFICES
```

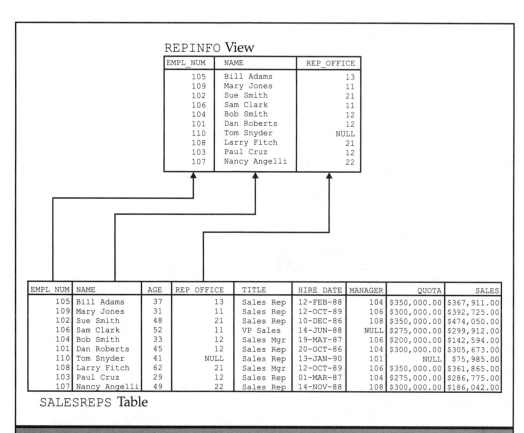

Figure 14-4. *A vertical view of the SALESREPS table*

Define a view of the CUSTOMERS table that includes only customer names and their assignment to salespeople.

```
CREATE VIEW CUSTINFO AS
    SELECT COMPANY, CUST_REP
        FROM CUSTOMERS
```

In each of these examples, the view is derived from a single source table. The select list in the view definition determines which columns of the source table are visible in the view. Because these are vertical views, every row of the source table is represented in the view, and the view definition does not include a WHERE clause.

Row/Column Subset Views

When you define a view, SQL does not restrict you to purely horizontal or vertical slices of a table. In fact, the SQL language does not include the notion of horizontal and vertical views. These concepts merely help you to visualize how the view presents the information from the source table. It's quite common to define a view that slices a source table in both the horizontal and vertical dimensions, as in this example:

Define a view that contains the customer number, company name, and credit limit of all customers assigned to Bill Adams (employee number 105).

```
CREATE VIEW BILLCUST AS
    SELECT CUST_NUM, COMPANY, CREDIT_LIMIT
        FROM CUSTOMERS
      WHERE CUST_REP = 105
```

The data visible through this view is a row/column subset of the CUSTOMERS table. Only the columns explicitly named in the select list of the view and the rows that meet the search condition are visible through the view.

Grouped Views

The query specified in a view definition may include a GROUP BY clause. This type of view is called a *grouped view,* because the data visible through the view is the result of a grouped query. Grouped views perform the same function as grouped queries; they group related rows of data and produce one row of query results for each group, summarizing the data in that group. A grouped view makes these grouped query results into a virtual table, allowing you to perform further queries on them.

Here is an example of a grouped view:

Define a view that contains summary order data for each salesperson.

```
CREATE VIEW ORD_BY_REP (WHO, HOW_MANY, TOTAL, LOW, HIGH, AVERAGE) AS
     SELECT REP, COUNT(*), SUM(AMOUNT), MIN(AMOUNT), MAX(AMOUNT),
          AVG(AMOUNT)
       FROM ORDERS
      GROUP BY REP
```

As this example shows, the definition of a grouped view always includes a column name list. The list assigns names to the columns in the grouped view, which are derived from column functions such as SUM() and MIN(). It may also specify a modified name for a grouping column. In this example, the REP column of the ORDERS table becomes the WHO column in the ORD_BY_REP view.

Once this grouped view is defined, it can be used to simplify queries. For example, this query generates a simple report that summarizes the orders for each salesperson:

Show the name, number of orders, total order amount, and average order size for each salesperson.

```
SELECT NAME, HOW_MANY, TOTAL, AVERAGE
   FROM SALESREPS, ORD_BY_REP
  WHERE WHO = EMPL_NUM
  ORDER BY TOTAL DESC
```

NAME	HOW_MANY	TOTAL	AVERAGE
Larry Fitch	7	$58,633.00	$8,376.14
Bill Adams	5	$39,327.00	$7,865.40
Nancy Angelli	3	$34,432.00	$11,477.33
Sam Clark	2	$32,958.00	$16,479.00
Dan Roberts	3	$26,628.00	$8,876.00
Tom Snyder	2	$23,132.00	$11,566.00
Sue Smith	4	$22,776.00	$5,694.00
Mary Jones	2	$7,105.00	$3,552.50
Paul Cruz	2	$2,700.00	$1,350.00

Unlike a horizontal or vertical view, the rows in a grouped view do not have a one-to-one correspondence with the rows in the source table. A grouped view is not just a filter on its source table that screens out certain rows and columns. It is a summary of the source tables; therefore, a substantial amount of DBMS processing is required to maintain the illusion of a virtual table for grouped views.

Grouped views can be used in queries just like other, simpler views. A grouped view cannot be updated, however. The reason should be obvious from the example. What would it mean to update the average order size for salesrep number 105? Because each row in the grouped view corresponds to a *group* of rows from the source table, and because the columns in the grouped view generally contain calculated data, there is no way to translate the update request into an update against the rows of the source table. Grouped views thus function as read-only views, which can participate in queries but not in updates.

Grouped views are also subject to the SQL restrictions on nested column functions. Recall from Chapter 8 that nested column functions, such as:

```
MIN(MIN(A))
```

are not legal in SQL expressions. Although the grouped view hides the column functions in its select list from the user, the DBMS still knows about them and enforces the restriction. Consider this example:

For each sales office, show the range of average order sizes for all salespeople who work in the office.

```
SELECT REP_OFFICE, MIN(AVERAGE), MAX(AVERAGE)
  FROM SALESREPS, ORD_BY_REP
 WHERE EMPL_NUM = WHO
 GROUP BY REP_OFFICE

Error: Nested column function reference
```

This query produces an error, even though it appears perfectly reasonable. It's a two-table query that groups the rows of the ORD_BY_REP view based on the office to which the salesperson is assigned. But the column functions MIN() and MAX() in the select list cause a problem. The argument to these column functions, the AVERAGE column, is itself the result of a column function. The "actual" query being requested from SQL is:

```
SELECT REP_OFFICE, MIN(AVG(AMOUNT)), MAX(AVG(AMOUNT))
  FROM SALESREPS, ORDERS
 WHERE EMPL_NUM = REP
 GROUP BY REP
 GROUP BY REP_OFFICE
```

This query is illegal because of the double GROUP BY and the nested column functions. Unfortunately, as this example shows, a perfectly reasonable grouped

SELECT statement may, in fact, cause an error if one of its source tables turns out to be a grouped view. There's no way to anticipate this situation; you must just understand the cause of the error when SQL reports it to you.

Joined Views

One of the most frequent reasons for using views is to simplify multitable queries. By specifying a two-table or three-table query in the view definition, you can create a *joined view* that draws its data from two or three different tables and presents the query results as a single virtual table. Once the view is defined, you can often use a simple single-table query against the view for requests that would otherwise each require a two-table or three-table join.

For example, suppose that Sam Clark, the vice president of sales, often runs queries against the ORDERS table in the sample database. However, Sam doesn't like to work with customer and employee numbers. Instead, he'd like to be able to use a version of the ORDERS table that has names instead of numbers. Here is a view that meets Sam's needs:

Create a view of the ORDERS table with names instead of numbers.

```
CREATE VIEW ORDER_INFO (ORDER_NUM, COMPANY, REP_NAME, AMOUNT) AS
     SELECT ORDER_NUM, COMPANY, NAME, AMOUNT
       FROM ORDERS, CUSTOMERS, SALESREPS
      WHERE CUST = CUST_NUM
        AND REP = EMPL_NUM
```

This view is defined by a three-table join. As with a grouped view, the processing required to create the illusion of a virtual table for this view is considerable. Each row of the view is derived from a combination of one row from the ORDERS table, one row from the CUSTOMERS table, and one row from the SALESREPS table.

Although it has a relatively complex definition, this view can provide some real benefits. Here is a query against the view that generates a report of orders, grouped by salesperson:

Show the total current orders for each company for each salesperson.

```
SELECT REP_NAME, COMPANY, SUM(AMOUNT)
  FROM ORDER_INFO
 GROUP BY REP_NAME, COMPANY

REP_NAME       COMPANY            SUM(AMOUNT)
------------   ----------------   -----------
Bill Adams     Acme Mfg.           $35,582.00
Bill Adams     JCP Inc.             $3,745.00
Dan Roberts    First Corp.          $3,978.00
```

```
Dan Roberts   Holm & Landis          $150.00
Dan Roberts   Ian & Schmidt       $22,500.00
Larry Fitch   Midwest Systems      $3,608.00
Larry Fitch   Orion Corp.          $7,100.00
Larry Fitch   Zetacorp            $47,925.00
       .
       .
       .
```

Note that this query is a single-table SELECT statement, which is considerably simpler than the equivalent three-table SELECT statement for the source tables:

```
SELECT NAME, COMPANY, SUM(AMOUNT)
  FROM SALESREPS, ORDERS, CUSTOMERS
 WHERE REP = EMPL_NUM
   AND CUST = CUST_NUM
 GROUP BY NAME, COMPANY
```

Similarly, it's easy to generate a report of the largest orders, showing who placed them and who received them, with this query against the view:

Show the largest current orders, sorted by amount.

```
SELECT COMPANY, AMOUNT, REP_NAME
  FROM ORDER_INFO
 WHERE AMOUNT > 20000.00
 ORDER BY AMOUNT DESC
```

```
COMPANY                     AMOUNT  REP_NAME
-----------------  ----------- -------------
Zetacorp            $45,000.00 Larry Fitch
J.P. Sinclair       $31,500.00 Sam Clark
Chen Associates     $31,350.00 Nancy Angelli
Acme Mfg.           $27,500.00 Bill Adams
Ace International   $22,500.00 Tom Snyder
Ian & Schmidt       $22,500.00 Dan Roberts
```

The view makes it much easier to see what's going on in the query than if it were expressed as the equivalent three-table join. Of course, the DBMS must work just as hard to generate the query results for the single-table query against the view as it would to generate the query results for the equivalent three-table query. In fact, the DBMS must perform slightly more work to handle the query against the view.

However, for the human user of the database, it's much easier to write and understand the single-table query that references the view.

Updating a View

What does it mean to insert a row of data into a view, delete a row from a view, or update a row of a view? For some views, these operations can obviously be translated into equivalent operations against the source table(s) of the view. For example, consider once again the EASTREPS view, defined earlier in this chapter:

Create a view showing Eastern region salespeople.

```
CREATE VIEW EASTREPS AS
    SELECT *
      FROM SALESREPS
     WHERE REP_OFFICE IN (11, 12, 13)
```

This is a straightforward horizontal view, derived from a single source table. As shown in Figure 14-5, it makes sense to talk about inserting a row into this view; it means the new row should be inserted into the underlying SALESREPS table from which the view is derived. It also makes sense to delete a row from the EASTREPS view; this would delete the corresponding row from the SALESREPS table. Finally, updating a row of the EASTREPS view makes sense; this would update the corresponding row of the SALESREPS table. In each case, the action can be carried out against the corresponding row of the source table, preserving the integrity of both the source table and the view.

However, consider the ORD_BY_REP grouped view, as it was defined earlier in the section "Grouped Views":

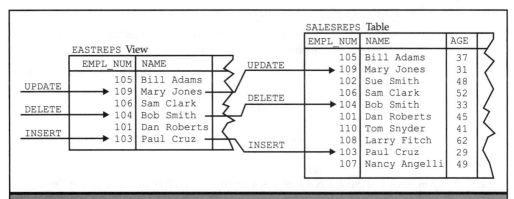

Figure 14-5.   *Updating data through a view*

Define a view that contains summary order data for each salesperson.

```
CREATE VIEW ORD_BY_REP (WHO, HOW_MANY, TOTAL, LOW, HIGH, AVERAGE) AS
     SELECT REP, COUNT(*), SUM(AMOUNT), MIN(AMOUNT), MAX(AMOUNT),
          AVG(AMOUNT)
      FROM ORDERS
     GROUP BY REP
```

There is no one-to-one correspondence between the rows of this view and the rows of the underlying ORDERS table, so it makes no sense to talk about inserting, deleting, or updating rows of this view. The ORD_BY_REP view is not updateable; it is a read-only view.

The EASTREPS view and the ORD_BY_REP view are two extreme examples in terms of the complexity of their definitions. There are views more complex than EASTREPS where it still makes sense to update the view, and there are views less complex than ORD_BY_REP where updates do not make sense. In fact, which views can be updated and which cannot has been an important relational database research problem over the years.

View Updates and the ANSI/ISO Standard

The ANSI/ISO SQL1 standard specifies the views that must be updateable in a database that claims conformance to the standard. Under the standard, a view can be updated if the query that defines the view meets all of these restrictions:

- DISTINCT must not be specified; that is, duplicate rows must not be eliminated from the query results.

- The FROM clause must specify only one updateable table; that is, the view must have a single source table for which the user has the required privileges. If the source table is itself a view, then that view must meet these criteria.

- Each select item must be a simple column reference; the select list cannot contain expressions, calculated columns, or column functions.

- The WHERE clause must not include a subquery; only simple row-by-row search conditions may appear.

- The query must not include a GROUP BY or a HAVING clause.

The basic concept behind the restrictions is easier to remember than the rules themselves.

For a view to be updateable, the DBMS must be able to trace any row of the view back to its source row in the source table. Similarly, the DBMS must be able to trace each individual column to be updated back to its source column in the source table.

If the view meets this test, then it's possible to define meaningful INSERT, DELETE, and UPDATE operations for the view in terms of the source table(s).

View Updates in Commercial SQL Products

The SQL1 standard rules on view updates are very restrictive. Many views can be theoretically updated but do not satisfy all of the restrictions. In addition, some views can support some of the update operations but not others, and some views can support updates on certain columns but not others. Most commercial SQL implementations have view update rules that are considerably more permissive than the SQL1 standard. For example, consider this view:

Create a view showing the sales, quota, and the difference between the two for each salesperson.

```
CREATE VIEW SALESPERF (EMPL_NUM, SALES, QUOTA, DIFF) AS
    SELECT EMPL_NUM, SALES, QUOTA, (SALES - QUOTA)
        FROM SALESREPS
```

The SQL1 standard disallows all updates to this view because its fourth column is a calculated column. However, note that each row in the view can be traced back to a single row in the source table (SALESREPS). For this reason, DB2 (and several other commercial SQL implementations) allows DELETE operations against this view. Further, DB2 allows UPDATE operations on the EMPL_NUM, SALES, and QUOTA columns because they are directly derived from the source table. Only the DIFF column cannot be updated. DB2 does not allow the INSERT statement for the view because inserting a value for the DIFF column would be meaningless.

The specific rules that determine whether a view can be updated vary from one brand of DBMS to another, and they are usually fairly detailed. Some views, such as those based on grouped queries, cannot be updated by any DBMS because the update operations simply do not make sense. Other views may be updateable in one brand of DBMS, partially updateable in another brand, and not updateable in a third brand. The SQL2 standard recognized this and includes a broader definition of updateable views along with considerable latitude for variation among DBMS brands. The best way to find out about updateability of views in your particular DBMS is to consult the user's guide or experiment with different types of views.

Checking View Updates (CHECK OPTION)

If a view is defined by a query that includes a WHERE clause, only rows that meet the search condition are visible in the view. Other rows may be present in the source table(s) from which the view is derived, but they are not visible through the view. For example, the EASTREPS view, described in the "Horizontal Views" section earlier in this chapter, contains only those rows of the SALESREPS table with specific values in the REP_OFFICE column:

Create a view showing Eastern region salespeople.

```
CREATE VIEW EASTREPS AS
    SELECT *
      FROM SALESREPS
     WHERE REP_OFFICE IN (11, 12, 13)
```

This is an updateable view for most commercial SQL implementations. You can add a new salesperson with this INSERT statement:

```
INSERT INTO EASTREPS (EMPL_NUM, NAME, REP_OFFICE, AGE, SALES)
    VALUES (113, 'Jake Kimball', 11, 43, 0.00)
```

The DBMS will add the new row to the underlying SALESREPS table, and the row will be visible through the EASTREPS view. But consider what happens when you add a new salesperson with this INSERT statement:

```
INSERT INTO EASTREPS (EMPL_NUM, NAME, REP_OFFICE, AGE, SALES)
    VALUES (114, 'Fred Roberts', 21, 47, 0.00)
```

This is a perfectly legal SQL statement, and the DBMS will insert a new row with the specified column values into the SALESREPS table. However, the newly inserted row doesn't meet the search condition for the view. Its REP_OFFICE value (21) specifies the Los Angeles office, which is in the Western region. As a result, if you run this query immediately after the INSERT statement:

```
SELECT EMPL_NUM, NAME, REP_OFFICE
  FROM EASTREPS

EMPL_NUM NAME          REP_OFFICE
-------- ------------  -----------
     105 Bill Adams            13
     109 Mary Jones            11
     106 Sam Clark             11
     104 Bob Smith             12
     101 Dan Roberts           12
     103 Paul Cruz             12
```

the newly added row doesn't show up in the view. The same thing happens if you change the office assignment for one of the salespeople currently in the view. This UPDATE statement:

```
UPDATE EASTREPS
   SET REP_OFFICE = 21
 WHERE EMPL_NUM = 104
```

modifies one of the columns for Bob Smith's row and immediately causes it to disappear from the view. Of course, both of the vanishing rows show up in a query against the underlying table:

```
SELECT EMPL_NUM, NAME, REP_OFFICE
   FROM SALESREPS
```

EMPL_NUM	NAME	REP_OFFICE
105	Bill Adams	13
109	Mary Jones	11
102	Sue Smith	21
106	Sam Clark	11
104	Bob Smith	21
101	Dan Roberts	12
110	Tom Snyder	NULL
108	Larry Fitch	21
103	Paul Cruz	12
107	Nancy Angelli	22
114	Fred Roberts	21

The fact that the rows vanish from the view as a result of an INSERT or UPDATE statement is disconcerting, at best. You probably want the DBMS to detect and prevent this type of INSERT or UPDATE from taking place through the view. SQL allows you to specify this kind of integrity checking for views by creating the view with a *check option*. The check option is specified in the CREATE VIEW statement, as shown in this redefinition of the EASTREPS view:

```
CREATE VIEW EASTREPS AS
     SELECT *
       FROM SALESREPS
      WHERE REP_OFFICE IN (11, 12, 13)
 WITH CHECK OPTION
```

When the check option is requested for a view, SQL automatically checks each INSERT and each UPDATE operation for the view to make sure that the resulting row(s) meet the search criteria in the view definition. If an inserted or modified row would not meet the condition, the INSERT or UPDATE statement fails, and the operation is not carried out.

The SQL2 standard specifies one additional refinement to the check option: the choice of CASCADED or LOCAL application of the check option. This choice applies when a view is created, and its definition is based not on an underlying table, but on one or more other views. The definitions of these underlying views might, in turn, be based on still other views, and so on. Each of the underlying views might or might not have the check option specified.

If the new view is created WITH CASCADED CHECK OPTION, any attempt to update the view causes the DBMS to go down through the entire hierarchy of view definitions on which it is based, processing the check option for each view where it is specified. If the new view is created WITH LOCAL CHECK OPTION, then the DBMS checks only that view; the underlying views are not checked. The SQL2 standard specifies CASCADED as the default, if the WITH CHECK OPTION clause is used without specifying LOCAL or CASCADED.

It's probably clear from the discussion that the check option can add significant overhead to the INSERT and UPDATE operations, especially if you are updating a view that is defined based on several layers of underlying view definitions. However, the check option plays an important role to ensure the integrity of the database. After all, if the update was intended to apply to data not visible through the view or to effectively switch a row of data from one view to another, then logically, the update should be made through an underlying view or base table. When you create an updateable view as part of a security scheme, it's almost always a good idea to specify the check option. It prevents modifications made through the view from affecting data that isn't accessible to the user in the first place.

Dropping a View (DROP VIEW)

Recall that the SQL1 standard treated the SQL Data Definition Language (DDL) as a static specification of the structure of a database, including its tables and views. For this reason, the SQL1 standard did not provide the ability to drop a view when it was no longer needed. However, all major DBMS brands have provided this capability for some time. Because views behave like tables and a view cannot have the same name as a table, some DBMS brands used the DROP TABLE statement to drop views as well. Other SQL implementations provided a separate DROP VIEW statement.

The SQL2 standard formalized support for dropping views through a DROP VIEW statement. It also provides for detailed control over what happens when a user attempts to drop a view when the definition of another view depends on it. For example, suppose two views on the SALESREPS table have been created by these two CREATE VIEW statements:

```
CREATE VIEW EASTREPS AS
    SELECT *
      FROM SALESREPS
     WHERE REP_OFFICE IN (11, 12, 13)

CREATE VIEW NYREPS AS
    SELECT *
      FROM EASTREPS
     WHERE REP_OFFICE = 11
```

For purposes of illustration, the NYREPS view is defined in terms of the EASTREPS view, although it could just as easily have been defined in terms of the underlying table. Under the SQL2 standard, the following DROP VIEW statement removes both of the views from the database:

```
DROP VIEW EASTREPS CASCADE
```

The CASCADE option tells the DBMS to delete not only the named view, but also any views that depend on its definition. In contrast, this DROP VIEW statement:

```
DROP VIEW EASTREPS RESTRICT
```

fails with an error, because the RESTRICT option tells the DBMS to remove the view only if no other views depend on it. This provides an added precaution against unintentional side-effects of a DROP VIEW statement. The SQL2 standard requires that either RESTRICT or CASCADE be specified. But many commercial SQL products support a version of the DROP VIEW statement without an explicitly specified option for backward compatibility with earlier versions of their products released before the publication of the SQL2 standard. The specific behavior of dependent views in this case depends on the particular DBMS brand.

Materialized Views *

Conceptually, a view is a *virtual* table within a database. The row/column data in the view is not physically stored in the database: it is derived from actual data in the underlying source tables. If the view definition is relatively simple (for example, if the view is a simple row/column subset of a single table, or a simple join based on foreign key relationships), it is fairly easy for the DBMS to translate database operations on the view into operations on the underlying tables. In this situation, the DBMS will perform this translation on the fly, operation by operation as it processes database queries or updates. In general, operations that update the database through a view (INSERT,

UPDATE, or DELETE operations) will always be carried out in this way—by translating the operation into one or more operations on the source tables.

If the view definition is more complicated, the DBMS may need to actually materialize the view to carry out a query against it. That is, the DBMS will actually carry out the query that defines the view and store the query results in a temporary table within the database. Then the DBMS carries out the requested query against this temporary table to obtain the requested results. When the query processing has finished, the DBMS discards the temporary table. Figure 14-6 shows this materialization process. Clearly, materializing the view contents can be a very high-overhead operation. If the typical database workload contains many queries that require view materialization, the total throughput capacity of the DBMS can be dramatically reduced.

To address this problem, some commercial DBMS products support *materialized views*. When you define a view as a materialized view, the DBMS will carry out the query that defines the view once (typically when the materialized view is defined), store the results (i.e., the data that appears in the view) within the database, and then permanently maintain this copy of the view data. To maintain the accuracy of the materialized view data, the DBMS must automatically examine every change to the data in the underlying

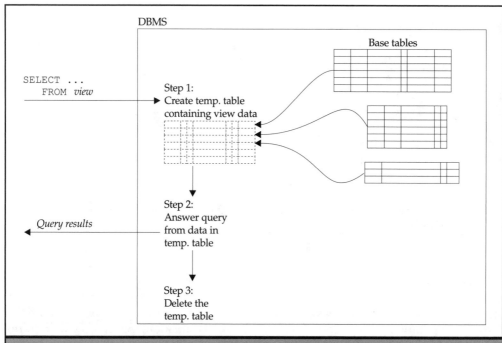

Figure 14-6. *Materializing a view for query processing*

source tables and make the corresponding changes in the materialized view data. When the DBMS must process a query against the materialized view, it has the data already at hand and can process the query very efficiently. Figure 14-7 shows DBMS operation with a materialized view.

Materialized views provide a trade-off between the efficiency of updates on the data contained in the view and the efficiency of queries on the view data. In a nonmaterialized view, updates to the source tables for a view are unaffected by the view definition; they proceed at normal DBMS processing speed. However, queries against a nonmaterialized view are much less efficient than queries against ordinary database tables, since the DBMS must do a great deal of on-the-fly work to process the queries.

Materialized views reverse this balance of work. When a materialized view is defined, updates to the source tables for the view are much less efficient than updates to ordinary database tables, since the DBMS must calculate the impact of the updates and change the materialized view data accordingly. However, queries against a materialized view can proceed at the same speed as queries against actual database tables, since the materialized view is represented within the database in the same form as a real table. Thus, a materialized view is most useful when the volume of updates to the underlying data is relatively small, and the volume of queries against the view is relatively high.

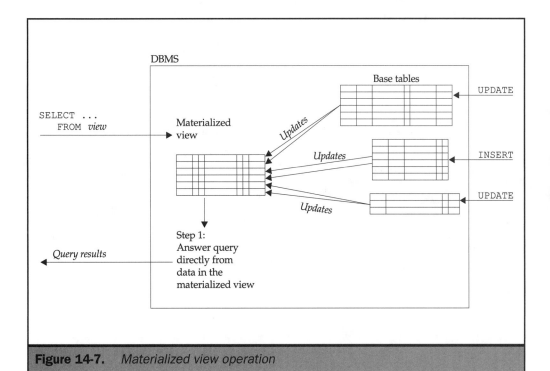

Figure 14-7. *Materialized view operation*

Summary

Views allow you to redefine the structure of a database, giving each user a personalized view of the database structure and contents:

■ A view is a virtual table defined by a query. The view appears to contain rows and columns of data, just like a real table, but the data visible through the view is, in fact, the results of the query.

■ A view can be a simple row/column subset of a single table, it can summarize a table (a grouped view), or it can draw its data from two or more tables (a joined view).

■ A view can be referenced like a real table in a SELECT, INSERT, DELETE, or UPDATE statement. However, more complex views cannot be updated; they are read-only views.

■ Views are commonly used to simplify the apparent structure of a database, to simplify queries, and to protect certain rows and/or columns from unauthorized access.

■ Materialized views can improve the efficiency of database processing in situations where there is a very high volume of query activity and relatively low update activity.

The Complete Reference

Chapter 15

SQL Security

When you entrust your data to a database management system, the security of the stored data is a major concern. Security is especially important in an SQL-based DBMS because interactive SQL makes database access very easy. The security requirements of a typical production database are many and varied:

- The data in any given table should be accessible to some users, but access by other users should be prevented.

- Some users should be allowed to update data in a particular table; others should be allowed only to retrieve data.

- For some tables, access should be restricted on a column-by-column basis.

- Some users should be denied interactive SQL access to a table but should be allowed to use application programs that update the table.

The SQL security scheme described in this chapter provides these types of protection for data in a relational database.

SQL Security Concepts

Implementing a security scheme and enforcing security restrictions are the responsibility of the DBMS software. The SQL language defines an overall framework for database security, and SQL statements are used to specify security restrictions. The SQL security scheme is based on three central concepts:

- **Users**. The actors in the database. Each time the DBMS retrieves, inserts, deletes, or updates data, it does so on behalf of some user. The DBMS permits or prohibits the action depending on which user is making the request.

- **Database objects**. The items to which SQL security protection can be applied. Security is usually applied to tables and views, but other objects such as forms, application programs, and entire databases can also be protected. Most users will have permission to use certain database objects but will be prohibited from using others.

- **Privileges**. The actions that a user is permitted to carry out for a given database object. A user may have permission to SELECT and INSERT rows in a certain table, for example, but may lack permission to DELETE or UPDATE rows of the table. A different user may have a different set of privileges.

Figure 15-1 shows how these security concepts might be used in a security scheme for the sample database.

To establish a security scheme for a database, you use the SQL GRANT statement to specify which users have which privileges on which database objects. For example, here is a GRANT statement that lets Sam Clark retrieve and insert data in the OFFICES table of the sample database:

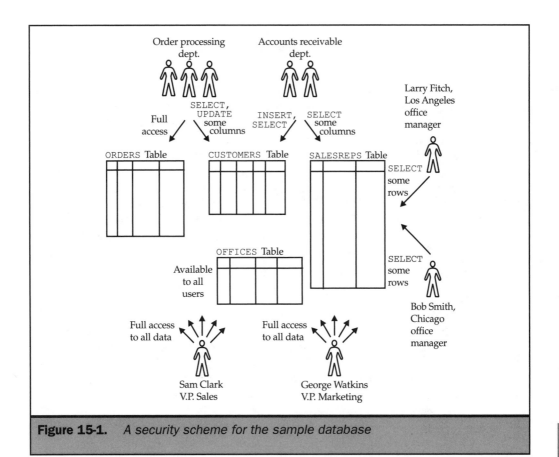

Figure 15-1.   *A security scheme for the sample database*

Let Sam Clark retrieve and insert data in the OFFICES table.

```
GRANT SELECT, INSERT
   ON OFFICES
   TO SAM
```

The GRANT statement specifies a combination of a user-id (SAM), an object (the OFFICES table), and privileges (SELECT and INSERT). Once granted, the privileges can be rescinded later with this REVOKE statement:

Take away the privileges granted earlier to Sam Clark.

```
REVOKE SELECT, INSERT
    ON OFFICES
  FROM SAM
```

The GRANT and REVOKE statements are described in detail later in this chapter, in the sections "Granting Privileges" and "Revoking Privileges."

User-Ids

Each user of a SQL-based database is typically assigned a *user-id*, a short name that identifies the user to the DBMS software. The user-id is at the heart of SQL security. Every SQL statement executed by the DBMS is carried out on behalf of a specific user-id. The user-id determines whether the statement will be permitted or prohibited by the DBMS. In a production database, user-ids are assigned by the database administrator. A personal computer database may have only a single user-id, identifying the user who created and who owns the database. In special-purpose databases (for example, those designed to be embedded within an application or a special-purpose system), there may be no need for the additional overhead associated with SQL security. These databases typically operate as if there were a single user-id.

In practice, the restrictions on the names that can be chosen as user-ids vary from implementation to implementation. The SQL1 standard permitted user-ids of up to 18 characters and required them to be valid SQL names. In some mainframe DBMS systems, user-ids may have no more than eight characters. In Sybase and SQL Server, user-ids may have up to 30 characters. If portability is a concern, it's best to limit user-ids to eight or fewer characters. Figure 15-2 shows various users who need access to the sample database and typical user-ids assigned to them. Note that all of the users in the order-processing department can be assigned the same user-id because they are to have identical privileges in the database.

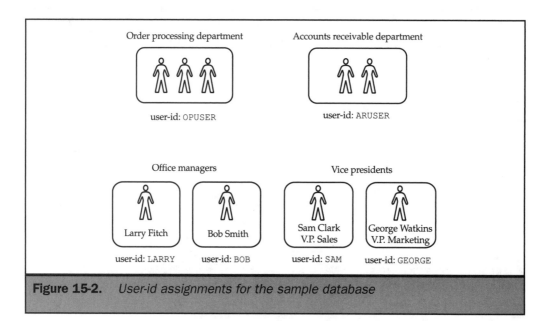

Figure 15-2. *User-id assignments for the sample database*

The ANSI/ISO SQL standard uses the term *authorization-id* instead of user-id, and you will occasionally find this term used in other SQL documentation. Technically, authorization-id is a more accurate term because the role of the ID is to determine authorization or privileges in the database. There are situations, as in Figure 15-2, where it makes sense to assign the same user-id to different users. In other situations, a single person may use two or three different user-ids. In a production database, authorization-ids may be associated with programs and groups of programs, rather than with human users. In each of these situations, authorization-id is a more precise and less confusing term than user-id. However, the most common practice is to assign a different user-id to each person, and most SQL-based DBMS use the term user-id in their documentation.

User Authentication

The SQL standard specifies that user-ids provide database security; however, the specific mechanism for associating a user-id with a SQL statement is outside the scope of the standard because a database can be accessed in many different ways. For example, when you type SQL statements into an interactive SQL utility, how does the DBMS determine which user-id is associated with the statements? If you use a forms-based data entry or query program, how does the DBMS determine your user-id? On a database server, a report-generating program might be scheduled to run at a preset time every evening; what is the user-id in this situation, where there is no human user? Finally, how are user-ids handled when you access a database across a network, where your user-id on the system where you are actively working might be different than the user-id established on the system where the database resides?

Most commercial SQL implementations establish a user-id for each database *session*. In interactive SQL, the session begins when you start the interactive SQL program, and it lasts until you exit the program. In an application program using programmatic SQL, the session begins when the application program connects to the DBMS, and it ends when the application program terminates. All of the SQL statements used during the session are associated with the user-id specified for the session.

Usually, you must supply both a user-id and an associated password at the beginning of a session. The DBMS checks the password to verify that you are, in fact, authorized to use the user-id that you supply. Although user-ids and passwords are common across most SQL products, the specific techniques used to specify the user-id and password vary from one product to another.

Some DBMS brands, especially those that are available on many different operating system platforms, implement their own user-id/password security. For example, when you use Oracle's interactive SQL program, called SQLPLUS, you specify a user name and associated password in the command that starts the program, like this:

```
SQLPLUS SCOTT/TIGER
```

The Sybase interactive SQL program, called ISQL, also accepts a user name and password, using this command format:

```
ISQL /USER=SCOTT /PASSWORD=TIGER
```

In each case, the DBMS validates the user-id (SCOTT) and the password (TIGER) before beginning the interactive SQL session.

Many other DBMS brands, including Ingres and Informix, use the user names of the host computer's operating system as database user-ids. For example, when you log in to a UNIX-based computer system, you must supply a valid UNIX user name and password to gain access. To start the Ingres interactive SQL utility, you simply give the command:

```
ISQL SALESDB
```

where SALESDB is the name of the Ingres database you want to use. Ingres automatically obtains your UNIX user name and makes it your Ingres user-id for the session. Thus, you don't have to specify a separate database user-id and password. DB2's interactive SQL, running under MVS/TSO, uses a similar technique. Your TSO login name automatically becomes your DB2 user-id for the interactive SQL session.

SQL security also applies to programmatic access to a database, so the DBMS must determine and authenticate the user-id for every application program that tries to access the database. Again, the techniques and rules for establishing the user-id vary from one brand of DBMS to another. For widely used utility programs, such as a data entry or an inquiry program, it is common for the program to ask the user for a user-id and password at the beginning of the session, via a screen dialog. For more specialized or custom-written programs, the appropriate user-id may be obvious from the application to be performed and hard-wired into the program.

The SQL2 standard also allows a program to use an authorization-id associated with a specific set of SQL statements (called a *module*), rather than the user-id of the particular person running the program. With this mechanism, a program may be given the ability to perform very specific operations on a database on behalf of many different users, even if those users are not otherwise authorized to access the target data. This is a convenient capability that is finding its way into mainstream SQL implementations. The specifics of SQL security for database access programs are described in Chapter 17, which covers programmatic SQL.

User Groups

A large production database often has groups of users with similar needs. In the sample database, for example, the three people in the order-processing department form a natural user group, and the two people in the accounts receivable department form another natural group. Within each group, all of the users have identical needs for data access and should have identical privileges.

Under the ANSI/ISO SQL security scheme, you can handle groups of users with similar needs in one of two ways:

- You can assign the same user-id to every person in the group, as shown in Figure 15-2. This scheme simplifies security administration because it allows you to specify data access privileges once for the single user-id. However, under this scheme, the people sharing the user-id cannot be distinguished from one another in system operator displays and DBMS reports.

- You can assign a different user-id to every person in the group. This scheme lets you differentiate between the users in reports produced by the DBMS, and it lets you establish different privileges for the individual users later. However, you must specify privileges for each user individually, making security administration tedious and error-prone.

The scheme you choose depends on the trade-offs in your particular database and application.

Several DBMS brands, including Sybase and SQL Server, offer a third alternative for dealing with groups of similar users. They support group-ids, which identify groups of related user-ids. Privileges can be granted both to individual user-ids and to group-ids, and a user may carry out a database action if it is permitted by either the user-id or group-id privileges. Group-ids thus simplify the administration of privileges given to groups of users. However, they are nonstandard, and a database design using them may not be portable to another DBMS brand.

DB2 also supports groups of users but takes a different approach. The DB2 database administrator can configure DB2 so that when you first connect to DB2 and supply your user-id (known as your *primary authorization-id*), DB2 automatically looks up a set of additional user-ids (known as *secondary authorization-ids*) that you may use. When DB2 later checks your privileges, it checks the privileges for all of your authorization-ids, primary and secondary. On an IBM mainframe system, the DB2 database administrator normally sets up the secondary authorization-ids so that they are the same as the user group names used by ResourceAccess Control Facility (RACF), the IBM mainframe security facility. Thus, the DB2 approach effectively provides group-ids but does so without adding to the user-id mechanism.

Security Objects

SQL security protections apply to specific *objects* contained in a database. The SQL1 standard specified two types of security objects—tables and views. Thus, each table and view can be individually protected. Access to a table or view can be permitted for certain user-ids and prohibited for other user-ids. The SQL2 standard expanded security protections to include other objects, including domains and user-defined character sets, and added a new type of protection for table or view access.

DATABASE STRUCTURE

Most commercial SQL products support additional security objects. In a SQL Server database, for example, a stored procedure is an important database object. The SQL security scheme determines which users can create and drop stored procedures and which users are allowed to execute them. In IBM's DB2, the physical tablespaces where tables are stored are treated as security objects. The database administrator can give some user-ids permission to create new tables in a particular tablespace and deny that permission to other user-ids. Other SQL implementations support other security objects. However, the underlying SQL security scheme—of specific privileges applied to specific objects, granted or revoked through the same SQL statements—is almost universally applied.

Privileges

The set of actions that a user can carry out against a database object are called the *privileges* for the object. The SQL1 standard specifies four basic privileges for tables and views:

- The SELECT privilege allows you to retrieve data from a table or view. With this privilege, you can specify the table or view in the FROM clause of a SELECT statement or subquery.

- The INSERT privilege allows you to insert new rows into a table or view. With this privilege, you can specify the table or view in the INTO clause of an INSERT statement.

- The DELETE privilege allows you to delete rows of data from a table or view. With this privilege, you can specify the table or view in the FROM clause of a DELETE statement.

- The UPDATE privilege allows you to modify rows of data in a table or view. With this privilege, you can specify the table or view as the target table in an UPDATE statement. The UPDATE privilege can be restricted to specific columns of the table or view, allowing updates to these columns but disallowing updates to any other columns.

These four privileges are supported by virtually all commercial SQL products.

SQL2 Extended Privileges

The SQL2 standard expanded the basic SQL1 privileges in several dimensions. It added new capabilities to the SQL1 INSERT and UPDATE privileges. It added a new REFERENCES privilege that restricts a user's ability to create a reference to a table from a foreign key in another table. It also added a new USAGE privilege that controls access to the new SQL2 database structures of domains, character sets, collation sequences, and translations.

The SQL2 extensions to the INSERT and UPDATE privileges are straightforward. These privileges may now be granted for a specific column or columns within a table, instead of applying to the entire table. The sample database provides a simple example of how this capability can be useful. Suppose you wanted to give your human resources manager the responsibility to insert new employees into the SALESREPS table, once the hiring paperwork is complete. The HR manager should supply the employee number, name, and similar information. But it should be the responsibility of the sales VP to set the QUOTA column for the new employee. Adjustments to the SALES column for existing employees would be similarly restricted.

Using the new SQL2 capabilities, you could implement this scheme by giving the HR manager INSERT privileges on the appropriate columns. The other columns (such as SALES and QUOTA) for any newly inserted employees would initially have the NULL value. With the UPDATE privilege on the other columns, the sales VP can then set the appropriate quota. Without the ability to specify these privileges on specific columns, you would have to either relax the restrictions on column access or define extraneous views on the table simply to restrict access.

The SQL2 standard does not allow the SELECT privilege to be applied to specific columns like the new INSERT and UPDATE capabilities; it must still be specified for an entire table. Theoretically, this capability isn't really needed, since you can achieve the same effect by defining a view on the table, limiting the view to specific columns, and then defining the appropriate privileges on the view. However, a column-specific SELECT privilege can be a much more straightforward approach. It keeps the structure of the database simpler (fewer view definitions) and concentrates the security scheme more tightly in one place (the GRANT statements). Several major DBMS brands, including Sybase and SQL Server, allow you to specify column-specific SELECT privileges, using the same syntax as for the column-specific UPDATE and INSERT. The SQL2 standard includes a note that this capability is also intended to be considered for future updates of the standard.

The new SQL2 REFERENCES privilege deals with a more subtle SQL security issue posed by the SQL2 capabilities of foreign keys and check constraints. Using the sample database as an example, suppose an employee has the ability to create a new table in the database (for example, a table containing new product information) but does not have any access to the employee information in the SALESREPS table. You might assume, given this security scheme, that there is no way for him to determine the employee numbers being used or whether a new employee has been hired.

However, this isn't strictly true. The employee could create a new table, with a column that is defined as a foreign key to the SALESREPS table. (Recall that this means the only legal values for this column are primary key values for the SALESREPS table— that is, valid employee numbers.) With this new table, the employee can simply try to insert new rows with different values in the foreign key column. The INSERT statements that succeed tell the employee that that he has discovered a valid employee number; those that fail represent invalid employee numbers.

Even more serious problems can be created by a new table defined with a check constraint on a column. For example, suppose the employee tries to execute this CREATE TABLE statement:

```
CREATE TABLE XYZ (TRYIT MONEY,
     CHECK ((SELECT QUOTA
                FROM SALESREPS
                WHERE TITLE = 'VP Sales')
   BETWEEN 400000 AND 500000))
```

Because of the column constraint linked to a value from the SALESREPS table, if this statement succeeds, it means the VP of sales has a quota in the specified range. If it doesn't, the employee can keep trying similar CREATE TABLE statements until he has determined the appropriate quota.

To eliminate this backdoor access to data, the SQL2 standard specifies a new REFERENCES privilege. Like the INSERT and UPDATE privileges, the REFERENCES privilege is granted for specific columns of a table. Only if a user has the REFERENCES privilege for a column is he or she allowed to create a new table that refers to that existing column in any way (for example, as the target of a foreign key reference, or in a check constraint, as in the previous examples). In databases that don't yet implement the REFERENCES privilege but do support foreign keys or check constraints, the SELECT privilege is sometimes used in this role.

Finally, the SQL2 standard specifies the USAGE privilege to control access to domains (sets of legal column values), user-defined character sets, collating sequences, and translations. The USAGE privilege is a simple on/off switch that either allows or disallows the use of these SQL2 database objects, by name, for individual user-ids. For example, with the USAGE privilege on a domain, you can define a new table with a column whose data type is defined as that domain. Without the privilege, you cannot create such a column definition. These privileges are directed mostly toward simplifying administration of large corporate databases that are used and modified by many different development teams. They typically do not present the same kinds of security issues as the table and column access privileges.

Ownership Privileges

When you create a table with the CREATE TABLE statement, you become its owner and receive full privileges for the table (SELECT, INSERT, DELETE, UPDATE, and any other privileges supported by the DBMS). Other users initially have no privileges on the newly created table. If they are to be given access to the table, you must explicitly grant privileges to them, using the GRANT statement.

When you create a view with the CREATE VIEW statement, you become the owner of the view, but you do not necessarily receive full privileges on it. To create the view successfully, you must already have the SELECT privilege on each of the source tables for the view; therefore, the DBMS gives you the SELECT privilege for the view automatically. For each of the other privileges (INSERT, DELETE, and UPDATE), the DBMS gives you the privilege on the view only if you hold that same privilege on *every* source table for the view.

Other Privileges

Many commercial DBMS products offer additional table and view privileges beyond the basic SELECT, INSERT, DELETE, and UPDATE privileges. For example, Oracle and the IBM mainframe databases support an ALTER and an INDEX privilege for tables. A user with the ALTER privilege on a particular table can use the ALTER TABLE statement to modify the definition of the table; a user with the INDEX privilege can create an index for the table with the CREATE INDEX statement. In DBMS brands that do not support the ALTER and INDEX privileges, only the owner may use the ALTER TABLE and CREATE INDEX statements.

Additional privileges are frequently supported for DBMS security objects other than tables and views. For example, Sybase and SQL Server support an EXECUTE privilege for stored procedures, which determines whether a user is allowed to execute a stored procedure. DB2 supports a USE privilege for tablespaces, which determines whether a user can create tables in a specific tablespace.

Views and SQL Security

In addition to the restrictions on table access provided by the SQL privileges, views also play a key role in SQL security. By carefully defining a view and giving a user permission to access the view but not its source tables, you can effectively restrict the user's access to only selected columns and rows. Views thus offer a way to exercise very precise control over what data is made visible to which users.

For example, suppose you wanted to enforce this security rule in the sample database:

Accounts receivable personnel should be able to retrieve employee numbers, names, and office numbers from the SALESREPS table, but data about sales and quotas should not be available to them.

You can implement this security rule by defining a view as follows:

```
CREATE VIEW REPINFO AS
    SELECT EMPL_NUM, NAME, REP_OFFICE
      FROM SALESREPS
```

and giving the SELECT privilege for the view to the ARUSER user-id, as shown in Figure 15-3. This example uses a vertical view to restrict access to specific columns.

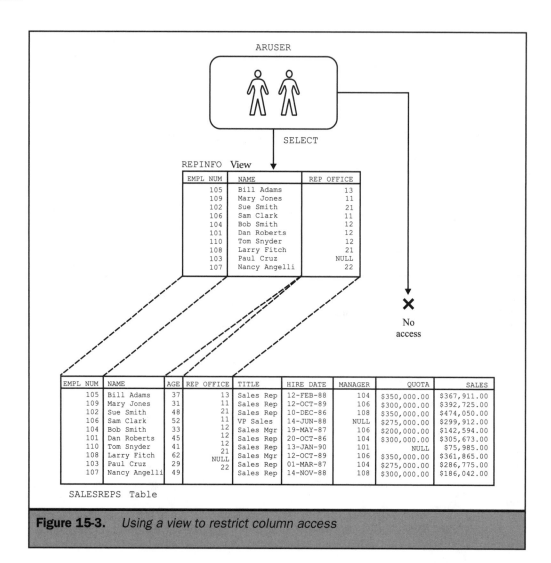

Figure 15-3. *Using a view to restrict column access*

Horizontal views are also effective for enforcing security rules such as this one:

The sales managers in each region should have full access to SALESREPS data for the salespeople assigned to that region.

As shown in Figure 15-4, you can define two views, EASTVIEWS and WESTVIEWS, containing SALESREPS data for each of the two regions, and then grant each office manager access to the appropriate view.

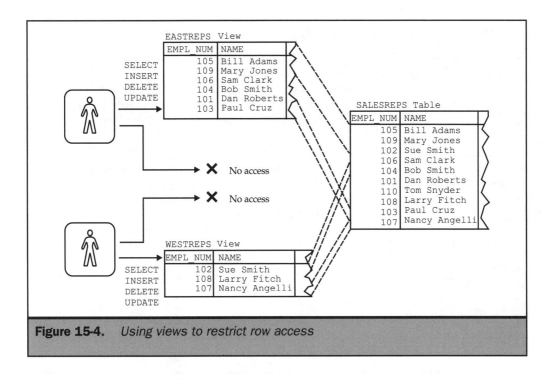

Figure 15-4.   *Using views to restrict row access*

Of course, views can be much more complex than the simple row and column subsets of a single table shown in these examples. By defining a view with a grouped query, you can give a user access to summary data but not to the detailed rows in the underlying table. A view can also combine data from two or more tables, providing precisely the data needed by a particular user and denying access to all other data. The usefulness of views for implementing SQL security is limited by the two fundamental restrictions described earlier in Chapter 14:

- **Update restrictions**. The SELECT privilege can be used with read-only views to limit data retrieval, but the INSERT, DELETE, and UPDATE privileges are meaningless for these views. If a user must update the data visible in a read-only view, the user must be given permission to update the underlying tables and must use INSERT, DELETE, and UPDATE statements that reference those tables.

- **Performance**. Because the DBMS translates every access to a view into a corresponding access to its source tables, views can add significant overhead to database operations. Views cannot be used indiscriminately to restrict database access without causing overall database performance to suffer.

Granting Privileges (GRANT)

The basic GRANT statement, shown in Figure 15-5, is used to grant security privileges on database objects to specific users. Normally, the GRANT statement is used by the owner of a table or view to give other users access to the data. As shown in the figure, the GRANT statement includes a specific list of the privileges to be granted, the name of the table to which the privileges apply, and the user-id to which the privileges are granted.

The GRANT statement shown in the syntax diagram conforms to the ANSI/ISO SQL standard. Many DBMS brands follow the DB2 GRANT statement syntax, which is more flexible. The DB2 syntax allows you to specify a list of user-ids and a list of tables, making it simpler to grant many privileges at once. Here are some examples of simple GRANT statements for the sample database:

Give order-processing users full access to the ORDERS table.

```
GRANT SELECT, INSERT, DELETE, UPDATE
    ON ORDERS
    TO OPUSER
```

Figure 15-5. *The GRANT statement syntax diagram*

Let accounts receivable users retrieve customer data and add new customers to the
CUSTOMERS table, but give order-processing users read-only access.

```
GRANT SELECT, INSERT
    ON CUSTOMERS
    TO ARUSER

GRANT SELECT
    ON CUSTOMERS
    TO OPUSER
```

Allow Sam Clark to insert or delete an office.

```
GRANT INSERT, DELETE
    ON OFFICES
    TO SAM
```

For convenience, the GRANT statement provides two shortcuts that you can use when granting many privileges or when granting them to many users. Instead of specifically listing all of the privileges available for a particular object, you can use the keywords ALL PRIVILEGES. This GRANT statement gives Sam Clark, the vice president of sales, full access to the SALESREPS table:

Give all privileges on the SALESREPS table to Sam Clark.

```
GRANT ALL PRIVILEGES
    ON SALESREPS
    TO SAM
```

Instead of giving privileges to every user of the database one-by-one, you can use the keyword PUBLIC to grant a privilege to every authorized database user. This GRANT statement lets anyone retrieve data from the OFFICES table:

Give all users SELECT acces to the OFFICES table.

```
GRANT SELECT
    ON OFFICES
    TO PUBLIC
```

Note that this GRANT statement grants access to all present and future authorized users, not just to the user-ids currently known to the DBMS. This eliminates the need for you to explicitly grant privileges to new users as they are authorized.

Column Privileges

The SQL1 standard allows you to grant the UPDATE privilege for individual columns of a table or view, and the SQL2 standard allows a column list for INSERT and REFERENCES privileges as well. The columns are listed after the UPDATE, INSERT, or REFERENCES keyword and enclosed in parentheses. Here is a GRANT statement that allows the order-processing department to update only the company name and assigned salesperson columns of the CUSTOMERS table:

Let order-processing users change company names and salesperson assignments.

```
GRANT UPDATE (COMPANY, CUST_REP)
    ON CUSTOMERS
    TO OPUSER
```

If the column list is omitted, the privilege applies to all columns of the table or view, as in this example:

Let accounts receivable users change any customer information.

```
GRANT UPDATE
    ON CUSTOMERS
    TO ARUSER
```

The ANSI/ISO standard does not permit a column list for the SELECT privilege; it requires that the SELECT privilege apply to all of the columns of a table or view. In practice, this isn't a serious restriction. To grant access to specific columns, you first define a view on the table that includes only those columns and then grant the SELECT privilege only for the view. However, views defined solely for security purposes can clog the structure of an otherwise simple database. For this reason, some DBMS brands allow a column list for the SELECT privilege. For example, the following GRANT statement is legal for the Sybase, SQL Server, and Informix DBMS brands:

Give accounts receivable users read-only access to the employee number, name, and sales office columns of the SALESREPS table.

```
GRANT SELECT (EMPL_NUM, NAME, REP_OFFICE)
    ON SALESREPS
    TO ARUSER
```

This GRANT statement eliminates the need for the REPINFO view defined in Figure 15-3, and in practice, it can eliminate the need for many views in a production database. However, the use of a column list for the SELECT privilege is unique to certain SQL dialects, and it is not permitted by the ANSI/ISO standard or by the IBM SQL products.

Passing Privileges (GRANT OPTION)

When you create a database object and become its owner, you are the only person who can grant privileges to use the object. When you grant privileges to other users, they are allowed to use the object, but they cannot pass those privileges on to other users. In this way, the owner of an object maintains very tight control both over who has permission to use the object and over which forms of access are allowed.

Occasionally, you may want to allow other users to grant privileges on an object that you own. For example, consider again the EASTREPS and WESTREPS views in the sample database. Sam Clark, the vice president of sales, created these views and owns them. He can give the Los Angeles office manager, Larry Fitch, permission to use the WESTREPS view with this GRANT statement:

```
GRANT SELECT
    ON WESTREPS
    TO LARRY
```

What happens if Larry wants to give Sue Smith (user-id SUE) permission to access the WESTREPS data because she is doing some sales forecasting for the Los Angeles office? With the preceding GRANT statement, he cannot give her the required privilege. Only Sam Clark can grant the privilege, because he owns the view.

If Sam wants to give Larry discretion over who may use the WESTREPS view, he can use this variation of the previous GRANT statement:

```
GRANT SELECT
    ON WESTREPS
    TO LARRY
  WITH GRANT OPTION
```

Because of the WITH GRANT OPTION clause, this GRANT statement conveys, along with the specified privileges, the right to grant those privileges to other users.

Larry can now issue this GRANT statement:

```
GRANT SELECT
    ON WESTREPS
    TO SUE
```

which allows Sue Smith to retrieve data from the WESTREPS view. Figure 15-6 graphically illustrates the flow of privileges, first from Sam to Larry, and then from Larry to Sue. Because the GRANT statement issued by Larry did not include the WITH GRANT OPTION clause, the chain of permissions ends with Sue; she can retrieve the WESTREPS data but cannot grant access to another user. However, if Larry's grant of

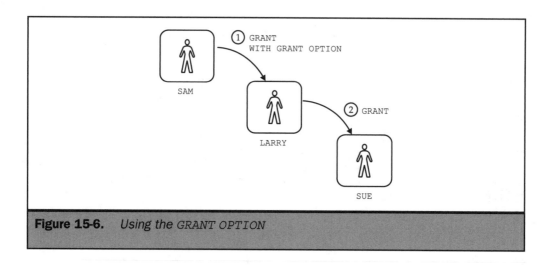

Figure 15-6. *Using the GRANT OPTION*

privileges to Sue had included the GRANT OPTION, the chain could continue to another level, allowing Sue to grant access to other users.

Alternatively, Larry might construct a view for Sue including only the salespeople in the Los Angeles office and give her access to that view:

```
CREATE VIEW LAREPS AS
     SELECT *
       FROM WESTREPS
       WHERE OFFICE = 21

GRANT ALL PRIVILEGES
    ON LAREPS
    TO SUE
```

Larry is the owner of the LAREPS view, but he does not own the WESTREPS view from which this new view is derived. To maintain effective security, the DBMS requires that Larry not only have the SELECT privilege on WESTREPS, but also requires that he have the GRANT OPTION for that privilege before allowing him to grant the SELECT privilege on LAREPS to Sue.

Once a user has been granted certain privileges with the GRANT OPTION, that user may grant those privileges *and* the GRANT OPTION to other users. Those other users can, in turn, continue to grant both the privileges and the GRANT OPTION. For this reason, you should use great care when giving other users the GRANT OPTION. Note that the GRANT OPTION applies only to the specific privileges named in the GRANT statement. If you want to grant certain privileges with the GRANT OPTION and grant other privileges without it, you must use two separate GRANT statements, as in this example:

> *Let Larry Fitch retrieve, insert, update, and delete data from the WESTREPS table,*
> *and let him grant retrieval permission to other users.*

```
GRANT SELECT
    ON WESTREPS
    TO LARRY
 WITH GRANT OPTION

GRANT INSERT, DELETE, UPDATE
    ON WESTREPS
    TO LARRY
```

Revoking Privileges (REVOKE)

In most SQL-based databases, the privileges that you have granted with the GRANT statement can be taken away with the REVOKE statement, shown in Figure 15-7. The REVOKE statement has a structure that closely parallels the GRANT statement,

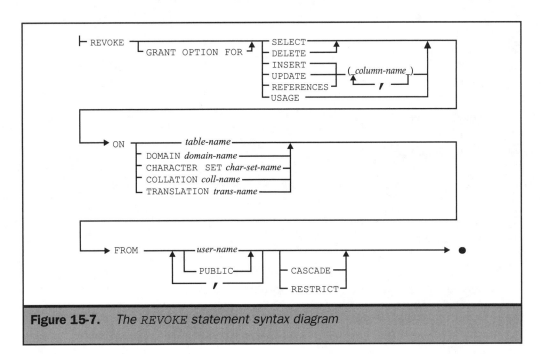

Figure 15-7. *The REVOKE statement syntax diagram*

specifying a specific set of privileges to be taken away, for a specific database object, from one or more user-ids.

A REVOKE statement may take away all or some of the privileges that you previously granted to a user-id. For example, consider this statement sequence:

Grant and then revoke some SALESREPS table privileges.

```
GRANT SELECT, INSERT, UPDATE
    ON SALESREPS
    TO ARUSER, OPUSER

REVOKE INSERT, UPDATE
     ON SALESREPS
   FROM OPUSER
```

The INSERT and UPDATE privileges on the SALESREPS table are first given to the two users and then revoked from one of them. However, the SELECT privilege remains for both user-ids. Here are some other examples of the REVOKE statement:

Take away all privileges granted earlier on the OFFICES table.

```
REVOKE ALL PRIVILEGES
     ON OFFICES
   FROM ARUSER
```

Take away UPDATE and DELETE privileges for two user-ids.

```
REVOKE UPDATE, DELETE
     ON OFFICES
   FROM ARUSER, OPUSER
```

Take away all privileges on the OFFICES that were formerly granted to all users.

```
REVOKE ALL PRIVILEGES
     ON OFFICES
   FROM PUBLIC
```

When you issue a REVOKE statement, you can take away only those privileges that *you* previously granted to another user. That user may also have privileges that were granted by other users; those privileges are not affected by your REVOKE statement. Note specifically that if two different users grant the same privilege on the same object to a user and one of them later revokes the privilege, the second user's grant will still allow the user to access the object. This handling of overlapping grants of privileges is illustrated in the following example sequence.

Suppose that Sam Clark, the sales vice president, gives Larry Fitch SELECT privileges for the SALESREPS table and SELECT and UPDATE privileges for the ORDERS table, using the following statements:

```
GRANT SELECT
    ON SALESREPS
    TO LARRY

GRANT SELECT, UPDATE
    ON ORDERS
    TO LARRY
```

A few days later George Watkins, the marketing vice president, gives Larry the SELECT and DELETE privileges for the ORDERS table and the SELECT privilege for the CUSTOMERS table, using these statements:

```
GRANT SELECT, DELETE
    ON ORDERS
    TO LARRY

GRANT SELECT
    ON CUSTOMERS
    TO LARRY
```

Note that Larry has received privileges on the ORDERS table from two different sources. In fact, the SELECT privilege on the ORDERS table has been granted by both sources. A few days later, Sam revokes the privileges he previously granted to Larry for the ORDERS table:

```
REVOKE SELECT, UPDATE
    ON ORDERS
    FROM LARRY
```

After the DBMS processes the REVOKE statement, Larry still retains the SELECT privilege on the SALESREPS table, the SELECT and DELETE privileges on the ORDERS table, and the SELECT privilege on the CUSTOMERS table, but he has lost the UPDATE privilege on the ORDERS table.

REVOKE and the GRANT OPTION

When you grant privileges with the GRANT OPTION and later revoke these privileges, most DBMS brands will *automatically* revoke all privileges derived from the original grant. Consider again the chain of privileges in Figure 15-6, from Sam Clark, the sales vice president, to Larry Fitch, the Los Angeles office manager, and then to Sue Smith. If Sam now revokes Larry's privileges for the WESTREPS view, Sue's privilege is automatically revoked as well.

The situation gets more complicated if two or more users have granted privileges and one of them later revokes the privileges. Consider Figure 15-8, a slight variation on the last example. Here, Larry receives the SELECT privilege with the GRANT OPTION from both Sam (the sales vice president) and George (the marketing vice president) and then grants privileges to Sue. This time when Sam revokes Larry's privileges, the grant of privileges from George remains. Furthermore, Sue's privileges also remain because they can be derived from George's grant.

However, consider another variation on the chain of privileges, with the events slightly rearranged, as shown in Figure 15-9. Here, Larry receives the privilege with

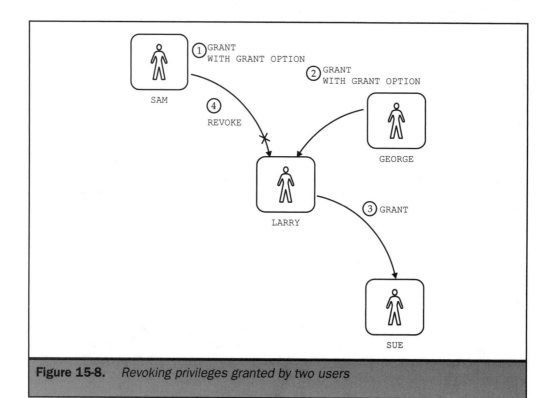

Figure 15-8. *Revoking privileges granted by two users*

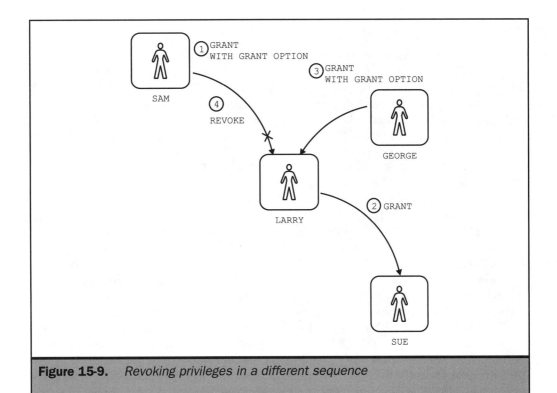

Figure 15-9. *Revoking privileges in a different sequence*

the GRANT OPTION from Sam, grants the privilege to Sue, and *then* receives the grant, with the GRANT OPTION, from George. This time when Sam revokes Larry's privileges, the results are slightly different, and they may vary from one DBMS to another. As in Figure 15-8, Larry retains the SELECT privilege on the WESTREPS view because the grant from George is still intact. But in a DB2 or SQL/DS database, Sue automatically loses her SELECT privilege on the table. Why? Because the grant from Larry to Sue was clearly derived from the grant from Sam to Larry, which has just been revoked. It could not have been derived from George's grant to Larry because that grant had not yet taken place when the grant from Larry to Sue was made.

In a different brand of DBMS, Sue's privileges might remain intact because the grant from George to Larry remains intact. Thus, the time sequence of GRANT and REVOKE statements, rather than just the privileges themselves, can determine how far the effects of a REVOKE statement will cascade. Granting and revoking privileges with the GRANT OPTION must be handled very carefully, to ensure that the results are those you intend.

REVOKE and the ANSI/ISO Standard

The SQL1 standard specified the GRANT statement as part of the SQL Data Definition Language (DDL). Recall from Chapter 13 that the SQL1 standard treated the DDL as a separate, static definition of a database and did not require that the DBMS permit dynamic changes to database structure. This approach applies to database security as well. Under the SQL1 standard, accessibility to tables and views in the database is determined by a series of GRANT statements included in the database schema. There is no mechanism for changing the security scheme once the database structure is defined. The REVOKE statement is therefore absent from the SQL1 standard, just as the DROP TABLE statement is missing from the standard.

Despite its absence from the SQL1 standard, the REVOKE statement was provided by virtually all commercial SQL-based DBMS products since their earliest versions. As with the DROP and ALTER statements, the DB2 dialect of SQL has effectively set the standard for the REVOKE statement. The SQL2 standard includes a specification for the REVOKE statement based on the DB2 statement with some extensions. One of the extensions gives the user more explicit control over how privileges are revoked when the privileges have, in turn, been granted to others. The other provides a way to revoke the GRANT OPTION without revoking the privileges themselves.

To specify how the DBMS should handle the revoking of privileges that have been in turn granted to others, the SQL2 standard requires that a CASCADE or RESTRICT option be specified in a REVOKE statement. (A similar requirement applies to many of the DROP statements in the SQL2 standard, as described in Chapter 13.) Suppose that SELECT and UPDATE privileges have previously been granted to Larry on the ORDERS table, with the GRANT OPTION, and that Larry has further granted these options to Bill. Then this REVOKE statement:

```
REVOKE SELECT, UPDATE
    ON ORDERS
    FROM LARRY CASCADE
```

revokes not only Larry's privileges, but Bill's as well. The effect of the REVOKE statement thus cascades to all other users whose privileges have flowed from the original GRANT.

Now, assume the same circumstances and this REVOKE statement:

```
REVOKE SELECT, UPDATE
    ON ORDERS
    FROM LARRY RESTRICT
```

In this case, the REVOKE fails. The RESTRICT option tells the DBMS not to execute the statement if it will affect any other privileges in the database. The resulting error calls the user's attention to the fact that there are (possibly unintentional) side-effects of the REVOKE statement and allows the user to reconsider the action. If the user wants to go ahead and revoke the privileges, the CASCADE option can be specified.

The SQL2 version of the REVOKE statement also gives a user more explicit, separate control over privileges and the GRANT OPTION for those privileges. Suppose again that Larry has been granted privileges on the ORDERS table, with the GRANT OPTION for those privileges. The usual REVOKE statement for those privileges:

```
REVOKE SELECT, UPDATE
    ON ORDERS
  FROM LARRY
```

takes away both the privileges and the ability to grant those privileges to others. The SQL2 standard permits this version of the REVOKE statement:

```
REVOKE GRANT OPTION FOR SELECT, UPDATE
    ON ORDERS
  FROM LARRY CASCADE
```

If the statement is successful, Larry will lose the ability to grant these privileges to other users, but he will not lose the privileges themselves. As before, the SQL2 standard requires the CASCADE or the RESTRICT option to specify how the DBMS should handle the statement if Larry has, in turn, granted the GRANT OPTION to other users.

Summary

The SQL language is used to specify the security restrictions for a SQL-based database:

- The SQL security scheme is built around privileges (permitted actions) that can be granted on specific database objects (such as tables and views) to specific user-ids (users or groups of users).

- Views also play a key role in SQL security because they can be used to restrict access to specific rows or specific columns of a table.

- The GRANT statement is used to grant privileges; privileges that you grant to a user with the GRANT OPTION can in turn be granted by that user to others.

- The REVOKE statement is used to revoke privileges previously granted with the GRANT statement.

DATABASE STRUCTURE

Chapter 16

The System Catalog

459

A database management system must keep track of a great deal of information about the structure of a database to perform its data management functions. In a relational database, this information is typically stored in the *system catalog,* a collection of system tables that the DBMS maintains for its own use. The information in the system catalog describes the tables, views, columns, privileges, and other structural features of the database.

Although the DBMS maintains the system catalog primarily for its own internal purposes, the system tables or views based on them are usually accessible to database users as well, through standard SQL queries. A relational database is thus self-describing; using queries against the system tables, you can ask the database to describe its own structure. General-purpose database front-ends, such as query tools and report writers, use this self-describing feature to generate lists of tables and columns for user selection, simplifying database access.

This chapter describes the system catalogs provided by several popular SQL-based DBMS products and the information that the catalogs contain. It also describes the system catalog capabilities specified by the ANSI/ISO SQL2 standard.

What Is the System Catalog?

The system catalog is a collection of special tables in a database that are owned, created, and maintained by the DBMS itself. These *system tables* contain data that describes the structure of the database. The tables in the system catalog are automatically created when the database is created. They are usually gathered under a special system user-id with a name like SYSTEM, SYSIBM, MASTER, or DBA.

The DBMS constantly refers to the data in the system catalog while processing SQL statements. For example, to process a two-table SELECT statement, the DBMS must:

- Verify that the two named tables actually exist.

- Ensure that the user has permission to access them.

- Check whether the columns referenced in the query exist.

- Resolve any unqualified column names to one of the tables.

- Determine the data type of each column.

By storing structural information in system tables, the DBMS can use its own access methods and logic to rapidly and efficiently retrieve the information it needs to perform these tasks.

If the system tables were used only internally to the DBMS, they would be of little interest to database users. However, the DBMS generally makes the system tables available for user access as well. If the system tables themselves are not made available, the DBMS generally provides views based on the system tables that offer a set of user-retrievable catalog information. User queries against the system catalogs or views are almost always permitted by personal computer and workgroup class databases. These queries are also supported by mainframe and enterprise DBMS products, but the database administrator may restrict system catalog access to provide an additional measure of database security. By querying the system catalogs, you can discover information about the structure of a database, even if you have never used it before.

User access to the system catalog is read-only. The DBMS prevents users from directly updating or modifying the system tables because such modifications would destroy the integrity of the database. Instead, the DBMS itself takes care of inserting, deleting, and updating rows of the system tables as it modifies the structure of a database. Data Definition Language (DDL) statements such as CREATE, ALTER, DROP, GRANT, and REVOKE produce changes in the system tables as a byproduct of their actions. In some DBMS products, even DML statements that modify the database, such as INSERT and DELETE, may produce changes in the system tables, which keep track of how many rows are in each table.

The Catalog and Query Tools

One of the most important benefits of the system catalog is that it makes possible user-friendly query tools, as shown in Figure 16-1. The objective of such tools is to let users simply and transparently access the database without learning the SQL language. Typically, a tool leads the user through a series of steps like this one:

1. The user gives a name and password for database access.

2. The query tool displays a list of available tables.

3. The user chooses a table, causing the query tool to display a list of the columns it contains.

4. The user chooses columns of interest, perhaps by clicking their names as they appear on a PC screen.

5. The user chooses columns from other tables or restricts the data to be retrieved with a search condition.

6. The query tool retrieves the requested data and displays it on the user's screen.

A general-purpose query tool like the one in Figure 16-1 will be used by many different users, and it will be used to access many different databases. The tool cannot possibly know in advance the structure of the database that it will access during any given session. Thus, it must be able to dynamically learn about the tables and columns of a database. The tool uses system catalog queries for this purpose.

The Catalog and the ANSI/ISO Standard

The ANSI/ISO SQL1 standard did not specify the structure and contents of the system catalog. In fact, the SQL1 standard does not require a system catalog at all. However, all of the major SQL-based DBMS products provide a system catalog in one form or another. The structure of the catalog and the tables it contains vary considerably from one brand of DBMS to another.

DATABASE STRUCTURE

Figure 16-1. *A user-friendly query tool*

Because of the growing importance of general-purpose database tools that must access the system catalog, the SQL2 standard includes a specification of a set of views that provide standardized access to information typically found in the system catalog. A DBMS system that conforms to the SQL2 standard must support these views, which are collectively called the INFORMATION_SCHEMA. Because this schema is more complex than the actual system catalogs used by commercial DBMS products, and is only slowly being supported, it is described in a separate section near the end of this chapter titled "The SQL2 Information Schema."

Catalog Contents

Each table in the system catalog contains information about a single kind of structural element in the database. Although the details vary, almost all commercial SQL products include system tables that describe each of these five entities:

- **Tables**. The catalog describes each table in the database, identifying its table name, its owner, the number of columns it contains, its size, and so on.

■ **Columns**. The catalog describes each column in the database, giving the column's name, the table to which it belongs, its data type, its size, whether NULLs are allowed, and so on.

■ **Users**. The catalog describes each authorized database user, including the user's name, an encrypted form of the user's password, and other data.

■ **Views**. The catalog describes each view defined in the database, including its name, the name of its owner, the query that defines the view, and so on.

■ **Privileges**. The catalog describes each set of privileges granted in the database, including the names of the grantor and grantee, the privileges granted, the object on which the privileges have been granted, and so on.

Table 16-1 shows the names of the system tables that provide this information in each of the major SQL-based DBMS products. The remainder of this chapter describes some typical system tables in more detail and gives examples of system catalog access. Because of the wide variations in system catalogs among DBMS brands, a complete description of the system catalogs and complete examples for all of the major DBMS brands is beyond the scope of this book. With the information provided here, you should be able to consult the system documentation for your DBMS brand and construct the appropriate system catalog queries.

DBMS	Tables	Columns	Users	Views	Privileges
DB2[1]	SCHEMATA TABLES REFERENCES KEYCOLUSE	COLUMNS	DBAUTH	VIEWS VIEWDEP	SCHEMAAUTH TABAUTH COLAUTH
Oracle	USER_ CATALOG USER_TABLES ALL_TABLES USER_ SYNONYMS	USER_TAB_ COLUMNS ALL_TAB_ COLUMNS	ALL_USERS	USER_VIEWS ALL_VIEWS	USER_TAB_ PRIVS USER_COL_ PRIVS USER_SYS_ PRIVS
Informix	SYSTABLES SYSREFER ENCES SYSSYNONYMS	SYSCOLUMNS	SYSUSERS	SYSVIEWS SYSDEPEND	SYSTABAUTH SYSCOLAUTH

Table 16-1.   *Selected System Tables in Popular SQL-Based Products*

DBMS	Tables	Columns	Users	Views	Privileges
Sybase	SYSDATA-BASES SYSOBJECTS SYSKEYS	SYSCOLUMNS	SYSUSERS	SYSOBJECTS SYSCOMMENTS	
SQL Server	SYSDATA-BASES SYSOBJECTS SYSFOREIGN-KEYS SYSREFERENCES	SYSCOLUMNS	SYSUSERS SYSLOGINS SYSMEMBERS	SYSOBJECTS SYSDEPENDS SYSCOMMENTS	SYSPROTECTS

---

[1] DB2 tables have the qualifier SYSCAT (e.g., SYSCAT.TABLES).

Table 16-1. *Selected System Tables in Popular SQL-Based Products* (continued)

Table Information

Each of the major SQL products has a system table or view that keeps track of the tables in the database. In DB2, for example, this information is provided by a system catalog view named SYSCAT.TABLES. (All of the DB2 system catalog views are part of a schema named SYSCAT, so they all have qualified table/view names of the form SYSCAT.*xxx*.)

Table 16-2 shows some of the columns of the SYSCAT.TABLES view. It contains one row for each table, view, or alias defined in the database. The information in this view is typical of that provided by the corresponding views in other major DBMS products.

Column Name	Data Type	Information
TABSCHEMA	CHAR(8)	Schema containing the table, view, or alias
TABNAME	VARCHAR(18)	Name of the table, view, or alias
DEFINER	CHAR(8)	User-id of table/view/alias creator
TYPE	CHAR(1)	T = table, V = view, A = alias

Table 16-2. *The SYSCAT.TABLES View (DB2)*

Column Name	Data Type	Information
STATUS	CHAR(1)	Status of object (system use)
BASE_TABSCHEMA	CHAR(8)	Schema of base table for an alias
BASE_TABNAME	VARCHAR(18)	Name of base table for an alias
CREATE_TIME	TIMESTAMP	Time of object creation
STATS_TIME	TIMESTAMP	Time when last statistics computed
COLCOUNT	SMALLINT	Number of columns in table
TABLEID	SMALLINT	Internal table-id number
TBSPACEID	SMALLINT	ID of primary tablespace for this table
CARD	INTEGER	Number of rows in table (cardinality)
NPAGES	INTEGER	Number of disk pages containing table data
FPAGES	INTEGER	Total number of disk pages for table
OVERFLOW	INTEGER	Number of overflow records for table
TBSPACE	VARCHAR(18)	Primary tablespace for storing table data
INDEX_TBSPACE	VARCHAR(18)	Tablespace for storing table indexes
LONG_TBSPACE	VARCHAR(18)	Tablespace for storing large object data
PARENTS	SMALLINT	Number of parent tables for this table
CHILDREN	SMALLINT	Number of child tables for this table
SELFREFS	SMALLINT	Number of self-references for this table
KEYCOLUMNS	SMALLINT	Number of columns in table's primary key
KEYINDEXID	SMALLINT	Internal ID for primary key index
KEYUNIQUE	SMALLINT	Number of unique constraints for table
CHECKCOUNT	SMALLINT	Number of check constraints for table
DATACAPTURE	CHAR(1)	Table is replicated? (Yes/No)
CONST_CHECKED	CHAR(32)	Constraint-checking flags
PMAP_ID	SMALLINT	Internal ID for table's partitioning map
PARTITION_MODE	CHAR(1)	Mode for partitioned database tables

Table 16-2. *The SYSCAT.TABLES View (DB2)* (continued)

Column Name	Data Type	Information
LOG_ATTRIBUTE	CHAR(1)	Whether logging is initially enabled for table
PCTFREE	SMALLINT	Percentage of page to reserve for future data
REMARKS	VARCHAR(254)	User-provided comments for table

Table 16-2.   *The SYSCAT.TABLES View (DB2)* (continued)

You can use queries like the following examples to find out information about the tables in a DB2 database. Similar queries, using different table and column names, can be used to obtain the same information from other DBMS brands.

List the names and owners of all tables in the database.

```
SELECT DEFINER, TABNAME
  FROM SYSCAT.TABLES
 WHERE TYPE = 'T'
```

List the names of all tables, views, and aliases in the database.

```
SELECT TABNAME
  FROM SYSCAT.TABLES
```

List the names and creation times of only my tables.

```
SELECT TABNAME, CREATE_TIME
  FROM SYSCAT.TABLES
 WHERE TYPE = 'T'
   AND DEFINER = USER
```

In an Oracle database, a pair of system views named USER_TABLES and ALL_TABLES perform a similar function to the DB2 SYSCAT.TABLES view. The USER_TABLES view contains one row for each database table that is owned by the current user. The ALL_TABLES view contains one row for each table to which the current user has access. The ALL_TABLES view thus will include all of the rows from USER_TABLES, plus additional rows representing tables owned by other users to which the current user has been granted at least one of the access privileges. Here is a typical query against these Oracle system catalog views:

List the names and owners of all tables to which I have access.

```
SELECT TABLE_NAME, OWNER
  FROM ALL_TABLES
```

The SQL Server equivalent of the DB2 SYSCAT.TABLES view is a system table named SYSOBJECTS, described in Table 16-3. The SYSOBJECTS table stores information about SQL Server tables and views and other SQL Server objects such as stored procedures, rules, and triggers. Note also how the SYSOBJECTS table uses an internal ID number instead of a name to identify the table owner.

The Informix Universal Server system table that gives information about tables is named SYSTABLES. Like the DB2 catalog, it contains information only about tables, views, and aliases; other database objects are described in other system tables. Here is a typical query against this Informix system table:

List the name, owner, and creation date of all tables in the database.

```
SELECT TABNAME, OWNER, CREATED
  FROM SYSTABLES
 WHERE TABTYPE = 'T'
```

Column Name	Data Type	Information
Name	SYSNAME	Name of the object
Id	INT	Internal object ID number
Uid	SMALLINT	User-id of object owner
Type	CHAR(2)	Object type code[1]
crdate	DATETIME	Date/time object was created
deltrig	INT	Procedure ID of DELETE trigger
instrig	INT	Procedure ID of INSERT trigger
updtrig	INT	Procedure ID of UPDATE trigger

[1] S = system table, U = user table, V = view, L = log, P = stored procedure, TR = trigger, and so on

Table 16-3.   *Selected Columns of the SYSOBJECTS Table (SQL Server)*

As these examples show, the queries to obtain table information have a similar structure across DBMS brands. However, the specific names of the system table(s) or view(s) containing the information, and the relevant columns, vary considerably across brands.

Column Information

All of the major SQL products have a system table that keeps track of the columns in the database. There is one row in this table for each column in each table or view in the database. Most DBMS brands restrict access to this base system table, but provide user column information through a view that shows only columns in tables owned by, or accessible to, the current user. In an Oracle database, two system catalog views provide this information—USER_TAB_COLUMNS, which includes one row for each column in each table owned by the current user, and ALL_TAB_COLUMNS, which contains one row for each column in each table accessible to the current user.

Most of the information in the system columns table or view stores the definition of a column—its name, its data type, its length, whether it can take NULL values, and so on. In addition, the table sometimes includes information about the distribution of data values found in each column. This statistical information helps the DBMS decide how to carry out a query in the optimal way.

Here is a typical query you could use to find out about the columns in an Oracle database:

List the names and data types of the columns in my OFFICES table.

```
SELECT COLUMN_NAME, DATA_TYPE
  FROM USER_TAB_COLUMNS
 WHERE TABLE_NAME = 'OFFICES'
```

Like the table information in the system catalog, the column information varies across DBMS brands. Table 16-4 shows the contents of the SYSCAT.COLUMNS system table, which contains column information in the DB2 catalog. Here are some queries that apply to this DBMS brand:

Find all columns in the database with a DATE data type.

```
SELECT TABSCHEMA, TABNAME, COLNAME
  FROM SYSCAT.COLUMNS
 WHERE TYPESCHEMA = 'SYSIBMD' AND TYPENAME = 'DATE'
```

List the owner, view name, column name, data type, and length for all text columns longer than ten characters defined in views.

```
SELECT DEFINER, COLS.TABNAME, COLNAME, TYPENAME, LENGTH
  FROM SYSCAT.COLUMNS COLS, SYSCAT.TABLES TBLS
 WHERE TBLS.TABSCHEMA = COLS.TABSCHEMA
   AND TBLS.TBLNAME = COLS.TBLNAME
   AND (TYPENAME = 'VARCHAR' OR TYPENAME = 'CHARACTER')
   AND LENGTH > 10
   AND TYPE = 'V'
```

Column Name	Data Type	Information
TABSCHEMA	CHAR(8)	Schema of table containing the column
TABNAME	VARCHAR(18)	Name of table containing the column
COLNAME	VARCHAR(18)	Name of the column
COLNO	SMALLINT	Position of column in table (first column = 0)
TYPESCHEMA	CHAR(8)	Schema of column's domain (or SYSIBM)
TYPENAME	VARCHAR(18)	Name of data type or domain for column
LENGTH	INTEGER	Maximum data length for variable-length types
SCALE	SMALLINT	Scale for DECIMAL data types
DEFAULT	VARCHAR(254)	Default value for column
NULLS	CHAR(1)	Whether NULLs are allowed (Y/N)
CODEPAGE	SMALLINT	Code page for extended character types
LOGGED	CHAR(1)	Whether logging is enabled (Y/N) for large object columns
COMPACT	CHAR(1)	Whether large object column is compacted (Y/N)
COLCARD	INTEGER	Number of distinct data values (cardinality)
HIGH2KEY	VARCHAR(33)	Second-highest column value in table
LOW2KEY	VARCHAR(33)	Second-lowest column value in table

Table 16-4.   *The* SYSCAT.COLUMNS *View (DB2)*

Column Name	Data Type	Information
AVGCOLLEN	INTEGER	Average data length for variable-length types
KEYSEQ	SMALLINT	Column position within primary key (or 0)
PARTKEYSEQ	SMALLINT	Column position within partitioning key (or 0)
NQUANTILES	SMALLINT	Number of quantiles in column statistics
NMOSTFREQ	SMALLINT	Number of frequent values in column statistics
REMARKS	VARCHAR(254)	User-supplied comments for column

Table 16-4. *The SYSCAT.COLUMNS View (DB2)* (continued)

There is considerable variation in the way that the column definition is provided by the system catalogs of various DBMS brands. For comparison, Table 16-5 shows the definition of the Informix Universal Server SYSCOLUMNS table. Some of the differences between the column information in the tables are simply matters of style:

- The names of the columns in the two tables are completely different, even when they contain similar data.

- The DB2 catalog uses a combination of the schema name and table name to identify the table containing a given column; the Informix catalog uses an internal table-id number, which is a foreign key to its SYSTABLES table.

- The DB2 specifies data types in text form (for example, CHARACTER); the Informix catalog uses integer data type codes.

Other differences reflect the different capabilities provided by the two DBMS brands:

- DB2 allows you to specify up to 254 characters of remarks about each column; Informix does not provide this feature.

- The Informix system table keeps track of the minimum and maximum length of actual data values stored in a variable-length column; this information is not available directly from the DB2 system catalog.

Column Name	Data Type	Information
COLNAME	CHAR(18)	Name of the column
TABID	INTEGER	Internal table-id of table containing column
COLNO	SMALLINT	Position of column in table
COLTYPE	SMALLINT	Data type of column and whether NULLs are allowed
COLLENGTH	SMALLINT	Column length
COLMIN	INTEGER	Second smallest column data value
COLMAX	INTEGER	Second largest column data value
MINLEN	INTEGER	Minimum actual data length
MAXLEN	INTEGER	Maximum actual data length
EXTENDED_ID	INTEGER	Internal ID of extended data type

Table 16-5.   *The SYSCOLUMNS Table (Informix)*

View Information

The definitions of the views in a database are usually stored by the DBMS in the system catalog. The DB2 catalog contains two system tables that keep track of views. The SYSCAT.VIEWS table, described in Table 16-6, contains the SQL text definition of each view. If the definition exceeds 3600 characters, it is stored in multiple rows, with sequence numbers 1, 2, 3, and so on.

The DB2 SYSCAT.VIEWDEP table, described in Table 16-7, shows how each view depends on other tables or views. There is one row in the table for each dependency, so a view with three source tables will be represented by three rows.

Using these two tables, you can see the definitions of the views in the database and quickly determine which tables in the database serve as the source tables for a view. As with many mainstream DBMS products, information about views is tightly linked to the information about tables in the DB2 catalog. This means there is often more than one way to find the answer to a catalog inquiry. For example, here is a direct query

Column Name	Data Type	Information
VIEWSCHEMA	CHAR(8)	Schema containing the view
VIEWNAME	VARCHAR(18)	Name of the view
DEFINER	CHAR(8)	User-id of person who created the view
SEQNO	SMALLINT	Sequence number for this row of SQL text
VIEWCHECK	CHAR(1)	Type of view checking
READONLY	CHAR(1)	Whether view is read-only (Y/N)
VALID	CHAR(1)	Whether view definition is valid (Y/N)
FUNC_PATH	VARCHAR(254)	Path for resolving function calls in view
TEXT	VARCHAR(3600)	SQL text of view definition ("SELECT...")

Table 16-6. *The SYSCAT.VIEWS View (DB2)*

Column Name	Data Type	Information
VIEWSCHEMA	CHAR(8)	Schema containing the view
VIEWNAME	VARCHAR(18)	Name of the view
DEFINER	CHAR(8)	User-id of person who created the view
BTYPE	CHAR(1)	Type of object on which view depends (T = table, V = view, A = alias, and so on)
BSCHEMA	CHAR(8)	Schema containing the object on which view depends
TABAUTH	SMALLINT	Flags indicating privileges on the object on which view depends

Table 16-7. *The SYSCAT.VIEWDEP View (DB2)*

against the DB2 VIEWS system table to obtain the names and creators of all views
defined in the database:

List the views defined in the database.

```
SELECT DISTINCT VIEWSCHAME, VIEWNAME, DEFINER
  FROM SYSCAT.VIEWS
```

Note the use of DISTINCT to eliminate duplicate rows that would be present for
views with long text definitions. Perhaps an easier way to obtain the same information
is to query the DB2 TABLES system table directly, selecting only rows representing
views, as indicated by the TYPE value:

List the views defined in the database.

```
SELECT TABSCHEMA, TABNAME, DEFINER
  FROM SYSCAT.TABLES
 WHERE TYPE = 'V'
```

Most of the major DBMS products treat views in this same way within their system
catalog structure. Informix Universal Server, for example, has a system table named
SYSVIEWS that contains view definitions. Each of its rows holds a 64-character chunk
of the SQL SELECT statement that defines a view. View definitions that span multiple
rows are handled by sequence numbers, as with DB2. The Informix SYSVIEWS table
includes only one other column—the table-id that links the SYSVIEWS table to the
corresponding row in the SYSTABLES table. Thus, Informix duplicates less information
between the SYSTABLES and SYSVIEWS tables, but you must explicitly join the tables
for the most common view information requests.

Oracle takes a similar approach by making the SQL text that defines a view available
via system views. As with table and column information, there are two system views
of interest: USER_VIEWS, which contains information about all views created and
owned by the current user, and ALL_VIEWS, which also includes information about
views accessible to the current user but created by other users. Unlike the DB2 and
Informix approaches, which split the SQL text defining the view into multiple rows
with sequence numbers if it is lengthy, Oracle's system views contain only one row
per view. The SQL text defining the view is held in a LONG (large object) column and
can conceivably run to thousands of characters. A length column tells the length of

the stored SQL text definition of the view. Here is a query to obtain Oracle view information:

List the current user's views and their definitions.

```
SELECT VIEW_NAME, TEXT_LENGTH, TEXT
   FROM USER_VIEWS
```

Note that most interactive SQL products (including Oracle's) truncate the text containing the view definition if it is too long to be displayed effectively. The actual text stored in the database is complete.

Remarks

IBM's DB2 products allow you to associate up to 254 characters of *remarks* with each table, view, and column defined in the database. The remarks allow you to store a brief description of the table or data item in the system catalog. The remarks are stored in the SYSCAT.TABLES and SYSCAT.COLUMNS system tables of the system catalog. Unlike the other elements of table and column definitions, the remarks and labels are not specified by the CREATE TABLE statement. Instead, the COMMENT statement is used. Its syntax is shown in Figure 16-2. Here are some examples:

Define remarks for the OFFICES table.

```
COMMENT ON TABLE OFFICES
      IS 'This table stores data about our sales offices'
```

Associate some remarks with the TARGET and SALES columns of the OFFICES table.

```
COMMENT ON OFFICES
(TARGET IS 'This is the annual sales target for the office',
  SALES IS 'This is the year-to-date sales for the office')
```

Because this is a capability carried forward from some of the earliest IBM SQL products, Oracle also supports the COMMENT ON statement for attaching comments to tables and columns. The comments are not stored inline with other table and column information, however. They are accessible via the Oracle system views USER_TAB_COMMENTS and USER_COL_COMMENTS. The DB2 COMMENT capability has been expanded over the years to allow comments on constraints, stored procedures, schemas, tablespaces, triggers, and other DB2 database objects. This capability is not part of the SQL standard and has generally not been adopted by other major DBMS products.

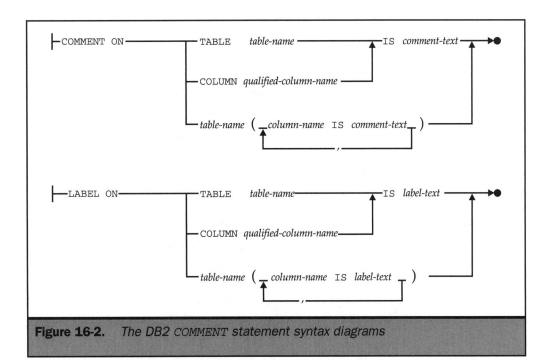

Figure 16-2.   *The DB2* COMMENT *statement syntax diagrams*

Relationship Information

With the introduction of referential integrity into the major enterprise DBMS products during the mid-1990s, system catalogs were expanded to describe primary keys, foreign keys, and the parent/child relationships that they create. In DB2, which was among the first to support referential integrity, the description is provided by the SYSCAT. REFERENCES system catalog table, described in Table 16-8. Every parent/child relationship between two tables in the database is represented by a single row in the SYSCAT.REFERENCES table. The row identifies the names of the parent and child tables, the name of the relationship, and the delete and update rules for the relationship. You can query it to find out about the relationships in the database:

List all of the parent/child relationships among my tables, showing the name of the relationship, the name of the parent table, the name of the child table, and the delete rule for each one.

```
SELECT CONSTNAME, REFTABNAME, TABNAME, DELETERULE
  FROM SYSCAT.REFERENCES
 WHERE DEFINER = USER
```

DATABASE STRUCTURE

Column Name	Data Type	Information
CONSTNAME	VARCHAR(18)	Name of constraint described by this row
TABSCHEMA	CHAR(8)	Schema containing the constraint
TABNAME	VARCHAR(18)	Table to which constraint applies
DEFINER	CHAR(8)	Creator of table to which constraint applies
REFKEYNAME	VARCHAR(18)	Name of parent key
REFTABSCHEMA	CHAR(8)	Schema containing parent table
REFTABNAME	VARCHAR(18)	Name of parent table
COLCOUNT	SMALLINT	Number of columns in the foreign key
DELETERULE	CHAR(1)	Delete rule for foreign key constraint (A = no action, C = cascade, R = restrict, and so on)
UPDATERULE	CHAR(1)	Update rule for foreign key constraint (A = no action, R = restrict)
CREATE_TIME	TIMESTAMP	Creation time of constraint
FK_COLNAMES	VARCHAR(320)	Names of foreign key columns
PK_COLNAMES	VARCHAR(320)	Names of primary key columns

Table 16-8. *The SYSCAT.REFERENCES View (DB2)*

List all of the tables related to the *SALESREPS* table as either a parent or a child.

```
SELECT REFTABNAME
  FROM SYSCAT.REFERENCES
 WHERE TABNAME = 'SALESREPS'
 UNION
SELECT TABNAME
  FROM SYSCAT.REFERENCES
 WHERE REFTABNAME = 'SALESREPS'
```

The names of the foreign key columns and the corresponding primary key columns are listed (as text) in the FK_COLNAMES and PK_COLNAMES columns of the REFERENCES system table. A second system table, SYSCAT.KEYCOLUSE, shown in Table 16-9, provides a somewhat more useful form of the information. There is one row in this system table for each column in each foreign key, primary key, or uniqueness constraint defined in the database. A sequence number defines the order of the columns in a compound key. You can use this system table to find out the names of the columns that link a table to its parent, using a query like this one:

List the columns that link ORDERS to PRODUCTS in the relationship named ISFOR.

```
SELECT COLNAME, COLSEQ
  FROM SYSCAT.KEYCOLUSE
 WHERE CONSTNAME = 'ISFOR'
 ORDER BY COLSEQ
```

The primary key of a table and the parent/child relationships in which it participates are also summarized in the SYSCAT.TABLES and SYSCAT.COLUMNS system tables, shown previously in Tables 16-2 and 16-4. If a table has a primary key, the KEYCOLUMNS column in its row of the SYSCAT.TABLES system table is nonzero, and tells how many columns make up the primary key (one for a simple key; two or more for a composite key). In the SYSCAT.COLUMNS system table, the rows for the columns that make up the primary key have a nonzero value in their KEYSEQ column.

Column Name	Data Type	Information
CONSTNAME	VARCHAR(18)	Name of constraint (unique, primary key, or foreign key) described by this row
TABSCHEMA	CHAR(8)	Schema containing the constraint
TABNAME	VARCHAR(18)	Table to which constraint applies
COLNAME	VARCHAR(18)	Name of column in the constraint
COLSEQ	SMALLINT	Position of column within the constraint

Table 16-9.   *The SYSCAT.KEYCOLUSE View (DB2)*

The value in this column indicates the position (1, 2, and so on) of the primary key column within the primary key.

You can query the SYSCAT.COLUMNS table to find a table's primary key:

List the columns that form the primary key of the PRODUCTS table.

```
SELECT COLNAME, KEYSEQ, TYPENAME, REMARKS
  FROM SYSCAT.COLUMNS
 WHERE TABNAME = 'PRODUCTS'
   AND KEYSEQ > 0
 ORDER BY KEYSEQ
```

The DB2 catalog support for primary and foreign keys is typical of that found in other major SQL products. The Oracle system view USER_CONSTRAINTS, for example, provides the same information as the DB2 SYSCAT.REFERENCES system table. Information about the specific columns that make up a foreign key or primary key appears in the Oracle USER_CONS_COLUMNS system view, which is analogous to the DB2 SYSCAT.KEYCOLUSE system table. Microsoft SQL Server has a similar system catalog structure, with foreign key information divided between the SYSFOREIGNKEYS and SYSREFERENCES system tables.

Informix Universal Server takes a similar approach to the DB2 catalog, but with the same types of differences previously illustrated in its table information and column information support. Each constraint defined within the database generates one row in the Informix SYSCONSTRAINTS system table, which defines the name of the constraint and its type (check constraint, primary key, referential, and so on). This system table also assigns an internal constraint-id number to identify the constraint within the catalog. The table to which the constraint applies is also identified by table-id (which serves as a foreign key to the SYSTABLES system table).

Further information about the referential constraints (foreign keys) is contained in a SYSREFERENCES system table. Again in this table, the constraint, the primary key, and the parent table are identified by internal IDs that link the foreign key information to the SYSCONSTRAINTS and SYSTABLES system tables. The SYSREFERENCES table contains information about the delete rule and update rule that apply to the foreign key relationship and similar information.

User Information

The system catalog generally contains a table that identifies the users who are authorized to access the database. The DBMS may use this system table to validate the user name and password when a user first attempts to connect to the database. The table may also store other data about the user.

SQL Server stores user information in its SYSUSERS system table, shown in Table 16-10. Each row of this table describes a single user or user group in the SQL Server security scheme. Informix takes a similar approach, with a system table that is also called SYSUSERS. The corresponding Oracle table is called ALL_USERS. Following are two equivalent queries that list the authorized users for SQL Server and Oracle:

List all the user-ids known to SQL Server.

```
SELECT NAME
  FROM SYSUSERS
 WHERE UID <> GID
```

List all the user-ids known to Oracle.

```
SELECT USERNAME
  FROM ALL_USERS
```

The DB2 system catalog table that contains user names also contains the information about their roles and privileges within the database (that is, whether they are a database administrator, whether they can create tables, whether they can create programs that access the database). Here is the equivalent query to the preceding queries for retrieving user names from the DB2 catalog:

List all the user-ids known to DB2.

```
SELECT DISTINCT GRANTEE
  FROM SYSCAT.DBAUTH
 WHERE GRANTEETYPE = 'U'
```

Column Name	Data Type	Information
uid	SMALLINT	Internal user-id number in this database
gid	SMALLINT	Internal user group-id number in this database
name	SYSNAME	User or group name

Table 16-10.   *Selected Columns of the SYSUSERS Table (SQL Server)*

DATABASE STRUCTURE

Privileges Information

In addition to storing database structure information, the system catalog generally stores the information required by the DBMS to enforce database security. As described in Chapter 15, various DBMS products offer different variations on the basic SQL privileges scheme. These variations are reflected in the structure of the system catalogs for the various DBMS brands.

DB2 has one of the most comprehensive schemes for user privileges, extending down to the individual columns of a table. Table 16-11 shows the DB2 system catalogs that store information about privileges and briefly describes the role of each one.

The authorization scheme used by SQL Server is more fundamental and streamlined than that of DB2. It treats databases, tables, stored procedures, triggers, and other entities uniformly as objects to which privileges apply. This streamlined structure is reflected in the system table, SYSPROTECTS, shown in Table 16-12, which implements the entire privileges scheme for SQL Server. Each row in the table represents a single GRANT or REVOKE statement that has been issued.

System Table	Role
TABAUTH	Implements table-level privileges by telling which users have permissions to access which tables, for which operations (SELECT, INSERT, DELETE, UPDATE, ALTER, and INDEX)
COLAUTH	Implements column-level privileges by telling which users have permission to update or to reference which columns of which tables
DBAUTH	Determines which users have permission to connect to the database, to create tables, and to perform various database administration functions
SCHEMAAUTH	Implements schema-level privileges by telling which users have permission to create, drop, or alter objects (tables, views, domains, and so on) within a schema
INDEXAUTH	Implements index-level privileges by telling which users have control privileges over various indexes
PACKAGEAUTH	Implements programmatic access privileges by telling which users have the ability to control, bind (create), and execute various database access programs ("packages")

Table 16-11. *DB2 System Catalog Views that Implement Permissions*

Column Name	Data Type	Information
id	INT	Internal ID of protected object
uid	SMALLINT	Internal ID of user or group with privilege
action	TINYINT	Numerical privilege code
protecttype	TINYINT	Numerical code for grant or revoke
columns	VARBINARY(32)	Bitmap for column-level update privileges

Table 16-12. *Selected Columns of the SYSPROTECTS Table (SQL Server)*

The SQL2 Information Schema

The SQL2 standard does not directly specify the structure of a system catalog that must be supported by DBMS implementations. In practice, given the widely differing features supported by different DBMS brands and the major differences in the system catalogs that were already being used by commercial SQL products when the SQL2 standard was adopted, it would have been impossible to reach an agreement on a standard catalog definition. Instead, the writers of the SQL2 standard defined an idealized system catalog that a DBMS vendor might design if he or she were building a DBMS to support the SQL2 standard from scratch. The tables in this idealized system catalog (called the *definition schema* in the standard) are summarized in Table 16-13.

System Table	Contents
USERS	One row for each user ("authorization-id") in the catalog cluster
SCHEMATA	One row for each schema in the catalog cluster
DATA_TYPE_DESCRIPTOR	One row for each domain or column defined with a data type
DOMAINS	One row for each domain
DOMAIN_CONSTRAINTS	One row for each domain constraint

Table 16-13. *Idealized System Catalog Used by the SQL2 Standard*

DATABASE STRUCTURE

System Table	Contents
TABLES	One row for each table or view
VIEWS	One row for each table or view
COLUMNS	One row for each column in each table or view definition
VIEW_TABLE_USAGE	One row for each table referenced in each view definition (if a view is defined by a query on multiple tables, there will be a row for each table)
VIEW_COLUMN_USAGE	One row for each column referenced by a view
TABLE_CONSTRAINTS	One row for each table constraint specified in a table definition
KEY_COLUMN_USAGE	One row for each column specified in each primary key, each foreign key, and each uniqueness constraint (if multiple columns are specified in a key definition or uniqueness constraint, there will be multiple rows representing that constraint)
REFERENTIAL_ CONSTRAINTS	One row for each foreign key definition specified in a table definition
CHECK_CONSTRAINTS	One row for each check constraint specified in a table definition
CHECK_TABLE_USAGE	One row for each table referenced in each check constraint, domain constraint, or assertion
CHECK_COLUMN_USAGE	One row for each column referenced in each check constraint, domain constraint, or assertion
ASSERTIONS	One row for each assertion defined
TABLE_PRIVILEGES	One row for each privilege granted on each table
COLUMN_PRIVILEGES	One row for each privilege granted on each column
CHARACTER_SETS	One row for each character set defined
COLLATIONS	One row for each collation defined
TRANSLATIONS	One row for each translation defined
SQL_LANGUAGES	One row for each language (e.g., COBOL, C, and so on) supported by this DBMS brand

Table 16-13. *Idealized System Catalog Used by the SQL2 Standard* (continued)

The SQL2 standard does not require a DBMS to actually support the system catalog tables in Table 16-13, or any system catalog at all. Instead, it defines a series of views on these catalog tables that identify database objects that are accessible to the current user. (These catalog views are called an *Information Schema* in the standard.) Any DBMS that claims the Intermediate or Full conformance level to the SQL2 standard must support these views. This effectively gives a user a standardized way to find out about the objects in the database that are available to him or her by issuing standard SQL against the catalog views. Note that support for the catalog views is not required for the Entry conformance level to the SQL2 standard.

In practice, major commercial SQL implementations have been slowly moving to support the SQL2 Information Schema, typically by defining corresponding views on the tables in their own system catalogs. In most cases, the information in the DBMS' own system catalogs is similar enough to that required by the standard that the first 90 percent of the conformance to the SQL2 standard is relatively easy. The last 10 percent has proven to be much more difficult, given the variations among DBMS brands and the degree to which even the SQL2 catalog views expose the specific features and capabilities of the underlying DBMS.

As a result, full support for the SQL2 catalog views has usually been implemented in conjunction with a major new version of a DBMS product, accompanied by underlying changes in the core of the DBMS software. The catalog views required by the SQL2 standard are summarized in Table 16-14, along with a brief description of the information contained in each view. Here are some sample queries that can be used to extract information about database structure from the SQL2-defined system catalog views:

List the names of all tables and views owned by the current user.

```
SELECT TABLE_NAME
  FROM TABLES
```

List the name, position, and data type of all columns in all views.

```
SELECT TABLE_NAME, C.COLUMN_NAME, ORDINAL_POSITION, DATA_TYPE
  FROM COLUMNS
 WHERE (COLUMNS.TABLE_NAME IN (SELECT TABLE_NAME FROM VIEWS))
```

Determine how many columns are in the table named `OFFICES`.

```
SELECT COUNT(*)
  FROM COLUMNS
 WHERE (TABLE_NAME = 'OFFICES')
```

System Catalog View	Contents
INFORMATION_SCHEMA_ CATALOG_NAME	A single row specifying the name of the database for each user (*"catalog"* in the language of the SQL2 standard) described by this Information Schema
SCHEMATA	One row for each schema in the database that is owned by the current user specifying the schema name, default character set, and so on
DOMAINS	One row for each domain accessible by the current user specifying the name of the domain, the underlying data type, character set, maximum length, scale, precision, and so on
DOMAIN_CONSTRAINTS	One row for each domain constraint specifying the name of the constraint and its deferability characteristics
TABLES	One row for each table or view accessible to the current user specifying its name and type (table or view)
VIEWS	One row for each view accessible to the current user specifying its name, check option, and updateability
COLUMNS	One row for each column accessible to the current user specifying its name, the table or view that contains it, its data type, precision, scale, character set, and so on
TABLE_PRIVILEGES	One row for each privilege on a table granted to or by the current user specifying the table type, the type of privilege, the grantor and grantee, and whether the privilege is grantable by the current user
COLUMN_PRIVILEGES	One row for each privilege on a column granted to or by the current user specifying the table and the column, the type of privilege, the grantor and grantee, and whether the privilege is grantable by the current user
USAGE_PRIVILEGES	One row for each usage granted to or by the current user

Table 16-14.   *Catalog Views Mandated by the SQL2 Standard*

System Catalog View	Contents
TABLE_CONSTRAINTS	One row for each table constraint (primary key, foreign key, uniqueness constraint, or check constraint) specified on a table owned by the current user, specifying the name of the constraint, the table, the type of constraint, and its deferability
REFERENTIAL_CONSTRAINTS	One row for each referential constraint (foreign key definition) for a table owned by the current user specifying the names of the constraint and the child and parent tables
CHECK_CONSTRAINTS	One row for each check constraint for a table owned by the current user
KEY_COLUMN_USAGE	One row for each column specified in each primary key, each foreign key, and each uniqueness constraint in a table owned by the current user, specifying the column and table names, and the position of the column in the key
ASSERTIONS	One row for each assertion owned by the current user, specifying its name and its deferability
CHARACTER_SETS	One row for each character set definition accessible to the current user
COLLATIONS	One row for each collation definition accessible to the current user
TRANSLATIONS	One row for each translation definition accessible to the current user
VIEW_TABLE_USAGE	One row for each table referenced in each view definition owned by the current user, specifying the name of the table
VIEW_COLUMN_USAGE	One row for each column referenced by a view owned by the current user, specifying its name and the table containing it
CONSTRAINT_TABLE_USAGE	One row for each table referenced in each check constraint, uniqueness constraint, foreign key definition, and assertion owned by the current user

Table 16-14. *Catalog Views Mandated by the SQL2 Standard* (continued)

System Catalog View	Contents
CONSTRAINT_COLUMN_ USAGE	One row for each column referenced in each check constraint, uniqueness constraint, foreign key definition, and assertion owned by the current user
SQL_LANGUAGES	One row for each language (i.e., COBOL, C, and so on) supported by this DBMS brand, specifying its level of conformance to the SQL2 standard, the type of SQL supported, and so on

Table 16-14. *Catalog Views Mandated by the SQL2 Standard* (continued)

The standard also defines three domains that are used by the catalog views and are also available to users. These domains are summarized in Table 16-15. Appendix E contains a complete summary of the major SQL2 catalog views and their contents.

System Domain	Values
SQL_INDENTIFIER	The domain of all variable-length character strings that are legal SQL identifiers under the SQL2 standard. A value drawn from this domain is a legal table name, column name, and so forth
CHARACTER_DATA	The domain of all variable-length character strings with a length between zero and the maximum length supported by this DBMS. A value drawn from this domain is a legal character string.
CARDINAL_NUMBER	The domain of all non-negative numbers, from zero up to the maximum number represented by an INTEGER for this DBMS. A value drawn from this is zero or a legal positive number.

Table 16-15. *Domains Defined by the SQL2 Standard*

Other Catalog Information

The system catalog is a reflection of the capabilities and features of the DBMS that uses it. Because of the many SQL extensions and additional features offered by popular DBMS products, their system catalogs always contain several tables unique to the DBMS. Here are just a few examples:

- DB2 and Oracle support aliases and synonyms (alternate names for tables). DB2 stores alias information with other table information in the SYSCAT.TABLES system table. Oracle makes synonym information available through its USER_SYNONYMS system view.

- SQL Server supports multiple named databases. It has a system table called SYSDATABASES that identifies the databases managed by a single server.

- Many DBMS brands now support stored procedures, and the catalog contains one or more tables that describes them. Sybase stores information about stored procedures in its SYSPROCEDURES system table.

- Ingres supports tables that are distributed across several disk volumes. Its IIMULTI_LOCATIONS system table keeps track of the locations of multivolume tables.

Summary

The system catalog is a collection of system tables that describe the structure of a relational database:

- The DBMS maintains the data in the system tables, updating it as the structure of the database changes.

- A user can query the system tables to find out information about tables, columns, and privileges in the database.

- Front-end query tools use the system tables to help users navigate their way through the database in a user-friendly way.

- The names and organization of the system tables differ widely from one brand of DBMS to another; and there are even differences among different DBMS products from the same vendor, reflecting the different internal structures and capabilities of the products.

- The SQL2 standard does not require that a DBMS actually have a set of system catalog tables, but it does define a set of standard catalog views for products that claim higher levels of SQL2 conformance.

DATABASE STRUCTURE

The
Complete
Reference

Part V

Programming with SQL

In addition to its role as an interactive data access language, SQL supports database access by application programs. Chapters 17–19 describe the special SQL features and techniques that apply to programmatic SQL. Chapter 17 describes embedded SQL, the oldest programmatic SQL technique, and one still supported by many SQL products. Dynamic SQL, an advanced form of embedded SQL that isused to build general-purpose database tools, is described in Chapter 18. Chapter 19 describes an alternative to embedded SQL—the function call interface provided by several popular DBMS products, which has been gaining in popularity.

The Complete Reference

Chapter 17

Embedded SQL

SQL is a *dual-mode language.* It is both an interactive database language used for ad hoc queries and updates and a programmatic database language used by application programs for database access. For the most part, the SQL language is identical in both modes. The dual-mode nature of SQL has several advantages:

- It is relatively easy for programmers to learn how to write programs that access the database.

- Capabilities available through the interactive query language are also automatically available to application programs.

- The SQL statements to be used in a program can be tried out first using interactive SQL and then coded into the program.

- Programs can work with tables of data and query results instead of navigating their way through the database.

This chapter summarizes the types of programmatic SQL offered by the leading SQL-based products and then describes the programmatic SQL used by the IBM SQL products, which is called *embedded SQL.*

Programmatic SQL Techniques

SQL is a language and can be used programmatically, but it would be incorrect to call SQL a programming language. SQL lacks even the most primitive features of real programming languages. It has no provision for declaring variables, no GOTO statement, no IF statement for testing conditions, no FOR, DO, or WHILE statements to construct loops, no block structure, and so on. SQL is a database *sublanguage* that handles special-purpose database management tasks. To write a program that accesses a database, you must start with a conventional programming language, such as COBOL, PL/I, FORTRAN, Pascal, or C and then add SQL to the program.

The initial ANSI/ISO SQL standard was concerned exclusively with this programmatic use of SQL. In fact, the standard did not even include the interactive SELECT statement described in Chapters 6 through 9. It only specified the programmatic SELECT statement described later in the section "Data Retrieval in Embedded SQL." The SQL2 standard, published in 1992, expanded its focus to include interactive SQL (called *direct invocation of SQL* in the standard) and more advanced forms of programmatic SQL (the *dynamic SQL* capabilities described in Chapter 20).

Commercial SQL database vendors offer two basic techniques for using SQL within an application program:

- **Embedded SQL.** In this approach, SQL statements are embedded directly into the program's source code, intermixed with the other programming language statements. Special embedded SQL statements are used to retrieve data into the program. A special SQL precompiler accepts the combined source code and, along with other programming tools, converts it into an executable program.

■ **Application program interface**. In this approach, the program communicates with the DBMS through a set of function calls called an *application program interface,* or API. The program passes SQL statements to the DBMS through the API calls and uses API calls to retrieve query results. This approach does not require a special precompiler.

The initial IBM SQL products used an embedded SQL approach, and most commercial SQL products adopted it in the 1980s. The original ANSI/ISO SQL standard specified only an awkward module language for programmatic SQL, but commercial SQL products continued to follow the IBM de facto standard. In 1989, the ANSI/ISO standard was extended to include a definition of how to embed SQL statements within the Ada, C, COBOL, FORTRAN, Pascal, and PL/I programming languages, this time following the IBM approach. The SQL2 standard continued this specification.

In parallel with this evolution of embedded SQL, several DBMS vendors who were focused on minicomputer systems introduced callable database APIs in the 1980s. When the Sybase DBMS was introduced, it offered *only* a callable API. Microsoft's SQL Server, derived from the Sybase DBMS, also used the API approach exclusively. Soon after the debut of SQL Server, Microsoft introduced Open Database Connectivity (ODBC), another callable API. ODBC is roughly based on the SQL Server API, but with the additional goals of being database independent and permitting concurrent access to two or more different DBMS brands through a common API.

More recently, Java Database Connectivity (JDBC) has emerged as an important API for accessing a relational database from within programs written in Java. With the growing popularity of callable APIs, the callable and embedded approaches are both in active use today. In general, programmers using older languages, such as COBOL and Assembler, will tend to favor the embedded SQL approach. Programmers using newer languages, such as C++ and Java, will tend to favor the callable API approach.

The following table summarizes the programmatic interfaces offered by some of the leading SQL-based DBMS products:

DBMS	Callable API	Embedded SQL Language Support
DB2	ODBC, JDBC	APL, Assembler, BASIC, COBOL, FORTRAN, Java, PL/I
Informix	ODBC, JDBC	C, COBOL
Microsoft SQL Server	DB Library (dblib), ODBC	C

DBMS	Callable API	Embedded SQL Language Support
MySQL	C-api (proprietary), ODBC, JDBC, Perl, PHP, Tcl…	None
Oracle	Oracle Call Interface (OCI), ODBC, JDBC	C, COBOL, FORTRAN, Pascal, PL/I, Java
Sybase	DB Library (dblib), ODBC, JDBC	C, COBOL

The basic techniques of embedded SQL, called *static* SQL, are described in this chapter. Some advanced features of embedded SQL, called *dynamic* SQL, are discussed in Chapter 20. Callable SQL APIs, including the Sybase/SQL Server API, ODBC, and JDBC, are discussed in Chapter 21.

DBMS Statement Processing

To understand any of the programmatic SQL techniques, it helps to understand a little bit more about how the DBMS processes SQL statements. To process a SQL statement, the DBMS goes through a series of five steps, shown in Figure 17-1:

1. The DBMS begins by *parsing* the SQL statement. It breaks the statement up into individual words, makes sure that the statement has a valid verb, legal clauses, and so on. Syntax errors and misspellings can be detected in this step.

2. The DBMS *validates* the statement. It checks the statement against the system catalog. Do all the tables named in the statement exist in the database? Do all of the columns exist, and are the column names unambiguous? Does the user have the required privileges to execute the statement? Semantic errors are detected in this step.

3. The DBMS *optimizes* the statement. It explores various ways to carry out the statement. Can an index be used to speed a search? Should the DBMS first apply a search condition to Table A and then join it to Table B, or should it begin with the join and use the search condition afterward? Can a sequential search through a table be avoided or reduced to a subset of the table? After exploring alternatives, the DBMS chooses one of them.

4. The DBMS then generates an *application plan* for the statement. The application plan is a binary representation of the steps that are required to carry out the statement; it is the DBMS equivalent of executable code.

5. Finally, the DBMS carries out the statement by executing the application plan.

Note that the steps in Figure 17-1 vary in the amount of database access they require and the amount of CPU time they take. Parsing a SQL statement does not require access to the database and typically can be done very quickly. Optimization, on the other hand, is a very CPU-intensive process and requires access to the database's system catalog. For a complex, multitable query, the optimizer may explore more than a dozen different ways of carrying out the query. However, the cost in computer processing time of doing the query the wrong way is usually so high compared to the cost of doing it the right way (or at least a better way) that the time spent in optimization is more than gained back in increased query execution speed.

When you type a SQL statement to interactive SQL, the DBMS goes through all five steps while you wait for its response. The DBMS has little choice in the matter—it doesn't know which statement you are going to type until you type it, so none of the processing can be done ahead of time. In programmatic SQL, however, the situation is quite different. Some of the early steps can be done at *compile-time*, when the programmer is developing the program. This leaves only the later steps to be done at *runtime*, when the program is executed by a user. When you use programmatic SQL, all DBMS products try to move as much processing as possible to compile-time, because once the final version of the program is developed, it may be executed thousands of times by users in a production application. In particular, the goal is to move optimization to compile-time if at all possible.

Figure 17-1. *How the DBMS processes a SQL statement*

Embedded SQL Concepts

The central idea of embedded SQL is to blend SQL language statements directly into a program written in a host programming language, such as C, Pascal, COBOL, FORTRAN, PL/I, or Assembler. Embedded SQL uses the following techniques to embed the SQL statements:

- SQL statements are intermixed with statements of the host language in the source program. This embedded SQL source program is submitted to a SQL precompiler, which processes the SQL statements.

- Variables of the host programming language can be referenced in the embedded SQL statements, allowing values calculated by the program to be used by the SQL statements.

- Program language variables are also used by the embedded SQL statements to receive the results of SQL queries, allowing the program to use and process the retrieved values.

- Special program variables are used to assign NULL values to database columns and to support the retrieval of NULL values from the database.

- Several new SQL statements that are unique to embedded SQL are added to the interactive SQL language, to provide for row-by-row processing of query results.

Figure 17-2 shows a simple embedded SQL program, written in C. The program illustrates many, but not all, of the embedded SQL techniques. The program prompts the user for an office number, retrieves the city, region, sales, and target for the office, and displays them on the screen.

Don't worry if the program appears strange, or if you can't understand all of the statements that it contains before reading the rest of this chapter. One of the disadvantages of the embedded SQL approach is that the source code for a program becomes an impure blend of two different languages, making the program hard to understand without training in both SQL and the programming language. Another disadvantage is that embedded SQL uses SQL language constructs not used in interactive SQL, such as the WHENEVER statement and the INTO clause of the SELECT statement—both used in this program.

Developing an Embedded SQL Program

An embedded SQL program contains a mix of SQL and programming language statements, so it can't be submitted directly to a compiler for the programming language. Instead, it moves through a multistep development process, shown in

```
main()
{
   exec sql include sqlca;
   exec sql begin declare section;
      int   officenum;           /* office number (from user) */
      char  cityname[16];        /* retrieved city name */
      char  regionname[11];      /* retrieved region name */
      float targetval;           /* retrieved target and sales */
      float salesval;            /* retrieved target and sales */
   exec sql end declare section;

   /* Set up error processing */
   exec sql whenever sqlerror goto query_error;
   exec sql whenever not found goto bad_number;

   /* Prompt the user for the employee number */
   printf("Enter office number:");
   scanf("%d", &officenum);

   /* Execute the SQL query */
   exec sql select city, region, target, sales
             from offices
            where office = :officenum
              into :cityname, :regionname, :targetval, :salesval;

   /* Display the results */
   printf("City:   %s\n", cityname);
   printf("Region: %s\n", regionname);
   printf("Target: %f\n", targetval);
   printf("Sales:  %f\n", salesval);
   exit();

query_error:
   printf("SQL error: %ld\n", sqlca.sqlcode);
   exit();

bad_number:
   printf("Invalid office number.\n");
   exit();
}
```

Figure 17-2. *A typical embedded SQL program*

Figure 17-3. The steps in the figure are actually those used by the IBM mainframe databases (DB2, SQL/DS), but all products that support embedded SQL use a similar process:

1. The embedded SQL source program is submitted to the SQL precompiler, a programming tool. The precompiler scans the program, finds the embedded SQL statements, and processes them. A different precompiler is required for each programming language supported by the DBMS. Commercial SQL products typically offer precompilers for one or more languages, including C, Pascal, COBOL, FORTRAN, Ada, PL/I, RPG, and various assembly languages.

2. The precompiler produces two files as its output. The first file is the source program, stripped of its embedded SQL statements. In their place, the precompiler substitutes calls to the private DBMS routines that provide the runtime link between the program and the DBMS. Typically, the names and calling sequences of these routines are known only to the precompiler and the DBMS; they are not a public interface to the DBMS. The second file is a copy of all the embedded SQL statements used in the program. This file is sometimes called a *database request module,* or DBRM.

3. The source file output from the precompiler is submitted to the standard compiler for the host programming language (such as a C or COBOL compiler). The compiler processes the source code and produces object code as its output. Note that this step has nothing in particular to do with the DBMS or with SQL.

4. The *linker* accepts the object modules generated by the compiler, links them with various library routines, and produces an executable program. The library routines linked into the executable program include the private DBMS routines described in Step 2.

5. The database request module generated by the precompiler is submitted to a special BIND program. This program examines the SQL statements, parses, validates, and optimizes them, and produces an application plan for each statement. The result is a combined application plan for the entire program, representing a DBMS-executable version of its embedded SQL statements. The BIND program stores the plan in the database, usually assigning it the name of the application program that created it.

The program development steps in Figure 17-3 correlate with the DBMS statement processing steps in Figure 17-1. In particular, the precompiler usually handles statement parsing (the first step), and the BIND utility handles verification, optimization, and plan generation (the second, third, and fourth steps). Thus, the first four steps of Figure 17-1 all take place at compile-time when you use embedded SQL. Only the fifth step, the actual execution of the application plan, remains to be done at runtime.

The embedded SQL development process turns the original embedded SQL source program into two executable parts:

Figure 17-3.   *The embedded SQL development process*

- ■ **An executable program**. Stored in a file on the computer in the same format as any executable program

- ■ **An executable application plan**. Stored within the database in the format expected by the DBMS

The embedded SQL development cycle may seem cumbersome, and it is more awkward than developing a standard C or COBOL program. In most cases, all of the steps in Figure 17-3 are automated by a single command procedure, so the individual steps are made invisible to the application programmer. The process does have several major advantages from a DBMS point of view, shown next.

■ The blending of SQL and programming language statements in the embedded SQL source program is an effective way to merge the two languages. The host programming language provides flow of control, variables, block structure, and input/output functions; SQL handles database access and does not have to provide these other constructs.

■ The use of a precompiler means that the compute-intensive work of parsing and optimization can take place during the development cycle. The resulting executable program is very efficient in its use of CPU resources.

■ The database request module produced by the precompiler provides portability of applications. An application program can be written and tested on one system, and then its executable program and DBRM can be moved to another system. After the BIND program on the new system creates the application plan and installs it in the database, the application program can use it without being recompiled itself.

■ The program's actual runtime interface to the private DBMS routines is completely hidden from the application programmer. The programmer works with embedded SQL at the source-code level and does not have to worry about other, more complex interfaces.

Running an Embedded SQL Program

Recall from Figure 17-3 that the embedded SQL development process produces two executable components, the executable program itself and the program's application plan, stored in the database. When you run an embedded SQL program, these two components are brought together to do the work of the application:

1. When you ask the computer system to run the program, the computer loads the executable program in the usual way and begins to execute its instructions.

2. One of the first calls generated by the precompiler is a call to a DBMS routine that finds and loads the application plan for the program.

3. For each embedded SQL statement, the program calls one or more private DBMS routines, requesting execution of the corresponding statement in the application plan. The DBMS finds the statement, executes that part of the plan, and then returns control to the program.

4. Execution continues in this way, with the executable program and the DBMS cooperating to carry out the task defined by the original embedded SQL source program.

Runtime Security

When you use interactive SQL, the DBMS enforces its security based on the user-id you supply to the interactive SQL program. You can type any SQL statement you want, but the privileges granted to your user-id determine whether the DBMS will or will not execute the statement you type. When you run a program that uses embedded SQL, there are two user-ids to consider:

- The user-id of the person who developed the program, or more specifically, the person who ran the BIND program to create the application plan
- The user-id of the person who is now executing the program and the corresponding application plan

It may seem strange to consider the user-id of the person who ran the BIND program (or more generally, the person who developed the application program or installed it on the computer system), but in fact, DB2 and several other commercial SQL products use both user-ids in their security scheme. To understand how the security scheme works, suppose that user JOE runs the ORDMAINT order maintenance program, which updates the ORDERS, SALES, and OFFICES tables. The application plan for the ORDMAINT program was originally bound by user-id OPADMIN, which belongs to the order-processing administrator.

In the DB2 scheme, each application plan is a database object, protected by DB2 security. To execute a plan, JOE must have the EXECUTE privilege for it. If he does not, execution fails immediately. As the ORDMAINT program executes, its embedded INSERT, UPDATE, and DELETE statements update the database. The privileges of the OPADMIN user determine whether the plan will be allowed to perform these updates. Note that the plan may update the tables even if JOE does not have the required privileges. However, the updates that can be performed are *only* those that have been explicitly coded into the embedded SQL statements of the program. Thus, DB2 provides very fine control over database security. The privileges of users to access tables can be very limited, without diminishing their ability to use canned programs.

Not all DBMS products provide security protection for application plans. For those that do not, the privileges of the user executing an embedded SQL program determine the privileges of the program's application plan. Under this scheme, the user must have privileges to perform all of the actions performed by the plan, or the program will fail. If the user is not to have these same permissions in an interactive SQL environment, access to the interactive SQL program itself must be restricted, which is a disadvantage of this approach.

Automatic Rebinding

Note that an application plan is optimized for the database structure as it exists at the time the plan is placed in the database by the BIND program. If the structure changes later (for example, if an index is dropped or a column is deleted from a table), any application plan that references the changed structures may become invalid. To handle this situation, the DBMS usually stores, along with the application plan, a copy of the original SQL statements that produced it.

The DBMS also keeps track of all the database objects upon which each application plan depends. If any of these objects are modified by a DDL statement, the DBMS can find the plans that depend on it and automatically marks those plans as invalid. The next time the program tries to use the plan, the DBMS can detect the situation, and in most cases, it will automatically rebind the statements to produce a new bind image. Because the DBMS has maintained a great deal of information about the application plan, it can make this automatic rebinding completely transparent to the application program. However, a SQL statement may take much longer to execute when its plan is rebound than when the plan is simply executed.

Although the DBMS can automatically rebind a plan when one of the structures upon which it depends is changed, the DBMS will usually not automatically detect changes in the database that may make a better plan possible. For example, suppose a plan uses a sequential scan of a table to locate particular rows because no appropriate index existed when it was bound. It's possible that a subsequent CREATE INDEX statement will create an appropriate index. To take advantage of the new structure, you must explicitly run the BIND program to rebind the plan.

Simple Embedded SQL Statements

The simplest SQL statements to embed in a program are those that are self-contained and do not produce any query results. For example, consider this interactive SQL statement:

Delete all salespeople with sales under $150,000.

```
DELETE FROM SALESREPS
 WHERE SALES < 150000.00
```

Figures 17-4, 17-5, and 17-6 show three programs that perform the same task as this interactive SQL statement, using embedded SQL. The program in Figure 17-4 is written in C, the program in Figure 17-5 is written in COBOL, and the program in Figure 17-6 is written in FORTRAN. Although the programs are extremely simple, they illustrate the most basic features of embedded SQL:

■ The embedded SQL statements appear in the midst of host programming language statements. It usually doesn't matter whether the SQL statement is written in uppercase or lowercase; the most common practice is to follow the style of the host language.

■ Every embedded SQL statement begins with an *introducer* that flags it as a SQL statement. The IBM SQL products use the introducer EXEC SQL for most host languages, and the ANSI/ISO SQL2 standard specifies it as well. Some embedded SQL products still support other introducers, for backward compatibility with their earlier versions.

- If an embedded SQL statement extends over multiple lines, the host language strategy for statement continuation is used. For COBOL, PL/I, and C programs, no special continuation character is required. For FORTRAN programs, the second and subsequent lines of the statement must have a continuation character in column 6.

- Every embedded SQL statement ends with a *terminator* that signals the end of the SQL statement. The terminator varies with the style of the host language. In COBOL, the terminator is the string END-EXEC., which ends in a period like other COBOL statements. For PL/I and C, the terminator is a semicolon (;), which is also the statement termination character in those languages. In FORTRAN, the embedded SQL statement ends when no more continuation lines are indicated.

```c
main()
{
   exec sql include sqlca;
   exec sql declare salesreps table
                  (empl_num integer not null,
                       name varchar(15) not null,
                        age integer
                 rep_office integer,
                      title varchar(10),
                  hire_date date not null,
                    manager integer,
                      quota money,
                      sales money not null);

   /* Display a message for the user */
   printf("Deleting salesreps with low quota.\n");

   /*Execute the SQL statement */
   exec sql delete from salesreps
           where sales < 150000.00;

   /* Display another message */
   printf("Finished deleting.\n");
   exit();
}
```

Figure 17-4.   *An embedded SQL program written in C*

```
        IDENTIFICATION DIVISION.
        PROGRAM-ID. SAMPLE.
        ENVIRONMENT DIVISION.
        DATA DIVISION.
        FILE SECTION.
        WORKING-STORAGE SECTION.
                EXEC SQL INCLUDE SQLCA.
                EXEC SQL DECLARE SALESREPS TABLE
                                (EMPL_NUM INTEGER NOT NULL,
                                     NAME VARCHAR(15) NOT NULL,
                                      AGE INTEGER,
                                REP_OFFICE INTEGER,
                                    TITLE VARCHAR(10),
                                HIRE_DATE DATE NOT NULL,
                                  MANAGER INTEGER,
                                    QUOTA MONEY,
                                    SALES MONEY NOT NULL)
                END-EXEC.
        PROCEDURE DIVISION.
        *
        *       DISPLAY A MESSAGE FOR THE USER
                DISPLAY "Deleting salesreps with low quota.".
        *
        *       EXECUTE THE SQL STATEMENT
                EXEC SQL DELETE FROM SALESREPS
                        WHERE QUOTA < 150000
                END EXEC.
        *
        *       DISPLAY ANOTHER MESSAGE
                DISPLAY "Finished deleting.".
```

Figure 17-5.   *An embedded SQL program written in COBOL*

The embedding technique shown in the three figures works for any SQL statement that (a) does not depend on the values of host language variables for its execution and (b) does not retrieve data from the database. For example, the C program in Figure 17-7 creates a new REGIONS table and inserts two rows into it, using exactly the same embedded SQL features as the program in Figure 17-4. For consistency, all of the remaining program examples in the book will use the C programming language, except when a particular host language feature is being illustrated.

```
            PROGRAM SAMPLE
      100 FORMAT (' ',A35)
            EXEC SQL INCLUDE SQLCA
            EXEC SQL DECLARE SALESREPS TABLE
      C                       (EMPL_NUM INTEGER NOT NULL,
      C                         NAME VARCHAR(15) NOT NULL,
      C                          AGE INTEGER,
      C                    REP_OFFICE INTEGER,
      C                         TITLE VARCHAR(10),
      C                     HIRE_DATE DATE NOT NULL,
      C                       MANAGER INTEGER,
      C                         QUOTA MONEY,
      C                         SALES MONEY NOT NULL)
      *
      *     DISPLAY A MESSAGE FOR THE USER
            WRITE (6,100) 'Deleting salesreps with low quota.'
      *
      *     EXECUTE THE SQL STATEMENT
            EXEC SQL DELETE FROM REPS
      C           WHERE QUOTA < 150000
      *
      *     DISPLAY ANOTHER MESSAGE
            WRITE (6,100) 'Finished deleting.'
            RETURN
            END
```

Figure 17-6.   *An embedded SQL program written in FORTRAN*

Declaring Tables

In the IBM SQL products, the embedded DECLARE TABLE statement, shown in
Figure 17-8, declares a table that will be referenced by one or more embedded SQL
statements in your program. This is an optional statement that aids the precompiler
in its task of parsing and validating the embedded SQL statements. By using the
DECLARE TABLE statement, your program explicitly specifies its assumptions about
the columns in the table and their data types and sizes. The precompiler checks the
table and column references in your program to make sure they conform to your table
declaration.

The programs in Figures 17-4, 17-5, and 17-6 all use the DECLARE TABLE statement.
It's important to note that the statement appears purely for documentation purposes
and for the use of the precompiler. It is not an executable statement, and you do not

```
    main()
    {
      exec sql include sqlca;

      /* Create a new REGIONS table */
      exec sql create table regions
                      (name char(15),
                   hq_city char(15),
                   manager integer,
                    target money,
                     sales money,
              primary key name,
              foreign key manager
                references salesreps);
      printf("Table created.\n");

      /* Insert two rows; one for each region */
      exec sql insert into regions
                  values ('Eastern', 'New York', 106, 0.00, 0.00);
      exec sql insert into regions
                  values ('Western', 'Los Angeles', 108, 0.00, 0.00);
      printf("Table populated.\n");

      exit();
    }
```

Figure 17-7.   *Using embedded SQL to create a table*

need to explicitly declare tables before referring to them in embedded DML or DDL
statements. However, using the DECLARE TABLE statement does make your program
more self-documenting and simpler to maintain. The IBM-developed SQL products all
support the DECLARE TABLE statement, but most other SQL products do not support
it, and their precompilers will generate an error message if you use it.

Error Handling

When you type an interactive SQL statement that causes an error, the interactive SQL
program displays an error message, aborts the statement, and prompts you to type a
new statement. In embedded SQL, error handling becomes the responsibility of the
application program. Actually, embedded SQL statements can produce two distinct
types of errors:

Figure 17-8. *The DECLARE TABLE statement syntax diagram*

- **Compile-time errors**. Misplaced commas, misspelled SQL keywords, and similar errors in embedded SQL statements are detected by the SQL precompiler and reported to the programmer. The programmer can fix the errors and recompile the application program.

- **Runtime errors**. An attempt to insert an invalid data value or lack of permission to update a table can be detected only at runtime. Errors such as these must be detected and handled by the application program.

In embedded SQL programs, the DBMS reports runtime errors to the application program through a returned error code. If an error is detected, a further description of the error and other information about the statement just executed is available through additional diagnostic information. The earliest IBM-embedded SQL implementations defined an error-reporting mechanism that was adopted, with variations, by most of the major DBMS vendors. The central part of this scheme—an error status variable named SQLCODE—was also defined in the original ANSI/ISO SQL standard. The SQL2 standard, published in 1992, defined an entirely new, parallel error-reporting mechanism, built around an error status variable named SQLSTATE. These mechanisms are described in the next two sections.

Error Handling with SQLCODE

Under this scheme, pioneered by the earliest IBM products, the DBMS communicates status information to the embedded SQL program through an area of program storage called the *SQL Communications Area,* or SQLCA. The SQLCA is a data structure that contains error variables and status indicators. By examining the SQLCA, the application program can determine the success or failure of its embedded SQL statements and act accordingly.

Notice in Figures 17-4, 17-5, 17-6, and 17-7 that the first embedded SQL statement in the program is INCLUDE SQLCA. This statement tells the SQL precompiler to include a SQL Communications Area in this program. The specific contents of the SQLCA vary slightly from one brand of DBMS to another, but the SQLCA always provides the same type of information. Figure 17-9 shows the definition of the SQLCA used by the IBM databases. The most important part of the SQLCA, the SQLCODE variable, is supported by all of the major embedded SQL products and was specified by the ANSI/ISO SQL1 standard.

As the DBMS executes each embedded SQL statement, it sets the value of the variable SQLCODE in the SQLCA to indicate the completion status of the statement:

```
struct sqlca {
    unsigned char sqlcaid[8];        /* the string "SQLCA  " */
    long          sqlcabc;           /* length of SQLCA, in bytes */
    long          sqlcode;           /* SQL status code */
    short         sqlerrml;          /* length of sqlerrmc array data */
    unsigned char sqlerrmc[70];      /* name(s) of object(s) causing error */
    unsigned char sqlerrp[8];        /* diagnostic information */
    long          sqlerrd[6];        /* various counts and error code */
    unsigned char sqlwarn[8];        /* warning flag array */
    unsigned char sqlext[8];         /* extension to sqlwarn array */
}

#define SQLCODE  sqlca.sqlcode       /* SQL status code */

/* A 'W' in any of the SQLWARN fields signals a warning condition;
   otherwise these fields each contain a blank */

#define SQLWARN0 sqlca.sqlwarn[0]  /* master warning flag */
#define SQLWARN1 sqlca.sqlwarn[1]  /* string truncated */
#define SQLWARN2 sqlca.sqlwarn[2]  /* NULLs eliminated from column function */
#define SQLWARN3 sqlca.sqlwarn[3]  /* too few/too many host variables */
#define SQLWARN4 sqlca.sqlwarn[4]  /* prepared UPDATE/DELETE without WHERE */
#define SQLWARN5 sqlca.sqlwarn[5]  /* SQL/DS vs DB2 incompatibility */
#define SQLWARN6 sqlca.sqlwarn[6]  /* invalid date in arithmetic expr */
#define SQLWARN7 sqlca.sqlwarn[7]  /* reserved */
```

Figure 17-9.   *The SQL Communications Area (SQLCA) for IBM databases*

- A SQLCODE of zero indicates successful completion of the statement, without any errors or warnings.

- A negative SQLCODE value indicates a serious error that prevented the statement from executing correctly. For example, an attempt to update a read-only view would produce a negative SQLCODE value. A separate negative value is assigned to each runtime error that can occur.

- A positive SQLCODE value indicates a warning condition. For example, truncation or rounding of a data item retrieved by the program would produce a warning. A separate positive value is assigned to each runtime warning that can occur. The most common warning, with a value of +100 in most implementations and in the SQL1 standard, is the out-of-data warning returned when a program tries to retrieve the next row of query results and no more rows are left to retrieve.

Because every executable embedded SQL statement can potentially generate an error, a well-written program will check the SQLCODE value after every executable embedded SQL statement. Figure 17-10 shows a C program excerpt that checks the SQLCODE value. Figure 17-11 shows a similar excerpt from a COBOL program.

```
        .
        .
        .
    exec sql delete from salesreps
            where quota < 150000;
if (sqlca.sqlcode < 0)
    goto error_routine;
        .
        .
        .


error_routine:
    printf("SQL error: %ld\n, sqlca.sqlcode);
    exit();
        .
        .
        .
```

Figure 17-10. *A C program excerpt with SQLCODE error checking*

```
             .
             .
             .
   01   PRINT_MESSAGE.
          02   FILLER     PIC X(11) VALUE 'SQL error:'.
          02   PRINT-CODE PIC SZ(9).
             .
             .
             .

          EXEC SQL DELETE FROM SALESREPS
                   WHERE QUOTA < 150000
          END EXEC.
          IF SQLCODE NOT = ZERO GOTO ERROR-ROUTINE.
             .
             .
             .

   ERROR-ROUTINE.
          MOVE SQLCODE TO PRINT-CODE.
          DISPLAY PRINT_MESSAGE.
             .
             .
             .
```

Figure 17-11. *A COBOL program excerpt with SQLCODE error checking*

Error Handling with SQLSTATE

By the time the SQL2 standard was being written, virtually all commercial SQL products were using the SQLCODE variable to report error conditions in an embedded SQL program. However, there was no standardization of the error numbers used by the different products to report the same or similar error conditions. Further, because of the significant differences among SQL implementations permitted by the SQL1 standard, considerable differences in the errors could occur from one implementation to another. Finally, the definition of the SQLCA varied in significant ways from one DBMS brand to another, and all of the major brands had a large installed base of applications that would be broken by any change to their SQLCA structure.

Instead of tackling the impossible task of getting all of the DBMS vendors to agree to change their SQLCODE values to some standard, the writers of the SQL2 standard took a different approach. They included the SQLCODE error value, but identified it as a *deprecated* feature, meaning that it was considered obsolete and would be removed from the standard at some future time. To take its place, they introduced a new error variable, called SQLSTATE. The standard also specifies, in detail, the error conditions that can be reported through the SQLSTATE variable, and the error code assigned to each error. To conform to the SQL2 standard, a SQL product must report errors using both the SQLCODE and SQLSTATE error variables. In this way, existing programs that use SQLCODE will still function, but new programs can be written to use the standardized SQLSTATE error codes.

The SQLSTATE variable consists of two parts:

■ A two-character *error class* that identifies the general classification of the error (such as a connection error, an invalid data error, or a warning).

■ A three-character *error subclass* that identifies a specific type of error within a general error class. For example, within the invalid data class, the error subclass might identify a divide by zero error, an invalid numeric value error, or invalid datetime data.

Errors specified in the SQL2 standard have an error class code that begins with a digit from zero to four (inclusive) or a letter between *A* and *H* (inclusive). For example, data errors are indicated by error class 22. A violation of an integrity constraint (such as a foreign key definition) is indicated by error class 23. A transaction rollback is indicated by error class 40. Within each error class, the standard subclass codes also follow the same initial number/letter restrictions. For example, within error class 40 (transaction rollback), the subclass codes are 001 for serialization failure (that is, your program was chosen as the loser in a deadlock), 002 for an integrity constraint violation, and 003 for errors where the completion status of the SQL statement is unknown (for example, when a network connection breaks or a server crashes before the statement completes). Figure 17-12 shows the same C program as Figure 17-10, but uses the SQLSTATE variable for error checking instead of SQLCODE.

The standard specifically reserves error class codes that begin with digits from five to nine (inclusive) and letters between *I* and *Z* (inclusive) as implementation-specific errors that are not standardized. While this allows differences among DBMS brands to continue, all of the most common errors caused by SQL statements are included in the standardized error class codes. As commercial DBMS implementations move to support the SQLSTATE variable, one of the most troublesome incompatibilities between different SQL products is gradually being eliminated.

The SQL2 standard provides additional error and diagnostics information through a new GET DIAGNOSTICS statement, shown in Figure 17-13. The statement allows an embedded SQL program to retrieve one or more items of information about the SQL statement just executed, or about an error condition that was just raised. Support for the GET DIAGNOSTICS statement is required for Intermediate SQL or Full SQL conformance to the standard but is not required or allowed in Entry SQL. Figure 17-14 shows a C program excerpt like that in Figure 17-12, extended to include the GET DIAGNOSTICS statement.

```
                    .
                    .
                    .
          exec sql delete from salesreps
                      where quota < 150000;
          if (strcmp(sqlca.sqlstate,"00000"))
             goto error_routine;
                    .
                    .
                    .

          error_routine:
             printf("SQL error: %s\n",sqlca.sqlstate);
             exit();
                    .
                    .
                    .
```

Figure 17-12.   *A C program excerpt with* SQLSTATE *error checking*

The WHENEVER Statement

It quickly becomes tedious for a programmer to write programs that explicitly check
the SQLCODE value after each embedded SQL statement. To simplify error handling,
embedded SQL supports the WHENEVER statement, shown in Figure 17-15. The
WHENEVER statement is a directive to the SQL precompiler, not an executable
statement. It tells the precompiler to automatically generate error-handling code
following every executable embedded SQL statement and specifies what the generated
code should do.

You can use the WHENEVER statement to tell the precompiler how to handle three
different exception conditions:

■ WHENEVER SQLERROR tells the precompiler to generate code to handle errors
(negative SQLCODEs).

■ WHENEVER SQLWARNING tells the precompiler to generate code to handle
warnings (positive SQLCODEs).

■ WHENEVER NOT FOUND tells the precompiler to generate code that handles a
particular warning—the warning generated by the DBMS when your program
tries to retrieve query results when no more are remaining. This use of the
WHENEVER statement is specific to the singleton SELECT and the FETCH
statements, and is described in the section "Single-Row Queries."

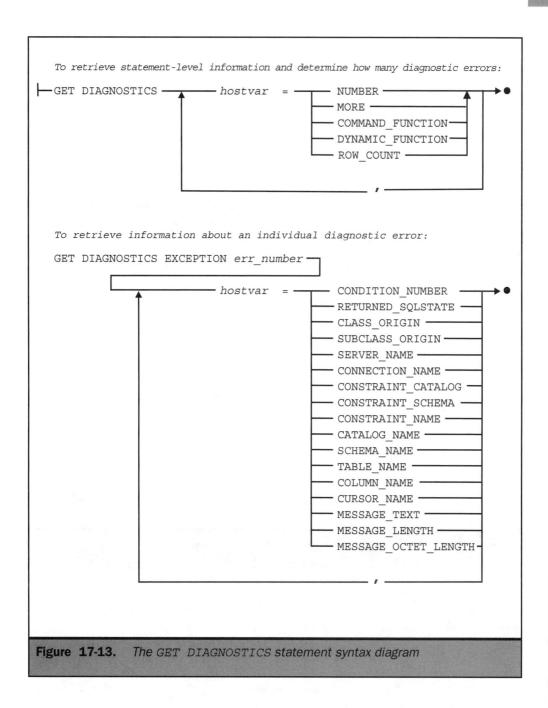

Figure 17-13. *The GET DIAGNOSTICS statement syntax diagram*

Note that the SQL2 standard does not specify the SQLWARNING form of the WHENEVER statement, but most commercial SQL products support it.

```
                     .
                     .
                     .
          /* execute the DELETE statement & check for errors */
          exec sql delete from salesreps
                   where quota < 150000;
          if (strcmp(sqlca.sqlstate,"00000"))
             goto error_routine;

          /* DELETE successful; check how many rows deleted */
          exec sql get diagnostics :numrows = ROW_COUNT;
          printf("%ld rows deleted\n",numrows);
                     .
                     .
                     .

       error_routine:
          /* Determine how many errors reported */
          exec sql get diagnostics :count = NUMBER;
          for (i=1; i<count; i++) {
             exec sql get diagnostics EXCEPTION :I
                        :err = RETURNED_SQLSTATE,
                        :msg = MESSAGE_TEXT;
             printf("SQL error # %d: code: %s message: %s\n",
                     i, err, msg);
          }
          exit();
                     .
                     .
                     .
```

Figure 17-14.   *A C program excerpt with* GET DIAGNOSTICS *error checking*

For any of these three conditions, you can tell the precompiler to generate code that takes one of two actions:

- WHENEVER/GOTO tells the precompiler to generate a branch to the specified *label*, which must be a statement label or statement number in the program.

- WHENEVER/CONTINUE tells the precompiler to let the program's flow of control proceed to the next host language statement.

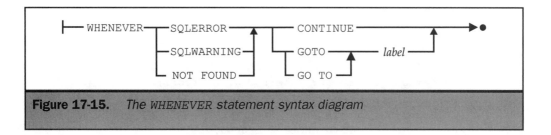

Figure 17-15.   *The WHENEVER statement syntax diagram*

The WHENEVER statement is a directive to the precompiler, and its effect can be superseded by another WHENEVER statement appearing later in the program text. Figure 17-16 shows a program excerpt with three WHENEVER statements and four executable SQL statements. In this program, an error in either of the two DELETE statements results in a branch to error1 because of the first WHENEVER statement. An error in the embedded UPDATE statement flows directly into the following statements of the program. An error in the embedded INSERT statement results in a branch to error2. As this example shows, the main use of the WHENEVER/CONTINUE form of the statement is to cancel the effect of a previous WHENEVER statement.

The WHENEVER statement makes embedded SQL error handling much simpler, and it is more common for an application program to use it than to check SQLCODE or SQLSTATE directly. Remember, however, that after a WHENEVER/GOTO statement appears, the precompiler will generate a test and a branch to the specified label for *every* embedded SQL statement that follows it. You must arrange your program so that the specified label is a valid target for branching from these embedded SQL statements, or use another WHENEVER statement to specify a different destination or cancel the effects of the WHENEVER/GOTO.

Using Host Variables

The embedded SQL programs in the previous figures don't provide any real interaction between the programming statements and the embedded SQL statements. In most applications, you will want to use the value of one or more program variables in the embedded SQL statements. For example, suppose you wanted to write a program to adjust all sales quotas up or down by some dollar amount. The program should prompt the user for the amount and then use an embedded UPDATE statement to change the QUOTA column in the SALESREPS table.

Embedded SQL supports this capability through the use of *host variables*. A host variable is a program variable declared in the host language (for example, a COBOL or C variable) that is referenced in an embedded SQL statement. To identify the host variable, the variable name is prefixed by a colon (:) when it appears in an embedded SQL statement. The colon allows the precompiler to distinguish easily between host variables and database objects (such as tables or columns) that may have the same name.

```
                    .
                    .
                    .
        exec sql whenever sqlerror goto error1;

        exec sql delete from salesreps
                where quota < 150000;

        exec sql delete from customers
                where credit_limit < 20000;

        exec sql whenever sqlerror continue;

        exec sql update salesreps
                set quota = quota * 1.05;

        exec sql whenever sqlerror goto error2;

        exec sql insert into salesreps (empl_num, name, quota)
                values (116, 'Jan Hamilton', 100000.00);
            .
            .
            .
    error1:
        printf("SQL DELETE error: %dl\n", sqlca.sqlcode);
        exit();

    error2:
        printf("SQL INSERT error: %ld\n", sqlca.sqlcode);
        exit();
            .
            .
            .
```

Figure 17-16. *Using the WHENEVER statement*

Figure 17-17 shows a C program that implements the quota adjustment application using a host variable. The program prompts the user for the adjustment amount and stores the entered value in the variable named amount. This host variable is referenced in the embedded UPDATE statement. Conceptually, when the UPDATE statement is executed, the value of the amount variable is obtained, and that value is substituted for the host variable in the SQL statement. For example, if you enter the amount 500 in response to the prompt, the DBMS effectively executes this UPDATE statement:

```
exec sql update salesreps
        set quota = quota + 500;
```

A host variable can appear in an embedded SQL statement wherever a constant can appear. In particular, a host variable can be used in an assignment expression:

```
exec sql update salesreps
        set quota = quota + :amount;
```

A host variable can appear in a search condition:

```
exec sql delete from salesreps
        where quota < :amount;
```

A host variable can also be used in the VALUES clause of an INSERT statement:

```
exec sql insert into salesreps (empl_num, name, quota)
        values (116, 'Bill Roberts', :amount);
```

In each case, note that the host variable is part of the program's input to the DBMS; it forms part of the SQL statement submitted to the DBMS for execution. Later, in the section "Data Retrieval in Embedded SQL," you will see how host variables are also used to receive output from the DBMS; they receive query results returned from the DBMS to the program.

Note that a host variable cannot be used instead of a SQL identifier. This attempted use of the host variable colname is illegal:

```
char *colname = "quota";

exec sql insert into salesreps (empl_num, name, :colname)
        values (116, 'Bill Roberts', 0.00);
```

Declaring Host Variables

When you use a host variable in an embedded SQL statement, you must declare the variable using the normal method for declaring variables in the host programming language. For example, in Figure 17-17, the host variable amount is declared using the

```
main()
{
    exec sql include sqlca;
    exec sql begin declare section;
        float amount;                      /* amount (from user) */
    exec sql end declare section;

    /* Prompt the user for the amount of quota increase/decrease */
    printf("Raise/lower quotas by how much:");
    scanf("%f", &amount);

    /* Update the QUOTA column in the SALESREPS table */
    exec sql update salesreps
            set quota = quota + :amount;

    /* Check results of statement execution */
    if (sqlqa.sqlcode != 0)
        printf("Error during update.\n");
    else
        printf("Update successful.\n");

    exit();
}
```

Figure 17-17. *Using host variables*

normal C language syntax (`float amount;`). When the precompiler processes the
source code for the program, it notes the name of each variable it encounters, along with
its data type and size. The precompiler uses this information to generate correct code
later when it encounters a use of the variable as a host variable in a SQL statement.

The two embedded SQL statements BEGIN DECLARE SECTION and END DECLARE
SECTION bracket the host variable declarations, as shown in Figure 17-17. These two
statements are unique to embedded SQL, and they are not executable. They are directives
to the precompiler, telling it when it must pay attention to variable declarations and
when it can ignore them.

In a simple embedded SQL program, it may be possible to gather together all of the
host variable declarations in one declare section. Usually, however, the host variables
must be declared at various points within the program, especially in block-structured

languages such as C, Pascal, and PL/I. In this case, each declaration of host variables must be bracketed with a BEGIN DECLARE SECTION/END DECLARE SECTION statement pair.

The BEGIN DECLARE SECTION and END DECLARE SECTION statements are relatively new to the embedded SQL language. They are specified in the ANSI/ISO SQL standard, and DB2 requires them in its newer embedded SQL implementations. However, DB2 and many other DBMS brands did not historically require declare sections, and some SQL precompilers do not yet support the BEGIN DECLARE SECTION and END DECLARE SECTION statements. In this case, the precompiler scans and processes all variable declarations in the host program.

When you use a host variable, the precompiler may limit your flexibility in declaring the variable in the host programming language. For example, consider the following C language source code:

```
#define BIGBUFSIZE 256
    .
    .
    .
exec sql begin declare section;
    char bigbuffer[BIGBUFSIZE+1];
exec sql end declare section;
```

This is a valid C declaration of the variable bigbuffer. However, if you try to use bigbuffer as a host variable in an embedded SQL statement like this:

```
exec sql update salesreps
        set quota = 300000
        where name = :bigbuffer;
```

many precompilers will generate an error message, complaining about an illegal declaration of bigbuffer. The problem is that some precompilers don't recognize symbolic constants like BIGBUFSIZE. This is just one example of the special considerations that apply when using embedded SQL and a precompiler. Fortunately, the precompilers offered by the major DBMS vendors are being improved steadily, and the number of special case problems like this one is decreasing.

Host Variables and Data Types

The data types supported by a SQL-based DBMS and the data types supported by a programming language such as C or FORTRAN are often quite different. These differences impact host variables because they play a dual role. On the one hand, a host variable is a program variable, declared using the data types of the programming language and manipulated by programming language statements. On the other hand, a host variable is used in embedded SQL statements to contain database data.

Consider the four embedded UPDATE statements in Figure 17-18. In the first UPDATE statement, the MANAGER column has an INTEGER data type, so hostvar1 should be declared as a C integer variable. In the second statement, the NAME column has a VARCHAR data type, so hostvar2 should contain string data. The program should declare hostvar2 as an array of C character data, and most DBMS products will expect the data in the array to be terminated by a null character (0). In the third UPDATE statement, the QUOTA column has a MONEY data type. There is no corresponding data type in C, and C does not support a packed decimal data type. For most DBMS brands, you can declare hostvar3 as a C floating point variable, and the DBMS will automatically translate the floating point value into the DBMS MONEY format. Finally, in the fourth UPDATE statement, the HIRE_DATE column has a DATE data type in the database. For most DBMS brands, you should declare hostvar4 as an array of C character data and fill the array with a text form of the date acceptable to the DBMS.

As Figure 17-18 shows, the data types of host variables must be chosen carefully to match their intended use in embedded SQL statements. Table 17-1 shows the SQL data types specified in the ANSI/ISO SQL2 standard and the corresponding data types used in four of the most popular embedded SQL programming languages, as specified in the standard. The standard specifies data type correspondences and embedded SQL rules for the Ada, C, COBOL, FORTRAN, MUMPS, Pascal, and PL/I languages.

Note, however, that in many cases, there is not a one-to-one correspondence between data types. In addition, each brand of DBMS has its own data type idiosyncrasies and its own rules for data type conversion when using host variables. Before counting on a specific data conversion behavior, consult the documentation for your particular DBMS brand and carefully read the description for the particular programming language you are using.

Host Variables and NULL Values

Most programming languages do not provide SQL-style support for unknown or missing values. A variable in COBOL, C, or FORTRAN, for example, always has a value. There is no concept of the value being NULL or missing. This causes a problem when you want to store NULL values in the database or retrieve NULL values from the database using programmatic SQL. Embedded SQL solves this problem by allowing each host variable to have a companion *host indicator variable*. In an embedded SQL statement, the host variable and the indicator variable together specify a single SQL-style value, as follows:

■ An indicator value of zero means that the host variable contains a valid value and that this value is to be used.

■ A negative indicator value means that the host variable should be assumed to have a NULL value; the actual value of the host variable is irrelevant and should be disregarded.

SQL Type	C Type	COBOL Type	FORTRAN Type	PL/I Type
SMALLINT	short	PIC S9 (4) COMP	INTEGER*2	FIXED BIN (15)
INTEGER	long	PIC S9 (9) COMP	INTEGER*4	FIXED BIN (31)
REAL	float	COMP-1	REAL*4	BIN FLOAT (21)
DOUBLE PRECISION	double	COMP-2	REAL*8	BIN FLOAT (53)
NUMERIC (p,s) DECIMAL (p,s)	double[1]	PIC S9 $(p-s)$ V9 (s) COMP-3	REAL*8[1]	FIXED DEC (p, s)
CHAR (n)	char x [n+1][2]	PIC X (n)	CHARACTER*n	CHAR (n)
VARCHAR (n)	char x [n+1][2]	Req. conv.[4]	Req. conv.[4]	CHAR (n) VAR
BIT (n)	char x [1][3]	PIC X (1)	CHARACTER*L3	BIT (n)
BIT VARYING (n)	char x [1][3]	Req. conv.[4]	Req. conv.[4]	BIT (n) VAR
DATE	Req. conv.[5]	Req. conv.[5]	Req. conv.[5]	Req. conv.[5]
TIME	Req. conv.[5]	Req. conv.[5]	Req. conv.[5]	Req. conv.[5]
TIMESTAMP	Req. conv.[5]	Req. conv.[5]	Req. conv.[5]	Req. conv.[5]
INTERVAL	Req. conv.[5]	Req. conv.[5]	Req. conv.[5]	Req. conv.[5]

Notes:

[1] Host language does not support packed decimal data; conversion to or from floating point data may cause truncation or round-off errors.

[2] The SQL standard specifies a C string with a null terminator; older DBMS implementations returned a separate length value in a data structure.

[3] The length of the host character string (l) is the number of bits (n), divided by the bits-per-character for the host language (typically 8), rounded up.

[4] Host language does not support variable-length strings; most DBMS brands will convert to fixed-length strings.

[5] Host languages do not support native date/time data types; requires conversion to/from host language character string data types with text date, time, and interval representations.

Table 17-1.   *SQL Data Types*

■ A positive indicator value means that the host variable contains a valid value, which may have been rounded off or truncated. This situation occurs only when data is retrieved from the database, and is described later in the section "Retrieving NULL Values."

```
              .
              .
              .
              exec sql begin declare section;
                  int    hostvar1  = 106;
                  char  *hostvar2 = "Joe Smith";
                  float  hostvar3  = 150000.00;
                  char  *hostvar4 = "01-JUN-1990";
              exec sql end declare section;

              exec sql update salesreps
                      set manager = :hostvar1
                      where empl_num = 102;

              exec sql update salesreps
                      set name = :hostvar2
                      where empl_num = 102:

              exec sql update salesreps
                      set quota = :hostvar3
                      where empl_num = 102;

              exec sql update salesreps
                      set hire_date = :hostvar4
                      where empl_num = 102;
              .
              .
              .
```

Figure 17-18.   *Host variables and data types*

When you specify a host variable in an embedded SQL statement, you can follow
it immediately with the name of the corresponding indicator variable. Both variable
names are preceded by a colon. Here is an embedded UPDATE statement that uses the
host variable amount with the companion indicator variable amount_ind:

```
exec sql update salesreps
        set quota = :amount :amount_ind, sales = :amount2
      where quota < 20000.00;
```

If amount_ind has a nonnegative value when the UPDATE statement is executed, the DBMS treats the statement as if it read:

```
exec sql update salesreps
         set quota = :amount, sales = :amount2
      where quota < 20000.00;
```

If amount_ind has a negative value when the UPDATE statement is executed, the DBMS treats the statement as if it read:

```
exec sql update salesreps
         set quota = NULL, sales = :amount2
      where quota < 20000.00;
```

A host variable/indicator variable pair can appear in the assignment clause of an embedded UPDATE statement (as shown here) or in the values clause of an embedded INSERT statement. You cannot use an indicator variable in a search condition, so this embedded SQL statement is illegal:

```
exec sql delete from salesreps
      where quota = :amount :amount_ind;
```

This prohibition exists for the same reason that the NULL keyword is not allowed in the search condition—it makes no sense to test whether QUOTA and NULL are equal, because the answer will always be NULL (unknown). Instead of using the indicator variable, you must use an explicit IS NULL test. This pair of embedded SQL statements accomplishes the intended task of the preceding illegal statement:

```
if (amount_ind < 0) {
   exec sql delete from salesreps
           where quota is null;
}
else {
   exec sql delete from salesreps
           where quota = :amount;
}
```

Indicator variables are especially useful when you are retrieving data from the database into your program and the retrieved data values may be NULL. This use of indicator variables is described later in the section "Retrieving NULL Values."

Data Retrieval in Embedded SQL

Using the embedded SQL features described thus far, you can embed any interactive SQL statement except the SELECT statement in an application program. Retrieving data with an embedded SQL program requires some special extensions to the SELECT statement. The reason for these extensions is that there is a fundamental mismatch between the SQL language and programming languages such as C and COBOL: a SQL query produces an entire table of query results, but most programming languages can manipulate only individual data items or individual records (rows) of data.

Embedded SQL must build a bridge between the table-level logic of the SQL SELECT statement and the row-by-row processing of C, COBOL, and other host programming languages. For this reason, embedded SQL divides SQL queries into two groups:

- **Single-row queries**. You expect the query results to contain a single row of data. Looking up a customer's credit limit or retrieving the sales and quota for a particular salesperson are examples of this type of query.

- **Multirow queries**. You expect that the query results may contain zero, one, or many rows of data. Listing the orders with amounts over $20,000 or retrieving the names of all salespeople who are over quota are examples of this type of query.

Interactive SQL does not distinguish between these two types of queries; the same interactive SELECT statement handles them both. In embedded SQL, however, the two types of queries are handled very differently. Single-row queries are simpler to handle and are discussed in the next section. Multirow queries are discussed shortly.

Single-Row Queries

Many useful SQL queries return a single row of query results. Single-row queries are especially common in transaction-processing programs, where a user enters a customer number or an order number and the program retrieves relevant data about the customer or order. In embedded SQL, single-row queries are handled by the singleton SELECT statement, shown in Figure 17-19. The singleton SELECT statement has a syntax much like that of the interactive SELECT statement. It has a SELECT clause, a FROM clause, and an optional WHERE clause. Because the singleton SELECT statement returns a single row of data, there is no need for a GROUP BY, HAVING, or ORDER BY clause. The INTO clause specifies the host variables that are to receive the data retrieved by the statement.

Figure 17-20 shows a simple program with a singleton SELECT statement. The program prompts the user for an employee number and then retrieves the name, quota, and sales of the corresponding salesperson. The DBMS places the three retrieved data items into the host variables repname, repquota, and repsales, respectively.

Figure 17-19. *The singleton SELECT statement syntax diagram*

Recall that the host variables used in the INSERT, DELETE, and UPDATE statements in the previous examples were input host variables. In contrast, the host variables specified in the INTO clause of the singleton SELECT statement are output host variables. Each host variable named in the INTO clause receives a single column from the row of query results. The select list items and the corresponding host variables are paired in sequence, as they appear in their respective clauses, and the number of query results columns must be the same as the number of host variables. In addition, the data type of each host variable must be compatible with the data type of the corresponding column of query results.

Most DBMS brands will automatically handle reasonable conversions between DBMS data types and the data types supported by the programming language. For example, most DBMS products will convert MONEY data retrieved from the database into packed decimal (COMP-3) data before storing it in a COBOL variable, or into floating point data before storing it in a C variable. The precompiler uses its knowledge of the host variable's data type to handle the conversion correctly.

Variable-length text data must also be converted before being stored in a host variable. Typically, a DBMS converts VARCHAR data into a null-terminated string for C programs and into a variable-length string (with a leading character count) for Pascal

```
main()
{
   exec sql   begin declare section;
      int      repnum;                  /* employee number (from user) */
      char     repname[16];             /* retrieved salesperson name */
      float    repquota;                /* retrieved quota */
      float    repsales;                /* retrieved sales */
   exec sql   end declare section;

   /* Prompt the user for the employee number */
   printf("Enter salesrep number: ");
   scanf("%d", &repnum);

   /* Execute the SQL query */
   exec sql select name, quota, sales
            from salesreps
            where empl_num = :repnum
             into :repname, :repquota, :repsales;

   /* Display the retrieved data */
   if (sqlca.sqlcode = = 0) {
      printf("Name:  %s\n", repname);
      printf("Quota: %f\n", repquota);
      printf("Sales: %f\n", repsales);
   }
   else if (sqlca.sqlcode = = 100)
      printf("No salesperson with that employee number.\n");
   else
      printf("SQL error: %ld\n", sqlca.sqlcode);

   exit();
}
```

Figure 17-20. *Using the singleton* SELECT *statement*

programs. For COBOL and FORTRAN programs, the host variable must generally be declared as a data structure with an integer count field and a character array. The DBMS returns the actual characters of data in the character array, and it returns the length of the data in the count field of the data structure.

If a DBMS supports date/time data or other data types, other conversions are necessary. Some DBMS products return their internal date/time representations into an integer host variable. Others convert the date/time data to text format and return it into a string host variable. Table 17-1 summarized the data type conversions typically provided by DBMS products, but you must consult the embedded SQL documentation for your particular DBMS brand for specific information.

The NOT FOUND Condition

Like all embedded SQL statements, the singleton SELECT statement sets the values of the SQLCODE and SQLSTATE variables to indicate its completion status:

■ If a *single* row of query results is successfully retrieved, SQLCODE is set to zero and SQLSTATE is set to 00000; the host variables named in the INTO clause contain the retrieved values.

■ If the query produced an *error*, SQLCODE is set to a negative value and SQLSTATE is set to a nonzero error class (the first two characters of the five-digit SQLSTATE string); the host variables do not contain retrieved values.

■ If the query produced *no* rows of query results, a special NOT FOUND warning value is returned in SQLCODE, and SQLSTATE returns a NO DATA error class.

■ If the query produced *more than one* row of query results, it is treated as an error, and a negative SQLCODE is returned.

The SQL1 standard specifies the NOT FOUND warning condition, but it does not specify a particular value to be returned. DB2 uses the value +100, and most other SQL products follow this convention, including the other IBM SQL products, Ingres, and SQLBase. This value is also specified in the SQL2 standard, but as noted previously, SQL2 strongly encourages the use of the new SQLSTATE error variable instead of the older SQLCODE values.

Retrieving NULL Values

If the data to be retrieved from a database may contain NULL values, the singleton SELECT statement must provide a way for the DBMS to communicate the NULL values to the application program. To handle NULL values, embedded SQL uses indicator variables in the INTO clause, just as they are used in the VALUES clause of the INSERT statement and the SET clause of the UPDATE statement.

When you specify a host variable in the INTO clause, you can follow it immediately with the name of a companion host indicator variable. Figure 17-21 shows a revised version of the program in Figure 17-20 that uses the indicator variable repquota_ind with the host variable repquota. Because the NAME and SALES columns are declared NOT NULL in the definition of the SALESREPS table, they cannot produce NULL output values, and no indicator variable is needed for those columns.

```
main()
{
   exec sql include sqlca;
   exec sql begin declare section;
      int    repnum;                  /* employee number (from user) */
      char   repname[16];             /* retrieved salesperson name */
      float  repquota;                /* retrieved quota */
      float  repsales;                /* retrieved sales */
      short  repquota_ind;            /* null quota indicator */
   exec sql end declare section;

   /* Prompt the user for the employee number */
   printf("Enter salesrep number: ");
   scanf("%d", &repnum);

   /* Execute the SQL query */
   exec sql select name, quota, sales
            from salesreps
          where empl_num = :repnum
            into :repname, :repquota, :repquota_ind, :repsales;

   /* Display the retrieved data */
   if (sqlca.sqlcode = = 0) {
      printf("Name:  %s\n", repname);
      if (repquota_ind < 0)
         printf("quota is NULL\n");
      else
         printf("Quota: %f\n", repquota);
      printf("Sales: %f\n", repsales);
   }
   else if (sqlca.sqlcode = = 100)
      printf("No salesperson with that employee number.\n");
   else
      printf("SQL error: %ld\n", sqlca.sqlcode);

   exit();
}
```

Figure 17-21. *Using singleton SELECT with indicator variables*

After the SELECT statement has been executed, the value of the indicator variable tells the program how to interpret the returned data:

- An indicator value of zero means the host variable has been assigned a retrieved value by the DBMS. The application program can use the value of the host variable in its processing.

- A negative indicator value means the retrieved value was NULL. The value of the host variable is irrelevant and should not be used by the application program.

- A positive indicator value indicates a warning condition of some kind, such as a rounding error or string truncation.

Because you cannot tell in advance when a NULL value will be retrieved, you should *always* specify an indicator variable in the INTO clause for any column of query results that may contain a NULL value. If the SELECT statement produces a column containing a NULL value and you have not specified an indicator variable for the column, the DBMS will treat the statement as an error and return a negative SQLCODE. Thus, indicator variables must be used to successfully retrieve rows containing NULL data.

Although the major use of indicator variables is for handling NULL values, the DBMS also uses indicator variables to signal warning conditions. For example, if an arithmetic overflow or division by zero makes one of the query results columns invalid, DB2 returns a warning SQLCODE of +802 and sets the indicator variable for the affected column to -2. The application program can respond to the SQLCODE and examine the indicator variables to determine which column contains invalid data.

DB2 also uses indicator variables to signal string truncation. If the query results contain a column of character data that is too large for the corresponding host variable, DB2 copies the first part of the character string into the host variable and sets the corresponding indicator variable to the full length of the string. The application program can examine the indicator variable and may want to retry the SELECT statement with a different host variable that can hold a larger string.

These additional uses of indicator variables are fairly common in commercial SQL products, but the specific warning code values vary from one product to another. They are not specified by the ANSI/ISO SQL standard. Instead, the SQL2 standard specifies error classes and subclasses to indicate these and similar conditions, and the program must use the GET DIAGNOSTICS statement to determine more specific information about the host variable causing the error.

Retrieval Using Data Structures

Some programming languages support *data structures*, which are named collections of variables. For these languages, a SQL precompiler may allow you to treat the entire data structure as a single, composite host variable in the INTO clause. Instead of specifying a separate host variable as the destination for each column of query results, you can specify a data structure as the destination for the entire row. Figure 17-22 shows the program from Figure 17-21, rewritten to use a C data structure.

```
main()
{
   exec sql include sqlca;
   exec sql begin declare section;
      int repnum;                        /* employee number (from user) */
      struct {
         char   name[16];                /* retrieved salesperson name */
         float quota;                    /* retrieved quota */
         float sales;                    /* retrieved sales */
      } repinfo;
      short rep_ind[3];                  /* null indicator array */
   exec sql end declare section;

   /* Prompt the user for the employee number */
   printf("Enter salesrep number: ");
   scanf("%d", &repnum);

   /* Execute the SQL query */
   exec sql select name, quota, sales
            from salesreps
            where empl_num = :repnum
             into :repinfo :rep_ind;

   /* Display the retrieved data */
   if (sqlca.sqlcode = = 0) {
      printf("Name:  %s\n", repinfo.name);
      if (rep_ind[1] < 0)
         printf("quota is NULL\n");
      else
         printf("Quota: %f\n", repinfo.quota);
      printf("Sales: %f\n", repinfo.sales);
   }
   else if (sqlca.sqlcode = = 100)
      printf("No salesperson with that employee number.\n");
   else
      printf("SQL error: %ld\n", sqlca.sqlcode);

   exit();
}
```

Figure 17-22.   *Using a data structure as a host variable*

When the precompiler encounters a data structure reference in the INTO clause, it replaces the structure reference with a list of the individual variables in the structure, in the order they are declared within the structure. Thus, the number of items in the structure and their data types must correspond to the columns of query results. The use of data structures in the INTO clause is, in effect, a shortcut. It does not fundamentally change the way the INTO clause works.

Support for the use of data structures as host variables varies widely among DBMS brands. It is also restricted to certain programming languages. DB2 supports C and PL/I structures but does not support COBOL or assembly language structures, for example.

Input and Output Host Variables

Host variables provide two-way communication between the program and the DBMS. In the program shown in Figure 17-21, the host variables repnum and repname illustrate the two different roles played by host variables:

- The repnum host variable is an input host variable, used to pass data from the program to the DBMS. The program assigns a value to the variable before executing the embedded statement, and that value becomes part of the SELECT statement to be executed by the DBMS. The DBMS does nothing to alter the value of the variable.

- The repname host variable is an output host variable, used to pass data back from the DBMS to the program. The DBMS assigns a value to this variable as it executes the embedded SELECT statement. After the statement has been executed, the program can use the resulting value.

Input and output host variables are declared the same way and are specified using the same colon notation within an embedded SQL statement. However, it's often useful to think in terms of input and output host variables when you're actually coding an embedded SQL program. Input host variables can be used in any SQL statement where a constant can appear. Output host variables are used only with the singleton SELECT statement and with the FETCH statement, described in the next section of this chapter.

Multirow Queries

When a query produces an entire table of query results, embedded SQL must provide a way for the application program to process the query results one row at a time. Embedded SQL supports this capability by defining a new SQL concept, called a *cursor*, and adding several statements to the interactive SQL language. Here is an overview of embedded SQL techniques for multirow query processing and the new statements it requires:

1. The DECLARE CURSOR statement specifies the query to be performed and associates a cursor name with the query.

2. The OPEN statement asks the DBMS to start executing the query and generating query results. It positions the cursor before the first row of query results.

3. The FETCH statement advances the cursor to the first row of query results and retrieves its data into host variables for use by the application program. Subsequent FETCH statements move through the query results row by row, advancing the cursor to the next row of query results and retrieving its data into the host variables.

4. The CLOSE statement ends access to the query results and breaks the association between the cursor and the query results.

Figure 17-23 shows a program that uses embedded SQL to perform a simple multirow query. The numbered callouts in the figure correspond to the numbers in the preceding steps. The program retrieves and displays, in alphabetical order, the name, quota, and year-to-date sales of each salesperson whose sales exceed quota. The interactive SQL query that prints this information is:

```
SELECT NAME, QUOTA, SALES
  FROM SALESREPS
 WHERE SALES > QUOTA
 ORDER BY NAME
```

Notice that this query appears, word for word, in the embedded DECLARE CURSOR statement in Figure 17-23. The statement also associates the cursor name repcurs with the query. This cursor name is used later in the OPEN CURSOR statement to start the query and position the cursor before the first row of query results.

The FETCH statement inside the for loop fetches the next row of query results each time the loop is executed. The INTO clause of the FETCH statement works just like the INTO clause of the singleton SELECT statement. It specifies the host variables that are to receive the fetched data items—one host variable for each column of query results. As in previous examples, a host indicator variable (repquota_ind) is used when a fetched data item may contain NULL values.

When no more rows of query results are to be fetched, the DBMS returns the NOT FOUND warning in response to the FETCH statement. This is exactly the same warning code that is returned when the singleton SELECT statement does not retrieve a row of data. In this program, the WHENEVER NOT FOUND statement causes the precompiler to generate code that checks the SQLCODE value after the FETCH statement. This generated code branches to the label done when the NOT FOUND condition arises, and to the label error if an error occurs. At the end of the program, the CLOSE statement ends the query and terminates the program's access to the query results.

```
main()
{
    exec sql include sqlca;
    exec sql begin declare section;
        char   repname[16];              /* retrieved salesperson name */
        float  repquota;                 /* retrieved quota */
        float  repsales;                 /* retrieved sales */
        short  repquota_ind;             /* null quota indicator */
    exec sql end declare section;

    /* Declare the cursor for the query */
    exec sql declare repcurs cursor for ◄──────────────────  ①
            select name, quota, sales
              from salesreps
             where sales > quota
             order by name;

    /* Set up error processing */
    whenever sqlerror goto error;
    whenever not found goto done;

    /* Open the cursor to start the query */
    exec sql open repcurs; ◄──────────────────────────────  ②

    /* Loop through each row of query results */
    for (;;) {

        /* Fetch the next row of query results */
        exec sql fetch repcurs ◄──────────────────────────  ③
                into :repname, :repquota, :repquota_ind, repsales;

        /* Display the retrieved data */
        printf("Name: %s\n", repname);
        if (repquota_ind < 0)
            printf("Quota is NULL\n");
        else
            printf("Quota: %f\n", repquota);
        printf("Sales: %f\n", repsales);
    }

error:
    printf("SQL error: %ld\n", sqlca.sqlcode);
    exit();

done:
    /* Query complete; close the cursor */
    exec sql close repcurs; ◄─────────────────────────────  ④
    exit();
}
```

Figure 17-23.   *Multirow query processing*

Cursors

As the program in Figure 17-23 illustrates, an embedded SQL cursor behaves much like a filename or file handle in a programming language such as C or COBOL. Just as a program opens a file to access the file's contents, it opens a cursor to gain access to the query results. Similarly, the program closes a file to end its access and closes a cursor to end access to the query results. Finally, just as a file handle keeps track of the program's current position within an open file, a cursor keeps track of the program's current position within the query results. These parallels between file input/output and SQL cursors make the cursor concept relatively easy for application programmers to understand.

Despite the parallels between files and cursors, there are also some differences. Opening a SQL cursor usually involves much more overhead than opening a file, because opening the cursor actually causes the DBMS to begin carrying out the associated query. In addition, SQL cursors support only sequential motion through the query results, like sequential file processing. In most current SQL implementations, there is no cursor analog to the random access provided to the individual records of a file.

Cursors provide a great deal of flexibility for processing queries in an embedded SQL program. By declaring and opening multiple cursors, the program can process several sets of query results in parallel. For example, the program might retrieve some rows of query results, display them on the screen for its user, and then respond to a user's request for more detailed data by launching a second query. The following sections describe in detail the four embedded SQL statements that define and manipulate cursors.

The DECLARE CURSOR Statement

The DECLARE CURSOR statement, shown in Figure 17-24, defines a query to be performed. The statement also associates a cursor name with the query. The cursor name must be a valid SQL identifier. It is used to identify the query and its results in other embedded SQL statements. The cursor name is specifically *not* a host language variable; it is declared by the DECLARE CURSOR statement, not in a host language declaration.

The SELECT statement in the DECLARE CURSOR statement defines the query associated with the cursor. The SELECT statement can be any valid interactive SQL SELECT statement, as described in Chapters 6 through 9. In particular, the SELECT statement must include a FROM clause and may optionally include WHERE, GROUP BY, HAVING, and ORDER BY clauses. The SELECT statement may also include the UNION operator, as described in Chapter 6. Thus, an embedded SQL query can use any of the query capabilities that are available in the interactive SQL language.

DECLARE *cursor-name* CURSOR FOR *select-statement*

Figure 17-24. *The DECLARE CURSOR statement syntax diagram*

The query specified in the DECLARE CURSOR statement may also include input host variables. These host variables perform exactly the same function as in the embedded INSERT, DELETE, UPDATE, and singleton SELECT statements. An input host variable can appear within the query anywhere that a constant can appear. Note that output host variables cannot appear in the query. Unlike the singleton SELECT statement, the SELECT statement within the DECLARE CURSOR statement has no INTO clause and does not retrieve any data. The INTO clause appears as part of the FETCH statement, described shortly.

As its name implies, the DECLARE CURSOR statement is a declaration of the cursor. In most SQL implementations, including the IBM SQL products, this statement is a directive for the SQL precompiler; it is not an executable statement, and the precompiler does not produce any code for it. Like all declarations, the DECLARE CURSOR statement must physically appear in the program before any statements that reference the cursor that it declares. Most SQL implementations treat the cursor name as a global name that can be referenced inside any procedures, functions, or subroutines that appear after the DECLARE CURSOR statement.

It's worth noting that not all SQL implementations treat the DECLARE CURSOR statement strictly as a declarative statement, and this can lead to subtle problems. Some SQL precompilers actually generate code for the DECLARE CURSOR statement (either host language declarations or calls to the DBMS, or both), giving it some of the qualities of an executable statement. For these precompilers, the DECLARE CURSOR statement must not only physically precede the OPEN, FETCH, and CLOSE statements that reference its cursor, but it must sometimes precede these statements in the flow of execution or be placed in the same block as the other statements.

In general, you can avoid problems with the DECLARE CURSOR statement by following these guidelines:

- Place the DECLARE CURSOR statement right before the OPEN statement for the cursor. This placement ensures the correct physical statement sequence, it puts the DECLARE CURSOR and the OPEN statements in the same block, and it ensures that the flow of control passes through the DECLARE CURSOR statement, if necessary. It also helps to document just what query is being requested by the OPEN statement.

- Make sure that the FETCH and CLOSE statements for the cursor follow the OPEN statement physically as well as in the flow of control.

The OPEN Statement

The OPEN statement, shown in Figure 17-25, conceptually opens the table of query results for access by the application program. In practice, the OPEN statement actually causes the DBMS to process the query, or at least to begin processing it. The OPEN statement thus causes the DBMS to perform the same work as an interactive SELECT statement, stopping just short of the point where it produces the first row of query results.

Figure 17-25. *The OPEN statement syntax diagram*

The single parameter of the OPEN statement is the name of the cursor to be opened. This cursor must have been previously declared by a DECLARE CURSOR statement. If the query associated with the cursor contains an error, the OPEN statement will produce a negative SQLCODE value. Most query-processing errors, such as a reference to an unknown table, an ambiguous column name, or an attempt to retrieve data from a table without the proper permission, will be reported as a result of the OPEN statement. In practice, very few errors occur during the subsequent FETCH statements.

Once opened, a cursor remains in the open state until it is closed with the CLOSE statement. The DBMS also closes all open cursors automatically at the end of a transaction (that is, when the DBMS executes a COMMIT or ROLLBACK statement). After the cursor has been closed, it can be reopened by executing the OPEN statement a second time. Note that the DBMS restarts the query from scratch each time it executes the OPEN statement.

The FETCH Statement

The FETCH statement, shown in Figure 17-26, retrieves the next row of query results for use by the application program. The cursor named in the FETCH statement specifies which row of query results is to be fetched. It must identify a cursor previously opened by the OPEN statement.

The FETCH statement fetches the row of data items into a list of host variables, which are specified in the INTO clause of the statement. An indicator variable can be associated with each host variable to handle retrieval of NULL data. The behavior of

Figure 17-26. *The FETCH statement syntax diagram*

the indicator variable and the values that it can assume are identical to those described earlier in the "Single-Row Queries" section for the singleton SELECT statement. The number of host variables in the list must be the same as the number of columns in the query results, and the data types of the host variables must be compatible, column by column, with the columns of query results.

As shown in Figure 17-27, the FETCH statement moves the cursor through the query results, row by row, according to these rules:

■ The OPEN statement positions the cursor before the first row of query results. In this state, the cursor has no current row.

■ The FETCH statement advances the cursor to the next available row of query results, if there is one. This row becomes the current row of the cursor.

■ If a FETCH statement advances the cursor past the last row of query results, the FETCH statement returns a NOT FOUND warning. In this state, the cursor again has no current row.

■ The CLOSE statement ends access to the query results and places the cursor in a closed state.

If there are no rows of query results, the OPEN statement still positions the cursor before the (empty) query results and returns successfully. The program cannot detect that the OPEN statement has produced an empty set of query results. However, the very first FETCH statement produces the NOT FOUND warning and positions the cursor after the end of the (empty) query results.

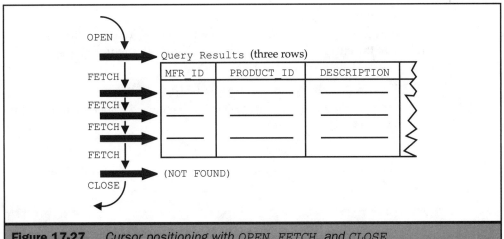

Figure 17-27. *Cursor positioning with OPEN, FETCH, and CLOSE*

The CLOSE Statement

The CLOSE statement, shown in Figure 17-28, conceptually closes the table of query results created by the OPEN statement, ending access by the application program. Its single parameter is the name of the cursor associated with the query results, which must be a cursor previously opened by an OPEN statement. The CLOSE statement can be executed any time after the cursor has been opened. In particular, it is not necessary to FETCH all rows of query results before closing the cursor, although this will usually be the case. All cursors are automatically closed at the end of a transaction. Once a cursor is closed, its query results are no longer available to the application program.

Scroll Cursors

The SQL1 standard specifies that a cursor can only move forward through the query results. Until the last few years, most commercial SQL products also supported only this form of forward, sequential cursor motion. If a program wants to reretrieve a row once the cursor has moved past it, the program must CLOSE the cursor and reOPEN it (causing the DBMS to perform the query again), and then FETCH through the rows until the desired row is reached.

In the early 1990s, a few commercial SQL products extended the cursor concept with the concept of a *scroll cursor*. Unlike standard cursors, a scroll cursor provides random access to the rows of query results. The program specifies which row it wants to retrieve through an extension of the FETCH statement, shown in Figure 19-28:

- FETCH FIRST retrieves the first row of query results.

- FETCH LAST retrieves the last row of query results.

- FETCH PRIOR retrieves the row of query results that immediately precedes the current row of the cursor.

- FETCH NEXT retrieves the row of query results that immediately follows the current row of the cursor. This is the default behavior if no motion is specified and corresponds to the standard cursor motion.

- FETCH ABSOLUTE retrieves a specific row by its row number.

- FETCH RELATIVE moves the cursor forward or backward a specific number of rows relative to its current position.

CLOSE *cursor-name*

Figure 17-28. *The CLOSE statement syntax diagram*

Scroll cursors can be especially useful in programs that allow a user to browse database contents. In response to the user's request to move forward or backward through the data a row or a screenful at a time, the program can simply fetch the required rows of the query results. However, scroll cursors are also a great deal harder for the DBMS to implement than a normal, unidirectional cursor. To support a scroll cursor, the DBMS must keep track of the previous query results that it provided for a program, and the order in which it supplied those rows of results. The DBMS must also ensure that no other concurrently executing transaction modifies any data that has become visible to a program through a scroll cursor, because the program can use the extended FETCH statement to reretrieve the row, even after the cursor has moved past the row.

If you use a scroll cursor, you should be aware that certain FETCH statements on a scroll cursor may have a very high overhead for some DBMS brands. If the DBMS brand normally carries out a query step by step as your program FETCHes its way down through the query results, your program may wait a much longer time than normal if you request a FETCH NEXT operation when the cursor is positioned at the first row of query results. It's best to understand the performance characteristics of your particular DBMS brand before writing programs that depend on scroll cursor functionality for production applications.

Because of the usefulness of scroll cursors, and because a few DBMS vendors had begun to ship scroll cursor implementations that were slightly different from one another, the SQL2 standard was expanded to include support for scroll cursors. The Entry SQL level of the standard requires only the older-style, sequential forward cursor, but conformance at the Intermediate SQL or Full SQL levels requires full support for the scroll cursor syntax shown in Figure 17-29. The standard also specifies that if any motion other than FETCH NEXT (the default) is used on a cursor, its DECLARE CURSOR statement must explicitly identify it as a scroll cursor. Using the SQL2 syntax, the cursor declaration in Figure 17-22 would appear as:

```
exec sql declare repcurs scroll cursor for
        select name, quota, sales
          from salesreps
         where sales > quota
         order by name;
```

Cursor-Based Deletes and Updates

Application programs often use cursors to allow the user to browse through a table of data row by row. For example, the user may ask to see all of the orders placed by a particular customer. The program declares a cursor for a query of the ORDERS table and displays each order on the screen, possibly in a computer-generated form, waiting for a signal from the user to advance to the next row. Browsing continues in this fashion until the user reaches the end of the query results. The cursor serves as a

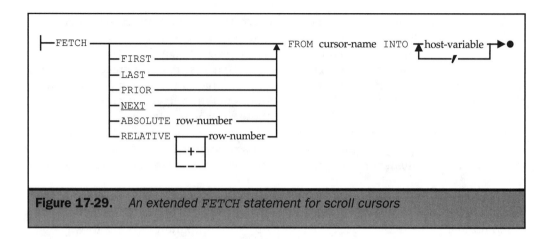

Figure 17-29.   *An extended FETCH statement for scroll cursors*

pointer to the current row of query results. If the query draws its data from a single table and it is not a summary query, as in this example, the cursor implicitly points to a row of a database table, because each row of query results is drawn from a single row of the table.

While browsing the data, the user may spot data that should be changed. For example, the order quantity in one of the orders may be incorrect, or the customer may want to delete one of the orders. In this situation, the user wants to update or delete this order. The row is not identified by the usual SQL search condition; rather, the program uses the cursor as a pointer to indicate which particular row is to be updated or deleted.

Embedded SQL supports this capability through special versions of the DELETE and UPDATE statements, called the *positioned* DELETE and *positioned* UPDATE statements, respectively.

The positioned DELETE statement, shown in Figure 17-30, deletes a single row from a table. The deleted row is the current row of a cursor that references the table. To process the statement, the DBMS locates the row of the base table that corresponds to the current row of the cursor and deletes that row from the base table. After the row is deleted, the cursor has no current row. Instead, the cursor is effectively positioned in the empty space left by the deleted row, waiting to be advanced to the next row by a subsequent FETCH statement.

The positioned UPDATE statement, shown in Figure 17-31, updates a single row of a table. The updated row is the current row of a cursor that references the table. To process the statement, the DBMS locates the row of the base table that corresponds to the current row of the cursor and updates that row as specified in the SET clause. After the row is updated, it remains the current row of the cursor. Figure 17-32 shows an order-browsing program that uses the positioned UPDATE and DELETE statements:

```
├──DELETE FROM cursor-name  WHERE  CURRENT  OF   cursor-name──────►●
```

Figure 17-30. *The positioned* DELETE *statement syntax diagram*

1. The program first prompts the user for a customer number and then queries the ORDERS table to locate all of the orders placed by that customer.

2. As it retrieves each row of query results, it displays the order information on the screen and asks the user what to do next.

3. If the user types an *N*, the program does not modify the current order, but moves directly to the next order.

4. If the user types a *D*, the program deletes the current order using a positioned DELETE statement.

5. If the user types a *U*, the program prompts the user for a new quantity and amount, and then updates these two columns of the current order using a positioned UPDATE statement.

6. If the user types an *X*, the program halts the query and terminates.

Although it is primitive compared to a real application program, the example in Figure 17-32 shows all of the logic and embedded SQL statements required to implement a browsing application with cursor-based database updates.

The SQL1 standard specifies that the positioned DELETE and UPDATE statements can be used only with cursors that meet these very strict criteria:

■ The query associated with the cursor must draw its data from a single source table; that is, there must be only one table named in the FROM clause of the query specified in the DECLARE CURSOR statement.

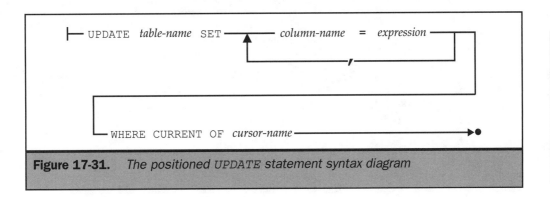

Figure 17-31. *The positioned* UPDATE *statement syntax diagram*

```
main()
{
    exec sql include sqlca;
    exec sql begin declare section;
        int    custnum;                    /* customer number entered by user*/
        int    ordnum;                     /* retrieved order number */
        char   orddate[12];                /* retrieved order date */
        char   ordmfr[4];                  /* retrieved manufacturer-id */
        char   ordproduct[6];              /* retrieved product-id */
        int    ordqty;                     /* retrieved order quantity */
        float  ordamount;                  /* retrieved order amount */
    exec sql end declare section;
    char inbuf[101]                        /* character entered by user */

    /* Declare the cursor for the query */
    exec sql declare ordcurs cursor for
            select order_num, ord_date, mfr, product, qty, amount
              from orders
             where cust = cust_num
             order by order_num
               for update of qty, amount;

    /* Prompt the user for a customer number */
    printf("Enter customer number: ");  ──────────────── ①
    scanf("%d", &custnum);

    /* Set up error processing */
    whenever sqlerror goto error;
    whenever not found goto done;

    /* Open the cursor to start the query */
    exec sql open ordcurs;  ───────────────────────

    /* Loop through each row of query results */
    for (;;) {

        /* Fetch the next row of query results */
        exec sql fetch ordcurs  ──────────────────── ②
                into :ordnum, :orddate, :ordmfr, :ordproduct,
                    :ordqty, :ordamount;

    /* Display the retrieved data */
    printf("Order Number: %d\n", ordnum);
    printf("Order Date:   %s\n", orddate);  ─────────
    printf("Manufacturer: %s\n", ordmfr);
```

Figure 17-32.   *Using the positioned DELETE and UPDATE statements*

- The query cannot specify an ORDER BY clause; the cursor must not identify a sorted set of query results.

- The query cannot specify the DISTINCT keyword.

- The query must not include a GROUP BY or a HAVING clause.

- The user must have the UPDATE or DELETE privilege (as appropriate) on the base table.

The IBM databases (DB2, SQL/DS) extended the SQL1 restrictions a step further. They require that the cursor be explicitly declared as an updateable cursor in the DECLARE CURSOR statement. The extended IBM form of the DECLARE CURSOR statement is shown in Figure 17-33. In addition to declaring an updateable cursor, the FOR UPDATE clause can optionally specify particular columns that may be updated through the cursor. If the column list is specified in the cursor declarations, positioned UPDATE statements for the cursor may update only those columns.

In practice, all commercial SQL implementations that support positioned DELETE and UPDATE statements follow the IBM SQL approach. It is a great advantage for the DBMS to know, in advance, whether a cursor will be used for updates or whether its data will be read-only, because read-only processing is simpler. The FOR UPDATE clause provides this advance notice and can be considered a de facto standard of the embedded SQL language.

Because of its widespread use, the SQL2 standard includes the IBM-style FOR UPDATE clause as an option in its DECLARE CURSOR statement. However, unlike the IBM products, the SQL2 standard automatically assumes that a cursor is opened for update unless it is a scroll cursor or it is explicitly declared FOR READ ONLY. The FOR READ ONLY specification in the SQL2 DECLARE CURSOR statement appears in exactly the same position as the FOR UPDATE clause and explicitly tells the DBMS that the program will not attempt a positioned DELETE or UPDATE operation using the cursor. Because they can significantly affect database overhead and performance, it can be very

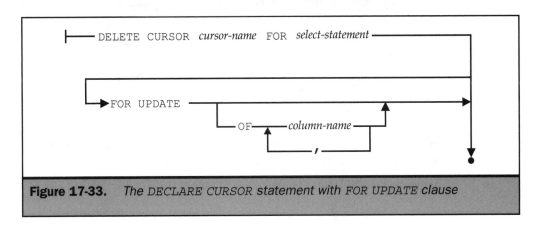

Figure 17-33. *The DECLARE CURSOR statement with FOR UPDATE clause*

PROGRAMMING
WITH SQL

important to understand the specific assumptions that your particular DBMS brand makes about the updateability of cursors and the clauses or statements that can be used to override them. In addition, programs that explicitly declare whether their intention is to allow updates via an opened cursor are more maintainable.

Cursors and Transaction Processing

The way your program handles its cursors can have a major impact on database performance. Recall from Chapter 12 that the SQL transaction model guarantees the consistency of data during a transaction. In cursor terms, this means that your program can declare a cursor, open it, fetch the query results, close it, reopen it, and fetch the query results again—and be guaranteed that the query results will be identical both times. The program can also fetch the same row through two different cursors and be guaranteed that the results will be identical. In fact, the data is guaranteed to remain consistent until your program issues a COMMIT or ROLLBACK to end the transaction. Because the consistency is not guaranteed across transactions, both the COMMIT and ROLLBACK statements automatically close all open cursors.

Behind the scenes, the DBMS provides this consistency guarantee by locking all of the rows of query results, preventing other users from modifying them. If the query produces many rows of data, a major portion of a table may be locked by the cursor. Furthermore, if your program waits for user input after fetching each row (for example, to let the user verify data displayed on the screen), parts of the database may be locked for a very long time. In an extreme case, the user might leave for lunch in mid-transaction, locking out other users for an hour or more!

To minimize the amount of locking required, you should follow these guidelines when writing interactive query programs:

- Keep transactions as short as possible.

- Issue a COMMIT statement immediately after every query and as soon as possible after your program has completed an update.

- Avoid programs that require a great deal of user interaction or that browse through many rows of data.

- If you know that the program will not try to refetch a row of data after the cursor has moved past it, use one of the less restrictive isolation modes described in Chapter 12. This allows the DBMS to unlock a row as soon as the next FETCH statement is issued.

- Avoid the use of scroll cursors unless you have taken other actions to eliminate or minimize the extra database locking they will cause.

- Explicitly specify a READ ONLY cursor, if possible.

Summary

In addition to its role as an interactive database language, SQL is used for programmatic access to relational databases:

- The most common technique for programmatic use of SQL is embedded SQL, where SQL statements are embedded into the application program, intermixed with the statements of a host programming language such as C or COBOL.

- Embedded SQL statements are processed by a special SQL precompiler. They begin with a special introducer (usually EXEC SQL) and end with a terminator, which varies from one host language to another.

- Variables from the application program, called host variables, can be used in embedded SQL statements wherever a constant can appear. These input host variables tailor the embedded SQL statement to the particular situation.

- Host variables are also used to receive the results of database queries. The values of these output host variables can then be processed by the application program.

- Queries that produce a single row of data are handled with the singleton SELECT statement of embedded SQL, which specifies both the query and the host variables to receive the retrieved data.

- Queries that produce multiple rows of query results are handled with cursors in embedded SQL. The DECLARE CURSOR statement defines the query, the OPEN statement begins query processing, the FETCH statement retrieves successive rows of query results, and the CLOSE statement ends query processing.

- The positioned UPDATE and DELETE statements can be used to update or delete the row currently selected by a cursor.

Chapter 18

Dynamic SQL [*]

The embedded SQL programming features described in Chapter 17 are collectively known as *static SQL*. Static SQL is adequate for writing all of the programs typically required in a data processing application. For example, in the order-processing application of the sample database, you can use static SQL to write programs that handle order entry, order updates, order inquiries, customer inquiries, customer file maintenance, and programs that produce all types of reports. In every one of these programs, the pattern of database access is decided by the programmer and hard-coded into the program as a series of embedded SQL statements.

There is an important class of applications, however, where the pattern of database access cannot be determined in advance. A graphic query tool or a report writer, for example, must be able to decide at runtime which SQL statements it will use to access the database. A personal computer spreadsheet that supports host database access must also be able to send a query to the host DBMS for execution on the fly. These programs and other general-purpose database front-ends cannot be written using static SQL techniques. They require an advanced form of embedded SQL, called *dynamic SQL*, described in this chapter.

Limitations of Static SQL

As the name *static SQL* implies, a program built using the embedded SQL features described in Chapter 17 (host variables, cursors, and the DECLARE CURSOR, OPEN, FETCH, and CLOSE statements) has a predetermined, fixed pattern of database access. For each embedded SQL statement in the program, the tables and columns referenced by that statement are determined in advance by the programmer and hard-coded into the embedded SQL statement. Input host variables provide some flexibility in static SQL, but they don't fundamentally alter its static nature. Recall that a host variable can appear anywhere a constant is allowed in a SQL statement. You can use a host variable to alter a search condition:

```
exec sql select name, quota, sales
         from salesreps
         where quota > :cutoff_amount;
```

You can also use a host variable to change the data inserted or updated in a database:

```
exec sql update salesreps
         set quota = quota + :increase
         where quota >:cutoff_amount;
```

However, you cannot use a host variable in place of a table name or a column reference. The attempted use of the host variables which_table and which_column in these statements is illegal:

```
exec sql update :which_table
        set :which_column = 0;

exec sql declare cursor cursor7 for
        select *
            from :which_table;
```

Even if you could use a host variable in this way (and you cannot), another problem would immediately arise. The number of columns produced by the query in the second statement would vary, depending on which table was specified by the host variable. For the OFFICES table, the query results would have six columns; for the SALESREPS table, they would have nine columns. Furthermore, the data types of the columns would be different for the two tables. But to write a FETCH statement for the query, you must know in advance how many columns of query results there will be and their data types, because you must specify a host variable to receive each column:

```
exec sql fetch cursor7
        into :var1, :var2, :var3;
```

As this discussion illustrates, if a program must be able to determine at runtime which SQL statements it will use, or which tables and columns it will reference, static SQL is inadequate for the task. Dynamic SQL overcomes these limitations.

Dynamic SQL has been supported by the IBM SQL products since their introduction, and it has been supported for many years by the minicomputer-based and UNIX-based commercial RDBMS products. However, dynamic SQL was not specified by the original ANSI/ISO SQL1 standard; the standard defined only static SQL. The absence of dynamic SQL from the SQL1 standard is ironic, given the popular notion that the standard allowed you to build front-end database tools that are portable across many different DBMS brands. In fact, such front-end tools must almost always be built using dynamic SQL.

In the absence of an ANSI/ISO standard, DB2 set the de facto standard for dynamic SQL. The other IBM databases of the day (SQL/DS and OS/2 Extended Edition) were nearly identical to DB2 in their dynamic SQL support, and most other SQL products also followed the DB2 standard. In 1992, the SQL2 standard added official support for dynamic SQL, mostly following the path set by IBM. The SQL2 standard does not require dynamic SQL support at the lowest level of compliance (Entry), but dynamic SQL support is required for products claiming the Intermediate or Full compliance levels to the SQL standard.

Dynamic SQL Concepts

The central concept of dynamic SQL is simple: don't hard-code an embedded SQL statement into the program's source code. Instead, let the program build the text of a SQL statement in one of its data areas at runtime. The program then passes the statement text to the DBMS for execution on the fly. Although the details get quite complex, all of dynamic SQL is built on this simple concept, and it's a good idea to keep it in mind.

To understand dynamic SQL and how it compares with static SQL, it's useful to consider once again the process the DBMS goes through to execute a SQL statement, originally shown in Figure 17-1 and repeated here in Figure 18-1. Recall from Chapter 17 that a static SQL statement goes through the first four steps of the process at compile-time. The BIND utility (or the equivalent part of the DBMS runtime system) analyzes the SQL statement, determines the best way to carry it out, and stores the application plan for the statement in the database as part of the program development process. When the static SQL statement is executed at runtime, the DBMS simply executes the stored application plan.

In dynamic SQL, the situation is quite different. The SQL statement to be executed isn't known until runtime, so the DBMS cannot prepare for the statement in advance. When the program is actually executed, the DBMS receives the text of the statement to

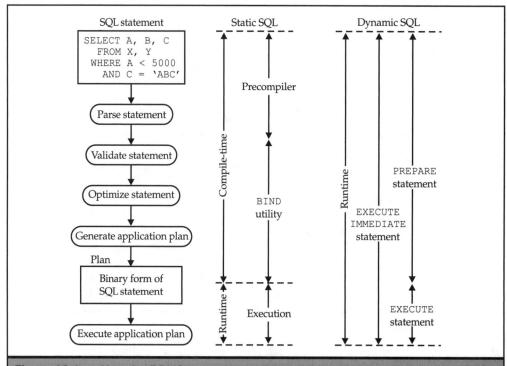

Figure 18-1. *How the DBMS processes a SQL statement*

be dynamically executed (called the *statement string*) and goes through all five of the steps shown in Figure 18-1 at runtime.

As you might expect, dynamic SQL is less efficient than static SQL. For this reason, static SQL is used whenever possible, and many application programmers never need to learn about dynamic SQL. However, dynamic SQL has grown in importance as more and more database access has moved to a client/server, front-end/back-end architecture over the last ten years. Database access from within personal computer applications such as spreadsheets and word processors has grown dramatically, and an entire set of PC-based front-end data entry and data access tools has emerged. All of these applications require the features of dynamic SQL.

More recently, the emergence of Internet-based three-tier architectures—with applications logic executing on one (mid-tier) system and the database logic executing on another (back-end) system—have added new importance to capabilities that have grown out of dynamic SQL. In most of these three-tier environments, the applications logic running in the middle tier is quite dynamic. It must be changed frequently to respond to new business conditions and to implement new business rules. This frequently changing environment is at odds with the very tight coupling of applications programs and database contents implied by static SQL. As a result, most three-tier architectures use a callable SQL API (described in Chapter 19) to link the middle tier to back-end databases. These APIs explicitly borrow the key concepts of dynamic SQL (for example, separate PREPARE and EXECUTE steps and the EXECUTE IMMEDIATE capability) to provide their database access. A solid understanding of dynamic SQL concepts is thus important to help a programmer understand what's going on behind the scenes of the SQL API. In performance-sensitive applications, this understanding can make all the difference between an application design that provides good performance and response times and one that does not.

Dynamic Statement Execution (EXECUTE IMMEDIATE)

The simplest form of dynamic SQL is provided by the EXECUTE IMMEDIATE statement, shown in Figure 18-2. This statement passes the text of a dynamic SQL statement to the DBMS and asks the DBMS to execute the dynamic statement immediately. To use this statement, your program goes through the following steps:

1. The program constructs a SQL statement as a string of text in one of its data areas (usually called a *buffer*). The statement can be almost any SQL statement that does not retrieve data.

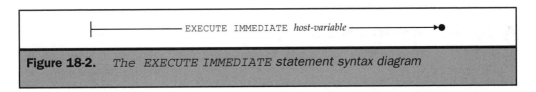

Figure 18-2. *The EXECUTE IMMEDIATE statement syntax diagram*

2. The program passes the SQL statement to the DBMS with the EXECUTE IMMEDIATE statement.

3. The DBMS executes the statement and sets the SQLCODE/SQLSTATE values to indicate the completion status, exactly as if the statement had been hard-coded using static SQL.

Figure 18-3 shows a simple C program that follows these steps. The program prompts the user for a table name and a SQL search condition, and builds the text of a DELETE statement based on the user's responses. The program then uses the EXECUTE IMMEDIATE statement to execute the DELETE statement. This program cannot use a static SQL-embedded DELETE statement, because neither the table name nor the search condition are known until the user enters them at runtime. It must use dynamic SQL. If you run the program in Figure 18-3 with these inputs:

```
Enter table name:         staff
Enter search condition: quota < 20000
Delete from staff successful.
```

the program passes this statement text to the DBMS:

```
delete from staff
 where quota < 20000
```

If you run the program with these inputs:

```
Enter table name:         orders
Enter search condition: cust = 2105
Delete from orders successful
```

the program passes this statement text to the DBMS:

```
delete from orders
 where cust = 2105
```

The EXECUTE IMMEDIATE statement thus gives the program great flexibility in the type of DELETE statement that it executes.

The EXECUTE IMMEDIATE statement uses exactly one host variable—the variable containing the entire SQL statement string. The statement string itself cannot include host variable references, but there's no need for them. Instead of using a static SQL statement with a host variable like this:

```
exec sql delete from orders
        where cust = :cust_num;
```

```
main()
{
   /* This program deletes rows from a user-specified table
      according to a user-specified search condition.
   */

   exec sql include sqlca;
   exec sql begin declare section;
      char stmtbuf[301];              /* SQL text to be executed */
   exec sql end declare section;

   char tblname[101];                 /* table name entered by user */
   char search_cond[101];             /* search condition entered by user */

   /* Start building the DELETE statement in stmtbuf */
   strcpy(stmtbuf,"delete from ");

   /* Prompt user for table name; add it to the DELETE statement text */
   printf("Enter table name:      ");
   gets(tblname);
   strcat(stmtbuf, tblname);

   /* Prompt user for search condition; add it to the text */
   printf("Enter search condition:");
   gets(search_cond);
   if (strlen(search_cond) > 0) {
      strcat(stmtbuf, " where ");
      strcat(stmtbuf, search_cond);
   }

   /* Now ask the DBMS to execute the statement */
   exec sql execute immediate :stmtbuf;
   if (sqlca.sqlcode < 0)
      printf("SQL error: %ld\n", sqlca.sqlcode);
   else
      printf("Delete from %s successful.\n", tblname);

   exit();
}
```

Figure 18-3.   *Using the EXECUTE IMMEDIATE statement*

a dynamic SQL program achieves the same effect by building the *entire* statement in a buffer and executing it:

```
sprintf(buffer, "delete from orders where cust = %d", cust_num)
exec sql execute immediate :buffer;
```

The EXECUTE IMMEDIATE statement is the simplest form of dynamic SQL, but it is very versatile. You can use it to dynamically execute most DML statements, including INSERT, DELETE, UPDATE, COMMIT, and ROLLBACK. You can also use EXECUTE IMMEDIATE to dynamically execute most DDL statements, including the CREATE, DROP, GRANT, and REVOKE statements.

The EXECUTE IMMEDIATE statement does have one significant limitation, however. You cannot use it to dynamically execute a SELECT statement, because it does not provide a mechanism to process the query results. Just as static SQL requires cursors and special-purpose statements (DECLARE CURSOR, OPEN, FETCH, and CLOSE) for programmatic queries, dynamic SQL uses cursors and some new special-purpose statements to handle dynamic queries. The dynamic SQL features that support dynamic queries are discussed later in the section "Dynamic Queries."

Two-Step Dynamic Execution

The EXECUTE IMMEDIATE statement provides one-step support for dynamic statement execution. As described previously, the DBMS goes through all five steps of Figure 18-1 for the dynamically executed statement. The overhead of this process can be very significant if your program executes many dynamic statements, and it's wasteful if the statements to be executed are identical or very similar. In practice, the EXECUTE IMMEDIATE statement should be used only for one-time statements that will be executed once by a program and then never executed again.

To deal with the large overhead of the one-step approach, dynamic SQL offers an alternative, two-step method for executing SQL statements dynamically. In practice, this two-step approach, separating statement preparation and statement execution, is used for *all* SQL statements in a program that is executed more than once, and especially for those that are executed repeatedly, hundreds or thousands of times, in response to user interaction. Here is an overview of the two-step technique:

1. The program constructs a SQL statement string in a buffer, just as it does for the EXECUTE IMMEDIATE statement. A question mark (?) can be substituted for a constant anywhere in the statement text to indicate that a value for the constant will be supplied later. The question mark is called a *parameter marker*.

2. The PREPARE statement asks the DBMS to parse, validate, and optimize the statement and to generate an application plan for it. This is Step 1 of the DBMS interaction. The DBMS sets the SQLCODE/SQLSTATE values to indicate any errors found in the statement and retains the application plan for later execution. Note that the DBMS does *not* execute the plan in response to the PREPARE statement.

3. When the program wants to execute the previously prepared statement, it uses the EXECUTE statement and passes a value for each parameter marker to the DBMS. This is Step 2 of the DBMS interaction. The DBMS substitutes the parameter values, executes the previously generated application plan, and sets the SQLCODE/SQLSTATE values to indicate its completion status.

4. The program can use the EXECUTE statement repeatedly, supplying different parameter values each time the dynamic statement is executed. The DBMS can simply repeat Step 2 of the interaction, since the work in Step 1 has already been done, and the results of that work (the application plan for execution) will still be valid.

Figure 18-4 shows a C program that uses these steps, which are labeled by the callouts in the figure. The program is a general-purpose table update program. It prompts the

```
main()
{
   /* This is a general-purpose update program. It can be used
      for any update where a numeric column is to be updated in
      all rows where a second numeric column has a specified
      value. For example, you can use it to update quotas for
      selected salespeople or to update credit limits for
      selected customers.
   /*

   exec sql include sqlca;
   exec sql begin declare section;
      char   stmtbuf[301]              /* SQL text to be executed */
      float search_value;             /* parameter value for searching */
      float new_value;                /* parameter value for update */
   exec sql end declare section;

   char tblname[31];                  /* table to be updated */
   char searchcol[31];                /* name of search column */
   char updatecol[31];                /* name of update column */
   char yes_no[31];                   /* yes/no response from user */

   /* Prompt user for tablename and column name * /
   printf("Enter name of table to be updated:   ");
   gets(tblname);
```

Figure 18-4.   *Using the PREPARE and EXECUTE statements*

```
        printf("Enter name of column to be searched: ");
        gets(searchcol);
        printf("Enter name of column to be updated:   ");
        gets(updatecol);


        /* Build SQL statement in buffer; ask DBMS to compile it */
        sprintf(stmtbuf, "update %s set %s = ? where %s = ?",    ◄──────── ①
                        tblname, searchcol, updatecol);
        exec sql prepare mystmt from :stmtbuf;   ◄────────────────────── ②
        if (sqlca.sqlcode) {
            printf("PREPARE error: %ld\n", sqlca.sqlcode);
            exit();
        }
        /* Loop prompting user for parameters and performing updates */
        for ( ; ; ) {
            printf("\nEnter search value for %s: ", searchcol);
            scanf("%f", &search_value);
            printf("Enter new value for %s: ", updatecol);
            scanf("%f", &new_value);


            /* Ask the DBMS to execute the UPDATE statement */
            execute mystmt using :search_value, :new_value;   ◄────── ③
            if (sqlca.sqlcode) {
                printf("EXECUTE error: %ld\n", sqlca.sqlcode);
                exit();
            }


            /*Ask user if there is another update */
            printf("Another (y/n)? ");   ◄───────────────────────── ④
            gets(yes_no);
            if (yes_no[0] == 'n')
                break;
        }

    printf("\nUpdates complete.\n");

    exit();
}
```

Figure 18-4. *Using the PREPARE and EXECUTE statements* (continued) user for a table name and two column names, and constructs an UPDATE statement for the table that looks like this:

```
update table-name
    set second-column-name = ?
 where first-column-name = ?
```

The user's input thus determines the table to be updated, the column to be updated, and the search condition to be used. The search comparison value and the updated data value are specified as parameters, to be supplied later when the UPDATE statement is actually executed.

After building the UPDATE statement text in its buffer, the program asks the DBMS to compile it with the PREPARE statement. The program then enters a loop, prompting the user to enter pairs of parameter values to perform a sequence of table updates. This user dialog shows how you could use the program in Figure 18-4 to update the quotas for selected salespeople:

```
Enter name of table to be updated:   staff
Enter name of column to be searched: empl_num
Enter name of column to be updated:  quota

Enter search value for empl_num: 106
Enter new value for quota: 150000.00
Another (y/n)? y

Enter search value for empl_num: 102
Enter new value for quota: 225000.00
Another (y/n)? y

Enter search value for empl_num: 107
Enter new value for quota: 215000.00
Another (y/n)? n

Updates complete.
```

This program is a good example of a situation where two-step dynamic execution is appropriate. The DBMS compiles the dynamic UPDATE statement only once but executes it three times, once for each set of parameter values entered by the user. If the program had been written using EXECUTE IMMEDIATE instead, the dynamic UPDATE statement would have been compiled three times and executed three times. Thus, the two-step dynamic execution of PREPARE and EXECUTE helps to eliminate some of the performance disadvantage of dynamic SQL. As mentioned earlier, this same two-step approach is used by all of the callable SQL APIs described in Chapter 19.

The PREPARE Statement

The PREPARE statement, shown in Figure 18-5, is unique to dynamic SQL. It accepts a host variable containing a SQL statement string and passes the statement to the DBMS. The DBMS compiles the statement text and prepares it for execution by generating an application plan. The DBMS sets the SQLCODE/SQLSTATE variables to indicate any errors detected in the statement text. As described previously, the statement string can contain a parameter marker, indicated by a question mark, anywhere that a constant can appear. The parameter marker signals the DBMS that a value for the parameter will be supplied later, when the statement is actually executed.

As a result of the PREPARE statement, the DBMS assigns the specified *statement name* to the prepared statement. The statement name is a SQL identifier, like a cursor name. You specify the statement name in subsequent EXECUTE statements when you want to execute the statement. DBMS brands differ in how long they retain the prepared statement and the associated statement name. For some brands, the prepared statement can be reexecuted only until the end of the current transaction (that is, until the next COMMIT or ROLLBACK statement). If you want to execute the same dynamic statement later during another transaction, you must prepare it again. Other brands relax this restriction and retain the prepared statement throughout the current session with the DBMS. The ANSI/ISO SQL2 standard acknowledges these differences and explicitly says that the validity of a prepared statement outside of the current transaction is implementation dependent.

The PREPARE statement can be used to prepare almost any executable DML or DDL statement, including the SELECT statement. Embedded SQL statements that are actually precompiler directives (such as the WHENEVER or DECLARE CURSOR statements) cannot be prepared, of course, because they are not executable.

The EXECUTE Statement

The EXECUTE statement, shown in Figure 18-6, is unique to dynamic SQL. It asks the DBMS to execute a statement previously prepared with the PREPARE statement. You can execute any statement that can be prepared, with one exception. Like the EXECUTE IMMEDIATE statement, the EXECUTE statement cannot be used to execute a SELECT statement, because it lacks a mechanism for handling query results.

If the dynamic statement to be executed contains one or more parameter markers, the EXECUTE statement must provide a value for each of the parameters. The values can be provided in two different ways, described in the next two sections. The ANSI/ISO SQL2 standard includes both of these methods.

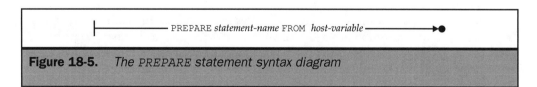

Figure 18-5. *The PREPARE statement syntax diagram*

Figure 18-6. *The EXECUTE statement syntax diagram*

EXECUTE with Host Variables

The easiest way to pass parameter values to the EXECUTE statement is by specifying a list of host variables in the USING clause. The EXECUTE statement substitutes the values of the host variables, in sequence, for the parameter markers in the prepared statement text. The host variables thus serve as input host variables for the dynamically executed statement. This technique was used in the program shown in Figure 18-4. It is supported by all of the popular DBMS brands that support dynamic SQL and is included in the ANSI/ISO SQL2 standard for dynamic SQL.

The number of host variables in the USING clause must match the number of parameter markers in the dynamic statement, and the data type of each host variable must be compatible with the data type required for the corresponding parameter. Each host variable in the list may also have a companion host indicator variable. If the indicator variable contains a negative value when the EXECUTE statement is processed, the corresponding parameter marker is assigned the NULL value.

EXECUTE with SQLDA

The second way to pass parameters to the EXECUTE statement is with a special dynamic SQL data structure called a *SQL Data Area,* or SQLDA. You must use a SQLDA to pass parameters when you don't know the number of parameters to be passed and their data types at the time that you write the program. For example, suppose you wanted to modify the general-purpose update program in Figure 18-4 so that the user could select more than one column to be updated. You could easily modify the program to generate an UPDATE statement with a variable number of assignments, but the list of host variables in the EXECUTE statement poses a problem; it must be replaced with a variable-length list. The SQLDA provides a way to specify such a variable-length parameter list.

Figure 18-7 shows the layout of the SQLDA used by the IBM databases, including DB2, which set the de facto standard for dynamic SQL. Most other DBMS products also use this IBM SQLDA format or one very similar to it. The ANSI/ISO SQL2 standard provides a similar structure, called a *SQL Descriptor Area.* The types of information contained in the ANSI/ISO SQL Descriptor Area and the DB2-style SQLDA are the same, and both structures play the same role in dynamic SQL processing. However, the details of use—how program locations are associated with SQL statement parameters,

```
struct sqlda {
   unsigned char sqldaid[8];
   long          sqldabc;
   short         sqln;
   short         sqld;
   struct sqlvar {
      short          sqltype;
      short          sqllen;
      unsigned char *sqldata;
      short          *sqlind;
      struct sqlname {
         short          length;
         unsigned char data[30];
      } sqlname;
   } sqlvar[1];
} ;
```

Figure 18-7.   *The SQL Data Area (SQLDA) for IBM databases*

how information is placed into the descriptor area and retrieved from it, and so on—
are quite different. In practice, the DB2-style SQLDA is the more important, because
dynamic SQL support appeared in most major DBMS brands, modeled on the DB2
implementation, long before the SQL2 standard was written.

The SQLDA is a variable-size data structure with two distinct parts:

■ The *fixed part* is located at the beginning of the SQLDA. Its fields identify the
   data structure as a SQLDA and specify the size of this particular SQLDA.

■ The *variable part* is an array of one or more SQLVAR data structures. When you
   use a SQLDA to pass parameters to an EXECUTE statement, there must be one
   SQLVAR structure for each parameter.

The fields in the SQLVAR structure describe the data being passed to the EXECUTE
statement as a parameter value:

■ The SQLTYPE field contains an integer *data type code* that specifies the data type
   of the parameter being passed. For example, the DB2 data type code is 500 for
   a 2-byte integer, 496 for a 4-byte integer, and 448 for a variable-length character
   string.

■ The SQLLEN field specifies the *length* of the data being passed. It will contain a
   two for a 2-byte integer and a four for a 4-byte integer. When you pass a character
   string as a parameter, SQLLEN contains the number of characters in the string.

■ The SQLDATA field is a pointer to the *data area* within your program that contains the parameter value. The DBMS uses this pointer to find the data value as it executes the dynamic SQL statement. The SQLTYPE and SQLLEN fields tell the DBMS which type of data is being pointed to and its length.

■ The SQLIND field is a pointer to a 2-byte integer that is used as an *indicator variable* for the parameter. The DBMS checks the indicator variable to determine whether you are passing a NULL value. If you are not using an indicator variable for a particular parameter, the SQLIND field must be set to zero.

The other fields in the SQLVAR and SQLDA structures are not used to pass parameter values to the EXECUTE statement. They are used when you use a SQLDA to retrieve data from the database, as described later in the "Dynamic Queries" section.

Figure 18-8 shows a dynamic SQL program that uses a SQLDA to specify input parameters. The program updates the SALESREPS table, but it allows the user to select the columns that are to be updated at the beginning of the program. Then it enters a loop, prompting the user for an employee number and then prompting for a new value

```
main()
{
   /* This program updates user-specified columns of the
      SALESREPS table. It first asks the user to select the
      columns to be updated, and then prompts repeatedly for the
      employee number of a salesperson and new values for the
      selected columns.
   */

   #define COLCNT 6                    /* six columns in SALESREPS table */

   exec sql include sqlca;
   exec sql include sqlda;
   exec sql begin declare section;
      char stmtbuf[2001];             /* SQL text to be executed */
   exec sql end declare section;

   char *malloc()
   struct {
      char  prompt[31];               /* prompt for this column */
      char  name[31];                 /* name for this column */
      short typecode;                 /* its data type code */
      short buflen;                   /* length of its buffer */
      char  selected;                 /* "selected" flag (y/n) */
   } columns[] = { "Name",     "NAME",        449, 16, 'n',
                   "Office",   "REP_OFFICE", 497,  4, 'n',
```

Figure 18-8. *Using EXECUTE with a SQLDA*

```
                        "Manager",  "MANAGER",    497, 4, 'n',
                        "Hire Date","HIRE_DATE",   449, 12, 'n',
                        "Quota",     "QUOTA",      481, 8, 'n',
                        "Sales",     "SALES",      481, 8, 'n'};

     struct sqlda  *parmda;              /* SQLDA for parameter values */
     struct sqlvar *parmvar;             /* SQLVAR for current parm value */
     int           parmcnt;              /* running parameter count */
     int           empl_num;             /* employee number entered by user
*/
     int           i;                    /* index for columns[] array */
     int           j;                    /* index for sqlvar array in sqlda
*/
     char          inbuf[101];           /* input entered by user */

     /* Prompt the user to select the columns to be updated */
     printf("*** Salesperson Update Program ***\n\n");
     parmcnt = 1;
     for (i = 0; i < COLCNT; i++) {

        /* Ask about this column */
        printf("Update %s column (y/n)? ");
        gets(inbuf);
        if (inbuf[0] == 'y') {
           columns[i].selected = 'y';
           parmcnt += 1;
        }
     }

     /* Allocate a SQLDA structure to pass parameter values */
     parmda = malloc(16 = (44 * parmcnt));      ◄──────────────── ①
     strcpy(parmda -> sqldaid, "SQLDA  ");
     parmda->sqldabc = (16 = (44 * parmcnt));
     parmda->sqln = parmcnt;

     /* Start building the UPDATE statement in statement buffer */
     strcpy(stmtbuf, "update orders set ");

     /* Loop through columns, processing the selected ones */
     for (i = 0; j = 0; i++; i < COLCNT) {      ◄──────────────── ②

        /* Skip over non-selected columns */
        if (columns[i].selected == 'n')
           continue;

        /* Add an assignment to the dynamic UPDATE statement */
```

Figure 18-8. *Using EXECUTE with a SQLDA* (continued)

```
      if (parmcnt > 0) strcat(stmtbuf, ", ");
      strcat(stmtbuf, columns[i].name);
      strcat(stmtbuf, " = ?");

      /* Allocate space for data and indicator variable, and */
      /* fill in the SQLVAR with information for this column */
      parmvar = parmda -> sqlvar + j;
      parmvar -> sqltype = columns[i].typecode;        <────────────── 3
      parmvar -> sqllen  = columns[i].buflen;          <────────── 4
      parmvar -> sqldata = malloc(columns[i].buflen);  <──────── 5
      parmvar -> sqlind  = malloc920;                  <────── 6
      strcpy(parmvar -> sqlname.data, columns[i].prompt);
      j += 1;
   }
/* Fill in the last SQLVAR for parameter in the WHERE clause */
strcat(stmbuf, " where empl_num = ?");
parmvar = parmda + parmcnt;
parmvar->sqltype = 496;
parmvar->sqllen  = 4;
parmvar->sqldata = &empl_num;
parmvar->sqlind  = 0;
parmda->sqld = parmcnt;>     <──────────────────────────── 7

/* Ask the DBMS to compile the complete dynamic UPDATE statement */
exec sql prepare updatestmt from :stmtbuf;
if (sqlca.sqlcode < 0) {
   printf("PREPARE error: %ld\n", sqlca.sqlcode);
   exit();
}

/* Now loop, prompting for parameters and doing UPDATEs */
for ( ; ; ) {

   /* Prompt user for order number of order to be updated */
   printf("\nEnter Salesperson's Employee Number: ");
   scanf("%ld", &empl_num);
   if (empl_num == 0) break;

   /* Get new values for the updated columns */
   for (j = 0; j < (parmcnt-1); j++) {
      parmvar = parmda + j;
      printf("Enter new value for %s: ", parmvar->sqlname.data);
      gets(inbuf);     <──────────────────────────── 8
      if (inbuf[0] == '*') {
         /* If user enters '*', set column to a NULL value */
         *(parmvar -> sqlind) = -1;
```

Figure 18-8. *Using EXECUTE with a SQLDA* (continued)

PROGRAMMING
WITH SQL

```
                    continue;
                }
            else {
                /* Otherwise, set indicator for non-NULL value */
                *(parmvar -> sqlind) = 0;

                switch(parmvar -> sqltype) {

                case 481:
                    /* Convert entered data to 8-byte floating point */
                    sscanf(inbuf, "%lf", parmvar -> sqldata);          ◄─────  ⑧
                    break;

                case 449:
                    /* Pass entered data as variable-length string */
                    stccpy(parmvar -> sqldata, inbuf, strlen(inbuf));
                    parmvar -> sqllen = strlen(inbuf);
                    break;

                case 501:
                    /* Convert entered data to 4-byte integer */
                    sscanf(inbuf, "%ld", parmvar->sqldata);          ◄─────────┘
                    break;
                }
            }
        }

            /* Execute the statement */
            exec sql execute updatestmt using :parmda;          ◄──────────────  ⑨
            if (sqlca.sqlcode < 0)      {
                printf("EXECUTE error: %ld\n", sqlca.sqlcode);
                exit();
            }
        }

        /* All finished with updates */
        exec sql execute immediate "commit work";
        if (sqlca.sqlcode)
            printf("COMMIT error: %ld\n", sqlca.sqlcode);
        else
            printf("\nAll updates committed.\n");

        exit();
    }
```

Figure 18-8.   *Using EXECUTE with a SQLDA* (continued)

for each column to be updated. If the user types an asterisk (*) in response to the new value prompt, the program assigns the corresponding column a NULL value.

Because the user can select different columns each time the program is run, this program must use a SQLDA to pass the parameter values to the EXECUTE statement. The program illustrates the general technique for using a SQLDA, indicated by callouts in Figure 18-8:

1. The program allocates a SQLDA large enough to hold a SQLVAR structure for each parameter to be passed. It sets the SQLN field to indicate how many SQLVARs can be accommodated.

2. For each parameter to be passed, the program fills in one of the SQLVAR structures with information describing the parameter.

3. The program determines the data type of a parameter and places the correct data type code in the SQLTYPE field.

4. The program determines the length of the parameter and places it in the SQLLEN field.

5. The program allocates memory to hold the parameter value and puts the address of the allocated memory in the SQLDATA field.

6. The program allocates memory to hold an indicator variable for the parameter and puts the address of the indicator variable in the SQLIND field.

7. The program sets the SQLD field in the SQLDA header to indicate how many parameters are being passed. This tells the DBMS how many SQLVAR structures within the SQLDA contain valid data.

8. The program prompts the user for data values and places them into the data areas allocated in Steps 5 and 6.

9. The program uses an EXECUTE statement with the USING DESCRIPTOR clause to pass parameter values via the SQLDA.

Note that this particular program copies the prompt string for each parameter value into the SQLNAME structure. The program does this solely for its own convenience; the DBMS ignores the SQLNAME structure when you use the SQLDA to pass parameters. Here is a sample user dialog with the program in Figure 18-8:

```
*** Salesperson Update Program ***

Update Name column (y/n)? y
Update Office column (y/n)? y
Update Manager column (y/n)? n
Update Hire Date column (y/n)? n
Update Quota column (y/n)? y
Update Sales column (y/n)? n
```

```
Enter Salesperson's Employee Number: 106
Enter new value for Name: Sue Jackson
Enter new value for Office: 22
Enter new value for Quota: 175000.00

Enter Salesperson's Employee Number: 104
Enter new value for Name: Joe Smith
Enter new value for Office: *
Enter new value for Quota: 275000.00

Enter Salesperson's Employee Number: 0

All updates committed.
```

Based on the user's response to the initial questions, the program generates this dynamic UPDATE statement and prepares it:

```
update salesreps
   set name = ?, office = ?, quota = ?
 where empl_num = ?
```

The statement specifies four parameters, and the program allocates a SQLDA big enough to handle four SQLVAR structures. When the user supplies the first set of parameter values, the dynamic UPDATE statement becomes:

```
update salesreps
   set name = 'Sue Jackson', office = 22, quota = 175000.00
 where empl_num = 106
```

and with the second set of parameter values, it becomes:

```
update salesreps
   set name = 'Joe Smith', office = NULL, quota = 275000.00
 where empl_num = 104
```

This program is somewhat complex, but it's simple compared to a real general-purpose database update utility. It also illustrates all of the dynamic SQL features required to dynamically execute statements with a variable number of parameters.

Dynamic Queries

The EXECUTE IMMEDIATE, PREPARE, and EXECUTE statements as described thus far support dynamic execution of most SQL statements. However, they can't support dynamic queries because they lack a mechanism for retrieving the query results. To support dynamic queries, SQL *combines* the dynamic SQL features of the PREPARE and EXECUTE statements with extensions to the static SQL query-processing statements, and adds a new statement. Here is an overview of how a program performs a dynamic query:

1. A dynamic version of the DECLARE CURSOR statement declares a cursor for the query. Unlike the static DECLARE CURSOR statement, which includes a hard-coded SELECT statement, the dynamic form of the DECLARE CURSOR statement specifies the statement name that will be associated with the dynamic SELECT statement.

2. The program constructs a valid SELECT statement in a buffer, just as it would construct a dynamic UPDATE or DELETE statement. The SELECT statement may contain parameter markers like those used in other dynamic SQL statements.

3. The program uses the PREPARE statement to pass the statement string to the DBMS, which parses, validates, and optimizes the statement and generates an application plan. This is identical to the PREPARE processing used for other dynamic SQL statements.

4. The program uses the DESCRIBE statement to request a description of the query results that will be produced by the query. The DBMS returns a column-by-column description of the query results in a SQL Data Area (SQLDA) supplied by the program, telling the program how many columns of query results there are, and the name, data type, and length of each column. The DESCRIBE statement is used exclusively for dynamic queries.

5. The program uses the column descriptions in the SQLDA to allocate a block of memory to receive each column of query results. The program may also allocate space for an indicator variable for the column. The program places the address of the data area and the address of the indicator variable into the SQLDA to tell the DBMS where to return the query results.

6. A dynamic version of the OPEN statement asks the DBMS to start executing the query and passes values for the parameters specified in the dynamic SELECT statement. The OPEN statement positions the cursor before the first row of query results.

7. A dynamic version of the FETCH statement advances the cursor to the first row of query results and retrieves the data into the program's data areas and indicator variables. Unlike the static FETCH statement, which specifies a list of host variables to receive the data, the dynamic FETCH statement uses the SQLDA to tell the DBMS where to return the data. Subsequent FETCH statements move through the query results row by row, advancing the cursor to the next row of query results and retrieving its data into the program's data areas.

8. The CLOSE statement ends access to the query results and breaks the association between the cursor and the query results. This CLOSE statement is identical to the static SQL CLOSE statement; no extensions are required for dynamic queries.

The programming required to perform a dynamic query is more extensive than the programming for any other embedded SQL statement. However, the programming is typically more tedious than complex. Figure 18-9 shows a small query program that uses dynamic SQL to retrieve and display selected columns from a user-specified table. The callouts in the figure identify the eight steps in the preceding list.

```
main()
{
   /* This is a simple general-purpose query program. It prompts
      the user for a table name, and then asks the user which
      columns of the table are to be included in the query.
      After the user's selections are complete, the program runs
      the requested query and displays the results.
   */

   exec sql include sqlca;
   exec sql include sqlda;
   exec sql begin declare section;
      char stmtbuf[2001];              /* SQL text to be executed */
      char querytbl[32];               /* user-specified table */
      char querycol[32];               /* user-specified column */
   exec sql end declare section;

   /* Cursor for system catalog query that retrieves column names */
   exec sql declare tblcurs cursor for
           select colname from system.syscolumns
              where tblname = :querytbl and owner = user;

   exec sql declare qrycurs cursor for querystmt;  ◄───────────── ①

   /* Data structures for the program */
   int            colcount = 0;        /* number of columns chosen */
   struct sqlda  *qry_da;              /* allocated SQLDA for query */
   struct sqlvar *qry_var;             /* SQLVAR for current column */
   int            i;                   /* index for SQLVAR array in SQLDA
*/
   char           inbuf[101];          /* input entered by user */

   /* Prompt the user for which table to query */
   printf("*** Mini-Query Program ***\n\n")
   printf("Enter name of table for query: ");
   gets(querytbl);

   /* Start the SELECT statement in the buffer */
```

Figure 18-9. *Data retrieval with dynamic SQL*

```
      strcpy(stmtbuf, "select ");  ◄─────────────────────────── ②

   /* Set up error processing */
   exec sql whenever sqlerror goto handle_error;
   exec sql whenever not found goto no_more_columns;

   /* Query the system catalog to get column names for the table */
   exec sql open tblcurs;
   for ( ; ; ) {

      /* Get name of next column and prompt the user */
      exec sql feth tblcurs into :querycol;
      printf("Include column %s (y/n)? ", querycol);
      gets(inbuf);
      if (inbuf[0] == 'y') {
         /* User wants the column; add it to the select list */
         if (colcount++ > 0)
            strcat(stmtbuf, ", ");
         strcat(stmtbuf, querycol);  ◄────────────────────── ②
      }
   }

no_more_columns:
   exec sql close tblcurs;

   /* Finish the SELECT statement with a FROM clause */
   strcat(stmtbuf, "from ");
   strcat(stmtbuf, querytbl);

   /* Allocate SQLDA for the dynamic query */
   query_da = (SQLDA *)malloc(sizeof(SQLDA) + colcount * sizeof(SQLVAR));
   query_da->sqln = colcount;

   /* Prepare the query and ask the DBMS to describe it */
   exec sql prepare querystmt from :stmtbuf;  ◄────────────── ③
   exec sql describe querystmt into qry_da;  ◄────────────── ④

   /* Loop through SQLVARs, allocating memory for each column */
   for (i = 0; i < colcount; i++) {
     qry_var = qry_da->sqlvar + i;
     qry_var->sqldat = malloc(qry_var->sqllen);  ◄────────── ⑤
     qry_var->sqlind = malloc(sizeof(short));
   }

   /* SQLDA is all set; do the query and retrieve the results! */
```

Figure 18-9. *Data retrieval with dynamic SQL* (continued)

```
                                                            ┌─── 6
   exec sql open qrycurs; ◄────────────────────────────────┘
   exec sql whenever not found goto no_more_data;
   for ( ; ; ) {

      /* Fetch the row of data into our buffers */    ┌─── 7
      exec sql fetch sqlcurs using descriptor qry_da; ◄┘
      printf("\n");

      /* Loop printing data for each column of the row */
      for (i = 0; i < colcount; i++) {

         /* Find the SQLVAR for this column; print column label */
         qry_var = qry_da->sqlvar + i;
         printf(" Column # %d (%s): ", i+1, qry_var->sqlname);

         /* Check indicator variable for NULL indication */
         if (*(qry_var -> sqlind)) != 0) {
            puts("is NULL!\n");
            continue;
         }

         /* Actual data returned; handle each type separately */
         switch (qry_var -> sqltype) {

         case 448:
         case 449:
            /* VARCHAR data -- just display it */
            puts(qry_var -> sqldata);
            break;

         case 496:
         case 497:
            /* Four-byte integer data -- convert & display it */
            printf("%ld", *((int *) (qry_var->sqldata)));
            break;
         case 500:
         case 501:
            /* Two-byte integer data -- convert & dispay it */
            printf("%d", *((short *) (qry_var->sqldata)));
            break;

         case 480:
         case 481:
            /* Floating-point data -- convert & display it */
```

Figure 18-9. *Data retrieval with dynamic SQL* (continued)

```
                printf("%lf", *((double *)(qry_var->sqldat)));
                break;
            }
        }
    }

 no_more_data:
    printf("\nEnd of data.\n");

    /* Clean up allocated storage */
    for (i = 0; i < colcount; i++) {
        qry_var = qry_da->sqlvar + i;
        free(qry_var->sqldata);
        free(qry_var->sqlind);
    }
    free(qry_da);
    close qrycurs;  ◄─────────────────────────────────── ⑧

    exit();
}
```

Figure 18-9.   *Data retrieval with dynamic SQL* (continued)

The program in the figure begins by prompting the user for the table name and then queries the system catalog to discover the names of the columns in that table. It asks the user to select the column(s) to be retrieved and constructs a dynamic SELECT statement based on the user's responses. The step-by-step mechanical construction of a select list in this example is very typical of database front-end programs that generate dynamic SQL. In real applications, the generated select list might include expressions or aggregate functions, and there might be additional program logic to generate GROUP BY, HAVING, and ORDER BY clauses. A graphical user interface would also be used instead of the primitive user prompting in the sample program. However, the programming steps and concepts remain the same. Notice that the generated SELECT statement is identical to the interactive SELECT statement that you would use to perform the requested query.

The handling of the PREPARE and DESCRIBE statements and the method of allocating storage for the retrieved data in this program are also typical of dynamic query programs. Note how the program uses the column descriptions placed in the SQLVAR array to allocate a data storage block of the proper size for each column. This program also allocates space for an indicator variable for each column. The program places the address of the data block and indicator variable back into the SQLVAR structure.

The OPEN, FETCH, and CLOSE statements play the same role for dynamic queries as they do for static queries, as illustrated by this program. Note that the FETCH statement specifies the SQLDA instead of a list of host variables. Because the program has previously filled in the SQLDATA and SQLIND fields of the SQLVAR array, the DBMS knows where to place each retrieved column of data.

As this example shows, much of the programming required for a dynamic query is concerned with setting up the SQLDA and allocating storage for the SQLDA and the retrieved data. The program must also sort out the various types of data that can be returned by the query and handle each one correctly, taking into account the possibility that the returned data will be NULL. These characteristics of the sample program are typical of production applications that use dynamic queries. Despite the complexity, the programming is not too difficult in languages like C, C++, Pascal, PL/I, or Java. Languages such as COBOL and FORTRAN, which lack the capability to dynamically allocate storage and work with variable-length data structures, cannot be used for dynamic query processing.

The following sections discuss the DESCRIBE statement and the dynamic versions of the DECLARE CURSOR, OPEN, and FETCH statements.

The DESCRIBE Statement

The DESCRIBE statement, shown in Figure 18-10, is unique to dynamic queries. It is used to request a description of a dynamic query from the DBMS. The DESCRIBE statement is used after the dynamic query has been compiled with the PREPARE statement but before it is executed with the OPEN statement. The query to be described is identified by its statement name. The DBMS returns the query description in a SQLDA supplied by the program.

The SQLDA is a variable-length structure with an array of one or more SQLVAR structures, as described earlier in the section "EXECUTE with SQLDA," and shown in Figure 18-7. Before passing the SQLDA to the DESCRIBE statement, your program must fill in the SQLN field in the SQLDA header, telling the DBMS how large the SQLVAR array is in this particular SQLDA. As the first step of its DESCRIBE processing, the DBMS fills in the SQLD field in the SQLDA header with the number of columns of query results. If the size of the SQLVAR array (as specified by the SQLN field) is too small to hold all of the column descriptions, the DBMS does not fill in the remainder of the SQLDA. Otherwise, the DBMS fills in one SQLVAR structure for each

Figure 18-10. The DESCRIBE statement syntax diagram

column of query results, in left-to-right order. The fields of each SQLVAR describe the corresponding column:

- The SQLNAME structure specifies the name of the column (with the name in the DATA field and the length of the name in the LENGTH field). If the column is derived from an expression, the SQLNAME field is not used.

- The SQLTYPE field specifies an integer data type code for the column. The data type codes used by different brands of DBMS vary. For the IBM SQL products, the data type code indicates both the data type and whether NULL values are allowed, as shown in Table 18-1.

- The SQLLEN field specifies the length of the column. For variable-length data types (such as VARCHAR), the reported length is the maximum length of the data; the length of the columns in individual rows of query results will not exceed this length. For DB2 (and many other SQL products), the length returned for a DECIMAL data type specifies both the size of the decimal number (in the upper byte) and the scale of the number (in the lower byte).

- The SQLDATA and SQLIND fields are not filled in by the DBMS. Your application program fills in these fields with the addresses of the data buffer and indicator variable for the column before using the SQLDA later in a FETCH statement.

Data Type	NULL Allowed	NOT NULL
CHAR	452	453
VARCHAR	448	449
LONG VARCHAR	456	457
SMALLINT	500	501
INTEGER	496	497
FLOAT	480	481
DECIMAL	484	485
DATE	384	385
TIME	388	389
TIMESTAMP	392	393
GRAPHIC	468	469
VARGRAPHIC	464	465

Table 18-1. *If SQLDA Data Type Codes for DB2*

A complication of using the DESCRIBE statement is that your program may not know in advance how many columns of query results there will be, and therefore, it may not know how large a SQLDA must be allocated to receive the description. One of three strategies is typically used to ensure that the SQLDA has enough space for the returned descriptions.

- If the program has generated the select list of the query, it can keep a running count of the select items as it generates them. In this case, the program can allocate a SQLDA with exactly the right number of SQLVAR structures to receive the column descriptions. This approach was used in the program shown in Figure 18-9.

- If it is inconvenient for the program to count the number of select list items, it can initially DESCRIBE the dynamic query into a minimal SQLDA with a one-element SQLVAR array. When the DESCRIBE statement returns, the SQLD value tells the program how large the SQLDA must be. The program can then allocate a SQLDA of the correct size and reexecute the DESCRIBE statement, specifying the new SQLDA. There is no limit to the number of times that a prepared statement can be described.

- Alternatively, the program can allocate a SQLDA with a SQLVAR array large enough to accommodate a typical query. A DESCRIBE statement using this SQLDA will succeed most of the time. If the SQLDA turns out to be too small for the query, the SQLD value tells the program how large the SQLDA must be, and it can allocate a larger one and DESCRIBE the statement again into that SQLDA.

The DESCRIBE statement is normally used for dynamic queries, but you can ask the DBMS to DESCRIBE any previously prepared statement. This feature is useful, for example, if a program needs to process an unknown SQL statement typed by a user. The program can PREPARE and DESCRIBE the statement and examine the SQLD field in the SQLDA. If the SQLD field is zero, the statement text was not a query, and the EXECUTE statement can be used to execute it. If the SQLD field is positive, the statement text was a query, and the OPEN/FETCH/CLOSE statement sequence must be used to execute it.

The DECLARE CURSOR Statement

The dynamic DECLARE CURSOR statement, shown in Figure 18-11, is a variation of the static DECLARE CURSOR statement. Recall from Chapter 17 that the static DECLARE CURSOR statement literally specifies a query by including the SELECT statement as one of its clauses. By contrast, the dynamic DECLARE CURSOR statement specifies the query indirectly, by specifying the statement name associated with the query by the PREPARE statement.

Like the static DECLARE CURSOR statement, the dynamic DECLARE CURSOR statement is a directive to the SQL precompiler rather than an executable statement. It must appear before any other references to the cursor that it declares. The cursor name declared by

---

DECLARE *cursor-name* CURSOR FOR *statement-name* ────→●

Figure 18-11. *The dynamic DECLARE CURSOR statement syntax diagram*

---

this statement is used in subsequent OPEN, FETCH, and CLOSE statements to process the results of the dynamic query.

The Dynamic OPEN Statement

The dynamic OPEN statement, shown in Figure 18-12, is a variation of the static OPEN statement. It causes the DBMS to begin executing a query and positions the associated cursor just before the first row of query results. When the OPEN statement completes successfully, the cursor is in an open state and is ready to be used in a FETCH statement.

The role of the OPEN statement for dynamic queries parallels the role of the EXECUTE statement for other dynamic SQL statements. Both the EXECUTE and the OPEN statements cause the DBMS to execute a statement previously compiled by the PREPARE statement. If the dynamic query text includes one or more parameter markers, then the OPEN statement, like the EXECUTE statement, must supply values for these parameters. The USING clause is used to specify parameter values, and it has an identical format in both the EXECUTE and OPEN statements.

If the number of parameters that will appear in a dynamic query is known in advance, the program can pass the parameter values to the DBMS through a list of host variables in the USING clause of the OPEN statement. As in the EXECUTE statement, the number of host variables must match the number of parameters, the data type of each host variable must be compatible with the type required by the corresponding parameter, and an indicator variable can be specified for each host variable, if necessary. Figure 18-13 shows a program excerpt where the dynamic query has three parameters whose values are specified by host variables.

If the number of parameters is not known until runtime, the program must pass the parameter values using a SQLDA structure. This technique for passing parameter values

Figure 18-12. *The dynamic OPEN statement syntax diagram*

```
           .
           .
           .
     /* Program has previously generated and prepared a SELECT
        statement like this one:

             SELECT A, B, C ...
               FROM SALESREPS
               WHERE SALES BETWEEN ? AND ?

        with two parameters to be specified
     */


     /* Prompt the user for low & high values and do the query */
     printf("Enter low end of sales range: ");
     scanf("%f", &low_end);
     printf("Enter high end of sales range: ");
     scanf("%f", &high_end);

     /* Open the cursor to start the query, passing parameters */
     exec sql open qrycursor using :low_end, :high_end;
           .
           .
           .
     ..    .        .
           .
```

Figure 18-13.   *OPEN statement with host variable parameter passing*

was described for the EXECUTE statement earlier in the section "EXECUTE with SQLDA."
The same technique is used for the OPEN statement. Figure 18-14 shows a program excerpt
like the one in Figure 18-13, except that it uses a SQLDA to pass parameters.

Note carefully that the SQLDA used in the OPEN statement has absolutely *nothing* to
do with the SQLDA used in the DESCRIBE and FETCH statements:

■ The SQLDA in the OPEN statement is used to pass parameter values *to* the DBMS
  for dynamic query execution. The elements of its SQLVAR array correspond to
  the parameter markers in the dynamic statement text.

■ The SQLDA in the DESCRIBE and FETCH statements receives descriptions of the
  query results columns *from* the DBMS and tells the DBMS where to place the
  retrieved query results. The elements of its SQLVAR array correspond to the
  columns of query results produced by the dynamic query.

```
       .
       .
       .

/* Program has previously generated and prepared a SELECT
   statement like this one:

       SELECT A, B, C ...
         FROM SALESREPS
         WHERE EMPL_NUM IN (?, ?, ... ?)

   with a variable number of parameters to be specified. The
   number of parameters for this execution is stored in the
   variable parmcnt.
*/

char    *malloc()
SQLDA  *parmda;
SQLVAR *parmvar;
long    parm_value[101];

/* Allocate a SQLDA to pass parameter values */
parmda = (SQLDA *)malloc(sizeof(SQLDA) + parmcnt * sizeof(SQLVAR));
parmda->sqln = parmcnt;

/*Prompt the user for parameter values */
for (i = 0; i < parmcnt; i++) {
   printf("Enter employee number: ");
   scanf("%ld", &(parm_value[i]));
   parmvar = parmda -> sqlvar + i;
   parmvar->sqltype = 496;
   parmvar->sqllen  = 4;
   parmvar->sqldata = &(parm_value[i]);
   parmvar->sqlind  = 0;
}

/* Open the cursor to start the query, passing parameters */
exec sql open qrycursor using descriptor :parmda;

       .
       .
       .
```

Figure 18-14.   *OPEN statement with SQLDA parameter passing*

The Dynamic FETCH Statement

The dynamic FETCH statement, shown in Figure 18-15, is a variation of the static FETCH statement. It advances the cursor to the next available row of query results and retrieves the values of its columns into the program's data areas. Recall from Chapter 17 that the static FETCH statement includes an INTO clause with a list of host variables that receive the retrieved column values. In the dynamic FETCH statement, the list of host variables is replaced by a SQLDA.

Before using the dynamic FETCH statement, it is the application program's responsibility to provide data areas to receive the retrieved data and indicator variable for each column. The application program must also fill in the SQLDATA, SQLIND, and SQLLEN fields in the SQLVAR structure for each column, as follows:

- The SQLDATA field must point to the data area for the retrieved data.

- The SQLLEN field must specify the length of the data area pointed to by the SQLDATA field. This value must be correctly specified to make sure the DBMS does not copy retrieved data beyond the end of the data area.

- The SQLIND field must point to an indicator variable for the column (a 2-byte integer). If no indicator variable is used for a particular column, the SQLIND field for the corresponding SQLVAR structure should be set to zero.

Normally, the application program allocates a SQLDA, uses the DESCRIBE statement to get a description of the query results, allocates storage for each column of query results, and sets the SQLDATA and SQLIND values, all before opening the cursor. This same SQLDA is then passed to the FETCH statement. However, there is no requirement that the same SQLDA be used or that the SQLDA specify the same data areas for each FETCH statement. It is perfectly acceptable for the application program to change the SQLDATA and SQLIND pointers between FETCH statements, retrieving two successive rows into different locations.

The Dynamic CLOSE Statement

The dynamic form of the CLOSE statement is identical in syntax and function to the static CLOSE statement shown in Figure 17-25. In both cases, the CLOSE statement ends

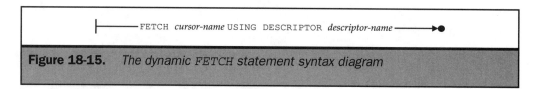

Figure 18-15. *The dynamic FETCH statement syntax diagram*

access to the query results. When a program closes a cursor for a dynamic query, the program normally should also deallocate the resources associated with the dynamic query, including:

- The SQLDA allocated for the dynamic query and used in the DESCRIBE and FETCH statements

- A possible second SQLDA, used to pass parameter values to the OPEN statement

- The data areas allocated to receive each column of query results retrieved by a FETCH statement

- The data areas allocated as indicator variables for the columns of query results

It may not be necessary to deallocate these data areas if the program will terminate immediately after the CLOSE statement.

Dynamic SQL Dialects

Like the other parts of the SQL language, dynamic SQL varies from one brand of DBMS to another. In fact, the differences in dynamic SQL support are more serious than for static SQL, because dynamic SQL exposes more of the nuts and bolts of the underlying DBMS—data types, data formats, and so on. As a practical matter, these differences make it impossible to write a single, general-purpose database front-end that is portable across different DBMS brands using dynamic SQL. Instead, database front-end programs must include a translation layer, often called a *driver,* for each brand of DBMS that they support to accommodate the differences.

The early front-end products usually shipped with a separate driver for each of the popular DBMS brands. The introduction of ODBC as a uniform SQL API layer made this job simpler, since an ODBC driver could be written once for each DBMS brand, and the front-end program could be written to solely use the ODBC interface. In practice, however, ODBC's least-common-denominator approach meant that the front-end programs couldn't take advantage of the unique capabilities of the various supported DBMS systems, and it limited the performance of the application. As a result, most modern front-end programs and tools still include a separate, explicit driver for each of the popular DBMS brands. An ODBC driver is usually included to provide access to the others.

A detailed description of the dynamic SQL features supported by all of the major DBMS brands is beyond the scope of this book. However, it is instructive to examine the dynamic SQL support provided by SQL/DS and by Oracle as examples of the kinds of differences and extensions to dynamic SQL that you may find in your particular DBMS.

Dynamic SQL in Oracle *

The Oracle DBMS preceded DB2 into the market and based its dynamic SQL support on IBM's System/R prototype. For this reason, the Oracle support for dynamic SQL differs somewhat from the IBM SQL standard. Although Oracle and DB2 are broadly compatible, they differ substantially at the detail level. These differences include Oracle's use of parameter markers, its use of the SQLDA, the format of its SQLDA, and its support for data type conversion. The Oracle differences from DB2 are similar to those you may encounter in other DBMS brands. For that reason, it is instructive to briefly examine Oracle's dynamic SQL support and its points of difference from DB2.

Named Parameters

Recall that DB2 does not allow host variable references in a dynamically prepared statement. Instead, parameters in the statement are identified by question marks (parameter markers), and values for the parameters are specified in the EXECUTE or OPEN statement. Oracle allows you to specify parameters in a dynamically prepared statement using the syntax for host variables. For example, this sequence of embedded SQL statements is legal for Oracle:

```
exec sql begin declare section;
    char   stmtbuf[1001];
    int    employee_number;
exec sql end declare section;
    .
    .
    .
strcpy(stmtbuf, "delete from salesreps
                  where empl_num = :rep_number;");
exec sql prepare delstmt from :stmtbuf;
exec sql execute delstmt using :employee_number;
```

Although rep_number appears to be a host variable in the dynamic DELETE statement, it is in fact a *named parameter.* As shown in the example, the named parameter behaves exactly like the parameter markers in DB2. A value for the parameter is supplied from a real host variable in the EXECUTE statement. Named parameters are a real convenience when you use dynamic statements with a variable number of parameters.

The DESCRIBE Statement

The Oracle DESCRIBE statement is used, like the DB2 DESCRIBE statement, to describe the query results of a dynamic query. Like DB2, Oracle returns the descriptions in a SQLDA. The Oracle DESCRIBE statement can also be used to request a description of the named parameters in a dynamically prepared statement. Oracle also returns these parameter descriptions in a SQLDA.

This Oracle DESCRIBE statement requests a description of the columns of query results from a previously prepared dynamic query:

```
exec sql describe select list for qrystmt into qry_sqlda;
```

It corresponds to the DB2 statement:

```
exec sql describe qrystmt into qry_sqlda;
```

This Oracle DESCRIBE statement requests a description of the named parameters in a previously prepared dynamic statement. The statement might be a query or some other SQL statement:

```
exec sql describe bind list for thestmt into the_sqlda;
```

This Oracle statement has no DB2 equivalent. Following this DESCRIBE statement, your program would typically examine the information in the SQLDA, fill in the pointers in the SQLDA to point to the parameter values the program wants to supply, and then execute the statement using the SQLDA form of the OPEN or EXECUTE statement:

```
exec sql execute thestmt using descriptor the_sqlda;
exec sql open qrycursor using descriptor the_sqlda;
```

The information returned by both forms of the Oracle DESCRIBE statement is the same, and is described in the next section.

The Oracle SQLDA

The Oracle SQLDA performs the same functions as the DB2 SQLDA, but its format, shown in Figure 18-16, differs substantially from that of DB2. The two important fields in the DB2 SQLDA header both have counterparts in the Oracle SQLDA:

■ The N field in the Oracle SQLDA specifies the size of the arrays used to hold column definitions. It corresponds to the SQLN field in the DB2 SQLDA.

■ The F field in the Oracle SQLDA indicates how many columns are currently described in the arrays of the SQLDA. It corresponds to the SQLD field in the DB2 SQLDA.

```
struct sqlda {
    int      N;  /* number of entries in the SQLDA arrays */
    char    **V;  /* pointer to array of pointers to data areas */
    int      *L;  /* pointer to array of buffer lengths */
    short    *T;  /* pointer to array of data type codes */
    short   **I;  /* pointer to array of pointers to indicator variables */
    int       F;  /* number of active entries in the SQLDA arrays */
    char    **S;  /* pointer to array of pointers to column/parameter names
*/
    short    *M;  /* pointer to array of name buffer lengths */
    short    *C;  /* pointer to array of current lengths of names */
    char    **X;  /* pointer to array of pointers to indicator parameter names
*/
    short    *Y;  /* pointer to array of indicator name buffer lengths */
    short    *Z;  /* pointer to array of current lengths of indicator names */
} ;
```

Figure 18-16.   *The Oracle SQLDA*

Instead of DB2's single array of SQLVAR structures that contain column descriptions, the Oracle SQLDA contains pointers to a series of arrays, each of which describes one aspect of a column:

- The T field points to an array of integers that specify the data type for each query results column or named parameter. The integers in this array correspond to the SQLTYPE field in each DB2 SQLVAR structure.

- The V field points to an array of pointers that specify the buffer for each column of query results or each passed parameter value. The pointers in this array correspond to the SQLDATA field in each DB2 SQLVAR structure.

- The L field points to an array of integers that specify the length of each buffer pointed to by the V array. The integers in this array correspond to the SQLLEN field in each DB2 SQLVAR structure.

- The I field points to an array of data pointers that specify the indicator variable for each query results column or named parameter. The pointers in this array correspond to the SQLIND field in each DB2 SQLVAR structure.

- The S field points to an array of string pointers that specify the buffers where Oracle is to return the name of each query results column or named parameter. The buffers pointed to by this array correspond to the SQLNAME structure in each DB2 SQLVAR structure.

- The M field points to an array of integers that specify the size of each buffer pointed to by the S array. For DB2, the SQLNAME structure has a fixed-length buffer, so there is no equivalent to the M field.

- The C field points to an array of integers that specify the actual lengths of the names pointed to by the S array. When Oracle returns the column or parameter names, it sets the integers in this array to indicate their actual lengths. For DB2, the SQLNAME structure has a fixed-length buffer, so there is no equivalent to the C field.

- The X field points to an array of string pointers that specify the buffers where Oracle is to return the name of each named indicator parameter. These buffers are used only by the Oracle DESCRIBE BLIND LIST statement; they have no DB2 equivalent.

- The Y field points to an array of integers specifying the size of each buffer pointed to by the X array. There is no DB2 equivalent.

- The Z field points to an array of integers specifying actual lengths of the indicator parameter names pointed to by the X array. When Oracle returns the indicator parameter names, it sets the integers in this array to indicate their actual lengths. There is no DB2 equivalent.

Data Type Conversions

The data type formats that DB2 uses to receive parameter values and return query results are those supported by the IBM S/370 architecture mainframes that run DB2. Because it was designed as a portable DBMS, Oracle uses its own internal data type formats. Oracle automatically converts between its internal data formats and those of the computer system on which it is running when it receives parameter values from your program and when it returns query results to your program.

Your program can use the Oracle SQLDA to control the data type conversion performed by Oracle. For example, suppose your program uses the DESCRIBE statement to describe the results of a dynamic query and discovers (from the data type code in the SQLDA) that the first column contains numeric data. Your program can request conversion of the numeric data by changing the data type code in the SQLDA before it fetches the data. If the program places the data type code for a character string into the SQLDA, for example, Oracle will convert the first column of query results and return it to your program as a string of digits.

The data type conversion feature of the Oracle SQLDA provides excellent portability, both across different computer systems and across different programming languages. A similar feature is supported by several other DBMS brands, but not by the IBM SQL products.

Dynamic SQL and the SQL2 Standard

The SQL1 standard did not address dynamic SQL, so the de facto standard for dynamic SQL, as described in the preceding sections, was set by IBM's implementation in DB2. The SQL2 standard explicitly included a standard for dynamic SQL, specified in a separate chapter of the standard that is nearly 50 pages long. In the simplest areas of dynamic SQL, the new SQL2 standard closely follows the dynamic SQL currently used by commercial DBMS products. But in other areas, including even the most basic dynamic SQL queries, the new standard introduces incompatibilities with existing DBMS products, which will require the rewriting of applications. The next several sections describe the SQL2 standard for dynamic SQL in detail, with an emphasis on the differences from the DB2-style dynamic SQL described in the preceding sections.

In practice, support for SQL2-style dynamic SQL is appearing slowly in commercial DBMS products, and most dynamic SQL programming still requires the use of the old, DB2-style dynamic SQL. Even when a new version of a DBMS product supports the new SQL2 statements, the DBMS vendor always provides a precompiler option that accepts the old dynamic SQL structure used by the particular DBMS. Often, this is the default option for the precompiler, because with thousands and thousands of SQL programs already in existence, the DBMS vendor has an absolute requirement that new DBMS versions do not break old programs. Thus, the migration to portions of SQL2 that represent incompatibilities with current practice will be a slow and evolutionary one.

Basic Dynamic SQL2 Statements

The SQL2 statements that implement basic dynamic SQL statement execution (that is, dynamic SQL that does not involve database queries) are shown in Figure 18-17. These statements closely follow the DB2 structure and language. This includes the single-step and two-step methods of executing dynamic SQL statements.

The SQL2 EXECUTE IMMEDIATE statement has an identical syntax and operation to that of its DB2 counterpart. It immediately executes the SQL statement passed to the DBMS as a character string. Thus, the EXECUTE IMMEDIATE statement in Figure 18-3 conforms to the SQL2 standard.

The SQL2 PREPARE and EXECUTE statements also operate identically to their DB2-style counterparts. The PREPARE statement passes a text string containing a SQL statement to the DBMS and causes the DBMS to analyze the statement, optimize it, and build an application plan for it. The EXECUTE statement causes the DBMS to actually execute a previously prepared statement. Like the DB2 version, the SQL2 EXECUTE statement optionally accepts host variables that pass the specific values to be used when executing the SQL statement. The PREPARE and EXECUTE statements in Figure 18-4 (called out as item 2) thus conform to the SQL2 standard.

Two useful extensions to the PREPARE/EXECUTE structure are a part of the Full compliance level SQL2 standard specification (neither is part of the Entry or Intermediate compliance levels). The first is a useful companion to the PREPARE statement that unprepares a previously compiled dynamic SQL statement. The

Figure 18-17. *SQL2 dynamic SQL statements*

DEALLOCATE PREPARE statement provides this capability. When the DBMS processes this statement, it can free the resources associated with the compiled statement, which will usually include some internal representation of the application plan for the statement. The statement named in the DEALLOCATE PREPARE statement must match the name specified in a previously executed PREPARE statement.

In the absence of a capability like that provided by DEALLOCATE PREPARE, the DBMS has no way of knowing whether a previously prepared statement will be executed again or not, and so must retain all of the information associated with the statement. In practice, some DBMS brands maintain the compiled version of the statement only until the end of a transaction; in these systems, a statement must be reprepared for each subsequent transaction where it is used. Because of the overhead involved in this process, other DBMS brands maintain the compiled statement information indefinitely. The DEALLOCATE PREPARE can play a more important role in these systems, where a database session might last for hours. Note, however, that the SQL2 standard explicitly says that whether a prepared statement is valid outside of the transaction in which it is prepared is implementation dependent.

The SQL2 extension to the DB2-style EXECUTE statement may be even more useful in practice. It allows the EXECUTE statement to be used to process simple singleton SELECT statements that return a single row of query results. Like the DB2 EXECUTE statement, the SQL2 statement includes a USING clause that names the host variables that supply the values for parameters in the statement being executed. But the SQL2 statement also permits an optional INTO clause that names the host variables that *receive* the values *returned* by a single-row query.

Suppose you have written a program that dynamically generates a query statement that retrieves the name and quota of a salesperson, with the salesperson's employee number as an input parameter. Using DB2-style dynamic SQL, even this simple query involves the use of a SQLDA, cursors, a FETCH statement loop, and so on. Using SQL2 dynamic SQL, the statement can be executed using the simple two-statement sequence:

```
PREPARE qrystmt FROM :statement_buffer;

EXECUTE qrystmt USING :emplnum INTO :name, :quota;
```

As with any prepared statement, this single-row query could be executed repeatedly after being prepared once. It still suffers from the restriction that the number of returned columns, and their data types, must know when the program is written, since they must match exactly the number and data types of the host variables in the INTO clause. This restriction is removed by allowing the use of a SQLDA-style descriptor area instead of a list of host variables, as described in the next section.

SQL2 and the SQLDA

Although its support for PREPARE/EXECUTE processing closely parallels that of DB2 dynamic SQL, the SQL2 standard diverges substantially from DB2 style in the area of dynamic query processing. In particular, the SQL2 standard includes major changes to the DB2 SQL Data Area (SQLDA), which is at the heart of dynamic multirow queries. Recall that a SQL Data Area (SQLDA) provides two important functions:

- A flexible way to pass parameters to be used in the execution of a dynamic SQL statement (passing data from the host program to the DBMS), as described earlier in the section "EXECUTE with SQLDA."

- The way that the query results are returned to the program in the execution of a dynamic SQL query (passing data from the DBMS back to the host program), as described earlier in the section "The Dynamic FETCH Statement."

The DB2-style SQLDA handles these functions with flexibility, but it has some serious disadvantages. It is a very low-level data structure, which tends to be specific to a particular programming language. For example, the variable-length structure of a DB2-style SQLDA makes it very difficult to represent in the FORTRAN language. The SQLDA structure also implicitly makes assumptions about the memory of the computer system on which the dynamic SQL program is running, how data items in a structure are aligned on such a system, and so on. For the writers of the SQL2 standard, these low-level dependencies were unacceptable barriers to portability. Therefore, they replaced the

DB2 SQLDA structure with a set of statements for manipulating a more abstract structure called a dynamic SQL *descriptor.*

The structure of a SQL2 descriptor is shown in Figure 18-18. Conceptually, the SQL2 descriptor is parallel to, and plays exactly the same role as, the DB2-style SQLDA shown in Figure 18-7. The fixed part of the SQL2 descriptor specifies a count of the number of items in the variable part of the descriptor. Each item in the variable part contains information about a single parameter being passed, such as its data type, its length, an indicator telling whether a NULL value is being passed, and so on.

But unlike the DB2 SQLDA, the SQL2 descriptor is not an actual data structure within the host program. Instead, it is a collection of data items owned by the DBMS software. The host program manipulates SQL2 descriptors—creating them, destroying

---

Fixed part

COUNT	number of items described

Variable part—one occurrence per item (parameter or query results column):

TYPE	data type of item
LENGTH	length of item
OCTET_LENGTH	length of item (in 8-bit octets)
RETURNED_LENGTH	length of returned data item
RETURNED_OCTET_LENGTH	length of returned data (in 8-bit octets)
PRECISION	precision of data item
SCALE	scale of data item
DATETIME_INTERVAL_CODE	type of date/time interval data
DATETIME_INTERVAL_PRECISION	precision of date/time interval data
NULLABLE	can item be NULL?
INDICATOR	is data item NULL? (indicator value)
DATA	data item itself
NAME	name of data item
UNNAMED	is data item unnamed?

Figure 18-18.   *SQL2 descriptor structure*

them, placing data items into them, extracting data from them—via a new set of dynamic SQL statements specially designed for that purpose. Figure 18-19 summarizes these SQL2 descriptor management statements.

To understand how the SQL2 descriptor management statements work, it's instructive to reexamine the dynamic SQL update program in Figure 18-8. This program illustrates the use of a DB2-style SQLDA in an EXECUTE statement. The flow of the program remains identical if a SQL2 descriptor is used instead, but the specifics change quite a lot.

Before using the descriptor, the program must create it, using the statement:

```
ALLOCATE DESCRIPTOR parmdesc WITH MAX :parmcnt;
```

This statement replaces the allocation of storage for the parmda data structure at callout 1 in Figure 18-8. The descriptor (named parmdesc) will perform the same functions as the parmda. Note that the program in Figure 18-8 had to calculate how much storage would be required for the parmda structure before allocating it. With the

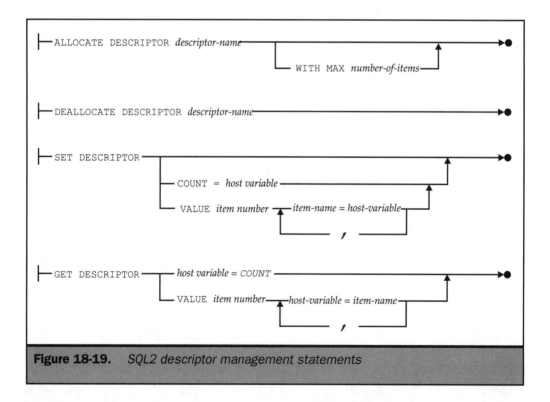

Figure 18-19. SQL2 descriptor management statements

SQL2 descriptor, that calculation is eliminated, and the host program simply tells the DBMS how many items the variable part of the descriptor must be able to hold.

The next step in the program is to set up the descriptor so that it describes the parameters to be passed—their data types, lengths, and so on. The loop at callout 2 of the program remains intact, but again, the details of how the descriptor is initialized differ from those for the SQLDA. At callout 3 and callout 4, the data type and length for the parameter are specified with a form of the SET DESCRIPTOR statement, with this code excerpt:

```
typecode = columns[i].typecode;
length = columns[i].buflen;
SET DESCRIPTOR parmdesc VALUE (:i + 1) TYPE = :typecode
SET DESCRIPTOR parmdesc VALUE (:i + 1) LENGTH = :length;
```

The differences from Figure 18-8 are instructive. Because the descriptor is maintained by the DBMS, the data type and length must be passed to the DBMS, through the SET DESCRIPTOR statement, using host variables. In this particular example, the simple variables typecode and length are used. Additionally, the data type codes in Figure 18-8 were specific to DB2. The fact that each DBMS vendor used different codes to represent different SQL data types was a major source of portability problems in dynamic SQL. The SQL2 standard specifies integer data type codes for all of the data types specified in the standard, eliminating this issue. The SQL2 data type codes are summarized in Table 18-2. So, in addition to the other changes, the data type codes in the columns structure of Figure 18-8 would need to be modified to use these SQL2 standard data type codes.

Data Type	Code
Data Type Codes (TYPE)	
INTEGER	4
SMALLINT	5
NUMERIC	2
DECIMAL	3
FLOAT	6

Table 18-2. *SQL2 Data Type Codes*

Data Type	Code
REAL	7
DOUBLE PRECISION	8
CHARACTER	1
CHARACTER VARYING	12
BIT	14
BIT VARYING	15
DATE/TIME/TIMESTAMP	9
INTERVAL	10
Date/Time Subcodes (Interval_Code)	
DATE	1
TIME	2
TIME WITH TIME ZONE	4
TIMESTAMP	3
TIMESTAMP WITH TIME ZONE	5
Date/Time Subcodes (Interval_Precision)	
YEAR	1
MONTH	2
DAY	3
HOUR	4
MINUTE	5
SECOND	6
YEAR – MONTH	7
DAY – HOUR	8
DAY – MINUTE	9
DAY – SECOND	10

Table 18-2. *SQL2 Data Type Codes* (continued)

The statements at callouts 5 and 6 in Figure 18-8 were used to bind the SQLDA structure to the program buffers used to contain the parameter data and the corresponding indicator variable. Effectively, they put pointers to these program buffers into the SQLDA for the use of the DBMS. With SQL2 descriptors, this type of binding is not possible. Instead, the data value and indicator value are specifically passed as host variables, later in the program. Thus, the statements at callouts 5 and 6 would be eliminated in the conversion to SQL2.

The statement at callout 7 in Figure 18-8 sets the SQLDA to indicate how many parameter values are actually being passed to the DBMS. The SQL2 descriptor must similarly be set to indicate the number of passed parameters. This is done with a form of the SET DESCRIPTOR statement:

```
SET DESCRIPTOR parmdesc COUNT = :parmcnt;
```

Strictly speaking, this SET DESCRIPTOR statement should probably be placed earlier in the program and should be executed before those for the individual items. The SQL2 standard specifies a complete set of rules that describe how setting values in some parts of the descriptor causes values in other parts of the descriptor to be reset. For the most part, these rules simply specify the natural hierarchy of information.

For example, if you set the data type for a particular item to indicate an integer, the standard says that the corresponding information in the descriptor that tells the length of the same item will be reset to some implementation-dependent value. Normally this doesn't impact your programming, but it does mean that you can't assume that just because you set some value within the descriptor previously, that it still retains the same value. It's best to fill the descriptor hierarchically, starting with higher-level information (for example, the number of items and their data types) and then proceeding to lower-level information (data type lengths, subtypes, whether NULL values are allowed, and so on).

The flow of the program in Figure 18-8 can now continue unmodified. The PREPARE statement compiles the dynamic UPDATE statement, and its form does not change for SQL2. The program then enters the for loop, prompting the user for parameters. Here again, the concepts are the same, but the details of manipulating the SQLDA structure and the SQL2 descriptor differ.

If the user indicates that a NULL value is to be assigned (by typing an asterisk in response to the prompt), the program in Figure 18-8 sets the parameter indicator buffer appropriately with the statement:

```
* (parmvar->sqlind) = -1;
```

and if the value is not NULL, the program again sets the indicator buffer with the statement:

```
* (parmvar->sqlind) = 0;
```

For the SQL2 descriptor, these statements would again be converted to a pair of SET DESCRIPTOR statements:

```
SET DESCRIPTOR parmdesc VALUE(:j + 1) INDICATOR = -1;
SET DESCRIPTOR parmdesc VALUE (:j + 1) INDICATOR = 0;
```

Note again the use of the loop control variable to specify which item in the descriptor is being set, and the direct passing of data (in this case, constants) rather than the use of pointers to buffers in the SQLDA structure.

Finally, the program in Figure 18-8 passes the actual parameter value typed by the user to the DBMS, via the SQLDA. The statements at callout 8 accomplish this for data of different types, by first converting the typed characters into binary representations of the data and placing the binary data into the data buffers pointed to by the SQLDA. Again, the conversion to SQL2 involves replacing these pointers and direct SQLDA manipulation with a SET DESCRIPTOR statement. For example, these statements pass the data and its length for a variable-length character string:

```
length = strlen(inbuf);
SET DESCRIPTOR parmdesc VALUE (:j + 1) DATA = :inbuf;
SET DESCRIPTOR parmdesc VALUE (:j + 1) LENGTH = :length;
```

For data items that do not require a length specification, passing the data is even easier, since only the DATA form of the SET DESCRIPTOR statement is required. It's also useful to note that SQL2 specifies implicit data type conversions between host variables (such as inbuf) and SQL data types. Following the SQL standard, it would be necessary for the program in Figure 18-8 to perform all of the data type conversion in the sscanf() functions. Instead, the data could be passed to the DBMS as character data, for automatic conversion and error detection.

With the SQLDA finally set up as required, the program in Figure 18-8 executes the dynamic UPDATE statement with the passed parameters at callout 9, using an EXECUTE statement that specifies a SQLDA. The conversion of this statement to a SQL2 descriptor is straightforward; it becomes:

```
EXECUTE updatestmt USING SQL DESCRIPTOR parmdesc;
```

The keywords in the EXECUTE statement change slightly, and the name of the descriptor is specified instead of the name of the SQLDA.

Finally, the program in Figure 18-8 should be modified like this to tell the DBMS to deallocate the SQL2 descriptor. The statement that does this is:

```
DEALLOCATE DESCRIPTOR parmdesc;
```

In a simple program like this one, the DEALLOCATE is not very necessary, but in a more complex real-world program with multiple descriptors, it's a very good idea to deallocate the descriptors when the program no longer requires them.

SQL2 and Dynamic SQL Queries

In the dynamic SQL statements of the preceding sections, the SQL2 descriptor, like the SQLDA it replaces, is used to pass parameter information from the host program to the DBMS, for use in dynamic statement execution. The SQL2 standard also uses the SQL descriptor in dynamic query statements where, like the SQLDA it replaces, it controls the passing of query result from the DBMS back to the host program. Figure 18-9 lists a DB2-style dynamic SQL query program. It's useful to examine how the program in Figure 18-9 would change to conform to the SQL2 standard. Again, the flow of the program remains identical under SQL2, but the specifics change quite a lot. The SQL2 forms of the dynamic SQL query-processing statements are shown in Figure 18-20.

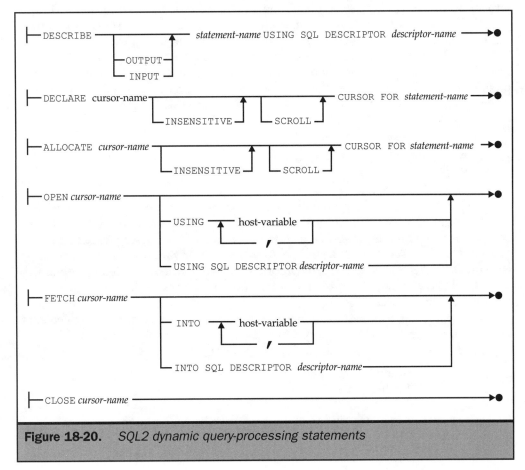

Figure 18-20.   *SQL2 dynamic query-processing statements*

The declaration of the cursor for the dynamic query, in callout 1 of Figure 18-9, remains unchanged under SQL2. The construction of the dynamic SELECT statement in callout 2 is also unchanged, as is the PREPARE statement of callout 3. The changes to the program begin at callout 4, where the program uses the DESCRIBE statement to obtain a description of the query results, which is returned in a SQLDA named qry_da. For SQL2, this DESCRIBE statement must be modified to refer to a SQL2 descriptor, which must have been previously allocated. Assuming the descriptor is named qrydesc, the statements would be:

```
ALLOCATE DESCRIPTOR qrydesc WITH MAX :colcount;
DESCRIBE querystmt USING SQL DESCRIPTOR qrydesc;
```

The SQL2 form of the DESCRIBE statement has a parallel effect on the one it replaces. Descriptions of the query result columns are returned, column by column, into the SQL2 descriptor, instead of into the SQLDA. Because the descriptor is a DBMS structure, rather than an actual data structure in the program, the host program must retrieve the information from the descriptor, piece by piece, as required. The GET DESCRIPTOR statement performs this function, just as the SET DESCRIPTOR function performs the opposite function of putting information into the SQL2 descriptor. In the program of Figure 18-9, the statements at callout 5, which obtains the length of a particular column of query results from a SQLDA, would be replaced with this statement:

```
GET DESCRIPTOR qrydesc VALUE (:i + 1) :length = LENGTH;
qry_var -> sqldat = malloc(length);
```

The statement at callout 5 that allocates buffers for each item of query results is still needed, but the method for telling the DBMS where to put the results changes for SQL2. Instead of placing the address of the program destination for each item into the SQLDA, the program must place these addresses into the SQL2 descriptor, using the SET DESCRIPTOR statement. The buffers for the indicator variables are not needed with the SQL2 descriptor. Instead, the information about whether a column contains a NULL value can be obtained from the descriptor for each row as it is fetched, as seen later in the program example.

In this particular example, the number of columns in the query results are calculated by the program as it builds the query. The program could also obtain the number of columns from the SQL2 descriptor with this form of the GET DESCRIPTOR statement:

```
GET DESCRIPTOR qrydesc :colcount = COUNT;
```

Having obtained the description of the query results, the program performs the query by opening the cursor at callout 6. The simple form of the OPEN statement, without any input parameters, conforms to the SQL2 standard. If the dynamic query specified parameters, they could be passed to the DBMS either as a series of host variables or via a SQL2 descriptor. The SQL2 OPEN statement using host variables is identical to the DB2 style, shown in the program in Figure 18-13. The SQL2 OPEN statement using a descriptor is parallel to the SQL2 EXECUTE statement using a descriptor, and differs from the DB2 style. For example, the OPEN statement of Figure 18-14:

```
OPEN qrycursor USING DESCRIPTOR :parmda;
```

is changed for SQL2 into this OPEN statement:

```
OPEN qrycursor USING SQL DESCRIPTOR parmdesc;
```

The technique for passing input parameters to the OPEN statement via the SQL2 descriptor is exactly the same as that described earlier for the EXECUTE statement.

Like the Oracle implementation of dynamic SQL, the SQL2 standard provides a way for the host program to obtain a description of the parameters in a dynamic query as well as a description of the query results. For the program fragment in Figure 18-14, this DESCRIBE statement:

```
DESCRIBE INPUT querystmt USING SQL DESCRIPTOR parmdesc;
```

will return, in the SQL2 descriptor named parmdesc, a description of each of the parameters that appears in the dynamic query. The number of parameters can be obtained with the GET DESCRIPTOR statement, retrieving the COUNT item from the descriptor. As with the Oracle implementation, the SQL2 standard can have two descriptors associated with a dynamic query. The input descriptor, obtained with the DESCRIBE INPUT statement, contains descriptions of the parameters. The output descriptor contains descriptions of the query results columns. The standard allows you to explicitly ask for the output description:

```
DESCRIBE OUTPUT querystmt USING SQL DESCRIPTOR qrydesc;
```

but the DESCRIBE OUTPUT form of the statement is the default, and the most common practice is to omit the keyword OUTPUT.

Returning to the dynamic query example of Figure 18-9, the cursor has been opened at callout 7, and it's time to fetch rows of query results at callout 8. Again, the SQL2 form of the FETCH statement is slightly modified to use the SQL2-style descriptor:

```
FETCH sqlcurs USING SQL DESCRIPTOR qrydesc;
```

The FETCH statement advances the cursor to the next row of query results and brings the values for that row into the program buffers, as specified within the descriptor structure. The program must still use the descriptor to determine information about each column of returned results, such as its length or whether it contains a NULL value. For example, to determine the returned length of a column of character data, the program might use the statement:

```
GET DESCRIPTOR qrydesc VALUE(:i + 1) :length = RETURNED_LENGTH;
```

To determine whether the value in the column was NULL, the program can use the statement:

```
GET DESCRIPTOR qrydesc VALUE(:i + 1) :indbuf = INDICATOR;
```

and similarly to determine the data type of the column, the program can use the statement:

```
GET DESCRIPTOR qrydesc VALUE(:i + 1) :type = TYPE;
```

As you can see, the details of row-by-row query processing within the for loop of the program will differ dramatically from those in Figure 18-9.

Having processed all rows of query results, the program closes the cursor at callout 8. The CLOSE statement remains unchanged under SQL2. Following the closing of the cursor, it would be good practice to deallocate the SQL2 descriptor(s), which would have been allocated at the very beginning of the program.

The changes required to the dynamic SQL programs in Figures 18-8, 18-9, and 18-14 to make them conform to the SQL2 standard illustrate, in detail, the new features specified by the standard and the degree to which they differ from common dynamic SQL usage today. In summary, the changes from DB2-style dynamic SQL are:

- The SQLDA structure is replaced with a named SQL2 descriptor.

- The ALLOCATE DESCRIPTOR and DEALLOCATE DESCRIPTOR statements are used to create and destroy descriptors, replacing allocation and deallocation of host program SQLDA data structures.

- Instead of directly manipulating elements of the SQLDA, the program specifies parameter values and information through the SET DESCRIPTOR statement.

- Instead of directly manipulating elements of the SQLDA, the program obtains information about query results and obtains the query result data itself through the GET DESCRIPTOR statement.

- The DESCRIBE statement is used both to obtain descriptions of query results (DESCRIBE OUTPUT) and to obtain descriptions of parameters (DESCRIBE INPUT).

- The EXECUTE, OPEN, and FETCH statements are slightly modified to specify the SQL2 descriptor by name instead of the SQLDA.

Summary

This chapter described dynamic SQL, an advanced form of embedded SQL. Dynamic SQL is rarely needed to write simple data processing applications, but it is crucial for building general-purpose database front-ends. Static SQL and dynamic SQL present a classic trade-off between efficiency and flexibility, which can be summarized as follows:

- **Simplicity**. Static SQL is relatively simple; even its most complex feature, cursors, can be easily understood in terms of familiar file input/output concepts. Dynamic SQL is complex, requiring dynamic statement generation, variable-length data structures, and memory management, with memory allocation/deallocation, data type alignment, pointer management, and associated issues.

- **Performance**. Static SQL is compiled into an application plan at compile-time; dynamic SQL must be compiled at runtime. As a result, static SQL performance is generally much better than that of dynamic SQL. The performance of dynamic SQL is dramatically impacted by the quality of the application design; a design that minimizes the amount of compilation overhead can approach static SQL performance.

- **Flexibility**. Dynamic SQL allows a program to decide at runtime which specific SQL statements it will execute. Static SQL requires that all SQL statements be coded in advance, when the program is written, limiting the flexibility of the program.

Dynamic SQL uses a set of extended embedded SQL statements to support its dynamic features:

- The EXECUTE IMMEDIATE statement passes the text of a dynamic SQL statement to the DBMS, which executes it immediately.

- The PREPARE statement passes the text of a dynamic SQL statement to the DBMS, which compiles it into an application plan but does not execute it. The dynamic statement may include parameter markers whose values are specified when the statement is executed.

- The EXECUTE statement asks the DBMS to execute a dynamic statement previously compiled by a PREPARE statement. It also supplies parameter values for the statement that is to be executed.

- The DESCRIBE statement returns a description of a previously prepared dynamic statement into a SQLDA. If the dynamic statement is a query, the description includes a description of each column of query results.

- The DECLARE CURSOR statement for a dynamic query specifies the query by the statement name assigned to it when it was compiled by the PREPARE statement.

- The OPEN statement for a dynamic query passes parameter values for the dynamic SELECT statement and requests query execution.

- The FETCH statement for a dynamic query fetches a row of query results into program data areas specified by a SQLDA structure.

- The CLOSE statement for a dynamic query ends access to the query results.

The Complete Reference

Chapter 19

SQL APIs

The embedded SQL technique for programmatic access to SQL-based databases was pioneered by the early IBM relational database prototypes and was widely adopted by mainstream SQL products. However, several major DBMS products, led by Sybase's first SQL Server implementation, took a very different approach. Instead of trying to blend SQL with another programming language, these products provide a library of function calls as an application programming interface (API) for the DBMS. To pass SQL statements to the DBMS, an application program calls functions in the API, and it calls other functions to retrieve query results and status information from the DBMS.

For many programmers, a SQL API is a very straightforward way to use SQL. Most programmers have some experience in using function libraries for other purposes, such as string manipulation, mathematical functions, file input/output, and screen forms management. Modern operating systems, such as UNIX and Windows, extensively use API suites to extend the core capabilities provided by the OS itself. The SQL API thus becomes just another library for the programmer to learn.

Over the last several years, SQL APIs have become very popular, equaling if not surpassing the popularity of the embedded SQL approach for new applications development. This chapter describes the general concepts used by all SQL API interfaces. It also describes specific features of some of the proprietary APIs used by popular SQL-based DBMS systems, and both the ANSI/ISO SQL Call-Level Interface standard and Microsoft's Open Database Connectivity (ODBC) standard on which it is based. Finally, it describes JDBC, which is the API standard for SQL access from programs written in Java, and is used by all of the popular Internet application servers.

API Concepts

When a DBMS supports a function call interface, an application program communicates with the DBMS exclusively through a set of calls that are collectively known as an *application programming interface,* or API. The basic operation of a typical DBMS API is illustrated in Figure 19-1.

- The program begins its database access with one or more API calls that connect the program to the DBMS and often to a specific database.

- To send a SQL statement to the DBMS, the program builds the statement as a text string in a buffer and then makes an API call to pass the buffer contents to the DBMS.

- The program makes API calls to check the status of its DBMS request and to handle errors.

- If the request is a query, the program uses API calls to retrieve the query results into the program's buffers. Typically, the calls return data a row at a time or a column at a time.

- The program ends its database access with an API call that disconnects it from the DBMS.

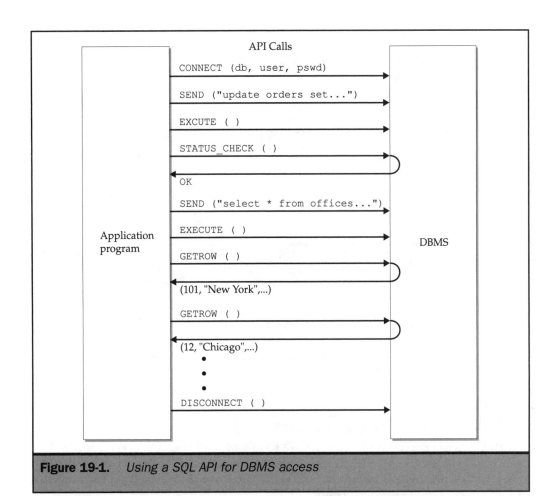

Figure 19-1. *Using a SQL API for DBMS access*

A SQL API is often used when the application program and the database are on two different systems in a client/server architecture, as shown in Figure 19-2. In this configuration, the code for the API functions is located on the client system, where the application program executes. The DBMS software is located on the server system, where the database resides. Calls from the application program to the API take place locally within the client system, and the API code translates the calls into messages that it sends to and receives from the DBMS over a network. A SQL API offers particular advantages for a client/server architecture because it can minimize the amount of network traffic between the API and the DBMS.

The early APIs offered by various DBMS products differed substantially from one another. Like many parts of the SQL language, proprietary SQL APIs proliferated long before there was an attempt to standardize them. In addition, SQL APIs tend to expose the underlying capabilities of the DBMS more than the embedded SQL approach,

Figure 19-2. *A SQL API in an client/server architecture*

leading to even more differences. Nonetheless, all of the SQL APIs available in commercial SQL products are based on the same fundamental concepts illustrated in Figures 19-1 and 19-2. These concepts also apply to the ODBC API and more recent ANSI/ISO standards based on it.

The `dblib` API (SQL Server)

The first major DBMS product to emphasize its callable API was SQL Server, in versions from both Sybase and Microsoft. For many years, the SQL Server callable API was the *only* interface offered by these products. Both Microsoft and Sybase now offer embedded SQL capabilities and have added newer or higher-level callable APIs, but the original SQL Server API remains a very popular way to access these DBMS brands. The SQL Server API also provided the model for much of Microsoft's ODBC API. SQL Server and its API are also an excellent example of a DBMS designed from the ground up around a client/server architecture. For all of these reasons, it's useful to begin our exploration of SQL APIs by examining the basic SQL Server API.

The original SQL Server API, which is called the *database library* or *dblib*, consists of about 100 functions available to an application program. The API is very comprehensive, but a typical program uses only about a dozen of the function calls, which are summarized in Table 19-1. The other calls provide advanced features, alternative methods of interacting with the DBMS, or single-call versions of features that otherwise would require multiple calls.

Function	Description
Database connection/disconnection	
dblogin()	Provides a data structure for login information
Dbopen()	Opens a connection to SQL Server
dbuse()	Establishes the default database
Dbexit()	Closes a connection to SQL Server
Basic statement processing	
dbcmd()	Passes SQL statement text to dblib
dbsqlexec()	Requests execution of a statement batch
dbresults()	Obtains results of next SQL statement in a batch
dbcancel()	Cancels the remainder of a statement batch
Error handling	
dbmsghandle()	Establishes a user-written message-handler procedure
dberrhandle()	Establishes a user-written error-handler procedure
Query results processing	
Dbbind()	Binds a query results column to a program variable
dbnextrow()	Fetches the next row of query results
dbnumcols()	Obtains the number of columns of query results
dbcolname()	Obtains the name of a query results column
dbcoltype()	Obtains the data type of a query results column
dbcollen()	Obtains the maximum length of a query results column
Dbdata()	Obtains a pointer to a retrieved data value
dbdatlen()	Obtains the actual length of a retrieved data value
dbcanquery()	Cancels a query before all rows are fetched

Table 19-1.   *Basic dblib API Functions*

Basic SQL Server Techniques

A simple SQL Server program that updates a database can use a very small set of dblib calls to do its work. The program in Figure 19-3 implements a simple quota update application for the SALESREPS table in the sample database. It is identical to

```
main()
{
    LOGINREC  *loginrec;        /* data structure for login information */
    DBPROCESS *dbproc;          /* data structure for connection */
    char      amount_str[31];   /* amount entered by user (as a string) */
    int       status;           /* dblib call return status */

    /* Get a login structure and set user name & password */
    loginrec = dblogin();                               ①
    DBSETLUSER(loginrec, "scott");
    DBSETLPWD (loginrec, "tiger");

    /* Connect to SQL Server */
    dbproc = dbopen(loginrec, "");                      ②

    /* Prompt the user for the amount of quota increase/decrease */
    printf("Raise/lower by how much: ");
    gets(amount_str);

    /* Pass SQL statement to dblib */
    dbcmd(dbproc, "update salesreps set quota = quota +");  ③
    dbcmd(dbproc, amount_str);

    /* Ask SQL Server to execute the statement */
    dbsqlexec(dbproc);                                  ④

    /* Get results of statement execution */
    status = dbresults(dbproc);                         ⑤
    if (status ! = SUCCEED)
        printf("Error during update.\n");
    else
        printf("Update successful.\n");

    /* Break connection to SQL Server */
    dbexit(dbproc);                                     ⑥
    exit();
}
```

Figure 19-3.   *A simple program using `dblib`*

the program in Figure 17-17, but uses the SQL Server API instead of embedded SQL.
The figure illustrates the basic interaction between a program and SQL Server:

1. The program prepares a login record, filling in the user name, password, and any other information required to connect to the DBMS.

2. The program calls dbopen() to establish a connection to the DBMS. A connection must exist before the program can send SQL statements to SQL Server.

3. The program builds a SQL statement in a buffer and calls dbcmd() to pass the SQL text to dblib. Successive calls to dbcmd() add to the previously passed text; there is no requirement that a complete SQL statement be sent in a single dbcmd() call.

4. The program calls dbsqlexec(), instructing SQL Server to execute the statement previously passed with dbcmd().

5. The program calls dbresults() to determine the success or failure of the statement.

6. The program calls dbexit() to close down the connection to SQL Server.

It's instructive to compare the programs in Figure 19-3 and Figure 17-17 to see the differences between the embedded SQL and the dblib approach:

■ The embedded SQL program either implicitly connects to the only available database (as in DB2), or it includes an embedded SQL statement for connection (such as the CONNECT statement specified by the SQL2 standard). The dblib program connects to a particular SQL Server with the dbopen() call.

■ The actual SQL UPDATE statement processed by the DBMS is identical in both programs. With embedded SQL, the statement is part of the program's source code. With dblib, the statement is passed to the API as a sequence of one or more character strings. In fact, the dblib approach more closely resembles the dynamic SQL EXECUTE IMMEDIATE statement than static SQL.

■ In the embedded SQL program, host variables provide the link between the SQL statements and the values of program variables. With dblib, the program passes variable values to the DBMS in the same way that it passes program text—as part of a SQL statement string.

■ With embedded SQL, errors are returned in the SQLCODE or SQLSTATE field of the SQLCA structure. With dblib, the dbresults() call retrieves the status of each SQL statement.

Overall, the embedded SQL program in Figure 17-17 is shorter and probably easier to read. However, the program is neither purely C nor purely SQL, and a programmer must be trained in the use of embedded SQL to understand it. The use of host variables means that the interactive and embedded forms of the SQL statement are different. In addition, the embedded SQL program must be processed both by the SQL precompiler and by the C compiler, lengthening the compilation cycle. In contrast, the SQL Server program is a plain vanilla C program, directly acceptable to the C compiler, and does not require special coding techniques.

Statement Batches

The program in Figure 19-3 sends a single SQL statement to SQL Server and checks its status. If an application program must execute several SQL statements, it can repeat the dbcmd() / dbsqlexec() / dbresults() cycle for each statement. Alternatively, the program can send several statements as a single *statement batch* to be executed by SQL Server.

Figure 19-4 shows a program that uses a batch of three SQL statements. As in Figure 19-3, the program calls dbcmd() to pass SQL text to dblib. The API simply

```
main()
{
    LOGINREC    *loginrec;        /* data structure for login information */
    DBPROCESS   *dbproc;          /* data structure for connection */
        .
        .
        .
    /* Delete salespeople with low sales */
    dbcmd(dbproc, "delete from salesreps where sales < 10000.00");

    /* Increase quota for salespeople with moderate sales */
    dbcmd(dbproc, "update salesreps set quota = quota + 10000.00");
    dbcmd(dbproc, "where sales <= 150000.00");

    /* Increase quota for salespeople with high sales */
    dbcmd(dbproc, "update salesreps set quota = quota + 20000.00");
    dbcmd(dbproc, "where sales > 150000.00");

    /* Ask SQL Server to execute the statement batch */
    dbsqlexec(dbproc);

    /* Check results of each of the three statements */
    if (dbresults(dbproc) != SUCCEED) goto do_error;
    if (dbresults(dbproc) != SUCCEED goto do_error;
    if (dbresults(dbproc) != SUCCEED goto do_error;
        .
        .
        .
}
```

Figure 19-4. *Using a dblib statement batch*

concatenates the text from each call. Note that it's the program's responsibility to include any required spaces or punctuation in the passed text. SQL Server does not begin executing the statements until the program calls `dbsqlexec()`. In this example, three statements have been sent to SQL Server, so the program calls `dbresults()` three times in succession. Each call to `dbresults()` advances the API to the results of the next statement in the batch and tells the program whether the statement succeeded or failed.

In the program shown in Figure 19-4, the programmer knows in advance that three statements are in the batch, and the programmer can code three corresponding calls to `dbresults()`. If the number of statements in the batch is not known in advance, the program can call `dbresults()` repeatedly until it receives the error code NO_MORE_RESULTS. The program excerpt in Figure 19-5 illustrates this technique.

Error Handling

The value returned by the `dbresults()` function tells the program whether the corresponding statement in the statement batch succeeded or failed. To get more detailed information about a failure, your program must provide its own message-handling

```
        .
        .
        .
    /* Execute statements previously with dbcmd() calls */
    dbsqlexec(dbproc);

    /* Loop checking results of each statement in the batch */
    while (status = dbresults(dbproc) != NO_MORE_RESULTS {
        if (status == FAIL)
            goto handle_error;
        else
            printf("Statement succeeded.\n");
    }

    /* Done with loop; batch completed successfully */
    printf("Batch complete.\n");
    exit();
        .
        .
        .
```

Figure 19-5. *Processing the results of a dblib statement batch*

function. The `dblib` software automatically calls the message-handling function when SQL Server encounters an error while executing SQL statements. Note that `dblib` calls the message-handling function during its processing of the `dbsqlexec()` or `dbresults()` function calls, before it returns to your program (i.e., it is a callback function, called back by the SQL Server software). This allows the message-handling function to do its own error processing.

Figure 19-6 shows an excerpt from a SQL Server program that includes a message-handling function called `msg_rtn()`. When the program begins, it activates the message-handling function by calling `msghandle()`. Suppose an error occurs later, while SQL Server is processing the DELETE statement. When the program calls

```
       •
       •
       •
   /* External variables to hold error information */
   int   errcode;                           /* saved error code */
   char errmsg[256];                        /* saved error message */

   /* Define our own message-handling function */
   int msg_rtn(dbproc, msgno, msgstate, severity, msgtext)
      DBPROCESS    *dbproc;
      DBINT         msgno;
      int           msgstate;
      int           severity;
      char         *msgtext;
      extern int    errcode;
      extern char *errmsg;
      {
          /* Print out the error number and message */
          printf("*** Error: %d Message: %s\n", msgno, msgtext);

          /* Save the error information for the application program */
          errcode = msgno;
          strcpy(errmsg, msgtext);

          /* Return to dlib to complete the API call */
          return(0);
      }
```

Figure 19-6.   *Error handling in a dblib program*

```
main()
{
    DBPROCESS *dbproc;              /* data structure for connection */
       •
       •
       •
    /* Install our own error handling function */
    dberrhandle(msg_rtn)
       •
       •
       •
    /* Execute a DELETE statement */
    dbcmd(dbproc, "delete from salesreps where quota < 100000.00");
    dbsqlexec(dbproc);
    dbresults(dbproc);
       •
       •
       •
```

Figure 19-6.   *Error handling in a dblib program* (continued)

dbsqlexec() or dbresults() and dblib receives the error message from SQL
Server, it upcalls the msg_rtn() routine in the program, passing it five parameters:

- **dbproc**. The connection on which the error occurred
- **msgno**. The SQL Server error number identifying the error
- **msgstate**. A parameter providing information about the error context
- **severity**. A number indicating the seriousness of the error
- **msgtext**. An error message corresponding to msgno

The msg_rtn() function in this program handles the message by printing it and
saving the error number in a program variable for use later in the program. When the
message-handling function returns to dblib (which called it), dblib completes its
own processing and then returns to the program with a FAIL status. The program can
detect this return value and perform further error processing, if appropriate.

The program excerpt in the figure actually presents a simplified view of SQL Server
error handling. In addition to SQL statement errors detected by SQL Server, errors can
also occur within the dblib API itself. For example, if the network connection to the
SQL Server is lost, a dblib call may time out waiting for a response from SQL Server,
resulting in an error. The API handles these errors by upcalling a separate error-handling
function, which operates much like the message-handling function described here.

A comparison of Figure 19-6 with Figures 17-10 and 17-13 illustrates the differences in error-handling techniques between dblib and embedded SQL:

■ In embedded SQL, the SQLCA structure is used to signal errors and warnings to the program. SQL Server communicates errors and warnings by upcalling special functions within the application program and returning a failure status for the API function that encountered the error.

■ In embedded SQL, error processing is synchronous. The embedded SQL statement fails, control returns to the program, and the SQLCODE or SQLSTATE value is tested. SQL Server error processing is asynchronous. When an API call fails, SQL Server calls the application program's error-handling or message-handling function *during* the API call. It returns to the application program with an error status later.

■ Embedded SQL has only a single type of error and a single mechanism for reporting it. The SQL Server scheme has two types of errors and two parallel mechanisms.

In summary, error handling in embedded SQL is simple and straightforward, but the application program can make only a limited number of responses when an error occurs. A SQL Server program has more flexibility in handling errors. However, the upcall scheme used by dblib is more sophisticated, and while it is familiar to systems programmers, it may be unfamiliar to application programmers.

SQL Server Queries

The SQL Server technique for handling programmatic queries is very similar to its technique for handling other SQL statements. To perform a query, a program sends a SELECT statement to SQL Server and uses dblib to retrieve the query results row by row. The program in Figure 19-7 illustrates the SQL Server query-processing technique.

1. The program uses the dbcmd() and dbsqlexec() calls to pass a SELECT statement to SQL Server and request its execution.

2. When the program calls dbresults() for the SELECT statement, dblib returns the completion status for the query and also makes the query results available for processing.

3. The program calls dbbind() once for each column of query results, telling dblib where it should return the data for that particular column. The arguments to dbbind() indicate the column number, the buffer to receive its data, the size of the buffer, and the expected data type.

4. The program loops, calling dbnextrow() repeatedly to obtain the rows of query results. The API places the returned data into the data areas indicated in the previous dbbind() calls.

```
main()
{
    LOGINREC   *loginrec;          /* data structure for login information */
    DBPROCESS  *dbproc;            /* data structure for connection */
    char        repname[16];       /* retrieved city for the office */
    short       repquota;          /* retrieved employee number of mgr */
    float       repsales;          /* retrieved sales for office */

    /* Open a connection to SQL Server */
    loginrec = dblogin();
    DBSETLUSER(loginrec, "scott");
    DBSETLPWD (loginrec, "tiger");
    dbproc = dbopen(loginrec, "");

    /* Pass query to dblib and ask SQL Server to execute it */
    dbcmd(dbproc, "select name, quota, sales from salesreps ");
    dbcmd(dbproc, "where sales > quota order by name ");   ◄──────────────①
    dbsqlexec(dbproc);                              ◄

    /* Get first statement in the batch */
    dbresults(dbproc);                       ◄──────────────────────────②

    /* Bind each column to a variable in this program */
    dbbind(dbproc, 1, NTBSTRINGBIND, 16, &repname);   ◄
    dbbind(dbproc, 2, FLT4BIND,       0, &repquota);  ◄───────────────────③
    dbbind(dbproc, 3, FLT4BIND,       0, &repsales);  ◄

    /* Loop retrieving rows of query results */
    while (status = dbnextrow(dbproc) == SUCCEED) {   ◄──────────────────④

        /* Print data for this salesperson */
        printf("Name:  %s\n",   repname);
        printf("Quota: %f\n\n", repquota);
        printf("Sales: %f\n",   repsales);
    }

    /* Check for errors and close connection */   ◄──────────────────────⑤
    if (status == FAIL) {
        printf("SQL error.\n");
    dbexit(dbproc);
    exit();
}
```

Figure 19-7. *Retrieving query results using* dblib

5. When no more rows of query results are available, the dbnextrow() call returns the value NO_MORE_ROWS. If more statements were in the statement batch following the SELECT statement, the program could call dbresults() to advance to the next statement.

Two of the dblib calls in Figure 19-7, dbbind() and dbnextrow(), support processing of the SQL Server query results. The dbbind() call sets up a one-to-one correspondence between each column of query results and the program variable that is to receive the retrieved data. This process is called *binding* the column. In the figure, the first column (NAME) is bound to a 16-byte character array and will be returned as a NULL-terminated string. The second and third columns, QUOTA and SALES, are both bound to floating point numbers. It is the programmer's responsibility to make sure that the data type of each column of query results is compatible with the data type of the program variable to which it is bound.

Once again, it is useful to compare the SQL Server query processing in Figure 19-7 with the embedded SQL queries in Figure 17-20 and Figure 17-23:

- Embedded SQL has two different query-processing techniques—one for single-row queries (singleton SELECT) and one for multirow queries (cursors). The dblib API uses a single technique, regardless of the number of rows of query results.

- To specify the query, embedded SQL replaces the interactive SELECT statement with the singleton SELECT statement or the DECLARE CURSOR statement. With SQL Server, the SELECT statement sent by the program is *identical* to the interactive SELECT statement for the query.

- With embedded SQL, the host variables that receive the query results are named in the INTO clause of the singleton SELECT or the FETCH statement. With SQL Server, the variables to receive query results are specified in the dbbind() calls.

- With embedded SQL, row-by-row access to query results is provided by special-purpose embedded SQL statements (OPEN, FETCH, and CLOSE). With SQL Server, access to query results is through dblib function calls (dbresults() and dbnextrow()), which keep the SQL language itself more streamlined.

Because of its relative simplicity and its similarity to the interactive SQL interface, many programmers find the SQL Server interface easier to use for query processing than the embedded SQL interface.

Retrieving NULL Values

The dbnextrow() and dbbind() calls shown in Figure 19-7 provide a simple way to retrieve query results, but they do not support NULL values. When a row retrieved by dbnextrow() includes a column with a NULL value, SQL Server replaces the NULL with a NULL substitution value. By default, SQL Server uses zero as a substitution value for numeric data types, a string of blanks for fixed-length strings, and an empty string for variable-length strings. The application program can change the default value for any data type by calling the API function dbsetnull().

In the program shown in Figure 19-7, if one of the offices had a NULL value in its QUOTA column, the dbnextrow() call for that office would retrieve a zero into the quota_value variable. Note that the program cannot tell from the retrieved data whether the QUOTA column for the row really has a zero value, or whether it is NULL. In some applications, the use of substitution values is acceptable, but in others, it is important to be able to detect NULL values. These latter applications must use an alternative scheme for retrieving query results, described in the next section.

Retrieval Using Pointers

With the basic SQL Server data retrieval technique, the dbnextrow() call copies the data value for each column into one of your program's variables. If there are many rows of query results or many long columns of text data, copying the data into your program's data areas can create a significant overhead. In addition, the dbnextrow() call lacks a mechanism for returning NULL values to your program.

To solve these two problems, dblib offers an alternate method of retrieving query results. Figure 19-8 shows the program excerpt from Figure 19-7, rewritten to use this alternate method:

1. The program sends the query to SQL Server and uses dbresults() to access the results, as it does for any SQL statement. However, the program does *not* call dbbind() to bind the columns of query results to program variables.

2. The program calls dbnextrow() to advance, row by row, through the query results.

3. For each column of each row, the program calls dbdata() to obtain a *pointer* to the data value for the column. The pointer points to a location within dblib's internal buffers.

4. If a column contains variable-length data, such as a VARCHAR data item, the program calls dbdatlen() to find out the length of the data item.

5. If a column has a NULL value, the dbdata() function returns a null pointer (0), and dbdatlen() returns 0 as the length of the item. These return values give the program a way to detect and respond to NULL values in the query results.

The program in Figure 19-8 is more cumbersome than the one in Figure 19-7. In general, it's easier to use the dbbind() function than the dbdata() approach, unless your program needs to handle NULL values or will be handling a large volume of query results.

```
main()
{
    LOGINREC    *loginrec;          /* data structure for login information */
    DBPROCESS   *dbproc;            /* data structure for connection */
    char        *namep;            /* pointer to NAME column data */
    int          citylen;          /* length of NAME column data */
    float       *quotap;           /* pointer to QUOTA column data */
    float       *salesp;           /* pointer to SALES column data */

    /* Open a connection to SQL Server */
    loginrec = dblogin();
    DBSETLUSER(loginrec, "scott");
    DBSETLPWD (loginrec, "tiger");
    dbproc = dbopen(loginrec, "");

    /* Pass query to dblib and ask SQL Server to execute it */
    dbcmd(dbproc, "select name, quota, sales from salesreps ");
    dbcmd(dbproc, "where sales > quota order by name ");
    dbsqlexec(dbproc);

    /* Get to first statement in the batch */    ◄───────────────①
    dbresults(dbproc);
    /* Retrieve the single row of query results */
    while (status = dbnextrow(dbproc) == SUCCEED) {    ◄─────────②

        /* Get the address of each data item in this row */
        namep   = dbdata(dbproc, 1);    ◄─────
        quotap  = dbdata(dbproc, 2);    ◄────────────────③
        salesp  = dbdata(dbproc, 3);    ◄─────
        namelen = dbdatlen(dbproc, 1);  ◄───────────────④

        /* Copy NAME value into our own buffer & null-terminate it */
        strncpy(namebuf, namep, namelen);
        *(namebuf + namelen) = (char) 0;
```

Figure 19-8.   *Retrieval using the* dbdata() *function*

```
        /* Print data for this salesperson */
        printf("Name:  %s\n", namebuf);
        if (quotap == 0)    ◄─────────────────────────────────── ⑤
            printf("Quota is NULL.\n");
        else
            printf("Quota: %f\n", *quotap);
        printf("Sales: %f\n", *salesp);
    }

    /* Check for successful completion */
    if (status == FAIL)
        printf("SQL error.\n");
    dbexit(dbproc);
    exit();
}
```

Figure 19-8.   *Retrieval using the* dbdata() *function* (continued)

Random Row Retrieval

A program normally processes SQL Server query results by moving through them sequentially using the dbnextrow() call. For browsing applications, dblib also provides limited random access to the rows of query results. Your program must explicitly enable random row access by turning on a dblib option. The dbgetrow() call can then be used to retrieve a row by its row number.

To support random row retrieval, dblib stores the rows of query results in an internal buffer. If the query results fit entirely within the dblib buffer, dbgetrow() supports random retrieval of any row. If the query results exceed the size of the buffer, only the initial rows of query results are stored. The program can randomly retrieve these rows, but a dbnextrow() call that attempts to retrieve a row past the end of the buffer returns the special BUF_FULL error condition. The program must then discard some of the saved rows from the buffer, using the dbclrbuf() call, to make room for the new row. Once the rows are discarded, they cannot be reretrieved with the dbgetrow() function. Thus, dblib supports random retrieval of query results within a limited window, dictated by the size of the row buffer, as shown in Figure 19-9. Your program can specify the size of the dblib row buffer by calling the dblib routine dbsetopt().

The random access provided by dbgetrow() is similar to the scroll cursors supported by several DBMS products and specified by the SQL2 standard. In both

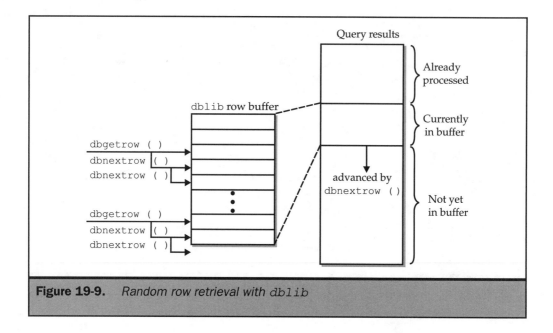

Figure 19-9. *Random row retrieval with* `dblib`

cases, random retrieval by row number is supported. However, a scroll cursor is a true pointer into the entire set of query results; it can range from the first to the last row, even if the query results contain thousands of rows. By contrast, the `dbgetrow()` function provides random access only within a limited window. This is adequate for limited browsing applications but cannot easily be extended to large queries.

Positioned Updates

In an embedded SQL program, a cursor provides a direct, intimate link between the program and the DBMS query processing. The program communicates with the DBMS row by row as it uses the `FETCH` statement to retrieve query results. If the query is a simple single-table query, the DBMS can maintain a direct correspondence between the current row of query results and the corresponding row within the database. Using this correspondence, the program can use the positioned update statements (`UPDATE...` `WHERE CURRENT OF` and `DELETE... WHERE CURRENT OF`) to modify or delete the current row of query results.

SQL Server query processing uses a much more detached, asynchronous connection between the program and the DBMS. In response to a statement batch containing one or more `SELECT` statements, SQL Server sends the query results back to the `dblib` software, which manages them. Row-by-row retrieval is handled by the `dblib` API calls, not by SQL language statements. As a result, early versions of SQL Server could not support positioned updates because its notion of a current row applied to query results within the `dblib` API, not to rows of the actual database tables.

Later versions of SQL Server (and Sybase) added complete support for standard SQL cursors, with their associated DECLARE/OPEN/FETCH/CLOSE SQL statements. Cursors actually operate within Transact-SQL stored procedures, and the action of the FETCH statement is to fetch data from the database into the stored procedure for processing—not to actually retrieve it into the application program that called the stored procedure. Stored procedures and their operation within various popular SQL DBMS products are discussed in Chapter 20.

Dynamic Queries

In the program examples thus far in this chapter, the queries to be performed were known in advance. The columns of query results could be bound to program variables by explicit dbbind() calls hard-coded in the program. Most programs that use SQL Server can be written using this technique. (This static column binding corresponds to the fixed list of host variables used in the static SQL FETCH statement in standard embedded SQL, described in Chapter 17.)

If the query to be carried out by a program is not known at the time the program is written, the program cannot include hard-coded dbbind() calls. Instead, the program must ask dblib for a description of each column of query results, using special API functions. The program can then bind the columns on the fly to data areas that it allocates at runtime. (This dynamic column binding corresponds to the use of the dynamic SQL DBNUMCOLS() statement and SQLDA, in dynamic embedded SQL, as described in Chapter 18.)

Figure 19-10 shows an interactive query program that illustrates the dblib technique for handling dynamic queries. The program accepts a table name entered by the user and then prompts the user to choose which columns are to be retrieved from the table. As the user selects the columns, the program constructs a SELECT statement and then uses these steps to execute the SELECT statement and display the data from the selected columns:

1. The program passes the generated SELECT statement to SQL Server using the dbcmd() call, requests its execution with the dbsqlexec() call, and calls dbresults() to advance the API to the query results, as it does for all queries.

2. The program calls dbnumcols() to find out how many columns of query results were produced by the SELECT statement.

3. For each column, the program calls dbcolname() to find out the name of the column, calls dbcoltype() to find out its data type, and calls dbcollen() to find out its maximum length.

4. The program allocates a buffer to receive each column of query results and calls dbbind() to bind each column to its buffer.

5. When all columns have been bound, the program calls dbnextrow() repeatedly to retrieve each row of query results.

```
main()
{
   /* This is a simple general-purpose query program. It prompts
      the user for a table name and then asks the user which columns
      of the table are to be included in the query. After the user's
      selections are complete, the program runs the requested query and
      displays the results.
   */

   LOGINREC  *loginrec;          /* data structure for login information */
   DBPROCESS *dbproc;            /* data structure for connection */
   char      stmbuf[2001];       /* SQL text to be executed */
   char      querytbl[32];       /* user-specified table */
   char      querycol[32];       /* user-specified column */
   int       status;            /* dblib return status */
   int       first_col = 0;      /* is this the first column chosen? */
   int       colcount;           /* number of columns of query results */
   int       i;                  /* index for columns */
   char      inbuf[101];         /* input entered by user */
   char      *item_name[100];    /* array to track column names */
   char      *item_data[100];    /* array to track column buffers */
   int       item_type[100];     /* array to track column data types */
   char      *address;           /* address of buffer for current column */
   int       length;             /* length of buffer for current column */

   /* Open a connection to SQL Server */
   loginrec = dblogin();
   DBSETLUSER(loginrec, "scott");
   DBSETLPWD (loginrec, "tiger");
   dbproc = dbopen(loginrec, "");

   /* Prompt the user for which table to query */
   printf("*** Mini-Query Program ***\n");
   printf("Enter name of table for query: ");
   gets(querytbl);

   /* Start the SELECT statement in the buffer */
   strcpy(stmbuf, "select ");
```

Figure 19-10.   *Using dblib for a dynamic query*

```
    /* Query the SQL Server system catalog to get column names */
    dbcmd(dbproc, "select name from syscolumns ");
    dbcmd(dbproc, "where id = (select id from sysobjects ");
    dbcmd(dbproc, "where type = 'U' and name = ");
    dbcmd(dbproc, querytbl);
    dbcmd(dbproc, ")");
    dbsqlexec(dbproc);

    /* Process the results of the query */
    dbresults(dbproc);
    dbbind(dbproc, querycol);
    while (status = dbnextrow(dbproc) == SUCCEED) {
        printf("Include column %s (y/n)? ", querycol);
        gets(inbuf);
        if (inbuf[0] == 'y') {
            /* User wants the column; add it to the select list */
            if (first_col++ > 0)  strcat(stmbuf, ", ");
            strcat(stmbuf, querycol);
        }
    }

    /* Finish the SELECT statement with a FROM clause */
    strcat(stmbuf, "from ");
    strcat(stmbuf, querytbl);

    /* Execute the query and advance to the query results */
    dbcmd(dbproc, stmbuf);                                        ①
    dbsqlexec(dbproc);
    dbresults(dbproc);

    /* Ask dblib to describe each column, allocate memory & bind it */
    colcount = dbnumcols(dbproc);                                 ②
    for (i = 0; i < colcount; i++) {
        item_name[i] = dbcolname(dbproc, i);                      ③
        type = dbcoltype(dbproc, i);
        switch(type) {

        case SQLCHAR:
        case SQLTEXT:
```

Figure 19-10.   *Using* dblib *for a dynamic query* (continued)

```
      case SQLDATETIME:
        length = dbcollen(dbproc, i) + 1;
        item_data[i] = address = malloc(length);
        item_type[i] = NTBSTRINGBIND;
        dbind(dbproc, i, NTBSTRINGBIND, length, address);
        break;

      case SQLINT1:
      case SQLINT2:
      case SQLINT4:
        item_data[i] = address = malloc(sizeof(long)):
        item_type[i] = INTBIND;
        dbbind(dbproc, i, INTBIND, sizeof(long), address);
        break;
      case SQLFLT8:
      case SQLMONEY:
        item_data[i] = address = malloc(sizeof(double));
        item_type[i] = FLT8BIND;
        dbbind(dbproc, i, FLT8BIND, sizeof(double), address);
        break;
      }
  }

  /* Fetch and display the rows of query results */
  while (status = dbnextrow(dbproc) == SUCCEED) {

    /* Loop, printing data for each column of the row */
    printf("\n");
    for (i = 0; i < colcount; i++) {

      /* Find the SQLVAR for this column; print column label */
      printf("Column # %d (%s): ", i+1, item_name[i];

      /* Handle each data type separately */
      switch(item_type[i]) {

      case NTBSTRINGBIND:
        /* Text data — just dispay it */
        puts(item_data[i]);
        break;
```

Figure 19-10. *Using* `dblib` *for a dynamic query* (continued)

```
        case INTBIND:
            /* Four-byte integer data — convert & display it */
            printf("%lf", *((double *) (item_data[i])));
            break;

        case FLT8BIND:
            /* Floating-point data — convert & display it */
            printf("%lf", *((double *) (item_data[i])));
            break;
        }
    }
}

printf("\nEnd of data.\n");

/* Clean up allocated storage */
for (i = 0; i < colcount; i++) {
    free(item_data[i]);
}
dbexit(dbproc);
exit();
}
```

Figure 19-10.   *Using dblib for a dynamic query* (continued)

The dblib-based program in Figure 19-10 performs exactly the same function as the dynamic embedded SQL program in Figure 18-9. It's instructive to compare the two programs and the techniques they use:

- For both embedded SQL and dblib, the program builds a SELECT statement in its buffers and submits it to the DBMS for processing. With dynamic SQL, the special PREPARE statement handles this task; with the SQL Server API, the standard dbcmd() and dbsqlexec() functions are used.

- For both interfaces, the program must request a description of the columns of query results from the DBMS. With dynamic SQL, the special DBNUMCOLS() statement handles this task, and the description is returned in a SQLDA data structure. With dblib, the description is obtained by calling API functions. Note that the program in Figure 19-10 maintains its own arrays to keep track of the column information.

■ For both interfaces, the program must allocate buffers to receive the query results and must bind individual columns to those buffer locations. With dynamic SQL, the program binds columns by placing the buffer addresses into the SQLVAR structures in the SQLDA. With SQL Server, the program uses the dbbind() function to bind the columns.

■ For both interfaces, the query results are returned into the program's buffers, row by row. With dynamic SQL, the program retrieves a row of query results using a special version of the FETCH statement that specifies the SQLDA. With SQL Server, the program calls dbnextrow() to retrieve a row.

Overall, the strategy used to handle dynamic queries is very similar for both interfaces. The dynamic SQL technique uses special statements and data structures that are unique to dynamic SQL; they are quite different from the techniques used for static SQL queries. In contrast, the dblib techniques for dynamic queries are basically the same as those used for all other queries. The only added features are the dblib functions that return information about the columns of query results. This tends to make the callable API approach easier to understand for the less-experienced SQL programmer.

ODBC and the SQL/CLI Standard

Open Database Connectivity (ODBC) is a database-independent callable API suite originally developed by Microsoft. Although Microsoft plays an important role as a database software vendor, its development of ODBC was motivated even more by its role as a major operating system developer. Microsoft wanted to make it easier for developers of Windows applications to incorporate database access. But the large differences between the various database systems and their APIs made this very difficult. If an application developer wanted a program to work with several different DBMS brands, it had to provide a separate, specially written database interface module (usually called a *driver*) for each one. Each application program that wanted to provide access to multiple databases had to provide a set of drivers.

Microsoft's solution to this problem was to create ODBC as a uniform, standardized database access interface, and incorporate it into the Windows operating system. For application developers, ODBC eliminated the need to write custom database drivers. For database vendors, ODBC provided a way to gain support from a broader range of application programs.

The Call-Level Interface Standardization

ODBC would have been important even as a Microsoft-only standard. However, Microsoft worked to make it a vendor-independent standard as well. A database vendor association called the SQL Access Group was working on standardizing client/server protocols for remote database access at about the same time as Microsoft's original development of ODBC. Microsoft persuaded the SQL Access Group to expand their focus and adopt ODBC as their standard for vendor-independent database access. Management of the SQL Access Group standard was eventually turned over to the European X/Open consortium, another standards organization, as part of its overall standards for a Common Application Environment (CAE).

With the growing popularity of call-level APIs for database access, the official SQL standards groups eventually turned their attention to standardization of this aspect of SQL. The X/Open standard (based on Microsoft's earlier ODBC work) was taken as a starting point and slightly modified to create an official ANSI/ISO standard. The resulting SQL/Call-Level Interface (SQL/CLI) standard was published in 1995 as ANSI/ISO/IEC 9075-3-1995. With a few modifications, SQL/CLI became Part 3 of the SQL:1999 standard.

Microsoft has evolved ODBC to conform to the official SQL/CLI standard. The CLI standard roughly forms the core level of Microsoft's ODBC 3 revision. Other, higher-level capabilities of ODBC 3 go beyond the CLI specification to provide more API functionality and to deal with the specific problems of managing ODBC as part of the Windows operating system. In practice, the core-level ODBC capabilities and the SQL/CLI specification form the effective callable API standard.

Because of its substantial advantages for both application developers and database vendors, ODBC/CLI has become a very widely supported standard. Virtually all SQL-based database systems provide an ODBC/CLI interface as one of their supported interfaces. Some DBMS brands have even adopted ODBC/CLI as their standard database API. Thousands of application programs support ODBC/CLI, including all of the leading programming tools packages, query- and forms-processing tools and report writers, and popular productivity software such as spreadsheets and graphics programs.

The SQL/CLI standard includes about 40 different API calls, summarized in Table 19-2. The calls provide a comprehensive facility for establishing connections to a database server, executing SQL statements, retrieving and processing query results, and handling errors in database processing. They provide all of the capabilities available through the standard's embedded SQL interface, including both static SQL and dynamic SQL capabilities.

The simple CLI program in Figure 19-11 repeats the program in Figure 19-3 and 17-14, but it uses the CLI functions. It follows the sequence of steps used by most CLI-based applications:

1. The program connects to the CLI and allocates data structures for its use.

2. It connects to a specific database server.

3. The program builds SQL statements in its memory buffers.

4. It makes CLI calls to request statement execution and check status.

5. Upon successful completion, it makes a CLI call to commit the database transaction.

6. It disconnects from the database and releases its data structures.

Function	Description
Resource and connection management	
SQLAllocHandle()	Allocates resources for environment, connection, descriptor, or statement
SQLFreeHandle()	Frees previously allocated resources
SQLAllocEnv()	Allocates resources for a SQL environment
SQLFreeEnv()	Frees resources for a SQL environment
SQLAllocConnect()	Allocates resources for a database connection
SQLFreeConnect()	Frees resources for a database connection
SQLAllocStmt()	Allocates resources for a SQL statement
SQLFreeStmt()	Frees resources for a SQL statement
SQLConnect()	Establishes a database connection
SQLDisconnect()	Ends an established database connection
Statement execution	
SQLExecDirect()	Directly executes a SQL statement
SQLPrepare()	Prepares a SQL statement for subsequent execution
SQLExecute()	Executes a previously prepared SQL statement
SQLRowCount()	Gets number of rows affected by last SQL statement
Transaction management	
SQLEndTran()	Ends a SQL transaction
SQLCancel()	Cancels execution of a SQL statement
Parameter handling	
SQLBindParam()	Binds program location to a parameter value
SQLParamData()	Processes deferred parameter values
SQLPutData()	Provides deferred parameter value or a portion of a character string value
Query results processing	
SQLSetCursorName()	Sets the name of a cursor
SQLGetCursorName()	Obtains the name of a cursor
SQLFetch()	Fetches a row of query results

Table 19-2. *SQL/CLI API Functions*

Function	Description
Query results processing (continued)	
SQLFetchScroll()	Fetches a row of query results with scrolling
SQLCloseCursor()	Closes an open cursor
SQLGetData()	Obtains the value of a query results column
Query results description	
SQLNumResultCols()	Determines the number of query results columns
SQLDescribeCol()	Describes a single query results column
SQLColAttribute()	Gets attribute of a query results column
SQLGetDescField()	Gets value of a descriptor field
SQLSetDescField()	Sets value of a descriptor field
SQLGetDescRec()	Gets values from a descriptor record
SQLSetDescRec()	Sets values in a descriptor record
SQLCopyDesc()	Copies descriptor area values
Error handling	
SQLError()	Obtains error information
SQLGetDiagField()	Gets value of a diagnostic record field
SQLGetDiagRec()	Gets value of the diagnostic record
Attribute management	
SQLSetEnvAttr()	Sets attribute value for a SQL environment
SQLGetEnvAttr()	Retrieves attribute value for a SQL environment
SQLSetStmtAttr()	Sets descriptor area to be used for a SQL statement
SQLGetStmtAttr()	Gets descriptor area for a SQL statement
Driver management	
SQLDataSources()	Gets a list of available SQL servers
SQLGetFunctions()	Gets information about supported features of a SQL implementation
SQLGetInfo()	Gets information about supported features of a SQL implementation

Table 19-2.   *SQL/CLI API Functions* (continued)

PROGRAMMING
WITH SQL

```
/* Program to raise all quotas by a user-specified amount */
#include <sqlcli.h>                    /* header file with CLI definitions */
main()
{
   SQLHENV    env_hdl;                 /* SQL-environment handle */
   SQLHDBC    conn_hdl;                /* connection handle */
   SQLHSTMT   stmt_hdl;                /* statement handle */
   SQLRETURN  status;                  /* CLI routine return status */
   char     *svr_name  = "demo";       /* server name */
   char     *user_name = "joe";        /* user name for connection */
   char     *user_pswd = "xyz";        /* user password for connection */
   char      amount_str[31];           /* amount entered by user */
   char      stmt_buf[128];            /* buffer for SQL statement */
   /* Allocate handles for SQL environment, connection, statement */
   SQLAllocHandle(SQL_HANDLE_ENV, SQL_NULL_HANDLE, &env_hdl);
   SQLAllocHandle(SQL_HANDLE_DBC, env_hdl, &conn_hdl);
   SQLAllocHandle(SQL_HANDLE_STMT, conn_hdl, &stmt_hdl);

   /* Connect to the database, passing server name, user, password */
   /* SQL_NTS says NULL-terminated string instead of passing length */
   SQLConnect(conn_hdl, svr_name, SQL_NTS,
                        user_name, SQL_NTS,
                        user_pswd, SQL_NTS);

   /* Prompt the user for the amount of quota increase/decrease */
   printf("Raise/lower quotas by how much: ");
   gets(amount_str);

   /* Assemble UPDATE statement and ask DBMS to execute it */
   strcpy(stmt_buf, "update salesreps set quota = quota + ");
   strcat(stmt_buf, amount_str);
   status = SQLExecDirect(stmt_hdl, stmt_buf, SQL_NTS);
   if (status)
      printf("Error during update\n");
   else
      printf("Update successful.\n");
```

Figure 19-11.   *A simple program using SQL/CLI*

```
     /* Commit updates and disconnect from database server */
     SQLEndTran(SQL_HANDLE_ENV, env_hdl, SQL_COMMIT);
     SQLDisconnect(conn_hdl);

     /* Deallocate handles and exit */
     SQLFreeHandle(SQL_HANDLE_STMT, stmt_hdl);
     SQLFreeHandle(SQL_HANDLE_DBC, conn_hdl);
     SQLFreeHandle(SQL_HANDLE_ENV, env_hdl);
     exit();
}
```

Figure 19-11.   *A simple program using SQL/CLI* (continued)

All of the CLI routines return a status code indicating either successful completion of the routine or some type of error or warning about its execution. The values for the CLI return status codes are summarized in Table 19-3. Some of the program examples in this book omit the checking of return status codes to shorten the example and focus on the specific features being illustrated. However, production programs that call CLI functions should always check the return value to ensure that the function was completed successfully. Symbolic constant names for the return status codes as well as many other values, such as data type codes and statement-id codes, are typically defined in a header file that is included at the beginning of a program that uses the CLI.

CLI Return Value	Meaning
0	Statement completed successfully
1	Successful completion with warning
100	No data found (when retrieving query results)
99	Data needed (required dynamic parameter missing)
−1	Error during SQL statement execution
−2	Error—invalid handle supplied in call

Table 19-3.   *CLI Return Status Codes*

CLI Structures

The CLI manages interactions between an application program and a supported database through a hierarchy of concepts, reflected in a hierarchy of CLI data structures:

- **SQL-environment.** The highest-level environment within which database access takes place. The CLI uses the data structure associated with a SQL-environment to keep track of the various application programs that are using it.

- **SQL-connection.** A logical connection to a specific database server. Conceptually, the CLI allows a single application program to connect to several different database servers concurrently. Each connection has its own data structure, which the CLI uses to track connection status.

- **SQL-statement.** An individual SQL statement to be processed by a database server. A statement may move through several stages of processing, as the DBMS prepares (compiles) it, executes it, processes any errors, and in the case of queries, returns the results to the application program. Conceptually, an application program may have multiple SQL statements moving through these processing stages in parallel. Each statement has its own data structure, which the CLI uses to track its progress.

The CLI uses a technique commonly used by modern operating systems and library packages to manage these conceptual entities. A symbolic pointer called a *handle* is associated with the overall SQL environment, with a SQL connection to a specific database server, and with the execution of a SQL statement. The handle identifies an area of storage managed by the CLI itself. Some type of handle is passed as one of the parameters in every CLI call. The CLI routines that manage handles are shown in Figure 19-12.

A handle is created (allocated) using the CLI SQLAllocHandle() routine. One of the parameters of the routine tells the CLI which type of handle is to be allocated. Another parameter returns the handle value to the application program. Once allocated, a handle is passed to subsequent CLI routines to maintain a context for the CLI calls. In this way, different threads of execution within a program or different concurrently running programs (processes) can each establish their own connection to the CLI and can maintain their own contexts, independent of one another. Handles also allow a single program to have multiple CLI connections to different database servers, and to process more than one SQL statement in parallel. When a handle is no longer needed, the application calls SQLFreeHandle() to tell the CLI.

In addition to the general-purpose handle management routines, SQLAllocHandle() and SQLFreeHandle(), the CLI specification includes separate routines to create and free an environment, connection, or statement handle. These routines (SQLAllocEnv(), SQLAllocStmt(), and so on) were a part of the original ODBC

```
/* Allocate a handle for use in subsequent CLI calls */
short SQLAllocHandle (
    short  HdlType,              /* IN:  integer handle type code */
    long   inHdl,               /* IN:  environment or conn handle */
    long   *rtnHdl)             /* OUT: returned handle */


/* Free a handle previously allocated by SQLAllocHandle() */
short SQLFreeHandle (
    short  HdlType,              /* IN:  integer handle type code */
    long   inHdl)               /* IN:  handle to be freed */


/* Allocate a handle for a new SQL-environment */
short SQLAllocEnv (
    long   *envHdl)             /* OUT: returned environment handle */


/* Free an environment handle previously allocated by SQLAllocEnv() */
short SQLFreeEnv (
    long   envHdl)              /* IN:  environment handle */


/* Allocate a handle for a new SQL-connection */
short SQLAllocConnect (
    long   envHdl,              /* IN:  environment handle */
    long   *connHdl)            /* OUT: returned handle */


/* Free a connection handle previously allocated */
short SQLFreeConnect (
    long   connHdl)            /* IN:  connection handle */


short SQLAllocStmt (
    long   envHdl,              /* IN:  environment handle */
    long   *stmtHdl)            /* OUT: statement handle */


/* Free a connection handle previously allocated */
short SQLFreeStmt (
    long   stmtHdl,            /* IN:  statement handle */
    long   option)             /* IN:  cursor and unbind options */
```

Figure 19-12.   *SQL/CLI handle management routines*

API and are still supported in current ODBC implementations for backward compatibility. However, Microsoft has indicated that the general handle-management routines are now the preferred ODBC functions, and the specific routines may be dropped in future ODBC releases. For maximum cross-platform portability, it's best to use the general-purpose routines.

SQL-Environment

The SQL-environment is the highest-level context used by an application program in its calls to the CLI. In a single-threaded application, there will typically be one SQL-environment for the entire program. In a multithreaded application, there may be one SQL-environment per thread or one overall SQL-environment, depending on the architecture of the program. The CLI conceptually permits multiple connections, possibly to several different database servers, from within one SQL-environment. A specific CLI implementation for a specific DBMS may or may not actually support multiple connections.

SQL-Connections

Within a SQL-environment, an application program may establish one or more SQL-connections. A SQL-connection is a linkage between the program and a specific SQL server (database server) over which SQL statements are processed. In practice, a SQL-connection often is actually a virtual network connection to a database server located on another computer system. However, a SQL-connection may also be a logical connection between a program and a DBMS located on the same computer system.

Figure 19-13 shows the CLI routines that are used to manage SQL-connections. To establish a connection, an application program first allocates a connection handle by calling SQLAllocHandle() with the appropriate handle type. It then attempts to connect to the target SQL server with a SQLConnect() call. SQL statements can subsequently be processed over the connection. The connection handle is passed as a parameter to all of the statement-processing calls to indicate which connection is being used. When the connection is no longer needed, a call to SQLDisconnect() terminates it, and a call to SQLFreeHandle() releases the associated connection handle in the CLI.

Normally, an application program knows the name of the specific database server (in terms of the standard, the "SQL server") that it wants to access. In certain applications (such as general-purpose query or data entry tools), it may be desirable to let the user choose which database server is to be used. The CLI SQLDataSources() call returns the names of the SQL servers that are known to the CLI—that is, the data sources that can be legally specified as server names in SQLConnect() calls. To obtain the list of server names, the application repeatedly calls SQLDataSources(). Each call returns a single server description, until the call returns an error indicating no more data. A parameter to the call can be optionally used to alter this sequential retrieval of server names.

```
/* Initiate a connection to a SQL-server */
short SQLConnect(
    long    connHdl,              /* IN:  connection handle */
    char    *svrName,             /* IN:  name of target SQL-server */
    short   svrnamlen,            /* IN:  length of SQL-server name */
    char    *userName,            /* IN:  user name for connection */
    short   usrnamlen,            /* IN:  length of user name */
    char    *passwd,              /* IN:  connection password */
    short   pswlen)               /* IN:  password length */

/* Disconnect from a SQL-server */
short SQLDisconnect(
    long    connHdl)              /* IN:  connection handle */

/* Get the name(s) of accessible SQL-servers for connection */
short SQLDataSources (
    long    envHdl,               /* IN:  environment handle */
    short   direction,            /* IN:  indicates first/next request */
    char    *svrname,             /* OUT: buffer for server name */
    short   buflen,               /* IN:  length of server name buffer */
    short   *namlen,              /* OUT: actual length of server name */
    char    *descrip,             /* OUT: buffer for description */
    short   buf2len,              /* IN:  length of description buffer */
    short   *dsclen)              /* OUT: actual length of description */
```

Figure 19-13.   *SQL/CLI connection management routines*

CLI Statement Processing

The CLI processes SQL statements using a technique very similar to that described for
dynamic embedded SQL in Chapter 18. The SQL statement is passed to the CLI in text
form, as a character string. It can be executed in a one- or two-step process.

Figure 19-14 shows the basic SQL statement-processing calls. The application program
must first call SQLAllocHandle() to obtain a statement handle, which identifies the
statement to the program and the CLI. All subsequent SQLExecDirect(), SQLPrepare(),
and SQLExecute() calls reference this statement handle. When the handle is no longer
needed, it is freed with a SQLFreeHandle() call.

For one-step execution, the application program calls SQL SQLExecDirect(),
passing the SQL statement text as one of the parameters to the call. The DBMS

```
/* Directly execute a SQL statement */
short SQLExecDirect (
   long    stmtHdl,        /* IN:  statement handle */
   char   *stmttext,       /* IN:  SQL statement text */
   short   textlen)        /* IN:  statement text length */

/* Prepare a SQL statement */
short SQLPrepare (
   long    stmtHdl,        /* IN:  statement handle */
   char   *stmttext,       /* IN:  SQL statement text */
   short   textlen)        /* IN:  statement text length */

/* Execute a previously-prepared SQL statement */
short SQLExecute (
   long    stmtHdl)        /* IN:  statement handle */

/* Bind a SQL statement parameter to a program data area */
short SQLBindParam (
   long    stmtHdl,        /* IN:  statement handle */
   short   parmnr,         /* IN:  parameter number (1,2,3...) */
   short   valtype,        /* IN:  data type of value supplied */
   short   parmtype,       /* IN:  data type of parameter */
   short   colsize,        /* IN:  column size */
   short   decdigits,      /* IN:  number of decimal digits */
   void   *value,          /* IN:  pointer to parameter value buf */
   long   *lenind)         /* IN:  pointer to length/indicator buf */

/* Get parameter-tag for next required dynamic parameter */
short SQLParamData (
   long    stmtHdl,        /* IN:  stmt handle w/dynamic parms */
   void   *prmtag)         /* OUT: returned parameter-tag value */

/* Obtain detailed info about an item described by a CLI descriptor
*/
short SQLPutData (
   long    stmtHdl,        /* IN:  stmt handle w/dynamic parms */
   void   *prmdata,        /* IN:  buffer with data for parameter */
   short   prmlenind)      /* IN:  parameter length or NULL ind */
```

Figure 19-14.   *CLI statement-processing routines*

processes the statement as a result of the call and returns the completion status of the statement. This one-step process was used in the simple example program in Figure 19-11. It corresponds to the one-step EXECUTE IMMEDIATE statement in embedded dynamic SQL, described in Chapter 18.

For two-step execution, the application program calls SQLPrepare(), passing the SQL statement text as one of the parameters to the call. The DBMS analyzes the statement, determines how to carry it out, and retains this information. It does not immediately carry out the statement. Instead, subsequent calls to the SQLExecute() routine cause the statement to actually be executed. This two-step process corresponds exactly to the PREPARE and EXECUTE embedded dynamic SQL statements described in Chapter 18. You should always use it for any SQL operations that will be carried out repeatedly, because it causes the DBMS to go through the overhead of statement analysis and optimization only once, in response to the SQLPrepare() call. Parameters can be passed through the CLI to tailor the operation of the multiple SQLExecute() calls that follow.

Statement Execution with Parameters

In many cases, a SQL statement must be repeatedly executed with only changes in some of the values that it specifies. For example, an INSERT statement to add an order to the sample database is identical for every order except for the specific information about the customer number, product and manufacturer, and quantity ordered. As described in Chapter 18, for dynamic embedded SQL, such statements can be processed efficiently by specifying the variable parts of the statement as input parameters. The statement text passed to the SQLPrepare() call has a parameter marker—a question mark (?)—in its text at each position where a parameter value is to be inserted. When the statement is later executed, values must be supplied for each of its input parameters.

The most straightforward way to supply input parameter values is with the SQLBindParam() call. Each call to SQLBindParam() establishes a linkage between one of the parameter markers in the SQL statement (identified by number) and a variable in the application program (identified by its memory address). In addition, an association is optionally established with a second application program variable (an integer) that provides the length of variable-length input parameters. If the parameter is a NULL-terminated string like those used in C programs, a special negative code value, defined in the header file as the symbolic constant SQL_NTS, can be passed, indicating that the string length can be obtained from the data itself by the CLI routines. Similarly, a negative code is used to indicate a NULL value for an input parameter. If there are three input parameter markers in the statement, there will be three calls to SQLBindParam(), one for each input parameter.

Once the association between application program variables (more accurately, program storage locations) and the statement parameters is established, the statement can be executed with a call to SQLExecute(). To change the parameter values for subsequent statements, it is only necessary to place new values in the application program buffer areas before the next call to SQLExecute(). Alternatively, the parameters can be rebound to different data areas within the application program by subsequent

```
/* Program to raise selected user-specified customer credit limits */
#include <sqlcli.h>                        /* header file with CLI defs */
main()
{
    SQLHENV     env_hdl;                   /* SQL-environment handle */
    SQLHDBC     conn_hdl;                  /* connection handle */
    SQLHSTMT    stmt_hdl;                  /* statement handle */
    SQLRETURN   status;                    /* CLI routine return status */
    char        *svr_name  = "demo";       /* server name */
    char        *user_name = "joe";        /* user name for connection */
    char        *user_pswd = "xyz";        /* user password for connection */
    char        amt_buf[31];               /* amount entered by user */
    int         amt_ind = SQL_NTS;         /* amount ind (NULL-term string) */
    char        cust_buf[31];              /* cust # entered by user */
    int         cust_ind = SQL_NTS;        /* cust # ind (NULL-term string) */
    char        stmt_buf[128];             /* buffer for SQL statement */

    /* Allocate handles for SQL environment, connection, statement */
    SQLAllocHandle(SQL_HANDLE_ENV, SQL_NULL_HANDLE, &env_hdl);
    SQLAllocHandle(SQL_HANDLE_DBC, env_hdl, &conn_hdl);
    SQLAllocHandle(SQL_HANDLE_STMT, conn_hdl, &stmt_hdl);

    /* Connect to the database, passing server name, user, password */
    /* SQL_NTS says NULL-terminated string instead of passing length */
    SQLConnect(conn_hdl, svr_name, SQL_NTS,
                         user_name, SQL_NTS,
                         user_pswd, SQL_NTS);

    /* Prepare an UPDATE statement with parameter markers */
    strcpy(stmt_buf, "update customers set credit_limit = ? ");
    strcat(stmt_buf, "where cust_num = ?");
    SQLPrepare(stmt_hdl, stmt_buf, SQL_NTS);
```

Figure 19-15.   *CLI program using input parameters*

```
      / * Bind parameters to the program's buffers */
      SQLBindParam(stmt_hdl,1,SQL_C_CHAR,SQL_DECIMAL,9,2,&amt_buf,&amt_ind);

SQLBindParam(stmt_hdl,2,SQL_C_CHAR,SQL_INTEGER,0,0,&cust_buf,&cust_ind);

      / * Loop to process each credit limit change */
      for ( ; ; ) {

          /* Prompt the user for the customer and new credit limit */
          printf("Enter customer number: ");
          gets(cust_buf);
          if (strlen(cust_buf) == 0)
             break;
          printf("Enter new credit limit: ");
          gets(amt_buf);

          / * Execute the statement with the parameters */
          status = SQLExecute(stmt_hdl);
          if (status)
             printf("Error during update\n");
          else
             printf("Credit limit change successful.\n");

          /* Commit the update */
          SQLEndTran(SQL_HANDLE_ENV, env_hdl, SQL_COMMIT);
      }

      / * Disconnect, deallocate handles and exit */
      SQLDisconnect(conn_hdl);
      SQLFreeHandle(SQL_HANDLE_STMT, stmt_hdl);
      SQLFreeHandle(SQL_HANDLE_DBC, conn_hdl);
      SQLFreeHandle(SQL_HANDLE_ENV, env_hdl);
      exit();
```

Figure 19-15. *CLI program using input parameters* (continued)

calls to SQLBindParam(). Figure 19-15 shows a program that includes a SQL statement with two input parameters. The program repeatedly prompts the user for a customer number and a new credit limit for the customer. The values provided by the user become the input parameters to an UPDATE statement for the CUSTOMERS table.

The SQLParamData() and SQLPutData() calls in Figure 19-15 provide an alternative method of passing parameter data at runtime, called *deferred parameter passing*. The selection of this technique for a particular statement parameter is indicated in the corresponding call to SQLBindParam(). Instead of actually supplying a program data location to which the parameter is bound, the SQLBindParam() call indicates that deferred parameter passing will be used and provides a value that will later be used to identify the particular parameter being processed in this way.

After statement execution is requested (by a SQLExecute() or SQLExecDirect() call), the program calls SQLParamData() to determine whether deferred parameter data is required by the statement. If so, the CLI returns a status code (SQL_NEED_DATA) along with an indicator of which parameter needs a value. The program then calls SQLPutData() to actually provide the value for the parameter. Typically, the program then calls SQLParamData() again to determine if another parameter requires dynamic data. The cycle repeats until all required dynamic data has been supplied, and SQL statement execution then continues normally.

This alternative parameter-passing method is considerably more complex than the straightforward process of binding parameters to application program locations. It has two advantages. The first is that the actual passing of data values (and the allocation of storage to contain those values) can be delayed until the last possible moment when the data is actually needed. The second advantage is that the technique can be used to pass very long parameter values piece by piece. For selected long data types, the CLI allows repeated calls to SQLPutData() for the same parameter, with each call passing the next part of the data. For example, the text of a document that is supplied as a parameter for the VALUES clause of an INSERT statement might be passed in 1000-character pieces through repeated SQLPutData() calls until all of the document has been passed. This avoids the need to allocate a single very large memory buffer within the application program to hold the entire parameter value.

CLI Transaction Management

The COMMIT and ROLLBACK functions for SQL transaction processing also apply to SQL operation via the CLI. However, because the CLI itself must be aware that a transaction is being completed, the COMMIT and ROLLBACK SQL statements are replaced by the CLI SQLEndTran() call, shown in Figure 19-16. This call was used to commit the transactions in the program examples of Figures 19-11 and 19-15. The same CLI routine is used to execute either a COMMIT or a ROLLBACK operation; the particular operation to be performed is specified by the completion type parameter to the call.

The CLI SQLCancel() call, also shown in Figure 19-16, does not actually provide a transaction management function, but in practice, it is almost always used in conjunction with a ROLLBACK operation. It is used to cancel the execution of a SQL statement that was previously initiated by a SQLExecDirect() or SQLExecute() call. This would be appropriate in a program that is using deferred parameter processing, as described in the previous section. If the program determines that it should cancel the statement execution instead of supplying a value for a deferred parameter, the program can call SQLCancel() to achieve this result.

```
/* COMMIT or ROLLBACK a SQL transaction */
short SQLEndTran (
    short   hdltype,            /* IN:  type of handle */
    long    txnHdl,             /* IN:  env, conn or stmt handle */
    short   compltype)          /* IN:  txn typ (COMMIT/ROLLBACK) */


/* Cancel a currently-executing SQL statement */
short SQLCancel (
    short   stmtHdl)            /* IN:  statement handle */
```

Figure 19-16.   *CLI transaction management routines*

The SQLCancel() call can also be used in a multithreaded application to cancel the effect of a SQLExecute() or SQLExecDirect() call that has not yet completed. In this situation, the thread making the original execute call will still be waiting for the call to complete, but another concurrently executing thread may call SQLCancel() using the same statement handle. The specifics of this technique, and how interruptible a CLI call is, tend to be very implementation dependent.

Processing Query Results with CLI

The CLI routines described thus far can be used to process SQL data definition statements or SQL data manipulation statements other than queries (that is, UPDATE, DELETE, and INSERT statements). For query processing, some additional CLI calls, shown in Figure 19-17, are required. The simplest way to process query results is with the SQLBindCol() and SQLFetch() calls. To carry out a query using these calls, the application program goes through the following steps (assuming a connection has already been established):

1. The program allocates a statement handle using SQLAllocHandle().

2. The program calls SQLPrepare(), passing the text of the SQL SELECT statement for the query.

3. The program calls SQLExecute() to carry out the query.

4. The program calls SQLBindCol() once for each column of query results that will be returned. Each call associates a program buffer area with a returned data column.

5. The program calls SQLFetch() to fetch a row of query results. The data value for each row in the newly fetched row is placed into the appropriate program buffer as indicated in the previous SQLBindCol() calls.

PROGRAMMING WITH SQL

6. If the query produces multiple rows, the program repeats Step 5 until the SQLFetch() call returns a value indicating that there are no more rows.

7. When all query results have been processed, the program calls SQLCloseCursor() to end access to the query results.

```
/* Bind a query results column to a program data area */
short SQLBindCol (
    long    stmtHdl,        /* IN:  statement handle */
    short   colnr,          /* IN:  column number to be bound */
    short   tgttype,        /* IN:  data type of program data area */
    void    value,          /* IN:  ptr to program data area */
    long    buflen,         /* IN:  length of program buffer */
    long    lenind)         /* IN:  ptr to length/indicator buffer */

/* Advance the cursor to the next row of query results */
short SQLFetch (
    long    stmtHdl)        /* IN:  statement handle */

/* Scroll the cursor up or down through the query results */
short SQLFetchScroll (
    long    stmtHdl,        /* IN:  statement handle */
    short   fetchdir,       /* IN:  direction (first/next/prev) */
    long    offset)         /* IN:  offset (number of rows) */

/* Get the data for a single column of query results */
short SQLGetData (
    long    stmtHdl,        /* IN:  statement handle */
    short   colnr,          /* IN:  column number to be retrieved */
    short   tgttype,        /* IN:  data type to return to program */
    void    *value,         /* IN:  ptr to buffer for column data */
    long    buflen,         /* IN:  length of program buffer */
    long    *lenind)        /* OUT: actual length and/or NULL ind */

/* Close a cursor to end access to query results */
short SQLCloseCursor (
    long    stmtHdl)        /* IN:  statement handle */
```

Figure 19-17.   *CLI query results processing routines*

```
/* Establish a cursor name for an open cursor */
short SQLSetCursorName (
    long    stmtHdl,        /* IN:  statement handle */
    char    cursname,       /* IN:  name for cursor */
    short   namelen)        /* IN:  length of cursor name */

/* Retrieve the name of an open cursor */
short SQLGetCursorName (
    long    stmtHdl,        /* IN:  statement handle */
    char    cursname,       /* OUT: buffer for returned name */
    short   buflen,         /* IN:  length of buffer */
    short   *namlen)        /* OUT: actual length of returned name */
```

Figure 19-17.   *CLI query results processing routines* (continued)

The program excerpt in Figure 19-18 shows a simple query carried out using this technique. The program is identical in function to the dblib-based program example in Figure 19-7. It's instructive to compare the two programs. The specifics of the calls

```
/* Program to display a report of sales reps over quota */
#include <sqlcli.h>                     /* header file with CLI definitions */
main()
{
    SQLHENV     env_hdl;                /* SQL-environment handle */
    SQLHDBC     conn_hdl;               /* connection handle */
    SQLHSTMT    stmt_hdl;               /* statement handle */
    SQLRETURN   status;                 /* CLI routine return status */
    char        *svr_name =  "demo";    /* server name */
    char        *user_name = "joe";     /* user name for connection */
    char        *user_pswd = "xyz";     /* user password for connection */
    char        repname[16];            /* retrieved salesperson's name */
    float       repquota;               /* retrieved quota */
    float       repsales;               /* retrieved sales */
    short       repquota_ind;           /* NULL quota indicator */
    char        stmt_buf[128];          /* buffer for SQL statement */
```

Figure 19-18.   *Retrieving CLI query results*

```
    /* Allocate handles and connect to the database */
    SQLAllocHandle(SQL_HANDLE_ENV, SQL_NULL_HANDLE, &env_hdl);
    SQLAllocHandle(SQL_HANDLE_DBC, env_hdl, &conn_hdl);
    SQLAllocHandle(SQL_HANDLE_STMT, conn_hdl, &stmt_hdl);
    SQLConnect(conn_hdl, svr_name, SQL_NTS,
                         user_name, SQL_NTS,
                         user_pswd, SQL_NTS);

    /* Request execution of the query */
    strcpy(stmt_buf, "select name, quota, sales from salesreps ");
    strcat(stmt_buf, "where sales > quota order by name");
    SQLExecDirect(stmt_hdl, stmt_buf, SQL_NTS);

    / * Bind retrieved columns to the program's buffers */
    SQLBindCol(stmt_hdl,1,SQL_C_CHAR,repname,15,NULL);
    SQLBindCol(stmt_hdl,2,SQL_C_FLOAT,&repquota,0,&quota_ind);
    SQLBindCol(stmt_hdl,3,SQL_C_FLOAT,&repsales,0,NULL);

    / * Loop through each row of query results */
    for ( ; ; ) {

       /* Fetch the next row of query results */
       if (SQLFetch(stmt_hdl) != SQL_SUCCESS)
          break;

       /* Display the retrieved data */
       printf("Name: %s\n", repname);
       if (repquota_ind < 0)
          printf("Quota is NULL\n");
       else
          printf("Quota: %f\n", repquota);
       printf("Sales: %f\n", repsales);
    }

    / * Disconnect, deallocate handles and exit */
    SQLDisconnect(conn_hdl);
    SQLFreeHandle(SQL_HANDLE_STMT, stmt_hdl);
    SQLFreeHandle(SQL_HANDLE_DBC, conn_hdl);
    SQLFreeHandle(SQL_HANDLE_ENV, env_hdl);
    exit();
```

Figure 19-18. *Retrieving CLI query results* (continued) and their parameters are quite different, but the flow of the programs and the logical sequence of calls that they make are the same.

Each call to SQLBindCol() establishes an association between one column of query results (identified by column number) and an application program buffer (identified by its address). With each call to SQLFetch(), the CLI uses this binding to copy the appropriate data value for the column into the program's buffer area. When appropriate, a second program data area is specified as the indicator-variable buffer for the column. Each call to SQLFetch() sets this program variable to indicate the actual length of the returned data value (for variable-length data) and to indicate when a NULL value is returned. When the program has finished processing all of the query results, it calls SQLCloseCursor().

The CLI routines in Figure 19-17 can also be used to implement an alternative method of processing query results. In this technique, the columns of query results are not bound to locations in the application program in advance. Instead, each call to SQLFetch() only advances the cursor to the next row of query results. It does not actually cause retrieval of data into host program data areas. Instead, a call to SQLGetData() is made to actually retrieve the data. One of the parameters of SQLGetData() specifies which column of query results is to be retrieved. The other parameters specify the data type to be returned and the location of the buffer to receive the data and an associated indicator variable value.

At the basic level, the SQLGetData() call is simply an alternative to the host-variable binding approach provided by SQLBindCol(), but SQLGetData() provides an important advantage when processing very large data items. Some databases support long binary or character-valued columns that can contain thousands or millions of bytes of data. It's usually impractical to allocate a program buffer to hold all of the data in such a column. Using SQLGetData(), the program can allocate a buffer of reasonable size and work its way through the data a few thousand bytes at a time.

It's possible to intermix the SQLBindCol() and SQLGetData() styles to process the query results of a single statement. In this case, the SQLFetch() call actually retrieves the data values for the bound columns (those for which a SQLBindCol() call has been made), but the program must explicitly call SQLGetData() to process the other columns. This technique may be especially appropriate if a query retrieves several columns of typical SQL data (names, dates, money amounts) and a column or two of long data, such as the text of a contract. Note that some CLI implementations severely restrict the ability to intermix the two styles of processing. In particular, some implementations require that all of the bound columns appear first in the left-to-right order of query results, before any columns retrieved using SQLGetData().

Scrolling Cursors

The SQL/CLI standard specifies CLI support for scrolling cursors that parallels the scrolling-cursor support originally included in the SQL2 standard for embedded SQL. The SQLFetchScroll() call, shown in Figure 19-17, provides the extended FETCH functions needed for forward/backward and random retrieval of query results. One of its parameters specifies the statement handle for the query, just as for the simple SQLFetch() call. The other two parameters specify the direction of FETCH motion (PREVIOUS, NEXT, and so on) and the offset for FETCH motions that require it (absolute and relative random row retrieval). The operation of SQLBindCol() and SQLGetData() for processing returned values is identical to that described for the SQLFetch() call.

Named Cursors

Note that the CLI doesn't include an explicit cursor declaration call to parallel the embedded SQL DECLARE CURSOR statement. Instead, SQL query text (that is, a SELECT statement) is passed to the CLI for execution in the same manner as any other SQL statement, using either a SQLExecDirect() call or SQLPrepare() / SQLExecute() call sequence. The results of the query are identified by the statement handle in subsequent SQLFetch(), SQLBindCol(), and similar calls. For these purposes, the statement handle takes the place of the cursor name used in embedded SQL.

A problem with this scheme arises in the case of positioned (cursor-based) updates and positioned deletes. As described in Chapter 17, a positioned database UPDATE or DELETE statement (UPDATE... WHERE CURRENT OF or DELETE... WHERE CURRENT OF) can be used to modify or delete the current (that is, just fetched) row of query results. These embedded SQL statements use the cursor name to identify the particular row to be processed, since an application program may have more than one cursor open at a time to process more than one set of query results.

To support positioned updates, the CLI provides the SQLSetCursorName() call shown in Figure 19-17. The call is used to assign a cursor name, specified as one of its parameters, to a set of query results, identified by the statement handle that produced them. Once the call has been made, the cursor name can be used in subsequent positioned UPDATE or DELETE statements, which can be passed to the CLI for execution. A companion call, SQLGetCursorName(), can be used to obtain a previously assigned cursor name, given its statement handle.

Dynamic Query Processing with CLI

If the columns to be retrieved by a SQL query are not known in advance when a program is developed, the program can use the query-processing calls in Figure 19-19 to determine the characteristics of the query results at runtime. These calls implement the same type of dynamic SQL query-processing capability that was described for

```
/* Determine the number of result columns in a query */
short SQLNumResultCols (
    long   stmtHdl,              /* IN:  statement handle */
    short *colcount)             /* OUT: returned number of columns */

/* Determine the characteristics of a column of query results */
short SQLDescribeCol (
    long   stmtHdl,              /* IN:  statement handle */
    short  colnr,                /* IN:  number of column to describe */
    char  *colname,              /* OUT: name of query results column */
    short  buflen,               /* IN:  length of column name buffer */
    short *namlen,               /* OUT: actual column name length */
    short *coltype,              /* OUT: returned column data type code */
    short *colsize,              /* OUT: returned column data length */
    short *decdigits,            /* OUT: returned # of digits in column */
    short *nullable)             /* OUT: can column have NULL values */

/* Obtain detailed info about a column of query results */
short SQLColAttribute (
    long   stmtHdl,              /* IN:  statement handle */
    short  colnr,                /* IN:  number of column to describe */
    short  attrcode,             /* IN:  code of attribute to retrieve */
    char  *attrinfo,             /* OUT: buffer for string attr. info */
    short  buflen,               /* IN:  length of col attribute buffer */
    short *actlen,               /* OUT: actual attribute info length */
    int   *numattr)              /* OUT: returned integer attr. info */

/* Retrieve frequently used info from a CLI descriptor */
short SQLGetDescRec (
    long   descHdl,              /* IN:  descriptor handle */
    short  recnr,                /* IN:  descriptor record number */
    char  *name,                 /* OUT: name of item being described */
    short  buflen,               /* IN:  length of name buffer */
    short *namlen,               /* OUT: actual length of returned name */
    short *datatype,             /* OUT: data type code for item */
    short *subtype,              /* OUT: data type subcode for item */
    short *length,               /* OUT: length of item */
    short *precis,               /* OUT: precision of item, if numeric */
    short *scale,                /* OUT: scale of item, if numeric */
    short *nullable)             /* OUT: can item have NULL values */
```

Figure 19-19. *CLI dynamic query-processing calls*

```
/* Set frequently used info in a CLI descriptor */
short SQLSetDescRec (
    long    descHdl,            /* IN:  descriptor handle */
    short   recnr,              /* IN:  descriptor record number */
    short   datatype,           /* IN:  data type code for item */
    short   subtype,            /* IN:  data type subcode for item */
    short   length,             /* IN:  length of item */
    short   precis,             /* IN:  precision of item, if numeric */
    short   scale,              /* IN:  scale of item, if numeric */
    void    *databuf,           /* IN:  data buffer address for item */
    short   buflen,             /* IN:  data buffer length */
    short   *indbuf)            /* IN:  indicator buffer addr for item */

/* Get detailed info about an item described by a CLI descriptor */
short SQLGetDescField (
    long    descHdl,            /* IN:  descriptor handle */
    short   recnr,              /* IN:  descriptor record number */
    short   attrcode,           /* IN:  code of attribute to describe */
    void    *attrinfo,          /* IN:  buffer for attribute info */
    short   buflen,             /* IN:  length of attribute info */
    short   *actlen)            /* OUT: actual length of returned info */

/* Set value of an item described by a CLI descriptor */
short SQLSetDescField (
    long    descHdl,            /* IN:  descriptor handle */
    short   recnr,              /* IN:  descriptor record number */
    short   attrcode,           /* IN:  code of attribute to describe */
    void    *attrinfo,          /* IN:  buffer with attribute value */
    short   buflen)             /* IN:  length of attribute info */

/* Copy a CLI descriptor contents into another descriptor */
short SQLCopyDesc (
    long    indscHdl,           /* IN:  source descriptor handle */
    long    outdscHdl)          /* IN:  destination descriptor handle */
```

Figure 19-19. *CLI dynamic query-processing calls* (continued)

dynamic embedded SQL in Chapter 18. Here are the steps for dynamic query
processing using CLI:

1. The program allocates a statement handle using SQLAllocHandle().

2. The program calls Prepare(), passing the text of the SQL SELECT statement
   for the query.

3. The program calls SQLExecute() to carry out the query.

4. The program calls SQLNumResultCols() to determine the number of
   columns of query results.

5. The program calls SQLDescribeCol() once for each column of returned
   query results to determine its data type, size, whether it may contain NULL
   values, and so on.

6. The program allocates memory to receive the returned query results and
   binds these memory locations to the columns by calling SQLBindCol()
   once for each column.

7. The program calls SQLFetch() to fetch a row of query results. The
   SQLFetch() call advances the cursor to the next row of query results and
   returns each column of results into the appropriate area in the application
   program, as specified in the SQLBindCol() calls.

8. If the query produces multiple rows, the program repeats Step 7 until the
   SQLFetch() call returns a value indicating that there are no more rows.

9. When all query results have been processed, the program calls
   SQLCloseCursor() to end access to the query results.

Figure 19-20 shows a program that uses these techniques to process a dynamic
query. The program is identical in its concept and purpose to the embedded dynamic
SQL query program shown in Figure 18-9 and the dblib-based dynamic SQL query
program shown in Figure 19-10. Once again, it's instructive to compare the program
examples to enhance your understanding of dynamic query processing. The API calls
have quite different names, but the sequence of functions calls for the dblib program
(Figure 19-10) and the CLI program (Figure 19-20) are nearly identical. The dbcmd() /
dbsqlexec() / dbresults() call sequence is replaced by SQLExecDirect().
(In this case, the query will be executed only once, so there's no advantage to using
SQLPrepare() and SQLExecute() separately.) The dbnumcols() call becomes
SQLNumResultCols(). The calls to obtain column information (dbcolname(),
dbcoltype(), dbcollen()) become a single call to SQLDescribeCol(). The
dbnextrow() call becomes SQLFetch(). All of the other changes in the program
are made to support these changes in the API functions.

```
main()
{
    /* This is a simple general-purpose query program.  It prompts
       the user for a table name, and then asks the user which
       columns of the table are to be included in the query.  After
       the user's selections are complete, the program runs the
       requested query and displays the results.
    */

    SQLHENV     env_hdl;                /* SQL-environment handle */
    SQLHDBC     conn_hdl;               /* connection handle */
    SQLHSTMT    stmt1_hdl;              /* statement handle for main query */
    SQLHSTMT    stmt2_hdl;              /* statement handle for col name query */
    SQLRETURN   status;                 /* CLI routine return status */
    char        *svr_name = "demo";     /* server name */
    char        *user_name = "joe";     /* user name for connection */
    char        *user_pswd = "xyz";     /* user password for connection */
    char        stmtbuf[2001];          /* main SQL query text to be executed */
    char        stmt2buf[2001];         /* SQL text for column name query */
    char        querytbl[32];           /* user-specified query table */
    char        querycol[32];           /* user-specified column */
    int         first_col = 0;          /* is this the first column chosen? */
    short       colcount;               /* number of columns of query results */
    char        *nameptr;               /* address for CLI to return column name */
    short       namelen;                /* returned CLI column name length */
    short       type;                   /* CLI data type code for column */
    short       size;                   /* returned CLI column size */
    short       digits;                 /* returned CLI column # digits */
    short       nullable;               /* returned CLI nullability */
    short       i;                      /* index for columns */
    char        inbuf[101];             /* inp ut entered by user */
    char        *item_name[100];        /* array to track column names */
    char        *item_data[100];        /* array to track column buffers */
    int         item_ind[100];          /* array of indicator variables */
    short       item_type[100];         /* array to track column data types */
    char        *dataptr;               /* address of buffer for current column */

    /* Open a connection to the demo database via CLI */
    SQLAllocHandle(SQL_HANDLE_ENV, SQL_NULL_HANDLE, &env_hdl);
    SQLAllocHandle(SQL_HANDLE_DBC, env_hdl, &conn_hdl);
    SQLAllocHandle(SQL_HANDLE_STMT, conn_hdl, &stmt1_hdl);
    SQLAllocHandle(SQL_HANDLE_STMT, conn_hdl, &stmt2_hdl);
    SQLConnect(conn_hdl, svr_name, SQL_NTS,
                            user_name, SQL_NTS,
                            user_pswd, SQL_NTS);
```

Figure 19-20.   *Using CLI for a dynamic query*

```
    /* Prompt the user for which table to query * /
    printf("*** Mini-Query Program ***\n");
    printf("Enter name of table for query: ");
    gets(querytbl);

    /* Start the SELECT statement in the buffer */
    strcpy(stmtbuf, "select ");

    /* Query the Information Schema to get column names */
    strcpy(stmt2buf, "select column_name from columns where table_name = ");
    strcat(stmt2buf, querytbl);
    SQLExecDirect(stmt2_hdl, stmt2buf, SQL_NTS);

    /* Process the results of the query */
    SQLBindCol(stmt2_hdl, 1, SQL_C_CHAR, querycol, 31, (int *)0);
    while (status = SQLFetch(stmt2_hdl) == SQL_SUCCESS) {
        printf("Include column %s (y/n)? ", querycol);
        gets(inbuf);
        if (inbuf[0] == 'y') {
            /* User wants the column, add it to the select list */
            if (first_col++ > 0) strcat(stmtbuf,", ");
            strcat(stmtbuf, querycol);
        }
    }

    /* Finish the SELECT statement with a FROM clause */
    strcat(stmtbuf, "from ");
    strcat(stmtbuf, querytbl);

    /* Execute the query and get ready to fetch query results */
    SQLExecDirect(stmt1_hdl, stmtbuf, SQL_NTS);

    /* Ask CLI to describe each column, allocate memory & bind it */
    SQLNumResultCols(stmt1_hdl, &colcount);
    for (i =0; i < colcount; i++) {
        item_name[i] = nameptr = malloc(32);
        indptr = &item_ind[i];
        SQLDescribeCol(stmt1_hdl, i, nameptr, 32, &namelen, &type, &size,
                                                  &digits, &nullable);

        switch(type) {

        case SQL_CHAR:
        case SQL_VARCHAR:
            /* Allocate buffer for string & bind the column to it */
            item_data[i] = dataptr = malloc(size+1);
```

Figure 19-20. *Using CLI for a dynamic query* (continued)

```
            item_type[i] = SQL_C_CHAR;
            SQLBindCol(stmt1_hdl, i, SQL_C_CHAR, dataptr, size+1, indptr);
            break;

    case SQL_TYPE_DATE:
    case SQL_TYPE_TIME:
    case SQL_TYPE_TIME_WITH_TIMEZONE:
    case SQL_TYPE_TIMESTAMP:
    case SQL_TYPE_TIMESTAMP_WITH_TIMEZONE:
    case SQL_INTERVAL_DAY:
    case SQL_INTERVAL_DAY_TO_HOUR:
    case SQL_INTERVAL_DAY_TO_MINUTE:
    case SQL_INTERVAL_DAY_TO_SECOND:
    case SQL_INTERVAL_HOUR:
    case SQL_INTERVAL_HOUR_TO_MINUTE:
    case SQL_INTERVAL_HOUR_TO_SECOND:
    case SQL_INTERVAL_MINUTE:
    case SQL_INTERVAL_MINUTE_TO_SECOND:
    case SQL_INTERVAL_MONTH:
    case SQL_INTERVAL_SECOND:
    case SQL_INTERVAL_YEAR:
    case SQL_INTERVAL_YEAR_TO_MONTH:
            /* Request ODBC/CLI conversion of these types to C-strings */
            item_data[i] = dataptr = malloc(31);
            item_type[i] = SQL_C_CHAR;
            SQLBindCol(stmt1_hdl, i, SQL_C_CHAR, dataptr, 31, indptr);
            break;

    case SQL_INTEGER:
    case SQL_SMALLINT:
            /* Convert these types to C long integers */
            item_data[i] = dataptr = malloc(sizeof(integer));
            item_type[i] = SQL_C_SLONG;
            SQLBindCol(stmt1_hdl, i, SQL_C_SLONG, dataptr, sizeof(integer), indptr);
            break;
    case SQL_NUMERIC:
    case SQL_DECIMAL:
    case SQL_FLOAT:
    case SQL_REAL:

    case SQL_DOUBLE:
            /* For illustration, convert these types to C double floats */
            item_data[i] = dataptr = malloc(sizeof(long));
            item_type[i] = SQL_C_DOUBLE;
            SQLBindCol(stmt1_hdl, i, SQL_C_DOUBLE, dataptr, sizeof(double), indptr);
            break;
```

Figure 19-20.   *Using CLI for a dynamic query* (continued)

```
      default:
         /* For simplicity, we don't handle bit strings, etc. */
         printf("Cannot handle data type %d\n", (integer)type);
         exit();
      }
   }

/* Fetch and display the rows of query results */
while (status = SQLFetch(stmt1_hdl) == SQL_SUCCESS) {

   /* Loop, printing data for each column of the row /
   printf("\n");
   for(i = 0; i < colcount; i++) {

      /* Print column label */
      printf("Column # %d (%s): ", i+1, item_name[i]);

      /* Check indicator variable for NULL indication */
      if (item_ind[i] == SQL_NULL_DATA){
         puts("is NULL!\n");
         continue;
      }

      /* Handle each returned (maybe converted) data type separately /
      switch(item_type[i]) {
      case SQL_C_CHAR:
         /* Returned as text data - just display it */
         puts(item_data[i]);
         break;

      case SQL_C_SLONG:
         /* Four-byte integer data - convert & display it */
         printf("%ld", *((int *)(item_data[i])));
         break;

      case SQL_C_DOUBLE:
         /* Floating-point data  convert & display it */
         printf("%lf", *((double *)(item_data[i])));
         break;

      }
   }
}
```

Figure 19-20.   *Using CLI for a dynamic query* (continued)

```
        printf("\nEnd of data.\n"):

        /* Clean up allocated storage */
        for (i = 0; i < colcount; i++) {
            free(item_data[i]);
            free(item_name[i]);
        }
        SQLDisconnect(conn_hdl);
        SQLFreeHandle(SQL_HANDLE_STMT, stmt1_hdl);
        SQLFreeHandle(SQL_HANDLE_STMT, stmt2_hdl);
        SQLFreeHandle(SQL_HANDLE_DBC, conn_hdl);
        SQLFreeHandle(SQL_HANDLE_ENV, env_hdl);

        exit();
    }
```

Figure 19-20.   *Using CLI for a dynamic query* (continued)

If you compare the program in Figure 19-20 with the corresponding embedded dynamic SQL program in Figure 18-9, one of the major differences is embedded SQL's use of the special SQL Data Area (SQLDA) for column binding and column description. The CLI splits these functions between the SQLNumResultCols(), SQLDescribeCol(), and SQLBindCol() functions, and most programmers find the CLI structure easier to use and understand. However, the CLI provides an alternative, lower-level method that offers capabilities like those provided by the embedded SQLDA.

The alternative CLI method for dynamic query processing involves CLI *descriptors*. A CLI descriptor contains low-level information about a statement parameter (a parameter descriptor) or a column of query results (a row descriptor). The information in the descriptor is like that contained in the variable area of the SQLDA—the column or parameter's name, data type and subtype, length, data buffer location, NULL indicator location, and so on. The parameter descriptors and row descriptors thus correspond to the input and output SQLDAs provided by some DBMS brands in their embedded dynamic SQL implementations.

CLI descriptors are identified by descriptor handles. The CLI provides a default set of descriptors for parameters and query results columns when a statement is prepared. Alternatively, the program can allocate its own descriptors and use them. The handles of the descriptors for a statement are considered statement attributes, and they are associated with a particular statement handle. The descriptor handle values can be retrieved and set by the application program using the attribute management routines, described later in the section "CLI Attributes."

Two calls are used to retrieve information from a descriptor, given its handle. The SQLGetDescField() call retrieves a particular field of a descriptor, which is identified by a code value. It is typically used to obtain the data type or length of a query results column, for example. The SQLGetDescRec() call retrieves many pieces of information in one call, including the column or parameter name, data type and subtype, length, precision and scale, and whether it may contain NULL values. A corresponding set of calls is used to place information into a descriptor. The SQLSetDescField() call sets the value of a single piece of information within a descriptor. The SQLSetDescRec() sets multiple values in a single call, including the data type and subtype, length, precision and scale, and nullability. For convenience, the CLI provides a SQLCopyDesc() call that copies all of the values from one descriptor to another.

CLI Errors and Diagnostic Information

Each CLI function returns a short integer value that indicates its completion status. If the completion status indicates an error, the error-handling CLI calls shown in Figure 19-21 can be used to obtain more information about the error and diagnose it. The most basic error-handling call is SQLError(). The application program passes the environment, connection, and statement handles and is returned the SQL2 SQLSTATE result code, the native error code of the subsystem producing the error, and an error message in text form.

The SQLError() routine actually retrieves specific, frequently used information from the CLI diagnostics area. The other error-handling routines provide more complete information through direct access to the diagnostic records created and maintained by the CLI. In general, a CLI call can produce multiple errors, which result in multiple diagnostic records. The SQLGetDiagRec() call retrieves an individual diagnostic record, by record number. Through repeated calls, the application program can retrieve complete information about all error records produced by a CLI call. Even more complete information can be obtained by interrogating individual diagnostic fields within the record. This capability is provided by the SQLGetDiagField() call.

Although not strictly an error-processing function, the SQLRowCount() function, like the error-handling functions, is called *after* a previous CLI SQLExecute() call. It is used to determine the impact of the previous statement when it was successful. A returned value indicates the number of rows of data affected by the previously executed statement. (For example, the value 4 would be returned for a searched UPDATE statement that updates four rows.)

CLI Attributes

The CLI provides a number of options that control some of the details of its processing. Some of these control relatively minor but critical details, such as whether the CLI should automatically assume that parameters passed as string values are NULL-terminated. Others control broader aspects of CLI operation, such as the scrollability of cursors.

The CLI gives application programs the capability to control these processing options through a set of CLI *attributes*. The attributes are structured in a hierarchy, paralleling the environment/connection/statement hierarchy of the CLI handle structure. Environment

```
/* Retrieve error information associated with a previous CLI call */
short SQLError (
    long    envHdl,             /* IN:  environment handle */
    long    connHdl,            /* IN:  connection handle */
    long    stmtHdl,            /* IN:  statement handle */
    char    *sqlstate,          /* OUT: five-character SQLSTATE value */
    long    *nativeerr,         /* OUT: returned native error code */
    char    *msgbuf,            /* OUT: buffer for err message text */
    short   buflen,             /* IN:  length of err msg text buffer */
    short   *msglen)            /* OUT: returned actual msg length */

/* Determine number of rows affected by previous SQL statement */
short SQLRowCount (
    long    stmtHdl,            /* IN:  statement handle */
    long    *rowcnt)            /* OUT: number of rows */

/* Retrieve info from one of the CLI diagnostic error records */
short SQLGetDiagRec (
    short   hdltype,            /* IN:  handle type code */
    long    inHdl,             /* IN:  CLI handle */
    short   recnr,             /* IN:  requested err record number */
    char    *sqlstate,         /* OUT: returned 5-char SQLSTATE code */
    long    *nativeerr,        /* OUT: returned native error code */
    char    *msgbuf,           /* OUT: buffer for err message text */
    short   buflen,            /* IN:  length of err msg text buffer */
    short   *msglen)           /* OUT: returned actual msg length */

/* Retrieve a field from one of the CLI diagnostic error records */
short SQLGetDiagField (
    short   hdltype,            /* IN:  handle type code */
    long    inHdl,             /* IN:  CLI handle */
    short   recnr,             /* IN:  requested err record number */
    short   diagid,            /* IN:  diagnostic field id */
    void    *diaginfo,         /* OUT: returned diagnostic info */
    short   buflen,            /* IN:  length of diagonal info buffer */
    short   *actlen)           /* OUT: returned actual info length */
```

Figure 19-21.   *CLI error-handling routines*

attributes control overall operational options. Connection options apply to a particular connection created by the SQLConnect() call but may vary from one connection to another. Statement attributes apply to the processing of an individual statement, identified by a CLI statement handle.

A set of CLI calls, shown in Figure 19-22, is used by an application program to control attributes. The get calls (SQLGetEnvAttr(), SQLGetConnectAttr(), and `SQLGetStmtAttr()`) obtain current attribute values. The `set` calls (`SQLSetEnvAttr()`, `SQLSetConnectAttr()`, and `SQLSetStmtAttr()`) modify the current attribute values. In all of the calls, the particular attribute being processed is indicated by a code value.

Although the CLI standard provides this elaborate attribute structure, it actually specifies relatively few attributes. The single environment attribute specified is NULL TERMINATION; it controls null-terminated strings. The single connection attribute specified controls whether the CLI automatically populates a parameter descriptor when a statement is prepared or executed. Statement-level attributes control the scrollability and sensitivity of cursors. Perhaps the most important of the CLI-specified attributes are the handles of the four CLI descriptors that may be associated with a statement (two parameter descriptors and two row descriptors). The calls in Figure 19-22 are used to obtain and set these descriptor handles when using descriptor-based statement processing.

The ODBC API, on which the SQL/CLI standard was originally based, includes many more attributes. For example, ODBC connection attributes can be used to specify a read-only connection, to enable asynchronous statement processing, to specify the timeout for a connection request, and so on. ODBC environment attributes control automatic translation of ODBC calls from earlier versions of the ODBC standard. ODBC statement attributes control transaction isolation levels, specify whether a cursor is scrollable, and limit the number of rows of query results that might be generated by a runaway query.

CLI Information Calls

The CLI includes three specific calls that can be used to obtain information about the particular CLI implementation. In general, these calls will not be used by an application program written for a specific purpose. They are needed by general-purpose programs (such as a query or report writing program) that need to determine the specific characteristics of the CLI they are using. The calls are shown in Figure 19-23.

The `SQLGetFunctions()` call is used to determine whether a specific implementation supports a particular CLI function call. It is called with a function code value corresponding to one of the CLI functions, and returns a parameter indicating whether the function is supported. The `SQLGetInfo()` call is used to obtain much more detailed information about a CLI implementation, such as the maximum lengths of table and user names, whether the DBMS supports outer joins or transactions, and whether SQL identifiers are case-sensitive.

The `SQLGetTypeInfo()` call is used to obtain information about a particular supported data type or about all types supported via the CLI interface. The call actually behaves as if it were a query against a system catalog of data type information. It produces a set of query results rows, each row containing information about one specific supported type. The supplied information indicates the name of the type, its size, whether it is nullable, whether it is searchable, and so on.

```
/* Obtain the value of a SQL-environment attribute */
short SQLGetEnvAttr(
    long    envHdl,           /* IN:  environment handle */
    long    attrCode,         /* IN:  integer attribute code */
    void    *rtnVal,          /* OUT: return value */
    long    bufLen,           /* IN:  length of rtnVal buffer */
    long    *strLen)          /* OUT: length of actual data */

/* Set the value of a SQL-environment attribute */
short SQLSetEnvAttr(
    long    envHdl,           /* IN:  environment handle */
    long    attrCode,         /* IN:  integer attribute code */
    void    *attrVal,         /* IN:  new attribute value */
    long    *strLen)          /* IN:  length of data */

/* Obtain the value of a SQL-connection attribute */
short SQLGetConnectAttr(
    long    connHdl,          /* IN:  connection handle */
    long    attrCode,         /* IN:  integer attribute code */
    void    *rtnVal,          /* OUT: return value */
    long    bufLen,           /* IN:  length of rtnVal buffer */
    long    *strLen)          /* OUT: length of actual data */

/* Set the value of a SQL-connection attribute */
short SQLSetConnectAttr(
    long    connHdl,          /* IN:  connection handle */
    long    attrCode,         /* IN:  integer attribute code */
    void    *attrVal,         /* IN:  new attribute value */
    long    *strLen)          /* IN:  length of data */

/* Obtain the value of a SQL-statement attribute */
short SQLGetStmtAttr(
    long    stmtHdl,          /* IN:  statement handle */
    long    attrCode,         /* IN:  integer attribute code */
    void    *rtnVal,          /* OUT: return value */
    long    bufLen,           /* IN:  length of rtnVal buffer */
    long    *strLen)          /* OUT: length of actual data */

/* Set the value of a SQL-statement attribute */
short SQLSetStmtAttr(
    long    stmtHdl,          /* IN:  statement handle */
    long    attrCode,         /* IN:  integer attribute code */
    void    *attrVal,         /* IN:  new attribute value */
    long    *strLen)          /* IN:  length of data */
```

Figure 19-22.   *CLI attribute management routines*

```
/* Retrieve detailed info about capabilities of a CLI implementation */
short SQLGetInfo (
    long    connHdl,            /* IN:  connection handle */
    short   infotype,           /* IN:  type of info requested */
    void   *infoval,            /* OUT: buffer for retrieved info */
    short   buflen,             /* IN:  length of info buffer */
    short  *infolen)            /* OUT: returned info actual length */

/* Determine number of rows affected by previous SQL statement */
short SQLGetFunctions (
    long    connHdl,            /* IN:  connection handle */
    short   functid,            /* IN:  function id code */
    short  *supported)          /* OUT: whether function supported */

/* Determine information about supported data types */
short SQLGetTypeInfo (
    long    stmtHdl,            /* IN:  statement handle */
    short   datatype)           /* IN:  ALL TYPES or type requested */
```

Figure 19-23.   *CLI implementation information routines*

The ODBC API

Microsoft originally developed the Open Database Connectivity (ODBC) API to
provide a database-brand-independent API for database access on its Windows
operating systems. The early ODBC API became the foundation for the SQL/CLI
standard, which is now the official ANSI/ISO standard for a SQL call-level interface.
The original ODBC API was extended and modified during the standardization
process to create the SQL/CLI specification. With the introduction of ODBC release 3.0,
Microsoft brought ODBC into conformance with the SQL/CLI standard. With this
revision, ODBC becomes a superset of the SQL/CLI specification.

   ODBC goes beyond the SQL/CLI capabilities in several areas, in part because
Microsoft's goals for ODBC were broader than simply creating a standardized database
access API. Microsoft also wanted to allow a single Windows application program to
be able to concurrently access several different databases using the ODBC API. It also
wanted to provide a structure where database vendors could support ODBC without
giving up their proprietary APIs, and where the software that provided ODBC support
for a particular brand of DBMS could be distributed by the database vendor and
installed on Windows-based client systems as needed. The layered structure of ODBC
and special ODBC management calls provide these capabilities.

PROGRAMMING
WITH SQL

The Structure of ODBC

The structure of ODBC as it is provided on Windows-based or other operating systems is shown in Figure 19-24. There are three basic layers to the ODBC software:

- **Callable API**. At the top layer, ODBC provides a single callable database access API that can be used by all application programs. The API is packaged as a dynamic-linked library (DLL), which is an integral part of the various Windows operating systems.

- **ODBC drivers**. At the bottom layer of the ODBC structure is a collection of ODBC drivers. There is a separate driver for each of the DBMS brands. The purpose of the driver is to translate the standardized ODBC calls into the appropriate call(s) for the specific DBMS that it supports. Each driver can be independently installed on a particular computer system. This allows the DBMS vendors to provide an ODBC driver for their particular brand of DBMS and distribute the driver independent of the Windows operating system software. If the database resides on the same system as the ODBC driver, the driver is usually linked directly to the database's native API code. If the database is to be accessed over a network, the driver may call a native DBMS client to handle the client/server connection, or the driver might handle the network connection itself.

- **Driver manager**. In the middle layer of the ODBC structure is the ODBC driver manager. Its role is to load and unload the various ODBC drivers, on request from application programs. The driver manager is also responsible for routing the API calls made by application programs to the appropriate driver for execution.

When an application program wants to access a database via ODBC, it goes through the same initiation sequence specified by the SQL/CLI standard. The program allocates an environment handle, then a connection handle, and then calls SQLConnect(), specifying the particular data source to be accessed. When it receives the SQLConnect() call, the ODBC driver manager examines the connection information provided and determines the appropriate ODBC driver that is needed. The driver manager loads the driver into memory if it's not already being used by another application program.

Subsequent calls by the application program on this particular CLI/ODBC connection are routed to this driver. The application program can, if appropriate, make other SQLConnect() calls for other data sources that will cause the driver manager to concurrently load other drivers for other DBMS brands. The application program can then use ODBC to communicate with two or more different databases, of different brands, using a uniform API.

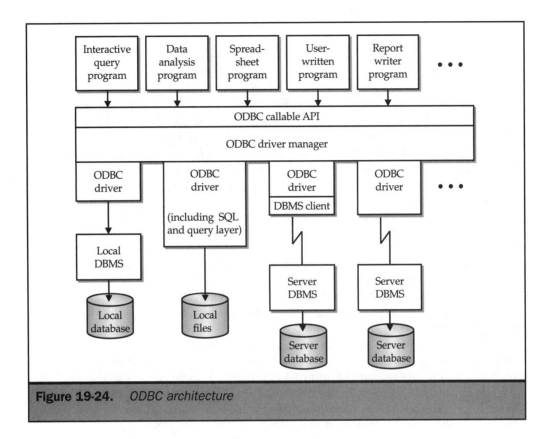

Figure 19-24. *ODBC architecture*

ODBC and DBMS Independence

By providing a uniform API and its driver manager architecture, ODBC goes a long way toward providing a cross-vendor API for database access, but it's impossible to provide fully transparent access. The ODBC drivers for the various database systems can easily mask cosmetic differences in their SQL dialects and API suites, but more fundamental differences are difficult or impossible to mask. ODBC provides a partial solution to this problem by providing several different levels of ODBC capability, and by making each ODBC driver self-describing through the ODBC/CLI calls that return information about general functionality, supported functions, and supported data types. However, the existence of different capability levels and profiles effectively pushes the DBMS differences right back into the application program, which must deal with this nonuniformity of ODBC drivers. In practice, the vast majority of application programs rely on only the basic, core set of ODBC functionality and don't bother with more advanced features or profiles.

ODBC Catalog Functions

One of the areas where ODBC offers capability beyond the SQL/CLI standard is the retrieval of information about the structure of a database from its system catalog. As a part of the ANSI/ISO SQL standard, the CLI assumes that this information (about tables, columns, privileges, and so forth) is available through the SQL2 Information Schema, as described in Chapter 16. ODBC doesn't assume the presence of an Information Schema. Instead, it provides a set of specialized functions, shown in Table 19-4, that provide information about the structure of a data source. By calling these functions and processing their results, an application program can determine, at runtime, information about the tables, columns, privileges, primary keys, foreign keys, and stored procedures that form the structure of a data source.

The ODBC catalog functions typically aren't needed by an application program that is written for a specific purpose. However, they are essential for a general-purpose program, such as a query program, report generator, or data analysis tool. The catalog functions can be called any time after a connection to a data source has been made. For example, a report writing program might call SQLConnect() and then immediately call SQLTables() to determine which tables are available in the target data source. The tables could then be presented in a list on the screen, allowing the user to select which table should be used to generate a report.

All of the catalog functions return their information as if they were a set of query results. The application program uses the techniques already described for CLI query processing to bind the columns of returned information to program variable areas. The program then calls SQLFetch() to work its way through the returned information. For example, in the results returned by the SQLTables() call, each SQLFetch() retrieves information about one table in the data source.

CLI Return Value	Meaning
0	Statement completed successfully
1	Successful completion with warning
100	No data found (when retrieving query results)
99	Data needed (required dynamic parameter missing)
−1	Error during SQL statement execution
−2	Error—invalid handle supplied in call

Table 19-4.   *ODBC Catalog Functions*

Extended ODBC Capabilities

ODBC provides a set of extended capabilities beyond those specified in the SQL/CLI standard. Many of the capabilities are designed to improve the performance of ODBC-based applications by minimizing the number of ODBC function calls an application program must make and/or the amount of network traffic generated by the ODBC calls. Other capabilities provide useful features for maintaining database independence or aid an application program in the database connection process. Some of the capabilities are provided through the additional set of ODBC function calls shown in Table 19-5. Others are provided through statement or connection attributes. Many of these additional capabilities were introduced in the 3.0 revision of ODBC and are not yet supported by most ODBC drivers or ODBC-based applications.

Function	Description
SQLBrowseConnect()	Supplies information about available ODBC data sources and the attributes required to connect to each
SQLDrivers()	Returns a list of the available drivers and driver attribute names
SQLDriverConnect()	Works as an extended form of the SQLConnect() call for passing additional connection information
SQLNumParams()	Returns the number of parameters in a previously prepared SQL statement
SQLBindParameter()	Provides extended functionality beyond the SQL/CLI SQLBindParam() call
SQLDescribeParam()	Returns information about a parameter
SQLBulkOperations()	Performs bulk insertion and bookmark operations
SQLMoreResults()	Determines whether more results are available for a statement
SQLSetPos()	Sets the cursor position within a retrieved set of query results for positioned operations
SQLNativeSQL()	Returns the native SQL translation of a supplied ODBC-compliant SQL statement text

Table 19-5. *Additional ODBC Functions*

Extended Connection Capabilities

Two of the extended ODBC features are focused on the connection process. *Connection browsing* is designed to simplify the data source connection process and make it more database independent. SQLBrowseConnect() supports an iterative style of connection for access to ODBC data sources. An application program first calls the function with basic information about the target data source, and the function returns additional connection attributes needed (such as a user name or password). The application program can obtain this information (for example, by prompting the user) and then recalls SQLBrowseConnect() with the additional information. The cycle continues until the application has determined all of the information required for a successful SQLConnect() call.

The *connection pooling* capability is designed to improve the efficiency of ODBC connect/disconnect processing in a client/server environment. When connection pooling is activated, ODBC does not actually terminate network connections upon receiving a SQLDisconnect() call. Instead, the connections are held open in an idle state for some period of time and reused if a SQLConnect() call is made for the same data source. This reuse of connections can significantly cut down the network and login/logout overhead in client/server applications that involve short transactions and high transaction rates.

SQL Dialect Translation

ODBC specifies not just a set of API calls, but also a standard SQL language dialect that is a subset of the SQL2 standard. It is the responsibility of ODBC drivers to translate the ODBC dialect into statements appropriate for the target data source (for example, modifying date/time literals, quote conventions, keywords, and so on). The SQLNativeSQL() call allows the application program to see the effect of this translation. ODBC also supports escape sequences that allow an application program to more explicitly direct the translation of SQL features that tend to be less consistent across SQL dialects, such as outer joins and pattern-matching search conditions.

Asynchronous Execution

An ODBC driver may support asynchronous execution of ODBC functions. When an application program makes an asynchronous mode ODBC call, ODBC initiates the required processing (usually statement preparation or execution) and then immediately returns control to the application program. The application program can proceed with other work and later resynchronize with the ODBC function to determine its completion status. Asynchronous execution can be requested on a per-connection or a per-statement basis. In some cases, asynchronously executing functions can be terminated with a SQLCancel() call, giving the application program a method for aborting long-running ODBC operations.

Statement-Processing Efficiency

Each ODBC call to execute a SQL statement can involve a significant amount of overhead, especially if the data source involves a client/server network connection. To reduce this overhead, an ODBC driver may support *statement batches.* With this capability, an application program can pass a sequence of two or more SQL statements as a batch to be executed in a single SQLExecDirect() or SQLExecute() call. For example, a series of a dozen INSERT or UPDATE statements could be executed as a batch in this way. It can significantly reduce network traffic in a client/server environment, but it complicates error detection and recovery, which tend to become driver-specific when statement batches are used.

Many DBMS products address the efficiency of multistatement transactions in a different way. They support stored procedures within the database itself, which can collect a sequence of SQL operations, together with the associated flow-control logic, and allow the statements to be invoked with a single call to the procedure. ODBC provides a set of capabilities that allow an application program to directly call a stored procedure in the target data source. For databases that allow stored procedure parameters to be passed by name, ODBC allows parameters to be bound by name instead of by position. For data sources that provide metadata information about stored procedure parameters, the SQLDescribeParam() call allows the application program to determine, at runtime, the required parameter data type. Output parameters of a stored procedure are supported either through SQLBindParam() (in which case, the application program's data buffer is modified upon return from the SQLExecute() or SQLExecDirect() call) or through SQLGetData(), which allows retrieval of long returned data.

Two other extended ODBC capabilities provide efficiency when a single SQL statement (such as an INSERT or UPDATE statement) is to be executed repeatedly. Both address the binding of parameters for this situation. With the *binding offset* feature, once a statement parameter has been bound and the statement has been executed, ODBC allows the application program to change its binding for the next statement execution by specifying a new memory location as an offset from the original location. This is an effective way of binding a parameter to individual items in an array for repeated statement execution. In general, modifying an offset value is much more efficient than rebinding the parameter with repeated calls to SQLBindParam().

ODBC *parameter arrays* provide an alternative mechanism for an application program to pass multiple sets of parameter values in a single call. For example, if an application program needs to insert multiple rows into a table, it can request execution of a parameterized INSERT statement and bind the parameters to arrays of data values. The effective result is as if multiple INSERT statements are performed—one for each set of parameter values. ODBC supports both row-wise parameter arrays (each array element holds one set of parameter values) or columnwise parameter arrays (each parameter value is bound to its own individual array, which holds its values).

Query-Processing Efficiency

In a client/server environment, the network overhead involved in fetching many rows of query results can be very substantial. To cut this overhead, an ODBC driver may support multirow fetches through the ODBC *block cursor* capability. With a block cursor, each SQLFetch() or SQLFetchScroll() call retrieves multiple rows (termed the *current rowset* of the cursor) from the data source. The application must bind the returned columns to arrays to hold the multiple rows of fetched data. Either row-wise or columnwise binding of the rowset data is supported, using the same techniques as those used for parameter arrays. In addition, the SQLSetPos() function may be used to establish one of the rows of the rowset as the current row for positioned update and delete operations.

ODBC *bookmarks* provide a different efficiency boost for an application program that needs to operate on retrieved rows of data. An ODBC bookmark is a database-independent unique row-id for SQL operations. (A driver may actually use primary keys or DBMS-specific row-ids or other methods to support bookmarks, but it is transparent to the application program.) When bookmarks are enabled, the bookmark (row-id) is returned for each row of query results. The bookmark can be used with scrolling cursors to return to a particular row. Additionally, it can be used to perform a positioned update or delete based on a bookmark.

Bookmarks can also be used to determine if a particular row retrieved by two different queries is, in fact, the same row or two different rows with the same data values. Bookmarks can make some operations much more efficient (for example, performing positioned updates via a bookmark rather than respecifying a complex search condition to identify the row). However, there can be substantial overhead for some DBMS brands and ODBC drivers in maintaining the bookmark information, so this trade-off must be considered carefully.

ODBC bookmarks form the basis for ODBC bulk operations, another efficiency-related feature. The SQLBulkOperations() call allows an application program to efficiently update, insert, delete or refetch multiple rows based on their bookmarks. It operates in conjunction with block cursors and works on the rows in the current rowset. The application program places the bookmarks for the rows to be affected into an array, and places into other arrays the values to be inserted or deleted. It then calls SQLBulkOperations() with a function code indicating whether the identified rows are to be updated, deleted, or refetched, or whether a set of new rows is to be added. This call completely bypasses the normal SQL statement syntax for these operations, and because it can operate on multiple rows in a single call, can be a very efficient mechanism for bulk insertion, deletion, or update of data.

The Oracle Call Interface (OCI)

The most popular programmatic interface to Oracle is embedded SQL. However, Oracle also provides an alternative callable API, known as the *Oracle Call Interface,* or OCI. OCI has been available for many years and remained fairly stable through a number of major Oracle upgrade cycles, including all of the Oracle7 versions. With the introduction of Oracle8, OCI underwent a major revision, and many of the original OCI calls were replaced by new, improved versions. Moving forward with Oracle9 and beyond, this "new OCI" (the Oracle8 version) is effectively *the* Oracle Call Interface for new programs.

The "old OCI"(from Oracle7 and before) is relevant only for legacy programs that were originally developed using it. For reference, the "old OCI" routines are summarized in Table 19-6, so that you can recognize a program that may be using this old version. Conceptually, the routines closely parallel the embedded dynamic SQL interface, described in Chapter 18.

The new OCI uses many of the same concepts as the SQL/CLI standard and ODBC, including the use of handles to identify interface objects. Several hundred routines are defined in the API, and a complete description of them is beyond the scope of this book. The following sections identify the major routines that will be used by most application programs and their functions.

OCI Handles

The new OCI uses a hierarchy of handles to manage interaction with an Oracle database, like the handle hierarchy of the SQL/CLI described earlier in the section "CLI Structures" The handles are:

- **Environment handle**. The top-level handle associated with an OCI interaction
- **Service context handle**. Identifies an Oracle server connection for statement processing
- **Server handle**. Identifies an Oracle database server (for multisession applications)
- **Session handle**. Identifies an active user session (for multisession applications)
- **Statement handle**. Identifies an Oracle-SQL statement being processed
- **Bind handle**. Identifies an Oracle statement input parameter
- **Define handle**. Identifies an Oracle query results column
- **Transaction handle**. Identifies a SQL transaction in progress
- **Complex object handle**. Retrieves data from an Oracle object
- **Error handle**. Reports and processes OCI errors

PROGRAMMING
WITH SQL

Function	Description
Database connection/disconnection	
olon()	Logs on to an Oracle database
oopen()	Opens a cursor (connection) for SQL statement processing
oclose()	Closes an open cursor (connection)
ologof()	Logs off from an Oracle database
Basic statement processing	
osql3()	Prepares (compiles) a SQL statement string
oexec()	Executes a previously compiled statement
oexn()	Executes with an array of bind variables
obreak()	Aborts the current Oracle call interface function
oermsg()	Obtains error message text
Statement parameters	
obndrv()	Binds a parameter to a program variable (by name)
obndrn()	Binds a parameter to a program variable (by number)
Transaction processing	
ocom()	Commits the current transaction
orol()	Rolls back the current transaction
ocon()	Turns on autocommit mode
ocof()	Turns off autocommit mode
Query results processing	
odsc()	Obtains a description of a query results column
oname()	Obtains the name of a query results column
odefin()	Binds a query results column to a program variable
ofetch()	Fetches the next row of query results
ofen()	Fetches multiple rows of query results into an array
ocan()	Cancels a query before all rows are fetched

Table 19-6. *Old Oracle Call Interface Functions (Oracle7 and Earlier)*

An application program manages OCI handles using the routines shown in Table 19-7. The allocate and free routines function like their SQL/CLI counterparts. The get attribute and set attribute functions operate like the similarly named SQL/CLI routines that get and set environment, connection, and statement attributes.

An error handle is used to pass information back from OCI to the application. The error handle to be used for error reporting is typically passed as a parameter to OCI calls. If the return status indicates an error, information about the error can be retrieved from the error handle using OCIErrorGet().

Oracle Server Connection

The initialization and connection sequence for OCI parallels those already illustrated for CLI/ODBC and dblib. The OCI routines associated with connection management are shown in Table 19-8. An application program first calls OCIInitialize() to initialize the Oracle Call Interface. This call also indicates whether OCI will be used in multithreaded mode, whether the application program will use OCI object-mode functions, and other options. After initialization, the application program calls OCIEnvInit() to initialize an environment handle. As with CLI/ODBC, all OCI interactions take place within the context of the environment defined by this handle.

After these initial steps, most applications call OCILogon() to establish a session with an Oracle database server. Subsequent OCI calls take place within the context of this session and use the supplied user-id to determine their privileges within the Oracle database. A call to OCILogoff() terminates the session. The other calls provide more advanced session management for multithreaded and multiconnection applications. The OCIServerVersion() call can be used to determine the version of the Oracle server software. The OCIChangePassword() call can be used to change an expired password.

Routine	Function
OCIHandleAlloc()	Allocates a handle for use
OCIHandleFree()	Frees a handle previously allocated
OCIAttrGet()	Retrieves a particular attribute of a handle
OCIAttrSet()	Sets the value of a particular handle attribute

Table 19-7. *OCI Handle Management Routines*

Routine	Function
OCIInitialize()	Initializes the Oracle Call Interface for use
OCIEnvInit()	Establishes an environment handle for OCI interaction
OCILogon()	Connects to an Oracle database server for an OCI session
OCILogoff()	Terminates a previous logon connection
OCIServerAttach()	Attaches to an Oracle server for multisession operations
OCIServerDetach()	Detaches from an Oracle server
OCIServerVersion()	Returns server version information
OCISessionBegin()	Begins a user session on a previously attached server
OCIPasswordChange()	Changes a user's password on the server
OCISessionEnd()	Ends a previously begun user session

Table 19-8. *OCI Initialization and Connection Management Routines*

Statement Execution

The OCI functions shown in Table 19-9 implement SQL statement execution. OCIStmtPrepare() and OCIStmtExecute() support the two-step prepare/execute process. The OCIStmtExecute() function can also be used to describe query results (similar to the embedded SQL DESCRIBE statement) without actually executing the query by passing a specific flag. OCI automatically provides a description of query results when OCIStmtExecute() is called in the normal statement execution mode. The description is available as an attribute of the statement handle for the executed query.

The OCIBindbyPos() and OCIBindbyName() functions are used to bind application program locations to statement parameters, using either parameter positions or parameter names. These calls automatically allocate bind handles for the parameters when they are called, or they may be called with explicitly allocated bind handles. The other calls implement more advanced binding techniques, including binding of multiple parameter values (arrays) and binding of complex object data types. They also provide execute-time parameter (and query results) processing, corresponding to the deferred parameter mode supported by CLI/ODBC and described earlier in the "CLI Statement Processing" section. The piece info calls support this mode of operation.

Routine	Function
OCIStmtPrepare()	Prepares a statement for execution
OCIStmtExecute()	Executes a previously prepared statement
OCIBreak()	Aborts current OCI operation on a server
OCIBindbyPos()	Binds a parameter based on its position
OCIBindbyName()	Binds a parameter based on its name
OCIStmtGetBindInfo()	Obtains the names of bind and indicator variables
OCIBindArrayOfStruct()	Sets up array binding for passing multiple parameter values
OCIBindDynamic()	Registers a callback routine for a previously bound parameter that will use runtime binding
OCIBindObject()	Provides additional information for a previously bound parameter with a complex object data type
OCIStmtGetPieceInfo()	Obtains information about a dynamic piecewise parameter value needed at execute-time by OCI (or a dynamic piecewise query results column being returned)
OCIStmtSetPieceInfo()	Sets information (buffer, length, indicator, etc.) for a dynamic piecewise parameter value being supplied at execute-time to OCI (or a dynamic piecewise query results column being accepted at runtime)

Table 19-9.   *OCI Statement-Processing and Parameter-Handling Routines*

Query Results Processing

The OCI functions shown in Table 19-10 are used to process query results. The
OCIDefineByPos() function is used to bind a query results column (identified by
column number) to an application program storage location. (The OCI terminology
refers to this as the *define* process; the term *binding* is reserved for input parameters.)
The other define calls support dynamic (execute-time) binding, array binding
(for multirow fetch operations), and binding of complex object data types. The
OCIStmtFetch() call retrieves a row of query results, and provides the SQL FETCH
statement functionality.

Routine	Function
OCIStmtFetch()	Fetches a row or rows of query results
OCIDefineByPos()	Binds a query results column
OCIDefineArrayofStruct()	Sets up array binding for multirow results retrieval
OCIDefineDynamic()	Registers a callback routine for dynamic processing of query results column
OCIDefineObject()	Provides additional information for a previously bound query results column with a complex object type

Table 19-10. *OCI Query Results Processing Routines*

Descriptor Handling

OCI uses *descriptors* to provide information about parameters, Oracle database objects (tables, views, stored procedures, and so on), large objects, complex objects, row-ids, and other OCI objects. A descriptor provides information to the application program and is used in some cases to manage the details of the processing of these objects. The routines shown in Table 19-11 are used to manage descriptors. They allocate and free the descriptors and retrieve and set individual data values within the descriptors.

Routine	Function
OCIDescriptorAlloc()	Allocates a descriptor or LOB locator
OCIDescriptorFree()	Frees a previously allocated descriptor
OCIParamGet()	Gets a descriptor for a parameter
OCIParamSet()	Sets a parameter descriptor in a complex object-retrieval handle

Table 19-11. *OCI Descriptor Management Routines*

Transaction Management

Application programs use the functions shown in Table 19-12 to implement SQL transaction management. The OCITransCommit() and OCITransRollback() calls provide the basic capability to commit and roll back transactions, and correspond to the usual SQL COMMIT and ROLLBACK statements. The other functions provide a very rich and complex transaction scheme, including the specification of read-only, serializable, and loosely or tightly coupled transactions, and control over distributed transactions. The transaction management routines take a service context handle that identifies a current connection as an input parameter.

Error Handling

The OCI functions return a status code indicating whether they completed successfully. In addition, most OCI functions accept an error handle as an input parameter. If an error occurs during processing, error information is associated with this handle. Upon return from the function, the application program can call OCIErrorGet() on the error handle to obtain further information about the error, including the error number and error message.

Catalog Information

The OCIDescribeAny() call provides access to Oracle system catalog information. An application program calls this routine with the name of a table, view, synonym, stored procedure, data type, or other Oracle schema object. The routine populates a descriptor (identified by a descriptor handle) with information about the attributes

Routine	Function
OCITransCommit()	Commits a transaction
OCITransRollback()	Rolls back a transaction
OCITransStart()	Initiates or reattaches a special transaction
OCITransPrepare()	Prepares to commit for a distributed transaction
OCITransForget()	Forgets a previously prepared transaction
OCITransDetach()	Detaches a distributed transaction

Table 19-12. *OCI Transaction Management Routines*

of the object. Subsequent calls to OCIAttrGet() on the descriptor handle can be used to obtain complete data about the object at runtime.

Large Object Manipulation

OCI includes a large group of routines, shown in Table 19-13, for processing Oracle large object (LOB) data types and large objects stored in files referenced in Oracle columns. Because large objects may be tens of thousands to millions of bytes in length, they typically cannot be bound directly to application program buffers in their entirety. Instead, OCI uses a LOB *locator*, which functions like a handle for the LOB data item. The locator is returned for LOB data in query results and used as an input parameter for LOB data being inserted or updated. The LOB handling routines support piece-by-piece processing of LOB data, allowing it to be transferred between an Oracle database and an application program. The routines accept one or more LOB locators as parameters.

Routine	Function
OCILobRead()	Reads a piece of a LOB into application program data area
OCILobWrite()	Writes data from an application program data area into a LOB
OCILobAppend()	Appends data to the end of a LOB
OCILobErase()	Erases data within a LOB
OCILobTrim()	Truncates data from the end of a LOB
OCILobGetLength()	Obtains the length of a LOB
OCILobLocatorIsInit()	Checks whether a LOB locator is valid
OCILobCopy()	Copies data from one LOB to another
OCILobAssign()	Assigns one LOB locator to another
OCILobIsEqual()	Compares two LOB locators
OCILobFileOpen()	Opens a file containing LOB data
OCILobFileClose()	Closes a previously opened LOB file
OCILobFileCloseAll()	Closes all previously opened LOB files

Table 19-13. *OCI Large Object Processing Routines*

Routine	Function
OCILobFileIsOpen()	Checks whether a LOB file is open
OCILobFileGetName()	Obtains the name of a LOB file, given a LOB locator
OCILobFileSetName()	Sets the name of a LOB file in a LOB locator
OCILobFileExists()	Checks if a LOB file exists
OCILobLoadFromFile()	Loads a LOB from a LOB file

Table 19-13. *OCI Large Object Processing Routines* (continued)

Java Database Connectivity (JDBC)

JDBC is a callable SQL API for the Java programming language. JDBC is both the official and de facto standard for SQL database access from Java. For the C programming language, the DBMS vendors developed their own proprietary APIs well before the development of ODBC or SQL-CLI API. For Java, the JDBC API was developed by Sun Microsystems as part of a suite of Java APIs, embodied in various Java editions. As a result, all of the major DBMS products provide Java support via JDBC; there are no important competing APIs.

JDBC History and Versions

The JDBC API has been through several major revisions since its original introduction. JDBC 1.0 provided the basic core of data access functionality, including a driver manager to arbitrate connections to multiple DBMS's, connection management to access individual databases, statement management to send SQL commands to the DBMS, and result set management to provide Java access to the query results.

The JDBC 2.0 API and its incremental versions extended JDBC 1.0, and divided the functionality into a Core API and Extensions API. The 2.0 version added:

- **Batch operations**. A Java program can pass many rows of data to be inserted or updated via a single API call, improving performance and efficiency of bulk operations.
- **Scrollable result sets**. Like the scrollable cursors provided in other APIs, this new capability permitted both forward and backward motion through query results.

■ **Updateable result sets**. A Java program can update the database by updating a specific row of query results or inserting a new row through the results.

■ **Connection pooling**. Connections to the database can be shared across Java programs, reducing the overhead of frequent connecting and disconnecting.

■ **Distributed transactions**. The API provides the capability to synchronize updates across multiple databases, with all or nothing transactions that span database boundaries.

■ **Data sources**. A new type of object encapsulates the details of a database connection, reducing the need for an application programmer to understand connection specifics.

■ **Rowsets**. An abstraction of query results, rowsets allow query results processing even when a program is disconnected from the source database and later resynchronization.

■ **Java Naming & Directory Interface (JNDI) support**. Databases and drivers can be named and cataloged in a network directory, and accessed via those directory entries.

The JDBC 3.0 API is a relatively new version of JDBC. It was finalized and formally announced by Sun in February 2002, and packaged as part of Java2 Standard Edition (J2SE) 1.4. New capabilities introduced in the 3.0 version include:

■ **Object-relational SQL extensions**. The API adds support for abstract data types and the associated capabilities that were added in the SQL:1999 standard.

■ **Savepoints**. The API allows a partial rollback to a specifically marked savepoint partway through a transaction.

■ **Cursor preservation**. API options allow cursors to remain open across transactions.

■ **Prepared statement metadata**. Programs can determine information about prepared statements, such as the number and data types of parameters and of query results columns.

JDBC Implementations and Driver Types

JDBC assumes a driver architecture like that provided by the ODBC standard, on which it is broadly based. Figure 19-25 shows the main building blocks. A Java program connects to the JDBC driver manager via the JDBC API. The JDBC system software is responsible for loading one or more JDBC drivers, typically on demand from Java programs that request them. Conceptually, each driver provides access to one particular DBMS brand, making whatever brand-specific API calls and sending the SQL statements needed to carry out the JDBC request. The JDBC software is delivered as a Java package, which is imported into a Java program that wants to use JDBC.

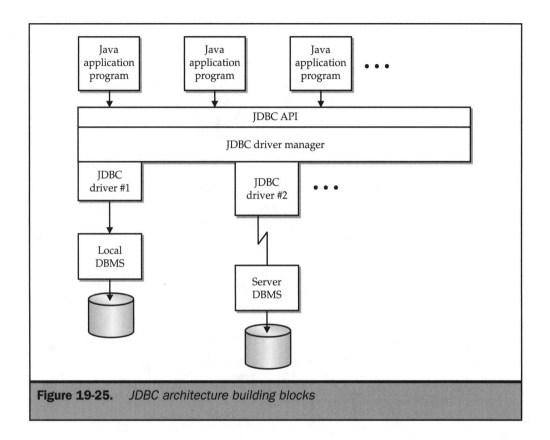

Figure 19-25.   *JDBC architecture building blocks*

The JDBC specification does not deal with the specific details of how a JDBC driver is implemented. However, since the introduction of JDBC, developers have tended to characterize JDBC drivers into four driver types. The type descriptions assume a client/server connection from the JDBC API (on the client system) to a database server. While this is a common enterprise deployment architecture, it's worth noting that JDBC is used to access local databases on systems as small as handheld devices; in this context, the driver types have less meaning. The driver types differ in how they translate JDBC calls (method invocations) into specific actions against the DBMS.

A *Type 1 driver* is also called a *JDBC/ODBC bridge,* shown in Figure 19-26. The driver translates JDBC calls into a vendor-neutral API, which in practice is always ODBC. The request passes to a specific ODBC driver for the target DBMS. (Optionally, the ODBC driver manager may be eliminated, since the ODBC API to the driver manager is the same as the API to the driver itself.) Ultimately, the ODBC driver calls the DBMS' proprietary API. If the database is on a local system, the DBMS carries out the request. If it's on a remote (server) system, the DBMS code on the client is a network access stub, which translates the request into a network message (proprietary to the DBMS) and sends it to the DBMS server.

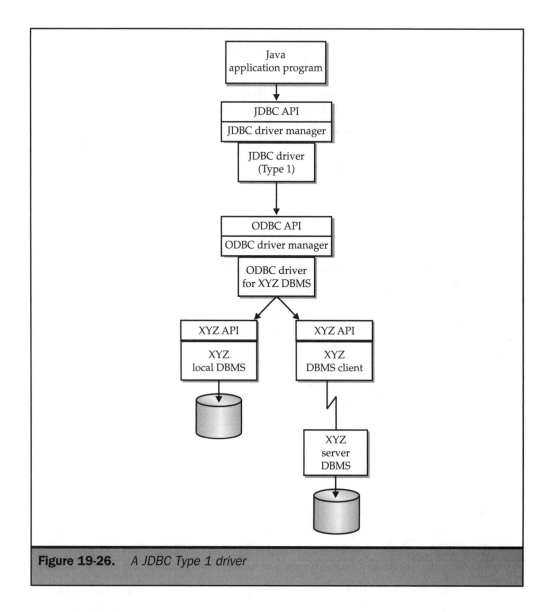

Figure 19-26. *A JDBC Type 1 driver*

A Type 1 driver has one significant advantage. Because nearly all popular DBMS products support ODBC, a single Type 1 driver can provide access to dozens of different DBMS brands. Type 1 drivers are widely available, including one that is distributed by Sun.

A Type 1 driver also has several disadvantages. Each JDBC request passes through many layers on its way to and from the DBMS, so a Type 1 driver typically carries a lot of computing overhead and its performance suffers as a result. The use of ODBC as an intermediate stage also may limit the functionality provided by the driver—features of the underlying DBMS that might be able to be delivered via the JDBC interface directly may not be accessible via ODBC. Finally, the ODBC driver required by a Type 1 driver will be delivered in binary form, not as a Java executable. Thus, any given Type 1 driver is specific to the client computer's hardware and operating system, and will lack the portability of Java.

A *Type 2 driver* is also called a *Native API driver.* The driver translates JDBC requests directly into the native API of the DBMS, as shown in Figure 19-27. Unlike the Type 1 driver, there is no ODBC or other vendor-neutral layer involved. If the database is located on the same system as the Java program, the Type 2 driver's calls to the native API will go directly to the DBMS. In a client/server network, the DBMS code on the client is again a network access stub, and the requests flow over the network in a DBMS-proprietary protocol, as in the Type 1 driver.

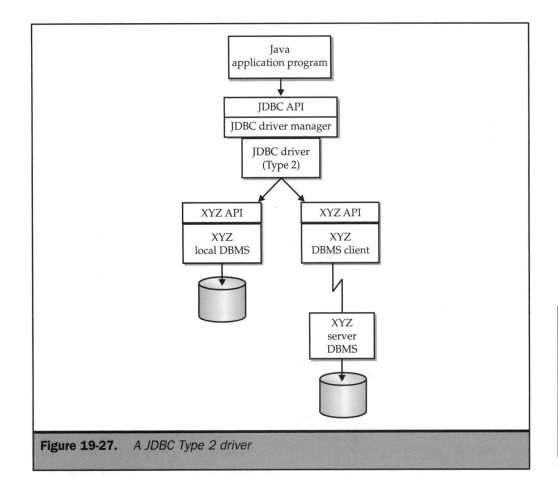

Figure 19-27.   *A JDBC Type 2 driver*

Type 2 drivers present a different set of trade-offs than Type 1 drivers. A Type 2 driver has fewer layers, so performance is typically higher. It still has the disadvantage of requiring binary code to be installed on the client system, so each Type 1 driver will still be specific to a hardware architecture and operating system. Unlike a Type 1 driver, a Type 2 driver is also specific to a DBMS brand. If you want to communicate with several different DBMS', you will need multiple drivers. Finally, it's worth noting that the Type 1/Type 2 distinction assumes that the native DBMS API is not ODBC. If a DBMS presents a native ODBC interface, then the use of ODBC does not imply an additional layer, and its Type 2 driver will, in fact, use ODBC to access the DBMS.

A *Type 3 driver* is a *Network-Neutral driver*. The driver translates JDBC requests into network messages in a vendor-neutral format, and sends them across the network to the server, as shown in Figure 19-28. On the server, a middleware layer receives the network requests and translates them into calls to the DBMS' native API. Query results are passed back across the network, again in a vendor-neutral format.

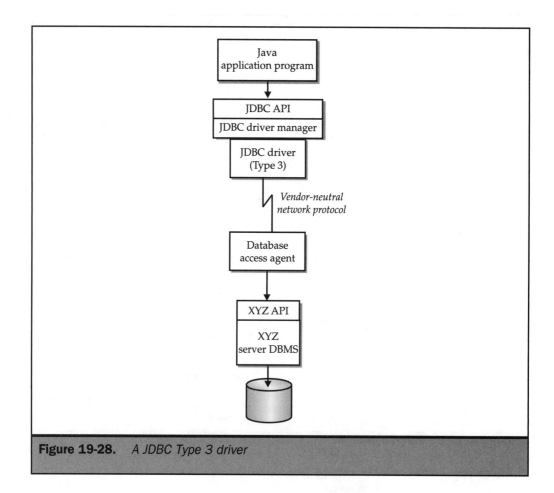

Figure 19-28. *A JDBC Type 3 driver*

Type 3 drivers once again present a different set of trade-offs. One major advantage claimed for the Type 3 architecture is that the client-side code can be written in Java, using the network interfaces provided by other Java APIs. Notice also that the client-side code is DBMS neutral; it does the same work no matter what the target DBMS on the server. This means that the client-side code is very portable, able to run on any system that supports a Java Virtual Machine (JVM) and Java network APIs. Type 3 drivers share one disadvantage with Type 1 drivers: the use of a vendor-neutral network layer, just like the use of a vendor-neutral ODBC layer, means that some capabilities of the underlying DBMS may be inaccessible through the intermediate layer. A Type 3 architecture also involves a double translation of each JDBC request, just as in Type 1; however, one of the translations takes place on the server system, minimizing the client-side impact.

A *Type 4 driver* is a *Network-Proprietary driver*. The driver translates JDBC requests into network messages, but this time in a DBMS-proprietary format, as shown in Figure 19-29. The driver is written in Java, and implements a network client for the DBMS' networking software, such as Oracle's SQL*Net. On the server, there is no need for a middleware layer, since the DBMS server already provides support for the DBMS

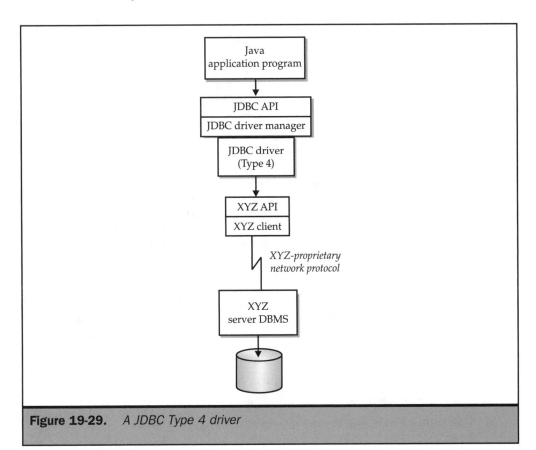

Figure 19-29. *A JDBC Type 4 driver*

		Database access	
		Via vendor-neutral (ODBC) API	Direct to vendor-proprietary API
DBMS API location	Client-side	Type 1 driver	Type 2 driver
	Server-side	Type 3 driver	Type 4 driver

Figure 19-30. *JDBC driver types and trade-offs*

vendor's own client/server networking. Query results flow back across the network, again in vendor-proprietary format, and supplied back to the requesting program.

Type 4 drivers preserve one of the important advantages of Type 3 drivers. They can be implemented in pure Java, so like Type 3, they are portable across computer hardware and operating systems. However, unlike Type 3 drivers, they are DBMS-specific, so different client-side code is required for each DBMS brand you want to access. A Type 4 architecture involves less overhead on the server system, and may therefore deliver slightly better performance. In practice, the overhead of the network messaging will almost always swamp this advantage, except in very high transaction rate applications.

Figure 19-30 summarizes the four JDBC driver types and shows how they relate to one another. The two columns divide the driver types based on whether they use a vendor-neutral intermediate layer (left column) or translate directly from the JDBC API to a DBMS-proprietary interface. The two rows divide the driver types based on whether the translation to a specific DBMS API occurs on the client side (left column) or on the server side. As the figure shows, each of these two decisions creates trade-offs, and they result in four (2×2) driver types.

The JDBC API

Java is an object-oriented language, so it's probably no surprise that JDBC organizes its API functions around a collection of database-related objects and the methods that they provide:

- **Driver Manager object**. The entry-point to JDBC
- **Connection objects**. Represent individual active connections to target databases
- **Statement objects**. Represent SQL statements to be executed

- **ResultSet objects**. Represent the results of a SQL query
- **MetaData objects**. Represent metadata about databases, query results, and statements
- **Exception objects**. Represent errors in SQL statement execution

These objects have the logical relationship shown in Figure 19-31, based on which objects provide methods to create other objects. The following sections describe each of these objects, and how their methods are used to connect to databases, execute SQL statements, and process query results. A complete explanation of the JDBC API is beyond the scope of this book, but the concepts described should allow you to make effective use of JDBC and to understand the documentation that is delivered with the package.

The DriverManager object is the main interface to the JDBC package. Some of the most important methods that it provides are shown in Table 19-14. After loading the JDBC driver class that you want to use (typically using the Class.forName()

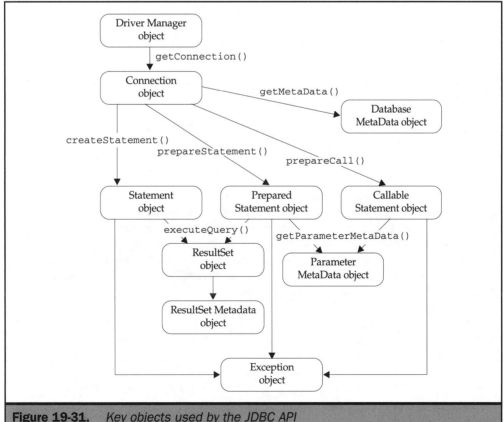

Figure 19-31. *Key objects used by the JDBC API*

Method	Description
getConnection()	Creates and returns a database connection object, given a URL for the datasource, and optionally a user name and password, and connection properties
registerDriver()	Registers a driver with JDBC driver manager
setLoginTimeout()	Sets timeout for connection login
getLoginTimeout()	Obtains login timeout value
setLogWriter()	Enables tracing of JDBC calls

Table 19-14. *DriverManager Object Methods*

method), your program will ask the DriverManager object to connect you to that specific driver and a specific database with the getConnection() method:

```
// Create a connection to the Oracle JDBC driver
String url = "… will vary depending on OS, etc."
String user = "Scott";
String pswd = "Tiger";
Connection dbconn =
    DriverManager.getConnection(url, user, pswd);
```

The getConnection() method returns an object, the Connection object, which embodies the connection that has just been created and the database on the other end of that connection. Other DriverManager methods provide programmatic control over connection timeouts, switch on JDBC call logging for debugging, and other utility functions. If it encounters an error while attempting to make the connection, the DriverManager object will throw an exception. Error handling is described in the "Error Handling in JDBC" section later in this chapter.

JDBC Basic Statement Processing

The major functions of the JDBC Connection object are to manage the connection to the database, to create SQL statements for processing by that database, and to manage transactions over the connection. Table 19-15 shows the Connection object methods that provide these functions. In most simple JDBC programs, the next step after a connection has been established will be to call the Connection object's createStatement() method to create a Statement object.

Method	Description
Close()	Closes the connection to the datasource
createStatement()	Creates a Statement object for the connection
prepareStatement()	Prepares a parameterized SQL statement into a PreparedStatement for execution
prepareCall()	Prepares a parameterized call to a stored procedure or function into a CallableStatement for execution
commit()	Commits the current transaction on the connection
rollback()	Rolls back the current transaction on the connection
setAutoCommit()	Sets/resets autocommit mode on the connection
getWarnings()	Retrieves SQL warning(s) associated with a connection
GetMetaData	Returns a DatabaseMetadata object with info about database

Table 19-15. *JDBC* Connection *Object Methods*

The major function of a Statement object is to actually execute SQL statements. Table 19-16 shows the Statement object methods that you use to control statement execution. There are several different execute() methods, depending on the specific type of SQL statement. Simple statements that do not produce query results (e.g., UPDATE, DELETE, INSERT, CREATE TABLE) can use the executeUpdate method. Queries use the executeQuery() method, because it provides a mechanism for returning the query results. Other execute methods support prepared SQL statements, statement parameters, and stored procedures.

To illustrate the basic use of Connection and Statement objects, here is a simple Java program excerpt that creates a connection to a database, performs two database updates, commits the changes, and then closes the connection.

```
// The connection object and strings we will use
Connection dbconn;         // the database connection
String str1 = "UPDATE OFFICES SET TARGET = 0";
String str2 = "DELETE FROM SALESREPS WHERE EMPL_NUM = 106";

  <code in here creates the connection>
```

```
// Create a statement object for executing SQL
Statement stmt = dbconn.createStatement();

// Update the OFFICES table with the statement object
stmt.executeUpdate(str1);

// Update the SALESREPS table with the statement object
stmt.executeUpdate(str2);

// Commit the changes to the database
dbconn.commit();

// Update the SALESREPS table using the same statement object
stmt.executeUpdate(str2);

// Finally, close the connection
dbconn.close();
```

As the example shows, the SQL transaction-processing operations (commit and rollback) are handled by method calls to the Connection object, rather than by

Method	Description
Basic statement execution	
executeUpdate()	Executes a nonquery SQL statement and returns the number of rows affected
executeQuery()	Executes a single SQL query and returns a result set
execute()	General-purpose execution of one or more SQL statements
Statement batch execution	
addBatch()	Stores previously supplied parameter values as part of a batch of values for execution
executeBatch()	Executes a sequence of SQL statements; returns an array of integers indicating the number of rows impacted by each one

Table 19-16.   *JDBC* Statement *Object Methods*

Method	Description
Query results limitation	
setMaxRows()	Limits number of rows retrieved by a query
getMaxRows()	Retrieves current maximum row limit setting
setMaxFieldSize()	Limits maximum size of any retrieved column
getMaxFieldSize()	Retrieves current maximum field size limit
setQueryTimeout()	Limits maximum time of query execution
getQueryTimeout()	Retrieves current maximum query time limit
Error handling	
getWarnings()	Retrieves SQL warning(s) associated with statement execution

Table 19-16. *JDBC* Statement *Object Methods* (continued)

executing COMMIT and ROLLBACK statements. This allows the JDBC driver to know the status of the transactions that it is processing without examining the specific SQL being executed. JDBC also supports an autocommit mode, in which every statement is treated as an individual transaction. A Connection object method also controls this option.

Note that the Connection and Statement methods called in this program excerpt can cause errors, and the excerpt does not show any error-handling code. If an error occurs, the JDBC driver will throw a SQLException exception. Normally, an excerpt like the previous one (or parts of it) will appear within a try / catch structure to handle the possible exception. For simplicity, the enclosing try / catch structure is suppressed in this and the next several examples. Error-handling techniques are described in the "Error Handling in JDBC" section later in this chapter.

Simple Query Processing

As with the other SQL APIs and embedded SQL, query processing requires an additional mechanism beyond those used for database updates to handle the returned query results. In JDBC, the ResultSet object provides that additional mechanism. To execute a simple query, a Java program invokes the executeQuery() method of a Statement object, passing the text of the query in the method call. The executeQuery() method returns a ResultSet object that embodies the query results. The Java program then invokes the methods of this ResultSet object to access the query results, row by row and column by column. Table 19-17 shows the methods provided by the ResultSet object.

Method	Description
Cursor motion	
next()	Moves cursor to next row of query results
close()	Ends query processing; closes the cursor
Basic column-value retrieval	
getInt()	Retrieves integer value from specified column
getShort()	Retrieves short integer value from specified column
getLong()	Retrieves long integer value from specified column
getFloat()	Retrieves floating point numeric value from specified column
getDouble()	Retrieves double-precision floating point value from specified column
getString()	Retrieves character string value from specified column
getBoolean()	Retrieves true/false value from specified column
getDate()	Retrieves date value from specified column
getTime()	Retrieves time value from specified column
getTimestamp()	Retrieves timestamp value from specified column
getByte()	Retrieves byte value from specified column
getBytes()	Retrieves fixed-length or variable-length BINARY data from specified column
getObject()	Retrieves any type of data from specified column
Large object retrieval	
getAsciiStream()	Gets input stream object for processing a character large object (CLOB) column
GetBinaryStream()	Gets input stream object for processing a binary large object (BLOB) column
Other functions	
getMetaData()	Returns a ResultSetMetaData object with meta data for query
getWarnings()	Retrieves SQL warnings associated with the ResultSet

Table 19-17. *JDBC ResultSet Object Methods*

Here is a very simple Java program excerpt that shows how the objects and methods you have seen so far combine to perform simple query processing. It retrieves and prints out the office number, city, and region for each office in the OFFICES table:

```
// The connection object, strings and variables
Connection dbconn;         // the database connection
Int num;               // returned office number
String city;           // returned city
String reg;            // returned region
String str1 = "SELECT OFFICE, CITY, REGION FROM OFFICES";

  <code in here creates the connection>

// Create a statement object for executing the query
Statement stmt = dbconn.createStatement();

// Carry out query - method returns a ResultSet object
ResultSet answer = stmt.executeQuery(str1);

// Loop through ResultSet a row at a time
while (answer.next()) {
    // Retrieve each column of data
    num  = answer.getInt("OFFICE");
    city = answer.getString("CITY");
    reg  = answer.getString(3);

    // Print the row of results
    System.out.println(city + "   " + num + "   " + reg);
}

// Explicitly close the cursor and connection
answer.close();
dbconn.close();
```

The methods used are straightforward and parallel the query-processing steps already seen for embedded SQL and C/C++ APIs. The ResultSet object maintains a cursor to note its current position within the query results. Its next method advances the cursor, row by row, through them. There is an explicit JDBC get method call to retrieve each column of data for each row. Java's strong typing and memory-protection schemes make this approach a requirement, but it carries significantly higher overhead than the C/C++ approach of binding program variables and having the database API automatically populate those variables when a next row is fetched. Finally, the close method call ends query processing.

The example also shows the two alternative methods for specifying which column's value should be retrieved by each get method call. You can specify the name of the column to be retrieved (used for the OFFICE and CITY columns), or its ordinal position within the columns of results (used for the REGION column). JDBC delivers this capability by overloading each of the get methods—one version takes a string (column name) argument; the other takes an integer (column number) argument.

Using Prepared Statements in JDBC

The executeQuery() and executeUpdate() methods of the Statement object provide a dynamic SQL capability. They parallel the SQLExecDirect() call in the CLI standard. The database on the other end of the JDBC connection doesn't know in advance which SQL text will be presented when the execute method is called. It must parse the statement on the fly and determine how to execute it. The dynamic SQL approach makes this part of the JDBC interface quite easy to use, but it creates the high overhead usually associated with dynamic SQL for the underlying DBMS. For high transaction rate applications where performance is important, an alternative prepared statement interface is more appropriate.

The prepared statement approach uses the same concepts as the PREPARE / EXECUTE statements of embedded dynamic SQL and the SQLPrepare() and SQLExecute() calls of the CLI standard. A SQL statement that is to be executed repeatedly (such as an UPDATE statement that will be used on many rows or a query that will be executed hundreds of times during a program) is first *prepared* by passing it to the DBMS for parsing and analysis. Later, the statement may be executed repeatedly with very little overhead. You can vary the specific values used by the statement during each execution by passing parameter values for the execution. For example, you can change the values to be used for each UPDATE operation, or change the value to be matched in the WHERE clause of a query using parameters.

To use a prepared statement with JDBC, your program invokes the prepareStatement() method on a connection instead of the createStatement() method. Unlike createStatement(), the prepareStatement() method takes an argument—a string containing the SQL statement that is to be prepared. Within the statement string, parameters to be supplied at statement execution are indicated by a question mark (?), which serves as a *parameter marker*. A parameter can be used within the statement anywhere that a constant could legally appear in the statement. The prepareStatement() method returns a PreparedStatement object, which includes some additional methods beyond those provided by a Statement object. Table 19-18 shows some of these additional methods, nearly all of which are for parameter processing.

The additional set() methods of the PreparedStatement object take two parameters. One indicates the parameter number for which a value is being supplied.

Method	Description
setInt()	Sets value of an integer parameter
setShort()	Sets value of a short integer parameter
setLong()	Sets value of a long integer parameter
setFloat()	Sets value of a floating point parameter
setDouble()	Sets value of a double-precision floating point parameter
setString()	Sets value of a string parameter
setBoolean()	Sets value of a BOOLEAN parameter
setDate()	Sets value of a DATE parameter
setTime()	Sets value of a TIME parameter
setTimeStamp()	Sets value of a TIMESTAMP parameter
setByte()	Sets value of a BYTE parameter
setBytes()	Sets value of a BINARY or VARBINARY parameter
setBigDecimal()	Sets value of a DECIMAL or NUMERIC parameter
setNull()	Sets a NULL value for a parameter
setObject()	Sets value of an arbitrary parameter
ClearParameters	Clears all parameter values
getParameterMetaData()	Returns ParameterMetaData object for a prepared statement (JDBC 3.0 only)

Table 19-18. *Additional Methods of a JDBC* PreparedStatement *Object*

The other provides the parameter value itself. With these methods, the typical sequence for JDBC prepared statement processing can be summarized as follows:

1. The Java program establishes a connection to the DBMS in the usual way.

2. The program calls the prepareStatement() method with the text of the statement to be prepared, including parameter markers. The DBMS analyzes the statement and creates an internal, optimized representation of the statement to be executed.

3. Later, when it's time to execute the parameter statement, the program calls one of the set methods in Figure 19-18 for each parameter, supplying a value for the parameter.

4. When all parameter values have been supplied, the program calls executeQuery or executeUpdate to execute the statement.

5. The program repeats Steps 3 and 4 over and over (typically dozens or hundreds of times or more), varying the parameter values. If a particular parameter's value does not change from one execution to the next, the set method does not need to be recalled.

Here is a program excerpt that illustrates the technique:

```
// The connection object, strings and variables
Connection dbconn;        // the database connection
String city;          // returned city
String str1 = "UPDATE OFFICES SET REGION = ? WHERE MGR = ?";

String str2 = "SELECT CITY FROM OFFICES WHERE REGION = ?";

  <code in here creates the connection>

// Prepare the UPDATE statement
PreparedStatement pstmt1 = dbconn.prepareStatement(str1);

// Prepare the query
PreparedStatement pstmt2 = dbconn.prepareStatement(str2);

// Set parameters for UPDATE statement & execute it
pstmt1.setString(1,"Central");
pstmt1.setInt(2,108);
pstmt1.executeUpdate();

// Reset one of the parameters and execute again, then commit
pstmt1.setInt(2,104);
pstmt1.executeUpdate();
dbconn.commit()/

// Set parameter for query & execute it
pstmt2.setString(1,"Central");
ResultSet answer = pstmt2.executeQuery();

// Loop through ResultSet a row at a time
while (answer.next()) {
    // Retrieve each column of data
    city = answer.getString(1);
```

```
        // Print the row of results
        System.out.println("Central city is " + city);
    }
    answer.close();

    // Set a different parameter for query & execute it
    pstmt2.setString(1,"Eastern");
    ResultSet answer = pstmt2.executeQuery();

    // Loop through ResultSet a row at a time
    while (answer.next()) {
        // Retrieve each column of data
        city = answer.getString(1);

        // Print the row of results
        System.out.println("Eastern city is " + city);
    }
    answer.close();

    // Done - close the connection
    dbconn.close();
```

Using Callable Statements in JDBC

The last several sections described how JDBC supports dynamic SQL statement execution (via the `Statement` object created by the `createStatement()` method) and prepared SQL statements (via the `PreparedStatement` object created by the `prepareStatement()` method). JDBC also supports the execution of stored procedures and stored functions through a third type of statement object, the `CallableStatement` object created by the `prepareCall()` method.

Here is how a Java program invokes a stored function or stored procedure using JDBC:

1. The Java program invokes the `prepareCall()` method, passing it a SQL statement that invokes the stored routine. Parameters to the call are indicated by parameter markers within the statement string, just as they are for a prepared statement.

2. The method returns a `CallableStatement` object.

3. The Java program uses the `set()` methods of the `CallableStatement` object to specify parameter values for the procedure or function call.

4. The Java program uses another method of the `CallableStatement` object to specify the data types of returned values from the stored procedure or function.

5. The Java program invokes one of the `CallableStatement` object's `execute()` methods to actually make the call to the stored procedure.

6. Finally, the Java program invokes one or more of the `CallableStatement` object's `get()` methods to retrieve the values returned by the stored procedure (if any) or the return value of the stored function.

A `CallableStatement` object provides all of the methods of a `PreparedStatement`, listed in Tables 19-16 and 19-18. The additional methods that it provides for registering the data types of output or input/output parameters, and for retrieving the returned values of those parameters after the call, are shown in Table 19-19.

Function	Description
`registerOutParameter()`	Registers data type for output (or input/output) parameter
`getInt()`	Retrieves integer returned value
`getShort()`	Retrieves short integer value from specified column
`getLong()`	Retrieves long integer value from specified column
`getFloat()`	Retrieves floating point numeric value from specified column
`getDouble()`	Retrieves double-precision floating point value from specified column
`getString()`	Retrieves character string value from specified column
`getBoolean()`	Retrieves true/false value from specified column
`getDate()`	Retrieves single date value from specified column
`getTime()`	Retrieves single time value from specified column
`getTimestamp()`	Retrieves single timestamp value from specified column
`getByte()`	Retrieves single byte value from specified column
`getBytes()`	Retrieves fixed-length or variable-length `BINARY` data
`getBigDecimal()`	Retrieves `DECIMAL` or `NUMERIC` data
`getObject()`	Retrieves any type of data

Table 19-19.   *Additional Methods of the `CallableStatement` Object*

A short example is the best way to illustrate the technique for calling a stored procedure and stored function. Suppose the sample database contains a stored procedure defined like this:

```
CREATE PROCEDURE CHANGE_REGION
    (IN OFFICE INTEGER,
    OUT OLD_REG VARCHAR(10),
     IN NEW_REG VARCHAR(10))
```

that changes the region of an office, as requested by the two input parameters, and returns the old region as an output parameter and a stored function, defined like this:

```
CREATE FUNCTION GET_REGION
    (IN OFFICE INTEGER)
        RETURNS VARCHAR(10)
```

that returns the region of an office, given its office number. This Java program excerpt shows how to invoke the stored procedure and stored function using JDBC:

```
// The connection object, strings and variables
Connection dbconn;        // the database connection
String str1 = "{CALL CHANGE_REGION(?, ?, ?)}";
String str2 = "{? = CALL GET_REGION(?)}";
String oldreg;           // returned former region
String ansreg;            // returned current region

  <code in here creates the connection>

// Prepare the two statements
CallableStatement cstmt1 = dbconn.prepareCall(str1);
CallableStatement cstmt2 = dbconn.prepareCall(str2);

// Specify param values & returned data types for stored procedure call
cstmt1.setInt(1,12);     // call with office number 12 (Chicago)
cstmt1.setString(3,"Central");  // and new Central region
cstmt1.registerOutParameter(2,Types.VARCHAR);  // returns a varchar param

// Go ahead and execute the call to the stored procedure
cstmt1.executeUpdate();
oldreg = cstmt.getString(2);  // returned (2nd) param is a string
```

```
// Specify param values & returned data type for stored function call
cstmt2.setInt(1,12);  // call with office number 12 (Chicago)
cstmt2.registerOutParameter(1,Types.VARCHAR);  // fcn returns a varchar

// Go ahead and execute the call to the stored function
cstmt2.executeUpdate();
ansreg = cstmt.getString(1); // returned value (1st param) is a string

// Done - close the connection
dbconn.close();
```

Note that the call invocations of the stored procedure or function in the statement strings are enclosed in curly brackets. The input parameters passed to a stored procedure or function are handled exactly the same way as parameters for a prepared statement. Output parameters from a stored procedure require some new machinery: the `registerOutParameter()` method call to specify their data types, and calls to the `get()` methods to retrieve their values after the call is complete. These are summarized in Table 19-19. Input/output parameters for a stored procedure require both that values be passed into the procedure call, using the `set()` methods, and that the output data type be specified with `registerOutParameter()` and the returned data be retrieved with the `get()` methods.

For a stored function, there are only input parameters, and the `set()` methods are once again used. The return value of the function is specified with a parameter marker in the prepared statement string. Its data type is registered, and its value is retrieved, just as if it were a regular output parameter.

Error Handling in JDBC

When an error occurs during JDBC operation, the JDBC interface throws a Java exception. Most SQL statement execution errors throw a `SQLException`. The error can be handled via the standard Java `try` / `catch` mechanism. When a SQLException error occurs, the `catch()` method is called with a `SQLException` object, some of whose methods are summarized in Table 19-20.

The `SQLException` methods allow you to retrieve the error message, `SQLSTATE` error code, and DBMS-specific error code associated with the error. It is possible for a single JDBC operation to create more than one error. In this case, the errors are available to your program in sequence. Calling `getNextException()` on the first reported error returns a `SQLException` for the second exception, and so on, until there are no more exceptions to be handled.

Scrollable and Updateable Cursors in JDBC

Just as scrollable cursors have been added to the ANSI/ISO SQL standards, scrollable cursors have been added to JDBC result sets in later versions of the specification. You indicate that you want a query to produce results that are scrollable through a parameter

Method	Description
getMessage()	Retrieves error message describing the exception
getSQLState()	Retrieves SQLSTATE value (5-char string, as described in Chapter 17)
getErrorCode()	Retrieves driver-specific or DBMS-specific error code
getNextException()	Moves to next SQL exception in a series

Table 19-20. *JDBC SQLException Methods*

to the executeQuery method. If you specify scrollability, the ResultSet returned by the executeQuery call offers some additional methods for cursor control. The important methods are listed in Table 19-21.

In addition to scrollable result sets, later versions of the JDBC specification added support for updateable result sets. This capability corresponds to the UPDATE...WHERE CURRENT OF capability in embedded SQL. It allows an update to specific columns of this row, which is indicated by the current position of a cursor. Updateable result sets also allow new rows of data to be inserted into a table via a result set.

Function	Description
Scrollable cursor motion	
previous()	Moves cursor to previous row of query results
beforeFirst()	Moves cursor before the start of the results
first()	Moves cursor to first row of query results
last()	Moves cursor to last row of query results
afterLast()	Moves cursor past end of the results
absolute()	Moves cursor to absolute row number indicated
relative()	Moves cursor to relative row number indicated

Table 19-21. *JDBC ResultSet Object Extended Cursor Methods*

Function	Description
Cursor position sensing	
isFirst()	Determines whether the current row is the first row of the result set
isLast()	Determines whether the current row is the last row of the result set
isBeforeFirst()	Determines whether the cursor is positioned before the beginning of the result set
isAfterLast()	Determines whether the cursor is positioned past the end of the result set
moveToInsertRow()	Moves cursor to "empty" row for inserting new data
moveToCurrentRow()	Moves cursor back to the current row before an insertion
Update a column of current row (via cursor)	
updateInt()	Updates an integer column value
updateShort()	Updates a short integer column value
updateLong()	Updates a long integer column value
updateFloat()	Updates a floating point column value
updateDouble()	Updates a double-precision floating point column value
updateString()	Updates a string column value
updateBoolean()	Updates a true/false column value
updateDate()	Updates a date column value
updateTime()	Updates a time column value
updateTimeStamp()	Updates a timestamp column value
updateByte()	Updates a byte column value
updateBytes()	Updates a fixed-length or variable-length column value
updateBigDecimal()	Updates a DECIMAL or NUMERIC column value
updateNull()	Updates a column to a NULL value
updateObject()	Updates an arbitrary column value

Table 19-21.   *JDBC ResultSet Object Extended Cursor Methods* (continued)

Retrieving Metadata with JDBC

The JDBC interface provides objects and methods for retrieving metadata about databases, query results, and parameterized statements. A JDBC `Connection` object provides access to metadata about the database that it represents. Invoking its `getMetaData()` method returns a `DatabaseMetaData` object, described in Table 19-22. Each method listed in the table returns a result set, containing information about a type of database entity: tables, columns, primary keys, and so on. The result set can be processed using the normal JDBC query results processing routines. Other metadata access methods provide information about the database product name supported on this connection, its version number, and similar information.

Metadata information about query results can also be very useful. A `ResultSet` object provides a `getMetaData` method that can be invoked to obtain a description of its query results. The method returns a `ResultSetMetaData` object, described in Table 19-23. The methods let you determine how many columns there are in the query results, and the name and data type of each column, identified by their ordinal position within the query results.

Finally, metadata information about the parameters used in a prepared SQL statement or a prepared call to a stored procedure can also be useful. The `PreparedStatement` and the `CallableStatement` objects both provide a `getParameterMetaData()` method that retrieves this information. The method returns a `ParameterMetaData` object, described in Table 19-24. Invoking the methods of this object provides information about how many parameters are used in the statement, their data types, whether each parameter is an input, output or input/output parameter, and similar information.

Function	Description
`getTables()`	Returns result set of table information of tables in database
`getColumns()`	Returns result set of column names and type info, given table name
`getPrimaryKeys()`	Returns result set of primary key info, given table name
`getProcedures()`	Returns result set of stored procedure info
`getProcedureColumns()`	Returns result set of info about parameters for a specific stored procedure

Table 19-22.   *DatabaseMetaData Methods for Database Information Retrieval*

Function	Description
getColumnCount()	Returns number of query results columns
getColumnName()	Retrieves name of specified results column
getColumnType()	Retrieves data type of specified results column

Table 19-23. *ResultSetMetaData Methods*

Advanced JDBC Capabilities

JDBC 2.0 and JDBC 3.0 introduced several capabilities that extend the basic database access functionality of JDBC. JDBC *data sources*, first introduced in JDBC 2.0, provide a higher-level method for finding available drivers and databases and connecting to them. They mask the details of making a connection from the Java application programmer. Basically, a data source is identified with some external directory or catalog that is able

Function	Description
getParameterClassName()	Returns name of the class (data type) for specified parameter
getParameterCount()	Returns number of parameters in the statement
getParameterMode()	Returns mode (IN, OUT, INOUT) of parameter
getParameterType()	Returns SQL data type of specified parameter
getParameterTypeName()	Returns DBMS data type of specified parameter
getPrecision()	Returns precision of specified parameter
getScale()	Returns scale of specified parameter
isNullable()	Determines whether the specified parameter is nullable
isSigned()	Determines whether the specified parameter is a signed number

Table 19-24. *JDBC ParameterMetaData Methods*

to translate logical entity names into specific details. Using a data source, the application programmer can specify a target database by an abstract name, and have the directory in conjunction with the JDBC software handle the details of connections.

JDBC *rowsets* are another advanced concept enhanced and extended in the JDBC revisions. A rowset extends the concept of a JDBC result set, which you will recall represents a set of query results. Beyond the query results themselves, a rowset encapsulates information about the underlying source database, the connection to the database, its user name and password, and so on. The rowset retains its identity independent of an active connection to the database. Thus, a rowset may exist in a disconnected state, and it can be used to reestablish a connection to the database. When connected to the database, the rowset can contain query results like a result set.

Rowsets have several other characteristics and capabilities. A rowset meets the requirement for a JavaBeans component, and when connected to a database, provides a way to make a result set look like an Enterprise Java Bean (EJB). Rowsets hold tabular row/column query results, and those results can be retrieved, navigated, and even updated whether the rowset is currently connected to the source database or not. If disconnected updates are made, resynchronization is implied when the rowset once again is connected to the source database. Finally, the concept of a rowset is not necessarily tied to SQL and relational databases. The data in a rowset can conceptually come from any tabular data source, such as a personal computer spreadsheet or even a table within a word processing document. A complete discussion of JDBC rowsets is beyond the scope of this book; see the JDBC documentation at http://www.java.sun.com/products/jdbc/ for more information about this and other JDBC capabilities.

Summary

Many SQL-based DBMS products provide a callable API for programmatic database access:

- Depending on the particular DBMS brand and its history, the callable API may be an alternative to an embedded SQL approach, or it may be the primary method by which an application program accesses the database.

- A callable interface puts query processing, parameter passing, statement compilation, statement execution, and similar tasks into the call interface, keeping the programmatic SQL language identical to interactive SQL. With embedded SQL, these tasks are handled by special SQL statements (OPEN, FETCH, CLOSE, PREPARE, EXECUTE, and so on) that are unique to programmatic SQL.

- Microsoft's ODBC is a widely supported, callable API that provides an effective way for an application program to achieve independence from a particular DBMS. However, differences between DBMS brands are reflected in varying support for ODBC functions and capabilities.

- The SQL/Call-Level Interface (SQL/CLI) standard is based on ODBC and is compatible with it at the core level. SQL/CLI provides a callable API to complement the embedded SQL interface specified in SQL2. Many DBMS vendors already support the SQL/CLI because of their historical support for ODBC.

- For Java programs, the JDBC interface is the de facto industry standard callable API, supported by all of the major DBMS products and defined as the database management API within the Java2 Enterprise Edition (J2EE) standard implemented by all of the major application server products.

- The proprietary callable APIs of the different DBMS brands remain important in the market (especially Oracle's OCI). All of them offer the same basic features, but they vary dramatically in the extended features that they offer and in the details of the calls and data structures that they use.

- In general, DBMS vendors put considerable performance-tuning work into their proprietary APIs and tend to offer ODBC and/or SQL/CLI support as a checkoff feature. Thus, applications with higher performance requirements tend to use the proprietary APIs, and are locked in to a particular DBMS brand when they do.

The Complete Reference

Part VI

SQL Today and Tomorrow

The influence of SQL continues to expand as new SQL capabilities and extensions to SQL address new types of data management requirements. Chapters 20 through 25 describe several of these newer areas. Chapter 20 describes stored procedures, which provide a processing capability within the DBMS itself for implementing business rules and creating well-defined database interactions. Chapter 21 describes SQL's role in analyzing data and the trend to create SQL-based data warehouses. Chapter 22 describes the role of SQL in creating interactive web sites, and especially its relationship to application server technology. Chapter 23 discusses how SQL is used to create distributed databases that tap the power of computer networks. Chapter 24 discusses one of the most important areas of SQL evolution—the interplay between SQL and object-oriented technologies and the new generation of object-relational databases. Chapter 25 focuses on the relationship between SQL and one of the most important of these technologies, XML, and the emerging Internet web services architecture based on XML. Finally, Chapter 26 highlights the key trends that will drive the evolution of SQL for the coming decade.

Chapter 20

Database Processing and Stored Procedures

701

The long-term trend in the database market is for databases to take on a progressively larger role in the overall data processing architecture. The prerelational database systems basically handled only data storage and retrieval; applications programs were responsible for navigating their way through the database, sorting and selecting data, and handling all processing of the data. With the advent of relational databases and SQL, the DBMS took on expanded responsibilities. Database searching and sorting were embodied in SQL language clauses and provided by the DBMS, along with the capability to summarize data. Explicit navigation through the database became unnecessary. Subsequent SQL enhancements such as primary and foreign keys and check constraints continued the trend, taking over data checking and data integrity functions that had remained the responsibility of application programs with earlier SQL implementations. At each step, having the DBMS take on more responsibility provided more centralized control and reduced the possibility of data corruption due to application programming errors.

In many information technology (IT) departments within large companies and organizations, this DBMS trend paralleled an organizational trend. The corporate database and the data it contains came to be viewed as a major corporate asset, and in many IT departments, a dedicated database administration (DBA) group emerged, with responsibility for maintaining the database, defining and updating the data it contained, and providing structured access to it. Other groups within the IT department, or elsewhere within the company, could develop application programs, reports, queries, or other logic that accessed the database. But the security of the database, the permitted forms of access, and in general, everything within the realm of the database, became the province of the DBA.

Two important features of modern enterprise-scale relational databases—stored procedures and triggers—have been a part of this trend. *Stored procedures* provide the capability to perform database-related application processing within the database itself. For example, a stored procedure might implement the application's logic to accept a customer order or to transfer money from one bank account to another. *Triggers* are used to automatically invoke the processing capability of a stored procedure based on conditions that arise within the database. For example, a trigger might automatically transfer funds from a savings account to a checking account if the checking account becomes overdrawn. This chapter describes the core concepts behind stored procedures and triggers, and their implementation in several popular DBMS brands.

The stored procedure and trigger capability of the popular DBMS products have been significantly expanded in their major revisions during the late 1990s and 2000s. A complete treatment of stored procedure and trigger programming is well beyond the scope of this book, but the concepts and comparisons here will give you an understanding of the core capabilities and a foundation for beginning to use the specific capabilities of your DBMS software. Stored procedures and triggers basically extend SQL into a more complete programming language, and this chapter assumes that you are familiar with basic programming concepts.

Stored Procedure Concepts

In its original form, SQL was not envisioned as a complete programming language. It was designed and implemented as a language for expressing database operations—creating database structures, entering data into the database, updating database data—and especially for expressing database queries and retrieving the answers. SQL could be used interactively by typing SQL statements at a keyboard, one by one. In this case, the sequence of database operations was determined by the human user. SQL could also be embedded within another programming language, such as COBOL or C. In this case, the sequence of database operations was determined by the flow of control within the COBOL or C program.

With stored procedures, several capabilities normally associated with programming languages are grafted onto the SQL language. Sequences of extended SQL statements are grouped together to form SQL programs or procedures. The specifics vary from one implementation to another, but generally, these capabilities are provided:

- **Conditional execution**. An IF...THEN...ELSE structure allows a SQL procedure to test a condition and carry out different operations depending on the result.

- **Looping**. A WHILE or FOR loop or similar structure allows a sequence of SQL operations to be performed repeatedly, until some terminating condition is met. Some implementations provide a special cursor-based looping structure to process each row of query results.

- **Block structure**. A sequence of SQL statements can be grouped into a single block and used in other flow-of-control constructs as if the statement block were a single statement.

- **Named variables**. A SQL procedure may store a value that it has calculated, retrieved from the database, or derived in some other way into a program variable, and later retrieve the stored value for use in subsequent calculations.

- **Named procedures**. A sequence of SQL statements may be grouped together, given a name, and assigned formal input and output parameters, like a subroutine or function in a conventional programming language. Once defined in this way, the procedure may be called by name, passing it appropriate values for its input parameters. If the procedure is a function returning a value, it may be used in SQL value expressions.

Collectively, the structures that implement these capabilities form a stored procedure language (SPL).

Stored procedures were first introduced by Sybase in the original Sybase SQL Server product. Much of the original enthusiasm for stored procedures was because of their performance impact in a client/server database architecture. Without stored procedures, every SQL operation requested by an application program (running on the client computer system) would be sent across the network to the database server, and would wait for a reply message to be returned across the network. If a logical transaction required six SQL operations, six network round trips were required. With stored procedures, the sequence of six SQL operations could be programmed into a procedure and stored in the database. The application program would simply request the execution of the stored procedure and await the results. In this way, six network round trips could be cut to one round trip—the request and reply for executing the stored procedure.

Stored procedures proved to be a natural fit for the client/server model, and Sybase used them to establish an early lead with this architecture. A competitive response quickly followed from many of the other DBMS vendors. Today, most enterprise DBMS products provide a stored procedure capability, and the benefits of stored procedures in corporate databases has expanded considerably beyond the early focus on network performance. Stored procedures are less relevant for other types of specialized DBMS systems, such as data warehousing systems or in-memory databases. Some DBMS products have modeled their SPL structures on C or Pascal language constructs. Others have tried to match the style of the SQL Data Manipulation Language (DML) and Data Definition Language (DDL) statements. As a result, while stored procedure concepts are very similar from one SQL dialect to another, the specific syntax varies considerably.

A Basic Example

It's easiest to explain the basics of stored procedures through an example. Consider the process of adding a customer to the sample database. Here are the steps that may be involved:

1. Obtain the customer number, name, credit limit, and target sales amount for the customer, as well as the assigned salesperson and office.

2. Add a row to the customer table containing the customer's data.

3. Update the row for the assigned salesperson, raising the quota target by the specified amount.

4. Update the row for the office, raising the sales target by the specified amount.

5. Commit the changes to the database, if all were successful.

Without a stored procedure capability, here is a SQL statement sequence that does this work for XYZ Corporation, new customer number 2137, with a credit limit of $30,000 and first-year target sales of $50,000 to be assigned to Paul Cruz (employee #103) of the Chicago office:

```
INSERT INTO CUSTOMERS (CUST_NUM, COMPANY, CUST_REP, CREDIT_LIMIT)
     VALUES (2137, 'XYZ Corporation', 103, 30000.00);
     UPDATE SALESREPS
        SET QUOTA = QUOTA + 50000.00
      WHERE EMPL_NUM = 103;
```

```
UPDATE OFFICES
   SET TARGET = TARGET + 50000.00
 WHERE CITY = 'Chicago';
COMMIT;
```

With a stored procedure, all of this work can be embedded into a single defined SQL routine. Figure 20-1 shows a stored procedure for this task, expressed in Oracle's PL/SQL stored procedure dialect. The procedure is named ADD_CUST, and it accepts six parameters—the customer name, number, credit limit, and target sales, the

```
/* Add a customer procedure */
create procedure add_cust (
   c_name   in varchar(20),          /* input customer name */
   c_num    in integer,              /* input customer number */
   cred_lim in number(16,2),         /* input credit limit */
   tgt_sls  in number(16,2),         /* input target sales */
   c_rep    in integer,              /* input salesrep emp # */
   c_offc   in varchar(15))          /* input office city */
as
begin
   /* Insert new row of CUSTOMERS table */
   insert into customers (cust_num, company, cust_rep,
credit_limit)
        values (c_num, c_name, c_rep, cred_lim);

   /* Update row of SALESREPS table */
   update salesreps
     set quota = quota + quota + tgt_sls
    where empl_num = c_rep;

   /* Update row of OFFICES table */
   update offices
     set target = target + tgt_sls
    where city = c_offc;

   /* Commit transaction and we are done */
   commit;
end;
```

Figure 20-1.   *A basic stored procedure in PL/SQL*

employee number of the assigned salesperson, and the city where the assigned sales office is located.

Once this procedure has been created in the database, a statement like this one:

```
ADD_CUST('XYZ Corporation', 2137, 30000.00, 50000.00, 103,'Chicago')
```

calls the stored procedure and passes it the six specified values as its parameters. The DBMS executes the stored procedure, carrying out each SQL statement in the procedure definition one by one. If the ADD_CUST procedure completes its execution successfully, a committed transaction has been carried out within the DBMS. If not, the returned error code and message indicates what went wrong.

Using Stored Procedures

The procedure defined in Figure 20-1 illustrates several of the basic structures common to all SPL dialects. Nearly all dialects use a CREATE PROCEDURE statement to initially define a stored procedure. A corresponding DROP PROCEDURE statement is used to discard procedures that are no longer needed. The CREATE PROCEDURE statement defines the following.

- The name of the stored procedure
- The number and data types of its parameters
- The names and data types of any local variables used by the procedure
- The sequence of statements executed when the procedure is called

The following sections describe these elements and the special SQL statements that are used to control the flow of execution within the body of a stored procedure.

Creating a Stored Procedure

In many common SPL dialects, the CREATE PROCEDURE statement is used to create a stored procedure and specify how it operates. The CREATE PROCEDURE statement assigns the newly defined procedure a name, which is used to call it. The name must typically follow the rules for SQL identifiers. (The procedure in Figure 20-1 is named ADD_CUST.) A stored procedure accepts zero or more parameters as its arguments. (This one has six parameters: C_NAME, C_NUM, CRED_LIMI, TGT_SLS, C_REP, and C_OFFC.) In all of the common SPL dialects, the values for the parameters appear in a comma-separated list, enclosed in parentheses, following the procedure name when the procedure is called. The header of the stored procedure definition specifies the names of the parameters and their data types. The same SQL data types supported by the DBMS for columns within the database can be used as parameter data types.

In Figure 20-1, all of the parameters are *input* parameters (signified by the IN keyword in the procedure header in the Oracle PL/SQL dialect). When the procedure is called, the parameters are assigned the values specified in the procedure call, and the statements in the procedure body begin to execute. The parameter names may appear within the procedure body (and particularly within standard SQL statements in the procedure body) anywhere that a constant may appear. When a parameter name appears, the DBMS uses its current value. In Figure 20-1, the parameters are used in the INSERT statement and the UPDATE statement, both as data values to be used in column calculations and search conditions.

In addition to input parameters, some SPL dialects also support *output* parameters. These allow a stored procedure to pass back values that it calculates during its execution. Output parameters aren't useful for stored procedures invoked from interactive SQL, but they provide an important capability for passing back information from one stored procedure to another stored procedure that calls it. Some SPL dialects support parameters that operate as *both* input and output parameters. In this case, the parameter passes a value to the stored procedure, and any changes to the value during the procedure execution are reflected in the calling procedure.

Figure 20-2 shows the same ADD_CUST procedure definition, expressed in the Sybase Transact-SQL dialect. (The Transact-SQL dialect is also used by Microsoft SQL Server; its basics are largely unchanged since the original Sybase SQL Server version, which was the foundation for both the Microsoft and Sybase product lines.) Note the differences from the Oracle dialect:

- The keyword PROCEDURE can be abbreviated to PROC.

- No parenthesized list of parameters follow the procedure name. Instead, the parameter declarations immediately follow the name of the stored procedure.

- The parameter names all begin with an at sign (@), both when they are declared at the beginning of the procedure and when they appear within SQL statements in the procedure body.

- There is no formal end-of-procedure body marker. Instead, the procedure body is a single Transact-SQL statement. If more than one statement is needed, the Transact-SQL block structure is used to group the statements.

Figure 20-3 shows the ADD_CUST procedure again, this time expressed in the Informix stored procedure dialect. The declaration of the procedure head itself and the parameters more closely follow the Oracle dialect. Unlike the Transact-SQL example, the local variables and parameters use ordinary SQL identifiers as their names, without any special identifying symbols. The procedure definition is formally ended with an END PROCEDURE clause, which makes the syntax less error-prone.

In all dialects that use the CREATE PROCEDURE statement, the procedure can be dropped when no longer needed by a corresponding DROP PROCEDURE statement:

```
DROP PROCEDURE ADD_CUST
```

```
/* Add a customer procedure */
create proc add_cust
   @c_name   varchar(20),              /* input customer name */
   @c_num    integer,                  /* input customer number */
   @cred_lim money,                    /* input credit limit */
   @tgt_sls  money,                    /* input target sales */
   @c_rep    integer,                  /* input salesrep emp # */
   @c_offc   varchar(15)               /* input office city */
as
begin
   /* Insert new row of CUSTOMERS table */
   insert into customers (cust_num, company, cust_rep, credit_limit)
       values (@c_num, @c_name, @c_rep, @cred_lim)

   /* Update row of SALESREPS table */
   update salesreps
      set quota = quota + quota + @tgt_sls
    where empl_num = @c_rep

   /* Update row of OFFICES table */
   update offices
      set target = target + @tgt_sls
    where city = @c_offc

   /* Commit transaction and we are done */
   commit trans
end
```

Figure 20-2.   *The ADD_CUST procedure in PL/SQL*

Calling a Stored Procedure

Once defined by the CREATE PROCEDURE statement, a stored procedure can be used.
An application program may request execution of the stored procedure, using the
appropriate SQL statement. Another stored procedure may call it to perform a specific
function. The stored procedure may also be invoked through an interactive SQL interface.

   The various SQL dialects differ in the specific syntax used to call a stored procedure.
Here is a call to the ADD_CUST procedure in the PL/SQL dialect:

```
EXECUTE ADD_CUST('XYZ Corporation', 2137, 30000.00, 50000.00, 103, 'Chicago')
```

```
/* Add a customer procedure */
create procedure add_cust (
    c_name    varchar(20),               /* input customer name */
    c_num     integer,                   /* input customer number */
    cred_lim money(16,2),                /* input credit limit */
    tgt_sls   money(16,2),               /* input target sales */
    c_rep     integer,                   /* input salesrep emp # */
    c_offc    varchar(15))               /* input office city */

    /* Insert new row of CUSTOMERS table */
    insert into customers (cust_num, company, cust_rep, credit_limit)
        values (c_num, c_name, c_rep, cred_lim);

    /* Update row of SALESREPS table */
    update salesreps
       set quota = quota + quota + tgt_sls
     where empl_num = c_rep;

    /* Update row of OFFICES table */
    update offices
       set target = target + tgt_sls
     where city = c_offc;

    /* Commit transaction and we are done */
    commit transaction;
  end procedure;
```

Figure 20-3.   *The ADD_CUST procedure in Informix SPL*

The values to be used for the procedure's parameters are specified, in order, in a list that is enclosed by parentheses. When called from within another procedure or a trigger, the EXECUTE statement may be omitted, and the call becomes simply:

```
ADD_CUST('XYZ Corporation', 2137, 30000.00, 50000.00, 103, 'Chicago')
```

In the Transact-SQL dialect, the call to the stored procedure becomes:

```
EXECUTE ADD_CUST 'XYZ Corporation', 2137, 30000.00, 50000.00, 103, 'Chicago'
```

The parentheses aren't required, and the values to be used for parameters again form a comma-separated list. The keyword EXECUTE can be abbreviated to EXEC, and the parameter names can be explicitly specified in the call, allowing you to specify the parameter values in any order you wish. Here is an alternative, equivalent Transact-SQL call to the ADD_CUST stored procedure:

```
EXEC ADD_CUST @C_NAME = 'XYZ Corporation',
              @C_NUM = 2137,
           @CRED_LIM = 30000.00,
            @C_OFFC = 'Chicago',
             @C_REP = 103,
            @TGT_SLS = 50000.00
```

The Informix SPL form of the same EXECUTE command is:

```
EXECUTE PROCEDURE ADD_CUST('XYZ Corporation', 2137, 30000.00, 50000.00, 103, 'Chicago')
```

Again, the parameters are enclosed in a comma-separated, parenthesized list. This form of the EXECUTE statement may be used in any context. For example, it may be used by an embedded SQL application program to invoke a stored procedure. Within a stored procedure itself, another stored procedure can be called using this equivalent statement:

```
CALL ADD_CUST('XYZ Corporation', 2137, 30000.00, 50000.00,103, 'Chicago')
```

Stored Procedure Variables

In addition to the parameters passed into a stored procedure, it's often convenient or necessary to define other variables to hold intermediate values during the procedure's execution. All stored procedure dialects provide this capability. Usually, the variables are declared at the beginning of the procedure body, just after the procedure header and before the list of SQL statements. The data types of the variables can be any of the SQL data types supported as column data types by the DBMS.

Figure 20-4 shows a simple Transact-SQL stored procedure fragment that computes the total outstanding order amount for a specific customer number, and sets up one of two messages depending on whether the total order amount is over or under $30,000. Note that Transact-SQL local variable names, like parameter names, begin with an at sign (@). The DECLARE statement declares the local variables for this procedure. In this case, there are two variables: one with the MONEY data type and one VARCHAR.

In Transact-SQL, the SELECT statement assumes the additional function of assigning values to variables. A simple form of this use of SELECT is the assignment of the message text:

```
SELECT @MSG_TEXT = "high order total"
```

```
/* Check order total for a customer */
create proc chk_tot
   @c_num integer       /* one input parameter */
as

   /* Declare two local variables */
   declare @tot_ord money, @msg_text varchar(30)

   begin
     /* Calculate total orders for customer */
     select @tot_ord = sum(amount)
       from orders
      where cust = @c_num

     /* Load appropriate message, based on total */
     if tot_ord < 30000.00
        select @msg_text = "high order total"
     else
        select @msg_text = "low order total"

     /* Do other processing for message text */
     . . .

   end
```

Figure 20-4.   *Using local variables in Transact-SQL*

The assignment of the total order amount at the beginning of the procedure body is a more complex example, where the SELECT is used both to assign a value and as the introducer of the query that generates the value to be assigned.

Figure 20-5 shows the Informix SPL version of the same stored procedure. There are several differences from the Transact-SQL version:

- Local variables are declared using the DEFINE statement. This example shows only a very limited subset of the options that are available.

- Variable names are ordinary SQL identifiers; there is no special first character.

- A specialized SELECT INTO statement is used within SPL to assign the results of a singleton SELECT statement into a local variable.

- The LET statement provides simple assignment of variable values.

```
/* Check order total for a customer */
create procedure chk_tot (c_num integer)

   /* Declare two local variables */
   define tot_ord money(16,2);
   define msg_text varchar(30);

   /* Calculate total orders for requested customer */
   select sum(amount) into tot_ord
     from orders
    where cust = c_num;

   /* Load appropriate message, based on total */
   if tot_ord < 30000.00
      let msg_text = "high order total"
   else
      let msg_text = "low order total"

   /* Do other processing for message text */
   . . .

end procedure;
```

Figure 20-5.   *Using local variables in Informix SPL*

Figure 20-6 shows the Oracle PL/SQL version of the same stored procedure. Again, there are several differences to note from the Transact-SQL and Informix SPL examples:

■ Local variable declarations occur in a separate DECLARE section. This section is actually an integral part of the Oracle BEGIN…END block structure; it declares local variables for use within the block.

■ The SELECT INTO statement has the same form as the Informix procedure; it is used to select values from a single-row query directly into local variables.

■ The assignment statements use Pascal-style (:=) notation instead of a separate LET statement.

Local variables within a stored procedure can be used as a source of data within SQL expressions anywhere that a constant may appear. The current value of the

```
/* Check order total for a customer */
create procedure chk_tot (c_num in integer)
as
declare
   /* Declare two local variables */
   tot_ord number(16,2);
   msg_text varchar(30);

begin
   /* Calculate total orders for requested customer */
   select sum(amount) into tot_ord
     from orders
    where cust = c_num;

   /* Load appropriate message, based on total */
   if tot_ord < 30000.00
      msg_text := 'high order total';
   else
      msg_text := 'low order total';

   /* Do other processing for message text */
   . . .

end;
```

Figure 20-6.   *Using local variables in Oracle PL/SQL*

variable is used in the execution of the statement. In addition, local variables may be destinations for data derived from SQL expressions or queries, as shown in the preceding examples.

Statement Blocks

In all but the very simplest stored procedures, it is often necessary to group a sequence of SQL statements together so that they will be treated as if they were a single statement. For example, in the IF...THEN...ELSE structure typically used to control the flow of execution within a stored procedure, most stored procedure dialects expect a single statement following the THEN keyword. If a procedure needs to perform a sequence of several SQL statements when the tested condition is true, it must group the statements together as a statement block, and this block will appear after THEN.

In Transact-SQL, a statement block has this simple structure:

```
/* Transact-SQL block of statements */
begin
   /* Sequence of SQL statements appears here */
   . . .

end
```

The sole function of the BEGIN...END pair is to create a statement block; they do not impact the scope of local variables or other database objects. The Transact-SQL procedure definition, conditional execution and looping constructs, and others, are all designed to operate with single SQL statements, so statement blocks are frequently used in each of these contexts to group statements together as a single unit.

In Informix SPL, a statement block includes not only a statement sequence, but may optionally declare local variables for use within the block and exception handlers to handle errors that may occur within the block. Here is the structure of an Informix SQL statement block:

```
/* Informix SPL block of statements */
/* Declaration of any local variables */
define . . .

/* Declare handling for exceptions */
on exception . . .

/* Define the sequence of SQL statements */
begin. . .

end
```

The variable declaration section is optional; we have already seen an example of it in the Informix stored procedure body in Figure 20-5. The exception-handling section is also optional; its role is described later in the "Handling Error Conditions" section. The BEGIN...END sequence performs the same function as it does for Transact-SQL. Informix also allows a single statement to appear in this position, if the block consists of just the other two components and a single SQL or SPL statement.

The Informix SQL language structures don't require the use of statement blocks as often as the Transact-SQL structures. In the Informix dialect, the looping conditional execution statements each include an explicit termination (IF...END IF, WHILE...END WHILE, FOR...END FOR). Within the structure, a single SQL statement or a sequence of statements (each ending with a semicolon) may appear. As a result, an explicit block structure is not always needed simply to group together a sequence of SQL statements.

The Oracle PL/SQL block structure has the same capabilities as the Informix structure. It offers the capability to declare variables and exception conditions, using this format:

```
/* Oracle PL/SQL statement block */
/* Declaration of any local variables */
declare . . .

/* Specify the sequence of statements */
begin . . .

/* Declare handling for exceptions */
exception . . .

end;
```

All three sections of the block structure are optional. It's common to see the structure used with only the BEGIN...END sequence to define a statement sequence, or with a DECLARE...BEGIN...END sequence to declare variables and a sequence of statements. As with Informix, the Oracle structures that specify conditional execution and looping have a self-defining end-of-statement marker, so sequences of statements within these structures do not necessarily need an explicit BEGIN...END statement block structure.

Returning a Value

In addition to stored procedures, most SPL dialects support a stored *function* capability. The distinction is that a stored function returns a value while a stored procedure does not. Here's a simple example of a stored function. Assume you want to define a stored procedure that, given a customer number, calculates the total current order amount for that customer. If you define the procedure as a function, the total amount can be returned as its value.

Figure 20-7 shows an Oracle stored function that calculates the total amount of current orders for a customer, given the customer number. Note the RETURNS clause in the procedure definition, which tells the DBMS the data type of the value being returned. In most DBMS products, if you enter a function call via the interactive SQL capability, the function value is displayed in response. Within a stored procedure, you can call a stored function and use its return value in calculations or store it in a variable.

Many SPL dialects also allow you to use a stored function as a user-defined function within SQL value expressions. This is true of the Oracle PL/SQL dialect, so this use of the function defined in Figure 20-7 within a search condition is legal:

```
SELECT COMPANY, NAME
  FROM CUSTOMERS, SALESREPS
 WHERE CUST_REP = EMPL_NUM
   AND GET_TOT_ORDS(CUST_NUM) > 10000.00
```

```
/* Return total order amount for a customer */
create function get_tot_ords(c_num in integer)
          return number(16,2)
as

/* Declare one local variable to hold the total */
declare tot_ord number(16,2);

begin
   /* Simple single-row query to get total */
   select sum(amount) into tot_ord
     from orders
    where cust = c_num;

   /* return the retrieved value as fcn value */
   return tot_ord;
end;
```

Figure 20-7.   *An Oracle PL/SQL stored function*

As the DBMS evaluates the search condition for each row of prospective query results, it uses the customer number of the current candidate row as an argument to the GET_TOT_ORDERS function and checks to see if it exceeds the $10,000 threshold. This same query could be expressed as a grouped query, with the ORDERS table also included in the FROM clause, and the results grouped by customer and salesperson. In many implementations, the DBMS carries out the grouped query more efficiently than the preceding one, which probably forces the DBMS to process the orders table once for each customer.

Figure 20-8 shows the Informix SPL definition for the same stored function shown in Figure 20-7. Except for stylistic variations, it differs very little from the Oracle version.

Transact-SQL does not have a stored function capability like the one illustrated in Figures 20-7 and 20-8. Transact-SQL stored procedures can explicitly return a status code, and they use a RETURN statement for this purpose. However, the returned value is always an integer status value. A zero return value indicates successful completion of the stored procedure; negative return values are used to indicate various types of errors. The system-defined stored procedures in Sybase Adaptive Server and Microsoft SQL Server all use this return status value convention. The return status of a called

```
/* Return total order amount for a customer */
create function get_tot_ords(c_num in integer)
     returning money(16,2)

/* Declare one local variable to hold the total */
define tot_ord money(16,2);

begin
   /* Simple single-row query to get total */
   select sum(amount) into tot_ord
     from orders
    where cust = c_num;

   /* Return the retrieved value as fcn value */
   return tot_ord;
end function;
```

Figure 20-8.   *An Informix SPL stored function*

procedure can be stored into a local variable by using this assignment form of the
EXECUTE statement:

```
declare sts_val int
execute sts_val = add_cust 'XYZ Corporation', 2137, 30000.00, 50000.00, 103, 'Chicago'
```

Returning Values via Parameters

The stored function capability provides only the ability to return a single value from a
stored routine. Several stored procedure dialects provide a method for returning more
than one value, by passing the values back to the calling routine through *output
parameters*. The output parameters are listed in the stored procedure's parameter list,
just like the input parameters seen in the previous examples. However, instead of being
used to pass data values *into* the stored procedure when it is called, the output parameters
are used to pass data back *out* of the stored procedure to the calling procedure.

Figure 20-9 shows a PL/SQL stored procedure to retrieve the name of a customer,
his or her salesperson, and the sales office to which the customer is assigned, given a

```
/* Get customer name, sales rep and office */
create procedure get_cust_info(c_num  in  integer,
                               c_name out varchar(20),
                               r_name out varchar(15),
                               c_offc out varchar(15))
as
begin
   /* Simple single-row query to get info */
   select company, name, city
     into c_name, r_name, c_offc
     from customers, salesreps, offices
    where cust_num = c_num
      and empl_num = cust_rep
      and office = rep_office;
end;
```

Figure 20-9.   *PL/SQL stored procedure with output parameters*

supplied customer number. The procedure has four parameters. The first one, CNUM, is an input parameter and supplies the requested customer number. The other three parameters are output parameters, used to pass the retrieved data values back to the calling procedure. In this simple example, the SELECT INTO form of the query places the returned variables directly into the output parameters. In a more complex stored procedure, the returned values might be calculated and placed into the output parameters with a PL/SQL assignment statement.

When a stored procedure with output parameters is called, the value passed for each output parameter must be an acceptable target that can receive a returned data value. The target may be a local variable, for example, or a parameter of a higher-level procedure that is calling a lower-level procedure to do some work for it. Here is a fragment of an Oracle PL/SQL procedure that makes an appropriate call to the GET_CUST_INFO procedure in Figure 20-9:

```
/* Get the customer info for customer 2111 */
declare the_name varchar(20),
        the_rep  varchar(15),
        the_city varchar(15);
execute get_cust_info(2111, the_name, the_rep, the_city);
```

Of course, it would be unusual to call this procedure with a literal customer number, but it's perfectly legal since that is an input parameter. The remaining three parameters have acceptable data assignment targets (in this case, they are PL/SQL variables) passed to them so that they can receive the returned values. Here is an illegal call to the same procedure:

```
/* Get the customer info for customer 2111 */
execute get_cust_info(2111, "XYZ Co", the_rep, the_city)
```

because the second parameter is an output parameter and cannot receive a literal value. In addition to input and output parameters, Oracle allows you to specify procedure parameters that are *both* input and output (INOUT) parameters. They must obey the same previously cited restrictions for output parameters, but in addition, their values are used as input by the procedure.

Figure 20-10 shows a version of the GET_CUST_INFO procedure defined in the Transact-SQL dialect. The way in which the output parameters are identified in the procedure header differs slightly from the Oracle version, and the single-row SELECT statement has a different form. Otherwise, the structure of the procedure and its operation are identical to the Oracle example.

```
/* Get customer name, sales rep and office */
create procedure get_cust_info(c_num   in   integer,
                                 c_name out varchar(20),
                                 r_name out varchar(15),
                                 c_offc out varchar(15))
as
begin
   /* Simple single-row query to get info */
   select company, name, city
     into c_name, r_name, c_offc
     from customers, salesreps, offices
    where cust_num = c_num
      and empl_num = cust_rep
      and office = rep_office;
end;
```

Figure 20-10.   *Transact-SQL stored procedure with output parameters*

When this procedure is called from another Transact-SQL procedure, the fact that the second, third, and fourth parameters are output parameters must be indicated in the call to the procedure, as well as in its definition. Here is the Transact-SQL syntax for calling the procedure in Figure 20-10:

```
/* Get the customer info for customer 2111 */
declare the_name varchar(20);
declare the_rep  varchar(15);
declare the_city varchar(15);
exec get_cust_info @c_num = 2111,
                   @c_name = the_name output,
                   @r_name = the_rep output,
                   @c_offc = the_city output
```

Figure 20-11 shows the Informix SPL version of the same stored procedure example. Informix takes a different approach to handling multiple return values. Instead of output parameters, Informix extends the definition of a stored function to allow multiple return values. Thus, the GET_CUST_INFO procedure becomes a function for the Informix dialect. The multiple return values are specified in the RETURNING clause of the procedure header, and they are actually returned by the RETURN statement.

```
/* Get customer name, sales rep and office */
create function get_cust_info(c_num integer)
     returning varchar(20), varchar(15), varchar(15)

  define c_name varchar(20);
  define r_name varchar(15);
  define c_offc varchar(15);

  /* Simple single-row query to get info */
  select company, name, city
    into cname, r_name, c_offc
    from customers, salesreps, offices
   where cust_num = c_num
     and empl_num = cust_rep
     and office = rep_office;

  /* Return the three values */
  return cname, r_name, c_offc;
end procedure;
```

Figure 20-11.   *Informix stored function with multiple return values*

The Informix CALL statement that invokes the stored function uses a special RETURNING clause to receive the returned values:

```
/* Get the customer info for customer 2111 */
define the_name varchar(20);
define the_rep  varchar(15);
define the_city varchar(15);
call get_cust_info (2111)
         returning the_name, the_rep, the_city;
```

As in the Transact-SQL dialect, Informix also allows a version of the CALL statement that passes the parameters by name:

```
call get_cust_info (c_num = 2111)
         returning the_name, the_rep, the_city;
```

Conditional Execution

One of the most basic features of stored procedures is an IF...THEN...ELSE construct for decision making within the procedure. Look back at the original ADD_CUST procedure defined in Figure 20-1 for adding a new customer. Suppose that the rules for adding new customers are modified so that there is a cap on the amount by which a salesperson's quota should be increased for a new customer. If the customer's anticipated first-year orders are $20,000 or less, that amount should be added to the quota, but if they are more than $20,000, the quota should be increased by only $20,000. Figure 20-12 shows a modified procedure that implements this new policy. The IF...THEN...ELSE logic operates exactly as it does in any conventional programming language.

All of the stored procedure dialects allow nested IF statements for more complex decision making. Several provide extended conditional logic to streamline multiway branching. For example, suppose you wanted to do three different things within the ADD_CUST stored procedure, depending on whether the customer's anticipated first-year orders are under $20,000, between $20,000 and $50,000, or over $50,000. In Oracle's PL/SQL, you could express the three-way decision this way:

```
/* Process sales target by range */
if tgt_sls < 20000.00
   then
   /* Handle low-target customers here */
   . . .
elsif tgt_sls < 50000.00
   then
   /* Handle mid-target customers here */
   . . .
else
   /* Handle high-target customers here */
   . . .
end if;
```

```
/* Add a customer procedure */
create procedure add_cust (
    c_name    in varchar(20),              /* input customer name */
    c_num     in integer,                  /* input customer number */
    cred_lim  in number(16,2),             /* input credit limit */
    tgt_sls   in number(16,2),             /* input target sales */
    c_rep     in integer,                  /* input salesrep empl # */
    c_offc    in varchar(15))              /* input office city */
as
begin
    /* Insert new row of CUSTOMERS table */
    insert into customers (cust_num, company, cust_rep, credit_limit)
        values (c_num, c_name, c_rep, cred_lim);

    if tgt_sales <= 20000.00
    then
       /* Update row of SALESREPS table */
       update salesreps
          set quota = quota + quota + tgt_sls
        where empl_num = c_rep;
    else
       /* Update row of SALESREPS table */
       update salesreps
          set quota = quota + quota + 20000.00
        where empl_num = c_rep;
    end if

    /* Update row of OFFICES table */
    update offices
       set target = target + tgt_sls
     where city = c_offc;

    /* Commit transaction and we are done */
    commit;
end;
```

Figure 20-12.   *Conditional logic in a stored procedure*

In the Informix dialect, the same multiway branch structure is allowed. The keyword ELSIF becomes ELIF, but all other aspects remain the same.

Repeated Execution

Another feature common to almost all stored procedure dialects is a construct for repeated execution of a group of statements (looping). Depending on the dialect, there may be support for Basic-style FOR loops (where an integer loop control value is counted up or counted down) or C-style WHILE loops with a test condition executed at the beginning or end of the loop.

In the sample database, it's hard to come up with an uncontrived example of simple loop processing. Assume you want to process some group of statements repeatedly, while the value of a loop-control variable, named ITEM_NUM, ranges from 1 to 10. Here is an Oracle PL/SQL loop that handles this situation:

```
/* Process each of ten items */
for item_num in 1..10 loop
   /* Process this particular item */
   . . .

   /* Test whether to end the loop early */
   exit when (item_num = special_item);
end loop;
```

The statements in the body of the loop are normally executed ten times, each time with a larger integer value of the ITEM_NUM variable. The EXIT statement provides the capability to exit an Oracle PL/SQL loop early. It can be unconditional, or it can be used with a built-in test condition, as in this example.

Here is the same loop structure expressed in Informix SPL, showing some of its additional capabilities and the dialectic differences from PL/SQL:

```
/* Process each of ten items */
for item_num = 1 to 10 step 1
   /* Process this particular item */
   . . .

   /* Test whether to end the loop early */
   if (item_num = special_item)
      then exit for;
end for;
```

The other common form of looping is when a sequence of statements is executed repeatedly while a certain condition exists or until a specified condition exists. Here is an Oracle PL/SQL loop construct that repeats indefinitely. Such a loop must, of course, provide a test within the body of the loop that detects a loop-terminating condition (in this case, a match of two variable values) and explicitly exits the loop:

```
/* Repeatedly process some data */
loop
   /* Do some kind of processing each time */
   . . .

   /* Test whether to end the loop early */
   exit when (test_value = exit_value);
end loop;
```

A more common looping construct is one that builds the test into the loop structure itself. The loop is repeatedly executed as long as the test is true. For example, suppose you want to reduce targets for the offices in the sample database until the total of the targets is less than $2,400,000. Each office's target is to be reduced by the same amount, which should be a multiple of $10,000. Here is a (not very efficient) Transact-SQL stored procedure loop that gradually lowers office targets until the total is below the threshold:

```
/* Lower targets until total below $2,400,000 */
while (select sum(target) from offices) < 2400000.00
   begin
      update offices
         set target = target - 10000.00
   end
```

The BEGIN...END block in this WHILE loop isn't strictly necessary, but most Transact-SQL WHILE loops include one. Transact-SQL repeats the single SQL statement following the test condition as the body of the WHILE loop. If the body of the loop consists of more than one statement, you must use a BEGIN...END block to group the statements. Here is the Oracle PL/SQL version of the same loop:

```
/* Lower targets until total below $2,400,000 */
select sum(target) into total_tgt from offices;
while (total_tgt < 2400000.00)
loop
   update offices
      set target = target - 10000.00;
   select sum(target) into total_tgt from offices;
end loop;
```

The subquery-style version of the SELECT statement from Transact-SQL has been replaced by the PL/SQL SELECT INTO form of the statement, with a local variable used to hold the total of the office targets. Each time the loop is executed, the OFFICES table is updated, and then the total of the targets is recalculated.

Here is the same loop once more, expressed using Informix SPL's WHILE statement:

```
/* Lower targets until total below $2,400,000 */
select sum(target) into total_tgt from offices;
while (total_tgt < 2400000.00)
   update offices
      set target = target - 10000.00;
   select sum(target) into total_tgt from offices;
end while;
```

Other variants of these loop-processing constructs are provided by the various dialects, but the capabilities and syntax are similar to these examples.

Other Flow-of-Control Constructs

Some stored procedure dialects provide statements to control looping and alter the flow of control. In Informix, for example, the EXIT statement interrupts the normal flow within a loop and causes execution to resume with the next statement following the loop itself. The CONTINUE statement interrupts the normal flow within the loop but causes execution to resume with the next loop iteration. Both of these statements have three forms, depending on the type of loop being interrupted:

```
exit for;
continue for;
exit while;
continue while;
exit foreach;
continue foreach;
```

In Transact-SQL, a single statement, BREAK, provides the equivalent of the Informix EXIT statement variants, and there is a single form of the CONTINUE statement as well. In Oracle, the EXIT statement performs the same function as for Informix, and there is no CONTINUE statement.

Additional control over the flow of execution within a stored procedure is provided by statement labels and the GOTO statement. In most dialects, the statement label is an identifier, followed by a colon. The GOTO statement names the label to which control should be transferred. There is typically a restriction that you cannot transfer control out of a loop or a conditional testing statement, and always a prohibition against transferring control into the middle of such a statement. As in structured programming languages, the use of GOTO statements is discouraged because it makes stored procedure code harder to understand and debug.

Cursor-Based Repetition

One common need for repetition of statements within a stored procedure is when the procedure executes a query and needs to process the query results, row by row. All of the major dialects provide a structure for this type of processing. Conceptually, the structures parallel the DECLARE CURSOR, OPEN CURSOR, FETCH, and CLOSE CURSOR statements in embedded SQL or the corresponding SQL API calls. However, instead of fetching the query results into the application program, in this case, they are being fetched into the stored procedure, which is executing within the DBMS itself. Instead of retrieving the query results into application program variables (host variables), the stored procedure retrieves them into local stored procedure variables.

To illustrate this capability, assume that you want to populate two tables with data from the ORDERS table. One table, named BIGORDERS, should contain customer name and order size for any orders over $10,000. The other, SMALLORDERS, should contain the salesperson's name and order size for any orders under $1000. The best and most efficient way to do this would actually be with two separate SQL INSERT statements with subqueries, but for purposes of illustration, consider this method instead:

1. Execute a query to retrieve the order amount, customer name, and salesperson name for each order.

2. For each row of query results, check the order amount to see whether it falls into the proper range for including in the BIGORDERS or SMALLORDERS tables.

3. Depending on the amount, INSERT the appropriate row into the BIGORDERS or SMALLORDERS table.

4. Repeat Steps 2 and 3 until all rows of query results are exhausted.

5. Commit the updates to the database.

Figure 20-13 shows an Oracle stored procedure that carries out this method. The cursor that defines the query is defined in the declare section of the procedure and assigned the name O_CURSOR. The variable CURS_ROW, defined in the same section, is defined as an Oracle *row type.* It is a structured Oracle *row variable* with individual components (like a C-language structure). By declaring it as having the same row type as the cursor, the individual components of CURS_ROW have the same data types and names as the cursor's query results columns.

The query described by the cursor is actually carried out by the cursor-based FOR loop. It basically tells the DBMS to carry out the query described by the cursor (equivalent to the OPEN statement in embedded SQL) before starting the loop processing. The DBMS then executes the FOR loop repeatedly, by fetching a row of query results at the top of the loop, placing the column values into the CURS_ROW variable, and then executing the statements in the loop body. When there are no more rows of query results to be fetched, the cursor is closed, and processing continues after the loop.

```
create procedure sort_orders()
declare
   /* Cursor for the query */
   cursor o_cursor is
   select amount, company, name
     from orders, customers, salesreps
    where cust = cust_num
      and rep = empl_num;

   /* Row variable to receive query results values */
   curs_row o_cursor%rowtype;

begin

   /* Loop through each row of query results */
   for curs_row in o_cursor
   loop

      /* Check for small orders and handle */
      if (curs_row.amount < 1000.00)
      then insert into smallorders
              values (curs_row.name, curs_row.amount);

      /* Check for big orders and handle */
      elsif (curs_row.amount > 10000.00)
      then insert into bigorders
              values (curs_row.company, curs_row.amount);
      end if;
   end loop;
```

Figure 20-13.   *A cursor-based FOR loop in PL/SQL*

Figure 20-14 shows an equivalent stored procedure with the specialized FOR loop structure of Informix SPL. In this case, the query results are retrieved into ordinary local variables; there is no special row data type used. The FOREACH statement incorporates several different functions. It defines the query to be carried out, through the SELECT expression that it contains. It marks the beginning of the loop that is to be executed for each row of query results. (The end of the loop is marked by the END FOREACH statement.) When the FOREACH statement is executed, it carries out the query

```
create procedure sort_orders()

    /* Local variables to hold query results */
    define ord_amt money(16,2);              /* order amount */
    define c_name varchar(20);               /* customer name */
    define r_name varchar(15);               /* salesrep name */

    /* Execute query and process each results row */
    foreach select amount, company, name
               into ord_amt, c_name, r_name
               from orders, customers, salesreps
             where cust = cust_num
               and rep = empl_num;
        begin

            /* Check for small orders and handle */
            if (ord_amt < 1000.00)
            then insert into smallorders
                      values (r_name, ord_amt);

            /* Check for big orders and handle */
            elif (ord_amt > 10000.00)
            then insert into bigorders
                      values (c_name, ord_amt);
            end if;
        end;
    end foreach;
end procedure;
```

Figure 20-14.   *A cursor-based FOREACH loop in Informix SPL*

and then fetches rows of query results repeatedly, putting their column values into the
local variables as specified in the statement. After each row is fetched, the body of
the loop is executed. When there are no more rows of query results, the cursor is
automatically closed, and execution continues with the next statement following the
FOREACH. Note that in this example, the cursor isn't even assigned a specific name
because all cursor processing is tightly specified within the single FOREACH statement.

The Transact-SQL dialect doesn't have a specialized FOR loop structure for cursor-
based query results processing. Instead, the DECLARE CURSOR, OPEN, FETCH, and
CLOSE statements of embedded SQL have direct counterparts within the Transact-SQL
language. Figure 20-15 shows a Transact-SQL version of the sort_orders procedure.

Note the separate DECLARE, OPEN, FETCH, and CLOSE statements for the cursor.
Loop control is provided by testing the system variable @@SQLSTATUS, which is the

```
create proc sort_orders()
as
/* Local variables to hold query results */
declare @ord_amt money(16,2);              /* order amount */
declare @c_name varchar(20);               /* customer name */
declare @r_name varchar(15);               /* salesrep name */

/* Declare cursor for the query */
declare o_curs cursor for
        select amount, company, name
          from orders, customers, salesreps
         where cust = cust_num
           and rep = empl_num

begin

   /* Open cursor and fetch first row of results */
   open o_curs
   fetch o_curs into @ord_amt, @c_name, @r_name

   /* If no rows, return immediately */
   if (@@sqlstatus = 2)
   begin
      close o_curs
      return
   end

   /* Loop through each row of query results */
   while (@@sqlstatus = 0)
   begin

      /* Check for small orders and handle */
      if (@ord_amt < 1000.00)
         insert into smallorders
               values (@r_name, @ord_amt)
```

Figure 20-15.   *A cursor-based WHILE loop in Transact-SQL*

```
        /* Check for big orders and handle */
        else if (curs_row.amount > 10000.00)
            insert into bigorders
                values (@c_name, @ord_amt)
    end

    /* Done with results; close cursor and return */
    close o_curs
end
```

Figure 20-15. *A cursor-based* WHILE *loop in Transact-SQL (continued)*

Transact-SQL equivalent of the SQLSTATE code. It receives a value of zero when a fetch is successful, and a nonzero value when there are no more rows to fetch.

Handling Error Conditions

When an application program uses Embedded SQL or a SQL API for database processing, the application program is responsible for handling errors that arise. Error status codes are returned to the application program, and more error information is typically available through additional API calls or access to an extended diagnostics area. When database processing takes place within a stored procedure, the procedure itself must handle errors.

Transact-SQL provides error handling through a set of global system variables. The specific error-handling variables are only a few of well over 100 system variables that provide information on the state of the server, transaction state, open connections, and other database configuration and status information. The two most useful global variables for error handling are:

- **@@@ERROR**. Contains error status of the most recently executed statement batch
- **@@@SQLSTATUS**. Contains status of the last fetch operation

The normal completion values for both variables are zero; other values indicate various errors and warnings. The global variables can be used in the same way as local variables within a Transact-SQL procedure. Specifically, their values can be checked for branching and loop control.

Oracle's PL/SQL provides a different style of error handling. The Oracle DBMS provides a set of system-defined exceptions, which are errors or warning conditions that can arise during SQL statement processing. Within an Oracle stored procedure (actually, any Oracle statement block), the EXCEPTION section tells the DBMS how it should handle any exception conditions that occur during the execution of the procedure. There are over a dozen different predefined Oracle-detected exception conditions. In addition, you can define your own exception conditions.

Most of the previous examples in this chapter don't provide any real error-handling capability. Figure 20-16 shows a revised version of the Oracle stored function in Figure 20-7. This improved version detects the specific situation where the supplied customer number does not have any associated orders (that is, where the query to calculate total orders returns a NO_DATA_FOUND exception). It responds to this situation by signaling back to the application program an application-level error and associated message. Any other exception conditions that arise are caught by the WHEN OTHERS exception handler.

```
/* Return total order amount for a customer */
create function get_tot_ords(c_num in integer)
        return number(16,2)
as

/* Declare one local variable to hold the total */
declare tot_ord number(16,2);

begin
   /* Simple single-row query to get total */
   select sum(amount) into tot_ord
     from orders
    where cust = c_num;

   /* return the retrieved value as fcn value */
   return tot_ord;

exception
   /* Handle the situation where no orders found */
   when no_data_found
   then raise_application_error (-20123, 'Bad cust#');

   /* Handle any other exceptions */
   when others
   then raise_application_error (-20199,'Unknown error');
end;
```

Figure 20-16.   *PL/SQL stored function with error handling*

The Informix SPL takes a similar approach to exception handling. Figure 20-17 shows the Informix version of the stored function, with Informix-style exception handling. The ON EXCEPTION statement is a declarative statement and specifies the sequence of SQL statements to be executed when a specific exception arises. A comma-separated list of exception numbers may be specified.

```
/* Return total order amount for a customer */
create function get_tot_ords(c_num in integer)
      returning money(16,2)

/* Declare one local variable to hold the total */
define tot_ord money(16,2);

/* Define exception handler for error #-123 and -121 */
on exception in (-121, -123)
   /* Do whatever is appropriate here */
   . . .
end exception;
on exception
   /* Handle any other exceptions in here */
   . . .
end exception;

begin
   /* Simple single-row query to get total */
   select sum(amount)
     into tot_ord
     from orders
    where cust = c_num;

   /* Return the retrieved value as fcn value */
   return tot_ord;

end function;
```

Figure 20-17. *Informix SPL stored function with condition handling*

Advantages of Stored Procedures

Stored procedures offer several advantages, both for database users and database administrators, including:

- **Runtime performance.** Many DBMS brands compile stored procedures (either automatically or at the user's request) into an internal representation that can be executed very efficiently by the DBMS at runtime. Executing a precompiled stored procedure can be much faster than running the equivalent SQL statements through the PREPARE/EXECUTE process.

- **Reusability.** Once a stored procedure has been defined for a specific function, that procedure may be called from many different application programs that need to perform the function, permitting very easy reuse of application logic and reducing the risk of application programmer error.

- **Reduced network traffic.** In a client/server configuration, sending a stored procedure call across the network and receiving the results in a reply message generates much less network traffic than using a network round trip for each individual SQL statement. This can improve overall system performance considerably in a network with heavy traffic or one that has lower-speed connections.

- **Security.** In most DBMS brands, the stored procedure is treated as a trusted entity within the database and executes with its own privileges. The user executing the stored procedure needs to have only permission to execute it, not permission on the underlying tables that the stored procedure may access or modify. Thus, the stored procedure allows the database administrator to maintain tighter security on the underlying data, while still giving individual users the specific data update or data access capabilities they require.

- **Encapsulation.** Stored procedures are a way to achieve one of the core objectives of object-oriented programming—the encapsulation of data values, structures, and access within a set of very limited, well-defined external interfaces. In object terminology, stored procedures can be the methods through which the objects in the underlying RDBMS are exclusively manipulated. To fully attain the object-oriented approach, all direct access to the underlying data via SQL must be disallowed through the RDBMS security system, leaving *only* the stored procedures for database access. In practice, few if any production relational databases operate in this restricted way.

- **Simplicity of access.** In a large enterprise database, a collection of stored procedures may be the main way in which application programs access the database. The stored procedures form a well-defined set of transactions and queries that applications can perform on the database. For most application programmers, a call to a simple, predefined function that checks an account balance, given a customer number, or one that adds an order, given a customer number, quantity, and product-id, is easier to understand than the corresponding SQL statements.

- **Business rules enforcement**. The conditional processing capabilities of stored procedures are often used to place business rules into the database. For example, a stored procedure used to add an order to the database might contain logic to check the credit of the customer placing the order and check whether there is enough inventory on hand to fill the order, and reject the order if these conditions cannot be met. A large company could quite easily have several different ways in which orders are taken and entered into the corporate database—one program for use by direct salespeople, one for people in the telesales department, another that accepts orders placed via the World Wide Web, and so on. Each of these would typically have its own order-acceptance program, usually written by different programmers at different times. But if all of the programs are forced to use the same stored procedure to add an order, the company can be assured that the business rules in that procedure are being uniformly enforced, no matter where the order originated.

Stored Procedure Performance

Different DBMS brands vary in the way they actually implement stored procedures. In several brands, the stored procedure text is stored within the database and is interpreted when the procedure is executed. This has the advantage of creating a very flexible stored procedure language, but it creates significant runtime overhead for complex stored procedures. The DBMS must read the statements that make up the stored procedure at runtime, parse and analyze them, and determine what to do on the fly.

Because of the overhead in the interpreted approach, some DBMS brands compile stored procedures into an intermediate form that is much more efficient to execute. Compilation may be automatic when the stored procedure is created, or the DBMS may provide the ability for the user to request stored procedure compilation. The disadvantage of compiled stored procedures is that the exact technique used to carry out the stored procedure is fixed when the procedure is compiled. Suppose, for example, that a stored procedure is created and compiled soon after a database is first created, and later some useful indexes are defined on the data. The compiled queries in the stored procedure won't take advantage of these indexes, and as a result, they may run much more slowly than if they were recompiled.

To deal with stale compiled procedures, some DBMS brands automatically mark any compiled procedures that may be affected by subsequent database changes as being in need of recompilation. The next time the procedure is called, the DBMS notices the mark and recompiles the procedure before executing it. Normally, this approach provides the best of both worlds—the performance benefits of precompilation while keeping the compiled procedure up to date. Its disadvantage is that it can yield unpredictable stored procedure execution times. When no recompile is necessary, the stored procedure may execute quickly; when a recompile is activated, it may produce a significant delay; and in most cases, the recompile delay is much longer than the disadvantage of using the old compiled version.

To determine the stored procedure compilation capabilities of a particular DBMS, you can examine its CREATE PROCEDURE and EXECUTE PROCEDURE statement options or look for other procedure management statements such as ALTER PROCEDURE.

System-Defined Stored Procedures

DBMS brands that support stored procedures sometimes provide built-in, system-defined stored procedures to automate database processing or management functions. Sybase SQL Server pioneered this use of system stored procedures. Today, hundreds of Transact-SQL system stored procedures provide functions such as managing users, database roles, job execution, distributed servers, replication, and others. Most Transact-SQL system procedures follow this naming convention:

- **SP_ADD_***something*. Adds a new object (user, server, replica, and so on)
- **SP_DROP_***something*. Drops an existing object
- **SP_HELP_***something*. Gets information about an object or objects

For example, the SP_HELPUSER procedure returns information about the valid users of the current database.

External Stored Procedures

Although stored procedures written in the extended SQL dialects of the major enterprise DBMS brands can be quite powerful, they have limitations. One major limitation is that they do not provide access to features outside the DBMS, such as the features of the operating system or other applications running on the same computer system. The extended SQL dialects also tend to be fairly high-level languages, with limited capability for the lower-level programming usually done in C or C++. To overcome these limitations, some DBMS brands provide access to external stored procedures.

An *external stored procedure* is a procedure written in a conventional programming language (such as C or Pascal) and compiled outside the DBMS itself. The DBMS is given a definition of the procedure's name and its parameters, along with other essential information such as the calling conventions used by the programming language in which the stored procedure was written. Once defined to the DBMS, the external stored procedure can be called as if it were a SQL stored procedure. The DBMS handles the call, turns over control to the external procedure, and then receives any return values and parameters.

Microsoft SQL Server provides a set of system-defined external stored procedures that provide access to selected operating system capabilities. The XP_SENDMAIL procedure can be used to send electronic mail to users, based on conditions within the DBMS:

```
XP_SENDMAIL @RECIPIENTS = 'Joe', 'Sam',
            @MESSAGE = 'Customer table nearly full';
```

Similarly, the XP_CMDSHELL external procedure can be called to pass commands to the underlying operating system on which SQL Server is operating. Beyond these predefined external procedures, SQL Server allows a user-written external procedure to be stored in a dynamic-linked library (DLL) and called from within SQL Server stored procedures.

Informix provides basic access to underlying operating system capabilities with a special SYSTEM statement. In addition, it supports user-written external procedures through its CREATE PROCEDURE statement. Where the statement block comprising the body of an Informix SPL procedure would appear, an EXTERNAL clause specifies the name, location, and language of the externally written procedure. With the procedure defined in this way, it can be called in the same way as native Informix SPL procedures. Newer versions of Oracle (Oracle8 and later) provide the same capability, also via the CREATE PROCEDURE statement. IBM's DB2 database family provides the same set of capabilities.

Triggers

As described at the beginning of this chapter, a trigger is a special set of stored procedure code whose activation is caused by modifications to the database contents. Unlike stored procedures created with a CREATE PROCEDURE statement, a trigger is not activated by a CALL or EXECUTE statement. Instead, the trigger is associated with a database table. When the data in the table is changed (by an INSERT, DELETE, or UPDATE statement), the trigger is *fired*, which means that the DBMS executes the SQL statements that make up the body of the trigger.

Triggers can be used to cause automatic updates of information within a database. For example, suppose you wanted to set up the sample database so that any time a new salesperson is inserted into the SALESREPS table, the sales target for the office where the salesperson works is raised by the new salesperson's quota. Here is an Oracle PL/SQL trigger that accomplishes this goal:

```
create trigger upd_tgt
   /* Insert trigger for SALESREPS */
   before insert on salesreps
   for each row
   when (new.quota is not null)
   begin
      update offices
         set target = target + new.quota;
   end;
```

The CREATE TRIGGER statement is used by most DBMS brands that support triggers to define a new trigger within the database. It assigns a name to the trigger (UPD_TGT for this one) and identifies the table the trigger is associated with (SALESREPS) and the update action(s) on that table that will cause the trigger to be executed (INSERT in this case). The body of this trigger tells the DBMS that for each new row inserted into the table, it should execute the specified UPDATE statement for the OFFICES table. The QUOTA value from the newly inserted SALESREPS row is referred to as NEW.QUOTA within the trigger body.

Advantages and Disadvantages of Triggers

Triggers can be extremely useful as an integral part of a database definition, and they can be used for a variety of different functions, including these:

- **Auditing changes**. A trigger can detect and disallow specific updates and changes that should not be permitted in the database.

- **Cascaded operations**. A trigger can detect an operation within the database (such as deletion of a customer or salesperson) and automatically cascade the impact throughout the database (such as adjusting account balances or sales targets).

- **Enforce interrelationships**. A trigger can enforce more complex interrelationships among the data in a database than those that can be expressed by simple referential integrity constraints or check constraints, such as those that require a sequence of SQL statements or IF...THEN...ELSE processing.

- **Stored procedure invocation**. A trigger can call one or more stored procedures or even invoke actions outside the DBMS itself through external procedure calls in response to database updates.

In each of these cases, a trigger embodies a set of business rules that govern the data in the database and modifications to that data. The rules are embedded in a single place in the database (the trigger definition). As a result, they are uniformly enforced across all applications that access the database. When they need to be changed, they can be changed once with the assurance that the change will be applied uniformly.

The major disadvantage of triggers is their potential performance impact. If a trigger is set on a particular table, then every database operation that attempts to update that table causes the DBMS to execute the trigger procedure. For a database that requires very high data insertion or update rates, the overhead of this processing can be considerable. This is especially true for bulk load operations, where the data may have already been prechecked for integrity. To deal with this disadvantage, some DBMS brands allow triggers to be selectively enabled and disabled, as appropriate.

Triggers in Transact-SQL

Transact-SQL provides triggers through a CREATE TRIGGER statement in both its Microsoft SQL Server and Sybase Adaptive Server dialects. Here is a Transact-SQL trigger definition for the sample database, which implements the same trigger function as the preceding Oracle PL/SQL example:

```
create trigger upd_tgt
   /* Insert trigger for SALESREPS */
   on salesreps
   for insert
   as
   if (@@rowcount = 1)
      begin
         update offices
            set target = target + inserted.quota
          from offices, inserted
         where offices.office = inserted.rep_office;
      end
   else
      raiserror 23456
```

The first clause names the trigger (UPD_TGT). The second clause is required and identifies the table to which the trigger applies. The third clause is also required and tells which database update operations cause the trigger to be fired. In this case, only an INSERT statement causes the trigger to fire. You can also specify UPDATE or DELETE operations, or a combination of two or three of these operations in a comma-separated list. Transact-SQL restricts triggers so that only one trigger may be defined on a particular table for each of the three data modification operations. The body of the trigger follows the AS keyword. To understand the body of a trigger like this one, you need to understand how Transact-SQL treats the rows in the target table during database modification operations.

For purposes of trigger operation, Transact-SQL defines two logical tables whose column structure is identical to the target table on which the trigger is defined. One of these logical tables is named DELETED, and the other is named INSERTED. These logical tables are populated with rows from the target table, depending on the data modification statement that caused the trigger to fire, as follows:

- **DELETE**. Each target table row that is deleted by the DELETE statement is placed into the DELETED table. The INSERTED table is empty.

- **INSERT**. Each target table row that is added by the INSERT statement is also placed into the INSERTED table. The DELETED table is empty.

- **UPDATE**. For each target table row that is changed by the UPDATE statement, a copy of the row before any modifications is placed into the DELETED table. A copy of the row after all modifications is placed into the INSERTED table.

These two logical tables can be referenced within the body of the trigger, and the data in them can be combined with data from other tables during the trigger's operation. In this Transact-SQL trigger, the trigger body first tests to make sure that only a single row of the SALESREPS table has been inserted, by checking the system variable @@ROWCOUNT. If this is true, then the QUOTA column from the INSERTED logical table is added to the appropriate row of the OFFICES table. The appropriate row is determined by joining the logical table to the OFFICES table based on matching office numbers.

Here is a different trigger that detects a different type of data integrity problem. In this case, it checks for an attempt to delete a customer when there are still orders outstanding in the database for that customer. If it detects this situation, the trigger automatically rolls back the entire transaction, including the DELETE statement that fired the trigger:

```
create trigger chk_del_cust
   /* Delete trigger for CUSTOMERS */
   on customers
   for delete
   as
   /* Detect any orders for deleted cust #'s */
   if (select count(*)
        from orders, deleted
      where orders.cust = deleted.cust_num) > 0
     begin
        rollback transaction
        print "Cannot delete; still have orders"
        raiserror 31234
     end
```

Transact-SQL triggers can be specified to fire on any UPDATE for a target table, or just for updates of selected columns. This trigger fires on inserts or updates to the

SALESREPS table and does different processing depending on whether the QUOTA or SALES column has been updated:

```
create trigger upd_reps
   /* Update trigger for SALESREPS */
   on salesreps
   for insert, update
   if update(quota)
      /* Handle updates to quota column */
      . . .
   if update (sales)
      /* Handle updates to sales column */
      . . .
```

Triggers in Informix SPL

Informix also supports triggers through a CREATE TRIGGER statement. As in the Transact-SQL dialect, the beginning of the CREATE TRIGGER statement defines the trigger name, the table on which the trigger is being defined, and the triggering actions. Here are statement fragments that show the syntax:

```
create trigger new_sls
   insert on salesreps . . .

create trigger del_cus_chk
   delete on customers . . .

create trigger ord_upd
   update on orders . . .

create trigger sls_upd
   update of quota, sales on salesreps . . .
```

The last example is a trigger that fires only when two specific columns of the SALESREPS table are updated.

Informix allows you to specify that a trigger should operate at three distinct times during the processing of a triggered change to the target table:

- **BEFORE**. The trigger fires before any changes take place. No rows of the target table have yet been modified.

- **AFTER**. The trigger fires after all changes take place. All affected rows of the target table have been modified.

■ **FOR EACH ROW.** The trigger fires repeatedly, once as each row affected by the change is being modified. Both the old and new data values for the row are available to the trigger.

An individual trigger definition can specify actions to be taken at one or more of these steps. For example, a trigger could execute a stored procedure to calculate the sum of all orders BEFORE an update, monitor updates to each ORDERS row as they occur with a second action, and then calculate the revised order total AFTER the update with a call to another stored procedure. Here is a trigger definition that does all of this:

```
create trigger upd_ord
    update of amount on orders
    referencing old as pre new as post

    /* Calculate order total before changes */
    before (execute procedure add_orders()
            into old_total;)

    /* Capture order increases and decreases */
    for each row
        when (post.amount < pre.amount)
            /* Write decrease data into table */
            (insert into ord_less
                values (pre.cust,
                        pre.order_date,
                        pre.amount,
                        post.amount);)
        when (post.amount > pre.amount)
            /* Write increase data into table */
            (insert into ord_more
                values (pre.cust,
                        pre.order_date,
                        pre.amount,
                        post.amount);)

    /* After changes, recalculate total */
    after (execute procedure add_orders()
            into new_total;)
```

The BEFORE clause in this trigger specifies that a stored procedure named ADD_ORDERS is to be called before any UPDATE statement processing occurs. Presumably, this procedure calculates the total orders and returns the total value into the local variable OLD_TOTAL. Similarly, the AFTER clause specifies that a stored procedure (in this case, the same one) is to be called after all UPDATE statement processing is complete. This time, the total orders amount is placed into a different local variable, NEW_TOTAL.

The FOR EACH ROW clause specifies the action to be taken as each affected row is updated. In this case, the requested action is an INSERT into one of two order tracking tables, depending on whether the order amount is being increased or decreased. These tracking tables contain the customer number, date, and both the old and new order amounts. To obtain the required values, the trigger must be able to refer to both the old (prechange) and the new (postchange) values of each row.

The REFERENCING clause provides names by which these two states of the currently-being-modified row of the ORDERS table can be used. In this example, the prechange values of the columns are available through the column name qualifier PRE, and the postchange values through the column name qualifier POST. These are not special names; any names can be used.

Informix is more limited than some other DBMS brands in the actions that can be specified within the trigger definition itself. These actions are available:

- An INSERT statement
- A DELETE statement
- An UPDATE statement
- An EXECUTE PROCEDURE statement

In practice, the last option provides quite a bit of flexibility. The called procedure can perform almost any processing that could be done inline within the trigger body itself.

Triggers in Oracle PL/SQL

Oracle provides a more complex trigger facility than either the Informix or Transact-SQL facility described in the preceding sections. It uses a CREATE TRIGGER statement to specify triggered actions. As in the Informix facility, a trigger can be specified to fire at specific times during specific update operations:

- **Statement-level trigger**. A statement-level trigger fires once for each data modification statement. It can be specified to fire either before the statement is executed or after the statement has completed its action.

- **Row-level trigger**. A row-level trigger fires once for each row being modified by a statement. In Oracle's structure, this type of trigger may also fire either before the row is modified or after it is modified.

- **Instead-of trigger**. An instead-of trigger takes the place of an attempted data modification statement. It provides a way to detect an attempted UPDATE, INSERT, or DELETE operation by a user or procedure, and substitute other processing instead. You can specify that a trigger should be executed instead of a statement, or that it should be executed instead of each attempted modification of a row.

```
create trigger bef_upd_ord
   before update on orders
   begin
      /* Calculate order total before changes */
      old_total = add_orders();
   end;
create trigger aft_upd_ord
   after update on orders
   begin
      /* Calculate order total after changes */
      new_total = add_orders();
   end;
create trigger dur_upd_ord
   before update of amount on orders
   referencing old as pre new as post

   /* Capture order increases and decreases */
   for each row
      when (post.amount != pre.amount)
         begin
            if (post.amount < pre.amount)
            then
               /* Write decrease data into table */
               insert into ord_less
                   values (pre.cust,
                           pre.order_date,
                           pre.amount,
                           post.amount);
            elsif (post.amount > pre.amount)
            then
               /* Write increase data into table */
               insert into ord_more
                   values (pre.cust,
                           pre.order_date,
                           pre.amount,
                           post.amount);
            end if;
         end;
```

These trigger structures and their options provide 14 different valid Oracle trigger types (12 resulting from a choice of INSERT/DELETE/UPDATE triggers for BEFORE or AFTER processing at the row or statement level (3×2×2), and two more from instead-of triggers at the statement or row level). In practice, relational databases built using Oracle don't tend to use instead-of triggers; they were introduced in Oracle8 to support some of its newer object-oriented features.

The code just shown is a PL/SQL trigger definition that implements the same processing as in the complex Informix example from the previous section. It has been split into three separate Oracle `CREATE TRIGGER` statements; one each for the `BEFORE` and `AFTER` statement-level triggers and one trigger that is executed for each update row.

Other Trigger Considerations

Triggers pose some of the same issues for DBMS processing that `UPDATE` and `DELETE` rules present. For example, triggers can cause a cascaded series of actions. A user's attempt to update a table may cause a trigger to fire. Within the body of that trigger is an `UPDATE` statement for another table. A trigger on that table causes the `UPDATE` of still another table, and so on. The situation is even worse if one of the fired triggers attempts to update the original target table that caused the firing of the trigger sequence in the first place! In this case, an infinite loop of fired triggers could result.

Various DBMS systems deal with this issue in different ways. Some impose restrictions on the actions that can be taken during execution of a trigger. Others provide built-in functions that allow a trigger's body to detect the level of nesting at which the trigger is operating. Some provide a system setting that controls whether cascaded trigger processing is allowed. Finally, some provide a limit on the number of levels of nested triggers that can fire.

One additional issue associated with triggers is the overhead that can result during very heavy database usage, such as when bulk data is being loaded into a database. Some DBMS brands provide the ability to selectively enable and disable trigger processing to handle this situation. Oracle, for example, provides this form of the `ALTER TRIGGER` statement:

```
ALTER TRIGGER BEF_UPD_ORD DISABLE;
```

A similar capability is provided within the `CREATE TRIGGER` statement of Informix.

Stored Procedures, Triggers, and the SQL Standard

The development of DBMS stored procedures and triggers has been largely driven by DBMS vendors and the competitive dynamics of the database industry. Sybase's initial introduction of stored procedures and triggers in SQL Server triggered a competitive response, and by the mid-1990s, many of the enterprise-class systems had added their own proprietary procedural extensions to SQL. Stored procedures were not a focus of the SQL2 standard, but became a part of the standardization agenda after the 1992 publication of the SQL2 standard. The work on stored procedure standards was split off from the broader object-oriented extensions that were proposed for SQL3, and was focused on a set of procedural extensions to the SQL2 language.

The result was a new part of the SQL standard, published in 1996 as SQL/Persistent Stored Modules (SQL/PSM), International Standard ISO/IEC 9075-4. The actual form of the standard specification is a collection of additions, edits, new paragraphs, and replacement paragraphs to the 1992 SQL2 standard (ISO/IEC 9075:1992). In addition to being a modification of the SQL2 standard, SQL/PSM was also drafted as a part of the planned follow-on standard, which was called SQL3 during its drafting. The development of the follow-on standard took longer than expected, but SQL/PSM eventually took its place as Part 4 of the SQL3 standard, officially known as SQL:1999. The SQL Call-Level Interface (CLI) standard, described in Chapter 19, was treated the same way; it is now Part 3 of the SQL:1999 standard. When the SQL:1999 standard was published, selected parts of SQL/PSM were moved to the core SQL/Foundation specification (Part 1), because they are also used by other parts of the standard.

The SQL/PSM standard published in 1996 addressed only stored procedures; it explicitly did *not* provide a specification of a trigger facility for the ISO SQL standard. The standardization of trigger functions was considered during the development of the SQL2 and SQL/PSM standards, but the standards groups determined that triggers were too closely tied to other object-oriented extensions proposed for SQL3. The SQL:1999 standard that resulted from the SQL3 work finally provided an ANSI/ISO standard trigger facility.

The publication of the SQL/PSM and SQL:1999 standards lagged the first commercial implementation of stored procedures and triggers by many years. By the time the standard was adopted, most enterprise DBMS vendors had responded to user enthusiasm and competitive pressure by introducing stored procedure and trigger capabilities in their products. Unlike some other SQL extensions where IBM's clout and a DB2 implementation had set a de facto standard, the major DBMS vendors implemented stored procedures and triggers in different, proprietary ways, and in some cases, competed with one another based on unique features of their implementations. As a result, the ANSI/ISO standardization of stored procedures and triggers has had little impact on the DBMS market to date. It's reasonable to expect that ANSI/ISO implementations will find their way into major DBMS products over time, but as a complement to, rather than a replacement for, the proprietary implementations.

The SQL/PSM Stored Procedures Standard

The capabilities specified in the SQL/PSM standard parallel the core features of the proprietary stored procedure capabilities of today's DBMS systems. They include SQL language constructs to:

- Define and name procedures and functions written in the extended SQL language
- Invoke (call) a previously defined procedure or function

- Pass parameters to a called procedure or function, and obtain the results of its execution

- Declare and use local variables within the procedure or function

- Group a block of SQL statements together for execution

- Conditionally execute SQL statements (IF...THEN...ELSE)

- Repeatedly execute a group of SQL statements (looping)

The SQL/PSM standard specifies two types of SQL-invoked routines. A *SQL-procedure* is a routine that does not return a value. It is called with a CALL statement:

```
CALL ADD_CUST('XYZ Corporation', 2137, 30000.00, 50000.00, 103, 'Chicago')
```

As with the proprietary stored procedure languages illustrated in the previous examples throughout this chapter, SQL/PSM stored procedures accept parameters passed via the CALL statement. SQL/PSM stored procedures can also pass data back to their caller via output parameters, again mirroring the capabilities of the proprietary stored procedure languages. SQL/PSM also supports combined input/output parameters, like some of the proprietary languages.

A SQL-function does return a value. It is called just like a built-in SQL function within a value expression:

```
SELECT COMPANY
  FROM CUSTOMERS
 WHERE GET_TOT_ORDS(CUST_NUM) > 10000.00
```

SQL/PSM restricts SQL-functions to only return a single value through the function-call mechanism. Output parameters and input/output parameters are not allowed in SQL-functions.

SQL routines are objects within the SQL-92 or SQL-99 database structure. SQL/PSM allows the creation of routines within a SQL-92 or SQL-99 schema (a schema-level routine) where it exists along with the tables, views, assertions, and other objects in the scheme. It also allows the creation of routines within a SQL2 module, which is the SQL procedure model carried forward from the SQL1 standard.

Creating a SQL Routine

Following the practice of most DBMS brands, the SQL/PSM standard uses the CREATE PROCEDURE and CREATE FUNCTION statements to specify the definitions of stored procedures and functions. Figure 20-18 shows simplified syntax for each of these

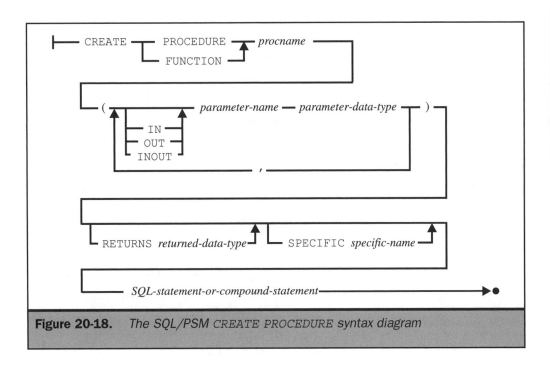

Figure 20-18. *The SQL/PSM* CREATE PROCEDURE *syntax diagram*

statements. In addition to the capabilities shown in the figure, the standard provides a capability to define external stored procedures, specifying the language they are written in, whether they can or cannot read or modify data in the database, their calling conventions, and other characteristics.

Flow-of-Control Statements

The SQL/PSM standard specifies the common programming structures that are found in most stored procedure dialects to control the flow of execution. Figure 20-19 shows the conditional branching and looping syntax. Note that the SQL statement lists specified for each structure consist of a sequence of SQL statements, each ending with a semicolon. Thus, explicit block structures are not required for simple multistatement sequences that appear in an IF...THEN...ELSE statement or a LOOP statement. The looping structures provide a great deal of flexibility for loop processing. There are forms that place the test at the top of the loop and at the bottom of the loop, as well as a form that provides infinite looping and requires the explicit coding of a test to break loop execution. Each of the program control structures is explicitly terminated by an END flag that matches the type of structure, making programming debugging easier.

Figure 20-19. *SQL/PSM flow-of-control statements syntax diagram*

Cursor Operations

The SQL/PSM standard extends the cursor manipulation capabilities specified in the SQL2 standard for embedded SQL into SQL routines. The DECLARE CURSOR, OPEN, FETCH, and CLOSE statements retain their roles and functions. Instead of using application program host variables to supply parameter values and to receive retrieved data, SQL routine parameters and variables can be used for these functions.

The SQL/PSM standard does introduce one new cursor-controlled looping structure, shown in Figure 20-20. Like the similar structures in the Oracle and Informix dialects

Figure 20-20. *SQL/PSM cursor-controlled loop syntax diagram*

described in the "Cursor-Based Repetition" section earlier in this chapter, it combines the cursor definition and the OPEN, FETCH, and CLOSE statements into a single loop definition that also specifies the processing to be performed for each row of retrieved query results.

Block Structure

Figure 20-21 shows the block structure specified by the SQL/PSM standard. It is quite a comprehensive structure, providing the following capabilities:

- Labels the block of statements with a statement label
- Declares local variables for use within the block
- Declares local user-defined error conditions
- Declares cursors for queries to be executed within the block
- Declares handlers to process error conditions that arise
- Defines the sequence of SQL statements to be executed

These capabilities resemble some of those described earlier in the "Statement Blocks" section of this chapter for the Informix and Oracle dialect stored procedure dialects.

Local variables within SQL/PSM procedures and functions (actually, within statement blocks) are declared using the DECLARE statement. Values are assigned

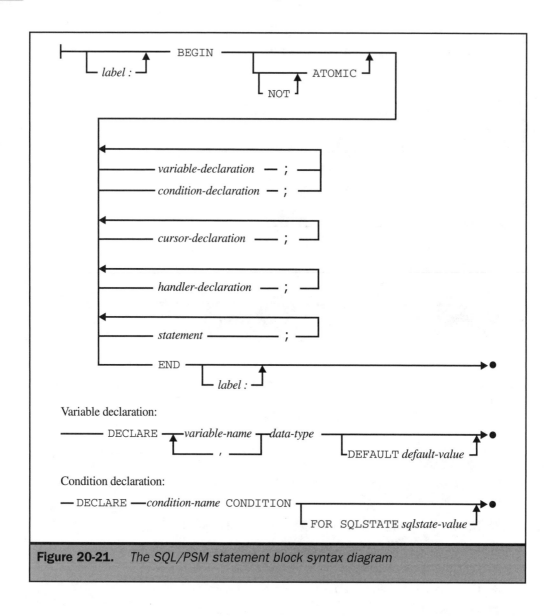

Figure 20-21. *The SQL/PSM statement block syntax diagram*

using the SET statement. Functions return a value using the RETURN statement. Here is a statement block that might appear within a stored function, with examples of these statements:

```
try_again:
  begin
```

```
    /* Declare some local variables */
    declare msg_text varchar(40);
    declare tot_amt decimal(16,2);

    /* Get the order total */
    set tot_amt = get_tot_ords();
    if (tot_amt > 0)
    then
       return (tot_amt);
    else
       return (0.00);
    end if
end try_again
```

Error Handling

The block structure specified by the SQL/PSM standard provides fairly comprehensive support for error handling. The standard specifies predefined conditions that can be detected and handled, including:

- **SQLWARNING**. One of the warning conditions specified in the SQL2 standard
- **NOT FOUND**. The condition that normally occurs when the end of a set of query results is reached with a FETCH statement
- **SQLSTATE values**. A test for specific SQLSTATE error codes
- **User-defined conditions**. A condition named by the stored procedure

Conditions are typically defined in terms of SQLSTATE values. Rather than using numerical SQLSTATE codes, you can assign the condition a symbolic name. You can also specify your own user-defined condition:

```
declare bad_err condition for sqlstate '12345';
declare my_err condition;
```

Once the condition has been defined, you can force the condition to occur through the execution of a SQL routine with the SIGNAL statement:

```
signal bad_err;
signal sqlstate '12345';
```

To handle error conditions that may arise, SQL/PSM allows you to declare a *condition handler*. The declaration specifies the list of conditions that are to be handled and the action to be taken. It also specifies the type of condition handling. The types differ in what happens to the flow of control after the handler is finished with its work:

- **CONTINUE type**. After the condition handler completes its work, control returns to the next statement following the one that caused the condition. That is, execution *continues* with the next statement.

- **EXIT type**. After the condition handler completes its work, control returns to the *end* of the statement block containing the statement that caused the condition. That is, execution effectively exits the block.

- **UNDO type**. After the condition handler completes its work, all modifications are undone to data in the database caused by statements within the same statement block as the statement causing the error. The effect is the same as if a transaction had been initiated at the beginning of the statement block and was being rolled back.

Here are some examples that show the structure of the handler definition:

```
/* Handle SQL warnings here, then continue */
declare continue handler for sqlwarning
    call my_warn_routine();

/* Handle severe errors by undoing effects */
declare undo handler for user_disaster
    begin
        /* Do disaster cleanup here */
        . . .
    end;
```

Error handling can get quite complex, and it's possible for errors to arise during the execution of the handler routine itself. To avoid infinite recursion on errors, the normal condition signaling does not apply during the execution of a condition handler. The standard allows you to override this restriction with the RESIGNAL statement. It operates just like the SIGNAL statement, but is used exclusively within condition-handler routines.

Routine Name Overloading

The SQL/PSM standard permits overloading of stored procedure and function names. Overloading is a common attribute in object-oriented systems and is a way to make stored routines more flexible in handling a wide variety of data types and situations. Using the overloading capability, several different routines can be given the same routine name. The multiple routines defined with the same name must differ from one another in the number of parameters that they accept or in the data types of the individual parameters. For example, you might define these three stored functions:

```
create function combo(a, b)
   a integer;
   b integer;
   returns integer;
   as return (a+b)

create function combo(a, b, c)
   a integer;
   b integer;
   c integer;
   returns integer;
   as return (a+b+c)

create procedure combo(a, b)
   a varchar(255);
   b varchar(255);
   returns varchar(255);
   as return (a || b)
```

The first COMBO function combines two integers by adding them and returns the sum. The second COMBO function combines three integers the same way. The third COMBO function combines two character strings by concatenating them. The standard allows both of these functions named COMBO to be defined at the same time within the database. When the DBMS encounters a reference to the COMBO function, it examines the number of arguments in the reference and their data types, and determines which version of the COMBO function to call. Thus, the overloading capability allows a SQL programmer to create a family of routines that logically perform the same function and have the same name, even though the specifics of their usage for different data types is different. In object-oriented terms, overloading is sometimes called *polymorphism*, meaning literally that the same function can take many different forms.

To simplify the management of a family of routines that share an overloaded name, the SQL/PSM standard has the concept of a *specific* name: a second name that is assigned to the routine that is unique within the database schema or module. It uniquely identifies a specific routine. The specific name is used to drop the routine, and it is reflected in the Information Schema views that describe stored routines. The specific name is not used to call the routine; that would defeat the primary purpose of the overloaded routine name. Support for specific names or some similar mechanism is a practical requirement for any system that permits overloading or polymorphism for objects and provides a capability to manage them by dropping or changing their definitions, since the system must be able to determine which specific object is being modified.

External Stored Procedures

The bulk of the SQL/PSM standard is concerned with the extensions to the SQL language that are used to define SQL-procedures and SQL-functions. Note, however, that the method used to invoke a SQL-procedure (the CALL statement) or a SQL-function (a reference to the function by name within a SQL statement) are not particular to procedures defined in the SQL language. In fact, the SQL/PSM standard provides for external stored procedures and functions, written in some other programming language such as C or Pascal. For external procedures, the CREATE PROCEDURE and CREATE FUNCTION statements are still used to define the procedure to the DBMS, specifying its name and the parameters that it accepts or returns. A special clause of the CREATE statement specifies the language in which the stored procedure or function is written, so that the DBMS may perform the appropriate conversion of data types and call the routine appropriately.

Other Stored Procedure Capabilities

The SQL/PSM standard treats SQL-procedures and SQL-functions as managed objects within the database, using extensions to the SQL statements used to manage other objects. You use a variation of the DROP statement to delete routines when they are no longer needed, and a variation of the ALTER statement to change the definition of a function or procedure. The SQL2 permissions mechanism is similarly extended with additional privileges. The EXECUTE privilege gives a user the ability to execute a stored procedure or function. It is managed by the GRANT and REVOKE statements in the same manner as other database privileges.

Because the stored routines defined by SQL/PSM are defined within SQL2 schemas, many routines can be defined in many different schemas throughout the database. When calling a stored routine, the routine name can be fully qualified to uniquely identify the routine within the database. The SQL/PSM standard provides an alternative method of searching for the definition of unqualified routine names through a new PATH concept.

The PATH is the sequence of schema names that should be searched to resolve a routine reference. A default PATH can be specified as part of the schema header in the CREATE SCHEMA statement. The PATH can also be dynamically modified during a SQL session through the SET PATH statement.

The SQL/PSM standard also lets the author of a stored procedure or function give the DBMS some hints about its operation to improve the efficiency of execution. One example is the ability to define a stored routine as DETERMINISTIC or NOT DETERMINISTIC. A DETERMINISTIC routine will always return the same results when it is called with the same parameter values. If the DBMS observes that a DETERMINISTIC routine is called repeatedly, it may choose to keep a copy of the results that it returns. Later, when the routine is called again, the DBMS does not need to actually execute the routine; it can simply return the same results that it returned the last time.

Another form of hint tells the DBMS whether an external stored procedure or function reads database contents and whether it modifies database contents. This not only allows the DBMS to optimize database access, but can also impose a security restriction on external routines from other sources. Other hints determine whether a SQL-function should be called if one of its parameters has a NULL value, and control how the DBMS selects the specific function or procedure to be executed when overloading is used.

Trigger Standards in SQL:1999

Triggers were addressed for standardization as part of the SQL3 effort, which led to the eventual publication of the SQL:1999 ANSI/ISO standard. By that time, many commercial DBMS products had already implemented triggers, and the standard synthesized the specific capabilities that had proven useful in practice. Like the commercial products, ANSI/ISO standard triggers are defined for a single, specific table. The standard permits trigger definitions only on tables, not on views.

The proprietary SQL Server, Oracle and Informix trigger mechanisms shown in the examples throughout this chapter provide a context for examining the ANSI/ISO standard mechanism. The standard does not provide any radical departure from the capabilities already described for the various DBMS products. Here is how the standard compares to them:

- **Naming**. The standard treats triggers as named objects within the database.

- **Types**. The standard provides INSERT, DELETE, and UPDATE triggers; UPDATE triggers can be associated with the update of a specific column or group of columns.

- **Timing**. The standard provides for triggers that operate before a database update statement or after the statement.

- **Row-level or statement-level operation**. The standard provides for both statement-level triggers (executed once per database-updating statement) and row-level triggers (executed repeatedly for each row of the table that is modified).

- **Aliases**. Access to the "before" and "after" values in a modified row or table is provided via an alias mechanism, like the table aliases used in the FROM clause.

You use the SQL:1999 CREATE TRIGGER statement, shown in Figure 20-22, to define a trigger. The statement clauses are familiar from the proprietary trigger examples throughout the earlier sections of this chapter.

One very useful extension provided by the standard is the WHEN clause that can be specified as part of a triggered action. The WHEN clause is optional, and it operates like a WHERE clause for determining whether a triggered action will be carried out. When

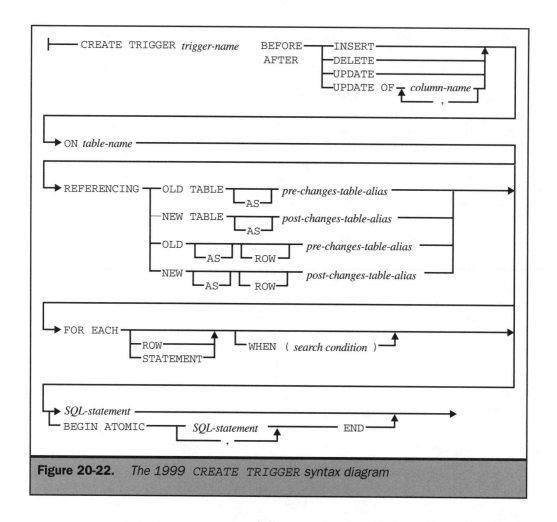

Figure 20-22. *The 1999* CREATE TRIGGER *syntax diagram*

DBMS executes the particular type of statement specified in the trigger definition, it evaluates the search condition specified in the WHEN clause. The form of the search condition is exactly like the search condition in a WHERE clause, and it will produce either a TRUE or FALSE result. The triggered action is carried out only if the result is TRUE.

To provide security for triggers, the SQL:1999 standard establishes a new TRIGGER privilege that may be granted for specific tables to specific users. With this privilege, a user may establish a trigger on the table. The owner of a table is always allowed to establish triggers on the table.

Summary

Stored procedures and triggers are two very useful capabilities for SQL databases used in transaction-processing applications:

- Stored procedures allow you to predefine common database operations, and invoke them simply by calling the stored procedure, for improved efficiency and less chance of error.

- Extensions to the basic SQL language give stored procedures the features normally found in programming languages. These features include local variables, conditional processing, branching, and special statements for row-by-row query results processing.

- Stored functions are a special form of stored procedure that return a value.

- Triggers are procedures whose execution is automatically initiated based on attempted modifications to a table. A trigger can be fired by an INSERT, DELETE, or UPDATE statement for the table.

- There is wide variation in the specific SQL dialects used by the major DBMS brands to support stored procedures and triggers.

- There is now an international standard for stored procedures (but not triggers); as one of the newer standards, it has not yet had a major impact on the actual implementation by leading DBMS vendors.

Chapter 21

SQL and Data Warehousing

One of the most important applications of SQL and relational database technology today is the rapidly growing area of data warehousing and business intelligence. The focus of data warehousing is to use accumulated data to provide information and insights for decision making. With the rising popularity of the World Wide Web and the direct interaction with customers that it provides, the amount of data available about customer behavior (reflected in their click-by-click journey through web pages) has literally exploded. Data warehousing advocates that this data be treated as a valuable asset, and that it be translated, through analysis, into competitive advantage. The complementary process of data mining involves in-depth analysis of historical and trend data to find valuable insights about customer behavior and cross-dependencies. SQL-based relational databases are a key technology underlying data warehousing applications.

Business intelligence applications have exploded in popularity over the last decade. Corporate IS surveys show that the majority of large corporations have some type of business analysis or data warehousing projects underway. In many ways, data warehousing represents relational databases coming full circle, back to their roots. When relational databases first appeared on the scene, the established databases (such as IBM's hierarchical IMS database) were squarely focused on business transaction-processing applications. Relational technology gained popularity by focusing on decision support applications and their ad hoc queries. As the popularity of these applications grew, most relational database vendors shifted their focus to compete for new transaction-processing applications. With data warehousing, attention has turned back to what was formerly called decision support, albeit with new terminology and much more powerful tools than those of 15 years earlier.

Data Warehousing Concepts

One of the foundations of data warehousing is the notion that databases for transaction processing and databases for business analysis serve very different needs. The core focus of an online transaction processing (OLTP) database is to support the basic day-to-day functions of an organization. In a manufacturing company, OLTP databases support the taking of customer orders, ordering of raw materials, management of inventory, billing of customers, and similar functions. Their heaviest users are the applications used by order-processing clerks, production workers, warehouse staff, and the like. By contrast, the core focus of a business intelligence (BI) database is to support business decision making through data analysis and reporting. Its heaviest users are typically product managers, production planners, and marketing professionals.

Table 21-1 highlights the significant differences in OLTP and business intelligence application profiles and the database workloads they produce. A typical OLTP transaction processing a customer's order might involve these database accesses:

- Read a row of the customer table to verify the proper customer number.

- Check the credit limit for that customer.
- Read a row of the inventory table to verify that a product is available.
- Insert a new row in an order table and an order-items table to record the customer's order.
- Update the row of the inventory table to reflect the decreased quantity available.

The workload presents a large volume of short, simple database requests that typically read, write, or update individual rows and then commit a transaction. The same type of workload is presented by all of the most frequent types of transactions, such as:

- Retrieving the price of a product
- Checking the quantity of product available
- Deleting an order
- Updating a customer address
- Raising a customer's credit limit

In contrast, a typical business analysis transaction (generating an order analysis report) might involve these database accesses:

- Join information from the orders, order-items, products, and customers tables
- Summarize the detail from the orders table by product in a summary query
- Compute the total order quantities for each product
- Sort the resulting information by customer

This workload presents a single, long-running query that is read-intensive. It processes many rows of the database (in this case, *every* order item) and involves computing totals and averages and summarizing data. These characteristics are typical of almost all business analysis queries, such as:

- Which regions had the best performance last quarter?
- How did sales by product last quarter compare to last year?
- What is the trend line for a particular product's sales?
- Which customers are buying the highest-growth products?
- Which characteristics do those customers share?

The difference between the business intelligence and the OLTP workloads is substantial and makes it difficult or impossible for a single DBMS to serve both types of applications.

Database Characteristic	OLTP Database	Data Warehouse Database
Data contents	Current data	Historical data
Data structure	Tables organized to align with transaction structure	Tables organized to be easy to understand and query
Typical table size	Thousands of rows	Millions of rows
Access patterns	Predetermined for each type of transaction to be processed	Ad hoc, depending on the particular decision to be made
Rows accessed per request	Tens	Thousands to millions
Row coverage per access	Individual rows	Groups (summary queries)
Access rate	Many business transactions per second or minute	Many minutes or hours per query
Access type	Read, insert, and update	Almost 100 percent read
Performance focus	Transaction throughput	Query completion time

Table 21-1.   *OLTP Versus Data Warehousing Database Attributes*

Components of a Data Warehouse

Figure 21-1 shows the architecture of a data warehousing environment. There are three key components:

- **Warehouse loading tools**. Typically, a suite of programs that extract data from corporate transaction-processing systems (relational databases, mainframe and minicomputer files, legacy databases), process the data, and load it into the warehouse. This process typically involves substantial cleanup of the transaction data, filtering it, reformatting it, and loading it on a bulk basis into the warehouse.

- **A warehouse database**. Typically, a relational database optimized for storing vast quantities of data, bulk loading data at high speeds, and supporting complex business analysis queries.

- **Data analysis tools**. Typically, a suite of programs for performing statistical and time series analysis, doing "what if" analysis, and presenting the results in graphical form.

Vendors in the data warehousing market have tended to concentrate in one of these component areas. Several vendors build product suites that focus on the warehouse-loading process and challenges. A different group of vendors have focused on data analysis. There has been some vendor consolidation in each of these areas, but both remain areas of focus for individual independent software companies, including several whose revenues are in the $100 million range.

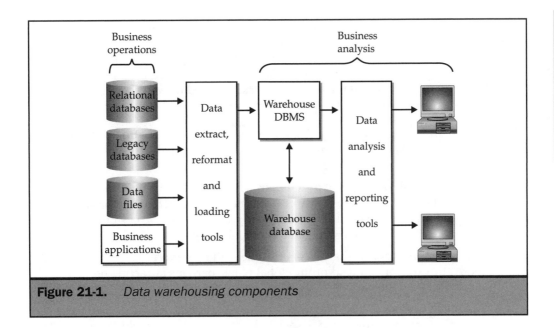

Figure 21-1. *Data warehousing components*

Specialized warehouse databases were also the target of several startup companies early in the data warehousing market. Over time, the major enterprise DBMS vendors also moved to address this area. Some developed their own specialized warehouse databases; others added warehouse databases to their product line by acquiring smaller companies that produced them. Today, the database component in the figure is almost always a specialized SQL-based warehouse DBMS supplied by one of the major enterprise database vendors.

The Evolution of Data Warehousing

The initial focus of data warehousing was the creation of huge, enterprisewide collections of all of the enterprise's accumulated data. By creating such a warehouse of data, almost any possible question about historical business practices could be posed. Many companies started down the road to creating warehouses with this approach, but success rates were low. Large, enterprisewide warehouses generally proved too difficult to create, too big, and too unwieldy to use in practice.

The focus eventually turned to smaller data warehouses focused on specific areas of a business that could most benefit from in-depth data analysis. The term *data mart* was coined to describe these smaller (but still often massive) data warehouses. With the advent of multiple data marts within enterprises, a recent area of focus has been on management of distributed data marts. In particular, there is a large potential for duplication of effort in the data cleansing and reformatting process when multiple marts are drawing data from the same production databases. The emerging answer seems to be a coordinated approach to data transformation for distributed marts, rather than a return to huge centralized warehouses.

Data warehousing, and more recently data marts, have grown to prominence in many different industries. They are most widely (and aggressively) used in industries where better information about business trends can be used to make decisions that save or generate large amounts of money. For example:

- **High-volume manufacturing**. Analysis of customer purchase trends, seasonality, and so on can help the company plan its production and lower its inventory levels, saving money for other purposes.

- **Packaged goods**. Analysis of promotions (coupons, advertising campaigns, direct mail, and so on) and the response of consumers with different demographics can help to determine the most effective way to reach prospective customers, saving millions of dollars in advertising and promotion costs.

- **Telecommunications**. Analysis of customer calling patterns can help to create more attractive pricing and promotional plans, perhaps attracting new customers from a competitor.

- **Airlines**. Analysis of customer travel patterns is critical to *yield management*, the process of setting airfares and associated restrictions on available airline seats to maximize profitability.

- **Financial services**. Analysis of customer credit factors and comparing them to historical customer profiles can help to make better decisions about which customers are creditworthy.

Database Architecture for Warehousing

The structure (schema) of a warehouse database is typically designed to make the information easy to analyze, since that is the major focus of its use. The structure must make it easy to slice and dice the data along various dimensions. For example, one day a business analyst may want to look at sales by product category by region, to compare the performance of different products in different areas of the country. The next day, the same analyst may want to look at sales trends over time by region, to see which regions are growing and which are not. The structure of the database must lend itself to this type of analysis along several different dimensions.

Fact Cubes

In most cases, the data stored in a warehouse can be accurately modeled as an N-dimensional cube (*N-cube*) of historical business facts. A simple three-dimensional cube of sales data is shown in Figure 21-2 to illustrate the structure. The fact in each cell of the cube is a dollar sales amount. Along one edge of the cube, one of the dimensions is the month during which the sales took place. Another dimension is the region where the sales occurred. The third dimension is the type of product that was sold. Each cell in the cube represents the sales for one combination of these three dimensions. The

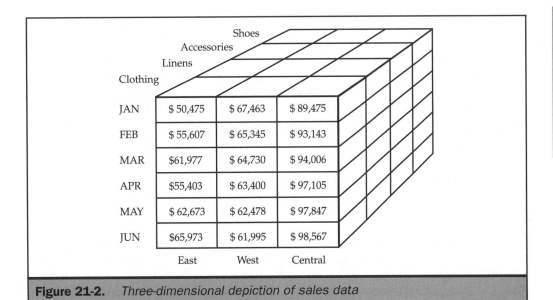

Figure 21-2.   *Three-dimensional depiction of sales data*

$50,475 amount in the upper-left front cell represents the sales amount for January, for clothing, in the East region.

Figure 21-2 shows a simple three-dimensional cube, but in many warehousing applications, there will be a dozen dimensions or more. Although a twelve-dimensional cube is difficult to visualize, the principles are the same as for the three-dimensional example. Each dimension represents some variable on which the data may be analyzed. Each combination of dimension values has one associated fact value, which is typically the historical business result obtained for that collection of dimension values.

To illustrate the database structures typically used in warehousing applications, we use a warehouse that might be found in a distribution company. The company distributes different types of products, made by various suppliers, to several hundred customers located in various regions of the country, through the efforts of its sales force. The company wants to analyze historical sales data along these dimensions, to discover trends and gain insights that will help it better manage its business. The underlying model for this analysis will be a five-dimensional fact cube with these dimensions:

- **Category**. The category of product that was sold, with values such as clothing, linens, accessories, and shoes. The warehouse has about two dozen product categories.

- **Supplier**. The supplier who manufactures the particular product sold. The company might distribute products from 50 different suppliers.

- **Customer**. The customer who purchased the products. The company has several hundred customers. Some of the larger customers purchase products centrally and are serviced by a single salesperson; others purchase on a local basis and are served by local salespeople.

- **Region**. The region of the country where the products were sold. Some of the company's customers operate in only one region of the country; others operate in two or more regions.

- **Month**. The month when the products were sold. For comparison purposes, the company has decided to maintain 36 months (three years) of historical sales data in the warehouse.

With these characteristics, each of the five dimensions is relatively independent of the others. Sales to a particular customer may be concentrated in a single region or in multiple regions. A specific category of product may be supplied by one or many different suppliers. The fact in each cell of the five-dimensional cube is the sales amount for that particular combination of dimension values. With the attributes just described, the fact cube contains over 35 million cells (24 categories × 50 suppliers × 300 customers × 3 regions × 36 months).

Star Schemas

In most data warehouses, the most effective way to model the N-dimensional fact cube is with a star schema. A star schema for the distributor warehouse in the previous example is shown in Figure 21-3. Each dimension of the cube is represented by a dimension table. There are five of them in the figure, named CATEGORIES, SUPPLIERS, CUSTOMERS, REGIONS, and MONTHS. There is one row in each dimension table for each possible value of that dimension. The MONTHS table has 36 rows, one for each month of sales history being stored. Three regions produce a three-row REGIONS table.

Dimension tables in a star schema often contain columns with descriptive text information or other attributes associated with that dimension (such as the name of the buyer for a customer, or the customer's address and phone number, or the purchasing terms for a supplier). These columns may be displayed in reports generated from the database. A dimension table always has a primary key that contains the value of the dimension. If the values of a dimension are numbers (such as a clothing size) or short text strings (such as a city name), the primary key may be this dimension value itself. It's more common for dimension values to be expressed in some type of code value. Three-letter airport codes and customer numbers are typical examples. In the sample warehouse of Figure 21-3, we assume that actual values are used as primary keys for REGIONS (East, West, and so on), CATEGORIES (clothing, shoes, and so on), and MONTHS. The other two dimensions use coded values (CUST_CODE for CUSTOMERS, SUPP_CODE for SUPPLIERS).

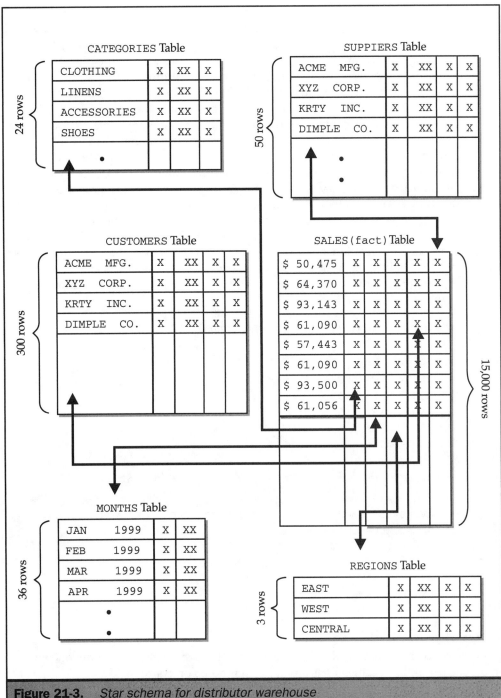

Figure 21-3.   *Star schema for distributor warehouse*

The largest table in the database is the fact table in the center of the schema. This table is named SALES in Figure 21-3. The fact table contains a column with the data values that appear in the cells of the N-cube in Figure 21-2. In addition, the fact table contains a column (or columns) that forms a foreign key for each of the dimension tables. In this example, there are five such foreign key columns. With this structure, each row represents the data for one cell of the N-cube. The foreign keys link the row to the corresponding dimension table rows for its position in the cube.

The fact table typically contains only a few columns, but many rows—hundreds of thousands or even millions of rows are not unusual in a production data warehouse. The fact column almost always contains numeric values, such as currency amounts, units shipped or received, or pounds processed. Virtually all reports from the warehouse involve summary data—totals, averages, high or low values, percentages—based on arithmetic computations on this numeric value.

The schema structure of Figure 21-3 is called a star schema for obvious reasons. The fact table is at the center of a star of data relationships. The dimension tables form the points of the star. The relationships created by the foreign keys in the fact table connect the center to the points. With the star-schema structure, most business analysis questions turn into queries that join the central fact table with one or more dimension tables. Here are some examples:

Show the total sales for clothing in January, by region.

```
SELECT SALES_AMOUNT, REGION
  FROM SALES, REGIONS
 WHERE MONTH = 01/1999
   AND PROD_TYPE = "Clothing"
   AND SALES.REGION = REGIONS.REGION
 ORDER BY REGION
```

Show the average sales for each CUSTOMER, by SUPPLIER, for each month.

```
SELECT AVG(SALES_AMOUNT), CUST_NAME, SUPPLIER_NAME, MONTH
  FROM SALES, CUSTOMERS, SUPPLIERS
 WHERE SALES.CUST_CODE = CUSTOMERS.CUST_CODE
   AND SALES.SUPP_CODE = SUPPLIERS.SUPP_CODE
 GROUP BY CUST_NAME, SUPP_NAME
 ORDER BY CUST_NAME, SUPP_NAME, MONTH
```

Multilevel Dimensions

In the star-schema structure of Figure 21-3, each of the dimensions has only one level. In practice, multilevel dimensions are quite common. For example:

- Sales data may in fact be accumulated for each sales office. Each office is a part of a sales district, and each district is a part of a sales region.

- Sales data is accumulated by month, but it may also be useful to look at quarterly sales results. Each month is a part of a particular quarter.

- Sales data may be accumulated for individual products ordered, and the products are associated with a particular supplier.

Multilevel dimensions such as these complicate the basic star schema, and in practice, there are several ways to deal with them:

- **Additional data in the dimension tables**. The geographic dimension table might contain information about individual offices, but also include columns indicating the district and region to which the office belongs. Aggregate data for these higher levels of the geographic dimension can then be obtained by summary queries that join the fact table to the dimension table and selected based on the district or region columns. This approach is conceptually simple, but it means that all aggregate (summary) data must be calculated query by query. This likely produces unacceptably poor performance.

- **Multiple levels within the dimension tables**. The geographic dimension table might be extended to include rows for offices, districts, and regions. Rows containing summary (total) data for these higher-level dimensions are added to the fact table when it is updated. This solves the runtime query performance problem by precalculating aggregate (summary) data. However, it complicates the queries considerably. Because every sale is now included in three separate fact table rows (one each for office, district, and region), any totals must be computed very carefully. Specifically, the fact table must usually contain a level column to indicate the level of data summarization provided by that row, and every query that computes totals or other statistics must include a search condition that restricts it to rows at only a specific level.

- **Precomputed summaries in the dimension tables**. Instead of complicating the fact table, summary data may be precomputed and stored in the dimension tables (for example, summary sales for a district stored in the district's row of the geographic dimension table). This solves the duplicate facts problem of the previous solution, but it works only for very simple precomputed amounts. The precalculated totals don't help with queries about products by district or district results by month, for example, without further complicating the dimension tables.

- **Multiple fact tables at different levels**. Instead of complicating the fact table, this approach creates multiple fact tables for different levels of summary data. To support cross-dimension queries (for example, district –results –by month), specialized fact tables that summarize data on this basis are needed. The resulting pattern of dimension tables and fact tables tends to have many interrelationships, creating a pattern resembling a snowflake; hence, this type of schema is often referred to as a *snowflake schema*. This approach solves the runtime performance problem and eliminates the possibility of erroneous data from a single fact table, but it can add significant complexity to the warehouse database design, making it harder to understand.

In practice, finding the right schema and architecture for a particular warehouse is a complicated decision, driven by the specifics of the facts and dimensions, the types of queries frequently performed, and other considerations. Many companies use specialized consultants to help them design data warehouses and deal with exactly these issues.

SQL Extensions for Data Warehousing

With a star-schema structure, a relational database conceptually provides a good foundation for managing data for business analysis. The capability to freely relate information within the database based solely on data values is a good match for the ad hoc, unstructured queries that typify business intelligence applications. But there are some serious mismatches between typical business intelligence queries and the capabilities of the core SQL language. For example:

- **Data ordering**. Many business intelligence queries deal explicitly or implicitly with data ordering—they pose questions like "What is the top 10 percent?" "What are the top 10?" or "Which are the worst performing?" As a set-oriented language, SQL manipulates unordered sets of rows. The only support for sorting and ordering data within standard SQL is the ORDER BY clause in the SELECT statement, which is applied only at the end of all other set-oriented processing.

- **Time series**. Many business intelligence queries compare values based on time—contrasting this year's results to last year's, or this month's results to the same month last year, or computing year-over-year growth rates, for example. It is very hard, and sometimes impossible, to get side-by-side comparisons of data from different time periods within a single row of standard SQL query results, depending on the structure of the underlying database.

- **Comparison to aggregate values**. Many business intelligence queries compare values for individual entities (for example, office sales results) to an overall total, or to subtotals (such as regional results). These comparisons are difficult to express in standard SQL. A report format showing line-item detail, subtotals, and totals is impossible to generate directly from SQL, since all rows of query results must have the same column structure.

To deal with these issues, DBMS products on data warehousing have tended to extend the core SQL language. For example, the DBMS from Red Brick, one of the data warehousing pioneers and now a part of Informix's product line (which has, in turn, been acquired by IBM), features these extensions as part of its Red Brick Intelligent SQL (RISQL) language:

- **Ranking**. Supports queries that ask for the top 10 and similar requests.

- **Moving totals and averages**. Supports queries that smooth raw data for time series analysis.

- **Running totals and averages**. Allows query responses that show results for individual months plus year-to-date totals, and similar requests.

- **Ratios**. Allows queries that very simply express the ratio of individual values to a total or subtotal without the use of complex subqueries.

- **Decoding**. Simplifies the translation of dimension-value codes (like the supplier-id in the example warehouse) into understandable names.

- **Subtotals**. Allow production of query results that combine detailed and summary data values, at various levels of summarization.

Other warehousing vendors provide similar extensions in their SQL implementations or provide the same capabilities built into their data analysis products. As with extensions in other areas of the SQL language, although the conceptual capabilities provided by several different DBMS brands may be similar, the specifics of the implementation differ substantially.

Warehouse Performance

The performance of a data warehouse is one of the keys to its usefulness. If business analysis queries take too long, people tend not to use the warehouse on an ad hoc basis for decision making. If it takes too long to load data into the warehouse, the corporate IS organization will probably resist frequent updates, and stale data may make the warehouse less useful. Achieving a good balance between load performance and runtime performance is one of the keys to successful warehouse deployment.

Load Performance

The process of loading a warehouse can be very time-consuming. It's common for warehouse data loads to take hours or even days for very large warehouses. Load processing typically involves these operations:

- **Data extraction**. The data to be loaded into the warehouse database typically comes from several different operational data sources. Some may be relational databases that support OLTP applications.

- **Data cleansing**. Operational data tends to be "dirty" in the sense that it contains significant errors. For example, older transaction-processing systems may not have strong integrity checks, permitting the entry of incorrect customer numbers or product numbers. The warehouse-loading process typically includes data integrity and data sanity checks.

■ **Data cross-checking.** In many companies, the data processing systems that support various business operations have been developed at different times and are not integrated. Changes that are processed by one system (for example, adding new product numbers to an order-processing application) may not automatically be reflected in other systems (for example, the inventory control system), or there may be delays in propagating changes. When data from these nonintegrated systems arrives at the warehouse, it must be checked for internal consistency.

■ **Data reformatting.** Data formats in the operational data stores may differ considerably from the warehouse database. Character data may need transformation from a mainframe's EBCDIC encoding to ASCII. Zoned decimal or packed decimal data may need reformatting. Date and time formats are another source of differences. Beyond these simple data format differences, data from one OLTP data source row may have to be broken apart into multiple warehouse tables, while data from multiple OLTP tables or files may have to be combined to create a warehouse table.

■ **Data insertion/update.** After the preprocessing, actual bulk loading of data into a warehouse database tends to be a specialized operation. High-volume data loaders typically operate in a batch-oriented mode, without transaction logic and with specialized recovery. Row loading or update rates of hundreds of megabytes per hour may be required.

■ **Index creation/update.** The specialized indexes used by the warehouse must be modified to reflect the revised warehouse contents. As with the actual data insertion and update, specialized handling is typically applied. In some cases, it is more efficient to rapidly re-create an entire index than to modify it incrementally as data rows are inserted or updated. Other index structures permit more incremental updates.

These tasks are typically performed by specialized warehouse-building programs on a batch-processing basis. Ad hoc query access to the warehouse is turned off during the update/refresh processing, allowing it to proceed at maximum speed without competition for DBMS cycles. Despite these optimizations, warehouse load times tend to grow as the amount of accumulated data grows, so the load-time versus runtime performance trade-off must be made on an ongoing basis. Warehouses with many indexes or precomputed summary values may offer much better runtime performance but at the expense of unacceptably long load times. Simpler structures with less loading work may increase the time required for ad hoc queries beyond an acceptable level. In practice, the warehouse administrator must find a good balance between loading and runtime query performance.

Query Performance

Database vendors focused on warehousing have invested considerable energy in optimizing their DBMS products to maximize query performance. As a result, warehousing performance has improved dramatically over the last several years. The growth in the size and complexity of warehouses has prevented some of this performance gain from actually being translated into perceived end-user benefit.

Several different techniques have evolved to maximize the performance of business analysis queries in a warehouse, including:

■ **Specialized indexing schemes**. Typical business analysis queries involve a subset of the data in the warehouse, selected on the basis of dimension values. For example, a comparison of this month's and last month's results involves only two of the 36 months of data in the example warehouse. Specialized indexing schemes have been developed to allow very rapid selection of the appropriate rows from the fact table and joining to the dimension tables. Several of these involve bitmap techniques, where the individual possible values for a dimension (or a combination of dimensions) are each assigned a single bit in an index value. Rows meeting a selection criteria can be very rapidly identified by bitwise logical operations, which a computer system can perform more rapidly than value comparisons.

■ **Parallel processing techniques**. Business analysis queries can often be broken up into parts that can be carried out in parallel, to reduce the overall time required to produce the final results. In a query joining four warehouse tables, for example, the DBMS might take advantage of a two-processor system by joining two of the tables in one process and two others in another. The results of these intermediate joins are then combined. Alternatively, the workload of processing a single table in the query might be split and carried out in parallel— for example, assigning rows for specific month ranges to specific processes. The use of multiprocessor systems in these cases is quite different than for OLTP databases. For OLTP, the focus of multiprocessor operations is to increase overall throughput. For warehousing, the focus is usually the improvement in overall execution time in response to a single complex query.

■ **Specialized optimizations**. When faced with a complex database query involving selection criteria and joins, the DBMS has many different sequences in which it can carry out the query. The optimizer for an OLTP database tends to benefit from the assumption that foreign key/primary key relationships should be exercised early in its processing, since they tend to cut down dramatically on the number of rows of intermediate results. The optimizer for a warehousing database may make a quite different decision, based on information accumulated during the load process about the distribution of data values within the database.

As with load-time performance, maximizing the runtime performance of a warehouse is an ongoing task for the database administrator. Newer revisions of DBMS software often provide performance benefits, as do higher-performance processors or more processors.

Summary

Data warehousing is a rapidly growing part of the market for SQL-based relational databases and is one with a set of specialized requirements:

- Warehouse databases are optimized for the workload of typical business analysis queries, which is quite different from OLTP workloads.

- Specialized utility programs provide high-performance loading of the warehouse and analysis tools for taking advantage of warehoused data.

- Specialized database schema structures, such as the star schema, are typically used in warehouse applications to support typical business analysis queries and optimize performance.

- SQL extensions are frequently used to support typical business analysis queries involving time series and trend analysis, rank orderings, and time-based comparisons.

- Careful design of a large warehouse is required to provide the correct balance between load-time performance and runtime performance.

Chapter 22

SQL and
Application Servers

Application servers are one of the major new computer technologies spawned by the growth of the Internet. Application servers form a key layer in most commercial web site architectures. As the name implies, application servers provide a platform for executing the application logic that drives user interaction on a web site. But application servers perform another important role—they act as mediators between the Internet-side components of a web site (the web servers and content management tools) and the IT-side components, such as legacy corporate applications and databases. In this role, application servers must work closely with DBMS software, and SQL is the language for that communication. This chapter explores the role of SQL in a multitier web site architecture built using application servers.

SQL and Web Sites: Early Implementations

Application servers did not always play a prominent role in web site architectures. The earliest web sites were focused almost exclusively on delivering content to their users, in the form of static web pages. The content of the web site was structured as a series of predefined web pages, stored in files. A web server accepted requests from user browsers (in the form of HTTP messages), located the particular page(s) requested, and sent them back to the browser for display, again using HTTP. The web page contents were expressed in HTML, the HyperText Markup Language. The HTML for a given page contained the text and graphics to be displayed on the page, and the links that supported navigation from this page to others.

It didn't take long before the demands for information to be delivered via the World Wide Web outstripped the static capabilities of predefined web pages. Companies began to use web sites to communicate with their customers, and needed to support basic capabilities like searching for specific products or accepting a customer order. The first step toward providing actual processing capability in conjunction with display of a web page was provided by the web servers themselves, as shown in Figure 22-1. Instead of accepting only requests for static web pages, web servers also accepted requests to execute a *script*: a series of instructions that determined which information to display.

Web server scripts were often written in specialized scripting languages, such as Perl. In its simplest form, a script might perform a very simple computation (such as retrieving the current date and time from the operating system) and output the result as part of a web page. In a slightly more complex form, the script might accept input typed by a user into a forms-oriented web page, perform a database query based on the input, and display the results. Because the output of the script could vary from one execution to the next, the resulting web page became *dynamic*: its contents could change from one viewing to the next, depending on the results of the script execution each time.

Scripting languages provided the earliest links between web sites and SQL databases. A script might, for example, submit a SQL query to a DBMS through a

Figure 22-1.   *Serving dynamic web content without an application server*

variation on the interactive SQL interface, and accept the results of the query for display on the web page. But there were many problems with scripting solutions for web site processing. Most of the script languages are interpreted, and executing a complex script can consume a lot of CPU cycles. Scripting facilities ran as separate processes on UNIX-based or Windows-based servers—a high-overhead structure if dozens or hundreds of scripts must be executed every second. These and other limitations of scripting solutions set the stage for an alternative approach and the emergence of application servers as a part of the web site architecture.

Application Servers and Three-Tier Web Site Architectures

The logical evolution from web server scripting was the definition of a separate role for an *application server*, resulting in a three-tier architecture shown in Figure 22-2. The web server retains its primary responsibility for locating and serving up static web pages and static pieces of web pages from its files. When application processing is required to determine which information to display or to process information supplied by the user, the web server invokes a separate application server to perform the processing. In a smaller, lower-volume web site, the application server may run as a separate process on the same physical server system as the web server. In the more general case, used by larger web sites, the web server and application server will run on two different

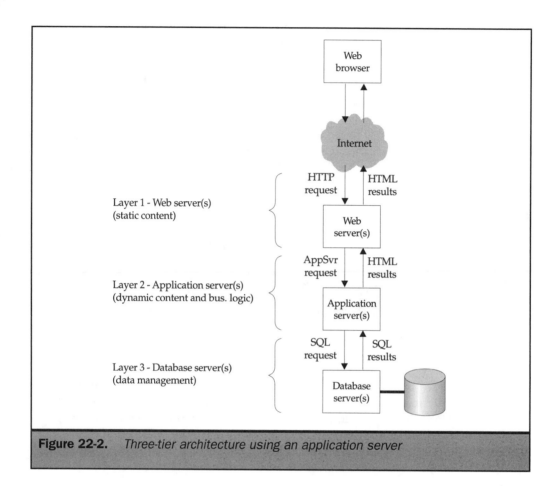

Figure 22-2. *Three-tier architecture using an application server*

server computers, typically connected by a high-speed local area network. In either configuration, the web server passes requests in the form of messages to the application server, and receives back responses in the form of HTML contents to be displayed on the page.

In the early days of application servers, there were a wide range of different application server products. Some servers required that applications be written in C or C++. Others required the use of Java. The interface between the application server and the web server was well defined by the APIs of the two leading web server vendors, Netscape and Microsoft. But all other aspects—from programming language to the supporting services provided by the application server to the API for database access—were not standardized.

Sun Microsystem's introduction of Enterprise Java Beans (EJBs) and the Java2 Enterprise Edition (J2EE) specification based on them began the standardization of application servers. EJBs built on the mushrooming popularity of Java as a programming language. The specification came from Sun, one of the leading server vendors and a company widely recognized for its leadership in Internet technologies. The specifications also contained a standardized API for database access, one of the most important functions provided by an application server, in the form of Java Database Connectivity (JDBC).

Within a short time, application servers based on the J2EE specification pulled ahead in the market. Vendors who had taken an alternative approach augmented their products with Java capability, and eventually abandoned their proprietary products for a J2EE-based strategy. A short time later, the application server market began a round of consolidation. Sun itself acquired NetDynamics, one of the pioneering J2EE application server vendors. BEA Systems, a leading vendor of software middleware for transaction processing, acquired WebLogic, another application server pioneer. Netscape, which provided one of the leading web servers, filled out its product line by acquiring Kiva, another early application server market leader.

Later, when AOL acquired Netscape and then formed a joint venture with Sun, both of these J2EE application server products came under common management at Sun, eventually merging into the Sun iPlanet application server (later rebranded the SunONE application server). Hewlett-Packard followed with its own acquisition of Bluestone, another application server vendor. IBM departed from the acquisition path by building its own application server, marketed under the WebSphere brand name. Oracle also introduced its own internally developed product, the Oracle Application Server, although much of its software was replaced by purchased third-party components over time as Oracle struggled to establish its position.

Over the course of several years of aggressive competition, the J2EE specification continued to evolve, including expanded features for application server database access. BEA's WebLogic and IBM's WebSphere emerged as the dominant players, with roughly equal market share. Products from Sun, Oracle, and a dozen smaller vendors divided up the remainder of the market. Every significant application server product complied with the J2EE specification, and provided JDBC-based facilities for database access.

Database Access from Application Servers

The convergence of the application server market around the J2EE specification effectively standardized the *external* interface between the application server and a DBMS around JDBC. Conceptually, an application server can automatically access any database product that offers a JDBC-compliant API, thus achieving DBMS independence. In practice, subtle differences between the DBMS systems in areas like SQL dialects and database naming still require some tweaking and testing, and manifest themselves in subtle dependencies within the code deployed on the application server. However, these differences tend to be minor, and adjusting for them is relatively straightforward.

The approach to data management for the application code running on the application server is a slightly more complicated story. While the application server does provide uniform services for data management, it provides these in several different architectures, using the different types of EJBs in the J2EE specification. The application designer must choose among these approaches, and in some cases, will mix and match them to achieve the requirements of the application. Here are some of the decisions that must be made:

- Will the application logic do direct database access from within a *session bean*, or will database contents be represented as entity beans, with database access logic encapsulated within them?

- If direct access from session beans is used, can the session bean remain stateless (which simplifies the coding of the bean and its management by the application server), or does the logic of database access require the bean to be stateful, preserving a context from one invocation to another?

- If entity beans are used to represent database contents, can the application rely on the container-managed persistence provided by the application server to manage database interaction, or does the application's logic require that the entity bean provide its own database access logic through bean-managed persistence?

- If entity beans are used to model database contents, do the beans correspond on a one-to-one basis to the tables in the underlying database (fine-grained modeling), or is it more appropriate for the beans to present a higher-level, more object-oriented view of the data, with the data within each bean drawn from multiple database tables (coarse-grained modeling)?

The trade-offs represented by these design questions provide an excellent perspective on the challenge of matching SQL and relational database technology to the demands of the World Wide Web and its stateless architecture, and the demands of application servers and object-oriented programming. The next several sections describe the basics of EJBs and the trade-offs among the different data access architectures they can support.

EJB Types

Within a J2EE-compliant application server, the user-developed Java applications code that implements the specific business logic is packaged and executes as a collection of EJBs. An EJB has a well-defined set of external interfaces (methods) that it must provide, and is written with an explicit set of class-specific public methods that define the external interface to the bean. The work done within the bean, and any private data variables that it maintains for its own use, can be encapsulated and hidden from other beans and from developers who do not need to know these internal details and should not write code that depends on them.

The EJBs execute on the application server within a *container*, which provides both a runtime environment for the beans and services for them. These range from general services, such as managing memory for the beans and scheduling their execution, to specific services like network access and database access (via JDBC). The container also provides persistence services, preserving the state of beans across activations.

EJBs come in two major types that are of interest from a data management perspective. The EJB types are graphically illustrated in Figure 22-3. The two major types of beans are:

- **Session beans**. These beans represent individual user sessions with the application server. Conceptually, there is a one-to-one association between each session bean and a current user. In the figure, users Mary, Joe, and Sam are each represented by their own session bean. If there are internal instance variables within the bean, these variable values represent the current state associated with the user during this particular session.

- **Entity beans**. These beans represent business objects, and logically correspond to individual rows of a database table. For example, for entity beans representing sales offices, there is a one-to-one association between each entity bean and a particular office, which is also represented in our sample database by a single row in the OFFICES table. If there are internal instance variables within the bean, these variable values represent the current state associated with the office, which is also represented by the column values in this row of the OFFICES table. This state is independent of any particular user session.

Either type of bean may access a database, but they will typically do it in quite different ways.

Session Bean Database Access

A session bean will typically access a database in a series of one or more JDBC calls on behalf of the user represented by the bean. An application server classifies session beans into two categories, depending on how the bean manages state:

- **Stateless session bean**. This type of bean does not maintain any status information across method invocations. It carries out its actions on behalf of one user at a time, and one request at a time. Each request to the bean is independent of the last. With this restriction, every invocation of the bean must carry with it (in the form of the parameters passed with the invocation) all of the information needed to carry out the request.

- **Stateful session bean**. This type of bean maintains status information across method invocations. The bean needs to "remember" information from its previous invocations (its state) to carry out the tasks requested by later invocations. It uses private instance variables to hold the information.

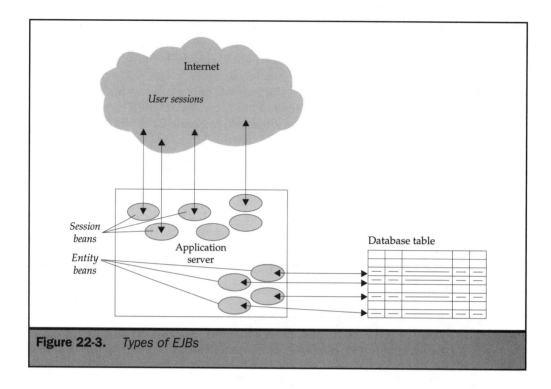

Figure 22-3. *Types of EJBs*

The next two sessions show examples of application tasks that are most easily implemented as each type of session bean. You specify whether a session bean is stateless or stateful in the deployment descriptor for the bean, which contains information supplied to the application server on which the bean is deployed.

An application server on a busy web site can easily have more session beans and other EJBs in use than it has main memory available to store them. In this situation, the application server will keep a limited number of session bean instances active in its main memory. If a user associated with a currently inactive session bean becomes active (i.e., one of his or her web site clicks must be processed), the application server chooses another instance of the same bean class and *passivates* it—that is, it saves the values of any instance variables defined for the bean and then reuses the bean to serve the user session needing activation.

Whether a session bean is stateful or stateless has a significant impact on this passivation and activation. Since a stateless session bean does not need its status preserved across method invocations, the application server does not need to save its instance variable values when it passivates the bean, and does not need to restore instance variable values when it reactivates the bean. But for a stateful session bean, the application server needs to copy its instance value variables to persistent storage (a disk file or a database) when it passivates the bean, and then restore those values when it reactivates the bean. Thus, stateful session beans can significantly diminish the performance and throughput of an application server on a busy site. Stateless beans are preferable for performance, but many applications are difficult or impossible to implement without using stateful beans.

Using JDBC from a Stateless Session Bean

Figure 22-4 shows a simple example of an application that can easily be handled with stateless session bean database access. A page on a web site displays the current price of a company's stock when the page is displayed. The page can't be static, since the displayed price will change minute by minute. So when the user's browser requests the page, the web server hands off the request to an application server, which eventually invokes a method of a session bean. The session bean can use JDBC to send a SQL SELECT statement to a database of current stock prices, and receives back the answer as one line of query results. The session bean reformats the stock quote as a fragment of a web page, and passes it back to the web server for display to the user.

Stateless session beans can perform more complex functions as well. Suppose the same company has a page on its web site where a user can request a product catalog by filling in the contents of a small form. When the form is filled in and the user clicks the Send button, the browser sends the data from the form to the web server, which again hands off the request to an application server. This time, a different method of the session bean is invoked, and receives the data from the form as parameters. The session bean can use JDBC to send a SQL INSERT statement to a database table holding pending catalog requests.

In each of these examples, all of the information that the session bean needs to carry out its task is passed to it with the method invocation. When the bean has completed its task, the information is not needed anymore. The next invocation again receives all of the information it needs with the next invocation, so there is no need to carry over status information. Even more important, the database activity on each invocation is completely independent from every other invocation. No database transaction spans multiple method invocations.

Using JDBC from a Stateful Session Bean

Many web interactions can't live with the limitations imposed by stateless session beans. Consider a more complex web-based form that spans four pages. As the user fills out each page and sends it to the web site, the session bean must accumulate the information and retain it across the four page clicks until all of the data is ready to be captured into a database. The need to retain information across method invocations calls for a stateful session bean.

Another example in which a stateful session bean is appropriate is a commercial web site where a user shops online and accumulates a list of items to be purchased in

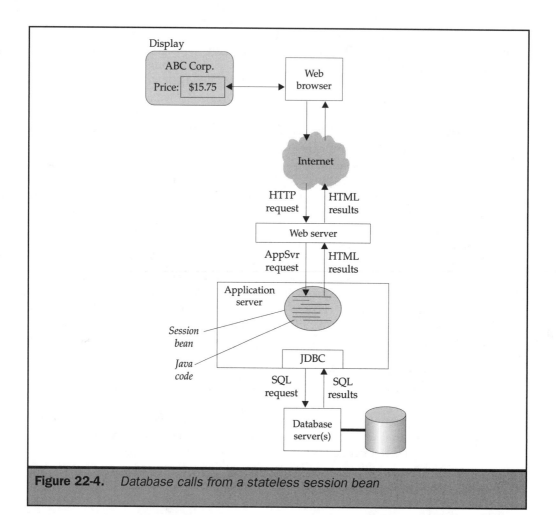

Figure 22-4. *Database calls from a stateless session bean*

an online shopping cart. After 40 or 50 clicks through the web site, the user may have accumulated five or six items in the shopping cart. If the user then clicks a button requesting display of the current shopping cart contents, those contents are probably most easily maintained as session bean state.

In both of these examples, the session bean requires continuity of database access to effectively accomplish its tasks. Figure 22-5 shows the pattern, and the contrast to the pattern of interactions in Figure 22-4. Even if the bean can be implemented without instance variables (for example, by storing all of its state information in a back-end database), it needs one continuous database session to carry out its database access. The client-side API for the DBMS maintains this session, and the API itself will need to maintain session-state information across session bean method invocations.

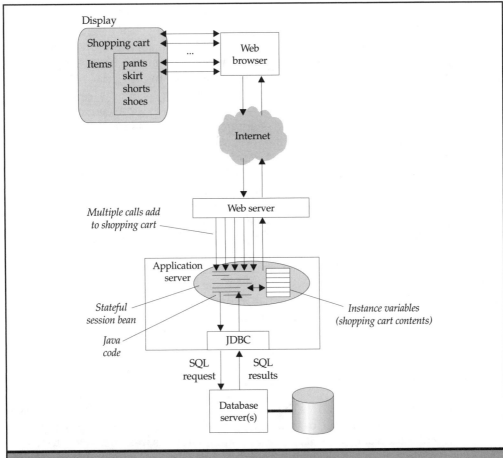

Figure 22-5. *Database calls from a stateful session bean*

Entity Bean Database Access

It's possible to implement complete, sophisticated web site applications using session beans deployed on a J2EE application server. However, programming an application using session beans tends to produce more procedural, and less object-oriented code. The object-oriented philosophy is to have object classes (in this case, EJB classes) represent real-world entities, such as customers or offices, and object instances represent individual customers or offices. But session beans don't represent any of those entities; they represent currently active user sessions. When database interaction is handled directly by session beans, the representation of real-world entities is basically left in the database; it doesn't have an object counterpart.

Entity beans provide the object counterpart for real-world entities and the rows in a database that represent them. Entity bean classes embody customers and offices; individual entity bean instances represent individual customers and individual offices. Other objects (such as session beans) within the application server can interact with customers and offices using object-oriented techniques, by invoking the methods of the entity beans that represent them.

To maintain this object-oriented model, there must be very close cooperation between the entity-bean representations of entities and their database representations. If a session bean invokes a customer entity bean method that changes a customer's credit limit, that change must be reflected in the database, so that an order-processing application using the database will use the new limit. Similarly, if an inventory management application adds to the quantity on hand for a particular product in the database, that product's entity bean in the application server must be updated.

Just as an application server will passivate and reactivate session beans as necessary, it will passivate and reactivate entity beans repeatedly in response to a heavy workload. Before the application server passivates an entity bean, the bean's state must be saved in a persistent way, by updating the database. Similarly, when the application server reactivates an entity bean, its instance variables must be set to their values just before it was passivated, by reloading those values from the database. The entity bean class defines callback methods that an entity bean must provide to implement this synchronization.

There is close correspondence between actions carried out on entity beans and database actions, as shown in Table 22-1. The J2EE specification provides two alternative ways to manage this coordination:

- **Bean-managed persistence.** The entity bean itself is responsible for maintaining synchronization with the database. The application programmer who develops the entity bean and codes its implementation methods must use JDBC to read and write data in the database when necessary. The application server container notifies the bean when it takes actions that require database interaction.

- **Container-managed persistence.** The EJB container provided by the application server is responsible for maintaining synchronization with the database. The container monitors interaction with the entity bean, and automatically uses JDBC to read and write data in the database and update the instance variables within the bean when needed. The application programmer who develops the entity bean and codes its implementation methods can focus on the business logic in the bean, and assumes that its instance variables will accurately represent the state of the data in the database.

Note that entity beans are always stateful—the distinction between these two bean types is not the difference between stateless and stateful beans, but rather, the difference between *who* is responsible for maintaining proper state. The next two sections discuss the practical issues associated with each type of entity bean, and the trade-offs between them.

Database Statement	EJB Method	EJB/Database Action
INSERT	ejbCreate(), ejbPostCreate()	Creates a new entity bean instance; initial state of the bean is specified by parameters in the create() call. A new row with these values must be inserted into the database.
SELECT	ejbLoad()	Loads instance variable values, reading them from the persistent data in the database.
UPDATE	EjbStore()	Stores instance variable values, saving them persistently in the database.
DELETE	ejbRemove()	Removes an entity bean instance; the corresponding row in the database must be deleted.

Table 22-1.   *Corresponding Database and EJB Activities*

Using Container-Managed Persistence

An entity bean's deployment descriptor specifies that an entity bean requires container-managed persistence. The deployment descriptor also specifies the mapping between instance variables of the bean and columns in the underlying database. The deployment descriptor also identifies the primary key that uniquely identifies the bean and the corresponding database row. The primary key value is used in the database operations that store and retrieve variable values from the database.

With container-managed persistence, the EJB container is responsible for maintaining synchronization between the entity bean and the database row. The container calls JDBC to store instance variable values into the database, to restore those values, to insert a new row into the database, and to delete a row—all as required by actions on the bean. The container will call the bean's ejbStore() callback method before it stores values in the database, to notify the bean that it must get its variable values into a consistent state. Similarly, the container will call the bean's ejbLoad() callback method after loading values from the database, to allow the bean to do appropriate post processing (for example, calculating a value that was not itself persisted, based on values that were). In the same way, the bean's ejbRemove() method will be called before the container deletes the row from the database, and ejbCreate() and `ejbPostCreate()` are called in conjunction with inserting a new row. For many entity beans, these callback methods will be empty, since the container handles the actual database operations.

Using Bean-Managed Persistence

If an entity bean's deployment descriptor specifies bean-managed persistence, the container assumes that the entity bean will handle its own database interaction. When a new entity bean is first created, the container calls the bean's `ejbCreate()` and `ejbPostCreate()` methods. The bean is responsible for processing the corresponding INSERT statement for the database. Similarly, when an entity bean is to be removed, the container calls the bean's `ejbRemove()` method. The bean is responsible for processing the corresponding DELETE statement for the database, and when the bean returns from the `ejbRemove()` method, the container is free to actually remove the bean itself and reuse its storage.

Bean loading is similarly handled by a container call to `ejbLoad()`, and storing by a call by the container to `ejbStore()`. The bean is similarly notified of passivation and activation by callbacks from the container. Of course, nothing limits the entity bean's database interaction to these callback methods. If the bean needs to access the database during the execution of one of its methods, the bean can make whatever JDBC calls it needs. The JDBC calls within the callback methods are strictly focused on managing bean persistence.

Container-Managed and Bean-Managed Trade-Offs

You might naturally ask why you would ever want to use bean-managed persistence when container-managed persistence eliminates the need to worry about synchronizing with the database. The answer is that container-managed persistence has some limitations:

- **Multiple databases**. For most application servers, entity beans must be mapped into a single database server. If entity bean data comes from multiple databases, then bean-managed persistence may be the only way to handle database synchronization.

- **Multiple tables per bean**. Container-managed persistence works well when all of the instance variables for an entity bean come from a single row of a single table—i.e., when there is a one-to-one correspondence between bean instances and table rows. If an entity bean needs to model a more complex object, such as an order header and individual line items of an order, which come from two different, related tables, bean-managed persistence is usually required, because the bean's own code must provide the intelligence to map to and from the database.

- **Performance optimizations**. With container-managed persistence, a container must make an all-or-nothing assumption about persisting instance variables. Every time the variables must be stored or loaded, all of the variables must be handled. In many applications, the entity bean may be able to determine that depending on its particular state, only a few of the variables need to be processed. If the entity bean holds a lot of data, the performance difference can be significant.

- **Database optimizations**. If the methods of an entity bean that implement its business logic involve heavy database access (queries and updates), then some of the database operations that the container will carry out in a container-managed persistence scheme may be redundant. If bean-managed persistence is used instead, the bean may be able to determine exactly when database operations are required for synchronization and when the database is already up to date.

In practice, these limitations often prevent the use of container-managed persistence in today's deployments. Enhancements in newer versions of the EJB specification are designed to address many of these shortcomings. However, bean-managed persistence remains a very important technique with the currently available application servers.

EJB 2.0 Enhancements

EJB 2.0 represents a major revision to the EJB specification. Many of the enhancements in EJB 2.0 were incompatible with the corresponding capabilities in EJB 1.x. To avoid breaking EJB 1.x-compatible beans, EJB 2.0 provides complementary capabilities in these areas, allowing side-by-side coexistence of EJB 1.x and EJB 2.0 beans. A complete description of the differences between EJB 1.x and EJB 2.0 is well beyond the scope of this book. However, several of the differences were motivated by difficulties in using container-managed persistence under the EJB 1.x specification, and those changes directly affect database processing within EJBs.

One difficulty with EJB 1.x has already been mentioned—the difficulty of modeling complex objects that draw their data from multiple database tables or that contain nonrelational structures like arrays and hierarchical data. With EJB 1.x, you could model a complex object as a family of inter-related entity beans, each drawn from one table. This approach allowed the use of container-managed persistence, but the relationships between pieces of the object need to be implemented in applications code within the bean. Ideally, these internal details within the complex object should be hidden from applications code. Alternatively, with EJB 1.x, you could model a complex object as a single entity bean, with data in the bean's instance variables drawn from multiple related tables. This achieves the desired application code transparency, but container-managed persistence could be used when an entity bean draws its data from multiple tables.

EJB 2.0 addresses this issue through the use of abstract *accessor methods,* which are used to set and retrieve every persistent instance variable within an entity bean. The container actually maintains the storage for the variables and the variable values. The bean explicitly calls a `get()` accessor method to retrieve an instance variable value and a `set()` accessor method to set its value. Similarly, there are `get()` and `set()` abstract accessor methods for every *relationship* that links the rows in the database that contribute data to the entity bean. Many-to-many relationships are easily handled by mapping them into Java collection variables.

With these new features, the container has complete knowledge of all the instance variables used by a bean, and every access that code within the bean makes to the instance variables. The entity bean can represent a complex object that draws data from multiple database tables, hiding the details from the applications code. But container-managed persistence can now be used, because the container "knows" all about the various parts of the object and the relationships among the parts.

Another problem with the EJB 1.x specification is that while database interactions were standardized, the *finder methods* that are used to search the active entity beans were not. The finder methods implement capabilities like searching for a particular entity bean by primary key, or searching for the set of beans that match a particular criterion. Without this standardization, portability across application servers was compromised, and searches of entity beans often required recourse to searching the underlying database.

EJB 2.0 addresses the searching limitations through the use of abstract *select methods* that search entity beans. The select methods use a newly defined EJB 2.0 Query Language (EJBQL). While the query language is based on SQL-92, it includes constructs such as path expressions that are decidedly nonrelational.

Finally, EJB 2.0 was designed to align with the SQL:1999 standard and its abstract data types. Support for these types somewhat simplifies the interaction between entity beans and the database for DBMS products that support abstract types. At this time, few DBMS products support them.

Application Server Caching

On a high-volume web site, database access can become a bottleneck to overall web site performance. Because of the EJB structure, the database access required by the business logic of the application is increased (perhaps substantially) by the database access required to support entity bean/database synchronization. If the web site implements heavy personalization of its user interaction (i.e., if a high percentage of its pages are dynamically generated based on the profile of the particular user who is viewing them), then the database access load can be even higher. At the extreme, every click on a highly personalized web site could require retrieval of user-profile data from the database to drive page generation. Finally, user interaction with a web site happens in real time, and is affected by peak-load activity. The average rate of click processing is less important than peak-load activity in determining whether users perceive the site as fast or sluggish.

The World Wide Web has already shown an effective architecture for dealing with these types of peak-load Internet volume demands—through web page caching and horizontal scaling. With caching, copies of heavily accessed web pages are pulled forward in the network and replicated. As a result, the total network capacity for serving web pages is increased, and the amount of network traffic associated with those page hits is reduced. With horizontal scaling, web site content is replicated across two or more web servers (up to dozens or even hundreds of servers), whose aggregate capacity for serving pages is much greater than any single server.

Similar caching and horizontal scaling architectures are used to increase the capacity of application servers. Most commercial application servers today implement *bean caching,* where copies of frequently used entity beans are kept in the application server's memory. In addition, application servers are often deployed in banks or clusters, with each application server providing identical business logic and application processing capability. In fact, many commercial application servers use horizontal scaling within a single server to take advantage of symmetric multiprocessing (SMP) configurations. It's typical for an eight-processor application server to be running up to eight independent copies of the application server software, operating in parallel. Figure 22-6 shows a typical application server configuration with three four-processor servers.

Unfortunately, horizontal scaling and caching tend to work against one another when dealing with stateful data such as that stored in an entity bean or a database. Without special cache synchronization logic, updates made to a bean stored in the cache of one server instance will not automatically appear in the other caches, with the potential to cause incorrect results. Consider, for example, what happens to quantity-on-hand data if three or four separate caches contain copies of an entity bean for a single product and the business logic of the application server updates those values. The caches will very quickly contain different values for quantity on hand, none of which are accurate. The cache synchronization logic required to detect and prevent such a situation unfortunately carries with it a great deal of overhead. Absolute synchronization requires a full two-phase commit protocol (described in Chapter 23) among the caches.

Database caches can address the problems of multiple bean caches within a single SMP server, as shown in Figure 22-7. By caching at the database level instead of the bean level, one database cache provides consistency across all of the application server instances on a single server. Synchronization across multiple physical servers is still

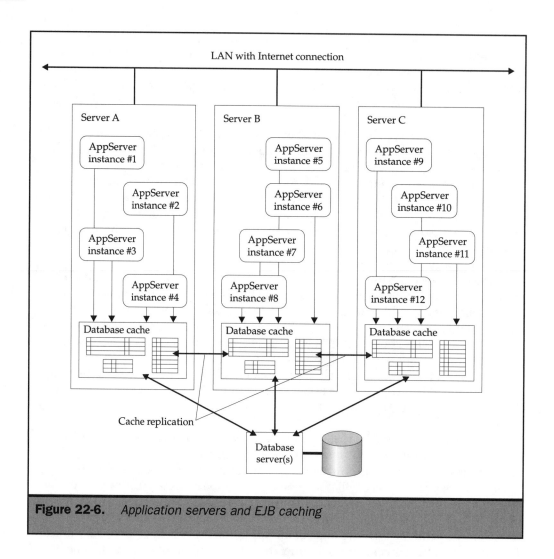

Figure 22-6. *Application servers and EJB caching*

required, however. If the ratio of database reads to database updates is high (as, for example, in a highly personalized web site), the overhead of cache synchronization will remain relatively low and the benefits of horizontal scaling can be significant.

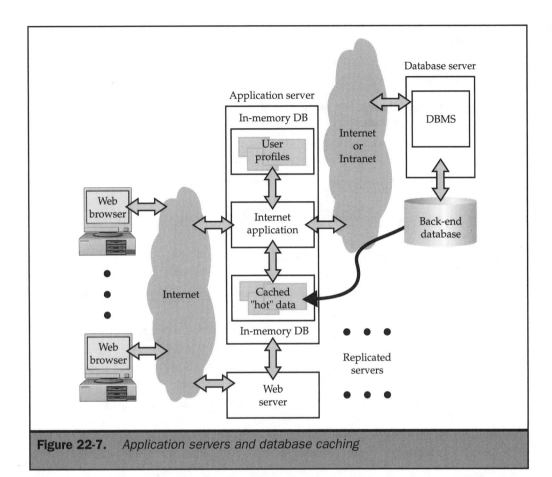

Figure 22-7.   *Application servers and database caching*

Oracle has used database caching within its own Oracle Application Server, and has attempted to use caching as a competitive advantage. IBM is naturally positioned to offer integrated database caching for its DB2 DBMS, but has not introduced such a capability at this writing. Several third-party products have been introduced as database caches for application servers, including products from several of the object-oriented database vendors and from in-memory database vendors. Whether database caching will substantially impact the application server market is still an open question.

Summary

This chapter described application servers and the role they play linking the World Wide Web to back-end enterprise systems, including enterprise databases:

- Popular application servers implement the J2EE specification, which standardizes database access through a JDBC API.

- Business logic within an application server is implemented by EJBs, which may be session beans or entity beans.

- Session beans embody user sessions. They can access databases directly through JDBC calls.

- Stateless session beans support very simple, one-transaction-per-invocation data access.

- Stateful beans support transactions that cross invocations, but their logic must handle the need to persist state across passivations and activations.

- Entity beans embody real-world objects, and correspond to rows in database tables. They are always stateful.

- Entity beans can use container-managed persistence, where the application server automatically handles entity bean/database synchronization.

- Alternatively, entity beans can take responsibility for their own database synchronization, under the bean-managed persistence scheme.

Chapter 23

SQL Networking and Distributed Databases

Over the last two decades, computer networking has radically transformed the landscape of corporate computing. In most companies, every personal computer is connected to a local area network (LAN). Powerful LAN-attached workgroup servers meet the computing needs of individual departments. Corporatewide networks interconnect the LANs within a building or campus, and connect them to divisional or corporate data centers. Additional links interconnect corporate locations around the world. The Internet provides a network of networks, linking companies to one another and to individual customers. Application programs run on computers at every level and at every location within this networked environment.

In this new, highly-networked environment, computer data does not reside on a single system under the control of a single DBMS. Instead, data within an organization is spread across many different systems, each with its own database manager. Often, the various computer systems and database management systems come from different manufacturers. As companies try to interconnect their data processing systems via the Internet, the challenge becomes even greater. Even if a company has managed to standardize on a single, companywide DBMS and on database structures, those standards won't apply to its suppliers or customers as it tries to build external links to conduct business electronically.

These trends have led to a strong focus in the computer industry and in the data management community on the problems of database management in a networked environment. This chapter discusses the challenges of managing distributed data, the variety of architectural approaches, and some of the products that DBMS vendors have offered to meet those challenges.

The Challenge of Distributed Data Management

When the foundations of relational database management and the SQL language were being laid in the 1970s, almost all commercial data processing happened on large, centralized computer systems. The company's data was stored on mass storage attached to the central system. The business programs that processed transactions and generated reports ran on the central system and accessed the data. Much of the workload of the central system was batch processing. Online users accessed the central system through "dumb" computer terminals with no processing power of their own. The central system formatted information to be displayed for the online user and accepted data typed by the user for processing.

In this environment, the roles of a relational database system and its SQL language were clear and well contained. The DBMS had responsibility for accepting, storing, and retrieving data based on requests expressed in the SQL language. The business-processing logic resided *outside* the database and was the responsibility of the business programs developed and maintained by the information systems staff. The programs and the DBMS software executed on the same centralized system where the data was stored, so the performance of the system was not affected by external factors like network traffic or outside system failures.

Commercial data processing in a modern corporation has evolved a long way from the centralized environment of the 1970s. Figure 23-1 shows a portion of a computer network that you might find in a manufacturing company, a financial services firm, or a distribution company today. Data is stored on a variety of computer systems in the network:

- **Mainframes**. The company's core data processing applications, such as accounting and payroll, run on an IBM mainframe. The oldest applications, developed and maintained over the last 20 or 30 years, still store their data in hierarchical IMS databases. The company has a strategy to migrate these applications to DB2 over time, and all new mainframe applications development uses DB2 as its database manager.

- **Workstations and UNIX-based servers**. The company's engineering organization uses UNIX-based workstations and servers (from Sun Microsystems) for engineering design, testing, and support. Engineering test results and specifications are stored in an Oracle database. The company also uses Oracle databases running on UNIX-based servers from Hewlett-Packard located in its six distribution centers to manage inventory and to process orders.

- **LAN servers**. All of the company's departments have individual PC LANs to share printers and files. Some of the departments also have local databases to support their work. For example, the personnel department has purchased a human resources management system software package, and it uses SQL Server on Windows NT to store its data. In the financial planning department, the data processing staff has built a custom-written corporate planning application, which uses Informix Universal Server.

- **Desktop personal computers**. All of the company's office workers use personal computers. Many of the administrative assistants and some of the senior managers maintain personal databases using Excel spreadsheets, Microsoft Access, or one of the lightweight DBMS products, such as Oracle Light. In a few cases, the databases are shared with other users, using LAN versions of these products.

- **Mobile laptop PCs**. The company recently purchased a sales force automation software package and equipped every salesperson with a laptop PC. The laptop runs sales presentations, sends and receives e-mail, and also holds a local lightweight database (SQL Anywhere from Sybase) with recent product pricing and availability data. The database also captures orders entered by the salesperson. At night, the laptop PC connects to the corporate network over a dialup connection, transmits its orders, and receives updated information for its local copy of the products database.

- **Handheld devices**. The company's management team has widely adopted handheld personal digital assistants (PDAs). In addition to the personal calendar and address-book functions, applications running on the PDA can use wireless network connections to check prices and enter customer orders. The wireless network can also be used to alert users, via their PDAs, of important database changes, such as price updates or product shortages.

- **Internet connections**. The company has an Internet web site where customers, dealers, and distributors can find out the latest information about its products and services. At first, this was an information-only web site, but competitors have recently begun accepting customer orders directly via the Internet. One of the corporate IS department's highest priorities is to respond to this competitive challenge by supporting e-commerce transactions on the company's web site.

Figure 23-1.   *DBMS usage in a typical corporate network*

With data spread over many different systems, it's easy to imagine requests that span more than one database and the possibility for conflicting data among the databases:

- An engineer needs to combine lab test results (on an engineering workstation) with production forecasts (on the mainframe) to choose among three alternative technologies.

- A financial planner needs to link financial forecasts (in an Informix database) to historical financial data (on the mainframe).

- A product manager needs to know how much inventory of a particular product is in each distribution center (data stored on six UNIX servers) to plan product obsolescence.

- Current pricing data needs to be downloaded daily from the mainframe to the distribution center servers, and also to all of the sales force's laptop computers.

- Orders need to be uploaded daily from the laptop systems and parceled out to the distribution centers; aggregate order data from the distribution centers must be uploaded to the mainframe so that the manufacturing plan can be adjusted.

- Salespeople may accept customer orders and make shipment date estimates for popular products based on their local databases, without knowing that other salespeople have made similar commitments. Orders must be reconciled and prioritized, and revised shipment estimates provided to customers.

- Engineering changes made in the workstation databases may affect product costs and pricing. These changes must be propagated through the mainframe systems and out to the web site, the distribution centers, and the sales force laptops.

- Managers throughout the company want to query the various shared databases using the PCs on their desktops.

As these examples suggest, effective ways of distributing data, managing distributed data, and providing access to distributed data have become critical as data processing has moved to a distributed computing model. The leading DBMS vendors are committed to delivering distributed database management, and currently offer a variety of products that solve some of the distributed data problems illustrated by these examples. Distributed data management has also been the focus of extensive university and corporate research, and many technical articles have been published about the theory of distributed data management and the trade-offs involved. There is general agreement among the researchers about the ideal characteristics that should be provided by a scheme to manage distributed databases:

- **Location transparency**. The user shouldn't have to worry about where the data is physically located. The DBMS should present all data as if it were local and be responsible for maintaining that illusion.

- **Heterogeneous systems**. The DBMS should support data stored on different systems, with different architectures and performance levels, including PCs, workstations, LAN servers, minicomputers, and mainframes.

- **Network transparency**. Except for differences in performance, the DBMS should work the same way over different networks, from high-speed LANs to low-speed telephone links.

- **Distributed queries**. The user should be able to join data from any of the tables in the (distributed) database, even if the tables are located on different physical systems.

- **Distributed updates**. The user should be able to update data in any table for which the user has the necessary privileges, whether that table is on the local system or on a remote system.

- **Distributed transactions**. The DBMS should support distributed transactions (using COMMIT and ROLLBACK) across system boundaries, maintaining the integrity of the (distributed) database even in the face of network failures and failures of individual systems.

- **Security**. The DBMS must provide a security scheme adequate to protect the entire (distributed) database from unauthorized forms of access.

- **Universal access**. The DBMS should provide universal, uniform access to all of the organization's data.

No current distributed DBMS product even comes close to meeting this ideal, and it's unlikely that any product ever will. In practice, formidable obstacles make it difficult to provide even simple forms of distributed database management. These obstacles include:

- **Performance**. In a centralized database, the path from the DBMS to the data has an access speed of a few milliseconds and a data transfer rate of millions of characters per second. Even on a fast local area network, access speeds lengthen to hundredths or tenths of a second, and transfer rates can fall to 100,000 characters per second or less. On a modem link, data access may take seconds or minutes, and a few thousand characters per second may be the maximum effective throughput. This vast difference in speeds can dramatically slow the performance of remote data access.

- **Integrity**. Distributed transactions require active cooperation by two or more independent copies of the DBMS software running on different computer systems if the transactions are to remain all-or-nothing propositions. Special two-phase commit transaction protocols must be used. These protocols generate a great deal of network traffic and lock parts of the databases that are participating in the distributed transaction for long periods of time.

- **Static SQL**. A static embedded SQL statement is compiled and stored in the database as an application plan. When a query combines data from two or more databases, where should its application plan be stored? Must there be two or more cooperating plans? If there is a change in the structure of one database, how do the application plans in the other databases get notified? Using dynamic SQL to solve these problems in a networked database environment almost always leads to unacceptably slow application performance, due to network overhead and delays.

■ **Optimization**. When data is accessed across a network, the normal rules for SQL optimization don't apply. For example, it may be more efficient to sequentially scan an entire local table than to use an index search on a remote table. The optimization software must know about the network(s) and their speeds. Generally speaking, optimization becomes both more critical and more difficult.

■ **Data compatibility**. Different computer systems support different data types, and even when two systems offer the same data type, they often use different formats. For example, a Windows PC and a Macintosh store 16-bit integers differently. IBM mainframes store EBCDIC character codes while UNIX-based servers and PCs use ASCII. A distributed DBMS must mask these differences.

■ **System catalogs**. As a DBMS carries out its tasks, it makes very frequent access to its system catalogs. Where should the catalog be kept in a distributed database? If it is centralized on one system, remote access to it will be slow, bogging down the DBMS. If it is distributed across many different systems, changes must be propagated around the network and synchronized.

■ **Mixed-vendor environment**. It's highly unlikely that all the data in an organization will be managed by a single brand of DBMS, so distributed database access will cross DBMS brand boundaries. This requires active cooperation between DBMS products from highly competitive vendors—an unlikely prospect. As the DBMS vendors scramble to extend the capabilities of their products with new features, capabilities, and data types, the ability to sustain a cross-vendor standard is even less likely.

■ **Distributed deadlocks**. When transactions on two different systems each try to access locked data on the other system, a deadlock can occur in the distributed database, even though the deadlock is not visible on either of the two systems. The DBMS must provide global deadlock detection for a distributed database. Again, this requires coordination of processing across a network and will typically lead to unacceptably slow application performance.

■ **Recovery**. If one of the systems running a distributed DBMS fails, the operator of that system must be able to run its recovery procedures independent of the other systems in the network, and the recovered state of the database must be consistent with that of the other systems.

Distributing Data: Practical Approaches

Because of the formidable obstacles to realizing the ideal distributed database, DBMS vendors have taken a step-by-step approach to databases and networking. They have focused on specific forms of network database access, data distribution, and distributed data management that are appropriate for particular application scenarios. For example, a DBMS vendor may first provide tools to rapidly extract subset data from a master database and send it across a network for loading into a slave database. Later, the vendor may enhance the tool to track updates to the master database since the last extract, and to extract and transmit only the changes to the master database.

A subsequent version of the tool may automate the entire process, providing a graphical user interface for specifying the data to be extracted and scripts to automate the periodic extract process. Similarly, a DBMS may provide initial support for distributed queries by allowing a user on one system to query a database located on another system. In subsequent releases, the DBMS may allow the remote query as a subquery within a query that accesses local database tables. Still later, the DBMS may allow distributed queries that more freely intermix data from local and remote databases.

Remote Database Access

One of the simplest approaches to managing data stored in multiple locations is remote data access. With this capability, a user of one database is given the ability to reach out across a network and retrieve information from a different database. In its simplest form, this may involve carrying out a single query against the remote database, as shown in Figure 23-2. It may also involve performing an INSERT, UPDATE, or DELETE statement to modify the remote database contents. This type of requirement often arises when the local database is a satellite database (such as a database in a local sales office or distribution center) and the remote database is a central, corporate database.

Figure 23-2.   *A remote database server access request*

In addition to the remote data access request, Figure 23-2 also shows a client/server request to the remote database from a (different) PC user. Note that, from the standpoint of the remote database, there is very little difference between processing the request from the PC client and processing the remote database access request. In both cases, a SQL request arrives across the network and the remote database determines that the user making the request has appropriate privileges and then carries it out. And, in both cases, the status of the SQL processing is reported back across the network.

The local database in Figure 23-2 must do some very different work than the process it normally uses to process local database requests, however. There are several complications for the local DBMS:

- It must determine which remote database the user wants to access, and how it can be accessed on the network.

- It must establish a connection to the remote database for carrying out remote requests.

- It must determine how the local user authentication and privilege scheme maps to the remote database. That is, does it simply pass the user name/password supplied for local database access to the remote database, or is a different remote user name/password supplied, or should some kind of automatic mapping be performed?

In effect, the local DBMS becomes an agent for the user making the remote access request. It becomes a client in a client/server connection to the remote DBMS.

Several of the leading enterprise DBMS vendors offer the kind of remote database access capability shown in Figure 23-2. They differ in the specific way that remote access is presented to the user and to the database administrator. In some cases, they involve extensions to the SQL language accepted by the DBMS. In others, the extra mechanisms for establishing remote access are mostly external to the SQL language.

Sybase offers a simple entry-level remote database access capability. While connected to a local Sybase installation, the user can issue a CONNECT TO SQL statement, naming a remote server that is known to the local server. For example, if a remote server named CENTRALHOST contains a copy of the sample database, then this statement:

```
CONNECT TO CENTRALHOST
```

makes that remote server the current server for the session. The local server in effect enters a passthrough mode, sending all SQL statements to the remote server. The remote database can now be processed directly over the connection, with standard, unmodified queries and data manipulation statements:

Get the names and sales numbers of all salespeople who are already over quota.

```
SELECT NAME, QUOTA, SALES
  FROM SALESREPS
 WHERE SALES > QUOTA
```

When the remote access is completed, a companion SQL statement:

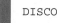

```
DISCONNECT
```

ends the passthrough mode, and the local server once again becomes the current server. Except for the CONNECT/DISCONNECT statement pair, the mechanism for managing remote access is external to the SQL language. The database administrator tells the local database about the existence, locations, and names of remote servers through the spaddserver() and spdropserver() system stored procedures. The current local user name and password are used by default for access to the remote server. Alternatively, the database administrator can specify a proxy user name/password that is used for remote server access, again through system stored procedures. Sybase offers other, more complex distributed database capabilities, but this basic capability has the advantage of maximum simplicity.

Oracle takes a somewhat different approach to remote database access, but one that is similar to the capabilities provided by other DBMS brands. It requires that Oracle's SQL*Net networking software be installed along with the Oracle DBMS on both the local and the remote system. The database administrator is responsible for establishing one or more named *database links* from the local database to remote databases. Each database link specifies:

- Network location of the target remote computer system
- Communications protocol to use
- Name of the Oracle database on the remote server
- Remote database user name and password

All remote database access occurs via a database link and is governed by the privileges of the supplied user name in the remote system. The database link thus embodies the answers to the "which database," "how to communicate," and "what privileges" questions raised earlier in this section. The database administrator assigns the database link a name. Links can be private (created for use by a specific user of the local system) or public (available for use by multiple users of the local system).

To access a remote database over a database link, the local system user uses standard SQL statements. The name of the database link is appended to the remote table and view names, following an at sign (@). For example, assume you are on a local computer system that is connected to a copy of the sample database on a remote system over a database link called CENTRALHOST. This SQL statement retrieves information from the remote SALESREPS table:

Get the names and sales numbers of all salespeople who are already over quota.

```
SELECT NAME, QUOTA, SALES
  FROM SALESREPS@CENTRALHOST
 WHERE SALES > QUOTA
```

Oracle supports nearly all of the query capabilities that are available for the local database against remote databases. The only restriction is that every remote database entity (table, view, and so on) must be suffixed with the database link name. Here is a two-table join, executed on the remote Oracle database:

Get the names and office cities of all salespeople who are already over quota.

```
SELECT NAME, CITY, QUOTA, SALES
  FROM SALESREPS@CENTRALHOST, OFFICES@CENTRALHOST
 WHERE SALES > QUOTA
   AND REP_OFFICE = OFFICE
```

Oracle also supports data definition and database update operations carried out in the remote database. Here is an example:

Create a new remote table of high-credit-limit customer info in the remote database and populate it with data from the CUSTOMERS table.

```
CREATE TABLE HIGHCUST@CENTRALHOST
   (CUST_NUM INTEGER NOT NULL,
      COMPANY VARCHAR(20) NOT NULL,
    REP_NAME VARCHAR(15))

INSERT INTO HIGHCUST@CENTRALHOST
    SELECT CUST_NUM, COMPANY, NAME
      FROM CUSTOMERS@CENTRALHOST, SALESREPS@CENTRALHOST
     WHERE CREDIT_LIMIT > 50000.00
       AND CUST_REP = EMPL_NUM
```

Informix Universal Server provides capabilities that are similar to those offered by Oracle, but uses a different mechanism for identifying remote databases and a different SQL syntax extension. The Informix architecture differentiates between a remote database *server* and a remote *database* that is managed by the remote server, since it tends to provide rich support for multiple, named databases per server. Suppose an Informix copy of the sample database is called SAMPLE and it resides on a remote database server called CENTRALHOST. Then this query is equivalent to the previous Oracle and Sybase examples:

Get the names and sales numbers of all salespeople who are already over quota.

```
SELECT NAME, QUOTA, SALES
  FROM SAMPLE@CENTRALHOST:SALEREPS
 WHERE SALES > QUOTA
```

The database name appears at the *beginning* of the table name (as an additional qualifier before the colon). If the database is remote, then the server name appears following the at sign (@) after the database name.

Remote Data Transparency

With any of the remote database-naming conventions that extend the usual SQL table and view names, the additional qualifiers can quickly become annoying or confusing. For example, if two tables in the remote database have columns with the same names, any query involving both tables must use qualified column names—and the table name qualifiers now have the remote database qualification as well. Here's a qualified Informix column name for the NAME column in the remote SALESREPS table owned by the user JOE in a remote database named SAMPLE on the remote Informix server CENTRALHOST:

```
SAMPLE@CENTRALHOST.JOE.SALESREPS.NAME
```

A single column reference has grown to half a line of SQL text! For this reason, table aliases are frequently used in SQL statements involving remote database access.

Synonyms and aliases (described in Chapter 16) are also very useful for providing more transparent access to remote databases. Here's an Informix synonym definition that could be established by a user or a database administrator:

```
CREATE SYNONYM REMOTE_REPS FOR SAMPLE@CENTRALHOST.JOE.SALESREPS
```

The equivalent Oracle synonym definition is:

```
CREATE SYNONYM REMOTE_REPS FOR JOE.SALESREPS@CENTRALHOST
```

With this synonym in place, the preceding qualified column name becomes simply:

```
REMOTE_REPS.NAME
```

Any query referencing the REMOTE_REPS table and its columns is actually a remote database query, but that fact is transparent to the user. In practice, most database installations with frequently accessed remote tables will have a set of synonyms defined for them. Most of the DBMS brands support both public synonyms (available to all users) and private synonyms that are created for a specific user or group of users. With this structure, synonyms can become an additional part of the remote access security mechanism, limited to only those users with a real need for remote access.

Several DBMS brands take the synonym capability for transparent database access one step further and permit *views* in the local database that are defined in terms of remote database tables. Here is an Oracle view definition that creates a view called

EAST_REPS in the local database. The view is a subset of information from the remote sample database:

Create a local view defined in terms of two remote tables.

```
CREATE VIEW EAST_REPS AS
     SELECT EMPL_NUM, NAME, AGE, CITY
       FROM SALESREPS@CENTRALHOST, OFFICES@CENTRALHOST
      WHERE REP_OFFICE = OFFICE
        AND REP_OFFICE BETWEEN 11 AND 19
```

After this view has been defined, a user can pose queries in terms of the EAST_REPS view, without worrying about database links or remote table names. The view not only provides transparent remote access, but also hides from the user the remote join operation between the OFFICES and SALESREPS tables.

Transparent access to remote data, provided by views and synonyms, is usually considered a very desirable characteristic. It does have one drawback, however. Because the remote aspect of the database access is now hidden, the network overhead created by the access is also hidden. Therefore, the possibility of a user or programmer inadvertently creating a great deal of network traffic through very large queries is increased. The database administrator must make this trade-off when deciding whether to permit remote transparent synonyms and views.

Transparent remote access also inevitably raises one additional question: since the remote tables now appear as if they are local, can the user pose queries that involve *both* remote and local tables? That is, can a join cross the database server boundaries and relate information from the remote database and the local database? Even more serious questions are posed when the SQL transaction scheme is considered. If a database permits transparent access to a remote database, then is a user allowed to update a row in the local database *and* insert a row in the remote database, and then decide to roll back the transaction? Since the remote resources have been made to appear as if they are local, it seems that the answer *should* be: "Of course—the local and remote databases together should appear as if they were just one local, integrated database."

In fact, supporting such distributed queries and transactions adds a major new level of complexity (and potentially huge network data transmission overhead) to the remote access. Because of this, although several commercial DBMS systems support distributed queries and transactions, they are not heavily used in practice. These capabilities, and their overhead implications, are more fully discussed later, in the "Distributed Database Access" section. The next section discusses a practical alternative—duplicating data, or database replication—that is much more frequently used in practice.

Table Extracts

Remote database access is very convenient for small remote queries and occasional remote database access. If an application requires heavy and frequent access to a remote database, however, the communications overhead of remote database access can become large. Once remote access grows beyond a certain point, it is often more efficient to maintain a local *copy* of the remote data in the local database. Many of the DBMS vendors provide tools to simplify the process of data extraction and distribution. In its simplest form, the process extracts the contents of a table in a master database, sends it across a network to another system, and loads it into a corresponding replica table in a slave database, as shown in Figure 23-3. In practice, the extract is performed periodically and during off-peak times of database activity.

This approach is very appropriate when the data in the replicated table changes slowly, or when changes to the table naturally occur in a batch. For example, suppose some tables of the sample database, located on a remote central computer system, are to be replicated in a local database. The contents of the OFFICES table hardly ever change. It would be an excellent candidate for replication onto distribution center or sales force automation databases. Once the initial (local) replica tables are set up and populated, they might need to be updated only once per month, or when a new sales office is opened.

The PRODUCTS table is also a good candidate for replication. Product price changes occur more frequently than office changes, but in most companies, they happen in batches, perhaps once a week or once a day. With this natural processing cycle, it would be very effective to extract a table of product price data just after each batch of updates, and send it to the distribution center databases and the sales force automation

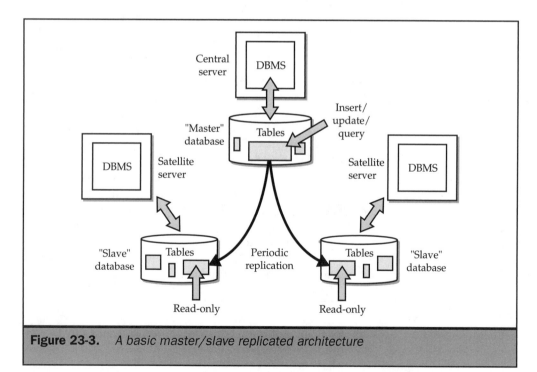

Figure 23-3.   *A basic master/slave replicated architecture*

central database. The price data in these databases does not need to be tightly linked to the mainframe database to insure that it is fresh. A weekly or daily extract/update cycle will make the data just as current, with substantially less processing workload.

It's possible to implement this type of replicated-table strategy without any support from the DBMS. You could write an application program that uses SQL on the mainframe to extract the product pricing data into a file. A file transfer program could transmit the file to the distribution centers, where another application program could read its contents and generate the appropriate DROP TABLE, CREATE TABLE, and INSERT statements to populate the replicated table.

The first step toward automating this strategy was the development of high-speed data extract and data loading programs. These utility programs, offered by the DBMS vendors, typically use proprietary, lower-level database access techniques to extract the data and load the data much more rapidly than is possible through SQL SELECT and INSERT statements. More recently, software companies have targeted this area as an opportunity for stand-alone software packages, independent of the DBMS vendors. This category of software, called Enterprise Application Integration (EAI) software, focuses on linking disparate computer systems, software packages, database systems, and file formats. Linking different DBMS systems is a small part of the total solution offered by these systems, which are extensively customized to meet an individual company's needs when they are installed. The EAI systems typically offer a graphical user interface for specifying the data extraction, an array of tools for reformatting data between the source and destination systems, a messaging capability for transmitting the data, perhaps a store-and-forward capability for staging extracted data before and after transmission, and utilities for managing and monitoring the overall process.

Table Replication

Several DBMS vendors have moved beyond their extract and load utility programs to offer support for table extraction within the DBMS itself. Oracle, for example, offers a snapshot facility to automatically create a local copy of a remote table. In its simplest form, the local table is a read-only replica of the remote master table, which is automatically refreshed by the Oracle DBMS periodically. Here is an Oracle SQL statement to create a local copy of product pricing data, assuming that the remote master database includes a PRODUCTS table like the one in the sample database:

Create a local replica of pricing information from the remote PRODUCTS table.

```
CREATE SNAPSHOT PRODPRICE
        AS SELECT MFR_ID, PRODUCT_ID, PRICE
            FROM PRODUCTS@REMOTE_LINK
```

This statement effectively creates a local Oracle table named PRODPRICE. It contains three columns, specified by the SELECT statement against the remote (master) database. The at sign and name REMOTE_LINK in the statement tell Oracle that the

PRODUCTS table from which the data is to be replicated is a remote table, accessible via the Oracle database link named REMOTE_LINK. The Oracle database administrator sets up these remote database links as part of the distributed Oracle capabilities that are required to use the snapshot feature. Finally, the CREATE SNAPSHOT statement will actually cause the local PRODPRICE snapshot table to be populated with data from the remote PRODUCTS table.

With this type of read-only snapshot, users are not allowed to change the snapshot table with INSERT, UPDATE, or DELETE statements. All database updates occur in the master (remote) table and are propagated to the replicated (snapshot) table by Oracle. The database administrator can manually refresh the snapshot table as desired. The CREATE SNAPSHOT statement also includes rather comprehensive facilities for specifying automatic refreshes. Here are some examples:

Create a local replica of pricing information from the remote PRODUCTS table. Refresh the data once per week, with a complete reload of the data.

```
CREATE SNAPSHOT PRODPRICE
       REFRESH COMPLETE START WITH SYSDATE NEXT SYSDATE+7
           AS SELECT MFR_ID, PRODUCT_ID, PRICE
               FROM PRODUCTS@REMOTE_LINK
```

Create a local replica of pricing information from the remote PRODUCTS table. Refresh the data once per day, sending only changes from the master table.

```
CREATE SNAPSHOT PRODPRICE
       REFRESH FAST START WITH SYSDATE NEXT SYSDATE+1
           AS SELECT MFR_ID, PRODUCT_ID, PRICE
               FROM PRODUCTS@REMOTE_LINK
```

In the latter example, the snapshot is refreshed by transmitting only changes from the remote PRODUCTS table. Oracle implements this capability by maintaining a log of changes (a snapshot log) on the remote system and updating the log every time an update to the PRODUCTS table would affect the snapshot replica. When the time for a refresh arrives, information from the snapshot log is used.

For applications like this one, where product price changes probably affect only a small percentage of the overall table, this strategy is effective. The additional overhead of maintaining the log for the master table is more than offset by the reduced network traffic of transmitting only changed data. In other applications, where a large percentage of the rows in the master table will be modified between refreshes, it may be more efficient to simply do a complete refresh and eliminate the overhead of maintaining the snapshot log.

By default, Oracle identifies rows (to determine whether they are changed) based on their primary key. If the primary key is not part of the replicated data, this can cause confusion about which rows have been updated; in this case, Oracle uses an internal row-id number to identify the modified rows for refreshes to the snapshot.

The SELECT statement that defines the snapshot table offers a very general capability for data extraction. It can include a SELECT clause to extract only selected rows of the master table:

Create a local replica of pricing information for high-priced products from the remote PRODUCTS table. Refresh the data once per day, sending only changes from the master table.

```
CREATE SNAPSHOT PRODPRICE
        REFRESH FAST START WITH SYSDATE NEXT SYSDATE+1
            AS SELECT MFR_ID, PRODUCT_ID, PRICE
                FROM PRODUCTS@REMOTE_LINK
                WHERE PRICE > 1000.00
```

Note that this makes maintaining the snapshot log more complex. Oracle does not need to add to the log all updates to the PRODUCTS table; only those that modify rows that meet the search criterion. The snapshot can also be created as a joined table, extracting its data from two or more master tables in the remote database:

Create a local replica of salesperson data, refreshed weekly.

```
CREATE SNAPSHOT SALESTEAM
        REFRESH FAST START WITH SYSDATE NEXT SYSDATE+7
            AS SELECT NAME, QUOTA, SALES, CITY
                FROM SALESREPS@REMOTE, OFFICES@REMOTE
                WHERE REP_OFFICE = OFFICE
```

Adding to the complexity, the snapshot can be defined by a grouped query:

Create a local summary of customer order volume, refreshed daily.

```
CREATE SNAPSHOT CUSTORD
        REFRESH FAST START WITH SYSDATE NEXT SYSDATE+1
            AS SELECT COMPANY, SUM(AMOUNT)
                FROM CUSTOMERS@REMOTE, ORDERS@REMOTE
                WHERE CUST = CUST_NUM
```

Of course, with each level of additional complexity, the overhead of managing the snapshot and the replication process increases. Regardless of how simple or complex the definition of the snapshot, however, the overall principles remain the same. Instead of having queries against the replicated data travel across the network to the remote database, the remote data is brought down into the snapshot. The refreshes to the snapshot still generate network traffic, but the day-to-day queries against the snapshot data are carried out locally and do not generate network traffic. For situations where the query workload is much higher than the overhead of maintaining the snapshot, this can be an effective way to improve overall database performance.

Updateable Replicas

In the simplest implementations, a table and its replicas have a strict master/slave relationship, as shown in Figure 23-3. The central/master copy contains the real data. It is always up to date, and all updates to the table must occur on this copy of the table. The other slave copies are populated by periodic updates, managed by the DBMS. Between updates, they may become slightly out of date, but if the database is configured in this way, then it is an acceptable price to pay for the advantage of having a local copy of the data. Updates to the slave copies are not permitted. If attempted, the DBMS returns an error condition.

By default, the Oracle CREATE SNAPSHOT statement creates this type of slave replica of a table. The master/slave relationship is implicit in the Microsoft SQL Server structure for replication. The SQL server architecture defines the master as the publisher of the data and the slaves as subscribers to the data. In the default configuration, there is a single (updateable) publisher, and there may be multiple (read-only) subscribers. The SQL Server architecture carries this analogy one step further, supporting both the notion of *push* updates (the publisher actively sends the update data to the subscribers) and *pull* updates (where the subscribers have primary responsibility for getting updates from the publisher).

There are some applications for which table replication is an excellent technique, but where the master/slave relationship does not apply. For example, applications that demand high availability use replicated tables to maintain identical copies of data on two different computer systems. If one system fails, the other contains current data and can carry on processing. An Internet application may demand very high database access rates, and achieve this scalability by replicating a table many times on different computer systems and then spreading out the workload across the systems. A sales force automation application will probably contain one central CUSTOMER table and hundreds of replicas on laptop systems, and individual salespeople should be able to enter new customers or change customer contact information on the laptop replicas. In these configurations (and others), the most efficient use of the computer resources is achieved if *all* of the replicas can accept updates to the table, as shown in Figure 23-4.

A replicated table where multiple copies can accept updates creates a new set of data integrity issues. What happens if the same row of the table is updated in one or more replicas? When the DBMS tries to synchronize the replicas, which of the two updates should apply, or should neither apply, or both? What happens if a row is deleted from one copy of the table, but it is updated in another copy of the table?

In DBMS systems that support updateable replicas, these issues are addressed by creating a set of conflict resolution rules that are applied by the replication system. For example, when replication is set up between a central CUSTOMER table and laptop versions of the table, the replication rule may say that changes to the central customer database always win over changes entered on a laptop system. Alternatively, the replication rule might say that the most recent update always wins. In addition to the built-in rules provided by the DBMS itself, the replication definition may include the capability to pass conflicts to a user-written procedure (such as a stored procedure within the database) for selection of the winner and loser replicas.

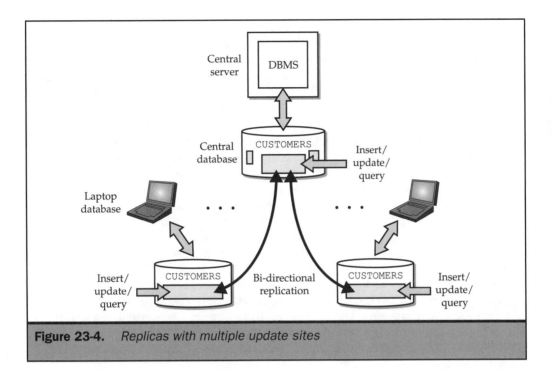

Figure 23-4.   *Replicas with multiple update sites*

Replication Trade-Offs

Practical replication strategies always involve a trade-off between the desire to keep data as current as possible and the desire to keep network traffic down to a practical level and provide adequate performance. These trade-offs usually involve not just technical considerations, but business practices and policies as well. For example, consider an order-processing application using the sample database, and assume that order processing is distributed across five different call centers that are geographically distributed around the world. Each call center has its own computer system and database. Incoming orders are checked against the PRODUCTS table to be certain that enough inventory is on hand to fill the order. The PRODUCTS table keeps track of product-on-hand quantities for all of the company's warehouses, worldwide.

Suppose the company's policy is that the order-processing clerk must be able to absolutely guarantee a customer that products can be shipped within 24 hours of the time an order is accepted. In this case, the PRODUCTS table must contain absolutely up-to-the-minute data, reflecting the inventory impact of orders taken just seconds earlier. There are only two possible designs for the database in this case. There could be a single, central copy of the PRODUCTS table, shared by all users at all five order-processing sites. Alternatively, there could be a fully mirrored copy of the PRODUCTS table at each of the five sites. The fully mirrored solution is almost certainly impractical because the frequent updates to the PRODUCTS table as each order is taken will cause excessive network traffic to keep the five copies of the table in perfect synchronization.

But suppose the company believes it can still maintain adequate customer satisfaction with a policy that is slightly less strict—for example, it promises to notify any customer within 24 hours if the order cannot be filled immediately and give the customer an opportunity to cancel the order. In this case, a replicated PRODUCTS table becomes an excellent solution. Once a day, updates to the PRODUCTS table can be downloaded to the replicated copy at each of the five sites. During the day, orders are verified against the *local copy* of the PRODUCTS table, but only the local PRODUCTS table is updated. This prevents the company from taking an order for which there was not adequate stock on hand at the beginning of the day, but it does not prevent orders taken at two or three different sites from exceeding the available stock. The next night, when data communications costs are lower than they are during the day, the orders from each site are transmitted to a central site, which processes them against a central copy of the PRODUCTS table. Orders that cannot be filled from inventory are flagged, and a report of them is generated. When processing is complete, the updated PRODUCTS table, along with the problem orders report, is transmitted back to each of the five sites to prepare for the next day's processing.

Which is the correct architecture for supporting the operation of this global business? As the example shows, it is not so much a database architecture question as a business policy question. The interdependence of computer systems architectures and business operations is one of the reasons why decisions about replication and data distribution inevitably make certain types of business operations easier and others harder.

Typical Replication Architectures

In many cases, it's possible to structure an application that involves replicated data so that conflicts between replica updates are avoided or greatly minimized. The DBMS conflict resolution rules are then applied as a last resort, when a conflict arises despite the design of the application. The next few sections describe some typical replicated table scenarios and the application structure that is often used in each scenario to minimize replication conflicts.

Horizontal Table Subsets

One efficient way to replicate parts of a table across a network is to divide the table horizontally, placing different rows of the table on different systems. Figure 23-5 shows a simple example where a horizontal table split is useful. In this application, a company operates three distribution centers, each with its own computer system and DBMS to manage an inventory database and order processing. A central database is also maintained for production-planning purposes.

To support this environment, the PRODUCTS table is split horizontally into three parts and expanded to include a LOCATION column that tells where the inventory is located. The central copy of the table contains all of the rows. The rows of the table that describe inventory in each distribution center are replicated in the local database managed by that center's DBMS.

Figure 23-5.   *Replication of horizontal table slices*

In this case, most updates to the PRODUCTS table take place at the distribution center itself, as it processes orders. Because distribution center replicas are mutually exclusive (that is, a row from the PRODUCTS table appears in only one distribution center replica), update conflicts are avoided. The replicas in the distribution center can periodically transmit updates to the central database to keep it up to date.

Vertical Table Subsets

Another efficient way to manage table replication is to divide the table vertically, replicating different columns of the table on different systems. Figure 23-6 shows a simple example of a vertical table split. The SALESREPS table has been expanded to include new columns of personnel information (phone number, marital status, and so on), and its information is needed in two databases—one in the order-processing department and the other in the personnel department. Most of the activity in each department focuses on one or two columns of the table, but many queries and reports use both personnel-related and order-related columns.

To accommodate this application, the SALESREPS table is replicated on both systems, but conceptually, it is split vertically into two parts. The columns of the table that store personnel data (NAME, AGE, HIRE_DATE, PHONE, MARRIED) are owned by the personnel system. It wins any conflicts related to updates on these columns. The other columns (EMPL_NUM, QUOTA, SALES, REP_OFFICE) are owned by the order-processing system. It wins update conflicts related to these columns. Because the entire table is replicated on

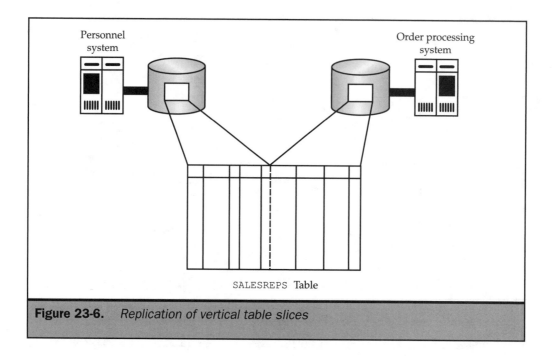

Figure 23-6.   *Replication of vertical table slices*

both systems, either system can be used to generate reports and handle ad hoc inquiries, and all of these can be processed locally. Only updates involve the replication mechanism, generate network traffic, and potentially require conflict resolution.

Mirrored Tables

When table replication is used to achieve high availability (that is, resistance to computer or database failure), the entire table is typically mirrored, as shown in Figure 23-7. The easiest way to implement this configuration is if one system is the active system and another is a hot standby. In this scheme, all database access normally flows to the active system (System A), which replicates any updates to the standby system (System B). Only in the event of system failure does the database access switch over to the standby system, but it has fresh data because of the replicated table. The disadvantage of this scheme is that it wastes the standby computer system under normal operation. The system must be paid for and maintained, but it doesn't add any data processing capacity.

For this reason, high-availability systems are often designed to also provide load balancing, as shown in Figure 23-8. In this configuration, some front-end software intercepts DBMS access requests and evenly distributes them between the two (or more) computer systems. Under normal operation, both (all) systems contribute data processing power; none is wasted. Furthermore, it's conceptually easy to grow the data processing power, simply by adding more computer systems with a copy of the replicated table.

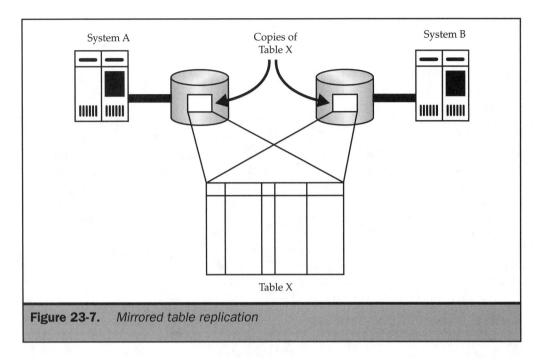

Figure 23-7. *Mirrored table replication*

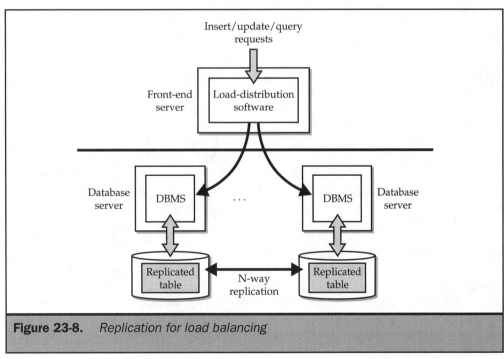

Figure 23-8. *Replication for load balancing*

This type of mirrored table approach can be highly effective if the ratio of database queries to database updates is very high (for example, 95 percent read access/5 percent update access). If the percentage of updates is higher, the potential for conflicts and the replication overhead can diminish the effectiveness and scalability of the overall configuration. Efficiency also decreases with each increase in the number of replicated systems, since the replication overhead rises.

One common way to get more efficiency out of a mirrored table configuration like the one in Figure 23-8 is to divide updates to the table based on some rule. For example, if the mirrored table is a customer table, the primary key may be the customer name. The front-end load-balancing software can then be written so that updates for customer names starting with *A* through *M* are routed to the one system and updates for customer names starting with *N* through *Z* are routed to the other system. This eliminates the possibility of update conflicts. Because the table remains fully replicated under this scenario, read access requests can still be distributed randomly between the two systems to balance the workload. This type of approach can be quite effective in achieving scalable database performance with replicated tables. It can be fairly easily extended from a two-way scheme to an N-way scheme, where updates are split among three or more database servers.

Distributed Database Access

Over the last several years, research into fully distributed database access has slowly but surely found its way into commercial products. Today, many of the mainstream enterprise database products offer at least some level of transparent distributed database access. As noted earlier in the "Remote Data Transparency" section, the performance implications of distributed database access and updates can be very substantial. Two very similar-looking queries can create massively different amounts of network traffic and overhead. A single query, carried out in a brute force method or an optimized method, can create the same differences, depending on the quality of the optimization done by the DBMS.

Because of these challenges, all of the vendors have taken a step-by-step approach to delivering distributed database access. When IBM first announced its blueprint for distributed data management in its SQL products, it defined a four-stage approach. IBM's four stages, shown in Table 23-1, provide an excellent framework for understanding distributed data management capabilities and their implications.

The IBM scheme provides a simple model for defining the distributed data access problem: a user of one computer system needs to access data stored on one or more other computer systems. The sophistication of the distributed access increases at each stage. Thus, the capabilities provided by a given DBMS can be described in terms of which stage it has reached. In addition, within each stage, a distinction can be made between read-only access (with the SELECT statement) and update access (with the INSERT, DELETE, and UPDATE statements). A DBMS product often provides read-only capability for a given stage before full update capability is provided.

Stage	Description
Remote request	Each SQL statement accesses a single remote database; each statement is a transaction.
Remote transaction	Each SQL statement accesses a single remote database; multistatement transactions are supported for a single database.
Distributed transaction	Each SQL statement accesses a single remote database; multistatement transactions are supported across multiple databases.
Distributed request	Each SQL statement may access multiple databases; multistatement transactions are supported across multiple databases.

Table 23-1.   *IBM's Four-Stage Approach for Distributed Database Access*

Remote Requests

The first stage of distributed data access, as defined by IBM, is a *remote request*, shown in Figure 23-9. In this stage, the PC user may issue a SQL statement that queries or updates data in a single remote database. Each individual SQL statement operates as its own transaction, similar to the autocommit mode provided by many interactive SQL programs. The user can issue a sequence of SQL statements for various databases, but the DBMS doesn't support multistatement transactions.

Remote requests are very useful when a PC user needs to query corporate data. Usually, the required data is located within a single database, such as a database of order-processing or manufacturing data. Using a remote request, the PC program can retrieve the remote data for processing by a PC spreadsheet, graphics program, or desktop publishing package.

The remote request capability is not powerful enough for most transaction-processing applications. For example, consider a PC-based order entry application that accesses a corporate database. To process a new order, the PC program must check inventory levels, add the order to the database, decrease the inventory totals, and adjust customer and sales totals, involving perhaps half a dozen different SQL statements. As explained in Chapter 11, database integrity can be corrupted if these statements do not execute as a single transaction. However, the remote request stage does not support multistatement transactions, so it cannot support this application.

Figure 23-9. *Distributed data access: remote requests*

Remote Transactions

The second stage of distributed data access, as defined by IBM, is a *remote transaction* (called a remote unit of work by IBM), shown in Figure 23-10. Remote transactions extend the remote request stage to include multistatement transaction support. The PC user can issue a series of SQL statements that query or update data in a remote database and then commit or roll back the entire series of statements as a single transaction. The DBMS guarantees that the entire transaction will succeed or fail as a unit, as it does for transactions on a local database. However, all of the SQL statements that make up the transaction must reference a single remote database.

Remote transactions open the door for distributed transaction-processing applications. For example, in an order-processing application, a PC-based order entry program can now perform a sequence of queries, updates, and inserts in the inventory database to process a new order. The program ends the statement sequence with a COMMIT or ROLLBACK for the transaction.

Remote transaction capability typically requires a DBMS (or at least transaction-processing logic) on the PC as well as the system where the database is located. The transaction logic of the DBMS must be extended across the network to ensure that the local and remote systems always have the same opinion about whether a transaction has been committed. However, the actual responsibility for maintaining database integrity remains with the remote DBMS.

Remote transaction capability is often the highest level of distributed database access provided by database gateways that link one vendor's DBMS to other DBMS brands. For example, most of the independent enterprise database vendors (Sybase, Oracle, Informix) provide gateways from their UNIX-based DBMS systems to IBM's mainframe DB2 implementation. Some gateway products go beyond the bounds of

Figure 23-10. *Distributed data access: remote transactions*

remote transactions, allowing a user to join, in a single query, tables from a local
database with tables from a remote database managed by a different brand of DBMS.
However, these gateways do not (and cannot, without support from the remote DBMS)
provide the underlying transaction logic required to support the higher stages of
distributed access as defined by IBM. The gateway can ensure the integrity of the local
and remote databases individually, but it cannot guarantee that a transaction will not
be committed in one and rolled back in the other.

Distributed Transactions

The third stage of distributed data access, as defined by IBM, is a *distributed transaction*
(a distributed unit of work in IBM parlance), shown in Figure 23-11. At this stage, each
individual SQL statement still queries or updates a single database on a single remote
computer system. However, the sequence of SQL statements within a transaction may
access two or more databases located on different systems. When the transaction is
committed or rolled back, the DBMS guarantees that all parts of the transaction on all
of the systems involved in the transaction will be committed or rolled back. The DBMS
specifically guarantees that there will not be a partial transaction, where the transaction
is committed on one system and rolled back on another.

Distributed transactions support the development of very sophisticated transaction-
processing applications. For example, in the corporate network of Figure 23-1, a PC
order-processing application can query the inventory databases on two or three different
distribution center servers to check the inventory of a scarce product and then update the
databases to commit inventory from multiple locations to a customer's order. The DBMS
ensures that other concurrent orders do not interfere with the remote access of the first
transaction.

Figure 23-11. *Distributed data access: distributed transactions*

Distributed transactions are much more difficult to provide than the first two stages of distributed data access. It's impossible to provide distributed transactions without the active cooperation of the individual DBMS systems involved in the transaction. For this reason, the DBMS brands that support distributed transactions almost always support them only for a homogeneous network of databases, all managed by the same DBMS brand (that is, an all-Oracle or all-Sybase network). A special transaction protocol, called the *two-phase commit* protocol, is used to implement distributed transactions and ensure that they provide the all-or-nothing requirement of a SQL transaction. The details of this protocol are described later in the section "The Two-Phase Commit Protocol."

Distributed Requests

The final stage of distributed data access in the IBM model is a *distributed request*, shown in Figure 23-12. At this stage, a single SQL statement may reference tables from two or more databases located on different computer systems. The DBMS is responsible for automatically carrying out the statement across the network. A sequence of distributed request statements can be grouped together as a transaction. As in the previous distributed transaction stage, the DBMS must guarantee the integrity of the distributed transaction on all systems that are involved.

The distributed request stage doesn't make any new demands on the DBMS transaction-processing logic, because the DBMS already had to support transactions across system boundaries at the previous distributed transaction stage. However, distributed requests pose major new challenges for the DBMS optimization logic. The optimizer must now consider network speed when it evaluates alternate methods for carrying out a SQL statement. If the local DBMS must repeatedly access part of a remote table (for example, when making a join), it may be faster to copy part of the table across the network in one large bulk transfer rather than repeatedly retrieving individual rows across the network.

Figure 23-12. *Distributed data access: distributed requests*

The relative sizes of the tables on the local and remote system are also relevant optimization factors, as well as the selectivity of any search conditions in the SELECT clause. For some queries, the search conditions may select only one or a few rows on the local system and hundreds of rows on the remote system, so they should be applied locally first. For other queries involving the same tables, the relative selectivity may be reversed, and the remote search condition should be applied. For still other queries, the join condition itself may limit the rows that participate in both the local and remote systems, and it may be most efficient to apply it first. In each case, the cost of the query is not just the cost of the database access but also the cost of shipping the results of intermediate query execution steps back and forth across the network.

The optimizer must also decide which copy of the DBMS should handle statement execution. If most of the tables are on a remote system, it may be a good idea for the remote DBMS on that system to execute the statement. However, that may be a bad choice if the remote system is heavily loaded. Thus, the optimizer's task is both more complex and much more important in a distributed request.

Ultimately, the goal of the distributed request stage is to make the entire distributed database look like one large database to the user. Ideally, the user would have full access to any table in the distributed database and could use SQL transactions without knowing anything about the physical location of the data. Unfortunately, this ideal scenario would quickly prove impractical in real networks. In a network of any size, the number of tables in the distributed database would quickly become very large, and users would find it impossible to find data of interest. The user-ids of every database in the organization would have to be coordinated to make sure that a given user-id uniquely identified a user in all databases. Database administration would also be very difficult.

In practice, therefore, distributed requests must be implemented selectively. Database administrators must decide which remote tables are to be made visible to local users and which will remain hidden. The cooperating DBMS copies must translate user-ids from one system to another, allowing each database to be administered autonomously while providing security for remote data access. Distributed requests that would consume too many DBMS or network resources must be detected and prohibited before they impact overall DBMS performance.

Because of their complexity, distributed requests are not fully supported by any commercial SQL-based DBMS today, and it will be some time before even a majority of their features are available. One major step toward distributed processing across database brands has been the standardization of a distributed transaction protocol. The XA protocol, originally developed to coordinate among multiple transaction monitors, is being actively applied to distributed database transactions as well. A Java version of the same capability, called Java Transaction Protocol (JTP), provides a distributed transaction interface for Java-based applications and application servers. Today, most commercial DBMS products designed to be used in a network environment support XA and JTA interfaces.

The Two-Phase Commit Protocol *

A distributed DBMS must preserve the all-or-nothing quality of a SQL transaction if it is to provide distributed transactions. The user of the distributed DBMS expects that a committed transaction will be committed on all of the systems where data resides, and that a rolled back transaction will be rolled back on all of the systems as well. Further, failures in a network connection or in one of the systems should cause the DBMS to abort a transaction and roll it back, rather than leaving the transaction in a partially committed state.

All commercial DBMS systems that support distributed transactions use a technique called *two-phase commit* to provide that support. You don't have to understand the two-phase commit scheme to use distributed transactions. In fact, the whole point of the scheme is to support distributed transactions without your knowing it. However, understanding the mechanics of a two-phase commit can help you plan efficient database access.

To understand why a special two-phase commit protocol is needed, consider the database in Figure 23-13. The user, located on System A, has updated a table on System B and a table on System C and now wants to commit the transaction. Suppose the DBMS software on System A tried to commit the transaction by simply sending a COMMIT message to System B and System C, and then waiting for their affirmative replies. This strategy works as long as Systems B and C can both successfully commit their part of the transaction.

But what happens if a problem such as a disk failure or a deadlock condition prevents System C from committing as requested? System B will commit its part of the transaction and send back an acknowledgment, System C will roll back its part of the transaction because of the error and send back an error message, and the user ends up with a partially committed, partially rolled back transaction. Note that System A can't change its mind at this point and ask System B to roll back the transaction. The transaction on System B has been committed, and other users may already have modified the data on System B based on the changes made by the transaction.

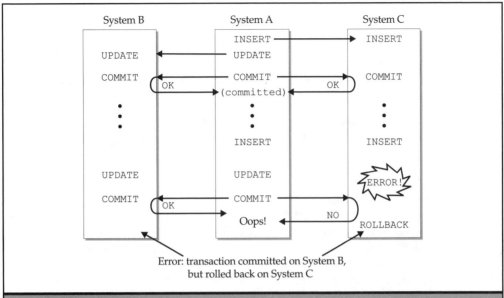

Error: transaction committed on System B,
but rolled back on System C

Figure 23-13.   *Problems with a broadcast commit scheme*

The two-phase commit protocol eliminates the problems of the simple strategy shown in Figure 23-13. Figure 23-14 illustrates the steps involved in a two-phase commit:

1. The program on System A issues a COMMIT for the current (distributed) transaction, which has updated tables on System B and System C. System A will act as the *coordinator* of the commit process, coordinating the activities of the DBMS software on Systems B and C.

2. System A sends a GET READY message to both System B and System C and notes the message in its own transaction log.

3. When the DBMS on System B or C receives the GET READY message, it must prepare to *either* commit or roll back the current transaction. If the DBMS can get into this "ready to commit" state, it replies YES to System A and notes that fact in its local transaction log; if it cannot get into this state, it replies NO.

4. System A waits for replies to its GET READY message. If all of the replies are YES, System A sends a COMMIT message to both System B and System C, and notes the decision in its transaction log. If any of the replies is NO, or if all of the replies are not received within some timeout period, System A sends a ROLLBACK message to both systems and notes that decision in its transaction log.

5. When the DBMS on System B or C receives the COMMIT or ROLLBACK message, it must do as it is told. The DBMS gave up the capability to decide the transaction's

fate autonomously when it replied YES to the GET READY message in Step 3. The DBMS commits or rolls back its part of the transaction as requested, writes the COMMIT or ROLLBACK message in its transaction log, and returns an OK message to System A.

6. When System A has received all the OK messages, it knows the transaction has been committed or rolled back and returns the appropriate SQLCODE value to the program.

This protocol protects the distributed transaction against any single failure in System B, System C, or the communications network. These two examples illustrate how the protocol permits recovery from failures:

■ Suppose a failure occurs on System C before it sends a YES message in Step 3. System A will not receive a YES reply and will broadcast a ROLLBACK message, causing System B to roll back the transaction. The recovery program on System C will not find the YES message or a COMMIT message in the local transaction log, and it will roll back the transaction on System C as part of the recovery process. All parts of the transaction will have b64een rolled back at this point.

Figure 23-14. *The two-phase commit protocol*

■ Suppose a failure occurs on System C after it sends a YES message in Step 3. System A will decide whether to commit or roll back the distributed transaction based on the reply from System B. The recovery program on System C will find the YES message in the local transaction log but will not find a COMMIT or ROLLBACK message to mark the end of the transaction. The recovery program then asks the coordinator (System A) what the final disposition of the transaction was and acts accordingly. Note that System A must maintain a record of its decision to commit or roll back the transaction until it receives the final OK from all of the participants, so that it can respond to the recovery program in case of failure.

The two-phase commit protocol guarantees the integrity of distributed transactions, but it generates a great deal of network traffic. If there are n systems involved in the transaction, the coordinator must send and receive a total of $(4 * n)$ messages to successfully commit the transaction. Note that these messages are in addition to the messages that actually carry the SQL statements and query results among the systems. However, there's no way to avoid the message traffic if a distributed transaction is to provide database integrity in the face of system failures.

Because of their heavy network overhead, distributed transactions can have a serious negative effect on database performance. For this reason, distributed databases must be carefully designed so that frequently accessed (or at least frequently updated) data is on a local system or on a single remote system. If possible, transactions that update two or more remote systems should be relatively rare.

Network Applications and Database Architecture

Innovations in computer networking have been closely linked to many of the innovations in relational database architectures and SQL over the years. Powerful minicomputers with mainframe network connections (such as Digital's VAX family) were the first popular platform for SQL-based databases. They offered a platform for decision support, based on data offloaded from mainframe systems. They also supported local data processing applications, for capturing business data and uploading it to corporate mainframe applications.

UNIX-based servers and powerful local area networks (such as Sun's server products) drove another wave of DBMS growth and innovation. This era of databases and networks gave birth to the client/server architecture that dominated enterprise data processing in the 1990s. Later, the rise of enterprisewide networks and applications (such as Enterprise Resource Planning) created a need for a new level of database scalability and distributed database capability. Today, the exploding popularity of the Internet is driving still another wave of innovation, as very high peak-load transaction rates and personalized user interaction drive database caching and main-memory database technologies.

Client/Server Applications and Database Architecture

When SQL-based databases were first deployed on minicomputer systems, the database and application architecture was very simple—all of the processing, from screen display (presentation) to calculation and data processing (business logic) to database access occurred on the minicomputer's CPU. The advent of powerful personal computers and server platforms drove a major change in that architecture, for several reasons.

The graphical user interface (GUI) of popular PC office automation software (spreadsheets, word processors, and so on) set a new standard for ease of use, and companies demanded the same style of interface from corporate applications. Supporting a GUI is processor-intensive and demands a high-bandwidth path from the processor to the display memory that holds the screen image. While some protocols emerged for running a GUI over the LAN (the X-windows protocol), the best place to run a production application's presentation-layer code was clearly on the PC itself.

Economics was also a factor. Personal computer systems were much cheaper, on a cost-per-processing-power basis, than minicomputers or UNIX-based servers. If more of the processing for a business application could take place on lower-cost PCs, the overall hardware cost of deploying an application would be reduced. This was an argument for moving not just the presentation layer, but much of the business logic layer, onto the PC as well.

Driven by these and other factors, the first client/server architectures emerged, shown in Figure 23-15. Many PC-based applications are still being deployed today using this architecture. SQL plays a key role as the client/server language. Requests are sent from the application logic (on the PC) to the DBMS (on the server) expressed in SQL statements. The answers come back across the network in the form of SQL completion status codes (for database updates) or SQL query results (for information requests).

Figure 23-15.   *Client/server applications architecture*

Client/Server Applications with Stored Procedures

Whenever an application is split across two or more networked computer systems, as in Figure 23-15, one of the major issues is the interface between the two halves of the split application. Each interaction across this interface now generates network traffic, and the network is always the slowest part of the overall system, both in its data transmission capacity (bandwidth) and in round-trip messaging delays (latency). With the architecture shown in Figure 23-15, each database access (that is, each SQL statement) generates at least one round trip across the network.

In an OLTP application, typical transactions may require as many as a dozen individual SQL statements. For example, to take a customer's order for a single product in the simple structure of the sample database, the order-processing application might:

- Retrieve the customer number based on the customer name (single-row SELECT)
- Retrieve the customer's credit limit to verify creditworthiness (single-row SELECT)
- Retrieve product information, such as price and quantity available (single-row SELECT)
- Add a row to the ORDERS table for the new order (INSERT)
- Update the product information to reflect the lower quantity available (UPDATE)
- Update the customer's credit limit, reducing the available credit (UPDATE)
- Commit the entire transaction (COMMIT)

for a total of seven round trips between the application and the database. In a real-world application, the number of database accesses might be two or three times this amount. As transaction volumes grow, the amount of network traffic can be very significant.

Database stored procedures provide an alternative architecture that can dramatically reduce the amount of network traffic, as shown in Figure 23-16. A stored procedure within the database itself incorporates the sequence of steps and the decision-making logic required to carry out all of the database operations associated with the transaction. Basically, part of the business logic that formerly resided within the application itself has been pushed across the network onto the database server. Instead of sending individual SQL statements to the DBMS, the application calls the stored procedure, passing the customer name, the product to be ordered, and the quantity desired. If all goes well, the stored procedure returns successfully. If a problem arises (such as lack of available product or a customer credit problem), a returned error code and message describes it. By using the stored procedure, the network traffic is reduced to a single client/server interaction.

There are several other advantages to using stored procedures, but the reduction in network traffic is one of the major ones. It was a major selling advantage of Sybase SQL Server when it was first introduced and helped to position Sybase as a DBMS specialized for high-performance OLTP applications. With the popularity of stored procedures, every major general-purpose enterprise DBMS now offers this capability.

Figure 23-16. *Client/server architecture with stored procedures*

Enterprise Applications and Data Caching

Today, major applications from the large packaged enterprise software vendors are all based on SQL and relational databases. Examples include large Enterprise Resource Planning (ERP), Supply Chain Management (SCM), Human Resources Management (HRM), Customer Relationship Management (CRM), financial management, and other packages from vendors such as SAP, BAAN, PeopleSoft, Vantive, Clarify, Siebel Systems, i2 Technologies, Manugistics, and others. These large-scale applications typically run on large UNIX-based server systems and place a heavy workload on the supporting DBMS. To isolate the applications and DBMS processing, and apply more total processing power to the application, they often use a three-tier architecture shown in Figure 23-17.

Even with the use of stored procedures to minimize network traffic, the network and database access demands of the most data-intensive of these enterprise applications can outstrip the available network bandwidth and DBMS transaction rates. For example, consider a supply chain planning application that helps a manufacturing company determine the parts that it must order from suppliers. To generate a complete plan, the application must examine *every* open order and apply the product bill-of-materials to it. A complex product might involve hundreds of parts, some of which are themselves subassemblies consisting of dozens or hundreds of parts.

If written using straightforward programming techniques, the planning application must perform a database inquiry to determine the parts makeup of every product, and then every subassembly, for every order, and it will accumulate the total needed information in the planning database for each of these parts. Using this technique, the application will take hours to process the hundreds of thousands of orders that may be currently on the books. In fact, the application will probably run so long that it cannot

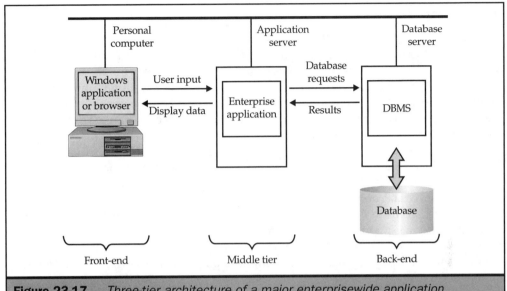

Figure 23-17. *Three-tier architecture of a major enterprisewide application*

possibly complete its work during the typical overnight low-volume batch processing window of time during which the company normally runs such applications.

To deliver acceptable performance, all data-intensive enterprise applications employ caching techniques, pulling the data forward out of the database server, closer to the application. In most cases, the application uses relatively primitive caching techniques. For example, it might read the bill-of-materials once and load it into main-memory data tables within the application program. By eliminating the heavily repeated product-structure queries, the program can dramatically improve its performance.

Recently, enterprise application vendors have begun to use more complex caching techniques. They may replicate the most heavily accessed data (the hot data) in a duplicate database table, on the same system as the application itself. Main-memory databases offer an even higher-performance alternative and are already being used where there is a relatively small amount of hot data (tens to hundreds of megabytes). With the advent of 64-bit operating system architectures and continuing declines in memory prices, it is becoming practical to cache larger amounts of data (several gigabytes or tens of gigabytes).

Advanced caching and replication will become more important in response to emerging business requirements. Leading-edge manufacturing companies want to move toward real-time planning, where incoming customer orders and changes immediately impact production plans. They want to offer more customized products, in more configurations, to more closely match customer desires. These and similar trends will continue to raise the volume and complexity of database access.

High-Volume Internet Data Management

High-volume Internet applications are also driving the trend to database caching and replication in networked database architectures. For example, financial services firms are competing for online brokerage clients by offering more and more advanced real-time stock reporting and analysis capabilities. The data management to support this application involves real-time data feeds (to insure that pricing and volume information in the database is current) and peak-load database inquiries of tens of thousands of transactions per second. Similar volume demands are found in applications for managing and monitoring high-volume Internet sites. The trend to personalize web sites (determining on the fly which banner ads to display, which products to feature, and so on) and measure the effectiveness of such personalization is another trend driving peak-load data access and data capture rates.

The Web has already shown to be an effective architecture for dealing with these types of peak-load Internet volume demands—through web site caching. Copies of heavily accessed web pages are pulled forward in the network and replicated. As a result, the total network capacity for serving web pages is increased, and the amount of network traffic associated with those page hits is reduced. Similar architectures are beginning to emerge for high-volume Internet database management, as shown in Figure 23-18. In this case, an Internet information services application caches hot data, such as the most recent news and financial information, in a very high-performance main-memory database from a vendor such as TimesTen Performance Software. It also stores summary user profile information in a main-memory database, which is used to personalize users' experiences as they interact with the web site.

As Figure 23-18 shows, the methods for handling high-performance data management are beginning to follow those already established for high-performance web page management. The issues for databases are more complex because of database integrity issues, but the emerging techniques are similar—replication, high-volume read access, memory-resident databases, and highly fault-tolerant architectures. These demands will only grow as Internet traffic and personalization continues to increase, leading to more advanced network database architectures.

Summary

This chapter described the distributed data management capabilities offered by various DBMS products and the trade-offs involved in providing access to remote data:

- A distributed database is implemented by a network of computer systems, each running its own copy of the DBMS software and operating autonomously for local data access. The copies of the DBMS cooperate to provide remote data access when required.

Figure 23-18. *Staging data for high-performance data management*

- The ideal distributed database is one in which the user doesn't know and doesn't care that the data is distributed; to the user, all of the relevant data appears as if it were on the local system.

- Because this ideal distributed DBMS is very difficult to provide and involves too many performance trade-offs, commercial DBMS products are providing distributed database capability in phases.

- Remote database access can be useful in situations where the remote access is a small part of total database activity; in this case, it's more practical to leave the data in the remote location and incur the network overhead for each database access.

■ Database replication is very useful in situations where there is relatively heavy access to data in multiple locations; it brings the data closer to the point of access, but at the cost of network overhead for replica synchronization and data that is not 100 percent up to date.

■ The particular trade-offs of remote data access and replication strategies have implications beyond technology decisions; they should reflect underlying trade-offs in business priorities as well.

■ Enterprisewide distributed applications, Internet-based applications, data warehousing, and other trends are increasing the complexity of the distributed data management environment. The N-tier architectures they use will require smart data caching and replication strategies to deliver adequate performance.

Chapter 24

SQL and Objects

The only serious challenge to the dominance of SQL and relational database management over the last few years has come from the emergence of an equally significant trend—the growing popularity of object-oriented technologies. Object-oriented programming languages (such as C++ and Java), object-oriented development tools, and object-oriented networking (including object request brokers, and more recently, Web Services) have emerged as foundation technologies for modern software development. Object technologies gained much of their initial popularity for building personal computer applications with graphical user interfaces. But their impact has grown, and they are being used today to build (and more importantly, to link together) enterprisewide network-based applications for large corporations.

In the early 1990s, a group of venture-backed object-oriented database companies was formed with the goal of applying object-oriented principles to database management. These companies believed that their object-oriented databases would supplant the outdated relational databases as surely as the relational model had supplanted earlier data models. However, they met with limited marketplace success in the face of entrenched relational technologies and SQL. In response to the object challenge, many relational database vendors moved aggressively to graft object technologies onto their relational systems, creating hybrid object-relational models. This chapter describes the object database challenge to SQL and the resulting object-relational features provided by some major DBMS vendors.

Object-Oriented Databases

Considerable academic research on database technology over the past decade has been focused on new, post-relational data models. Just as the relational model provided clear-cut advantages over the earlier hierarchical and network models, the goal of this research was to develop new data models that would overcome some of the disadvantages of the relational model. Much of this research has focused on how to merge the principles of object-oriented programming and design with traditional database characteristics, such as persistent storage and transaction management.

In addition to the academic research, in the early and mid-1990s, some large venture capital investments flowed into a group of startup software companies whose goal was to build a new generation of data management technologies. These companies typically started with the object data structures used by an object-oriented program to manage its in-memory data, and extended them for disk-based storage and multiuser access. Enthusiastic supporters of these object-oriented databases (OODBs) firmly believed that they would mount a serious challenge to the relational model and become the dominant database architecture by the end of the decade. That scenario proved far off the mark, but the object database vendors have had a significant impact on their relational rivals.

Object-Oriented Database Characteristics

Unlike the relational data model, where Codd's 1970 paper provided a clear, mathematical definition of a relational database, there is no single definition of an object-oriented database. However, the core principles embodied in most object-oriented databases include:

- **Objects**. In an object-oriented database, everything is an object and is manipulated as an object. The tabular, row/column organization of a relational database is replaced by the notion of collections of objects. Generally, a collection of objects is itself an object and can be manipulated in the same way that other objects are manipulated.

- **Classes**. Object-oriented databases replace the relational notion of atomic data types with a hierarchical notion of classes and subclasses. For example, VEHICLES might be a class of object, and individual members (instances) of that class would include a car, a bicycle, a train, or a boat. The VEHICLES class might include subclasses called CARS and BOATS, representing a more specialized form of vehicle. Similarly, the CARS class might include a subclass called CONVERTIBLES, and so on.

- **Inheritance**. Objects inherit characteristics from their class and from all of the higher-level classes to which they belong. For example, one of the characteristics of a vehicle might be "number of passengers." All members of the CARS, BOATS, and CONVERTIBLES classes also have this attribute, because they are subclasses of VEHICLES. The CARS class might also have the attribute "number of doors," and the CONVERTIBLES class would inherit this attribute. However, the BOATS class would not inherit the attribute.

- **Attributes**. The characteristics that an object possesses are modeled by its attributes. Examples include the color of an object, or the number of doors that it has, and its English-language name. The attributes are related to the object they describe in roughly the same way that the columns of a table relate to its rows.

- **Messages and methods**. Objects communicate with one another by sending and receiving *messages*. When it receives a message, an object responds by executing a *method*, a program stored within the object that determines how it processes the message. Thus, an object includes a set of behaviors described by its methods. Usually, an object shares many of the same methods with other objects in higher-level classes.

- **Encapsulation**. The internal structure and data of objects is hidden from the outside world (encapsulated) behind a limited set of well-defined interfaces. The only way to find out about an object, or to act on it, is through its methods, whose functions and behaviors are clearly specified. This makes the object more predictable and limits the opportunities for accidental data corruption.

■ **Object identity**. Objects can be distinguished from one another through unique object identifiers, usually implemented as an abstract pointer known as an object *handle*. Handles are frequently used to represent relationships among objects; an object points to a related object by storing the object's handle as one of its data items (attributes).

These principles and techniques make object-oriented databases well suited to applications involving complex data types, such as computer-aided design or compound documents that combine text, graphics, and spreadsheets. The database provides a natural way to represent the hierarchies that occur in complex data. For example, an entire document can be represented as a single object, composed of smaller objects (sections), composed of still smaller objects (paragraphs, graphs, and so on). The class hierarchy allows the database to track the type of each object in the document (paragraphs, charts, illustrations, titles, footnotes, and so on).

Finally, the message mechanism offers natural support for a graphical user interface. The application program can send a "draw yourself" message to each part of the document, asking it to draw itself on the screen. If the user changes the shape of the window displaying the document, the application program can respond by sending a "resize yourself" message to each document part, and so on. Each object in the document bears responsibility for its own display, so new objects can easily be added to the document architecture.

Pros and Cons of Object-Oriented Databases

Object-oriented databases have stirred up a storm of controversy in the database community. Proponents claim that object databases are essential to create a proper match between the programming and database data models. They claim that the rigid, fixed, row/column structure of relational tables is a holdover from the punch-card era of data processing with its fixed data fields and record orientation. A more flexible model, where classes of objects can be similar to one another (that is, share certain attributes) but also different from one another is essential, they claim, to effectively model real-world situations.

Another claim is that the multitable joins that are an integral part of the relational data model inherently create database overhead and make relational technology unsuitable for the ever-increasing performance demands of today's applications. Finally, since objects are well-established as the in-memory data model for modern programs, the proponents claim that the only natural data model is one that transparently extends the in-memory model to permanent, shared, disk-based, multiuser storage.

Opponents of object-oriented databases are just as adamant in their claims that object-oriented databases are unnecessary and offer no real, substantive advantages over the relational model. They claim that the handles of object-oriented databases are nothing more than the embedded database pointers of prerelational hierarchical and network databases, recycled with different names. They point out that, like these earlier database technologies, the object-oriented databases lack the strong underlying mathematical theory that forms the basis of relational databases. The lack of object database standards and the absence of a standardized query language like SQL are reflections of this deficiency, and have prevented the development of vendor-independent tools and applications that have been essential to the development of the database industry.

In response to claims of inferior performance, they point to the use of relational technology in some of the most performance-demanding enterprise applications. They are also careful to draw a distinction between the external relational model of data and the underlying implementation, which may well contain embedded pointers for performance acceleration. Finally, they claim that any mismatch between object-oriented programming and relational databases can be addressed by technologies like JDBC and other object-to-relational interfaces.

Objects and the Database Market

In the marketplace, pure object-oriented databases have gained some success in applications with very complex data models and those where the object-oriented model of classes and inheritance closely parallels the real world. However, the object database companies have had real difficulty breaking through into the mainstream. Many have not survived into the first decade of the twenty-first century. The survivors have had a hard time reaching the $100 million annual revenue mark, and achieving sustainable profits, and have experienced significant management changes. In contrast, the largest relational database vendors have continued to experience steady growth. The largest have annual revenues measured in billions of dollars per year, proving that relational database technology clearly continues to dominate the database market today.

Not surprisingly, the object-oriented and relational camps have had a substantial impact on one another. With the slow marketplace acceptance of object-oriented technology, the object-oriented vendors have focused on some of the factors that created the success of the relational generation two decades ago. They have formed standards groups, such as the Object Data Management Group (ODMG), to standardize object-oriented database technology. Several have added relational adapters, with standard interfaces such as ODBC and SQL, as optional layers for relational access to their databases. Several have focused on the international standards process and have worked to put strong object-oriented capabilities into the SQL3 standard. The net result has been a trend toward embracing or coexisting with the relational world, rather than competing with it.

The object-oriented challenge has had a significant impact on the relational mainstream as well. Several features that began as relational capabilities (for example, stored procedures) are now being touted as providing object-oriented advantages (for example, encapsulation). Vendors have also steadily added onto their relational databases selected object-oriented capabilities, such as abstract data types. The resulting object-relational databases provide a hybrid of relational and object capabilities. They stretch the relational model—some would say past the breaking point—to incorporate features such as tables within tables, which model the relationships between object classes.

One of the major vendors, Informix Software, gained its object-relational capabilities by acquisition, buying Illustra Software. Illustra's object-relational technology was based on the Postgres work at the University of California at Berkeley, a follow-up to the university's pioneering relational database system, Ingres. The Informix version of the Illustra product was renamed Informix Universal Server. Another of the major vendors, Oracle Corporation, evolved its own mainstream database system to include object-relational technologies. Oracle8, introduced in 1998, embodies several years of intensive Oracle development in this area, and Oracle9 further expanded it.

The object-oriented database vendors and the relational vendors' response to it have also had a major impact on the SQL standards efforts. The most significant change to the SQL2 standard addressed in the work on SQL3 was the addition of object capabilities. When the SQL3 work was finally approved as the SQL:1999 official standard, the new object-oriented capabilities nearly doubled the size of the SQL language specification in terms of page count. The acquisition and development of object-relational databases by the industry leaders, and the formal adoption of object extensions to SQL, signal the growing synergy between SQL and the world of object technology.

Object-Relational Databases

Object-relational databases typically begin with a relational database foundation, and add selected features that provide object-oriented capabilities. This approach simplifies the addition of object capabilities for the major RDBMS vendors, whose enterprise-class RDBMS products have been developed over the course of 15 or more years and would be tremendously costly to reproduce from scratch. It also recognizes the large installed base of relational systems and gives those customers a smoother upgrade path (not to mention an upgrade revenue stream for the vendors).

The object extensions that are commonly found in object-relational databases are:

- **Large data objects**. Traditional relational data types are small in size—integers, dates, short character strings; large data objects can store documents, audio and video clips, web pages, and other new media data types.

- **Structured/abstract data types**. Relational data types are atomic and indivisible; structured data types allow groups of individual data items to be grouped into higher-level structures that can be treated as entities of their own.

- **User-defined data types**. Relational databases typically provide a limited range of built-in data types; object-oriented systems and databases emphasize the user's ability to define his or her own new data types.

■ **Tables within tables**. Relational database columns store individual data items; object-relational databases allow columns to contain complex data items, such as structured types or even entire tables. This can be used to represent object hierarchies.

■ **Sequences, sets, and arrays**. In a traditional relational database, sets of data are represented by rows in their own table, linked to an owning entity by a foreign key; object-relational databases may allow the direct storage of collections of data items (sequences, sets, arrays) within a single column.

■ **Stored procedures**. Traditional relational databases provide set-based interfaces, such as SQL, for storing, selecting, and retrieving data; object-relational databases provide procedural interfaces, such as stored procedures, that encapsulate the data and provide strictly defined interactions.

■ **Handles and object-ids**. A pure relational database requires that data within each row of the database itself (the primary key) uniquely identifies the row; object-relational databases provide built-in support for row-ids or other unique identifiers for objects.

Large Object Support

Relational databases have traditionally focused on business data processing. They store and manipulate data items that represent money amounts, names, addresses, unit quantities, dates, times, and the like. These data types are relatively simple and require small amounts of storage space, from a few bytes for an integer that holds order or inventory quantities to a few dozen bytes for a customer name, employee address, or product description. Relational databases have been optimized to manage rows containing up to a few dozen columns of this type of data. The techniques they use to manage disk storage and to index data assume that data rows will occupy a few hundred to a few thousand bytes. The programs that store and retrieve data can easily hold dozens or hundreds of these types of data items in memory, and can easily store and retrieve entire rows of data at a time through reasonably sized memory buffers. The row-at-a-time processing techniques for relational query results work well.

Many modern types of data have quite different characteristics from traditional business data. A single high-resolution graphical image to be displayed on a PC screen can require hundreds of thousands of bytes of storage or more. A word processing document, such as a contract or the text of this book, can take even more storage. The HTML text that defines web pages and the PostScript files that define printed images are other examples of larger, document-oriented data items. Even a relatively short high-quality audio track can occupy millions of bytes, and video clips can run to hundreds of megabytes or even gigabytes of data. As multimedia applications have become more important, users have wanted to manage these types of data along with the other data in their databases. The capability to efficiently manage large objects, often called binary large objects (BLOBs), was one of the earliest advantages claimed for object-oriented databases.

BLOBs **in the Relational Model**

The first approach to supporting BLOBs in relational databases was through the underlying operating system and its file system. Each individual BLOB data item was stored in its own operating system file. The name of the file was placed in a character-valued column within a table, as a pointer to the file. The table's other columns could be searched to find rows that met certain criteria. When an application needed to manipulate the BLOB content associated with one of the rows, it read the name of the file and retrieved the BLOB data from it. Management of the file input/output was the responsibility of the application program. This approach worked, but it was error-prone and required that a programmer understand *both* the RDBMS and the file system interfaces. The lack of integration between the BLOB contents and the database was readily apparent. For example, you couldn't ask the database to compare two BLOB data items to see if they were the same, and the database couldn't provide even basic text searching capability for BLOB contents.

Today, most major enterprise-class DBMS systems provide direct support for one or more types of BLOB data. You can define a column as containing one of these BLOB data types and use it in certain situations in SQL statements. There are typically substantial restrictions on the BLOB data, such as not allowing its use in a join condition or a GROUP BY clause.

Sybase provides two large object data types. Its TEXT data type can store up to 2 billion bytes of variable-length text data. You can use a limited set of SQL capabilities (such as the LIKE text-search operator) to search the contents of TEXT columns. A companion IMAGE data type can store up to 2 billion bytes of variable-length binary data. Microsoft SQL Server supports these types, plus an NTEXT data type that allows up to 1 billion characters of 2-byte national language text.

IBM's DB2 provides a similar set of data types. A DB2 character large object (CLOB) type stores up to 2 billion bytes of text. A DB2 double-byte character large object (DBCLOB) type stores up to 1 billion 2-byte characters. A DB2 binary large object (BLOB) stores up to 2 billion bytes of binary data.

Oracle historically provided two large object data types. A LONG data type stored up to 2 billion bytes of text data. A LONG RAW data type stored up to 2 billion bytes of binary data. Oracle restricted the use of either LONG type to only a single column per table. With the introduction of Oracle8, support for BLOB data was expanded substantially:

- An Oracle BLOB type stores up to 4 gigabytes of binary data within the database.

- An Oracle CLOB type stores up to 4 gigabytes of single-byte character data within the database.

- An Oracle NCLOB type stores multibyte character data as a BLOB.

- An Oracle BFILE type stores long binary data in a file external to the database.

The BLOB, CLOB, and NCLOB types are tightly integrated into Oracle's operation, including transaction support. BFILE data is managed through a pointer within the database to an external operating system file. It is not supported by Oracle transaction semantics. Special Oracle PL/SQL functions are provided to manipulate BLOB, CLOB, and NCLOB data from within PL/SQL stored procedures, as described in the next section.

Informix Universal Server's support for large object data is similar to that of Oracle. It supports simple large objects and smart large objects:

- An Informix BYTE type is a simple large object that stores binary data.
- An Informix TEXT type is a simple large object that stores text data.
- An Informix BLOB type is a smart large object that stores binary data.
- An Informix CLOB type is a smart large object that stores text (character) data.

Informix simple large objects store up to 1 gigabyte of data. The entire large object must be retrieved or stored as a unit from the application program, or it can be copied between the database and an operating system file. Smart large objects can store up to 4 terabytes of data. Special Informix functions are provided to process smart large objects in smaller, more manageable chunks. These functions provide random access to the contents of an Informix smart object, similar to the random access typically provided for operating system files. Informix also provides advanced controls over logging, transaction management, and data integrity for smart large objects.

Specialized BLOB Processing

Because BLOBs can be very large in size compared to the data items typically handled by RDBMS systems, they pose special problems in several areas:

- **Data storage and optimization**. Storing a BLOB item in-line with the other contents of a table's row would destroy the optimization that the DBMS performs to fit database data neatly into pages that match the size of disk pages. For this reason, BLOB data is always stored out-of-line in separate storage areas. Most DBMS brands that support BLOBs provide special BLOB storage options, including named storage spaces that are specified when the BLOB type column is created.

- **Storing BLOB data in the database**. Because a BLOB can be tens or hundreds of megabytes in size, most programs can't hold the entire contents of a BLOB in a memory buffer at once. They process portions of the BLOB at a time (for example, pages of a long document or individual frames of a video clip). But Embedded SQL and normal SQL APIs are designed for row-at-a-time processing (through INSERT and UPDATE statements) that store the values for all columns in the row at once. Special techniques are required to put data into a database BLOB column piece by piece, through multiple API calls per BLOB column.

- **Retrieving BLOB data from the database**. This is the same issue as retrieving the data, but in reverse. Embedded SQL and normal SQL APIs are designed for SELECT statement or FETCH statement processing that retrieves data values for all columns of a row at once. But because a stored BLOB value can be tens or hundreds of megabytes in size, most programs can't possibly process it all at once in a memory buffer. Special techniques are required to retrieve the database BLOB column data, piece by piece, so that it can be processed by the application.

- **Transaction logging**. Most DBMS's support transactions by maintaining before and after images of modified data in a transaction log. Because of the potentially large size of BLOB data, the logging overhead could be extreme. For this reason, many DBMS's don't support logging for BLOB data, or they allow logging but provide the ability to turn it on and off.

Several DBMS's address these issues through extended APIs that specifically support BLOB manipulation. These calls provide random access to individual segments of the BLOB contents, allowing the program to retrieve or store the BLOB in manageable chunks. Oracle8 introduced this capability for manipulating its LOB data types (character and binary) within stored procedures written in the Oracle PL/SQL language. Its capabilities are similar to those provided by other object-relational databases, such as Informix Universal Server.

When a stored procedure reads an Oracle LOB column from a table, Oracle does not actually return the contents of the column. Instead, a *locator* for the LOB data (in object parlance, a *handle* for the LOB) is returned. The locator is used in conjunction with a set of nine special LOB-processing functions that the stored procedure can then use to manipulate the actual data stored in the LOB column of the database. Here is a brief description of each LOB-processing function:

- **dbms_lob.read**(*locator, length, offset, buffer*). Reads into the PL/SQL buffer the indicated number of bytes/characters from the LOB identified by the locator, starting at the offset.

- **dbms_lob.write**(*locator, length, offset, buffer*). Writes the indicated number of bytes/characters from the PL/SQL buffer into the LOB identified by the locator, starting at the offset.

- **dbms_lob.append**(*locator1, locator2*). Appends the entire contents of the LOB identified by *locator2* to the end of the contents of the LOB identified by *locator1*.

- **dbms_lob.erase**(*locator, length, offset*). Erases the contents of the LOB identified by the locator at *offset* for *length* bytes/characters; for character-based LOBs, spaces are inserted, and for binary LOBs, binary zeroes are inserted.

- **dbms_lob.copy**(*locator1, locator2, length, offset1, offset2*). Copies *length* bytes/characters from the LOB identified by *locator2* at *offset2* into the LOB identified by *locator1* at *offset1*.

- **dbms_lob.trim**(*locator1, length*). Trims the LOB identified by the locator to the indicated number of bytes/characters.

- **dbms_lob.substr**(*locator, length, offset*). Returns (as a text string return value) the indicated number of bytes/characters from the LOB identified by the locator, starting at the offset; the return value from this function may be assigned into a PL/SQL VARCHAR variable.

- **dbms_lob.getlength**(*locator*). Returns (as an integer value) the length in bytes/characters of the LOB identified by the locator.

- **dbms_lob.compare**(*locator1, locator2, length, offset1, offset2*). Compares the LOB identified by *locator1* to the LOB identified by *locator2*, starting at *offset1* and *offset2*, respectively, for *length* bytes/characters; returns zero if they are the same and nonzero if they are not.

- **dbms_lob.instr**(*locator, pattern, offset, i*). Returns (as an integer value) the position within the LOB identified by the locator where the *i*-th occurrence of *pattern* is matched; the returned value may be used as an offset in subsequent LOB processing calls.

Oracle imposes one further restriction on updates and modifications to LOB values that are performed through these functions. LOBs can impose an unacceptably high overhead on Oracle's transaction mechanisms, so Oracle normally does not lock the contents of a LOB data item when the row containing the LOB is read by an application program or a PL/SQL routine. If the LOB data is to be updated, the row must be explicitly locked prior to modifying it. This is done by including a FOR UPDATE clause in the SELECT statement that retrieves the LOB locator. Here is a PL/SQL fragment that retrieves a row containing a LOB that contains document text, and updates 100 characters in the middle of the LOB data:

```
declare
   lob     CLOB;
   textbuf varchar(255);

begin
   /* Put text to be inserted into buffer /
   . . .

   /* Get lob locator and lock LOB for update */
   select document_lob into lob
     from documents
    where document_id = '34218'
      for update;

   /* Write new text 500 bytes into LOB */
```

```
    dbms_lob.write(lob,100,500,textbuf);

    commit;
end;
```

Abstract (Structured) Data Types

The data types envisioned by the relational data model are simple, indivisible, atomic data values. If a data item such as an address is actually composed of a street address, city, state, and postal code, as a database designer, you have two choices. You can treat the address as four separate data items, each stored in its own column, so that you can search and retrieve the items individually. Or you can treat the address as a single unit, in which case, you cannot process its individual component parts within the database. There is no middle ground that allows you to treat the address as a unit for certain situations and access its component parts for others.

Many programming languages (including even nonobject-oriented languages like C or Pascal) do provide such a middle ground. They support compound data types or named data structures. The data structure is composed of individual data items or lower-level structures, which can be accessed individually. But the entire data structure can also be treated as a single unit when that is most convenient. Structured or composite data types in object-relational databases provide this same capability in a DBMS context.

Informix Universal Server supports abstract data types through its concept of *row data types.* You can think of a row type as a structured sequence of individual data items, called *fields.* Here is an Informix CREATE TABLE statement for a simple PERSONNEL table that uses a row data type to store both name and address information:

```
CREATE TABLE PERSONNEL (
    EMPL_NUM INTEGER,
        NAME ROW (
      F_NAME VARCHAR(15),
      M_INIT CHAR(1),
      L_NAME VARCHAR(20))
     ADDRESS ROW (
      STREET VARCHAR(35),
        CITY VARCHAR(15),
       STATE CHAR(2),
    POSTCODE ROW (
        MAIN INTEGER,
         SFX INTEGER)));
```

This table has three columns. The first one, EMPL_NUM, has an integer data type. The last two, NAME and ADDR, have a row data type, indicated by the keyword ROW, followed by a parenthesized list of the fields that make up the row. The NAME column's row data type has three fields within it. The ADDRESS column's row data type has four fields. The last of these four fields itself has a row data type and consists of two fields. In this simple example, the hierarchy is only two levels deep, but the capability can be (and often is) extended to additional levels.

Individual fields within the columns of the table are accessible in SQL statements through an extension of the SQL dot notation that is already used to qualify column names with table names and user names. Adding a dot *after* a column name allows you to specify the names of individual fields within a column. This SELECT statement retrieves the employee numbers and first and last names of all personnel with a specified main postal code:

```
SELECT EMPL_NUM, NAME.F_NAME, NAME.L_NAME
  FROM PERSONNEL
 WHERE ADDRESS.POSTCODE.MAIN = '12345';
```

Suppose another table within the database, named MANAGERS, had the same NAME structure as one of its columns. Then this query retrieves the employee numbers of employees who are also managers:

```
SELECT EMPL_NUM
  FROM PERSONNEL, MANAGERS
 WHERE PERSONNEL.NAME = MANAGERS.NAME;
```

In the first of these two queries, it makes sense to retrieve the individual fields within the NAME column. The second query shows a situation where it's more convenient to use the *entire* name column (all three fields) as the basis for comparison. It's clearly a lot more convenient to ask the DBMS to compare the two abstract data typed columns than it is to specify separate comparisons for each of the individual fields. Together, these examples show the advantages of the row data type in allowing access to the fields at any level of the hierarchy.

The row data type columns require special handling when inserting data into the database. The PERSONNEL table has three columns, so an INSERT statement for the table must have three items in its VALUES clause. The columns that have a row data type require a special ROW value-constructor to put together the individual data items into a row-type item that matches the data type of the column. Here is a valid INSERT statement for the table that illustrates the use of the ROW constructor:

```
INSERT INTO PERSONNEL
    VALUES (1234,
            ROW('John', 'J', 'Jones'),
            ROW('197 Rose St.', 'Chicago', 'IL',
            ROW(12345, 6789)));
```

Defining Abstract Data Types

With the Informix row data type capabilities illustrated so far, each individual structured column is defined in isolation. If two tables need to use the same row data type structure, it is defined within each table. This violates one of the key principles of object-oriented design, which is reusability. Instead of having each object (the two columns in the two different tables) have its own definition, the row data type should be defined once and then reused for the two columns. Informix Universal Server provides this capability through its *named row type* feature. (The row data types shown in previous examples are *unnamed* row data types.)

You create an Informix named row type with the CREATE ROW TYPE statement. Here are examples for the PERSONNEL table:

```
CREATE ROW TYPE NAME_TYPE (
    F_NAME VARCHAR(15),
    M_INIT CHAR(1),
    L_NAME VARCHAR(20));

CREATE ROW TYPE POST_TYPE (
    MAIN INTEGER,
     SFX INTEGER);

CREATE ROW TYPE ADDR_TYPE (
    STREET VARCHAR(35),
      CITY VARCHAR(15),
     STATE CHAR(2),
  POSTCODE POST_TYPE);
```

Note that the definition of a named row type can depend on other, previously created named row types, as shown by the ADDR_TYPE and POST_TYPE definitions. With these row data types defined, the name and address columns in the PERSONNEL table (and any other columns holding name or address data in other tables of the database) can be defined using it. The aggressive use of abstract data types can thus help to enforce uniformity in naming and data typing within an object-relational database. Here is the new Informix definition of the PERSONNEL table, using the just-defined abstract data types:

```
CREATE TABLE PERSONNEL (
    EMPL_NUM INTEGER,
        NAME NAME_TYPE,
     ADDRESS ADDR_TYPE);
```

PERSONNEL **Table**

	NAME			ADDRESS			POSTCODE	
EMPL NUM	F NAME	M INIT	L NAME	STREET	CITY	STATE	MAIN	SFX
1234	Sue	J.	Marsh	1803 Main St.	Alamo	NJ	31948	4567
1374	Sam	F.	Wilson	564 Birch Rd.	Marion	KY	82942	3524
1421	Joe	P.	Jones	13 High St.	Delano	NM	13527	2394
1532	Rob	G.	Mason	9123 Plain Av.	Franklin	PA	83624	2643

Figure 24-1. *PERSONNEL table using abstract data types*

Figure 24-1 shows some sample data for this table and the hierarchical column/ field structure created by the abstract data types.

Oracle supports abstract data types through a very similar structure, with slightly different SQL syntax. Here is the Oracle CREATE TYPE statement to create the same abstract data structure for names and addresses:

```
CREATE TYPE NAME_TYPE AS OBJECT (
    F_NAME VARCHAR(15),
    M_INIT CHAR(1),
    L_NAME VARCHAR(20));

CREATE TYPE POST_TYPE AS OBJECT (
      MAIN INTEGER,
       SFX INTEGER);

CREATE TYPE ADDR_TYPE AS OBJECT (
    STREET VARCHAR(35),
      CITY VARCHAR(15),
     STATE CHAR(2),
  POSTCODE POST_TYPE);
```

Oracle calls the abstract data type an object instead of a row type. In fact, the type is functioning as an object class in the usual object-oriented terminology. Extending the object-oriented terminology further, the individual components of an Oracle abstract data type are referred to as *attributes* (corresponding to the Informix *fields* described earlier). The ADDR_TYPE type has four attributes in this example. The fourth attribute, POSTCODE, is itself an abstract data type.

Both Oracle and Informix use the extended dot notation to refer to individual data elements within abstract data types. With nested abstract types, it takes several levels of dot-delimited names to identify an individual data item. The main postal code within the PERSONNEL table is identified as:

```
PERSONNEL.ADDRESS.POSTCODE.MAIN
```

If the table were owned by another user, Sam, the qualified name becomes even longer:

```
SAM.PERSONNEL.ADDRESS.POSTCODE.MAIN
```

Informix allows the use of row types to go one step beyond their role as data type templates for individual columns. You can use a row type to define the structure of an entire table. For example, with this row type definition:

```
CREATE ROW TYPE PERS_TYPE (
   EMPL_NUM INTEGER,
      NAME NAME_TYPE,
   ADDRESS ADDR_TYPE)
```

you can define the PERSONNEL table using the row type as a model:

```
CREATE TABLE PERSONNEL
     OF TYPE PERS_TYPE;
```

The columns of this PERSONNEL table will be exactly as they were in the previous CREATE TABLE examples, but now PERSONNEL is a typed table. The most basic use of the typed table capability is to formalize the object structure in the database. Each object class has its own row type, and the typed table that holds objects (rows) of that class is defined in terms of the row type. Beyond this usage, typed tables are also a key component of the Informix notion of table inheritance, described later in the "Inheritance" section.

Manipulating Abstract Data Types

Unfortunately, structured data types create new complexity for database update statements that must insert or modify their structured data values. Informix Universal Server is fairly liberal in its data type conversion requirements for unnamed row types. The data you assign into a row-type column must simply have the same number of fields, of the same data types. The ROW constructor is used, as shown in previous examples, to assemble individual data items into a row-type value for inserting or updating data.

For named row types, the requirement is more stringent; the data you assign into a named row-type column must actually have the same named row type. You can achieve this in the INSERT statement by explicitly casting the constructed row value to have the NAME_TYPE data type:

```
INSERT INTO PERSONNEL
    VALUES (1234,
            ROW('John', 'J', 'Jones')::NAME_TYPE,
            ROW('197 Rose St.', 'Chicago', 'IL',
            ROW(12345, 6789))));
```

The double-colon operator casts the constructed three-field row as a NAME_TYPE row and makes the VALUES clause compatible with the data types of the columns in the table.

Oracle uses a slightly different approach to constructing structured data items and inserting them into columns that have abstract data types. When you create an Oracle abstract data type (using the CREATE TYPE statement), Oracle automatically defines a *constructor method* for the type. You can think of the constructor method as a function that takes as its arguments the individual components of the abstract data type and returns an abstract data type value, with the individual components all packaged together. The constructor is used in the VALUES clause of the INSERT statement to glue the individual data item values together into a structured data value that matches the column definition. Here is an INSERT statement for the PERSONNEL table:

```
INSERT INTO PERSONNEL
    VALUES (1234,
            NAME_TYPE('John', 'J', 'Jones'),
            ADDR_TYPE('197 Rose St.', 'Chicago', 'IL',
            POST_TYPE(12345, 6789))));
```

The constructors (NAME_TYPE, ADDR_TYPE, POST_TYPE) perform the same functions as the ROW constructor does for Informix, and also provide the casting required to ensure strict data type correspondence.

Inheritance

Support for abstract data types gives the relational data model a foundation for object-based capabilities. The abstract data type can embody the representation of an object, and the values of its individual fields or subcolumns are its attributes. Another important feature of the object-oriented model is *inheritance*. With inheritance, new objects can be defined as being a particular type of an existing object type (class) and inherit the predefined attributes and behaviors of that type.

Figure 24-2 shows an example of how inheritance might work in a model of a company's employee data. All employees are members of the class PERSONNEL, and they all have the attributes associated with being an employee (employee number, name, and address). Some employees are salespeople, and they have additional attributes (such as a sales quota and the identity of their sales manager). Other employees are engineers, with a different set of attributes (such as the academic degrees they hold or the current project to which they are assigned). Each of these employee types has its own class, which is a subclass of PERSONNEL. The subclass inherits all of the characteristics of the class above it in the hierarchy (we want to track all of the core personnel data for engineers and salespeople, too). However, the subclasses have additional information that is unique to their type of object. In Figure 24-2, the class hierarchy goes down to a third layer for engineers, differentiating between technicians, developers, and managers.

Informix Universal Server's abstract data type inheritance mechanism provides an easy way to define abstract data types (Informix row types) that correspond to the natural hierarchy in Figure 24-2. Assume that the Informix PERS_TYPE row type has already been created, as in the example from the "Defining Abstract Data Types" section earlier in this chapter, and a typed table named PERSONNEL has been created based on this row type. Using the Informix inheritance capabilities, here are some CREATE ROW TYPE statements for other types in the hierarchy:

```
CREATE ROW TYPE SALES_TYPE (
    SLS_MGR INTEGER,              /* employee number of sales mgr */
    SALARY MONEY(9,2),            /* annual salary */
    QUOTA MONEY(9,2))
    UNDER 1PERS_TYPE;

CREATE ROW TYPE ENGR_TYPE (
    SALARY MONEY(9,2),            /* annual salary */
  YRS_EXPER INTEGER              /* years of experience */
    UNDER PERS_TYPE;

CREATE ROW TYPE MGR_TYPE (
    BONUS MONEY(9,2))            /* annual bonus */
    UNDER ENGR_TYPE;

CREATE ROW TYPE TECH_TYPE (
  WAGE_RATE MONEY(5,2))          /* hourly wage rate */
    UNDER ENGR_TYPE;
```

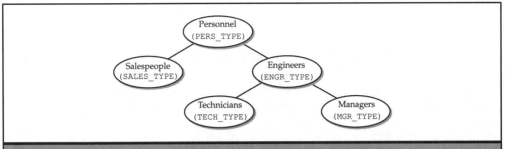

Figure 24-2. *Natural class hierarchy for a personnel application*

The type defined for technicians (TECH_TYPE) is a subtype (subclass) of the engineer type (ENGR_TYPE), so it inherits all of the fields for the personnel type (PERS_TYPE), plus the fields added at the ENGR_TYPE level, plus the additional field added in its own definition. An abstract type that is defined UNDER another type, and inherits its fields, is called a *subtype* of the higher-level type. Conversely, the higher-level type is a *supertype* of the lower-level types defined UNDER it.

With this type hierarchy defined, it's easy to create Informix typed tables that use them. Here are some Informix statements that create a table for engineers, separate tables for managers and technicians, and another table to hold salesperson data:

```
CREATE TABLE ENGINEERS
     OF TYPE ENGR_TYPE;
CREATE TABLE TECHNICIANS
     OF TYPE TECH_TYPE;
CREATE TABLE MANAGERS
     OF TYPE MGR_TYPE;
CREATE TABLE REPS
     OF TYPE SALES_TYPE;
```

The type hierarchy has pushed the complexity into the data type definitions and made the table structure very simple and easy to define. All other characteristics of the table can (and must) still be defined within the table definition. For example, the salesperson table contains a column that is actually a foreign key to the personnel table, so its table definitions should probably include a FOREIGN KEY clause like this:

```
CREATE TABLE REPS
     OF TYPE SALES_TYPE
 FOREIGN KEY (SLS_MGR)
  REFERENCES PERSONNEL(EMPL_NUM);
```

Type inheritance creates a relationship among the structure of the tables that are based on the defined row types, but the tables remain independent of one another in terms of the data that they contain. Rows inserted into the TECHNICIANS table don't automatically appear in the ENGINEERS table nor in the PERSONNEL table. Each is a table in its own right, containing its own data. A different kind of inheritance, *table inheritance,* provides a very different level of linkage between the table's contents, actually turning the tables into something much closer to object classes. It is described in the next section.

Table Inheritance: Implementing Object Classes

Informix Universal Server provides a capability called table inheritance that moves the table structure of a database away from the traditional relational model and makes it much closer to the concept of an object class. Using table inheritance, it's possible to create a hierarchy of typed tables (classes), such as the one shown in Figure 24-3. The tables are still based on a defined type hierarchy, but now the tables themselves have a parallel hierarchy.

Here is a set of CREATE TABLE statements that implements this table inheritance:

```
CREATE TABLE ENGINEERS
     OF TYPE ENGR_TYPE
        UNDER PERSONNEL;
CREATE TABLE TECHNICIANS
     OF TYPE TECH_TYPE
        UNDER ENGINEERS;
CREATE TABLE MANAGERS
     OF TYPE MGR_TYPE
        ENDER ENGINEERS;
CREATE TABLE REPS
     OF TYPE SALES_TYPE
        UNDER PERSONNEL;
```

When a table is defined in this way (as under another table), it inherits many more characteristics from its supertable than just the column structure. It inherits the foreign key, primary key, referential integrity, and check constraints of the supertable, any triggers defined on the supertable, as well as indexes, storage areas, and other Informix-specific characteristics. It's possible to override this inheritance by specifically including the overridden characteristics in the CREATE TABLE statements for the subtables.

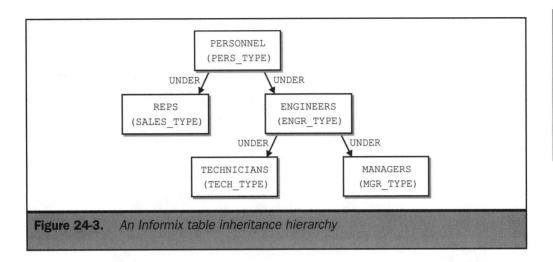

Figure 24-3. *An Informix table inheritance hierarchy*

A table type hierarchy has a profound impact on the way that the Universal Server DBMS treats the rows stored in the tables. The tables in the hierarchy now form a collection of nested *sets* of rows, as shown in Figure 24-4. When a row is inserted into

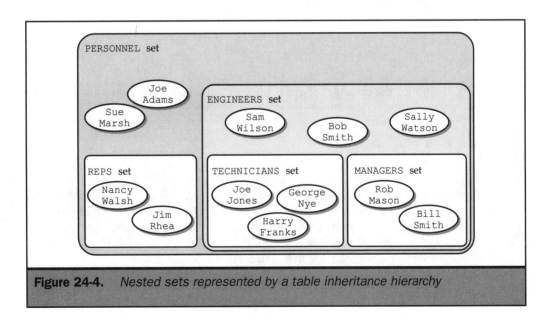

Figure 24-4. *Nested sets represented by a table inheritance hierarchy*

the table hierarchy, it is still inserted into a specific table. Joe Jones, for example, is in the TECHNICIANS table, while Sam Wilson is in the ENGINEERS table and Sue Marsh is in the PERSONNEL table.

SQL queries behave quite differently, however. When you perform a database query on one of the tables in the hierarchy, it returns rows not only from the table itself, but from *all* of the included subtables of that table. This query:

```
SELECT *
  FROM PERSONNEL;
```

returns rows from the PERSONNEL table and rows from the ENGINEERS, TECHNICIANS, and REPS tables. Similarly, this query:

```
SELECT *
  FROM ENGINEERS;
```

returns rows from TECHNICIANS and MANAGERS in addition to ENGINEERS. The DBMS is now treating the tables as a nested collection of rows, and a query on a table (rowset) applies to all rows included in the set. If you want to retrieve only the rows that appear in the top-level table itself, you must use the ONLY keyword:

```
SELECT *
  FROM ONLY(ENGINEERS);
```

The DBMS applies the same set-of-rows logic to DELETE operations. This DELETE statement:

```
DELETE FROM PERSONNEL
  WHERE EMPL_NUM = 1234;
```

successfully deletes the row for employee number 1234 regardless of which table in the hierarchy actually contains the row. The statement is interpreted as "Delete any rows from the PERSONNEL set that match these criteria." As with the queries, if you want to delete *only* rows that appear in the ENGINEERS table of the hierarchy, but not rows from any of its subtables, you can use this statement:

```
DELETE FROM ONLY(ENGINEERS)
  WHERE EMPL_NUM = 1234;
```

The same logic holds for UPDATE statements. This one changes the employee number, regardless of which table in the hierarchy actually holds the row for the employee:

```
UPDATE PERSONNEL
   SET L_NAME = 'Harrison'
 WHERE EMPL_NUM = 1234;
```

Again, the ONLY construct may be used to restrict the scope of the UPDATE operation to only rows that actually appear in the named table and not those that appear in its subtables.

Of course, when operating at a given level within the table hierarchy, your SQL statements can reference only columns that are defined at that level. You cannot use this statement:

```
DELETE FROM PERSONNEL
  WHERE SALARY < 20000.00;
```

because the SALARY column doesn't exist in the top-level PERSONNEL table (class). It is defined only for some of its subtables (subclasses). You can use this statement:

```
DELETE FROM MANAGERS
  WHERE SALARY < 20000.00;
```

because SALARY is defined at this level of the table (class) hierarchy.

As noted, table inheritance moves the operation of Informix Universal Server fairly far out of the relational database realm and into the object-oriented world. Relational purists point to examples like the previous ones to claim that object-relational databases bring with them dangerous inherent inconsistencies. They ask these typical kinds of questions: "Why should an INSERT of a row into one table cause it to suddenly appear in two other tables?" and "Why should a searched DELETE statement that doesn't match any rows of a table cause other rows in other tables to disappear?" Of course, the table hierarchy has stopped behaving strictly as if it were a set of relational tables, and instead has taken on many of the characteristics of an object class and object class hierarchy. Whether this is good or bad depends on your point of view. It does mean that you must be very careful about applying relational database assumptions blindly to an object-relational implementation.

Sets, Arrays, and Collections

In a relational database, tables are the *only* database structure used to represent a set of objects. For example, the set of engineers in our personnel database is represented by the rows in the ENGINEERS table. Suppose each engineer has a set of academic degrees (a B.S. in science from MIT, a Ph.D. in electrical engineering from Michigan, and so on) that are to be stored in the database. The number of degrees for each engineer will vary—from none for some engineers to perhaps half a dozen for others. In a pure relational database, there is only one correct way to add this information to the data model. A new table, DEGREES, must be created, as shown in Figure 24-5. Each row in the DEGREES table represents one individual academic degree held by one of the engineers. A column in the DEGREES table holds the employee number of the engineer holding the degree described by that particular row, and serves as a foreign key to the ENGINEERS table, linking the two tables in a parent/child relationship. The other columns in the DEGREES table describe the particulars of the degree.

You have seen the type of parent/child relational table structure shown in Figure 24-5 many times in the earlier chapters of this book, and it has been a basic construct of relational databases since the beginning. However, there are some disadvantages to

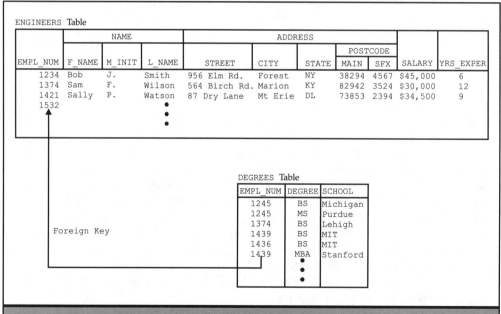

Figure 24-5.   *A relational modeling of engineers and their degrees*

having this be the only way in which sets of data attributes can be modeled. First, the database tends to have a great many tables and foreign key relationships and becomes hard to understand. Second, many common queries need to join three, four, or more tables to get the required answers. Third, with the implementations of relational joins provided by most DBMS systems, the performance of queries will deteriorate as they involve more and more joins.

An object-oriented model of the engineers and their degrees would tend to reject the table structure of Figure 24-5. It would claim that the degrees are not substantial objects in their own right and deserving of their own table. Instead, they are *attributes* of the engineer holding the degrees. True, a variable number of degrees are associated with each engineer, but the object-oriented model would have no problem with representing this situation as an array or a set of data within the engineer object.

The object-relational databases support this object-oriented view of data by supporting sets, arrays, or other collection data types. A column within a table can be defined to have one of these data types. It will then contain not a single data item value, but a *set* of data item values. Special SQL extensions allow a user, or more often a stored procedure, to manipulate the set of data items as a whole or to access individual members of the set.

Defining Collections

Informix Universal Server supports collections of attributes through its *collection data types*. Three different collection data types are supported:

- **Lists**. A *list* is an ordered collection of data items, all of which have the same type. Within a list, there is the concept of a first item, a last item, and the *n*-th item. The items in the list are not required to be unique. For example, a list of the first names of the employees hired in the last year, in order of hire, might be {'Jim', 'Mary', 'Sam', 'Jim', 'John'}.

- **Multisets**. A *multiset* is an unordered collection of data items, all of which have the same type. There is no concept of a sequencing to the items in a multiset; its items have no implied ordering. The items are not required to be unique. The list of employee first names could be considered a multiset if you didn't care about the order of hire: {'Jim', 'Sam', 'John', 'Jim', 'Mary'}.

- **Sets**. A *set* is an unordered collection of unique data items, all of which have the same type. As in a multiset, there is no concept of first or last; the set has no implied ordering. The items must have unique values. The first names in the previous examples wouldn't qualify, but the last names might: {'Johnson', 'Samuels', 'Wright', 'Jones', 'Smith'}.

To illustrate the concept of collection data, we will expand the tables in our example object-relational database as follows:

- The REPS table will include sales targets for each of the first, second, third, and fourth quarters. The quarterly targets can naturally be represented as a list column added to the REPS table. The quarters have a natural ordering (first through fourth), the quota for each quarter has the same data type (money), and the values are not necessarily unique (that is, the quotas for the first and second quarters might be the same).

- The ENGINEERS table will include information about the academic degrees that each engineer holds. Two items of data will actually be stored about each degree—the actual degree (B.S., Ph.D., MBA, and so on) and the school. This data will be stored as a multiset column added to the ENGINEERS table, because it's possible to have two identical entries—for example, an engineer may have a B.S. degree in engineering and a B.S. degree in business from the same school.

- The TECHNICIANS table will include information about the projects to which each technician is assigned. Each technician may be assigned to two or more projects, but each project has a unique name. This data will be stored as a set column added to the TECHNICIANS table. The data values must be unique, but no particular order is associated with them.

Here are some Informix ALTER TABLE statements that implement these changes to the previously defined tables:

```
ALTER TABLE REPS
        ADD QTR_TGT LIST(MONEY(9,2));   /* four quarterly targets */

ALTER TABLE TECHNICIANS
        ADD PROJECT SET(VARCHAR(15));   /* projects assigned */

ALTER TABLE ENGINEERS (
        ADD DEGREES MULTISET(ROW(       /* degree info */
    DEGREE VARCHAR(3),
    SCHOOL VARCHAR(15));
```

These collection column types create a row-within-a-row structure within the table that contains them, as shown in Figure 24-6. In the case of the ENGINEERS table, the structure might more accurately be described as a table within a table. Clearly, the relational model of row/column tables with atomic data items has been stretched considerably by the introduction of collection data types.

Informix Universal Server allows collections to be used quite generally and intermixed with other object-relational extensions. A collection can be a field of a row

SQL TODAY AND
TOMORROW

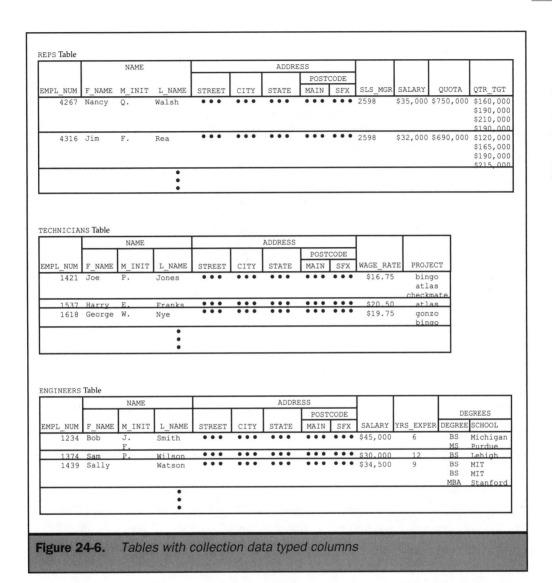

Figure 24-6.   *Tables with collection data typed columns*

data type. The items of a collection can be row data types. It's also possible to define collections within collections where that makes sense. For example, the projects in this example might have subprojects that must be tracked for each technician. At each level of additional complexity, the complexity of the stored procedure language (SPL) and SQL expressions that are required to manipulate the data items and process them increases accordingly.

Oracle also provides extensive support for collection-type data, through two different Oracle object-relational extensions:

- **Varying arrays**. A *varying array* is an ordered collection of data items, all having the same data type. There is no requirement that the items in the array be unique. You define the maximum number of data items that can occur when you specify a varying array type for a column. Oracle provides extensions to SQL to access the individual items within the array.

- **Nested tables**. A *nested table* is an actual table within a table. A column with a nested table type contains individual data items that are themselves tables. Oracle actually stores the nested table data separately from the main table that contains it, but it uses SQL extensions to process nested references to the inner table. Unlike a varying array, a nested table can contain any number of rows.

A column within a table can be declared to have a VARRAY (varying array) or TABLE OF (nested table) structure. Here are some Oracle CREATE TYPE and CREATE TABLE statements that use varying arrays and nested tables to achieve table structures like those shown in Figure 24-6:

```
CREATE TABLE REPS (
    EMPL_NUM INTEGER,
        NAME NAME_TYPE,
    ADDRESS ADDR_TYPE,
    SLS_MGR INTEGER,                            /* employee number of mgr */
     SALARY MONEY(9,2),                         /* annual salary */
      QUOTA MONEY(9,2),                         /* sales quota */
    QTR_TGT VARRAY(4) OF NUMBER(9,2));          /* four quarterly tgts */

CREATE TYPE DEGR_TYPE AS OBJECT ( (
    DEGREE VARCHAR(3),
    SCHOOL VARCHAR(15));

CREATE TABLE ENGINEERS (
    EMPL_NUM INTEGER,
        NAME NAME_TYPE,
    ADDRESS ADDR_TYPE,
     SALARY NUMBER(9,2),                        /* annual salary */
   YRS_EXPER INTEGER,                           /* years of experience */
    DEGREES TABLE OF DEGR_TYPE);
NESTED TABLE DEGREES STORE AS DEGREES_TABLE;
```

The quarterly target information for the REPS table is most easily represented as an Oracle varying array column. There will be exactly four quarters of information, so the maximum size of the array is known in advance. In this example, the varying array contains a simple data item as its element, but it's also common to define varying arrays whose items are themselves abstract (structured) data types.

The academic degree information for the ENGINEERS table is represented as a nested table. For a data item like this one, you could decide to place an upper limit on the number of rows and use a varying array structure instead, but in general, if the maximum number of items is unknown, a nested table is the right choice. In this case, the nested table has an abstract data type composed of two attributes. Each row of the nested table will contain information about a degree granted and the school that granted it.

Querying Collection Data

Collection-valued columns complicate the process of querying the tables that contain them. In the SELECT item list, they generate multiple data values for each row of query results. In search conditions, they don't contain individual data items, but it's sometimes convenient to treat them as sets of data. The object-relational databases typically provide a limited set of SQL extensions or extend existing SQL concepts to provide simple queries involving collection data. For more advanced queries, they require you to write stored procedure language programs with loop structures that process the collection data items one by one.

For query purposes, Informix treats the collection types as if they were a set of data values, like the values that might be returned by a subquery. You can match individual items within a collection using the SQL IN search condition. Here is a query that finds any technicians who work on a project named "bingo":

```
SELECT EMPL_NUM, NAME
  FROM TECHNICIANS
 WHERE 'bingo' IN (PROJECTS);
```

The name of the collection-valued column (in this case, the set-valued column PROJECTS) appears in parentheses. Informix treats the members of the collection as a set and applies the IN matching condition. In interactive SQL, you can put a collection-valued column in the select item list. Informix displays the collection of data as either a SET, LIST, or MULTISET in the displayed output. To process collection-valued data in the select list of a programmatic request (that is, from a program using ESQL or a call-level API), you must use special API extensions and/or extensions to the Informix stored procedure language.

Oracle provides additional capabilities for processing nested tables within SQL queries. A special THE keyword flattens the nested table, in effect, producing an unnested table with one row for each row of the nested table within each row of the main table. Here's a query that shows the schools from which one of the engineers has received degrees:

```
SELECT NEST.SCHOOL
  FROM THE (SELECT DEGREES
              FROM ENGINEERS
             WHERE EMPL_NUM = 1234) NEST;
```

The query within the inner parentheses is a query against the main (ENGINEERS) table. It selects the column containing the nested table, but it could select other columns as well. The THE operation, applied to the query results, flattens them out, creating a row for each nested row within each row of the main table. This flattened table is assigned an alias (NEST in this example), and it becomes the source of candidate query results rows from the FROM clause of the main, top-level query. With this table as a source, the main query in this example is quite simple; it selects one column that originated in the nested table.

The ability to flatten nested tables in this way and process them as if they were actually joined versions of two separate tables is actually quite powerful. It allows many queries to be expressed in high-level SQL that would otherwise require you to resort to stored procedures. However, the logic behind such queries and the task of actually constructing them correctly can be extremely complicated, as even this simple example begins to show.

Manipulating Collection Data

Extensions to standard SQL syntax are used to insert new rows into a table containing collection-valued columns. Informix provides a trio of constructors—the SET constructor, MULTISET constructor, and LIST constructor—for this purpose. They transform a list of data items into the corresponding collections to be inserted. Here is a pair of INSERT statements that illustrates their use with the tables in Figure 24-6:

```
INSERT INTO TECHNICIANS
    VALUES (1279,
            ROW('Sam', 'R', 'Jones'),
            ROW('164 Elm St.', 'Highland', 'IL', ROW(12345, 6789)),
            SET{'atlas', 'checkmate', 'bingo'}");
```

```
INSERT INTO ENGINEERS
    VALUES (1281,
            ROW('Jeff', 'R', 'Ames'),
            ROW('1648 Green St.', 'Elgin', 'IL', ROW(12345, 6789)),
            MULTISET{ROW('BS', 'Michigan'),
                    ROW('BS', 'Michigan'),
                    ROW('PhD','Stanford')}");
```

The first statement inserts a single row into the TECHNICIANS table with a three-item set in the PROJECTS column. The second inserts a single row into the ENGINEERS table with a three-item multiset in the DEGREES column. Because the members of this particular multiset are themselves row types, the row constructor must be used for each item.

Oracle uses a different approach to constructing the collection-valued data items for insertion into the table. Recall from the discussion of Oracle abstract data types that each Oracle abstract data type automatically has an associated *constructor method* that is used to build a data item of the abstract type out of individual data items. This concept is extended to varying arrays and nested tables. A constructor method is automatically supplied for each varying array or nested table, and it is used in the INSERT statements:

```
INSERT INTO TECHNICIANS
    VALUES (NAME_TYPE('Sam', 'R', 'Jones'),
            ADDR_TYPE('164 Elm St.', 'Highland', 'IL',
                    POST_TYPE(12345, 6789)),
            PROJECTS('atlas', 'checkmate', 'bingo'));

INSERT INTO ENGINEERS
    VALUES (NAME_TYPE('Jeff', 'R', 'Ames'),
            ADDR_TYPE('1648 Green St.', 'Elgin','IL',
                    POST_TYPE(12345, 6789)),
            DEGREES(DEGREE_TYPE('BS', 'Michigan'),
                    DEGREE_TYPE('BS', 'Michigan'),
                    DEGREE_TYPE('PhD', 'Stanford')));
```

Collections and Stored Procedures

Collections pose special problems for stored procedures that are retrieving and manipulating data in tables that contain them. Both Oracle and Informix provide special stored procedure language facilities for this purpose. In Informix, special SPL collection variables must be used. Here is an SPL stored procedure fragment that handles the PROJECTS collection column from the TECHNICIANS table:

```
define proj_coll collection;     /* holds project collection */
define a_project varchar(15);    /* holds individual project */
define proj_cnt  integer;        /* number of projects */
define empl_name name_type;      /* buffer for tech name */

/* Check how many projects the technician is supporting */
select cardinality(projects) into proj_cnt
  from technicians
 where empl_num = 1234;

/* If too many projects, then refuse to add a new one */
if (proj_cnt > 6) then . . .

/* Retrieve row, including project set for the technician */
select name, projects into empl_name, proj_coll
  from technicians
 where empl_num = 1234;

/* Add the 'gonzo' project to the list for this tech */
insert into table(proj_coll)
    values ('gonzo');

/* Search through project list one by one */
foreach proj_cursor for
 select * into a_project
   from table(proj_coll)

   if (a_project = 'atlas') then
     begin
        update table(proj_coll)(project)
          set project = 'bingo'
         where current of proj_cursor;
        exit foreach;
     end;
   end if;
end foreach;
```

```
/* Update the database row with modified project list */
update technicians
    set projects = proj_coll
 where empl_num = 1234;
```

The example shows several aspects of collection-handling in Informix SPL. First, the collection is retrieved from the database into an SPL variable as a collection data type. It would also be possible to retrieve it into a variable explicitly declared as having a SET type (or in other situations, a LIST or MULTSET type). The collection stored in the variable is then explicitly treated as a table for manipulating items within the collection. To add a new project, an INSERT is performed into the collection table. To find and modify a specific project, a cursor is used to search through the collection table, and a cursor-based UPDATE statement is used to change the value of one member of the collection. Note that the FOREACH loop retrieves each item of the collection into a variable so that the SPL routine can process it. Finally, the collection variable's contents are used to update the collection column within the table.

Oracle takes a similar approach to processing varying arrays. The individual elements of an array within an abstract data type are available through subscripted references within a structured data type. The typical Oracle PL/SQL process for accessing variable array elements is:

1. Retrieve the row from the table containing the varying array into a local variable whose data type is defined to match the row structure of the table, or of the particular columns being retrieved.

2. Execute a FOR loop with an index variable, n, that counts from 1 to the number of elements in the varying array. The number of elements is available through the value of a special attribute of the array column named COUNT.

3. Within the FOR loop, a subscript is used on the varying array name to access the n-th element of the varying array.

A similar technique can be used to process nested tables; however, it's usually not necessary. Instead, the THE operator is generally used to flatten the table in a SQL query, and the results are processed with a single cursor-driven FOR loop. The processing may still be complex. In particular, the stored procedure may need to detect whether a particular row coming from the query results is from the same main table row as the previous row and, upon detecting a change in main table rows, perform special processing such as computing subtotals. In this aspect, the processing of both varying arrays and nested tables begins to resemble the nested-loop processing typical of the COBOL report-writing programs of 30 years ago that handled master and detail records.

As the discussion in this section has illustrated, collection types and the processing of individual collection items tend to call for programmatic access through stored procedures rather than for ad hoc SQL use. One of the criticisms of object-oriented databases is that they are a regression from the simplicity of the relational model and reintroduce that need for explicit database navigation that was part of the prerelational databases. Examples like these provide evidence that there is at least a certain amount of truth in the criticism.

User-Defined Data Types

Object-relational data management systems generally provide a mechanism through which a user can extend the built-in data types provided by the DBMS with additional, user-defined data types. For example, a mapping application might need to operate on a LOCATION data type that consists of a pair of latitude and longitude measurements, each consisting of hours, minutes, and seconds. To effectively process location data, the application may need to define special functions, such as a DISTANCE(X,Y) function that computes the distance between two locations. The meanings of some built-in operations, such as a test for equality (=), will need to be redefined for location type data.

One way that Informix Universal Server supports user-defined data types is through its OPAQUE data type. An OPAQUE data type is (not surprisingly) opaque to the DBMS. The DBMS can store and retrieve data with this type, but it has no knowledge of the internal workings of the type. In object-oriented terms, the data is completely encapsulated. The user must explicitly provide (in external routines, written in C or some similar programming language) the data structure for the type, code to implement the functions or operations that can be performed on the type (such as comparing two data items of the type for equality), and code to convert the opaque type between internal and external representations. Thus, OPAQUE data types represent a low-level capability to extend the core functionality of the DBMS with data types that appear as if they were built-in.

A more basic user-defined data type capability is provided by the implementation of DISTINCT data types within Informix. A DISTINCT type is useful to distinguish among different types of data, all of which use one of the DBMS built-in data types. For example, the city and company name data items in a database might both be defined with the data type VARCHAR(20). Even though they share the same underlying DBMS data type, these data items really represent quite different types of data. You would never normally compare a city value to a company name, and yet the DBMS will let you do this because the two VARCHAR(20) columns are directly comparable.

To maintain a higher level of database integrity, you could define each of these three data items as having a DISTINCT data type:

```
CREATE DISTINCT TYPE CITY_TYPE AS VARCHAR(20);
CREATE DISTINCT TYPE CO_NAME_TYPE AS VARCHAR(20);
```

Now tables can be created containing city and customer name data items in terms of the CITY_TYPE and CO_NAME_TYPE data types. If you try to compare columns with these two different data types, the DBMS automatically detects the situation and generates an error. You can compare them, but only by explicitly casting the data type of one item to match the data type of the other. As a result, the distinct data types assigned to the different columns help to maintain the integrity of the database and prevent inadvertent errors in programs and ad hoc queries that use the database.

Methods and Stored Procedures

In object-oriented languages, objects encapsulate both the data and programming code that they contain; the details of the data structures within an object and the programming instructions that manipulate those data structures are explicitly hidden from view. The only way to manipulate the object and obtain information about it is through *methods*, which are explicitly defined procedures associated with the object (or more accurately with the object class). For example, one method associated with a customer object might obtain the customer's current credit limit. Another method might provide the ability to change the credit limit. The credit limit data itself is encapsulated, hidden within the customer object.

The data within the tables of a relational database is inherently not encapsulated. The data and its structure are directly visible to outside users. In fact, one of the main advantages of a relational database is that SQL can be used to carry out ad hoc queries against the database. When the system catalog of a relational database is considered, the contrast with the object-oriented ideal is even more extreme. With the catalog, the database is self-describing, so that even applications that don't know the internal structure of the database in advance can use SQL queries to find out what it is.

Stored procedures provide a way for relational databases to offer capabilities that resemble those of object-oriented methods. At the extreme, all users of a relational database could be granted permission only to execute a limited set of stored procedures, and no underlying data access permissions on the base tables at all. In this case, the users' access would approach the encapsulation of the object-oriented ideal. In practice, stored procedures are often used to provide application designers with the limited database access they need. However, the ad hoc capabilities of the database are almost always exploited by query tools or reporting programs.

Oracle formalizes the linkage between object methods and database stored procedures by allowing you to explicitly define a stored procedure as a *member function* of an abstract data type. Once defined in this way, the member function can be used in queries involving the abstract data type, just as if it were a built-in function of the DBMS designed to work on that type. Here is a redefinition of the ADDR_TYPE abstract data type that is used to store addresses, with a relatively simple member function, named GET_FULL_POST. The function takes the postal-code part of the address, which stores both a five-digit main postal code and a four-digit suffix as two separate numbers, and combines them into one nine-digit number, which it returns:

```
CREATE TYPE ADDR_TYPE AS OBJECT (
     STREET VARCHAR(35),
       CITY VARCHAR(15),
      STATE CHAR(2),
   POSTCODE POST_TYPE,
     MEMBER FUNCTION GET_FULL_POST(POSTCODE IN POST_TYPE)
     RETURN NUMBER,
     PRAGMA RESTRICT_REFERENCES(GET_FULL_POST, WNDS));

CREATE TYPE BODY ADDR_TYPE AS
     MEMBER FUNCTION GET_FULL_POST(POSTCODE POST_TYPE)
     RETURN NUMBER IS
      BEGIN
         RETURN((POSTCODE.MAIN * 10000) + POSTCODE.SFX);
      END;
      . . .
```

The member function is identified as such within the CREATE TYPE statement for the abstract data type, following the lines that describe the data items. The additional PRAGMA clause tells Oracle that the function does not modify the contents of the database, which is a requirement for a function that is to be used within query expressions. There are several more options, which are beyond the scope of this discussion. A separate CREATE TYPE BODY statement defines the actual procedural code for the function. After the first few words of the statement, it follows the same format as the standard CREATE PROCEDURE or CREATE FUNCTION statements. Once the member function is defined, it can be used in query expressions like this one, which finds employees living in postal code 12345-6789:

```
123456789;
```

Informix Universal Server doesn't have an extended mechanism like Oracle's to turn stored procedures into object-oriented methods. Instead, it's possible to use an Informix row type (corresponding to an Oracle object type) as the parameter of a stored function. When called, the function is passed a data item with the appropriate row type (such as the POSTCODE abstract data item in the preceding Oracle example) and can perform appropriate calculations on it. You could, for example, define an Informix stored function GET_FULL_POST() with a single parameter of type POST_TYPE. With that definition, the preceding Oracle SELECT statement could be used, unmodified, in the equivalent Informix database.

Another powerful feature associated with object-relational stored procedures is the *overloading* of procedure definitions to allow them to process different types of data. In an object class hierarchy, it's frequently necessary to define a method that carries out the same or very similar operations on different classes of objects. For example, you may want to define a GET_TGT_WAGES method (function) that can obtain the target total annual wages for any of the subclasses of the PERSONNEL class in our example database. The method (which will be implemented as a stored function) should return the target total wages for the employee to which it is applied. The particulars of the calculation differ, depending on the type (class) of employee:

- For technicians, total wages are the hourly rate times a normal 40-hour week × 52 weeks per year.

- For managers, total wages are equal to their annual salary plus bonus.

- For all other engineers, total wages are equal to their annual salary.

To solve this problem, a different GET_TGT_WAGES routine is defined for each class. The routine takes an object (a row of the TECHNICIANS, ENGINEERS, or MANAGERS table) as its parameter and returns the calculated amount. The three routines are identically named, which is the reason why the procedure name is said to be overloaded—a single name is associated with more than one actual stored procedure. When the routine is called, the DBMS looks at the particular data type of the argument (that is, the particular class of the object) and determines which of the routines is the appropriate one to call.

Informix Universal Server implements this stored procedure overloading capability without any additional object-oriented extensions. It allows you to define many different stored procedures with identical names, provided that no two of them have the identical number of arguments with identical data types. In the previous example, there would be three CREATE FUNCTION definitions like this:

```
/* Calculates target wages for a technician */
CREATE FUNCTION GET_TGT_WAGES(PERSON TECH_TYPE)
   RETURNS MONEY(9,2) AS RETURN (PERSON.WAGE_RATE * 40 * 52)
END FUNCTION;

/* Calculates target wages for a manager */
CREATE FUNCTION GET_TGT_WAGES(PERSON MGR_TYPE)
   RETURNS MONEY(9,2) AS RETURN (PERSON.SALARY + PERSON.BONUS)
END FUNCTION;

/* Calculates target wages for an engineer */
CREATE FUNCTION GET_TGT_WAGES(PERSON ENGR_TYPE)
   RETURNS MONEY(9,2) AS RETURN (PERSON.SALARY)
END FUNCTION;
```

With these definitions in place, you can invoke the GET_TGT_WAGES() function and pass it a row from the ENGINEERS, MANAGERS, or TECHNICIANS table. The DBMS automatically figures out which of the functions to use and returns the appropriate calculated value.

Stored procedures are made even more valuable for typed tables through Informix Universal Server's *substitutability* feature. If you call a stored procedure whose argument is a row type and pass it one of the rows from a typed table, Informix will first search for a stored procedure with the appropriate name whose argument data type is an exact match. For example, if you call a GET_LNAME() stored procedure to extract the last name from a TECH_TYPE row (probably from the TECHNICIANS table), Informix searches for a procedure written to process TECH_TYPE data. But if Informix doesn't find such a stored procedure, it does not immediately return with an error. Instead, it searches upwards in the type hierarchy, trying to find a procedure with the same name that is defined for a supertype of TECH_TYPE. If there is a GET_LNAME() stored procedure defined for the ENGR_TYPE type, Informix will execute that stored procedure to obtain the required information. If not, it will continue up the hierarchy, looking for a GET_LNAME() stored procedure defined for the PERS_TYPE type. Thus, substitutability means that you can define stored procedures (methods) for the highest-level type in the hierarchy to which they apply. The stored procedures are automatically available to process all subtypes of that type. (That is, all subclasses inherit the method from the class.)

Object Support in the SQL:1999 Standard

As mentioned at the beginning of this chapter, the largest area of SQL expansion in the SQL:1999 standard was object-relational support. The SQL:1999 standard specifies new statements, clauses, and expressions in the SQL language in these areas:

- User-defined data types
- Composite (abstract) data types
- Array values
- Overloaded (polymorphic) stored procedures
- Row constructors and table constructors supporting abstract types
- Row-valued and table-valued expressions supporting abstract types

The SQL:1999 extensions don't exactly match any of the major commercial object-relational DBMS products in their specifics, but the underlying concepts are the same as those illustrated in the earlier sections for specific products. It's likely that this area of SQL will follow the pattern of others with respect to the standard. Slowly, over a series of major releases, the major DBMS vendors will provide support for the SQL:1999 syntax where it can be added in parallel to their own, well-established proprietary syntax. This process has just begun for SQL:1999 object support. For the next several years, the object-relational capabilities that matter for real-world implementations will continue to be the vendor-proprietary capabilities.

Summary

Object-oriented databases will likely play an increasing role in specialized market segments, such as engineering design, compound document processing, and graphical user interfaces. They are not being widely adopted for mainstream enterprise data processing applications. However, hybrid object-relational databases are being offered by some of the leading enterprise DBMS vendors:

- The object-relational databases significantly extend the SQL and stored procedure languages with object-oriented statements, structures, and capabilities.

- Common object-relational structures include abstract/structured data types, tables within tables, and explicit support for object identifiers. These capabilities stretch the simple relational model a great deal and tend to add complexity for casual or ad hoc users.

- The object-relational extensions added by the various DBMS vendors are highly proprietary. There are significant conceptual differences in the approaches as well as differences in implementation approach.

- Object-relational capabilities are particularly well suited for more complex data models, where the overall design of the database may be simpler, even though individual tables/objects are more complex.

- Object-relational capabilities are a major focus of the SQL3 standards efforts, and more relational databases are likely to incorporate them in the future.

Chapter 25

SQL and XML

T he eXtensible Markup Language (XML) is one of the most important new technologies to come out of the evolution of the Internet and the World Wide Web. XML is a standard language for representing and exchanging *structured data.* SQL is a standard language for defining, accessing, and updating the structured data stored in relational databases. It seems obvious on the surface that there should be a relationship between XML and SQL. The natural question is what *is* the relationship, and are the two technologies naturally in conflict or complementary to one another? The answer is a little bit of both. This chapter provides an overview of XML basics, and then examines the evolving relationship of XML and SQL, and how XML is being integrated into major SQL products.

What Is XML?

As implied by its name, XML is a *markup language.* It shares many characteristics with its more familiar cousin, the HyperText Markup Language (HTML), which has become wildly popular as the core technology enabling the World Wide Web and web browsers. The languages have common origins in document *markup,* a technique that is as old as the printing and publishing business. When a complex document, such as this book or a newsletter or a magazine, is to be printed, it can be thought of as having two related logical parts. The *content* of the document, which usually consists of text and graphics, contains its meaning. The *structure* of the document (titles, subtitles, paragraphs, captions) and the accompanying formatting (fonts, indentations, page layouts) help to organize the contents and ensure that they are presented in a meaningful way. Since the earliest days of printing and publishing, editors have employed markup symbols and formatting marks, embedded within the contents of the document itself, to indicate the document's structure and how it should be formatted for printing.

When computerized publishing systems arrived on the scene, markup commands embedded within the contents of a document became instructions for the publishing software programs. Each type of publishing software or equipment had its own proprietary markup commands, making it difficult to move from one system to another. The Standard General Markup Language (SGML) was developed as a way to standardize markup languages, and eventually was adopted as an ISO standard. More precisely, SGML is a *metalanguage* for defining specific markup languages. Its inventors recognized that no single markup language could cover all of the possible markup requirements, but that all markup languages had common elements. By standardizing these common elements, a family of closely related markup languages could be created. HTML is one such markup language, focused especially on the use of hypertext to link documents together. XML is another such language, focused especially on strong typing and tight structuring of document contents. Their common roots in SGML make HTML and XML cousin languages, and account for their similarity.

Both HTML and XML are World Wide Web Consortium (W3C) recommendations, defined by specifications that are developed by, voted on, and then published by the W3C. The W3C is an independent, nonprofit consortium whose purpose is to develop and advocate the use of standards associated with the Internet and the World Wide

Web. W3C recommendations have "officially adopted" status; the terminology means that the W3C organization advocates and recommends their use. Through this process, HTML and XML are vendor-independent industry standards.

HTML was the first SGML-based language to gain widespread popularity. The contents of every web page on every web site on the World Wide Web are expressed as an HTML document. Special markup elements, called *tags* within an HTML document, indicate graphical elements, such as buttons to be displayed by a web browser. The tags also describe the hypertext links to other documents that the browser should follow when a button is clicked. Other tags identify graphical elements that are to be inserted into the HTML text when it is displayed.

As the use of the World Wide Web exploded in the 1990s, HTML was rapidly adapted to display much richer content on highly formatted web pages. HTML tags were quickly invented to control the formatting of web pages, directing the display of boldface or italic text, centering and indents, and text location within the page. In some cases, these tags were even unique to a specific web browser, such as the Netscape browser or Microsoft's Internet Explorer. Over time, a great deal of the markup within an HTML page became focused on formatting and presentation of information. This had the benefit that web page formatting was tightly specified, so pages tended to be displayed in the same way regardless of the browser or device on which it was displayed. It had the disadvantage that the logical structure of web page content tended to get lost in the formatting and presentation details.

An important original goal of SGML was that a given logical element, such as a page title or a web page subsection, could be consistently identified across hundreds of documents (for example, across hundreds of pages on a web site). A simple directive to the browser, such as "display all subsection titles in blue, boldfaced, 16-point Times New Roman font," would then ensure consistent presentation of all pages. Instead, web page authors tended to explicitly mark every element, such as those subsection titles, with its own detailed formatting instructions. These could easily become inconsistent, and worse, a change to the formatting instructions would require hundreds of individual page edits rather than being specified once for all pages.

One of the main driving forces behind the development of XML was to restore a more logical-level, rather than formatting-level, approach to markup. XML implements much more rigid rules about document structure than HTML. Most of its components and capabilities are squarely focused at representing logical document structure. Companion standards, such as XML Schema, which specifies types of documents, extend this focus of XML even farther.

XML Basics

To understand the interactions between XML and SQL, you need a basic understanding of XML and how it is used. If you already understand or use XML, feel free to skip this section and go on to the next. If you are not familiar with XML, this section provides a simple introduction, based on some examples of XML documents.

Figure 25-1 shows a typical XML representation of a text document, a portion of Part II of this book. This example has little to do with data processing or SQL, but it shows XML in its original environment, and it illustrates key XML concepts. Each *element* of the XML document in the figure—each component part—is represented by a corresponding XML element with the simple structure shown in Figure 25-2. The element is identified by an *opening tag,* which contains the name of the element type, enclosed between less-than (<) and greater-than (>) symbols.

In Figure 25-1, paragraphs are identified by an opening <para> tag, and headers are identified by an opening <header> tag. The end of each element is identified by a *closing tag,* which again contains the name of the element type, preceded by a slash (/) character, again enclosed between less-than and greater-than symbols. In Figure 25-1, paragraphs end with a </para> tag and headers end with a </header> tag. Between the opening and closing tags is the *content* of the element. Most of the content in Figure 25-1 is text, enclosed in quotes. You can use single or double quotes to enclose the text, as long as you use the same type of quotation mark for the beginning and ending of a piece of text.

Figure 25-1 shows the hierarchy of elements typical of most XML documents. At the top level is the para element. Its contents are not text, but other elements—a sequence of chapter elements. Each chapter element contains a title element, possibly some introductory para elements, and then a series of section elements. Each section element contains a header element and one or more para elements, possibly interspersed with some figure elements and some table elements. Each para element has only text as its contents.

In addition to the element hierarchy, Figure 25-1 shows some examples of *attributes,* another fundamental XML structure. An attribute is associated with a specific XML element, and describes some characteristic of the element. Each attribute has an attribute name and a value. In Figure 25-1, the chapter element has an attribute called chapNum whose value is the chapter number associated with that particular content. The chapter element has another attribute called revStatus whose value indicates whether the chapter is in its original draft, being rewritten, or in final form. Individual <header> elements in Figure 25-1 also have an attribute called hdrLevel that indicates whether the header is top level (level 1) or lower level (level 2 or 3).

The first line of the XML document in Figure 25-1 identifies it as an XML 1.0 document. Every other part of the document describes the element structure, element contents, or attributes of elements. XML documents can become considerably more complex, but these fundamental components are the ones that are important for XML/database interaction. Note that element names and attribute names are case-sensitive. An element named bookPart and one named bookpart are not considered the same element. This is different from the usual SQL convention for table and column names, which are usually case-insensitive.

One additional XML shorthand notation is not shown in Figure 25-1 for clarity, but is very useful in practice. For elements that have no content of their own but only attributes, the end of the element can be indicated within the same pair of less-than

```
<?xml version="1.0"?>
<bookPart partNum="2" title="Retrieving Data">
  <para>Queries are at the heart… used to handle complex queries.</para>
  <chapter chapNum = "5" revStatus="final">
    <title>SQL Basics</title>
    <para>This chapter begins… described in this chapter."</para>
    <section>
      <header hdrLevel="1">Statements</header>
      <para>The main body of… in Figure 5-1.</para>
      <para>Every SQL statement… constands, or expressions.</para>
      <figure figNum="5-1"></figure>
      <table tabNum="5-1"></table>
      <para>The ANSI/ISO SQL…. In Table 5-3.</para>
      <table tabNum="5-2"></table>
      <table tabNum="5-3"></table>
      <para>Throughout this book… in lowercase.</para>
      <figure figNum="5-2"></figure>
      <para>Variable items… is UNDERLINED.</para>
    </section>
    <section>
      <header hdrLevel="1">Names</header>
      <para>The objects in a… data entry forms (Ingres).</para>
      <para>The original… special characters.</para>
      <section>
        <header> hdrLevel=""2">Table Names</header>
        <para>When you specify… or designer.</para>
        <para>In a larger… table name</para>
              … etc …
      </section>
    </section>
  </chapter>
  <chapter chapNum="6">
    <title>Simple Queries</title>
    <para>In many ways … in the database.</para>
    <section>
              … etc …
    </section>
  </chapter>
              … etc …
</bookPart>
```

Figure 25-1. *XML document for part of a book*

Figure 25-2. *Anatomy of an XML element*

and greater-than symbols as the opening tag, indicated by a slash just before the greater-than symbol. Using this convention, this element from Figure 25-1:

```
<figure figNum="5-1"></figure>
```

can be instead represented as:

```
<figure figNum="5-2" />
```

The XML specification defines certain rules that every XML document should follow. It dictates that elements within an XML document must be strictly nested within one another. The closing tag for a lower-level element must appear before the closing tag for a higher-level element that contains it. The standard also dictates that an attribute must be uniquely named within its element; it is illegal to have two attributes with the same name attached to a single element. XML documents that obey the rules are described as *well-formed* XML documents.

XML for Data

Although the roots of XML are in documents and document processing, XML can be quite useful for representing the structured data commonly found in data processing applications as well. Figure 25-3 shows a typical XML document from the data processing world, a very simplified purchase order. This is quite a different type of document than the book excerpt in Figure 25-1, but the key components of the document are the same. Instead of a chapter, the top-level element is a purchaseOrder. Its contents, like those of the chapter, are subelements—a customerNumber, an orderNumber, an orderDate, and an orderItem. The orderItem in turn is composed of further subelements. Figure 25-3 also shows some business terms associated with the purchase order as attributes of the terms element. The ship attribute specifies how the order is to be shipped. The bill attribute specifies the credit terms for the order.

It should be obvious that the simple XML purchase order document in Figure 25-3 has a strong relationship to the ORDERS table in the sample database. You may want to compare it to the structure of the ORDERS table shown in Appendix A (Figure A-5). The lowest-level elements in the document mostly match the individual columns of the ORDERS table, except for the terms element. The top-level element in the document represents an entire row of the table. The transformation between a group of documents like the one in Figure 25-3 and a set of rows in the ORDERS table is a straightforward, mechanical one, which can be automatically performed by a simple computer program.

Unlike the ORDERS table, the XML document imposes one middle level of hierarchy, grouping together the information about the ordered product—the manufacturer ID, product ID, quantity, and total amount. In a real-world purchase order, this group of data items might be repeated several times, forming multiple line items on the order. The XML document could be easily extended to support this structure, by adding a second or third orderItem element after the first one. The sample database cannot

```
<?xml version="1.0"?>
<purchaseOrder>
  <customerNumber>2117</customerNumber>
  <orderNumber>112961</orderNumber>
  <orderDate>1989-12-17</orderDate>
  <repNumber>106</repNumber>
  <terms ship="ground" bill="Net30"></terms>
  <orderItem>
    <mfr>REI</mfr>
    <product>2A44L</product>
    <qty>7</qty>
    <amount>31500.00</amount>
  </orderItem>
</purchaseOrder>
```

Figure 25-3.   *XML document for a simple purchase order*

be so easily extended. To support orders with multiple line items, the ORDERS table would probably be split into two tables: one holding the order header information (order number, date, customer-ID, and so on), and the other holding individual order line items.

XML and SQL

The SGML origins give XML several unique and useful characteristics, which have strong parallels to the SQL language:

■ **Descriptive approach**. XML approaches document structure by telling what each element of a document is, rather than how to process it. You may recall this is also a characteristic of SQL, which focuses on which data is requested rather than how to retrieve it.

■ **Building blocks**. XML documents are built up from a very small number of basic building blocks, including two fundamental concepts, *elements* and *attributes*. There are some strong (but not perfect) parallels between an XML element and a SQL table, and between an XML attribute and a SQL column.

■ **Document types**. XML defines and validates documents as conforming to specific document types that parallel real-world documents, such as a purchase order document or a business reply letter document or a vacation request document. Again, there are strong parallels to SQL, where tables represent different types of real-world entities.

Although there are some strong parallels between XML and SQL, there are also some very strong differences:

- **Document vs. data orientation**. The core concepts of XML arise out of typical document structures. XML is text-centric, and it implements a strong distinction between the content itself (the elements of a document) and characteristics of the content (attributes). The core concepts of SQL arise out of typical data processing record structures. It is data-centric, with a range of data types (in their binary representations), and its structures (tables and columns) focus on content (data). This mismatch between the fundamental XML and SQL models can cause some conflicts or difficult choices when using them together.

- **Hierarchical vs. tabular structure**. Natural XML structures are hierarchical, reflecting the hierarchy of elements in most types of documents (for example, a book contains chapters, chapters contain sections, and sections contain a heading, paragraphs, and figures). The structures are also flexible and variable. One section may contain five paragraphs and a single figure, the next one three paragraphs and two figures, and the next one six paragraphs and no figures. In contrast, SQL structures are tabular, not hierarchical, and they reflect the records typical of data processing applications. SQL structures are also quite rigid. Every row of a table contains exactly the same columns, in the same order. Each column has the same data type in every row. There are no optional columns; every column must appear in every row. These differences can also cause conflicts when using XML and SQL together.

- **Objects vs. operations**. The core purpose of the XML language is to *represent* objects. If you take a meaningful piece of XML text and ask "What does this represent?" the answer will be an object: a paragraph, a purchase order, or a customer address, for example. The SQL language has a broader purpose, but most of it is focused on *manipulating* objects. If you take a meaningful piece of SQL text and ask "What does this represent?" the answer will usually be an *operation* on an object: creating an object, deleting an object, finding one or more objects, or updating object contents. These differences make the two languages fundamentally complementary in their purpose and use.

Elements vs. Attributes

The relational model offers only one way to represent data values within the database—as values of individual columns within individual rows of a table. The XML document model offers two ways to represent data:

- **Elements**. An element within an XML document has contents, and the contents can include a data value in the form of text for that element. When represented in this way, the data value is a fundamental part of the XML document hierarchy; the hierarchy is built up from elements. Often, an element containing a data value will be a leaf node in the XML document tree; that element will be a child of higher-level elements, but it will not itself have any children. This will almost always be true of elements that represent data that comes from a relational database. However, XML does support *mixed* elements, which contain a combination of text (content) and other subelements.

■ **Attributes**. An element within an XML document may have one or more named attributes, and each attribute has a text value. The attributes are attached to an element within the XML hierarchy but are not the content of the element. The names of different attributes of an element must be different, so you can't have two attributes with the same name. Also, XML treats the order of the attributes of an element as insignificant; they can appear in any order. This differs from the XML treatment of elements, which have a definite position within an XML document, and where the difference between the first, second, and third child elements of a higher-level element is significant.

The existence of two different ways to represent data in XML means that there are two different legitimate ways to express the contents of a relational database as XML. These two rows of data:

```
ORDER_NUM  MFR  PRODUCT  QTY     AMOUNT
---------  ---  -------  ----  ----------
   112963  ACI    41004    28  $3,276.00
   112983  ACI    41004     3    $702.00
```

might be represented by this XML document when elements are used to represent column values:

```
<?xml version="1.0"?>
<queryResults>
  <row>
    <orderNum>112963</orderNum>
    <mfr>ACI</mfr>
    <product>41004</product>
    <qty>28</qty>
    <amount>3276.00</amount>
  </row>
  <row>
    <orderNum>112983</orderNum>
    <mfr>ACI</mfr>
    <product>41004</product>
    <qty>3</qty>
    <amount>702.00</amount>
  </row>
</queryResults>
```

and would be represented by this XML document when attributes are used:

```
<?xml version="1.0"?>
<queryResults>
  <row orderNum="112963"
       mfr="ACI"
       product="41004"
       qty="28"
       amount="3276.00">
  </row>
  <row orderNum="112983"
       mfr="ACI"
       product="41004"
       qty="3"
       amount="702.00">
  </row>
</queryResults>
```

As you might expect, there are strong advocates for both the element-representation and the attribute-representation methods, with strongly held beliefs. Advocates of the element approach make these arguments:

■ Elements are more fundamental to the XML model than attributes; they are the carriers of content in all markup languages (HTML, XML, SGML, etc.), and the content of the database (column values) should be represented as content in XML.

■ Element order matters, and in some cases, so does the ordering of data in a DBMS (for example, when identifying a column by number in a query specification or when using a column number to retrieve query results with an API).

■ Elements provide a uniform way of representing column data, regardless of whether the column has a simple, atomic data type (integer, string) or more complex, compound, user-defined data types supported by the object-relational extensions and SQL3. Attributes don't provide this capability. (Attribute values are atomic.)

Advocates of the attribute approach make these arguments:

■ Attributes are a fundamental match for the columns in the relational model. Individual rows represent entities, so they should be mapped into elements. Column values describe attributes of the entity (row) in which they appear; they should be represented as attribute values in XML.

■ The restriction of unique attribute names within an element matches the uniqueness required of column names within a table. The unordered nature of attributes matches the unordered nature of columns in the fundamental relational model. (The places where column position is used are shortcuts for convenience, not fundamental to the underlying relations.)

■ The attribute representation is more compact, since column names appear only once in the XML form, not as both opening and closing tags. This is a practical advantage when storing or transmitting XML.

Both the element-centric and attribute-centric styles are found in today's XML and SQL products. The choice depends on the preferences of the document author and the conventions of the organization using XML with SQL. In addition, standards imposed by industry bodies for document exchange using XML may dictate one style or the other.

Using XML with Databases

With the rapidly growing popularity of XML, database product vendors have moved quickly to offer XML support in their products. The form of XML support varies, but tends to fall into one or more of these categories:

■ **XML output**. An XML document can easily represent the data in one or more rows of query results. With this support, the DBMS generates an XML document as its response to a SQL query instead of the usual row/column query results.

■ **XML input**. An XML document can easily represent the data to be inserted as one or more new rows of a table. It can also represent data to update a row of a table, or the identification of a row to be deleted. With this support, the DBMS accepts an XML document as input instead of a SQL request.

■ **XML data exchange**. XML is a natural way to express data that is to be exchanged between different DBMS systems or among DBMS servers. Data from the source database is transformed into an XML document and shipped to the destination database, where it is transformed back into a database format. This same style of data exchange is useful for moving data between relational databases and non-DBMS applications, such as corporate Enterprise Resource Planning (ERP) or Enterprise Application Integration (EAI) systems.

■ **XML storage**. A relational database can easily accept an XML document (which is a string of text characters) as a piece of variable-length character string (VARCHAR) or character large object (CLOB) data. At the most basic level of XML support, an entire XML document becomes the content of one column in one row of the database. Slightly stronger XML support may be possible if the DBMS allows the column to be declared with an explicit "XML-data" data type.

■ **XML data integration**. A more sophisticated level of integrated XML storage is possible if the DBMS can parse an XML document, decompose it into its component elements, and store the individual elements in individual columns. Ordinary SQL can then be used to search those columns, providing search support for elements within the XML document. In response to a query, the DBMS can recompose the XML document from its stored component elements.

XML Output

One of the most straightforward combinations of XML and database technology is to use XML as a format for SQL query results. Query results have a structured tabular format that can easily be translated into an XML representation. Consider this simple query from the sample database:

```
SELECT ORDER_NUM, MFR, PRODUCT, QTY, AMOUNT
  FROM ORDERS
 WHERE CUST = 2103;

ORDER_NUM  MFR  PRODUCT  QTY     AMOUNT
---------  ---  -------  ----  ----------
   112963  ACI    41004    28   $3,276.00
   112983  ACI    41004     3     $702.00
   113027  ACI    41002    54   $4,104.00
   112987  ACI    4100Y    11  $27,500.00
```

If the DBMS is instructed to output the query results in XML format instead, here is the output that might result:

```
SELECT ORDER_NUM, MFR, PRODUCT, QTY, AMOUNT
  FROM ORDERS
 WHERE CUST = 2103;

<?xml version="1.0"?>
<queryResults>
  <row>
    <order_num>112963</order_num>
    <mfr>ACI</mfr>
    <product>41004</product>
    <qty>28</qty>
    <amount>3276.00</amount>
  </row>
  <row>
    <order_num>112983</order_num>
    <mfr>ACI</mfr>
    <product>41004</product>
    <qty>3</qty>
    <amount>702.00</amount>
  </row>
  <row>
```

```
      <order_num>113027</order_num>
      <mfr>ACI</mfr>
      <product>41002</product>
      <qty>54</qty>
      <amount>4104.00</amount>
   </row>
   <row>
      <order_num>112987</order_num>
      <mfr>ACI</mfr>
      <product>4100Y</product>
      <qty>11</qty>
      <amount>27500.00</amount>
   </row>
</queryResults>
```

This is typical of the output you could actually receive from some of the popular DBMS products that currently support XML output. The query results are a well-formed, self-contained XML document. If you submit the results to an XML parser (parsers are described in the "Large Objects and Parsers" section later in this chapter), the parser will correctly interpret them as having:

■ One root element, `queryResults`

■ Four `row` subelements beneath the root

■ Five subelements beneath each row element, and in this case, all five subelements appearing for every row element, and in the same order

Having XML-formatted query output can be a significant advantage. The output can be sent directly to programs that accept XML documents as input, for further processing. The output can be sent across a network to another system, and because of its XML format, its elements are self-describing—*every* receiving system or application will interpret the query results in the same way—as four rows of five elements each. Because the output is in pure text format, it won't be misinterpreted because of differences in binary data representations between sending and receiving systems. Finally, if the XML is transmitted over an HTTP link using the Simple Object Access Protocol (SOAP) protocol standards, the XML-formatted message can typically move through corporate firewalls and link an originating application in one company with a receiving application in a different company.

The XML-formatted output also has some disadvantages. One is the raw size of the data. There are about four times as many characters in the XML-formatted results as in the tabular format. If the XML form is being stored on disk, it requires four times the storage. If it's being sent to another computer system over a network, it will take four times as long to transmit, or it will require a network with four times the bandwidth to preserve the same transmission time. These aren't serious problems for the small amount of data in the example, but they can be very significant for results with thousands or tens of thousands of rows, multiplied by hundreds of applications in an enterprise data center.

This simple XML output format also loses some information about the data. The currency symbol that appeared in the tabular display has disappeared, so it's impossible to determine, from the XML content itself, that the data has a currency type and what kind of currency it is. The XML Schema capability provides a way to gain back this information, as described later in the "XML Schema" section, but at the expense of still more increase in the size of the query results text.

XML Input

Just as XML can be used to represent a row of query results that is output from a database, XML can easily be used to represent a row of data to be inserted into a database. To process the XML data, the DBMS must analyze the XML document containing the data to be inserted and identify the individual data items (represented as either elements or attributes). The DBMS must then match (usually using column names) or translate (using a DBMS-specific scheme) the corresponding element or attribute names to columns in the target table that is to receive the new data. Conceptually, this simple INSERT statement:

```
INSERT INTO OFFICES (OFFICE, CITY, REGION, SALES)
    VALUES (23,'San Francisco','Western',0.00)
```

can be easily translated into an equivalent hybrid SQL/XML statement like this one:

```
INSERT INTO OFFICES (OFFICE, CITY, REGION, SALES)
    VALUES <?xml version="1.0"?>
            <row>
              <office>23</office>
              <city>San Francisco</city>
              <region>Western</region>
              <sales>0.00</sales>
            </row>
```

Updates to the database can be similarly handled. This simple UPDATE statement:

```
UPDATE OFFICES
   SET TARGET = 200000.00, MGR = 108
 WHERE OFFICE = 23
```

can be translated into this equivalent hybrid SQL/XML statement:

```
UPDATE OFFICES
  WHERE OFFICE = 23
        <?xml version="1.0"?>
          <update_info>
            <values>
              <target>200000.00</target>
              <mgr>108</mgr>
            </values>
            <where>office = 23</where>
          </update_info>
```

and a DELETE statement requires only the specification of the WHERE clause, using the
same conventions.

While several SQL DBMS brands have added the capability to process XML-based
INSERT, UPDATE, and DELETE operations using this type of approach, the specific
techniques for representing table and column names and data values in the XML text,
and for mapping them to corresponding database structures, are DBMS-specific. There
are no standards (yet) for the type of hybrid SQL/XML syntax in these examples.

Although representing input and update values as small XML documents is
conceptually straightforward, it represents some significant DBMS processing issues.
For example, the column list in a SQL INSERT statement appears to be redundant if
the XML document containing the data values to be inserted also contains the column
names as either element or attribute names. Why not simply drop the column list and
let the XML documents specify which columns to insert? For interactive SQL, there is
no problem in doing this, but the XML format is unlikely to be used for an interactive
SQL session. For programmatic use of SQL, the problem is that the XML document and
the data values that it contains will be supplied to the DBMS at runtime. If the column
names (or even the table name) are also supplied only in the XML document, then
the DBMS cannot know, until runtime, which tables and columns are affected. In this
situation, the DBMS must use dynamic SQL to handle the processing, as described in
Chapter 18, with all of its associated performance penalties.

Similar problems arise with the WHERE clause in an UPDATE or DELETE statement,
and the SET clause of the UPDATE statement. To get the performance and efficiency of
static SQL, the DBMS must know in advance (when the program is compiled) which
search conditions will be used and which columns will be updated. One approach to
this problem is to use the parameterized form of these statements. Here is the same
UPDATE example, using this approach:

```
UPDATE OFFICES
   SET TARGET = ?, MGR = ?
  WHERE OFFICE = ?
```

```
<?xml version="1.0"?>
  <update_info>
    <param>200000.00</param>
    <param>108</param>
    <param>23</param>
  </update_info>
```

With this style, the XML text and the SQL text are actually quite separate. The SQL text is self-contained, and can be processed at compile-time. The XML text is self-contained, and the DBMS can match its parameter values to the needed statement parameters at runtime. This example follows the usual SQL style of specifying parameters by position, but the XML document loses a lot of its self-describing qualities as a result. Depending on the DBMS, it may be possible to use named elements within the XML document and match them to named statement parameters at runtime.

XML Data Exchange

A DBMS can support XML data exchange in a simple form merely by supporting XML output for query results and XML input for INSERT operations. However, this requires the user or programmer to carefully construct the format of the generated query results in the source database to match the expected format for the INSERT operations in the destination database. XML data exchange is more useful if the DBMS provides more explicit built-in support.

Several commercial DBMS products now offer the ability to perform a bulk export of a table (or in a more sophisticated operation, the results of a query) into an external file, formatted as an XML document. At the destination end, these products offer the same ability to do a bulk import from this same type of file into a DBMS table. With this scheme, the XML document file becomes a standard way of representing table contents for the exchange.

Note that once XML-based table import/export capabilities are offered, their use is not restricted to database-to-database exchanges. The source of the XML document in the data exchange file could well be an enterprise application, such as a Supply Chain Management (SCM) system. The destination similarly could be an enterprise application. In addition, many EAI systems now support XML document files. These systems provide further processing and integration capabilities, such as eliminating duplicated data and combining data from multiple input files.

XML Storage and Integration

XML input, output, and data exchange capabilities offer a very effective way to integrate existing relational databases with the emerging world of XML. With these approaches, XML is used in the external world to represent structured data, but the data within the database itself retains its row/column, tabular, binary structure. As XML documents proliferate, a natural next step is to consider storing XML documents themselves within a database.

Simple XML Storage with Large Objects

Any SQL-based DBMS that supports large objects automatically contains basic support for XML document storage and retrieval. The section titled "Large Object Support" in Chapter 24 described how several commercial databases store and retrieve large text documents through character large object (CLOB) or binary large object (BLOB) data types. Many commercial products support documents of up to 4 gigabytes for CLOB or BLOB data, which is adequate for the vast majority of XML documents.

To store XML documents using BLOBs or CLOBs, you would typically define a table that contains one BLOB or CLOB column to contain the document text, and some auxiliary columns (using standard data types) that contain attributes that identify the document. For example, if a table is to store purchase order documents, you might define auxiliary columns to hold the customer number, order date, and purchase order number using INTEGER, VARCHAR, or DATE data, in addition to the CLOB column for the XML document. You can search the table of purchase orders based on customer numbers, order dates, or P.O. numbers, and use the CLOB processing techniques described in Chapter 24 to retrieve or store the XML document.

An advantage of this approach is that it is relatively simple to implement. It also maintains a clean separation between the SQL operations (such as query processing) and the XML operations. A disadvantage is that the level of XML/DBMS integration is fairly weak. In the simplest implementations, a stored XML document is completely opaque to the DBMS; the DBMS knows nothing about its contents. You cannot search for a document based on one of its attributes or its element values, unless that particular attribute or element has been extracted from the XML document and is also represented as a separate column in the table. If you can anticipate in advance which types of searches are likely, this is not a large restriction.

Some object-relational databases provide a more advanced search capability for CLOBs by extending the SQL WHERE clause with full-text search capability. These products allow you to search CLOB columns as text, using the type of text search capabilities typically found in word processors. This provides an expanded, but typically still limited, capability for searching XML documents stored as CLOB columns. Using full-text search, you could, for example, locate every purchase order where the phrase "Type 4 Widgets" occurred. However, it will be difficult or impossible to search for only those XML documents where "Type 4 Widgets" applies in an order item description element. Because the search software doesn't explicitly know about the structure of XML documents, it will probably also return rows where "Type 4 Widgets" occurred in a comments element or some other element.

Large Objects and Parsers

When exchanged between applications or stored in a file or in a DBMS CLOB column, XML documents are always in text form. This makes the contents very portable, but unwieldy for computer programs to handle. An XML *parser* is a piece of computer software that translates XML documents from their text form to a more program-friendly, internal representation. Any SQL-based DBMS that supports XML will have an XML parser as part of its software, for its own use in processing XML. If the DBMS brand supports CLOBs, it can provide further integration with XML by allowing an XML parser to operate directly on the CLOB column contents.

There are two popular types of XML parsers, which support two styles of XML processing:

- **Document Object Model (DOM).** DOM parsers transform an XML document into a hierarchical tree structure within a computer's main memory. A program can than make calls to the DOM API to navigate through the tree, moving up and down or sequentially through the element hierarchy. The DOM API makes the element structure of an XML document easily accessible to programmers and simplifies random access to portions of the document.

- **Simple XPI for XML (SAX).** SAX parsers transform an XML document into a series of *callbacks* to a program, which inform the program of each part of the XML document as it is encountered. A program can be structured to take certain actions when the beginning of a document section is encountered, or when a particular attribute is encountered. The SAX API imposes a more sequential style of processing on a program using it. The API's callback style matches well with an event-driven program structure.

Either type of XML parser will validate that an XML document is well formed, and can also validate an XML document against a schema, as described in the "XML Schema" section later in this chapter. A DOM parser is practical when the size of the stored XML document is fairly small; it will require double the memory space of the text XML document, because it generates a second, tree-structured representation of the entire document. For very large documents, a SAX parser makes it easy to process documents in small, discrete pieces. However, the fact that the entire document is not available at one time may require a program to make multiple passes through it, if the program needs to process various sections of the document out of sequential order.

XML Marshalling

Storing XML documents as large objects within a database is an excellent solution for some types of SQL/XML integration. If the XML documents are, for example, text-oriented business documents, or if they are text components of web pages, then there is really very little need for the DBMS to "understand" the internals of the XML documents themselves. Each document can probably be identified by one or more keywords or attributes, which can easily be extracted and stored as conventional columns for searching.

If the XML documents to be processed are really data processing records, however, the simple integration provided by large objects may be too primitive. You will probably want to process and access individual elements, and search based on their contents and attributes. The DBMS already provides these capabilities for its native row/column data. Why can't the DBMS automatically decompose an incoming XML document, transforming its element contents and attribute values into a corresponding set of internal row/column data for processing? On the outbound side, we have already seen how this approach can work to transform row/column query results into an XML document. The same technique could be used to recompose an XML document if it were once again needed in its external text form.

The challenge of transforming XML documents, which are an excellent external data representation, to and from internal data representations more useful for programs is not unique to database systems. The same problems occur, for example, in Java processing of XML, where it is very desirable to transform an XML document to and from a set of Java class instances for internal processing. The process of decomposing an XML document into its component elements and attributes in some internal, binary representation is called *unmarshalling* in the XML literature. Conversely, the process of reassembling these individual element and attribute representations into a complete text XML document is called *marshalling*.

For very simple XML documents, the marshalling and unmarshalling process is straightforward, and commercial DBMS products are moving to support it. Consider once again the simple purchase order document in Figure 25-3. Its elements map directly, one to one, onto individual columns of the ORDERS table. In the simplest case, the names of the elements (or attributes) will be identical to the names of the corresponding columns. The DBMS can receive an inbound XML document like the one in the figure, automatically turn its elements (or attributes, depending on the style used) into column values, using the element names (or attribute names) to drive the process. Reconstituting the XML document from a row of the table is also no problem at all.

The DBMS must do slightly more work if the element names in the XML document don't precisely match column names. In this case, some kind of mapping between element names (or attribute names) and column names must be specified. It's relatively straightforward to put such a mapping into the DBMS system catalog.

Many useful real-world XML documents do not map neatly into single rows of a table. Figure 25-4 shows a simple extension of the purchase order XML document from Figure 25-3, which supports the typical real-world requirement that a purchase order may contain multiple line items. How should this XML document be unmarshalled into the sample database? One solution is to make each line item from the purchase order into a separate row of the ORDERS table. (Ignore for the moment that each row in the ORDERS table must contain a unique order number because the order number is the primary key.) This would result in some duplication of data, since the same order number, order date, customer number, and salesperson number will appear in several rows. It would also make marshalling the data to reconstitute the document more complex—the DBMS would have to know that all of the rows with the same order number should be marshaled into one purchase order XML document with multiple line items. Clearly, the marshalling/unmarshalling of even this simple document requires a more complex mapping.

```
<?xml version="1.0"?>
<purchaseOrder>
  <customerNumber>2117</customerNumber>
  <orderNumber>112961</orderNumber>
  <orderDate>1989-12-17</orderDate>
  <repNumber>106</repNumber>
  <terms ship="ground" bill="Net30"></terms>
  <orderItem>
    <mfr>REI</mfr>
    <product>2A44L</product>
    <qty>7</qty>
    <amount>31500.00</amount>
  </orderItem>
  <orderItem>
    <mfr>ACI</mfr>
    <product>41003</product>
    <qty>10</qty>
    <amount>6520.00</amount>
  </orderItem>
</purchaseOrder>
```

Figure 25-4.   *A slightly expanded XML purchase order document*

The multiline purchase order merely scratches the surface of marshalling and unmarshalling XML documents. The more general situation is shown in Figure 25-5, where the DBMS must unmarshal an XML document into multiple rows of multiple, interrelated tables. To marshal the document, the DBMS must exercise the relationships between the tables to find the related rows and recompose the XML hierarchy. The underlying reason for this complexity is the mismatch between XML's natural hierarchical structure and the flat, normalized, row/column structure of a relational database.

Marshalling and unmarshalling is both simplified and made more complex if a DBMS supports object-relational extensions, such as structured data types. The translation to and from XML can be simpler because individual columns of a table can now have their own hierarchical structure. A higher-level XML element (such as a billing address composed of street, city, state, country, and postal code elements) can be mapped into a corresponding column with an abstract ADDRESS data type, with its own internal hierarchy. However, the translation to and from XML now involves more decisions in the database design, trading off the marshalling/unmarshalling simplicity of structured data types against the flexibility of a flattened row/column approach.

Several commercial products are beginning to offer marshalling/unmarshalling capabilities, or have announced plans to provide this capability in future releases. The

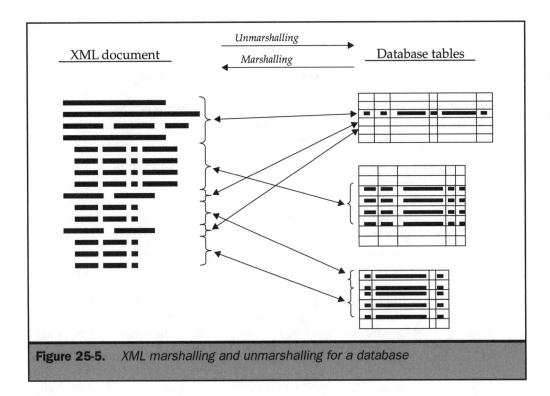

Figure 25-5.   *XML marshalling and unmarshalling for a database*

performance overhead of this translation can be very substantial, and it remains to be seen how popular these capabilities will be in practice. However, if an application is handling external data in XML form, the translation between XML and SQL data must occur at some point, and translation within the DBMS itself may be the most efficient approach.

XML and Metadata

One of the most powerful qualities of the relational model is its very rigid support for data types and data structure, implemented by the definitions of tables, columns, primary keys, foreign keys, and constraints. In addition, as shown in Chapter 16, the system catalog of a relational database contains *metadata*, or "data about the data" in the database. By querying the system catalog, you can discover the structure of the database, including the data types of its columns, the columns that comprise its tables, and intratable relationships.

In contrast, XML documents by themselves provide only very limited metadata. They impose a hierarchical element structure on their data, but the only real data about the structure is the names of the elements and attributes. An XML document can be well formed and still have quite an irregular structure. For example, there is nothing to prevent a well-formed XML document from having a named element that contains text data in one instance and subelements in another instance, or a named attribute that has an integer value for one element and a date value for another. Clearly, a document with this structure, while it may be well formed, does not represent data that is easily transformed to and from a relational database. When using XML for data processing documents, stronger support for data types and rigid structure is needed.

XML standards and products have addressed this need in multiple ways during the short history of XML technologies. These include:

- **Document Type Definition (DTD)**. A part of the original XML 1.0 specification, Document Type Definitions provided a way to specify and restrict the structure of a document. XML parsers can examine an XML document in the context of a DTD and determine whether it is a *valid document* (i.e., whether it conforms to the DTD restrictions).

- **XML-Data**. Submitted to the W3C in 1998, XML-Data was an early attempt to address some of the deficiencies in the DTD scheme. It never received W3C endorsement, but many of its ideas have carried forward into the XML Schema specification. Microsoft adapted its own form of XML-Data, called XML-Data Reduced (XDR), and implemented it as part of its BizTalk integration server and Internet Explorer 5.0 browser. The energy around the XML-Data proposal shifted in late 1999 and 2000 to the XML Schema proposal.

- **XML Schema**. A stand-alone specification that became a W3C recommendation in May 2001, XML Schema built on and extended the ideas in XML-Data. XML Schema provides much more rigorous data type support, and has the advantage that the schema definition (the document metadata) is itself expressed as an XML document, in much the same way that relational database metadata is provided via a standard relational table structure.

- **Industry group standards**. Various industry groups have banded together to define XML standards for specific types of documents that are important for data exchange within their industry. For example, financial services firms are working on standards to describe financial instruments (stocks, bonds, etc.) and market data. Manufacturing firms are working on standards to describe purchase order documents, order confirmations, and the like. These standards for specific industry-oriented documents are usually built on generic standards, such as DTD and XML Schema.

The area of XML metadata and document type standards is evolving rapidly. The W3C consortium provides a frequently updated web site at http://www.w3.org, which provides access to the various XML-related standards and information about their status. You can find information about industry-specific standards at http://www.xml.org, a site organized and hosted by the Organization for the Advancement of Structured Information Systems (OASIS). The site contains a registry of XML-based standards, classified by industry.

Document Type Definitions (DTDs)

The earliest attempt to standardize XML metadata was contained in the Document Type Definition (DTD) capability of the original XML 1.0 specification. DTD's are used to specify the form and structure of a particular type of document (such as a purchase order document or a transfer-of-funds document). Figure 25-6 shows a DTD that might be used for a simple purchase order document in Figure 25-5. This DTD demonstrates only a fraction of the full capabilities of DTDs, but it illustrates the key components of a typical DTD.

The !ELEMENT entries in the DTD define the element hierarchy that gives the document its basic form. DTDs provide for these different types of elements:

- **Text-only element.** The element contains only a text string, which can represent a data value from a single column of database data.

- **Element-only element.** The element's contents are other elements (subelements); it is the parent in a local parent/child hierarchy of elements. This type of element can be used to represent a row of a table, with subelements representing the columns.

- **Mixed-content element.** The element can contain a mixture of interspersed text contents and subelements. This type is not typically used for database contents, because this mix of subelements and data doesn't naturally appear in the row/column structure of tables.

- **Empty-content element.** The element has no content—neither subelements nor text content—but it may have attributes. This type of element can represent a row of a table when its attributes are used to represent individual column values.

```
<!ELEMENT purchaseOrder (customerNumber, orderNumber,
                         orderDate, terms, orderItem*)>
<!ELEMENT customerNumber (#PCDATA)>
<!ELEMENT orderDate (#PCDATA)>
<!ELEMENT repNumber (#PCDATA)>
<!ELEMENT terms EMPTY>
<!ATTLIST terms
  ship CDATA
  bill CDATA #REQUIRED>
<!ELEMENT orderItem (mfr, product, qty, amount)>
<!ELEMENT mfr (#PCDATA)>
<!ELEMENT product (#PCDATA)>
<!ELEMENT qty (#PCDATA)>
<!ELEMENT amount (#PCDATA)>
```

Figure 25-6. *DTD for a simple purchase order document*

■ **Any-content element**. The element has unrestricted content. The content may be empty, or may contain a mix of subelements and/or text. Like the mixed-content element, this type is typically not useful for XML documents used in database processing.

In the purchase order DTD of Figure 25-6, the top-level `purchaseOrder` element and the `orderItem` element have the element-only type. Their declarations list the subelements that they contain. The `customerNumber` and `OrderDate` elements are text-only elements, indicated by the `#PCDATA` definitions. The `TERMS` element is empty; it only has attributes. Both attributes have values that are character data (indicated by the `CDATA` type); one is required, and the other is optional, as indicated. Note that this DTD combines a data-as-elements style (for the customer information) and a data-as-attributes style (for the order terms) only for illustrative purposes. In practice, you would choose one style or the other of data representation and use it consistently, to simplify processing.

Document Type Definitions are critical to make XML actually useful in practice for representing structured documents for data exchange. They allow you to define the essential elements of a transactional document, such as a purchase order or an employee personnel action form or a request-for-quote form. With a DTD for such a document in place, it is straightforward to validate that a document that originates somewhere else within a company, or even outside a company, is a valid document of the specific type and can be processed. Any XML parser, whether based on the DOM API or the SAX API, is capable of validating an XML document against a supplied DTD. In addition, it's possible to explicitly declare the DTD to which an XML document should conform within the document itself.

Document Type Definitions have some drawbacks, however. They lack the strong data typing typically found in relational databases. There is no way to specify that an element must contain an integer or a date, for example. DTDs also lack good support for user-defined (or corporate-defined) types or subdocument structures. For example, it's possible that the `orderItem` element in Figure 25-6 will appear not only in a purchase order document, but also in a change order document, an order cancellation document, a backorder document, and an order acknowledgement document. It would be convenient to define the `orderItem` substructure once, give it a name, and then refer to it in these other document definitions, but DTDs don't provide this capability.

DTDs are also somewhat restrictive in the types of content structures that they allow, although in practice, they are usually rich enough to support the kinds of transactional documents needed for hybrid database/XML applications. Finally, the expressions used by DTDs to define document structure are an extended form of Backus Naur Form (BNF). (An example of this is the asterisk that appears after the `orderItem` declaration within the `purchaseOrder` element list in Figure 25-6, which means, "This element may be repeated zero or more times.")

While familiar to computer science students who deal with computer languages, this format is unfamiliar to people who approach XML from the document markup world of HTML. All of these deficiencies became visible soon after the adoption of XML 1.0, and work began to define a stronger metadata capability for XML documents. Eventually, these efforts resulted in the XML Schema specification, described in the next section.

XML Schema

XML Schema 1.0 became an official W3C recommendation in May 2001, and support for it is rapidly growing in commercial XML-related products. DTD's are still widely supported for backward compatibility, but XML Schema offers some compelling advantages, and addresses most of the shortcomings of DTD. Figure 25-7 shows the document schema for the purchase order document in Figure 25-5, this time defined using an XML Schema. It's useful to compare the XML Schema declaration in Figure 25-7 with the DTD declaration in Figure 25-6. Even this simple example shows the strong data type support in XML Schema; elements and attributes have data types that look very much like SQL data types. Also, the schema in Figure 25-7 is itself an XML document, so it is more readable for someone who is familiar with XML basics than the DTD in Figure 25-6.

```
<schema xmlns="http://www.w3.org/2001/XMLSchema">

  <element name="purchaseOrder" type="POType" />

  <complexType name="POType">
    <sequence>
      <element name="customerNumber" type="integer" />
      <element name="orderNumber" type="integer" />
      <element name="orderDate" type="date" />
      <element name="repNumber" type="integer" length="3" />
      <element name="terms">
        <attribute name="ship" type="string" />
        <attribute name="bill" type="string" />
      </element>
      <element name="orderItem" minOccurs="0" maxOccurs="unbounded">
        <complexType>
          <sequence>
            <element name="mfr" type="string" length="3" />
            <element name="product" type="string" />
            <element name="qty" type="integer" />
            <element name="amount" type="decimal" fractionDigits="2" />
          </sequence>
        </complextype>
      </element>
    </sequence>
  </complexType>
</schema>
```

Figure 25-7. *XML Schema for a simple purchase order document*

Data Types in XML Schema

From a database point of view, XML Schema's strong support for data types and data structures is one of its major advantages. XML Schema defines over 20 built-in data types, which correspond fairly closely to the defined SQL data types. Table 25-1 lists the most important XML Schema built-in data types for database processing.

XML Schema Data Type	Description
Numeric data	
Integer	Integer number
PositiveInteger	Positive integers only
NegativeInteger	Negative integers only
NonNegativeInteger	Zero or positive integers only
NonPositiveInteger	Zero or negative integers only
Int	32-bit signed integer
UnsignedInt	32-bit unsigned integer
Long	64-bit signed integer
UnsignedLong	64-bit unsigned integer
Short	16-bit signed integer
UnsignedShort	16-bit unsigned integer
Decimal	Numeric, with possible decimal places
Float	Standard precision floating point
Double	Double precision floating point
Character data	
String	Variable-length character string
NormalizedString	String, with newline, carriage return, and tab characters converted to spaces
Token	String, processed like normalizedString, plus leading/trailing space removal and multiple spaces collapsed to a single space

Table 25-1.   *XML Schema Built-In Data Types*

XML Schema Data Type	Description
Date and time data	
Time	Time of day (hr/min/seconds/thousandths)
DateTime	Day and time (equivalent to SQL TIMESTAMP)
Duration	Length of time (equivalent to SQL DURATION)
Date	Year/month/day only
Gmonth	Gregorian month (1 to 12)
Gyear	Gregorian year (0000 to 9999)
Gday	Gregorian day (1 to 31)
GmonthDay	Gregorian month/day
Other data	
Boolean	TRUE/FALSE value
Byte	Single byte data, with assumed sign bit
UnsignedByte	Single byte data, no sign bit
base64Binary	Binary data, expressed with base 64 notation
HexBinary	Binary data, expressed with hexadecimal notation
AnyURI	Internet URI, such as http://www.w3.org
Language	Valid XML language (English, French...)

Table 25-1. *XML Schema Built-In Data Types* (continued)

Like the SQL2 and SQL3 standards, XML Schema supports user-defined data types that are derived from these built-in types or from other user-defined types. You can specify a derived data type as a restriction on another XML type. For example, here is a definition for a derived repNumType type that restricts legal employee numbers to a range from 101 to 199:

```
<simpleType name="repNumType">
  <restriction base="integer">
    <minInclusive value="101" />
    <maxExclusive value="200" />
  </restriction>
</simpleType>
```

With this data type defined, you can declare entities or attributes in a schema as having a data type of `repNumType` and the restriction is automatically implemented. XML Schema provides a rich set of data type characteristics (called *facets*) on which you can build restrictions. These include data length (for strings and binary data), inclusive and exclusive data ranges, number of digits and fractional digits (for numeric data), and explicit lists of permitted values. There is even a built-in pattern-matching capability, where data values can be restricted using a regular expression syntax like that used in the Perl scripting language.

XML Schema also gives you the ability to define complex data types, which are user-defined structures. For example, here is a definition for a complex `custAddrType` type that is comprised of familiar subelements:

```
<complexType name="custAddrType">
  <sequence>
    <element name="street" type="string" />
    <element name="city" type="string" />
    <element name="state" type="string" />
    <element name="postCode" type="integer" />
  </sequence>
</complexType>
```

You can also create a user-defined data type that is a list of data items with another type. For example, here is a definition for a complex `repListType` type, which is a list of salesperson employee numbers:

```
<simpleType name=repListType">
  <list itemType="repNumType" />
</simpleType>
```

XML Schema also allows you to overload a user-defined data type, allowing it to take on one of several different underlying data types depending on the specific need. For example, in the preceding `custAddrType` definition, the postal code portion of the address is defined as an integer. This works for US-style five-digit zip codes (except that it doesn't preserve the leading zero), but not for Canadian six-digit postal codes, which include letters and digits. A more international approach is to declare the U.S. and Canadian versions, and then a more universal postal code, which may be *any* of the types:

```
<simpleType name="usZip5Type">

  <restriction base="integer">
    <totalDigits value=5 />
```

```
    </restriction>
  </simpleType>
  <simpleType name="canPost6Type">

    <restriction base="string">
      <length value=6 />
    </restriction>
  </simpleType>
  <simpleType name="intlPostType">
    <union memberTypes="usZip5Type canPost6Type" />
  </simpleType>
```

With user-defined data type definitions in place, you can more easily define larger, more complex structures. For example, here is part of the purchase order document in Figure 25-7, expanded to include a bill-to and ship-to address, and to permit a list of sales representatives:

```
<complexType name="purchaseOrderType">
    ... other element declarations go here ...
    <element name="billAddr" type="custAddrType" />
    <element name="shipAddr" type="custAddrType" />
    <element name="repNums" type="repListType" />
    ... other element declarations continue...
```

Elements and Attributes in XML Schema

Building on its support for a rich data type structure, XML Schema also provides a rich vocabulary for specifying the legal structure of a document type and the permitted elements and attributes that comprise it. XML Schema supports the same basic element types defined in the DTD model:

- **Simple content.** The element contains only text content (although as explained in the preceding section, the text can be restricted to data of a specific type like a date or a numeric value). Content of this type is defined using a `simpleContent` element.

- **Element-only content.** The element contains only subelements. Content of this type is defined using a `complexType` element.

- **Mixed content.** The element contains a mix of subelements and its own text content. Unlike the DTD mixed-content model, XML Schema requires that the sequence of elements and text content be rigidly defined, and valid documents must conform to the defined sequence. Content of this type is defined using a `mixed` attribute on a `complexType` element.

- **Empty content**. The element contains only attributes, and no text content of its own. XML Schema treats this as a special case of element-only content, with no declared elements.

- **Any content**. The element contains any mix of content and subelements, in any order. Content of this type is defined using the XML Schema data type anyType as the data type of the element.

These basic element types can appear individually in the declarations of elements within a schema. You can also specify that an element may occur multiple times within a document, and optionally, specify a minimum and a maximum number of occurrences. XML Schema also supports SQL-style NULL values for elements, to indicate that element contents are unknown. The XML terminology is nil values, but the concept is the same. This capability simplifies mapping of data between XML document elements and database columns that can contain NULL values.

XML Schema lets you define a logical group of elements that are typically used together, and give the element group a name. Subsequent element declarations can then include the entire named group of elements as a unit. Grouped elements also provide additional flexibility for element structure. The group can specify a *sequence* of elements, which must all be present, in the specified order. Alternatively, it can specify a *choice* of elements, indicating that only one of a set of defined element types must appear.

XML Schema provides similar control over attributes. You can specify an individual attribute as optional or required. You can specify a default attribute value, to be used if an explicit value is not provided in the document instance, or a fixed attribute value, which forces the attribute to *always* have the specified value in an instance document. Attribute groups allow you to define and name a group of attributes that are typically used together. The entire group of attributes can be declared for an element in a schema simply by naming the attribute group.

Finally, XML Schema provides extensive support for XML *namespaces,* which are used to store and manage different XML *vocabularies*—that is, different collections of data type definitions and data structure declarations that are used for different purposes. In a large organization, it will be useful to define standardized XML representations for common basic business objects, such as an address, a product number, or a customer-id, and collect these in a common repository. Higher-level XML declarations for documents such as purchase orders, vacation time requests, payment authorization forms, and the like will also be useful, but should typically be collected together in groups based on shared usage.

XML namespaces support these capabilities by allowing you to collect together related XML definitions and declarations, store them in a file, and identify them by name. An XML schema for a new type of document can then draw its basic data definitions and structures from one or more namespaces by referencing the namespaces in the schema header. In fact, the standard XML vocabulary and many of the built-in data types are defined in a namespace maintained on the W3C organization web site. An Internet-style URL identifies the source file for an XML namespace.

If an XML Schema declaration incorporates definitions from more than one XML namespace, the potential for name conflict exists. The same name could easily have been chosen by the developers of two different namespaces to represent two quite different XML structures or data types. To remove the potential ambiguity, XML data types and structure definitions can be specified using *qualified* names, using a technique that closely parallels the use of qualified column names in SQL. Each namespace that is identified in a schema header can be assigned a *prefix name*, which is then used to qualify references to items within that namespace. For clarity, the prefix names have been omitted from the schema examples in this chapter. Here is a more typical schema header and excerpt from a schema body that uses prefix names and qualification to reference the main XML Schema namespace (maintained by W3C) and a corporate namespace:

```
<schema xmlns:xsd="http://www.w3.org/2001/XMLSchema"
        xmlns:corp="http://www.mycompany.com/schemas/purchasing" >
  <complexType name="purchaseOrderType">
    ... other element declarations go here ...
    <element name-="orderDate" type="xsd:date" />
    <element name="billAddr" type="corp:custAddrType" />
    <element name="shipAddr" type="corp:custAddrType" />
    <element name="repNums" type="corp:repListType" nillable="true" />
  ... other element declarations continue...
```

In this example, the corporate XML namespace is identified by the prefix corp and the main XML Schema namespace by the prefix xsd. All of the data type references are qualified by one of these prefixes, and as a result, they are unambiguous. Because qualified references can become quite cumbersome, it's also possible to specify default namespaces that minimize the need for prefixes. The complete XML Schema naming system is quite a bit more sophisticated than the capabilities outlined here, but the capabilities are clearly directed toward supporting the creation of very complex document type specifications by large groups of people.

As with DTDs, the power of XML Schema is that it allows you to specify well-defined document types against which individual document instances can be validated. All of the popular XML parsers, whether they implement the SAX API or the DOM API, provide XML Schema–based validation. You can specify the schema to which an XML document claims conformance within the XML document itself, but you can also ask a parser to validate an arbitrary XML document against an arbitrary schema.

XML and Queries

SQL provides a powerful and very useful query facility for finding, transforming, and retrieving structured data from relational databases, so it's natural to seek a similar query capability for finding, transforming, and retrieving structured data from XML documents. The earliest efforts to define a query and transformation capability were embodied in a pair of specifications—eXtensible Stylesheet Language Transformation (XSLT) and XML Path Language (XPath). Like XML itself, these specifications have their roots in document processing

XSLT focuses on transforming an XML document, as shown in Figure 25-8. A stylesheet governs the transformation, selecting which elements of the input XML document are to be transformed and dictating how they are modified and combined with other elements to produce the output XML document. One popular use for XSLT is to transform a single, generic version of a web page into various forms that are appropriate for rendering on different screen sizes and display devices.

Within the XSLT language, it is often necessary to select individual elements or groups of elements to be transformed, or to navigate through the element hierarchy to specify data to be combined from parent and child elements. XPath originally emerged as a part of the XSLT language for element selection and navigation. It quickly became apparent that XPath was useful for other applications as well, and the specification was split out of XSLT to stand on its own. In the early days of XML, XPath was the de facto query capability for XML documents.

More recently, industry attention has focused on some of the deficiencies of XPath as a full query language. A W3C working group was formed to specify a query facility under the working name XML Query, or XQuery. As the specification passed through

Figure 25-8.   *Transforming an XML document with XSLT*

various drafts, the XSL working group (responsible for XSLT and XPath) and the XQuery working groups joined forces. At this writing, both XQuery 1.0 and XPath 2.0 are in Working Draft stage, and the two languages are tightly linked, with common syntax and semantics wherever possible.

A full description of XQuery and XPath is beyond the scope of this book. Because XQuery 1.0 has only Working Draft and not Official Recommendation status, it is still subject to change as it is reviewed by the W3C membership. However, a brief review of XQuery concepts and a few examples will illustrate the relationship to SQL, and these fundamentals are unlikely to change as XQuery 1.0 moves toward official standard status.

XQuery Concepts

If the underlying data model beneath the SQL language is the row/column table, the underlying data model beneath XQuery is a tree-structured hierarchy of nodes that represent an XML document. XQuery actually uses a finer-grained tree structure than the element hierarchy of XML documents and XML Schema. These XQuery nodes are relevant for database-style queries:

- **Element node**. This type of XQuery node represents an element itself.

- **Text node**. This type of node represents element contents. It is a child of the corresponding element node.

- **Attribute node**. This type of node represents an attribute and attribute value for an element. It is a child of the corresponding element node.

- **Document node**. This is a specialized element node that represents the top, or *root* level, of a document.

To navigate through an item tree and identify one or more items for processing, XQuery uses a *path expression*. In many ways, a path expression plays the same role for XQuery as the SQL3 query expression, described in Chapter 24, plays for SQL. A path expression identifies an individual node in the XQuery item tree by specifying the sequence of steps through the tree hierarchy that is needed to reach the node. XQuery path expressions come in two types:

- **Rooted path expression**. A rooted path expression starts at the top (the root) of the item tree, and steps down through the hierarchy to reach the target node. Within the book document in Figure 25-1, the rooted path expression /bookPart/ chapter/section/para navigates down to an individual paragraph within a section of a chapter.

- **Relative path expression**. A relative path expression starts the current node of the item tree (the node where processing is currently focused) and steps up and/or down through the hierarchy to reach the target node. Within the book document in Figure 25-1, the relative path expression section/para navigates down to a specific paragraph if the current node is a chapter node.

The steps within a path can specify motion downward within the node tree to child nodes that represent subelements, element contents, or element attributes. The steps can also specify upward motion to the parent of a node. With each step, you can specify a *node test* that must be passed to continue on the path to the target element. Table 25-2 shows some typical path expressions and the navigation path that they specify.

Path Expression	Navigation
section/para	Move down to a child section element, and down from there to a child para element.
/book/part/chapter	Start at the top of the hierarchy, and move down through book, then part children, to a chapter child.
..	Move up from the current node to its parent.
../chapter	Move up to the parent of the current node, then down to a chapter child node.
.//para	Select any child para node that appears anywhere below the current node in the hierarchy.
@hdrLevel	Select the hdrLevel attribute of the current node.
/header@hdrLevel	Select the hdrLevel attribute of a child header node.
para[3]	Select the third child element with a para type.
*	Select all children of the current node.
*/para	Select all para grandchildren of the current node.
chapter[@revStatus="draft"]	Select all chapter children of the current node that have an attribute named status with value draft.

Table 25-2. *Some Typical XQuery Path Expressions*

Like SQL, XQuery is a set-oriented language. It is optimized to work on an XQuery *sequence*, an ordered collection of zero or more items. The items themselves might be elements, attributes, or data values. XQuery operations tend to take sequences as their input and produce sequences as their output. A simple atomic data item is usually treated as if it were a one-item sequence.

XQuery also resembles SQL in being a strongly typed language. The working draft of the XQuery specification is evolving to align the XQuery data types with those specified in XML Schema, which were described earlier in this chapter in the "XML Schema" section. Like SQL3, XQuery provides constructors to build up more complex data values.

XQuery differs substantially from SQL in being an expression-oriented rather than a statement-oriented language. Casually stated, everything in XQuery is an expression, which is evaluated to produce a value. Path expressions are one type of XQuery expression, and they produce a sequence of nodes as their result. Other expressions may combine literal values, function calls, arithmetic and Boolean expressions, and the typical parenthesized combinations of these to form arbitrarily complex expressions. Expressions can also combine sequences of nodes, using set operations like the union or intersection of sets, which match the corresponding SQL set operations.

Named variables in XQuery are denoted by a leading dollar sign ($) in their names. For example, $orderNum, $currentOffice, and $c would be valid XQuery variable names. Variables can be used freely in XQuery expressions to combine their variables with literals and other variable values and node values. Variables receive new values through function calls, and by assignment in `for` or `let` expressions.

Query Processing in XQuery

XQuery path expressions can provide the XML equivalent of the simple SQL SELECT statement with a WHERE clause. Assume that a collection of XML documents contains the XML equivalent of the contents of the sample database, with the top-level documents named with the names of the tables in the sample database and the individual row structures named with the singular equivalents of those names (e.g., the OFFICES document contains individual OFFICE elements to represent the rows of the OFFICES table, and so on). Here are some query requests and their corresponding path expressions:

Identify the offices managed by employee number 108.

```
/offices/office[mgr=108]
```

Find all offices with sales over target.

```
/offices/office[sales > target]
```

Find all orders for manufacturer ACI with amounts over $30,000.

```
/orders/order[mfr = 'ACI' and amount > 35000.00]
```

Because the sample database is a shallow row/column structure, the XML hierarchy is only three levels deep. To illustrate the query possibilities in more hierarchical XML documents, consider once again the book document in Figure 25-1. Here are some query requests and their corresponding path expressions:

Find all components of chapters that have draft status.

```
/book/part/chapter[revStatus='draft']/*
```

Get the third paragraph of the second chapter of part 2.

```
/book/part[2]/chapter[2]/para[3]
```

These expressions don't give you the same control over query results as the SELECT list provides in SQL queries. They also don't provide the equivalent of SQL cursors for row-by-row processing. XQuery provides both of these capabilities through For/Let/Where/Returns expressions (FLWR expressions, pronounced "flower"). An example is the best way to illustrate the capability. Once again, assume a set of XML documents structured to resemble the sample database, as in the previous examples. This query implements a two-table join and generates three specific columns of query results:

List the salesperson's name, order date, and amount of all orders under $5000, sorted by amount.

```
<smallOrders> {
   for $o in document("orders.xml")//order[amount < 5000.00],
      $r in
document("salesreps.xml")//salesreps[empl_num=$o/order/rep]
   return
     <smallOrder> {
       $r/name,
       $o/order_date,
       $o/amount
     }
     </smallOrder>
   sortby(amount)
   }
</smallOrders>
```

At the outer level, the contents of the smallOrders element are specified by the XQuery expression enclosed in the outer braces. The for expression uses two variables to iterate through two documents, corresponding to the ORDERS and SALESREPS tables. These two variables effectively implement a join between the two tables (documents). The predicates at the end of each line following the for keyword correspond to the SQL WHERE clause. The predicate in the first line restricts the query to orders with amounts over $5000. The predicate in the second row implements the join, using the $o variable to link rows in the SALESREPS table (document) with rows in the ORDERS table (document).

The return part of the for expression specifies which elements should be returned as the results of the expression evaluation. It corresponds to the select list in a SQL query. The returned value will be an XML sequence of smallOrder elements, and each element comes from one corresponding element in the source tables (documents). Once again, the iteration variables are used to qualify the specific path to the element whose contents are to be returned. Finally, the sortby part of the expression functions in the same way as the corresponding ORDER BY clause of a SQL query.

There are a few additional query-processing capabilities not illustrated in this example. You can use a let expression within the for iteration to capture additional variable values within the for loop that you may need in predicates or other expressions. An if...then...else expression supports conditional execution. Aggregate functions support grouped XQuery queries, corresponding to the SQL summary queries described in Chapter 8. With these capabilities, the flexibility of XQuery is comparable to that of SQL query expressions. However, as you can see from the example, the style of the query expression is quite different, reflecting both the expression orientation and the very strong navigational orientation of XQuery and XML documents.

XML Databases

With the proliferation of XML usage and XML documents, several venture-backed startup companies have been formed to commercialize native XML databases. Typically, these databases store and model their data contents as XML documents. The actual database contents may be stored in native form as XML text, or in some parsed form such as that maintained by a DOM XML parser. Most of the XML database products currently support XPath as a core query capability, and many of them have added proprietary extensions to XPath to make it a more complete query language. They typically pledge support for XQuery as a replacement for XPath or as a second, complementary query language, as soon as the XQuery specification is finalized.

The vendors of native XML databases tend to make the same arguments in favor of their products that the object-oriented database vendors made a decade earlier. With external data increasingly represented as XML, the best match is a database that carries the same underlying data model. The choice of XML documents as a native format reduces the overhead of XML marshalling and unmarshalling, but provides the same level of individual element and attribute access and navigation. Finally, they argue that with a growing body of users trained in HTML and XML, an XML database can be more accessible to more people than SQL-based relational databases.

The native XML databases are relatively new to the market at this writing, and it is too soon to judge their eventual market success and impact. It seems likely that a native XML database may be a good match for data management needs within an XML-based web site for storing, accessing, and transforming XML documents. However, the previous history of pure object-oriented databases suggests that relational database vendors are capable of extending their core products to incorporate the most important features of new data models at a pace that is fast enough to retain their dominant market shares. It seems very likely that relational databases will remain the dominant native database type for data processing applications. But within these products, XML integration will grow tighter over time and relational products will offer more and more XML-oriented features.

Summary

This chapter described the relationships between XML and SQL, and between XML documents and the relational databases processed by each language:

- XML has its origins in printing and publishing; it was originally designed as a way to indicate and specify document contents.

- XML's document orientation produces a natural hierarchical view of data. The mismatch between XML hierarchies and SQL row/column tables is one of the biggest challenges when integrating the two technologies.

- XML documents are comprised of a hierarchy of elements. Elements can carry contents, they can have named attributes, and they can have other elements as children.

- XML integration with relational databases can take several forms, including XML query output, XML input, XML data exchange, and the storage and retrieval of XML data within the database itself.

- XML Schema, and an older standard, XML DTDs, define rigid structures for specific types of documents. They are useful to restrict document contents to a standard form acceptable for data processing applications.

- XQuery is an emerging query language for XML documents. It has some parallels to SQL, but its focus on expressions and path navigation make it quite different in style from SQL.

- Native XML databases have been introduced, and are moving to adopt XQuery as a native query language. They pose a challenge to the relational model, but major DBMS vendors are moving quickly to provide XML extensions to their relational products.

The Complete Reference

Chapter 26

The Future of SQL

SQL and SQL-based relational databases are one of the most important foundation technologies of the computer market today. From its first commercial implementation about two decades ago, SQL has grown to become *the* standard database language. In its first decade, the backing of IBM, the blessing of standards bodies, and the enthusiastic support of DBMS vendors made SQL a dominant standard for enterprise-class data management. In its second decade, the dominance of SQL extended to personal computer and workgroup environments and to new, database-driven market segments, such as data warehousing. In the early part of its third decade, SQL stands as the standard database technology for Internet-based computing. The market evidence clearly shows the importance of SQL:

- The world's second-largest software company, Oracle, has been built on the success of SQL-based relational data management, through both its flagship database servers and tools and its SQL-based enterprise applications.

- IBM, the world's largest computer company, offers its SQL-based DB2 product line as a common foundation across all of its product lines and for use on competitor's systems as well, and has expanded its commitment to SQL with the acquisition of Informix's SQL DBMS.

- Microsoft, the world's largest software company, uses SQL Server as a critical part of its strategy to penetrate the enterprise computing market with server editions of its Windows operating systems, and a key part of its .NET architecture for delivering Internet web services.

- Every significant database company offers either a SQL-based relational database product or SQL-based access to its nonrelational products.

- All of the major packaged enterprise applications (Enterprise Resource Planning (ERP), Supply Chain Management (SCM), Human Resource Management (HRM), Sales Force Automation (SFA), Customer Relationship Management (CRM), and so on) are built on SQL-based databases.

- SQL is emerging as a standard for specialized databases in applications ranging from data warehousing to mobile laptop databases to embedded applications in telecomm and data communications networks.

- SQL-based access to databases is an integral feature of Windows, available on the vast majority of personal computer systems, and it is a built-in capability of popular PC software products such as spreadsheets and report writers.

- SQL-based access to databases is a standard part of Internet application servers, required by the J2EE specification.

This chapter describes some of the most important current trends and developments in the database market, and projects the major forces acting on SQL and database management over the next several years.

Database Market Trends

Today's market for database management products exceeds $12 billion per year in products and services revenues, up from about $5 billion per year a decade ago. On several occasions over the last decade, lower year-over-year growth in the quarterly revenues of the major database vendors has led analysts to talk about a maturing database market. Each time, a wave of new products or new data management applications has returned the market to double-digit growth. Client/server architecture, ERP applications, data warehousing and business intelligence, three-tier web site architectures—each of these spurred a new wave of database technology and a new wave of SQL-based database deployments. If the history of the last two decades is any indication, database technology will continue to find new applications and generate increasing revenues for years to come. The trends shaping the market bode well for its continued health and point to a continuing tension between market maturity and consolidation on the one hand, and exciting new database capabilities and applications on the other.

Enterprise Database Market Maturity

Relational database technology has become accepted as a core enterprise data processing technology, and relational databases have been deployed by virtually all large corporations. Because of the importance of corporate databases and years of experience in using relational technology, many, if not most, large corporations have selected a single DBMS brand as an enterprisewide database standard. Once such a standard has been established and widely deployed within a company, there is strong resistance to switching brands. Even though an alternative DBMS product may offer advantages for a particular application or may pioneer a new, useful feature, an announcement by the standard vendor that such features are planned for a future release will often forestall the loss of a customer by the established vendor.

The trend to corporate database standards has tended to reinforce and strengthen the market positions of the established major DBMS vendors. The existence of large direct sales forces, established customer support relationships, and multiyear volume purchase agreements has become as important as, or more important than, technology advantage. With this market dynamic, the large established players tend to concentrate on growing their business within their existing installed base instead of attempting to take customers away from competitors. In the late 1990s, industry analysts saw and predicted this tendency at both Informix and Sybase. Oracle, with a much larger share of the market, was forced to aggressively compete for new accounts in its attempt to maintain its database license revenue growth. Microsoft, as the upstart in the enterprise database market, was cast in the role of challenger, attempting to leverage its position in workgroup databases into enterprise-level prototypes and pilot projects as a way to pry enterprise business away from the established players.

One important impact of the trend to corporate DBMS vendor standardization has been a consolidation in the database industry. New startup database vendors tend to pioneer new database technology and grow by selling it to early adopters. These early adopters have helped to shape the technology and identified the solution areas where it can deliver real benefits. After a few years, when the advantages of the new technology have been demonstrated, the startup vendors are acquired by large established players. These vendors can bring the new technology into their installed base, and bring their marketing and sales muscle to bear in an attempt to win business in their competitor's accounts. The early 1990s saw this cycle play out with database vendor acquisitions of database tools vendors. In the late 1990s, the same cycle applied to mergers and acquisitions of database vendors. Informix's purchase of Illustra (a pioneering object-relational vendor), Red Brick (a pioneering data warehousing vendor), and Cloudscape (a pioneering pure Java database vendor) are three examples of the pattern. Just a few years later, Informix itself was acquired by IBM, continuing this particular chain of consolidation.

Market Diversity and Segmentation

Despite the maturing of some parts of the database market (especially the market for corporate enterprise-class database systems), it continues to develop new segments and niches that appear and then grow rapidly. For much of the 1990s, the most useful way to segment the database market has been based on database size and scale—there were PC databases, minicomputer databases, mainframe databases, and later, workgroup databases. Today's database market is much more diverse and is more accurately segmented based on target application and specialized database capabilities to address unique application requirements. Market segments that have appeared and have experienced high growth include:

- Data warehousing databases, focused on managing thousands of gigabytes of data, such as historical retail purchase data.

- Online analytic processing (OLAP) and relational online analytic processing (ROLAP) databases, focused on carrying out complex analyses of data to discover underlying trends (data mining), allowing organizations to make better business decisions.

- Mobile databases, in support of mobile workers such as salespeople, support personnel, field service people, consultants, and mobile professionals. Often, these mobile databases are tied back to a centralized database for synchronization.

- Embedded databases, which are an integral, transparent part of an application sold by an independent software vendor (ISV) or a value-added reseller (VAR). These databases are characterized by small footprints and very simple administration.

- Microdatabases, designed for appliance-type devices, such as smart cards, network computers, smart phones, and handheld PCs and organizers.

- In-memory databases, designed for ultra-high-performance OLTP applications, such as those embedded in telecomm and data communications networks and used to support customer interaction in very high-volume Internet applications.

- Clustered databases, designed to take advantage of powerful, low-cost servers used in parallel to perform database management tasks with high scalability and reliability.

Packaged Enterprise Applications

A decade or two ago, the vast majority of corporate applications were developed in-house by the company's information systems department. Decisions about database technology and vendor standardization were part of the company's IS architecture planning function. Leading-edge companies sometimes took a risk on new, relatively unproven database technologies in the belief that they could gain competitive advantage by using them. Sybase's rise to prominence in the financial services sector during the late 1980s and early 1990s is an example.

Today, most corporations have shifted from *make* to *buy* strategies for major enterprisewide applications. Examples include ERP applications, SCM applications, HRM applications, SFA applications, CRM applications, and others. All of these areas are now supplied as enterprise-class packaged applications, along with consulting, customization, and installation services, by groups of software vendors. Several of these vendors have reached multihundred-million-dollar annual revenues. All of these packages are built on a foundation of SQL-based relational databases.

The emergence of dominant purchased enterprise applications has had a significant effect on the dynamics of the database market. The major enterprise software package vendors have tended to support DBMS products from only two or three of the major DBMS vendors. For example, if a customer chooses to deploy SAP as its enterprisewide ERP application, the underlying database is restricted to those supported by the SAP packages. This has tended to reinforce the dominant position of the current top-tier enterprise database players and make it more difficult for newer database vendors. It has also tended to lower average database prices, as the DBMS is viewed more as a component part of an application-driven decision rather than a strategic decision in its own right.

The emergence of packaged enterprise software has also shifted the relative power of corporate IS organizations and the packaged software vendors. The DBMS vendors today have marketing and business development teams focused on the major enterprise application vendors to ensure that the latest versions of the applications support their DBMS and to support performance tuning and other activities. The largest independent DBMS vendor, Oracle Corporation, is playing both roles, supplying both DBMS software and major enterprise applications (that run on the Oracle DBMS, of course). Oracle's single-vendor approach has created some considerable tension between Oracle and the largest enterprise applications vendors, especially in the ranks of their field sales organizations. Some industry analysts attribute the growing DBMS market share of IBM and Microsoft to a tendency for enterprise application vendors to steer prospective customers away from Oracle's DBMS products as a result.

Hardware Performance Gains

One of the most important contributors to the rise of SQL has been a dramatic increase in the performance of relational databases. Part of this performance increase was due to advances in database technology and query optimization. However, most of the DBMS performance improvement came from gains in the raw processing power of the underlying computer systems, and changed in the DBMS software designed to capitalize on those gains. While the performance of mainframe systems steadily increased, the most dramatic performance gains have been in the UNIX-based and Windows-based server markets, where processing power has doubled or more year by year.

Some of the most dramatic advances in server performance come from the growth of symmetric multiprocessing (SMP) systems, where two, four, eight, or even dozens of processors operate in parallel, sharing the processing workload. A multiprocessor architecture can be applied to OLTP applications, where the workload consists of many small, parallel database transactions. Traditional OLTP vendors, such as Tandem, have always used a multiprocessor architecture, and the largest mainframe systems have used multiprocessor designs for more than a decade. In the 1990s, multiprocessor systems became a mainstream part of the UNIX-based server market, and somewhat later, an important factor at the high end of the PC server market.

With Intel's introduction of multiprocessor chipsets, SMP systems featuring two-way and four-way multiprocessing achieved near-commodity status in the LAN server market, and were available for well under $10,000. In the midrange of the UNIX-based server market, database servers from Sun, Hewlett-Packard, and IBM routinely have 8 or 16 processors and sell in the hundred-thousand-dollar price range. High-end UNIX servers today can be configured with more than 100 processors and tens of gigabytes of main memory. These systems, which rival the computing power of traditional mainframes, carry multimillion-dollar price tags.

SMP systems also provided performance benefits in decision support and data analysis applications. As SMP servers became more common, the DBMS vendors invested in parallel versions of their systems that were able to take the work of a single complex SQL query and split it into multiple, parallel paths of execution. When a DBMS with parallel query capabilities is installed on a four-way or eight-way SMP system, a query that might have taken two hours on a single-processor system can be completed in less than an hour. Companies are taking advantage of this hardware-based performance boost in two ways: either by obtaining business analysis results in a fraction of the time previously required or by leaving the timeframe constant and carrying out much more complex and sophisticated analysis.

Operating system support for new hardware features (such as multiprocessor architectures) has often lagged the availability of the hardware capabilities—often by several quarters or even years. This has posed a special dilemma for DBMS vendors, who need to decide whether to bypass the operating system in an attempt to improve database performance. The Sybase DBMS, for example, when originally introduced, operated as a single process and took responsibility for its own task management, event handling, and input/output—functions that are usually handled by an operating system such as UNIX or VMS. In the short term, this gave Sybase a major performance advantage over rival DBMS products with less parallel processing capability.

But when operating system SMP support arrived, many of its benefits were automatically available to rival systems that had relied on the operating system for task management, while Sybase had the continuing burden of extending and enhancing its low-level performance-oriented software. This cycle has played out for SMP designs, with major database vendors now relying on operating systems for thread support and SMP scaling. But the same trade-offs continue to apply to new hardware features as they appear and require explicit strategic decisions on the part of the DBMS vendors.

Today, the quest for higher and higher database performance certainly shows no signs of stopping. With today's highest-performance servers featuring hundreds of multigigahertz processors, hardware advances have more than overcome the higher overhead of the relational data model, giving it performance equal to, or better than, the best nonrelational databases of the past. At the same time, of course, the demand for higher and higher transaction rates against larger and larger databases continues to grow. At the top end of the database market, it appears that one can never have too much database performance.

Database Server Appliances

Another hardware-based market trend in the 1980s and early 1990s was the emergence of companies that combined high-performance microprocessors, fast disk drives, and multiprocessor architectures to build dedicated systems that were optimized as database servers. These vendors argued that they could deliver much better database performance with a specially designed database engine than with a general-purpose computer system. In some cases, their systems included application-specific integrated circuits (ASICs) that implement some of the DBMS logic in hardware for maximum speed. Dedicated database systems from companies such as Teradata and Sharebase (formerly Britton-Lee) found some acceptance in applications that involve complex queries against very large databases. However, they have not become an important part of the mainstream database market, and these vendors eventually disappeared or were acquired by larger, general-purpose computer companies.

Interestingly, the notion of a packaged, all-in-one database server appliance was briefly rekindled at the end of the 1990s by Oracle Corporation and its CEO, Larry Ellison. Ellison argued that the Internet era had seen the success of other all-in-one products, such as networking equipment and web cache servers. Oracle announced partnerships with several server hardware vendors to build Oracle-based database appliances. Over time, however, these efforts had little market impact, and Oracle's enthusiasm for database appliances faded from media attention.

Several venture-backed startups have recently embraced the idea of database server appliances once again, this time in the form of database caching servers that reside in a network between the application and an enterprise database. These startups point to the widespread success of web page caching within the Internet architecture, and posit a similar opportunity for data caching. Unlike web pages, however, database contents tend to have an inherent transactional character, which makes the synchronization of cache contents with the main database both much more important (to insure that requests satisfied by the database cache come up with the right response) and much more difficult. Whether the notion of a database caching appliance will catch on or not remains an open question as of this writing.

Benchmark Wars

As SQL-based relational databases have moved into the mainstream of enterprise data processing, database performance has become a critical factor in DBMS selection. User focus on database performance, coupled with the DBMS vendors' interest in selling high-priced, high-margin, high-end DBMS configurations, has produced a series of benchmark wars among DBMS vendors. Virtually all of the DBMS vendors have joined the fray at some point over the last decade. Some have focused on maximum absolute database performance. Others emphasize price/performance and the cost-effectiveness of their DBMS solution. Still others emphasize performance for specific types of database processing, such as OLTP or OLAP. In every case, the vendors tout benchmarks that show the superior performance of their products while trying to discredit the benchmarks of competitors.

The early benchmark claims focused on vendor-proprietary tests, and then on two early vendor-independent benchmarks that emerged. The Debit/Credit benchmark simulated simple accounting transactions. The TP1 benchmark, first defined by Tandem, measured basic OLTP performance. These simple standardized benchmarks were still easy for the vendors to manipulate to produce results that cast them in the most favorable light.

In an attempt to bring more stability and meaning to the benchmark data, several vendors and database consultants banded together to produce standardized database benchmarks that would allow meaningful comparisons among various DBMS products. This group, called the Transaction Processing Council, defined a series of official OLTP benchmarks, known as TPC-A, TPC-B, and TPC-C. The Council has also assumed a role as a clearinghouse for validating and publishing the results of benchmarks run on various brands of DBMS and computer systems. The results of TPC benchmarks are usually expressed in transactions per minute (e.g., tpmC), but it's common to hear the results referred to simply by the benchmark name (e.g., "DBMS Brand X on hardware Y delivered 10,000 TPC-Cs").

The most recent TPC OLTP benchmark, TPC-C, attempts to measure not just raw database server performance, but the overall performance of a client/server configuration. Modern multiprocessor workgroup-level servers are delivering thousands or tens of thousands of transactions per minute on the TPC-C test. Enterprise-class UNIX-based SMP servers are delivering multiple tens of thousands of tpmC. The maximum results on typical commercially available systems (a multimillion-dollar 64-bit Alpha processor cluster) exceed 100,000 tpmC.

The Transaction Processing Council has branched out beyond OLTP to develop benchmarks for other areas of database performance. The TPC-D benchmark focuses on data warehousing applications. The suite of tests that comprise TPC-D are based on a database schema typical of warehousing environments, and they include more complex data analysis queries, rather than the simple database operations more typical of OLTP environments. Interestingly, the TPC benchmarks specify that the size of the database must increase as the claimed number of transactions per minute goes up. A TPC benchmark result of 5000 tpmC may reflect results on a database of hundreds of megabytes of data, for example, while a result of 20,000 tpmC on the same benchmark may reflect a test on a multigigabyte database. This provision of the TPC benchmarks is designed to add more realism to the benchmark results since the size of database and computer system needed to support an application with demands in the 5000 tpm range is typically much smaller than the scale required to support an application with 20,000 tpm demands.

In addition to raw performance, the TPC benchmarks also measure database price/ performance. The price used in the calculation is specified by the council as the five-year ownership cost of the database solution, including the purchase price of the computer system, the purchase price of the database software, five years of maintenance and support costs, and so on. The price/performance measure is expressed in dollar-per-TPC (e.g., "Oracle on a Dell four-way server broke through the $500-per- TPC-C barrier"). While higher numbers are better for transactions-per-minute results, lower numbers are better for price/performance measures.

Over the last several years, vendor emphasis on TPC benchmark results have waxed and waned. The existence of the TPC benchmarks, and the requirement that published TPC results be audited, have added a level of integrity and stability to benchmark claims. It appears that benchmarking and performance testing will be part of the database market environment for some time to come. In general, benchmark results can help with matching database and hardware configurations to the rough requirements of an application. On an absolute basis, small advantages in benchmark performance for one DBMS over another will probably be masked by other factors.

SQL Standardization

The adoption of an official ANSI/ISO SQL standard was one of the major factors that secured SQL's place as the standard relational database language in the 1980s. Compliance with the ANSI/ISO standard has become a checkoff item for evaluating DBMS products, so each DBMS vendor claims that its product is compatible with or based on the ANSI/ISO standard. Through the late 1980s and early 1990s, all of the popular DBMS products evolved to conform to the parts of the standard that represented common usage. Other parts, such as the module language, were effectively ignored. This produced slow convergence around a core SQL language in popular DBMS products.

As discussed in Chapter 3, the SQL1 standard was relatively weak, with many omissions and areas that are left as implementation choices. For several years, the standards committee worked on an expanded SQL2 standard that remedies these weaknesses and significantly extends the SQL language. Unlike the first SQL standard, which specified features that were already available in most SQL products, the SQL2 standard, when it was published in 1992, was an attempt to lead rather than follow the market. It specified features and functions that were not yet widely implemented in current DBMS products, such as scroll cursors, standardized system catalogs, much broader use of subqueries, and a new error message scheme. DBMS vendors are still in the process of evolving their products to support the full features of SQL2. In practice, proprietary extensions (such as enhanced support for multimedia data or stored procedures or object extensions) have often been more important to a DBMS vendor's success than higher levels of SQL2 compliance.

The progress of the SQL standards groups continued, with work on a SQL3 standard begun even before the SQL2 standard was published. As delays set in and the number of different areas to be addressed by the next standard grew, the work on SQL3 was divided into separate, parallel efforts, focused on the core of the language, a Call-Level Interface (CLI), persistent stored modules (stored procedures), distributed transaction capabilities, time-based data, and so fourth. Some of these efforts were published a few years later as enhancements to the 1992 SQL2 standard. A SQL2-compatible CLI standard was released in 1995, as SQL-CLI. A year later, in 1996, a standardized stored procedure capability was released as SQL-PLM. In 1998, object language bindings for SQL were standardized in the SQL-OLB specification. A basic set of OLAP capabilities were published in a SQL-OLAP standard in 2000.

While progress continued on these additions to the SQL2 standard, the work on the core language part of SQL3 (called the *foundation* part of the standard) focused on how to add object capabilities to SQL2. This quickly became a very controversial activity. Relational database theorists and purists took a strong stand against many of the proposed extensions. They claimed that the proposals confuse conceptual and architectural issues (e.g., adding substructure beyond the row/column tables) with implementation issues (e.g., performance issues of normalized databases and multitable joins). Proponents of the proposed SQL3 object extensions pointed to the popularity of object-oriented programming and development techniques, and insist that the rigid row/column structure of relational databases must be extended to embrace object concepts or it would be bypassed by the object revolution. Their argument was bolstered in the marketplace as the major relational DBMS vendors added object-oriented extensions to their products, to blunt the offensive from pure object-oriented databases, and were largely successful with this strategy.

The controversy over the SQL3 work was finally resolved after a seven-year effort, with the publication of the SQL:1999 standard. (The term *SQL3*, which was used during the development of the standard, has now been replaced by the official term *SQL:1999*.) The SQL:1999 standard is structured in a series of parts:

- **Part 1: Framework**. Describes the overall goals and structure of the standard, and the organization of its other parts.

- **Part 2: Foundation**. Is the main body of the standard, focused on the SQL language itself. SQL statements and clauses, transaction semantics, database structure, privileges, and similar capabilities are specified here. This part also contains the object-oriented extensions to SQL.

- **Part 3: Call-Level Interface**. Contains the SQL-CLI (1995) extensions to the SQL-92 standard, updated to conform to SQL:1999.

- **Part 4: Persistent Stored Modules**. Similarly contains the SQL-PSM (1996) extensions to the SQL-92 standard, updated to conform to SQL:1999.

- **Part 5: Host Language Bindings**. Deals with the interactions between procedural host languages (such as C or COBOL) and SQL.

- **Part 9: Management of External Data**. Describes how a SQL-based database should manage data external to the database itself.

- **Part 10: Object Language Bindings**. Deals with the same issues as Part 5, but for object-oriented languages.

Some parts of the standard are still under development at this writing, as indicated by the missing part numbers. In addition, other SQL-related standardization efforts have broken off into their own, separate standards activities. A separate standard is under development for SQL-based handling of multimedia data, such as full-text documents, audio, and video content. This is itself a multipart standard; some parts have already been published. Another separate standard makes official the embedded SQL for Java work known as SQLJ.

In the progression from SQL1 to SQL2, and then to SQL:1999, the official ANSI/ISO SQL standards have ballooned in scope. The original SQL1 standard was less than 100 pages; the Framework section (Part 1) of the SQL:1999 standard alone is nearly that large. The Foundation section of the SQL:1999 standard runs well over 1000 pages, and the currently published parts, taken together, run over 2000 pages. The broadly expanded scope of the SQL:1999 standard reflects the wide usefulness and applicability of SQL, but the challenge of implementing and conforming to such a voluminous set of standards is very formidable, even for large DBMS vendors with large development staffs.

It's worth noting that the SQL:1999 standard takes a very different approach to standards conformance claims than the SQL1 and SQL2 standards. The SQL2 standard defined three levels of conformance, Entry, Intermediate, and Full, and laid out the specific features of the standard that must be implemented to claim conformance at each level. In practice, DBMS vendors found *some* features at each level to be important to their customers, and others relatively unimportant. So virtually all current SQL implementations claim some form of compliance with SQL2, but very few, if any, implement all of the features required for formal Intermediate or Full conformance.

With this experience in mind, the SQL:1999 standards group instead defined only one Core SQL level of conformance, which corresponds roughly to the Entry level of SQL2 plus selected features from the Intermediate and Full levels. Beyond this Core SQL, additional features are grouped together in *packages*, to which conformance can individually be claimed. There is a package for the SQL-CLI capabilities, one for SQL-PSM, one for enhanced data integrity functions, one for enhanced date and time functions, and so on. This structure allows individual DBMS vendors to pick and choose the areas of the standard that are most important to the particular markets they serve, and makes conformance to parts of the standard more practical.

At this writing, the SQL:1999 standard is too new to fully gauge its impact on the DBMS market. If the experience with SQL2 is any guide, vendors will carefully evaluate individual new pieces of SQL:1999 functionality and seek feedback from their customer base about which ones are useful. With the very large new functionality required by SQL:1999 features such as user-defined types and recursive queries, implementation of some parts of SQL:1999 will be a multiyear project for even the largest DBMS vendors. In practice, the SQL1 (SQL-89) standard defines the core SQL capabilities supported by virtually all products; the SQL2 (SQL-92) standard represents the current state of the art in large enterprise database products, and the SQL:1999 standard is a roadmap for future development.

In addition to the official SQL standard, IBM's and Oracle's SQL products will continue to be a powerful influence on the evolution of SQL. As the developer of SQL and a major influencer of corporate IS management, IBM's SQL decisions have always had a major impact on other vendors of SQL products. Oracle's dominant market position has given it similar clout when it has added new SQL features to its products. When the IBM, Oracle, and ANSI SQL dialects have differed in the past, most independent DBMS vendors have chosen to follow the IBM or Oracle standards.

The likely future path of SQL standardization thus appears to be a continuation of the history of the last several years. The core of the SQL language will continue to be highly standard. More features will slowly become a part of the core, and will be defined as add-on packages or new standards in their own right. Database vendors will continue to add new, proprietary features in an ongoing effort to differentiate their products and offer customers a reason to buy.

SQL in the Next Decade

Predicting the path of the database market and SQL over the next five to ten years is a risky proposition. The computer market is in the midst of a major transition into an Internet-driven era. The early stages of that era, dominated by the World Wide Web and user/browser interaction, are giving way to a ubiquitous Internet used to deliver all communication services, information services, and e-business interaction. The emergence of the PC and its creation of the client/server era of the 1980s and 1990s illustrates how shifts in the underlying computer systems market can produce major changes in data management architectures. It's likely that the Internet will have at least as large, if not a larger, impact on the data management architectures of the next ten years. Nonetheless, several trends appear to be safe predictions for the future evolution of database management. They are discussed in the final sections of this chapter.

Distributed Databases

As more and more applications are used on an enterprisewide basis or beyond, the ability of a single, centralized database to support dozens of major applications and thousands of concurrent users will continue to erode. Instead, major corporate databases will become more and more distributed, with dedicated databases supporting the major applications and functional areas of the corporation. To meet the higher service levels required of enterprisewide or Internet-based applications, data must be distributed; but to ensure the integrity of business decisions and operations, the operation of these distributed databases must be tightly coordinated.

Another strain on centralized database architectures will be the continuing growth of mobile personal computers and other mobile information appliance devices. These devices are, by their nature, more useful if they can become an integral part of a distributed network. However, by their nature, they are also *occasionally connected*— they work in a sometimes-disconnected, sometimes-connected mode, using either wired or wireless networks. The databases at the heart of mobile applications must be able to operate in this occasionally connected environment.

These trends will drive heavy demand for data distribution, database integration, data synchronization, data caching, data staging, and distributed database technology. A one-size-fits-all model of distributed data and transaction is inadequate for the highly distributed, anywhere/anytime environment that will emerge. Instead, some transactions will require absolute synchronization with a centralized master database, while others will demand support for long-duration transactions where synchronization may take hours or days. Developing ways to create and operate these distributed environments, without having them become a database administrator's nightmare, will be a major challenge for DBMS vendors in the next decade, and a major source of revenues for the vendors that provide practical, relatively easy-to-use solutions.

Massive Data Warehousing

The last few years have demonstrated that companies that use database technology aggressively and treat their data as a valuable corporate asset can gain tremendous competitive advantage. The competitive success of WalMart, for example, is widely attributed to its use of information technology (led by database technology) to track its inventory and sales on a daily basis, based on cash register transaction data. This allowed the company to minimize its inventory levels and closely manage its supplier relationships. Data mining techniques have allowed companies to discover unexpected trends and relationships based on their accumulated data—including the legendary discovery by one retailer that late-night sales of diapers were highly correlated with sales of beer.

It seems clear that companies will continue to accumulate as much information as they can on their customers, sales, inventories, prices, and other business factors. The Internet creates enormous new opportunities for this kind of information-gathering. Literally every customer or prospective customer's interaction with a company's web site, click-by-click, provides potential clues to the customer's wants, needs and behavior. That type of click-by-click information can easily generate tens of gigabytes of data or more per day on a busy web site. The databases to manage these massive quantities of data will need to support multilevel storage systems. They will need to rapidly import vast quantities of new data, and rapidly peel off large data subsets for analysis. Despite the high failure rate of data warehousing projects, the large potential payoffs in reduced operating costs and more on-target marketing and sales activities will continue to drive data warehousing growth.

Beyond the collection and warehousing of data, pressure will build to perform business analyses in real time. IS consulting groups are writing about the zero-latency enterprise or the real-time enterprise to describe an architecture in which customer interactions translate directly into changes in business plans with zero or very little delay. To meet this challenge, database systems will continue to take advantage of processor speed advances and multiprocessing technologies.

Ultra-High-Performance Databases

The emergence of an Internet-centric architecture is exposing enterprise data processing infrastructures to new peak-load demands that dwarf the workloads of just a few years ago. When databases primarily supported in-house applications used by a few dozen employees at a time, database performance issues may have produced employee frustration, but they did not really impact customers. The advent of call centers and other customer support applications produced a closer coupling between data management and customer satisfaction, but applications were still limited to at most hundreds of concurrent users (the people manning the phones in the call center).

With the Internet, the connection between a customer and the company's databases becomes a direct one. Database performance problems translate directly into slow customer response times. Database unavailability translates directly into lost sales. Furthermore, databases and other parts of the data processing infrastructure are no longer buffered from peak-load transaction rates. If a financial services firm offers online trading or portfolio management, it will need to prepare for peak-load volumes on days of heavy stock price movement that may be 10 or 20 times the average daily volume. Similarly, an online retailer must gear up to support the heaviest end-of-year selling season, not just mid-March transaction rates.

The demands of e-commerce and real-time Internet information access are already producing peak-load transaction rates from the most popular Internet services that are one or two orders of magnitude higher than the fastest conventional disk-based RDBMS systems. To cope with these demands, companies will increasingly turn to distributed and replicated databases. They will pull hot data forward and cache it closer to the customer interaction within the network. To meet peak-load demands, they will use in-memory databases. This will, in turn, require new database support for deciding which data to cache, and which levels of synchronization and replication are appropriate. At first, these issues will apply only to the largest and highest-volume sites, but just as web page caching has become an accepted and then an essential technique for maintaining adequate web browser performance, hot data caching will become a mainstream Internet data management architecture as volumes grow.

Internet and Network Services Integration

In the Internet era, database management will increasingly become just one more network service, and one that must be tightly integrated with other services, such as messaging, transaction services, and network management. In some of these areas, standards are well established, such as the XA standard for distributed transaction management. In others, standards are in their infancy or are just emerging, such as the SOAP standard for sending XML data over the Internet's HTTP protocol and the UDDI standards for finding services in a distributed network environment.

The multitier architecture that is dominating Internet-centric applications also poses new questions about which roles should be played by the database manager and by other components of the overall information system. For example, when network transactions are viewed from the point of distributed databases, a two-phase commit protocol, implemented in a proprietary way by a DBMS vendor, may provide a solution. When network transactions involve a combination of legacy applications (e.g., mainframe CICS transactions), relational database updates, and interapplication messages, the transaction management problem moves outside the database, and external mechanisms are required.

A similar trade-off surrounds the emergence of Java-based application servers as a middle-tier platform for executing business logic. Before the Internet era, stored procedures became known as the accepted DBMS technique for embedding business logic within the database itself. More recently, Java has emerged as a viable stored procedure language, an alternative to earlier, vendor-proprietary languages. Now, application servers create an alternative platform for business logic written in Java, in this case, external to the database. It's not yet clear how these two trends will be rationalized, and whether business logic will continue its migration into the database or will settle in an application server layer. Whichever trend predominates, tighter integration between database servers and application servers will be required. Several of the DBMS vendors now produce their own application servers, and it seems likely that they will provide the best integration within their own product lines. Whether this approach will prevail against a best-of-breed approach remains another open question.

Embedded Databases

Relational database technology has reached into many parts of the computer industry, from small handheld devices to large mainframes. Databases underlie nearly all enterprise-class applications as the foundation for storing and managing their information. Lightweight database technology underlies an even broader range of applications. Directory services, a foundation technology for the new era of value-added data communications network services, are a specialized form of database technology. Lightweight, very-high-performance databases also form an integral part of telecommunications networks, enabling cellular networks, advanced billing schemes, smart messaging services, and similar capabilities.

These embedded database applications have traditionally been implemented using proprietary, custom-written data management code tightly integrated with the application. This application-specific approach produced the highest possible performance, but at the expense of an inflexible, hard-to-maintain data management solution. With declining memory prices and higher-performance processors, lightweight SQL-based relational databases are now able to economically support these applications.

The advantages of a standards-based embedded database are substantial. Without a serious compromise in performance, an application can be developed in a more modular fashion, changes in database structure can be handled transparently, and new services and applications can be rapidly deployed atop existing databases. With these advantages, embedded database applications appear destined to be a new area of growth potential for SQL and relational database technology. As in so many other areas of information technology, the ultimate triumph of SQL-based databases may be that they disappear into the fabric of other products and services—invisible as a stand-alone component, but vital to the product or service that contains them.

Object Integration

The most significant unknown in the future evolution of SQL is how it will integrate with object-oriented technologies. Modern application development tools and methodologies are all based on object-oriented techniques. Two object-oriented languages, C++ and Java, dominate serious software development, for both client-side and server-side software. The core row/column principles of the relational data model and SQL, however, are rooted in a much earlier COBOL era of records and fields, not objects and methods.

The object database vendors' solution to the relational/object mismatch has been the wholesale discarding of the relational model in favor of pure object database structures. But the lack of standards, steep learning curve, lack of simple query facilities, and other disadvantages have prevented pure object databases from having any significant market success to date. The relational database vendors have responded to the object database challenge by embracing object-oriented features, but the result has been a proliferation of nonstandard, proprietary database features and SQL extensions.

It's clear that relational database technology and object technology must be more tightly integrated if relational databases are to remain an integral part of the next generation of applications. Several trends are visible today:

- Java-based interfaces to RDBMS's, such as JDBC and embedded SQL for Java, will continue to grow rapidly in popularity.

- Java will become a more important stored procedure language for implementing business logic within a RDBMS. Virtually all of the major DBMS vendors have announced plans to support Java as an alternative to their proprietary stored procedure languages.

- DBMS products will expand support for abstract, complex data types that exhibit object-oriented capabilities such as encapsulation and inheritance. Beyond high-level agreement on the need to store objects within a row/column structure, the specifics (nested tables, arrays, complex columns) vary dramatically.

- The SQL:1999 standard for object-oriented extensions to SQL will influence vendor products, but slowly, as vendors continue to seek competitive advantages and user lock-in through proprietary object-oriented extensions.

- Message-oriented interfaces, including database triggers that produce messages external to the DBMS for integration with other applications, will grow in importance, as the database becomes a more active component for integrating systems together.

- XML will emerge as an important standard format for representing both data retrieved from a SQL database, and data to be entered into or updated in a database.

- DBMS vendors will offer SQL extensions to store and retrieve XML documents, and to search and retrieve their contents.

Whether these extensions to SQL and the relational model can successfully integrate the worlds of RDBMS and objects remains to be seen. The object-oriented database vendors continue to maintain that object capabilities bolted onto an RDBMS can't provide the kind of transparent integration needed. Most of them have enthusiastically embraced XML as the newest wave of object technology. The enterprise DBMS vendors have announced and added substantial object-relational capabilities, and more recently, XML integration products and features, but it's hard to determine how many of them are actually being used. In addition, the emergence of XML as an important Internet standard has given birth to a new round of database challengers, offering native XML databases. With all of these competing alternatives, the further integration of object technologies into the world of relational databases seems certain. The specific path that this evolution will take remains the largest unknown in the future of SQL.

Summary

SQL continues to play a major role in the computer industry, and appears poised to continue as an important core technology:

- SQL-based databases are flagship software products for the three largest software vendors in the world: Microsoft, Oracle, and IBM.
- SQL-based databases operate on all classes of computer systems, from mainframes and database servers to desktop computer clients, notebook computers, and handheld PDAs.
- All of the major enterprise applications used in large organizations rely on enterprise-class SQL databases to store and structure their data.
- SQL-based databases have responded successfully to the challenges of the object model, with SQL extensions in object/relational databases.
- SQL-based databases are responding to the needs of Internet-based architectures by incorporating XML and integrating with application servers.

The
Complete
Reference

SQL

Part VII

Appendixes

Appendix A

The Sample Database

M ost of the examples in this book are based on the sample database described in this appendix. The sample database contains data that supports a simple order processing application for a small distribution company. It consists of five tables:

- **CUSTOMERS**. Contains one row for each of the company's customers.

- **SALESREPS**. Contains one row for each of the company's ten salespeople.

- **OFFICES**. Contains one row for each of the company's five sales offices where the salespeople work.

- **PRODUCTS**. Contains one row for each type of product that is available for sale.

- **ORDERS**. Contains one row for each order placed by a customer. For simplicity, each order is assumed to be for a single product.

Figure A-1 graphically shows the five tables, the columns that they contain, and the parent/child relationships among them. The primary key of each table is shaded. The five tables in the sample database can be created using the CREATE TABLE statements shown here:

```
CREATE TABLE CUSTOMERS
    (CUST_NUM INTEGER NOT NULL,
      COMPANY VARCHAR(20) NOT NULL,
     CUST_REP INTEGER,
CREDIT_LIMIT MONEY,
 PRIMARY KEY (CUST_NUM),
 FOREIGN KEY HASREP (CUST_REP)
  REFERENCES SALESREPS
    ON DELETE SET NULL)

CREATE TABLE OFFICES
     (OFFICE INTEGER NOT NULL,
        CITY VARCHAR(15) NOT NULL,
      REGION VARCHAR(10) NOT NULL,
         MGR INTEGER,
      TARGET MONEY,
       SALES MONEY NOT NULL,
 PRIMARY KEY (OFFICE),
 FOREIGN KEY HASMGR (MGR)
  REFERENCES SALESREPS
    ON DELETE SET NULL)
```

```
CREATE TABLE SALESREPS
    (EMPL_NUM INTEGER NOT NULL,
         NAME VARCHAR(15) NOT NULL,
          AGE INTEGER,
   REP_OFFICE INTEGER,
        TITLE VARCHAR(10),
    HIRE_DATE DATE NOT NULL,
      MANAGER INTEGER,
        QUOTA MONEY,
        SALES MONEY NOT NULL,
  PRIMARY KEY (EMPL_NUM),
  FOREIGN KEY (MANAGER)
   REFERENCES SALESREPS
   ON DELETE SET NULL,
  FOREIGN KEY WORKSIN (REP_OFFICE)
   REFERENCES OFFICES
   ON DELETE SET NULL)

CREATE TABLE ORDERS
   (ORDER_NUM INTEGER NOT NULL,
   ORDER_DATE DATE NOT NULL,
         CUST INTEGER NOT NULL,
          REP INTEGER,
          MFR CHAR(3) NOT NULL,
      PRODUCT CHAR(5) NOT NULL,
          QTY INTEGER NOT NULL,
       AMOUNT MONEY NOT NULL,
  PRIMARY KEY (ORDER_NUM),
  FOREIGN KEY PLACEDBY (CUST)
   REFERENCES CUSTOMERS
   ON DELETE CASCADE,
  FOREIGN KEY TAKENBY (REP)
   REFERENCES SALESREPS
   ON DELETE SET NULL,
  FOREIGN KEY ISFOR (MFR, PRODUCT)
   REFERENCES PRODUCTS
   ON DELETE RESTRICT)
```

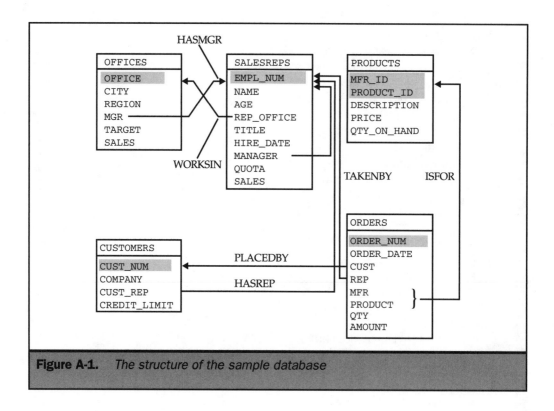

Figure A-1. *The structure of the sample database*

```
CREATE TABLE PRODUCTS
     (MFR_ID CHAR(3) NOT NULL,
  PRODUCT_ID CHAR(5) NOT NULL,
 DESCRIPTION VARCHAR(20) NOT NULL,
       PRICE MONEY NOT NULL,
QTY_ON_HAND INTEGER NOT NULL,
PRIMARY KEY (MFR_ID, PRODUCT_ID))
```

Figures A-2 through A-6 show the contents of each of the five tables in the sample database. The query results in examples throughout the book are based on the data shown in these figures.

CUST_NUM	COMPANY	CUST_REP	CREDIT_LIMIT
2111	JCP Inc.	103	$50,000.00
2102	First Corp.	101	$65,000.00
2103	Acme Mfg.	105	$50,000.00
2123	Carter & Sons	102	$40,000.00
2107	Ace International	110	$35,000.00
2115	Smithson Corp.	101	$20,000.00
2101	Jones Mfg.	106	$65,000.00
2112	Zetacorp	108	$50,000.00
2121	QMA Assoc.	103	$45,000.00
2114	Orion Corp.	102	$20,000.00
2124	Peter Brothers	107	$40,000.00
2108	Holm & Landis	109	$55,000.00
2117	J.P. Sinclair	106	$35,000.00
2122	Three-Way Lines	105	$30,000.00
2120	Rico Enterprises	102	$50,000.00
2106	Fred Lewis Corp.	102	$65,000.00
2119	Solomon Inc.	109	$25,000.00
2118	Midwest Systems	108	$60,000.00
2113	Ian & Schmidt	104	$20,000.00
2109	Chen Associates	103	$25,000.00
2105	AAA Investments	101	$45,000.00

Figure A-2. *The CUSTOMERS table*

EMPL_NUM	NAME	AGE	REP_OFFICE	TITLE	HIRE_DATE	MANAGER	QUOTA	SALES
105	Bill Adams	37	13	Sales Rep	12-FEB-88	104	$350,000.00	$367,911.00
109	Mary Jones	31	11	Sales Rep	12-OCT-89	106	$300,000.00	$392,725.00
102	Sue Smith	48	21	Sales Rep	10-DEC-86	108	$350,000.00	$474,050.00
106	Sam Clark	52	11	VP Sales	14-JUN-88	NULL	$275,000.00	$299,912.00
104	Bob Smith	33	12	Sales Mgr	19-MAY-87	106	$200,000.00	$142,594.00
101	Dan Roberts	45	12	Sales Rep	20-OCT-86	104	$300,000.00	$305,673.00
110	Tom Snyder	41	NULL	Sales Rep	13-JAN-90	101	NULL	$75,985.00
108	Larry Fitch	62	21	Sales Mgr	12-OCT-89	106	$350,000.00	$361,865.00
103	Paul Cruz	29	12	Sales Rep	01-MAR-87	104	$275,000.00	$286,775.00
107	Nancy Angelli	49	22	Sales Rep	14-NOV-88	108	$300,000.00	$186,042.00

Figure A-3. *The SALESREPS table*

OFFICE	CITY	REGION	MGR	TARGET	SALES
22	Denver	Western	108	$300,000.00	$186,042.00
11	New York	Eastern	106	$575,000.00	$692,637.00
12	Chicago	Eastern	104	$800,000.00	$735,042.00
13	Atlanta	Eastern	105	$350,000.00	$367,911.00
21	Los Angeles	Western	108	$725,000.00	$835,915.00

Figure A-4. *The OFFICES table*

ORDER_NUM	ORDER_DATE	CUST	REP	MFR	PRODUCT	QTY	AMOUNT
112961	17-DEC-89	2117	106	REI	2A44L	7	$31,500.00
113012	11-JAN-90	2111	105	ACI	41003	35	$3,745.00
112989	03-JAN-90	2101	106	FEA	114X	6	$1,458.00
113051	10-FEB-90	2118	108	QSA	XK47	4	$1,420.00
112968	12-OCT-89	2102	101	ACI	41004	34	$3,978.00
113036	30-JAN-90	2107	110	ACI	4100Z	9	$22,500.00
113045	02-FEB-90	2112	108	REI	2A44R	10	$45,000.00
112963	17-DEC-89	2103	105	ACI	41004	28	$3,276.00
113013	14-JAN-90	2118	108	BIC	41003	1	$652.00
113058	23-FEB-90	2108	109	FEA	112	10	$1,480.00
112997	08-JAN-90	2124	107	BIC	41003	1	$652.00
112983	27-DEC-89	2103	105	ACI	41004	6	$702.00
113024	20-JAN-90	2114	108	QSA	XK47	20	$7,100.00
113062	24-FEB-90	2124	107	FEA	114	10	$2,430.00
112979	12-OCT-89	2114	102	ACI	4100Z	6	$15,000.00
113027	22-JAN-90	2103	105	ACI	41002	54	$4,104.00
113007	08-JAN-90	2112	108	IMM	773C	3	$2,925.00
113069	02-MAR-90	2109	107	IMM	775C	22	$31,350.00
113034	29-JAN-90	2107	110	REI	2A45C	8	$632.00
112992	04-NOV-89	2118	108	ACI	41002	10	$760.00
112975	12-OCT-89	2111	103	REI	2A44G	6	$2,100.00
113055	15-FEB-90	2108	101	ACI	4100X	6	$150.00
113048	10-FEB-90	2120	102	IMM	779C	2	$3,750.00
112993	04-JAN-89	2106	102	REI	2A45C	24	$1,896.00
113065	27-FEB-90	2106	102	QSA	XK47	6	$2,130.00
113003	25-JAN-90	2108	109	IMM	779C	3	$5,625.00
113049	10-FEB-90	2118	108	QSA	XK47	2	$776.00
112987	31-DEC-89	2103	105	ACI	4100Y	11	$27,500.00
113057	18-FEB-90	2111	103	ACI	4100X	24	$600.00
113042	02-FEB-90	2113	101	REI	2A44R	5	$22,500.00

Figure A-5. *The ORDERS table*

MFR_ID	PRODUCT_ID	DESCRIPTION	PRICE	QTY_ON_HAND
REI	2A45C	Ratchet Link	$79.00	210
ACI	4100Y	Widget Remover	$2,750.00	25
QSA	XK47	Reducer	$355.00	38
BIC	41672	Plate	$180.00	0
IMM	779C	900-lb Brace	$1,875.00	9
ACI	41003	Size 3 Widget	$107.00	207
ACI	41004	Size 4 Widget	$117.00	139
BIC	41003	Handle	$652.00	3
IMM	887P	Brace Pin	$250.00	24
QSA	XK48	Reducer	$134.00	203
REI	2A44L	Left Hinge	$4,500.00	12
FEA	112	Housing	$148.00	115
IMM	887H	Brace Holder	$54.00	223
BIC	41089	Retainer	$225.00	78
ACI	41001	Size 1 Widget	$55.00	277
IMM	775C	500-lb Brace	$1,425.00	5
ACI	4100Z	Widget Installer	$2,500.00	28
QSA	XK48A	Reducer	$177.00	37
ACI	41002	Size 2 Widget	$76.00	167
REI	2A44R	Right Hinge	$4,500.00	12
IMM	773C	300-lb Brace	$975.00	28
ACI	4100X	Widget Adjuster	$25.00	37
FEA	114	Motor Mount	$243.00	15
IMM	887X	Brace Retainer	$475.00	32
REI	2A44G	Hinge Pin	$350.00	14

Figure A-6.   *The PRODUCTS table*

Appendix B

Database Vendor Profiles

The database systems vendors profiled in this appendix have been selected because of their unique positions within the broader database industry. They include the providers of the leading enterprise-class DBMS products, some smaller companies that are leaders in new technology areas, pioneers in newer segments of the database market, and vendors that focus on embeddable database technology. Any compilation like this cannot possibly be exhaustive, and the omission of a company does not mean that its products or capabilities are inferior to those of the vendors profiled here. Collectively, these companies and their profiles as presented, illustrate the landscape of today's multibillion-dollar database software and services market. The vendors are:

- A2i, Inc.
- Arbor Software (now Hyperion Solutions Corporation)
- Birdstep Technology
- Computer Associates (Jasmine, Ingres)
- Computer Corporation of America (Model 204)
- Empress Software
- eXcelon (ObjectStore, XIS)
- Gupta Technologies (SQLBase)
- Hewlett-Packard (NonStop SQL)
- IBM Corporation (DB2, Informix, Cloudscape)
- Informix Software (now part of IBM)
- Microsoft Corporation (SQL Server)
- MySQL AB
- Objectivity
- Oracle Corporation (Oracle, Rdb/VMS)
- Persistence Software
- Pervasive Software
- PointBase
- PostgreSQL
- Quadbase Systems
- Red Brick Systems (now part of Informix Software)
- Sybase, Inc.
- TimesTen Performance Software
- Versant Corporation

A2i, Inc. (www.a2i.com)

Founded in 1993, A2i develops and markets an integrated, database-driven, cross-media catalog publishing system that centralizes the management of catalog data, simplifies the catalog production process, and completely automates the catalog production workflow. The system includes tools for creating, designing, and publishing both printed and electronic catalogs; supports single source cross-media publishing to paper, CD-ROM, and the Web; and efficiently manages catalogs containing from hundreds to millions of items.

All of A2i's software products layer on top of a SQL-based DBMS. They include performance accelerators that improve catalog access by a factor of 10 to 1000 times that of SQL alone, and feature additional catalog-specific functionality that supports interactive browsing and sorting of large databases in ways that would otherwise be impossible using a traditional SQL-based DBMS alone. A2i's parametric search technology—an alternative to DBMS-style query forms that is intuitive, easy to use, and very, very fast—allows a user to search an entire catalog and locate any item or group of items in a matter of seconds, narrowing down from thousands or millions of items to one or several with just a few mouse clicks.

Arbor Software (www.hyperion.com)

Arbor was one of the early leaders in the development of Online Analytic Processing (OLAP) databases and tools. Arbor's flagship Essbase OLAP server was first introduced in 1992 and pioneered many of the capabilities that have now become commonplace in analytic systems. Large corporations typically use the Essbase product suite to create integrated reporting, analysis, and planning systems.

Current versions of the Essbase product support both client/server and web-based analytic processing and reporting. They also support both precalculated data (a hallmark of most OLAP systems) and dynamic, on-the-fly calculations. Another major enhancement of the Essbase product is distributed OLAP capability, which allows OLAP databases to be partitioned across computer networks. Essbase supports both its own proprietary multidimensional database formats and integrates with conventional relational databases. The latest version, marketed under the brand name Essbase XTD, is positioned as a business intelligence platform, and runs across a number of different operating systems.

In 1998, Arbor merged with Hyperion Solutions Corporation to create a $500 million company (annual revenue) focused on business reporting and analysis. The product line has grown to include a substantial business in integration products and customization services. It spans applications from single-user analysis on Windows workstations to enterprisewide web-based OLAP deployments for hundreds of users.

Birdstep Technology (www.birdstep.com)

Birdstep Technology is a Norwegian software company focused on wirelessly connected systems and embedded solutions. Birdstep entered the database business with its September 2001 acquisition of Raima Corporation. Raima, founded in 1982, was an early database vendor focused on the IBM PC database market. Its initial db_VISTA product was first released in 1984. It has been steadily enhanced over the years and combined with an object manager to create the Raima Database Manager (RDM) product, now marketed by Birdstep.

A newer Raima product, the Velocis Database Server, was first shipped in 1993. Velocis is a SQL-based relational database system with an ODBC interface. It is designed as an embeddable database, and the company targets it to professional application developers—independent software vendors (ISVs) and value-added resellers (VARs) who use it as a bundled database foundation. Velocis runs on Windows, Windows NT, OS/2, and many UNIX-based operating system variants.

A distinctive feature of the Velocis server is its explicit support for network data model's embedded pointers within a SQL-based database. A CREATE JOIN statement specifies an explicit relationship, implemented with network database-style pointers, which are stored within the database structure. These can then be exploited with SQL syntax, delivering very fast performance. Velocis supports C/C++, Java, Visual Basic, Delphi, and Perl language interfaces as well as the industry-standard ODBC interface.

Birdstep sells the Velocis product as a server edition of the Raima Data Engine. A complementary Mobile Edition is tuned for use in mobile devices with wireless connectivity. A third edition is focused on embedded applications.

Computer Associates (www.cai.com)

Computer Associates (CA) is one of the world's largest independent software companies. Initially focused on mainframe software, the company has steadily expanded its focus to provide an extensive line of software products and services for enterprise data processing. Computer Associates has been built largely through acquisition, taking advantage of its large direct sales force and well-established relationships with senior Fortune 500 information systems executives. Through its acquisitions, it has steadily added more products to its portfolio.

Ingres, one of the earliest relational database systems to appear on the market, is now a product of Computer Associates. It was originally developed at the University of California at Berkeley as a research project under the direction of Professor Michael Stonebreaker. The research project became the foundation of an independent company, which eventually changed its name to Ingres Corporation in the 1980s. Ingres and its native QUEL query language were an early competitor to SQL, which was backed by rival Oracle Corporation. Although most analysts gave Ingres clear claim to technical leadership, Oracle's aggressive marketing and sales efforts, coupled with IBM's backing of SQL, eventually led to SQL dominance in the market. Eventually, Ingres was adapted to support SQL, which emerged as the dominant standard. In the 1990s, Ingres was sold to the ASK Group, and eventually to Computer Associates.

The current version of the product, Advantage Ingres Enterprise Relational Database, is a comprehensive relational database management product suite. The core Ingres/DBMS is augmented by a capability that links the DBMS to the Web. The product includes standards-based ODBC access, a sophisticated distributed data manager, and built-in XML support. It runs on major UNIX server platforms and Windows server versions.

Computer Associates also offers Jasmine Object Database, a new object-oriented DBMS. Although touted as a complete DBMS solution with a modern object-oriented architecture, two major areas of focus for Jasmine are multimedia and Internet applications. The core DBMS is heavily object-oriented, featuring multiple inheritance, instance and class methods and properties, and set-level methods. Methods for the Jasmine object-oriented DBMS can be written in C, C++, or Java. Jasmine includes an extensive class library with support for multimedia data types (images, animation sequences, audio, video, rich text, page layouts). CA is clearly positioning Jasmine as a new-generation, pure object-oriented database. It is not positioned as having object/relational capabilities, and it does not offer any SQL access to its own data management capabilities. CA does tout Jasmine's integration with back-end relational databases (Oracle, Sybase, Informix, SQL Server, DB2) and mainframe files (VSAM and CA-IDMS). The linkage to an Ingres back-end is especially close, with tightly integrated transaction management, security, and replication management capabilities.

Computer Corporation of America (www.cca-int.com)

Computer Corporation of America (CCA) is one of the pioneering software companies, and has been involved in data management since its founding in 1965. It develops and sells one of the earliest DBMS systems: Model 204. The product has been substantially enhanced over the years, but the focus continues to be on mainframe systems.

Model 204 features an ANSI-compliant SQL interface, even though the underlying structure is a network database architecture. The network structure is manifested in Model 204's embedded table capability—essentially a table-within-a-table structure. Although network databases fell out of favor with the advent of SQL and the relational model, some of the same capabilities provided by the network systems are now appearing in highly touted new object-relational systems. The nested table structure offered by Model 204 is an example of such a capability, which appears in object-relational systems from Informix and in Oracle's flagship Oracle8 object-oriented extensions.

The current version of Model 204 includes multiprocessing and parallel query options for data warehousing applications. Over the years, its indexing structures have become quite sophisticated and now include bitmap, hashing, B-tree, and record list schemes. Another unique feature of Model 204 is support for iterative queries—queries that are carried out against the results of previous queries. SQL-based access to mainframe Model 204 databases is available through CCA's Connect* product, which offers ODBC and OLE-DB APIs for remote database access from Windows and UNIX-based client workstations.

CCA also provides System 1032, a high-performance database product for the OpenVMS operating system (the successor to Digital Equipment's popular VAX/VMS from the 1980s and 1990s). System 1032 focuses on high-performance query applications. Although not originally a relational database, it now offers access via ODBC and SQL.

Empress Software (www.empress.com)

Empress Software produces an ANSI SQL relational database system for embedded applications. The company was founded in 1979 in Toronto, Canada, and currently is headquartered outside Washington, DC. The Empress DBMS offers both an ODBC callable API and Embedded SQL interfaces. It also offers a low-level set of database access calls that come in below the SQL access layer. These calls provide direct access to the Empress storage manager layer for very high performance record insert, update, delete, and retrieve operations.

The Empress DBMS runs on many different UNIX-based systems, including several UNIX operating system variants that run on Intel processor-based systems. It also supports Windows, Windows NT, and a range of real-time operating systems typically used for embedded applications. It offers a rich collection of data types, plus user-definable functions and procedures. For Internet-based applications, Empress also offers script language interfaces for the popular Perl and Tcl/Tk scripting languages.

eXcelon (www.exln.com)

eXcelon was founded as Object Design, one of the early object database vendors in 1988 in Burlington, Massachusetts. The initial version of its ObjectStore object database system was shipped in 1990. The ObjectStore database can be used either as a stand-alone object-oriented database (OODB) or as a caching solution, providing fast, object-oriented access to data that has been pulled forward from a back-end relational database such as Oracle or DB2.

In the late 1990s, as the market momentum of the object-oriented databases stalled, Object Design invested in an XML database product, named eXcelon, and eventually renamed itself after this product in February 2000. After roughly a year, the company moved to reassure its installed base of ObjectStore customers by re-creating an Object Design division, responsible for the ObjectStore product line, which remains a major product of the company today. In May 2001, eXcelon again moved to broaden its offerings through a merger with C-bridge, a professional services company. Today, its products include the original ObjectStore OODB; an XML database named XIS; a caching product focused on application server data caching named Javlin; and professional services for solutions development and deployment based on these technologies.

Gupta Technologies (www.guptaworldwide.com)

Gupta Technologies was founded by a former manager of Oracle's microcomputer division, Umang Gupta. The company's initial focus was a DBMS and database development tools for PCs and PC local area networks. Renamed Centura Software in the late 1990s, the company has returned to its original name, and now focuses on embedded database software and development tools, primarily targeting independent software vendors and value-added resellers.

SQLBase, the company's flagship DBMS product, has evolved considerably since its origins as a stand-alone and client/server database for IBM PCs under MS-DOS. It has grown to support Windows NT and NetWare as database servers. Centura currently targets SQLBase for applications on PCs and sub-PC devices such as handheld PCs, RISC-based information appliances (e.g., smart phones), and even smart cards. It features a small footprint, zero-maintenance operation, and a scalable architecture. ODBC 3.0 and JDBC interfaces are provided. Companion products complement the core SQLBase offering with software development tools, report writing, mainframe database connectivity, and similar capabilities.

Hewlett Packard (www.hp.com)

Hewlett-Packard's NonStop SQL database products are a result of its merger with Compaq in 2002. Several years earlier, in 1997, Compaq (at the time a vendor of Intel-architecture PCs and servers) acquired Tandem Computers, an early leader in the market for fault-tolerant minicomputer systems. Many Tandem systems are used by financial services and transportation companies for use in online transaction processing applications that demand 24/7 nonstop operation. For example, Tandem systems run many of the major banks' ATM networks and many of the leading stock exchanges. Tandem's older systems ran the proprietary TXP operating system, and fault-tolerant applications are generally written in the proprietary Tandem Application Language (TAL). More recent Tandem systems are based on UNIX operating systems.

Database management for nonstop applications on Tandem systems has been provided for many years by a SQL-based Tandem-developed RDBMS, called NonStop SQL. Because of Tandem's heavy OLTP emphasis, NonStop SQL has pioneered several special techniques, such as disk mirroring. It also takes advantage of the inherent Tandem multiprocessor architecture and provides distributed database capabilities. The programmatic interface to NonStop SQL is through embedded SQL.

During the 1980s and early 1990s, virtually every minicomputer vendor had its own proprietary SQL-based implementation (Digital with Rdb/VMS, Hewlett-Packard with Allbase/SQL, Data General with DG-SQL, and so on). Over the years, all of the other systems vendors have concluded that the high cost of maintaining their own RDBMS with competitive features was prohibitive. They also had difficulty managing the dual roles of competing with the independent DBMS vendors (such as Oracle) and also working with them as ISV partners on their platforms. As a result, Hewlett-Packard (via its acquisition of the former Tandem product line) is the only remaining major system vendor (except for IBM) with its own proprietary SQL-based RDBMS.

NonStop SQL is still an important product for the Tandem customer base. It ships in two versions. NonStop SQL MP is a distributed, highly parallel database system, designed to run on systems with 2 to over 4000 processors. NonStop SQL MX is a version of NonStop SQL extended with object-relational capabilities.

IBM Corporation (www.ibm.com)

IBM, the largest computer company in the world, is also among the largest software vendors in the world. IBM researchers pioneered the relational database concept, invented the SQL language, and produced the first relational database prototype—System/R—in the 1970s. Over the next two decades, IBM's flagship relational database—DB2—for its mainframe systems, pioneered several relational capabilities that have since found their way into mainstream RDBMS products and into generations of SQL standards. During this same time, relational database technology proliferated onto other IBM computer system platforms, including time-sharing mainframes, minicomputers, UNIX-based workstations and servers, and personal computers. In the late 1990s, IBM moved aggressively to bring all of these IBM data management products under a single umbrella (using the DB2-Universal Database name), and to offer its DB2 relational database technology on non-IBM platforms from other leading UNIX system vendors.

In addition to its own database development, IBM expanded its database reach substantially with its 2001 acquisition of the database-related businesses of Informix Software. Informix had been a UNIX-based DBMS pioneer, with its internally developed flagship Informix product. Informix had also been an aggressive acquirer of other database companies and technologies, including object-relational database pioneer Illustra (1996), data warehousing pioneer Red Brick (1998), database vendor Ardent Software (1999), and Java database pioneer Cloudscape (1999). Many of these database products survive as part of IBM's data management software product line.

Today, DB2-Universal Database is a comprehensive, enterprise-class, SQL-based relational database system. DB2 implementations run on a very broad range of platforms, from desktop personal computers to the largest IBM mainframe clusters. DB2 can be characterized as a quite complete and comprehensive SQL implementation, especially in areas that have been traditional IBM strongholds, such as high availability, reliability, maintainability, and worldwide support (international character set). Adjunct products and tools support software development, distributed database capabilities, data warehousing, data replication and distribution, and most other major areas of database activity. Although IBM has made its products available on non-IBM platforms, the vast majority of IBM DB2 installations are on IBM computer systems and are sold as part of integrated IBM-based enterprise systems, and the core strength of DB2 is on IBM mainframe systems.

The pioneering object-relational DBMS, Illustra, survives in IBM's product line as the Informix Dynamic Server, and retains a significant market share on UNIX-based systems. The Cloudscape product is available from IBM, distinguished as a 100 percent Java database especially tuned for mobile computing applications. Red Brick data warehouse provides a specialized business intelligence server, but its functions overlap considerably with BI and OLAP tools in the DB2 product line. UniVerse is focused on client/server and web-based data management, with low management overhead, but also has considerable overlap with other IBM products. Finally, it's worth noting that IMS (a non-SQL, hierarchical database whose origins predate the relational model) remains a very significant IBM data management product, with ongoing development.

Informix Software (See IBM Corporation)

Informix was one of the original leaders in the UNIX-based relational database market. The company's first relational DBMS was implemented on UNIX-based microcomputer systems in the early 1980s, and was known for its efficiency and compactness. In 1985, Informix was rewritten as a SQL-based DBMS and introduced as Informix-SQL. It was subsequently ported to a wide range of systems, from IBM PCs under MS-DOS to Amdahl mainframes running UNIX. Informix was also one of the first database vendors to expand its product offerings beyond the core database engine to include development tools. Its Informix-4GL product family supports the development of forms-based interactive applications.

In the early 1990s, Informix expanded its product line into the office automation area, including among other products, a database-integrated spreadsheet named Wingz. This effort was not very successful against Microsoft's office suite juggernaut, and Informix refocused on its core database capabilities. One of its flagship products during the mid-1990s was Informix Parallel Server, the technology leader in so-called parallel query technology. Parallel Server splits the processing of a single complex query into multiple, parallel operations, which can take advantage of symmetric multiprocessing (SMP) servers. Later, Informix established a leadership position in object-relational technology through the acquisition of Illustra. Illustra was a venture-backed database software firm, led by Michael Stonebreaker (the same Berkeley professor who had led the development of Ingres years before). A side-effect of the Illustra acquisition was a proliferation of product lines and development teams within Informix, adding to some confusion among Informix customers.

As the enterprise database market turned into a three-horse race in the late 1990s, Informix found itself a much smaller competitor than the "Big 3" (Oracle, IBM, and Microsoft). Informix resources were also split between its original data management business and an emerging and faster-growing business in enterprise data integration tools. Informix sold the database part of its business to IBM in April 2001, for more than $1 billion. The data integration part of the business was renamed Ascential Software, and continues with a focus in that market.

Microsoft Corporation (www.microsoft.com)

Microsoft Corporation, the world's largest personal computer software company, is also a major vendor in the SQL-based database market. Microsoft's first foray into database products came in 1987 and began as a defensive move. With the announcement of OS/2 Extended Edition, IBM tried to establish built-in database management and data communications as key components of an enterprise-class PC operating system. In 1988, Microsoft responded with SQL Server, a version of the Sybase DBMS ported to OS/2. Although Microsoft later abandoned OS/2 in favor of its own Windows NT operating system, SQL Server continued as its flagship DBMS. Today, SQL Server is a major product in the workgroup database segment, and Microsoft is aggressively moving to establish it as an enterprise-class DBMS competing with Oracle and DB2.

Expanding on its early experience with SQL Server, Microsoft moved on several other fronts to expand its role as a database vendor. In the early 1990s, Microsoft acquired Foxbase Corporation, developer of the Foxbase DBMS. Foxbase had established itself as a very successful clone of dBASE, the most popular and widely used PC database product. Through the acquisition, Microsoft moved to challenge Borland International, which had acquired the rights to dBASE shortly before.

While the Foxbase acquisition was focused more on the PC-installed base and the relatively mature market for character-based, flat file PC databases, Microsoft's internal development focused on the new, growing market for graphical lightweight relational PC databases. After several false starts and abandoned development prototypes, the result product, Microsoft Access, was introduced. Microsoft Access continues today as both a stand-alone lightweight database product and a front-end for SQL-based production databases.

Microsoft also moved aggressively to enable Windows as a database access and database development platform. Its first major move in this area was the introduction of Open Database Connectivity (ODBC), a SQL-based API for database access. Microsoft built ODBC capability into Windows and successfully lobbied the SQL Access Group, a database vendor association, to adopt it as a callable database API standard. This early version of ODBC eventually made its way into the formal ISO standards as the SQL Call-Level Interface (CLI). Microsoft has continued to evolve ODBC and expand its capabilities.

Microsoft has also layered other database access APIs on top of ODBC. The first such step was to incorporate database access into Microsoft's Object Linking and Embedding (OLE) framework for linking applications together. The OLE/DB portion of the OLE suite provided source-independent data access, and relied on ODBC as its underlying architecture for working with relational databases. Later, with the recasting of OLE into the ActiveX component framework, another layer was added to the database access hierarchy. The Active Data Objects (ADO) set of components provide data access within Microsoft's Component Object Model (COM) architecture. Again, the ADO capabilities are layered on top of ODBC for relational database access.

Paralleling the evolution of the Windows database access capability, Microsoft has steadily expanded and enhanced the capabilities of SQL Server. SQL Server 7, introduced in 1998, represented a major step forward. SQL Server 2000 continued this trend, and came with a parallel marketing push to establish it as an enterprise-class database product. SQL Server features have grown to include an integrated OLAP server and business intelligence capabilities, putting Microsoft squarely into competition with the data warehousing vendors and the warehouse-oriented database capabilities of Oracle and DB2. The high-end Enterprise Edition package provides failover clustering, multiprocessing support for up to 32-way SMP systems, and much more extensive replication services for both online and offline distributed databases, and more recently, XML support as part of Microsoft's .NET web services initiative. The debate continues over SQL Server's readiness for enterprise-class data management, but Microsoft continues to work, release by release, toward that goal.

MySQL AB (www.mysql.com)

MySQL AB is the Swedish company that publishes and distributes the most popular open source SQL database, MySQL. Founded by two Swedes and a Finn (David Axmark, Allan Larsson, and Monty Widenius), the company's mission is to "make superior data management affordable to all." The company is owned primarily by its founding partners, and is firmly devoted to the open source model. The MySQL software, including source code, is free for noncommercial use under the GNU license.

The partners have grown MySQL into a virtual company, with employees distributed around the world. The company earns its revenues from support, training, and other services associated with MySQL, and from revenue-bearing commercial licenses. Several million free copies have been downloaded. The MySQL product is distinguished by being fairly compact in size, and delivering high performance. The capabilities of the product continue to grow, with an active user base that contributes enhancements. Monty Widenius, the principal author of the original MySQL product, acts as moderator for the contributions and orchestrates the formal releases from MySQL AB.

Objectivity (www.objectivity.com)

Objectivity was one of the early object-oriented database vendors, and has steadily enhanced its Objectivity/DB OODBMS over the years. It has added fault-tolerant and data-replication capabilities to its core object database engine. Access to Objectivity/DB is provided from C++, Java, and SmallTalk.

Although Objectivity remains firmly focused on an object-oriented architecture, it has moved to provide SQL-based access to its object database engine, through both ODBC and proprietary APIs. The SQL language used through these interfaces contains many extensions to accommodate access to object database structures. Unique object-ids within the Objectivity/DB database are automatically mapped to row-ids available via the SQL interface. Object associations within the OODB are available for use as SQL join criteria. Stored procedures and triggers are presented via extended SQL features. Extended SQL syntax is also provided to access elements of arrays and nested object structures, which appear as complex columns to the SQL user. These capabilities provide the advantages of SQL-based access to many of Objectivity/DB's object-oriented capabilities, but at the expense of very nonstandard SQL syntax.

The Objectivity/DB product is focused on managing complex data across a broad range of operating environments. It is deployed in large enterprise databases providing access for hundreds of users to terabytes of data. At the other extreme, Objectivity/DB is positioned as an embeddable component for data management within real-time systems.

Oracle Corporation (www.oracle.com)

Oracle Corporation was the first DBMS vendor to offer a commercial SQL product, preceding IBM's own announcement by almost two years. During the 1980s, Oracle grew to become the largest independent DBMS vendor. Today, it is the dominant enterprise DBMS competitor, selling its products through an aggressive direct sales force and through a variety of other channels.

The Oracle DBMS was originally implemented on Digital minicomputers, but the center of gravity of Oracle system sales shifted firmly to UNIX-based minicomputers and servers in the 1990s. One of the major advantages of Oracle is its portability. It is available on dozens of different computer systems, from Windows-based laptop computers through Sun, HP, and IBM UNIX-based systems to IBM mainframes. Using Oracle's networking software, many of these Oracle implementations can participate in a distributed network of Oracle systems. With these capabilities, Oracle has targeted enterprisewide database deployments and has been effective in leveraging its market leadership into a position as an IS-imposed corporatewide database standard in many organizations.

The Oracle DBMS was originally based on IBM's System/R prototype, and has remained generally compatible with IBM's SQL-based products. In recent years, Oracle has been aggressively marketing the OLTP performance of its DBMS, using benchmark results from multiprocessor systems to substantiate its claim as the OLTP performance leader. One round of advertisements in computer industry publications touted a breakthrough level of 100,000 TPC-C transactions per minute on a high-end cluster of SMP 64-bit Digital Alpha servers.

Oracle has consistently combined good technology with an aggressive sales force and high-profile marketing campaigns (including the high-profile presence of its flamboyant CEO and founder, Larry Ellison). It has expanded its product line to include not only DBMS software and database development and management tools, but also enterprise applications software for financial and business management applications. Oracle's core server products also include an application server for implementing multitier Internet applications.

Oracle also acquired the Rdb relational database from Digital Equipment Corporation, picking up a large installed base of Digital users that it is converting to its Oracle products. Consulting services and recurring maintenance revenues have also become a major part of its revenue. It has also announced that it will make several of its products available on an outsourced basis, effectively allowing customers to use them on a fee-for-services basis. Today, DBMS licensing revenues account for less than half of Oracle's annual revenues, but enterprise-class data management remains at the heart of the company's business.

Oracle8 and Oracle8i, introduced in 1998 and 1999, respectively, and Oracle 9i, introduced in late 2000, represented major steps forward in the evolution of the Oracle DBMS. They feature extensive object-relational capabilities, including abstract data types, object structures (such as nested tables, arrays, and sequences), Java APIs (both embedded SQL for Java and a JDBC callable API), and specialized capabilities for high-performance OLTP on SMP systems and data warehousing. To accommodate a broad range of systems, low-end DBMS capability continues to be provided by an Oracle Light product for notebook systems. Oracle 9i is specifically focused on integration of the Oracle DBMS with Internet technologies, such as web and application servers. In addition, marketing for Oracle9i has placed a strong focus on reliability and scalability, with claims of being unbreakable.

Oracle considers its major competitor to be Microsoft, and it embraces a network-centric enterprise computing architecture to combat Microsoft's PC-centric view. In the Oracle view, a centralized database system is the critical data store for all information within an organization, which should be accessible anytime and anywhere via the Internet. Easier central control and administration provided by this architecture are key selling points for Oracle to enterprise IS organizations.

Oracle is also aggressively pursuing a one-vendor approach to enterprise IT shops. With the introduction of the Oracle applications suites in the 1990s, Oracle became a competitor to enterprise application vendors like SAP, BAAN, and PeopleSoft. The addition of the Oracle application server put Oracle into competition with BEA and Sun's application server, as well as IBM's WebSphere. With its suite of application, database, and middleware products, Oracle's message to corporate IT organizations is that the best way to deliver applications to their company is with an all-Oracle approach.

Persistence Software (www.persistence.com)

Persistence Software was initially focused on software that bridged the gap between object-oriented development and messaging technologies (including object request brokers) and relational database technology. Its middleware products supported object-based data management structures and requests, and mapped them into relational databases stored in the major RDBMS systems. One of the primary target markets for Persistence products has been the financial services market.

Over time, Persistence enhanced its products and repositioned them as a transactional application server. The company's PowerTier server family includes versions designed to support C++ development or Java (via Enterprise JavaBeans). One of the major features of the PowerTier servers is in-memory caching of objects. Other capabilities of the servers include object transaction isolation and object triggers. The servers continue to offer database independence, integrating with the mainstream enterprise database engines of Oracle, Informix, Sybase, and Microsoft. Application development in C++, Java, and Visual Basic is supported.

More recently, Persistence has repurposed its caching technology and packaged it into two different products. Persistence Dynamai is a dynamic caching product designed to speed web browsing by caching dynamically generated web pages. Persistence EdgeXtend is a data cache for application servers, designed to speed their operation in database-intensive applications. It works with BEA WebLogic and IBM WebSphere.

Pervasive Software (www.pervasive.com)

Pervasive Software traces its roots back to the earliest days of personal computer databases. The storage manager that underlies the Pervasive products, Btrieve, was initially developed as a PC-based database for MS-DOS systems in the early 1980s. SoftCraft, the company that developed Btrieve, was acquired in 1987 by Novell, the vendor of the leading network operating system at the time (NetWare). As a result, Btrieve became a more tightly integrated part of the NetWare OS. Layered capabilities, including NetWare SQL, were developed as layers on top of the Btrieve storage manager.

In 1994, Novell decided to refocus on its core network operating system capabilities, and its database technologies were spun out into a new company, which was renamed Pervasive Software in 1996. Pervasive's focus is on cost-effective SQL-based databases for use by ISVs and VARs. Packaged software for accounting, inventory control, order processing, and similar functions use it as an underlying bundled database manager. These products are typically sold to small and medium-sized businesses, and to departments of big companies.

Pervasive's current product, Pervasive SQL, combines their Scalable SQL and Btrieve products. The emphasis is on features important to the small/medium business market. These include low database administration, scalability to support business volumes, a small DBMS footprint, and the capability to handle reasonable data volumes at low cost. Overwhelmingly, Pervasive SQL is used by an ISV or VAR and delivered as a bundled component of their software product, often invisible to the end-user.

PointBase (www.pointbase.com)

PointBase is the developer and marketer of the PointBase DBMS, a 100 percent Java SQL-based database. The company was founded in 1998 by Bruce Scott, who had already had a very successful career in the database business. In 1997, Scott was one of the founders of Oracle Corporation, involved in creating the first several major releases of Oracle. In 1984, he cofounded his second successful database company, Gupta Technologies, with its SQLBase product.

The PointBase products are focused on enabling mobile computing, with its special requirements—replication and synchronization of data and providing database capabilities in a very small memory footprint on the client side (e.g., in handheld devices). To serve this market, PointBase comes in three versions. A micro version provides the smallest footprint, and is appropriate for very constrained environments, such as battery-powered handheld devices. An embedded version increases the footprint for systems with a larger memory budget, but where the database is still invisibly embedded in the application. A server version provides the back-end.

PostgreSQL (www.postgresql.org)

The Postgres object-relational database traces its roots to the University of California at Berkeley, home of the pioneering Ingres relational database. From the late 1980s to the early 1990s, Professor Michael Stonebreaker and his colleagues worked on extending the relational model to include object-oriented capabilities, resulting in the Postgres prototypes. In the mid-1990s, Stonebreaker used the Postgres foundation as the basis for Illustra, a commercial object-relational product that eventually became the flagship Informix product after Illustra was sold to Informix. In parallel, a group of database experts at Berkeley continued to work on Postgres itself, adding SQL capabilities and distributing it to the research community as PostgreSQL.

With its university roots, Postgres was a natural fit for the open source movement, and began to build its own following as an open source database. PostgreSQL.org is the organization that was eventually formed to organize and coordinate PostgreSQL development. Today, it acts as distributor, support mechanism, and clearinghouse for PostgreSQL distributions, with contributions from a growing user community.

Quadbase Systems (www.quadbase.com)

Quadbase-SQL is a SQL-based client/server database system for IBM-compatible PCs. It was originally offered in the early 1990s as a DOS/Windows database with a fileserver architecture. It has since evolved into a client/server database, with support for NetWare, Windows, and Windows NT–based servers. The Quadbase

SQL implementation is ANSI SQL-92 compliant at the Entry level. It provides both Embedded SQL interfaces (for C, C++, and SmallTalk) and an ODBC callable API.

Quadbase supports a number of advanced SQL features including updateable scroll cursors and views. Its multiuser concurrency control offers the flexibility of multiple isolation levels for balancing database integrity requirements with performance concerns. Quadbase also supports read-only schemas that allow it to be used to create and access read-only databases on CD-ROMs. In recent years, the company has placed increased emphasis on its charting and reporting tools, and deemphasized its database management products.

Red Brick Systems (See IBM Corporation)

Red Brick (named after the red brick building where the company was founded in Los Gatos, California) was an early pioneer in the data warehousing market. Its founder, Ralph Kimball, remains a recognized expert in data warehousing. The company's core offering is a SQL-based DBMS that is heavily optimized for data warehousing applications.

Optimizations in the Red Brick system include high-performance data loading, with a parallel loader capability for exploiting SMP systems and high-performance data transformation, cleansing, and integrity checking. The Red Brick software also allows automatic precalculation of aggregate data values (sums, averages, minimum, and maximum values) during the table loading process.

The Red Brick DBMS also focused on a high-performance implementation of the star-schema structure often found in data warehousing applications. Its STARindex technology and associated STARjoin capability implement support for star schemas within the database structure itself. The DBMS also features adaptive bitmap indexing for rapid data selection from very large tables. SQL extensions within the RISQL language handle typical decision support query structures, such as selecting the top three or the 95th percentile of rows based on some numerical measure.

Despite its early lead in the data warehousing market and several early customer successes, Red Brick found its early momentum hard to sustain. Other, much larger database vendors, including Oracle Corporation, Sybase, IBM, and eventually Microsoft, saw data warehousing as a major market opportunity and announced (sometimes with much-delayed shipment) data warehousing capabilities for their product lines. Although its products retained acknowledged technical advantages, Red Brick saw customers decide to wait for their current DBMS vendor. The company was sold to Informix Corporation in 1998, and the Informix database management products were subsequently sold to IBM.

Sybase, Inc. (www.sybase.com)

Sybase was a hot mid-1980s DBMS startup company, funded by tens of millions of dollars in venture capital. The company's founding team and many of its early employees were alumni of other DBMS vendors, and for most of them, Sybase represented the second or third relational DBMS they had built. Sybase quite effectively positioned its product as the relational DBMS for online applications, and stressed the technical and architectural features that distinguished it from contemporary SQL-based DBMS products. These features included the following:

- A client/server architecture, with client software running on Sun and VAX workstations and IBM PCs and the server running on VAX/VMS or Sun systems

- A multithreaded server that handled its own task management and input/output for maximum efficiency

- A programmatic API, instead of the embedded SQL interface used by most other DBMS vendors at the time

- Stored procedures, triggers, and a Transact-SQL dialect that extended SQL into a complete programming language for building substantial parts of an application within the database itself

Aggressive marketing and a first-class roster of venture capital backers gained Sybase the attention of industry analysts, but it was a subsequent OEM deal with Microsoft (the leading PC software vendor) and Ashton-Tate (the leading PC database vendor) that positioned the company as an up-and-coming DBMS vendor. Renamed SQL Server, the Sybase DBMS was ported to OS/2 (at the time, both IBM's and Microsoft's strategic future PC operating system) to be marketed to computer systems vendors by Microsoft and through retail computer channels by Ashton-Tate. Sales from the alliance never met early expectations, but it propelled Sybase into the DBMS market as a serious player. Today, SQL Server (several generations later) continues to be Microsoft's strategic DBMS for Windows NT; Microsoft has split from Sybase, pursuing its own development path. Sybase remains a major DBMS vendor, but the positive impact of its formative alliance with Microsoft has long since passed.

The innovations that made the Sybase product unique in the late 1980s were eventually copied by the other DBMS vendors. Sybase's early lead cemented its leadership position in market segments that demanded high-performance OLTP, including especially financial services applications. These niches remain Sybase strongholds today. During the 1990s, Sybase expanded its product line to include development tools through a merger with PowerSoft, one of the leading DBMS tools vendors. Other mergers and acquisitions brought consulting services and other data management technologies.

Sybase's current product line has three distinct database engines, focused on three different segments of the database market:

- Sybase Adaptive Server IQ is focused on data warehousing. It features complex query optimization techniques that are claimed to improve performance by 100 times over conventional RDBMS's.

- SQL Anywhere is focused on mobile computing. It features a small footprint and integrated support for Java classes and objects as well as Java stored procedures.

- Sybase Adaptive Server Enterprise is the successor to the Sybase SQL Server products, optimized for OLTP workloads. It features flexible locking strategies and query performance improvements.

Together with the Sybase application server, other middleware products, database development tools, messaging products, and consulting services, these product lines make Sybase a multihundred-million-dollar database supplier.

TimesTen Performance Software (www.timesten.com)

TimesTen is a venture-backed database company focused on delivering ultra-high-performance in-memory database systems. The company was formed as a spinoff of a main-memory database project at Hewlett-Packard, and its underlying technology has been shipping as an embedded component of HP telecommunications systems since 1996. TimesTen's version of the technology began shipments in 1998. It features an ODBC and JDBC APIs and industry-standard SQL, and runs on Windows server operating systems, Linux, and UNIX-based servers from HP, Sun Microsystems, and IBM.

The TimesTen in-memory database is targeted at applications with high-performance requirements in telecomm/datacomm systems, high-volume Internet applications, and financial services applications. It has been deployed as a stand-alone data manager within cellular networks and datacomm applications. It has also been used as a high-performance data cache front-ending conventional disk-based RDBMS systems in Internet applications, and as a stand-alone database for stock trading and market data distribution applications

For typical OLTP applications, the TimesTen engine delivers at least ten times (1000 percent) the performance of a fully cached conventional RDBMS. TimesTen 4, the current version, supports 64-bit database addressing, allowing in-memory databases of tens of gigabytes. In addition to its RDBMS features, TimesTen offers N-way data replication capabilities for high-availability and load-sharing configurations and an event-publishing capability. The company's main-memory database products have been measured at transaction rates exceeding 10 million SQL read operations (read based on primary key) per minute.

Versant Corporation (www.versant.com)

Versant was one of the early object database vendors. Its first OODBMS product shipped in September 1990. The current version of its database product offers Java, C++, and SmallTalk interfaces. The object database engine is multisession and multithreaded, and it runs on Windows NT and UNIX platforms. One of its distinguishing characteristics is fault-tolerant capability with automatic failover.

Like all of the pure object database vendors, Versant initially presented itself as a next-generation DBMS system, rejecting the relational vendors and their systems as yesterday's technology. More recently, the company has opened its OODBMS to the relational world through the Versant SQL suite, providing SQL access and an ODBC API. The SQL facility, and a corresponding Interactive SQL utility, are available for Versant servers on Solaris, AIX, HP-UX, and Windows platforms. A caching version of the Versant product, named Versant enJin, provides an object-oriented data cache for use in conjunction with J2EE-based application servers.

The philosophy of the Versant SQL suite is to automatically present as much of the OODBMS capabilities in a relational model as possible. It automatically maps the Versant database's object schema to a corresponding SQL schema: for example, it transforms two object classes with many-to-many relationships into two base tables and an intersection table to represent relationships. SQL schema information is available through virtual SYSTABLES, SYSCOLUMNS, and SYSINDEXES catalog views. Embedded pointers within the object schema are exploited transparently to enhance query performance. In addition to the programmatic (ODBC) and interactive SQL interfaces, the SQL suite includes data loading and extraction tools to move information between the Versant OODBMS and conventional RDBMS systems.

Appendix C

SQL Syntax Reference

The ANSI/ISO SQL standard specifies the syntax of the SQL language using a formal BNF notation. Unfortunately, the standard is difficult to read and understand for several reasons. First, the standard specifies the language bottom-up rather than top-down, making it difficult to get the "big picture" of a SQL statement. Second, the standard uses unfamiliar terms (such as *table-expression* and *predicate*). Finally, the BNF in the standard is many layers deep, providing a very precise specification but masking the relatively simple structure of the SQL language.

This appendix presents a complete, simplified BNF for "standard" SQL as it is commonly implemented in the products of most DBMS vendors. Specifically:

■ The language described generally conforms to that required for entry-level conformance to the SQL2 standard, plus those intermediate-level and full-level conformance features that are commonly found in the major DBMS products.

■ The module language is omitted because it is replaced in virtually all SQL implementations by embedded SQL or a SQL API.

■ Components of the language are referred to by the common names generally used in DBMS vendor documentation, rather than by the technical names used in the standard.

The BNF in this appendix uses the following conventions:

■ SQL keywords appear in all UPPERCASE MONOSPACE characters.

■ Syntax elements are specified in *italics*.

■ The notation *element-list* indicates an *element* or a list of *elements* separated by commas.

■ Vertical bars (|) indicate a choice between two or more alternative syntax elements.

■ Square brackets ([ ]) indicate an optional syntax element enclosed within them.

■ Braces ({ }) indicate a choice among required syntax elements enclosed within them.

Data Definition Statements

These statements define the structure of a database, including its tables and views and the DBMS-specific "objects" that it contains:

```
CREATE TABLE table ( table-def-item-list )

DROP TABLE table [ drop-options ]
```

```
ALTER TABLE table alter-action

CREATE VIEW view [ ( column-list ) ]
   AS query-spec
 [ WITH CHECK OPTION ]

DROP VIEW view [ drop-options ]

CREATE db-object-type db-object-name [ db-object-spec ]

DROP db-object-type [ drop-options ]

ALTER db-object-type alter-action

GRANT { ALL PRIVILEGES | privilege-list }
   ON { table | db-object-type db-object-name }
   TO { PUBLIC | user-list }
 [ WITH GRANT OPTION ]

REVOKE { ALL PRIVILEGES | privilege-list }
   ON { table | db-object-type db-object-name }
   FROM { PUBLIC | user-list }
 [ WITH GRANT OPTION ]
```

The keywords used to specify database objects (*db-object-type*) depend on the specific DBMS. Typical "database objects" with associated privileges include TABLE, VIEW, SCHEMA, PROCEDURE, DOMAIN, INDEX, and the named storage areas maintained by the DBMS. The SQL syntax used to specify these objects is specific to the DBMS that supports them. The specific set of *alter-actions* that are supported are also DBMS-specific and object type-specific.

The language elements used in the CREATE, DROP, ALTER, GRANT, and REVOKE statements are:

Language Element   Syntax

table-def-item	*column-definition*	*table-constraint*

column-definition	column data-type
	    [DEFAULT { *literal*
		USER	NULL }]
			    [*column-constraint-list*]

Language Element Syntax

column-constraint	`[ CONSTRAINT constraint-name ]` `{ NOT NULL	uniqueness	foreign-key-ref	check-constr }` `[constraint-timing]`
table-constraint	`[ CONSTRAINT constraint-name ]` `{ uniqueness	foreign-key-constr	check-constr }` `[constraint-timing]`
uniqueness	`UNIQUE (col-list)	PRIMARY KEY (col-list)`
foreign-key-constr	`FOREIGN KEY ( col-list ) foreign-key-ref`
foreign-key-ref	`REFERENCES table [ ( col-list ) ]` `[MATCH FULL	PARTIAL]` `[ON DELETE ref-action]`
ref-action	`CASCADE	SET NULL	SET DEFAULT	NO ACTION`
check-constr	`CHECK ( search-condition )`
constraint-timing	`[INITIALLY IMMEDIATE	INITIALLY DEFERRED]` `[[NOT] DEFERRABLE]`

Privilege	`SELECT |`
	`  DELETE |`
	`  UPDATE [ ( colmn-list ) ]`
	`  INSERT [ ( colmn-list ) ]`

drop-options	`CASCADE	RESTRICT`

Basic Data Manipulation Statements

The "singleton SELECT" statement retrieves a single row of data into a set of host variables (embedded SQL) or stored procedure variables:

```
SELECT [ ALL | DISTINCT ] { select-item-list | * }
    INTO variable-list
    FROM table-ref-list
  [ WHERE search-condition ]
```

The "interactive SELECT" statement retrieves any number of rows of data in an interactive SQL session (multirow retrieval from embedded SQL or stored procedures requires cursor-based statements):

```
SELECT [ ALL | DISTINCT ] { select-item-list | * }
    INTO host-variable-list
```

```
   FROM table-ref-list
[ WHERE search-condition ]
[ GROUP BY column-ref-list ]
[ HAVING search-condition ]
[ ORDER BY sort-item-list ]
```

These statements modify the data in the database:

```
INSERT INTO table [ ( column-list ) ]
 { VALUES ( insert-item-list ) | query-expr }

DELETE FROM table [ WHERE search-condition ]

UPDATE table SET set-assignment-list [ WHERE search-condition ]
```

Transaction Processing Statements

These statements signal the end of a SQL transaction:

```
COMMIT [ WORK ]

ROLLBACK [ WORK ]
```

Cursor-Based Statements

These programmatic SQL statements support data retrieval and positioned update of data:

```
DECLARE cursor [ SCROLL ] CURSOR FOR query-expr
 [ ORDER BY sort-item-list ]
 [ FOR { READ ONLY | UPDATE [ OF column-list ] } ]

OPEN cursor

CLOSE cursor

FETCH [ [ fetch-dir ] FROM ] cursor INTO variable-list

DELETE FROM table WHERE CURRENT OF cursor

UPDATE table SET set-assignment-list WHERE CURRENT OF cursor
```

The optional fetch direction (*fetch-dir*) is specified as the following; and *row-nr* can be specified as a variable or a literal.

NEXT | PRIOR | FIRST | LAST | ABSOLUTE *row-nr* | RELATIVE *row-nr*

Query Expressions

The SQL2 standard provides a rich set of expressions for specifying queries, from simple queries to more complex query expressions that use relational database operations to combine the results of simpler queries.

The basic query specification has the form:

```
SELECT [ ALL | DISTINCT ] { select-item-list | * }
    FROM  table-ref-list
  [ WHERE  search-condition ]
  [ GROUP BY  column-ref-list ]
  [ HAVING  search-condition ]
```

The table references (*tbl-ref*) in the FROM clause can be:

■ A *simple table reference*, consisting of a (possibly qualified) *table name*.

■ A *derived table reference*, consisting of a subquery (see the text that follows) that produces a table-valued result. Not all DBMS brands allow table-valued subqueries to appear in the FROM clause.

■ A *joined table reference* (see the text that follows) that combines data from two or more tables using relational OUTER JOIN, INNER JOIN, or other join operators. Not all DBMS brands allow join specifications to appear in the FROM clause.

Joined tables are specified according to the SQL2 standard as follows; in practice, there is wide variation in the specific types of joins supported by individual DBMS brands and the syntax used to specify various join types:

Join Type	Syntax
joined-table	*inner-join* | *outer-join* | *union-join* | *cross-join* | (*joined-table*)

Join Type	Syntax
inner-join	*table-ref* [NATURAL] [INNER] JOIN *table-ref* | *table-ref* [INNER] JOIN *table-ref* [*join-spec*]
outer-join	*table-ref* [NATURAL] [LEFT|RIGHT|FULL] OUTER JOIN *table-ref* | *table-ref* [LEFT|RIGHT|FULL] OUTER JOIN *table-ref* [*join-spec*]
union-join	*table-ref* UNION JOIN *table-ref*
cross-join	*table-ref* CROSS JOIN *table-ref*
join-spec	ON *search-condition* | USING (*col-list*)

The SQL2 standard allows basic query specifications to be combined with one another using the set-oriented relational operations UNION, EXCEPT, and INTERSECT. The resulting *query-expression* provides the full relational set-processing power of the standard. Enclosed in parentheses, a query-expression becomes a subquery that can appear in various positions within SQL statements (for example, within certain search conditions in the WHERE clause).

Not all DBMS brands support all of these operations. A simplified form of the SQL2 syntax for the operations (without the details of operator precedence) is given by:

Expression	Syntax
query-expr	*Simple-table* | *joined-table* | *union-expr* | *except-expr* | *intersect-expr* | (*query-expr*)
union-expr	*query-expr* UNION [ALL] [*corresponding-spec*] *query-expr*
except-expr	*query-expr* EXCEPT [ALL] [*corresponding-spec*] *query-expr*
Intersect-expr	*query-expr* INTERSECT [ALL] [*corresponding-spec*] *query-expr*
corresponding-spec	CORRESPONDING [BY (*col-list*)]
subquery	(*query-expr*)

Search Conditions

These expressions select rows from the database for processing:

Language Element	Syntax
search-condition	*search-item* | *search-item* { AND | OR } *search-item*
search-item	[NOT] { *search-test* | (*search-condition*) }
search-test	*comparison-test* | *between-test* | *like-test* | *null-test* | *set-test* | *quantified-test* | *existence-test*
comparison-test	*expr* { = | <> | < | <= | > | >= } { *expr* | *subquery* }
between-test	*expr* [NOT] BETWEEN *expr* AND *expr*
like-test	*column-ref* [NOT] LIKE *value* [ESCAPE *value*]
null-test	*column-ref* IS [NOT] NULL
set-test	*expr* [NOT] IN { *value-list* | *subquery* }
quantified-test	*expr* { = | <> | < | <= | > | >= } [ALL | ANY | SOME] *subquery*
existence-test	EXISTS *subquery*

Expressions

These expressions are used in SQL select lists and search conditions:

Language Element	Syntax
expr	*expr-item* | *expr-item* { + | - | * | / } *expr-item*
expr-item	[+ | -] [*value* | *column-ref* | *function* | (*expr*) }
value	*literal* | USER | *host-variable* | *stored-proc-variable*
host-variable	*variable* [[INDICATOR] *variable*]
function	COUNT (*) | *distinct-fcn* | *all-fcn*
distinct-function	{ AVG | MAX | MIN | SUM | COUNT } (DISTINCT *column-ref*)
all-function	{ AVG | MAX | MIN | SUM | COUNT } ([ALL] *expr*)

Statement Elements

These elements appear in various SQL statements:

Language Element	Syntax
set-assignment	*column* = { *expr*	NULL	DEFAULT }
sort-item	{ *column-ref*	*integer* } [ASC	DESC]
insert-item	{ *value*	NULL }
select-item	*expr*
table-ref	*table* [*table-alias*]
column-ref	[{ *table*	*alias* } .] *column*

Simple Elements

The following are the basic names and constants that appear in SQL statements:

Language Element	Description
table	Table name
column	Column name
user	Database user name
variable	Host language or stored procedure variable name
literal	Number or a string literal enclosed in quotes
integer	Integer number
data-type	SQL data type
alias	SQL identifier
cursor	SQL identifier

Appendix D

SQL Call-Level Interface

For clarity, the routines are presented here with two differences from the standard. The names of the parameters of the routines are abbreviated in this appendix to make the routine headers easier to read and, in some cases, to clarify their function. In actual calls to the routines from an application program, you use the names of the application program variables to be used as input and output parameters instead of the parameter names. Also for clarity, the data types of the parameters are stated here in terms of the actual C-language data types (e.g., long, short, *char). The standard defines the parameters using defined symbolic constants (#define's in the C language) to represent these data types.

Appendix A.1 of the standard (ISO/IEC 9075-3:1995) is a C-language header file that defines symbolic constants for all of the constants and codes specified in the standard, and uses the full parameter variable names specified in the standard. The following is a summary of the routines, organized by function:

AllocHandle()	Allocates resources for environment, connection, descriptor, or statement
FreeHandle()	Frees previously allocated resources
AllocConnect()	Allocates resources for a database connection
FreeConnect()	Frees resources for a database connection
Connect()	Establishes a database connection
Disconnect()	Ends an established database connection
DataSources()	Gets a list of available SQL servers to which connection may be made
AllocEnv()	Allocates resources for a SQL environment
FreeEnv()	Frees resources for a SQL environment
SetEnvAttr()	Sets attribute value for a SQL environment
GetEnvAttr()	Retrieves attribute value for a SQL environment
AllocStmt()	Allocates resources for a SQL statement
FreeStmt()	Frees resources for a SQL statement
SetStmtAttr()	Sets descriptor area to be used for a SQL statement
GetStmtAttr()	Gets descriptor area for a SQL statement
ExecDirect()	Directly executes a SQL statement
Prepare()	Prepares a SQL statement for subsequent execution
Execute()	Executes a previously prepared SQL statement

EndTran()	Ends a SQL transaction
Cancel()	Cancels execution of a SQL statement
GetDescField()	Gets value of a descriptor field
SetDescField()	Sets value of a descriptor field
GetDescRec()	Gets values from a descriptor record
SetDescRec()	Sets values in a descriptor record
CopyDesc()	Copies descriptor area values
NumResultCols()	Determines the number of query results columns
DescribeCol()	Describes one column of query results
ColAttribute()	Gets attribute of a query results column
BindParam()	Binds program location to a parameter value
ParamData()	Processes deferred parameter values
PutData()	Provides deferred parameter value or portion of a character string value
SetCursorName()	Sets the name of a cursor
GetCursorName()	Obtains the name of a cursor
Fetch()	Fetches a row of query results
FetchScroll()	Fetches a row of query results with scrolling
GetData()	Obtains the value of a query results column
CloseCursor()	Closes an open cursor
Error()	Obtains error information
GetDiagField()	Gets value of a diagnostic record field
GetDiagRec()	Gets value of the diagnostic record
RowCount()	Gets number of rows affected by last SQL statement
GetFunctions()	Gets information about supported features of a SQL implementation
GetInfo()	Gets information about supported features of a SQL implementation
GetTypeInfo()	Gets information about supported data types

CLI Return Values

Every Call-Level Interface (CLI) routine returns a `short` value with one of the following values and meanings:

CLI Return Value	Meaning
0	Statement completed successfully
1	Successful completion with warning
	No data found (when retrieving query results)
99	Data needed (required dynamic parameter missing)
–1	Error during SQL statement execution
–2	Error—invalid handle supplied in call

General Handle Management Routines

These routines are used to allocate a handle for use by the CLI, and to free a previously allocated handle that is no longer needed. The allocation routine accepts an argument indicating which type of handle is to be allocated. In general, it may be preferable to use the routines that create and free the specific types of handles, described in their respective sections. These routines must be used to allocate and free application program descriptor handles.

```
/* Allocate a handle for use in subsequent CLI calls */
short SQLAllocHandle (
        short    hdlType,    /* IN:  integer handle type code */
        long     inHdl,      /* IN:  env or conn handle */
        long     *rtnHdl)    /* OUT: returned handle */

/* Free a handle previously allocated by SQLAllocHandle() */
short SQLFreeHandle (
        short    hdlType,    /* IN:  integer handle type code */
        long     inHdl)      /* IN:  handle to be freed */
```

SQL Environment Management Routines

These routines are used to allocate a handle for a new SQL environment, to free an environment handle when it is no longer needed, and to retrieve and set the value of attributes associated with the SQL environment.

```
/* Allocate a handle for a new SQL-environment */
short SQLAllocEnv (
       long    *envHdl)    /* OUT: returned env handle */

/* Free an environment handle previously allocated */
short SQLFreeEnv (
       long    envHdl)     /* IN:  environment handle */

/* Obtain the value of a SQL-environment attribute */
short SQLGetEnvAttr(
       long    envHdl,     /* IN:  environment handle */
       long    AttrCode,   /* IN:  integer attribute code*/
       void    *rtnVal,    /* OUT: return value */
       long    bufLen,     /* IN:  length of rtnVal buffer */
       long    *strLen)    /* OUT: length of actual data */

/* Set the value of a SQL-environment attribute */
short SQLSetEnvAttr(
       long    envHdl,     /* IN:  environment handle */
       long    AttrCode,   /* IN:  integer attribute code*/
       void    *attrVal,   /* IN:  new attribute value */
       long    *strLen)    /* IN:  length of data */
```

SQL Connection Management Routines

These routines are used to create, terminate, and manage a connection to a SQL server. They allocate and free the handles used to maintain connection status, set up and terminate connections, manage the attributes associated with a connection, and obtain a list of the SQL servers available for connection.

```
/* Allocate a handle for a new SQL-connection */
short SQLAllocConnect (
       long    envHdl,     /* IN:  environment handle */
       long    *connHdl)   /* OUT: returned connection handle */
```

APPENDIXES

```
/* Free a connection handle previously allocated */
short SQLFreeConnect (
        long    connHdl)     /* IN:  connection handle */


/* Initiate a connection to a SQL-server */
short SQLConnect(
        long    connHdl,     /* IN:  connection handle */
        char    *svrName,    /* IN:  name of target SQL-server */
        short   svrnamlen,   /* IN:  length of SQL-server name */
        char    *userName,   /* IN:  user name for connection */
        short   usrnamlen,   /* IN:  length of user name */
        char    *passwd,     /* IN:  connection password */
        short   pswlen)      /* IN:  password length */


/* Disconnect from a SQL-server */
short SQLDisconnect(
        long    connHdl)     /* IN:  connection handle */


/* Get the name(s) of accessible SQL-servers for connection */
short SQLDataSources (
        long    envHdl,      /* IN:  environment handle */
        short   direction,   /* IN:  indicates first/next rqst */
        char    *svrname,    /* OUT: buffer for server name */
        short   buflen,      /* IN:  length of server name buffer */
        short   *namlen,     /* OUT: actual length of server name */
        char    *descrip,    /* OUT: buffer for description */
        short   buf2len,     /* IN:  length of description buffer */
        short   *dsclen)     /* OUT: actual length of description */


/* Obtain the value of a SQL-connection attribute */
short SQLGetConnectAttr(
        long    connHdl,     /* IN:  connection handle */
        long    AttrCode,    /* IN:  integer attribute code*/
        void    *rtnVal,     /* OUT: return value */
        long    bufLen,      /* IN:  length of rtnVal buffer */
        long    *strLen)     /* OUT: length of actual data */


/* Set the value of a SQL-connection attribute */
short SQLSetConnectAttr(
        long    connHdl,     /* IN:  connection handle */
        long    AttrCode,    /* IN:  integer attribute code*/
        void    *attrVal,    /* IN:  new attribute value */
        long    *strLen)     /* IN:  length of data */
```

SQL Statement Management Routines

These routines are used to allocate and free the handle associated with a SQL statement, to pass SQL statement text for execution, and to request preparation and actual execution of the statement via the CLI.

```
/* Allocate a handle to manage processing of SQL statement(s) */
short SQLAllocStmt (
        long     envHdl,     /* IN:  environment handle */
        long     *stmtHdl)   /* OUT: statement handle */

/* Free a statement handle previously allocated */
short SQLFreeStmt (
        long     stmtHdl,    /* IN:  statement handle */
        long     option)     /* IN:  cursor & unbind options */

/* Bind a SQL statement parameter to a program data area */
short SQLBindParam (
        long     stmtHdl,    /* IN:  statement handle */
        short    parmnr,     /* IN:  parameter number (1,2,3...) */
        short    valtype,    /* IN:  data type of value supplied */
        short    parmtype,   /* IN:  data type of parameter */
        short    colsize,    /* IN:  column size */
        short    decdigits,  /* IN:  number of decimal digits */
        void     *value,     /* IN:  pointer to parm value buffer */
        long     *lenind)    /* IN:  ptr to length/indicator buffer */

/* Obtain the value of a SQL-statement attribute */
short SQLGetStmtAttr(
        long     stmtHdl,    /* IN:  statement handle */
        long     AttrCode,   /* IN:  integer attribute code*/
        void     *rtnVal,    /* OUT: return value */
        long     bufLen,     /* IN:  length of rtnVal buffer */
        long     *strLen)    /* OUT: length of actual data */

/* Set the value of a SQL-statement attribute */
short SQLSetStmtAttr(
        long     stmtHdl,    /* IN:  statement handle */
        long     AttrCode,   /* IN:  integer attribute code*/
        void     *attrVal,   /* IN:  new attribute value */
        long     *strLen)    /* IN:  length of data */
```

SQL Statement Execution Routines

These routines are used to pass SQL statement text to the CLI and to request SQL statement execution, either immediately or after being prepared. They also control the execution of SQL transactions and the cancellation of currently operating statements.

```
/* Pass SQL statement text and request its execution */
short SQLExecDirect (
        long    stmtHdl,      /* IN:  statement handle */
        char    *stmttext,    /* IN:  SQL statement text */
        short   textlen)      /* IN:  statement text length */

/* Prepare a SQL statement, passing it in SQL text form */
short SQLPrepare (
        long    stmtHdl,      /* IN:  statement handle */
        char    *stmttext,    /* IN:  SQL statement text */
        short   textlen)      /* IN:  statement text length */

/* Execute a previously prepared SQL statement */
short SQLExecute (
        long    stmtHdl)      /* IN:  statement handle */

/* COMMIT or ROLLBACK a SQL transaction */
short SQLEndTran (
        short   hdltype,      /* IN:  type of handle */
        long    txnHdl,       /* IN:  env, conn or stmt handle */
        short   compltype)    /* IN:  txn type (commit/rollback) */

/* Cancel a currently executing SQL statement */
short SQLCancel (
        short   stmtHdl)      /* IN:  statement handle */
```

Query Results Processing Routines

These routines are used to retrieve rows of query results and to specify the application program data areas that are to receive the returned query results.

```
/* Advance the cursor to the next row of query results */
short SQLFetch (
        long    stmtHdl)      /* IN:  statement handle */
```

```
/* Scroll the cursor up or down through the query results */
short SQLFetchScroll (
        long    stmtHdl,      /* IN:  statement handle */
        short   fetchdir,     /* IN:  direction (first/next/prev) */
        long    offset)       /* IN:  offset (number of rows) */

/* Get the data for a single column of query results */
short SQLGetData (
        long    stmtHdl,      /* IN:  statement handle */
        short   colnr,        /* IN:  column number to be retrieved */
        short   tgttype,      /* IN:  data type to return to program */
        void    *value,       /* IN:  ptr to buffer for column data */
        long    buflen,       /* IN:  length of program buffer */
        long    *lenind)      /* OUT: actual length and/or NULL ind */

/* Close a cursor to end access to query results */
short SQLCloseCursor (
        long    stmtHdl)      /* IN:  statement handle */

/* Establish a cursor name for an open cursor */
short SQLSetCursorName (
        long    stmtHdl,      /* IN:  statement handle */
        char    cursname,     /* IN:  name for cursor */
        short   namelen)      /* IN:  length of cursor name */

/* Retrieve the name of an open cursor */
short SQLGetCursorName (
        long    stmtHdl,      /* IN:  statement handle */
        char    cursname,     /* OUT: buffer for returned name */
        short   buflen,       /* IN:  length of buffer */
        short   *namlen)      /* OUT: actual length of returned name */

/* Bind a query results column to a program data area */
short SQLBindCol (
        long    stmtHdl,      /* IN:  statement handle */
        short   colnr,        /* IN:  column number to be bound */
        short   tgttype,      /* IN:  data type of program data area */
        void    value,        /* IN:  pointer to program data area */
        long    buflen,       /* IN:  length of program buffer */
        long    lenind)       /* IN:  ptr to length/indicator buffer */
```

Query Results Description Routines

These routines are used to obtain a description of the results of a query, including the number of columns of query results, the data type, and other attributes of each column.

```
/* Determine the number of result columns in a query */
short SQLNumResultCols (
        long    stmtHdl,       /* IN:  statement handle */
        short   *colcount)     /* OUT: returned number of columns */

/* Determine the characteristics of a column of query results */
short SQLDescribeCol (
        long    stmtHdl,       /* IN:  statement handle */
        short   colnr,         /* IN:  number of column to describe */
        char    *colname,      /* OUT: name of query results column */
        short   buflen,        /* IN:  length of column name buffer */
        short   *namlen,       /* OUT: actual column name length */
        short   *coltype,      /* OUT: returned column data type code */
        short   *colsize,      /* OUT: returned column data length */
        short   *decdigits,    /* OUT: returned # digits in column */
        short   *nullable)     /* OUT: can column have NULL values */

/* Obtain detailed info about a column of query results */
short SQLColAttribute (
        long    stmtHdl,       /* IN:  statement handle */
        short   colnr,         /* IN:  number of column to describe */
        short   attrcode,      /* IN:  code of attribute to retrieve */
        char    *attrinfo,     /* OUT: buffer for attribute info */
        short   buflen,        /* IN:  length of col attribute buffer */
        short   *actlen)       /* OUT: actual attribute info length */
```

Query Results Descriptor Management Routines

These routines are used to obtain a description of the results of a query using the CLI descriptor mechanism, and to manipulate the descriptors to manage the return of query results into application program data areas.

```
/* Retrieve frequently used info from a CLI descriptor */
short SQLGetDescRec (
        long    descHdl,       /* IN:  descriptor handle */
        short   recnr,         /* IN:  descriptor record number */
        char    *name,         /* OUT: name of item being described */
        short   buflen,        /* IN:  length of name buffer */
```

```
        short    *namlen,    /* OUT: actual length of returned name */
        short    *datatype,  /* OUT: data type code for item*/
        short    *subtype,   /* OUT: data type subcode for item */
        short    *length,    /* OUT: length of item */
        short    *precis,    /* OUT: precision of item, if numeric */
        short    *scale,     /* OUT: scale of item, if numeric */
        short    *nullable)  /* OUT: can item have NULL values */


/* Obtain detailed info for an item described by a CLI descriptor */
short SQLColAttribute (
        long     descHdl,   /* IN:  descriptor handle */
        short    recnr,     /* IN:  descriptor record number */
        short    attrcode,  /* IN:  code of attribute to describe */
        void     *attrinfo, /* OUT: buffer for attribute info */
        short    buflen,    /* IN:  length of col attribute buffer */
        short    *actlen)   /* OUT: actual attribute info length */

/* Set frequently used info in a CLI descriptor */
short SQLSetDescRec (
        long     descHdl,   /* IN:  descriptor handle */
        short    recnr,     /* IN:  descriptor record number */
        short    datatype,  /* IN: data type code for item*/
        short    subtype,   /* IN: data type subcode for item */
        short    length,    /* IN: length of item */
        short    precis,    /* IN: precision of item, if numeric */
        short    scale,     /* IN: scale of item, if numeric */
        void     *databuf,  /* IN: data buffer address for item */
        short    buflen,    /* IN: data buffer length */
        short    *indbuf)   /* IN: indicator buffer addr for item */

/* Set detailed info about an item described by a CLI descriptor */
short SQLColAttribute (
        long     descHdl,   /* IN:  descriptor handle */
        short    recnr,     /* IN:  descriptor record number */
        short    attrcode,  /* IN:  code of attribute to describe */
        void     *attrinfo, /* IN:  buffer with attribute info */
        short    buflen)    /* IN:  length of attribute info */

/* Copy a CLI descriptor contents into another descriptor */
short SQLCopyDesc (
        long     indscHdl,  /* IN:  source descriptor handle */
        long     outdscHdl) /* IN:  destination descriptor handle */
```

Deferred Dynamic Parameter Processing Routines

These routines are used to process deferred parameters when their values are requested by the CLI during execution of a SQL statement containing them.

```
/* Get param-tag for next required dynamic parameter */
short SQLParamData (
        long    stmtHdl,    /* IN:  stmt handle w/ dynamic params */
        void    *prmtag)    /* OUT: buffer for rtn param-tag value */

/* Obtain detailed info for an item described by a CLI descriptor */
short SQLPutData (
        long    stmtHdl,    /* IN:  stmt handle w/ dynamic params */
        void    *prmdata,   /* IN:  buffer with data for param */
        short   prmlenind)  /* IN:  param length or NULL ind */
```

Error, Status, and Diagnostic Routines

These routines are used to determine the reason for an error condition returned by the CLI, to determine the number of rows affected by successful statement execution, and to obtain detailed diagnostic information about error conditions.

```
/* Retrieve error information associated with a previous CLI call */
short SQLError (
        long    envHdl,     /* IN:  environment handle */
        long    connHdl,    /* IN:  connection handle */
        long    stmtHdl,    /* IN:  statement handle */
        char    *sqlstate,  /* OUT: five-character SQLSTATE value */
        long    *nativeerr, /* OUT: returned native error code */
        char    *msgbuf,    /* OUT: buffer for err message text */
        short   buflen,     /* IN:  length of err msg text buffer */
        short   *msglen)    /* OUT: returned actual msg length */

/* Determine number of rows affected by previous SQL statement */
short SQLRowCount (
        long    stmtHdl,    /* IN:  statement handle */
        long    *rowcnt)    /* OUT: number of rows */

/* Retrieve info from one of the CLI diagnostic error records */
short SQLGetDiagRec (
        short   hdltype,    /* IN:  handle type code */
        long    inHdl,      /* IN:  CLI handle */
```

```
        short    recnr,      /* IN:  requested err record number */
        char     *sqlstate,  /* OUT: returned 5-char SQLSTATE code */
        long     *nativeerr, /* OUT: returned native error code */
        char     *msgbuf,    /* OUT: buffer for err message text */
        short    buflen,     /* IN:  length of err msg text buffer */
        short    *msglen)    /* OUT: returned actual msg length */


/* Retrieve a field from one of the CLI diagnostic error records */
short SQLGetDiagField (
        short    hdltype,    /* IN:  handle type code */
        long     inHdl,      /* IN:  CLI handle */
        short    recnr,      /* IN:  requested err record number */
        short    diagid,     /* IN:  diagnostic field id */
        void     *diaginfo,  /* OUT: returned diagnostic info */
        short    buflen,     /* IN:  length of diag info buffer */
        short    *actlen)    /* OUT: returned actual info length */
```

CLI Implementation Information Routines

These routines return information about the specific CLI implementation, including the CLI calls, statements, and data types it supports.

```
/* Retrieve info about capabilities of a CLI implementation */
short SQLGetInfo (
        long     connHdl,    /* IN:  connection handle */
        short    infotype,   /* IN:  type of info requested */
        void     *infoval,   /* OUT: buffer for retrieved info */
        short    buflen,     /* IN:  length of info buffer */
        short    *infolen)   /* OUT: returned info actual length */


/* Determine number of rows affected by previous SQL statement */
short SQLGetFunctions (
        long     connHdl,    /* IN:  connection handle */
        short    functid,    /* IN:  function id code */
        short    *supported) /* OUT: whether function supported */


/* Determine information about supported data types */
short SQLGetTypeInfo (
        long     stmtHdl,    /* IN:  statement handle */
        short    datatype)   /* IN:  ALL TYPES or type requested */
```

CLI Parameter Value Codes

These codes are passed to or returned by the CLI as parameter values, to indicate handle types, data types, statement types, and so on.

Code	Value
Handle type codes	
SQL-environment handle	1
SQL-connection handle	2
SQL-statement handle	3
SQL-descriptor handle	4
SQL implementation data type codes	
CHARACTER	1
NUMERIC	2
DECIMAL	3
INTEGER	4
SMALLINT	5
FLOAT	6
REAL	7
DOUBLE	8
DATETIME	9
INTERVAL	10
VARCHAR	12
BIT	14
Implementation-defined	< 0
Application program language data type codes	
CHARACTER	1
NUMERIC	2
DECIMAL	3
INTEGER	4
SMALLINT	5

Code	Value
FLOAT	6
REAL	7
DOUBLE	8
Implementation-defined	< 0
DateTime subcodes for SQL data types	
DATE	1
TIME	2
TIMESTAMP	3
TIME w/ ZONE	4
TIMESTAMP w/ ZONE	5
DateTime interval codes for SQL DateTime types	
YEAR	1
MONTH	2
DAY	3
HOUR	4
MINUTE	5
SECOND	6
YEAR TO MONTH	7
DAY TO HOUR	8
DAY TO MINUTE	9
DAY TO SECOND	10
HOUR TO MINUTE	11
HOUR TO SECOND	12
MINUTE TO SECOND	13
Transaction termination codes	
COMMIT	0
ROLLBACK	1

Code	Value
FreeStmt () processing option codes	
CLOSE CURSOR	0
FREE HANDLE	1
UNBIND COLUMNS	2
UNBIND PARAMS	3
Fetch orientation codes	
NEXT	1
FIRST	2
LAST	3
PRIOR	4
ABSOLUTE	5
RELATIVE	6
GetData () data type codes	
CHARACTER	1
INTEGER	4
SMALLINT	5
REAL	7
DOUBLE	8
CLI routine codes for GetFunction () call	
AllocConnect	1
AllocEnv	2
AllocHandle	1001
AllocStmt	3
BindCol	4
BindParam	1002
Cancel	5
CloseCursor	1003

Code	Value
ColAttribute	6
Connect	7
CopyDesc	1004
DataSources	57
DescribeCol	8
Disconnect	9
EndTran	1005
Error	10
ExecDirect	11
Execute	12
Fetch	13
FetchScroll	1021
FreeConnect	14
FreeEnv	15
FreeHandle	1005
FreeStmt	16
GetConnectAttr	1007
GetCursorName	17
GetData	43
GetDescField	1008
GetDescRec	1009
GetDiagField	1010
GetDiagRec	1011
GetEnvAttr	1012
GetFunctions	44
GetInfo	45
GetStmtAttr	1014
GetTypeInfo	47

Code	Value
NumResultCols	18
ParamData	48
Prepare	19
PutData	49
RowCount	20
SetConnectAttr	1016
SetCursorName	21
SetDescField	1017
SetDescRec	1018
SetEnvAttr	1019
SetStmtAttr	1020
Concise data type codes	
CHARACTER	1
NUMERIC	2
DECIMAL	3
INTEGER	4
SMALLINT	5
FLOAT	6
REAL	7
DOUBLE	8
VARCHAR	12
BIT	14
VARBIT	15
DATE	91
TIME	92
TIMESTAMP	93
TIME W/ ZONE	94
TIMESTAMP W/ ZONE	95

Code	Value
INTERVAL YEAR	101
INTERVAL MONTH	102
INTERVAL DAY	103
INTERVAL HOUR	104
INTERVAL MINUTE	105
INTERVAL SECOND	106
INTERVAL YEAR TO MONTH	107
INTERFAL DAY TO HOUR	108
INTERVAL DAY TO MINUTE	109
INTERVAL DAY TO SECOND	110
INTERVAL HOUR TO MINUTE	111
INTERVAL HOUR TO SECOND	112
INTERVAL MINUTE TO SECOND	113

Appendix E

SQL Information Schema Standard

This appendix describes the Information Schema views specified by the SQL2 (SQL-92) standard. These views must be supported by any database system claiming Intermediate or Full conformance to the standard; they are not required for the Entry conformance level. In practice, support for the full Information Schema views is slowly making its way into enterprise DBMS products. The views make a SQL2-compliant database self-describing. By querying them, a user can determine relevant information about all of the database objects (schemas, tables, columns, views, constraints, domains, character sets, etc.) accessible to him or her.

The following table provides information about schemas, tables, and columns:

SCHEMATA   Describes all schemas owned by the current user

TABLES   Describes all tables accessible to the current user

COLUMNS   Describes all columns of those tables owned/ accessible
                to the current user

This table provides information about views:

VIEWS   Describes all views accessible to the current user

VIEW_TABLE_USAGE   Describes tables on which those views depend

VIEW_COLUMN_USAGE   Describes columns on which those views depend

This table provides information about constraints (unique, primary keys, foreign keys, check constraints, assertions):

TABLE_CONSTRAINTS   Describes all constraints on tables owned
                            by the user

REFERENTIAL_CONSTRAINTS   Describes all foreign key constraints owned
                            by the user

CHECK_CONSTRAINTS   Describes all check constraints owned by
                            the user

KEY_COLUMN_USAGE   Describes keys defined by the current user

ASSERTIONS   Describes all assertions owned by the
                            current user

CONSTRAINT_TABLE_USAGE   Describes all tables used by constraints

CONSTRAINT_COLUMN_USAGE   Describes columns used by constraints

This table provides information about privileges:

TABLE_PRIVILEGES	Describes privileges on tables
COLUMN_PRIVILEGES	Describes privileges on columns
USAGE_PRIVILEGES	Describes privileges on other database objects

This table provides information about domains:

DOMAINS	Describes domains accessible to the user
DOMAIN_CONSTRAINTS	Describes constraints that define those domains
DOMAIN_COLUMN_USAGE	Describes columns based on those domains

This table provides information about character sets:

CHARACTER_SETS	Describes character sets
COLLATIONS	Describes collating sequences
TRANSLATIONS	Describes translations between character sets

And here's information about supported programming languages:

SQL_LANGUAGES	Describes supported languages and SQL APIs

The specific contents of each Information Schema view are described on the following pages.

The SCHEMATA View

The SCHEMATA view contains one row for each schema that is owned by the current user. Its structure is shown in the following table:

Column Name	Data Type	Description
CATALOG_NAME	VARCHAR(*len*)	Name of catalog containing this schema
SCHEMA_NAME	VARCHAR(*len*)	Name of schema described by this row
SCHEMA_OWNER	VARCHAR(*len*)	Name of schema's creator

Column Name	Data Type	Description
DEFAULT_CHARACTER_ SET_CATALOG	VARCHAR(*len*)	Catalog of default character set for this schema
DEFAULT_CHARACTER_ SET_SCHEMA	VARCHAR(*len*)	Schema of default character set for this schema
DEFAULT_CHARACTER_ SET_NAME	VARCHAR(*len*)	Name of default character set for this schema

VARCHAR(*len*) is the data type for SQL identifiers; *len* is the maximum length defined by the SQL implementation.

The TABLES View

The TABLES view contains one row for each table defined in the current catalog that is accessible to the current user. Its structure is shown in the following table:

Column Name	Data Type	Description
TABLE_CATALOG	VARCHAR(*len*)	Name of catalog containing this table definition
TABLE_SCHEMA	VARCHAR(*len*)	Name of schema containing this table definition
TABLE_NAME	VARCHAR(*len*)	Name of table
TABLE_TYPE	VARCHAR(*maxlen*)	Type of table (BASE TABLE/ VIEW/GLOBAL TEMPORARY/ LOCAL TEMPORARY)

VARCHAR(*len*) is the data type for SQL identifiers; *len* is the maximum length defined by the SQL implementation.

VARCHAR(*maxlen*) is a VARCHAR data type with the largest maximum length permitted by the SQL implementation.

The COLUMNS View

The COLUMNS view contains one row for each column of each table defined in the current catalog that is accessible to the current user. Its structure is shown in the following table:

Column Name	Data Type	Description
TABLE_CATALOG	VARCHAR(*len*)	Name of catalog containing the table definition containing this column

Column Name	Data Type	Description
TABLE_SCHEMA	VARCHAR(*len*)	Name of schema containing the table definition containing this column
TABLE_NAME	VARCHAR(*len*)	Name of table containing this column
COLUMN_NAME	VARCHAR(*len*)	Name of column
ORDINAL_POSITION	INTEGER > 0	Position of column within this table
COLUMN_DEFAULT	VARCHAR(*maxlen*)	Text representation of default value for column
IS_NULLABLE	VARCHAR(*maxlen*)	Whether the column may contain NULL values (YES/NO)
DATA_TYPE	VARCHAR(*maxlen*)	SQL2 data type of column (text representation)
CHARACTER_MAXIMUM_LENGTH	INTEGER > 0	Maximum length, in characters, for variable-length columns
CHARACTER_OCTET_LENGTH	INTEGER > 0	Maximum length, in bytes, for variable-length columns
NUMERIC_PRECISION	INTEGER > 0	Precision for numeric data type columns
NUMERIC_PRECISION_RADIX	INTEGER > 0	Radix of the precision
NUMERIC_SCALE	INTEGER > 0	Scale for numeric data type columns
DATETIME_PRECISION	INTEGER > 0	Precision for DateTime data type columns
CHARACTER_SET_CATALOG	VARCHAR(*len*)	Catalog containing character set definition for this column
CHARACTER_SET_SCHEMA	VARCHAR(*len*)	Schema containing character set definition for this column
CHARACTER_SET_NAME	VARCHAR(*len*)	Name of character set for this column, if any
COLLATION_CATALOG	VARCHAR(*len*)	Catalog containing collation definition for this column

Column Name	Data Type	Description
COLLATION_SCHEMA	VARCHAR(*len*)	Schema containing collation definition for this column
COLLATION_NAME	VARCHAR(*len*)	Name of collation for this column, if any
DOMAIN_CATALOG	VARCHAR(*len*)	Catalog containing domain definition for this column
DOMAIN_SCHEMA	VARCHAR(*len*)	Schema containing domain definition for this column
DOMAIN_NAME	VARCHAR(*len*)	Name of domain for this column, if any

VARCHAR(*len*) is the data type for SQL identifiers; *len* is the maximum length defined by the SQL implementation.

VARCHAR(*maxlen*) is a VARCHAR data type with the largest maximum length permitted by the SQL implementation.

The VIEWS View

The VIEWS view contains one row for each view defined in the current catalog that is accessible to the current user. Its structure is shown in the following table:

Column Name	Data Type	Description
TABLE_CATALOG	VARCHAR(*len*)	Name of catalog containing this view definition
TABLE_SCHEMA	VARCHAR(*len*)	Name of schema containing this view definition
TABLE_NAME	VARCHAR(*len*)	Name of view
VIEW_DEFINITION	VARCHAR(*maxlen*)	Text of SQL SELECT statement defining the view
CHECK_OPTION	VARCHAR(*maxlen*)	Check option for this view (CASCADED/LOCAL/NONE)
IS_UPDATABLE	VARCHAR(*maxlen*)	Whether the view can be updated (YES/NO)

VARCHAR(*len*) is the data type for SQL identifiers; *len* is the maximum length defined by the SQL implementation.

VARCHAR(*maxlen*) is a VARCHAR data type with the largest maximum length permitted by the SQL implementation.

The `VIEW_TABLE_USAGE` View

The `VIEW_TABLE_USAGE` view contains one row for each table on which a view defined in the current catalog by the current user depends. Its structure is shown in the following table:

Column Name	Data Type	Description
VIEW_CATALOG	VARCHAR(*len*)	Name of catalog containing the view definition
VIEW_SCHEMA	VARCHAR(*len*)	Name of schema containing the view definition
VIEW_NAME	VARCHAR(*len*)	Name of view
TABLE_CATALOG	VARCHAR(*len*)	Catalog containing the definition of the table on which the view depends
TABLE_SCHEMA	VARCHAR(*len*)	Schema containing the definition of the table on which the view depends
TABLE_NAME	VARCHAR(*len*)	Name of table on which the view depends

VARCHAR(*len*) is the data type for SQL identifiers; *len* is the maximum length defined by the SQL implementation.

The `VIEW_COLUMN_USAGE` View

The `VIEW_COLUMN_USAGE` view contains one row for each column on which a view defined in the current catalog by the current user depends. Its structure is shown in the following table:

Column Name	Data Type	Description
VIEW_CATALOG	VARCHAR(*len*)	Name of catalog containing the view definition
VIEW_SCHEMA	VARCHAR(*len*)	Name of schema containing the view definition
VIEW_NAME	VARCHAR(*len*)	Name of view
TABLE_CATALOG	VARCHAR(*len*)	Catalog containing the definition of the column on which the view depends
TABLE_SCHEMA	VARCHAR(*len*)	Schema containing the definition of the column on which the view depends

Column Name	Data Type	Description
TABLE_NAME	VARCHAR(*len*)	Name of table containing the column on which the view depends
COLUMN_NAME	VARCHAR(*len*)	Name of column on which the view depends

VARCHAR(*len*) is the data type for SQL identifiers; *len* is the maximum length defined by the SQL implementation.

The TABLE_CONSTRAINTS View

The TABLE_CONSTRAINTS view contains one row for each table constraint defined for tables in the current catalog owned by the current user. Its structure is shown in the following table:

Column Name	Data Type	Description
CONSTRAINT_CATALOG	VARCHAR(*len*)	Name of catalog containing the constraint definition
CONSTRAINT_SCHEMA	VARCHAR(*len*)	Name of schema containing the constraint definition
CONSTRAINT_NAME	VARCHAR(*len*)	Name of constraint
TABLE_CATALOG	VARCHAR(*len*)	Name of catalog containing the table definition
TABLE_SCHEMA	VARCHAR(*len*)	Name of schema containing the table definition
TABLE_NAME	VARCHAR(*len*)	Name of table being constrained
CONSTRAINT_TYPE	VARCHAR(*maxlen*)	Type of constraint (UNIQUE/PRIMARY KEY/ FOREIGN KEY/CHECK)
IS_DEFERRABLE	VARCHAR(*maxlen*)	Whether the constraint is deferrable (YES/NO)
INITIALLY_DEFERRED	VARCHAR(*maxlen*)	Whether the constraint is initially deferred (YES/NO)

VARCHAR(*len*) is the data type for SQL identifiers; *len* is the maximum length defined by the SQL implementation.

VARCHAR(*maxlen*) is a VARCHAR data type with the largest maximum length permitted by the SQL implementation.

The `REFERENTIAL_CONSTRAINTS` View

The `REFERENTIAL_CONSTRAINTS` view contains one row for each referential constraint (foreign key/primary key relationship) defined for tables in the current catalog owned by the current user. Its structure is shown in the following table:

Column Name	Data Type	Description
CONSTRAINT_CATALOG	VARCHAR(*len*)	Name of catalog containing the constraint definition
CONSTRAINT_SCHEMA	VARCHAR(*len*)	Name of schema containing the constraint definition
CONSTRAINT_NAME	VARCHAR(*len*)	Name of constraint
UNIQUE_CONSTRAINT_ CATALOG	VARCHAR(*len*)	Name of catalog containing the unique or primary key constraint definition for the parent table
UNIQUE_CONSTRAINT_ SCHEMA	VARCHAR(*len*)	Name of schema containing the unique or primary key constraint definition for the parent table
UNIQUE_CONSTRAINT_ NAME	VARCHAR (*len*)	Name of unique or primary key constraint definition for the parent table
MATCH_OPTION	VARCHAR(*maxlen*)	Type of partial foreign key matching (NONE/ PARTIAL/FULL)
UPDATE_RULE	VARCHAR(*maxlen*)	Update rule for the referential constraint (CASCADE/ SET NULL/SET DEFAULT/ NO ACTION)
DELETE_RULE	VARCHAR(*maxlen*)	Delete rule for referential constraint (CASCADE/ SET NULL/SET DEFAULT/ NO ACTION)

VARCHAR(*len*) is the data type for SQL identifiers; *len* is the maximum length defined by the SQL implementation.

VARCHAR(*maxlen*) is a VARCHAR data type with the largest maximum length permitted by the SQL implementation.

The CHECK_CONSTRAINTS View

The CHECK_CONSTRAINTS view contains one row for each check constraint (check constraint, domain check constraint, or assertion definition) defined in the current catalog that is owned by the current user. Its structure is shown in the following table:

Column Name	Data Type	Description
CONSTRAINT_CATALOG	VARCHAR(*len*)	Name of catalog containing the constraint definition
CONSTRAINT_SCHEMA	VARCHAR(*len*)	Name of schema containing the constraint definition
CONSTRAINT_NAME	VARCHAR(*len*)	Name of constraint
CHECK_CLAUSE	VARCHAR(*maxlen*)	Text of SQL search condition that defines the check constraint

VARCHAR(*len*) is the data type for SQL identifiers; *len* is the maximum length defined by the SQL implementation.

VARCHAR(*maxlen*) is a VARCHAR data type with the largest maximum length permitted by the SQL implementation.

The KEY_COLUMN_USAGE View

The KEY_COLUMN_USAGE view contains one row for each column that participates in a key defined in the current catalog by the current user. Its structure is shown in the following table:

Column Name	Data Type	Description
CONSTRAINT_CATALOG	VARCHAR(*len*)	Name of catalog containing the key constraint definition
CONSTRAINT_SCHEMA	VARCHAR(*len*)	Name of schema containing the key constraint definition
CONSTRAINT_NAME	VARCHAR(*len*)	Name of key constraint
TABLE_CATALOG	VARCHAR(*len*)	Name of catalog containing the definition of the table containing the key
TABLE_SCHEMA	VARCHAR(*len*)	Name of schema containing the definition of the table containing the key
TABLE_NAME	VARCHAR(*len*)	Name of table containing the key column

Column Name	Data Type	Description
COLUMN_NAME	VARCHAR(*len*)	Name of column
ORDINAL_POSITION	INTEGER > 0	Position of column within the key

VARCHAR(*len*) is the data type for SQL identifiers; *len* is the maximum length defined by the SQL implementation.

The ASSERTIONS View

The ASSERTIONS view contains one row for each assertion defined in the current catalog that is owned by the current user. Its structure is shown in the following table:

Column Name	Data Type	Description
CONSTRAINT_CATALOG	VARCHAR(*len*)	Name of catalog containing the assertion definition
CONSTRAINT_SCHEMA	VARCHAR(*len*)	Name of schema containing the assertion definition
CONSTRAINT_NAME	VARCHAR(*len*)	Name of assertion
IS_DEFERRABLE	VARCHAR(*maxlen*)	Whether assertion is deferrable (YES/NO)
INITIALLY_DEFERRED	VARCHAR(*maxlen*)	Whether assertion is initially deferred (YES/NO)

VARCHAR(*len*) is the data type for SQL identifiers; *len* is the maximum length defined by the SQL implementation.

VARCHAR(*maxlen*) is a VARCHAR data type with the largest maximum length permitted by the SQL implementation.

The CONSTRAINT_TABLE_USAGE View

The CONSTRAINT_TABLE_USAGE view contains one row for each table used by a constraint (referential constraint, unique constraint, check constraint, or assertion) defined in the current catalog by the current user. Its structure is shown in the following table:

Column Name	Data Type	Description
TABLE_CATALOG	VARCHAR(*len*)	Name of catalog containing the table definition

Column Name	Data Type	Description
TABLE_SCHEMA	VARCHAR(*len*)	Name of schema containing the table definition
TABLE_NAME	VARCHAR(*len*)	Name of table
CONSTRAINT_CATALOG	VARCHAR(*len*)	Name of catalog containing the definition of the constraint
CONSTRAINT_SCHEMA	VARCHAR(*len*)	Name of schema containing the definition of the constraint
CONSTRAINT_NAME	VARCHAR(*len*)	Name of constraint

VARCHAR(*len*) is the data type for SQL identifiers; *len* is the maximum length defined by the SQL implementation.

The CONSTRAINT_COLUMN_USAGE View

The CONSTRAINT_COLUMN_USAGE view contains one row for each column used by a constraint (referential constraint, unique constraint, check constraint, or assertion) defined in the current catalog by the current user. Its structure is shown in the following table:

Column Name	Data Type	Description
TABLE_CATALOG	VARCHAR(*len*)	Name of catalog containing the column definition
TABLE_SCHEMA	VARCHAR(*len*)	Name of schema containing the column definition
TABLE_NAME	VARCHAR(*len*)	Name of table containing the column
COLUMN_NAME	VARCHAR(*len*)	Name of column
CONSTRAINT_CATALOG	VARCHAR(*len*)	Name of catalog containing the definition of the constraint
CONSTRAINT_SCHEMA	VARCHAR(*len*)	Name of schema containing the definition of the constraint
CONSTRAINT_NAME	VARCHAR(*len*)	Name of constraint

VARCHAR(*len*) is the data type for SQL identifiers; *len* is the maximum length defined by the SQL implementation.

The `TABLE_PRIVILEGES` View

The `TABLE_PRIVILEGES` view contains one row for each privilege on tables defined in the current catalog that has been granted to the current user, granted to all users, or granted by the current user. Its structure is shown in the following table:

Column Name	Data Type	Description
GRANTOR	VARCHAR(*len*)	Authorization-id of user granting the privilege
GRANTEE	VARCHAR(*len*)	Authorization-id of user being granted the privilege
TABLE_CATALOG	VARCHAR(*len*)	Name of catalog containing this view definition
TABLE_SCHEMA	VARCHAR(*len*)	Name of schema containing this view definition
TABLE_NAME	VARCHAR(*len*)	Name of view
PRIVILEGE_TYPE	VARCHAR(*maxlen*)	Type of privilege (SELECT/INSERT/DELETE/ UPDATE/ REFERENCES)
IS_GRANTABLE	VARCHAR(*maxlen*)	Whether privilege is granted with GRANT option (YES/NO)

VARCHAR(*len*) is the data type for SQL identifiers; *len* is the maximum length defined by the SQL implementation.

VARCHAR(*maxlen*) is a VARCHAR data type with the largest maximum length permitted by the SQL implementation.

The `COLUMN_PRIVILEGES` View

The `COLUMN_PRIVILEGES` view contains one row for each privilege on columns defined in the current catalog that has been granted to the current user, granted to all users, or granted by the current user. Its structure is shown in the following table:

Column Name	Data Type	Description
GRANTOR	VARCHAR(*len*)	Authorization-id of user granting the privilege
GRANTEE	VARCHAR(*len*)	Authorization-id of user being granted the privilege

Column Name	Data Type	Description
TABLE_CATALOG	VARCHAR(*len*)	Name of catalog containing the table definition containing this column
TABLE_SCHEMA	VARCHAR(*len*)	Name of schema containing the table definition containing this column
TABLE_NAME	VARCHAR(*len*)	Name of table containing this column
COLUMN_NAME	VARCHAR(*len*)	Name of column
PRIVILEGE_TYPE	VARCHAR(*maxlen*)	Type of privilege (SELECT/INSERT/DELETE/UPDATE/REFERENCES)
IS_GRANTABLE	VARCHAR(*maxlen*)	Whether privilege is granted with GRANT option (YES/NO)

VARCHAR(*len*) is the data type for SQL identifiers; *len* is the maximum length defined by the SQL implementation.

VARCHAR(*maxlen*) is a VARCHAR data type with the largest maximum length permitted by the SQL implementation.

The USAGE_PRIVILEGES View

The USAGE_PRIVILEGES view contains one row for each privilege on objects defined in the current catalog that has been granted to the current user, granted to all users, or granted by the current user. Its structure is shown in the following table:

Column Name	Data Type	Description
GRANTOR	VARCHAR(*len*)	Authorization-id of user granting the privilege
GRANTEE	VARCHAR(*len*)	Authorization-id of user being granted the privilege
OBJECT_CATALOG	VARCHAR(*len*)	Name of catalog containing the object definition
OBJECT_SCHEMA	VARCHAR(*len*)	Name of schema containing the object definition
OBJECT_NAME	VARCHAR(*len*)	Name of object

Column Name	Data Type	Description
OBJECT_TYPE	VARCHAR(*maxlen*)	Type of object (DOMAIN/ CHARACTER SET/ COLLATION/ TRANSLATION)
PRIVILEGE_TYPE	VARCHAR(*maxlen*)	Type of privilege (always the literal USAGE)
IS_GRANTABLE	VARCHAR(*maxlen*)	Whether privilege is granted with GRANT option (YES/NO)

VARCHAR(*len*) is the data type for SQL identifiers; *len* is the maximum length defined by the SQL implementation.

VARCHAR(*maxlen*) is a VARCHAR data type with the largest maximum length permitted by the SQL implementation.

The DOMAINS View

The DOMAINS view contains one row for each domain defined in the current catalog that is accessible to the current user. Its structure is shown in the following table:

Column Name	Data Type	Description
DOMAIN_CATALOG	VARCHAR(*len*)	Name of catalog containing this domain definition
DOMAIN_SCHEMA	VARCHAR(*len*)	Name of schema containing this domain definition
DOMAIN_NAME	VARCHAR(*len*)	Name of domain
DATA_TYPE	VARCHAR(*maxlen*)	SQL2 data type on which the domain definition is based (text representation)
CHARACTER_MAXIMUM_ LENGTH	INTEGER > 0	Maximum length, in characters, for variable-length character types
CHARACTER_OCTET_ LENGTH	INTEGER > 0	Maximum length of variable-length data type, in bytes
COLLATION_CATALOG	VARCHAR(*len*)	Name of catalog containing the definition of the collation for this domain
COLLATION_SCHEMA	VARCHAR(*len*)	Name of schema containing the collation for this domain

Column Name	Data Type	Description
COLLATION_NAME	VARCHAR(*len*)	Name of collation for this domain
CHARACTER_SET_ CATALOG	VARCHAR(*len*)	Name of catalog containing the definition of the character set for this domain
CHARACTER_SET_ SCHEMA	VARCHAR(*len*)	Name of schema containing the definition of the character set for this domain
CHARACTER_SET_NAME	VARCHAR(*len*)	Name of character set for this domain
NUMERIC_PRECISION	INTEGER > 0	Precision if this domain is based on a numeric data type
NUMERIC_PRECISION_ RADIX	INTEGER > 0	Radix of the precision
NUMERIC_SCALE	INTEGER > 0	Scale if this domain is based on a numeric type
DATATIME_PRECISION	INTEGER > 0	Precision if this domain is based on a DateTime data type
DOMAIN_DEFAULT	VARCHAR(*maxlen*)	Text representation of the default value for the domain

VARCHAR(*len*) is the data type for SQL identifiers; *len* is the maximum length defined by the SQL implementation.

VARCHAR(*maxlen*) is a VARCHAR data type with the largest maximum length permitted by the SQL implementation.

The DOMAIN_CONSTRAINTS View

The DOMAIN_CONSTRAINTS view contains one row for each domain constraint for a domain defined in the current catalog that is accessible to the current user. Its structure is shown in the following table:

Column Name	Data Type	Description
CONSTRAINT_CATALOG	VARCHAR(*len*)	Name of catalog containing this constraint definition
CONSTRAINT_SCHEMA	VARCHAR(*len*)	Name of schema containing this constraint definition

Column Name	Data Type	Description
CONSTRAINT_NAME	VARCHAR(*len*)	Name of constraint
DOMAIN_CATALOG	VARCHAR(*len*)	Name of catalog containing the domain definition to which constraint applies
DOMAIN_SCHEMA	VARCHAR(*len*)	Name of schema containing the domain definition to which constraint applies
DOMAIN_NAME	VARCHAR(*len*)	Maximum length of variable-length data type, in octets
IS_DEFERRABLE	VARCHAR(*maxlen*)	Whether constraint is deferrable (YES/NO)
INITIALLY_DEFERRED	VARCHAR(*maxlen*)	Whether constraint is initially deferred (YES/NO)

VARCHAR(*len*) is the data type for SQL identifiers; *len* is the maximum length defined by the SQL implementation.

VARCHAR(*maxlen*) is a VARCHAR data type with the largest maximum length permitted by the SQL implementation.

The DOMAIN_COLUMN_USAGE View

The DOMAIN_COLUMN_USAGE view contains one row for each column used by a domain defined in the current catalog by the current user. Its structure is shown in the following table:

Column Name	Data Type	Description
DOMAIN_CATALOG	VARCHAR(*len*)	Name of catalog containing the definition of the domain
DOMAIN_SCHEMA	VARCHAR(*len*)	Name of schema containing the definition of the domain
DOMAIN_NAME	VARCHAR(*len*)	Name of domain
TABLE_CATALOG	VARCHAR(*len*)	Name of catalog containing the column definition
TABLE_SCHEMA	VARCHAR(*len*)	Name of schema containing the column definition

Column Name	Data Type	Description
TABLE_NAME	VARCHAR(*len*)	Name of table containing the column
COLUMN_NAME	VARCHAR(*len*)	Name of column

VARCHAR(*len*) is the data type for SQL identifiers; *len* is the maximum length defined by the SQL implementation.

The CHARACTER_SETS View

The CHARACTER_SETS view contains one row for each character set defined in the current catalog that is accessible to the current user. Its structure is shown in the following table:

Column Name	Data Type	Description
CHARACTER_SET_ CATALOG	VARCHAR(*len*)	Name of catalog containing the character set definition
CHARACTER_SET_ SCHEMA	VARCHAR(*len*)	Name of schema containing the character set definition
CHARACTER_SET_ NAME	VARCHAR(*len*)	Name of character set
FORM_OF_USE	VARCHAR(*len*)	Form-of-use of the character set
NUMBER_OF_ CHARACTERS	INTEGER > 0	Number of characters in the character set
DEFAULT_COLLATE_ CATALOG	VARCHAR(*len*)	Name of catalog containing the default collation definition for this character set
DEFAULT_COLLATE_ SCHEMA	VARCHAR(*len*)	Name of schema containing the default collation definition for this character set
DEFAULT_COLLATE_ NAME	VARCHAR(*len*)	Name of default collation for this character set

VARCHAR(*len*) is the data type for SQL identifiers; *len* is the maximum length defined by the SQL implementation.

VARCHAR(*maxlen*) is a VARCHAR data type with the largest maximum length permitted by the SQL implementation.

The COLLATIONS View

The COLLATIONS view contains one row for each collation (sorting sequence) defined in the current catalog that is accessible to the current user. Its structure is shown in the following table:

Column Name	Data Type	Description
COLLATION_CATALOG	VARCHAR(*len*)	Name of catalog containing the collation definition
COLLATION_SCHEMA	VARCHAR(*len*)	Name of schema containing the collation definition
COLLATION_NAME	VARCHAR(*len*)	Name of collation
CHARACTER_SET_ CATALOG	VARCHAR(*len*)	Name of catalog containing the character set definition on which the collating sequence is defined
CHARACTER_SET_ SCHEMA	VARCHAR(*len*)	Name of schema containing the character set definition on which the collating sequence is defined
CHARACTER_SET_NAME	VARCHAR(*len*)	Name of character set on which the collating sequence is defined
PAD_ATTRIBUTE	VARCHAR(*maxlen*)	Character padding (PAD SPACE/NO PAD)

VARCHAR(*len*) is the data type for SQL identifiers; *len* is the maximum length defined by the SQL implementation.

VARCHAR(*maxlen*) is a VARCHAR data type with the largest maximum length permitted by the SQL implementation.

The TRANSLATIONS View

The TRANSLATIONS view contains one row for each translation (conversion from one character set to another) defined in the current catalog that is accessible to the current user. Its structure is shown in the following table:

Column Name	Data Type	Description
TRANSLATION_CATALOG	VARCHAR(*len*)	Name of catalog containing the translation definition
TRANSLATION_SCHEMA	VARCHAR(*len*)	Name of schema containing the translation definition

Column Name	Data Type	Description
TRANSLATION_NAME	VARCHAR(*len*)	Name of translation
SOURCE_CHARACTER_SET_CATALOG	VARCHAR(*len*)	Name of catalog containing the character set definition from which the translation occurs
SOURCE_CHARACTER_SET_SCHEMA	VARCHAR(*len*)	Name of schema containing the character set definition from which the translation occurs
CHARACTER_SET_NAME	VARCHAR(*len*)	Name of character set from which the translation occurs
TARGET_CHARACTER_SET_CATALOG	VARCHAR(*len*)	Name of catalog containing the character set definition to which the translation occurs
TARGET_CHARACTER_SET_SCHEMA	VARCHAR(*len*)	Name of schema containing the character set definition to which the translation occurs
TARGET_CHARACTER_SET_NAME	VARCHAR(*len*)	Name of character set to which the translation occurs

VARCHAR(*len*) is the data type for SQL identifiers; *len* is the maximum length defined by the SQL implementation.

The SQL_LANGUAGES View

The SQL_LANGUAGES view contains one row for each ANSI-standard language supported by this SQL implementation. Its structure is shown in the following table:

Column Name	Data Type	Description
SQL_LANGUAGE_SOURCE	VARCHAR(*maxlen*)	Text identifying source of language standard (e.g., ISO 9075)
SQL_LANGUAGE_YEAR	VARCHAR(*maxlen*)	Year in which standard was approved (e.g., 1987)
SQL_LANGUAGE_CONFORMANCE	VARCHAR(*maxlen*)	Conformance level (1/2)
SQL_LANGUAGE_INTEGRITY	VARCHAR(*maxlen*)	Integrity (YES/NO) or NULL

Column Name	Data Type	Description
SQL_LANGUAGE_ IMPLEMENTATION	VARCHAR(*maxlen*)	Implementation-defined character string or NULL
SQL_LANGUAGE_ BINDING_STYLE	VARCHAR(*maxlen*)	Binding style (e.g., EMBEDDED/ MODULE/DIRECT)
SQL_LANGUAGE_ PROGRAMMING_ LANGUAGE	VARCHAR(*maxlen*)	Name of the supported programming language (e.g., ADA/C/COBOL/FORTRAN/ PASCAL/PLI)

VARCHAR (*maxlen*) is a VARCHAR data type with the largest maximum length permitted by the SQL implementation.

The Complete Reference

Appendix F

CD-ROM
Installation Guide

The bonus CD-ROM that accompanies this book includes full-function Windows NT/2000 versions of these three leading brands of SQL-based DBMS:

- Microsoft SQL Server 2000
- IBM DB2
- MySQL

In addition, the last section of this appendix contains instructions on how to download a trial version of the Oracle DBMS.

These are *not* incomplete "demo" versions of the DBMS products. Rather, they are full-capability *evaluation* versions of the latest software from these leading database vendors, allowing you to learn SQL using a live DBMS, test out and compare each product, and find a SQL DBMS that best suits your specific needs.

The CD-ROM also includes data files that you can use to populate the DBMS products with the five tables of the sample database so that you can easily run the example queries in the book. The files reside in the root directory of the CD-ROM and are named:

- CUSTOMERS.DAT
- OFFICES.DAT
- ORDERS.DAT
- PRODUCTS.DAT
- SALESREPS.DAT

Enjoy this unique CD-ROM, which is available only with *SQL: The Complete Reference*, the most comprehensive book on SQL with the most comprehensive collection of valuable SQL DBMS software from the leading DBMS vendors.

 Note   *These products are subject to restricted use licenses, are for evaluation purposes only, and, in some cases, include expiration mechanisms that cause the software to cease operation 90 or 120 days after installation. See the tables in the sections that follow for specific details on each product.*

Installing the SQL DBMS Software

When you insert the bonus CD-ROM into your CD-ROM drive, Windows automatically launches the DBMS installation program on the CD-ROM. The program prompts you to accept the McGraw-Hill/Osborne license agreement and then allows you to select a DBMS for installation, as shown here:

The sections that follow contain detailed instructions for installing each brand of SQL DBMS.

Microsoft SQL Server 2000

The following table lists details and facts about the product and the company:

Product name	SQL Server 2000 Enterprise Edition
First shipment	1988
Platform	Windows NT/2000
Software limitations	Expires 120 days after installation
Vendor	Microsoft Corporation
Founded	1975
Annual sales	$27.7 billion

Hardware and Software Requirements

Microsoft SQL Server 2000 Enterprise Edition requires the following hardware and software:

Category	Requirements
Computer	Intel or compatible Pentium 166MHz or higher
Operating system	Microsoft Windows NT Workstation 4.0 with SP5 or later, Windows NT Server 4.0 with SP5 or later, Windows NT Server 4.0 Enterprise Edition with SP5 or later, Windows 2000 Professional, Windows 2000 Server, Windows 2000 Advanced Server, or Windows 2000 Datacenter Server operating system
Memory (RAM)	128MB or more recommended
Hard disk space	Approx. 250MB for typical installation
Internet software	Microsoft Internet Explorer version 5.0 or later
Network software	Windows 95, Windows 98, Windows Millennium Edition, Windows NT 4.0, or Windows 2000 built-in network software (additional network software is not required unless you are using Banyan VINES or AppleTalk ADSP; Novell NetWare IPX/SPX client support is provided by the NWLink protocol of Windows networking)

Installation Notes

The official Microsoft SQL Server 2000 evaluation CD-ROM has been pruned somewhat in order for the SQL Server 2000 software to fit onto the bonus CD-ROM. Therefore, you must choose precisely the selections indicated in the instructions in the next section or the installation may not proceed smoothly. In addition, do *not* attempt to install OLAP Analysis Services.

If you have any further questions about SQL Server 2000 installation, please refer to the SQL Server Installation Guide on the bonus CD-ROM. The file is located at \MSSQL\books\instsql.chm.

Finally, if you are installing SQL Server 2000 on the same computer alongside a previous version of SQL Server, back up your previous Microsoft SQL Server installation, and do *not* install SQL Server 2000 in the same directory as the previous installation.

SQL Server 2000 Installation

Perform the following steps to install SQL Server 2000:

1. Log on to the system as a member of the Administrators group.

2. Insert the bonus CD-ROM into your CD-ROM drive.

3. Windows automatically launches the DBMS installation program on the CD-ROM. If the installation program does not launch automatically, double-click SQLINSTALL.EXE in the root directory of the CD-ROM to launch it manually.

4. The installation program displays a dialog prompting you to accept the McGraw-Hill/Osborne license agreement. Indicate your acceptance of the agreement and click Next.

5. The installation program displays the DBMS selection dialog. Select Microsoft SQL Server 2000 Enterprise Edition from the list of DBMS choices and click Next.

6. The SQL Server installation Welcome dialog appears. Click Next to continue.

7. The Computer Name dialog appears. Click Next to accept the Local Computer selection.

8. The Installation Selection dialog appears. Click Next to accept the Create A New Instance Of SQL Server, or Install Client Tools selection.

9. The User Information dialog appears. Enter your name and company if they are different than the default values indicated and click Next.

10. The Software License Agreement dialog appears. Click Yes to accept the agreement.

11. The Installation Definition dialog appears. Click Next to accept the Server and Client Tools selection.

12. The Instance Name dialog appears. Click Next to accept the Default check box, or enter an Instance Name if you already have a previous SQL Server installation.

13. The Setup Type dialog appears. Leave the Typical choice selected. The dialog also indicates the default directories into which the SQL Server files will be copied. Accept the defaults or click Browse to specify different directories and click Next.

14. The Services Accounts dialog appears. Leave the Use The Same Account For Each Service. Auto Start SQL Server Service choice selected. Enter an existing user name and password to use for the SQL Server service, or select Use the Local System Account, and click Next.

15. The Authentication Mode dialog appears. Select Mixed Mode and enter a password for the sa login.

16. The Start Copying Files dialog appears. Click Next to continue.

17. If you are prompted to shut down running tasks, click Next to continue and click Finish to begin installation.

18. The installation program installs SQL Server on your hard disk. This may take several minutes.

19. When installation is complete, the Setup Complete dialog appears. Click Finish to return to Windows.

Starting SQL Server 2000

After you install SQL Server 2000, you must reboot your computer before you can begin to use the software. SQL server is started automatically after you reboot and each time you start your computer after that. Alternatively, to start SQL Server without rebooting, go into the SQL Server Service Manager and select Start/Continue.

Uninstalling SQL Server 2000

Perform the following steps to uninstall SQL Server 2000:

1. Choose Start | Settings | Control Panel from the Windows taskbar.

2. Double-click on the Add/Remove Programs application.

3. Select Microsoft SQL Server 2000 from the list of currently installed programs and click Change/Remove.

4. The Confirm File Deletion dialog appears. Click Yes to continue.

5. The Remove Shared File? dialog appears and asks you to confirm that you want to remove shared files that are no longer being used. Click Yes to All to remove these files and click Yes when the second confirmation dialog appears.

6. Windows removes all SQL Server 2000 programs from your system.

IBM DB2

The following table provides a variety of miscellaneous details about the product and the company:

Product name	DB2 Universal Database 7.2 Enterprise Edition
First shipment	1985
Platform	Windows NT/2000

Software limitations	Expires 90 days after installation
Vendor	IBM Corporation
Founded	1911
Annual sales	$83.4 billion

Hardware and Software Requirements

IBM DB2 Enterprise Edition requires the following hardware and software:

Category	Requirements
Computer	Pentium-based personal computer
Operating system	Microsoft Windows NT Version 4.0 SP5 or later, or Microsoft Windows 2000
Memory (RAM)	128MB or more recommended
Hard disk space	Approx. 245MB for typical installation
Network software	TCP/IP, IPX/SPX, Named Pipes, NetBios, and MPTN (APPC over TCP/IP)
Other	If you have the IBM Antivirus program installed on your computer, it must be disabled or uninstalled to perform the DB2 installation

Installation Notes

The official IBM DB2 evaluation CD-ROM has been pruned somewhat in order for the DB2 software to fit onto the bonus CD-ROM. Therefore, you must choose precisely the selections indicated in the instructions in the next section or the installation may not proceed smoothly. In addition, do *not* attempt to install OLAP Starter Kit.

If you have any further questions about DB2 installation, please refer to the DB2 Installation Guide on the bonus CD-ROM. The file is located at \IBMDB2\doc\en\db2i6\db2i6.htm.

DB2 Enterprise Edition Installation

Perform the following steps to install DB2 Universal Database Enterprise Edition:

1. Log on to the system as a user that meets the requirements for installing DB2. The account you are logged in as must (a) be defined locally, (b) belong to the Local Administrator's group, and (c) have the following advanced user rights:

   - Act as part of the operating system
   - Create token object

■ Increase quotas

■ Replace a process level token

2. Insert the bonus CD-ROM into your CD-ROM drive.

3. Windows automatically launches the DBMS installation program on the CD-ROM. If the installation program does not launch automatically, double-click SQLINSTALL.EXE in the root directory of the CD-ROM to launch it manually.

4. The installation program displays a dialog prompting you to accept the McGraw-Hill/Osborne license agreement. Indicate your acceptance of the agreement and click Next.

5. The installation program displays the DBMS selection dialog. Select IBM DB2 Universal Database 7.2 Enterprise Edition from the list of DBMS choices and click Next.

6. The installation program displays a dialog prompting you to accept the IBM Corporation license agreement. Indicate your acceptance of the agreement and click Next.

7. The Select Products dialog appears. Click Next to accept the DB2 Enterprise Edition selection.

8. The Select Installation Type dialog appears. Click Next to accept the Typical selection.

9. The Select Destination Location dialog appears and indicates the default directory into which the IBM DB2 files will be copied. Accept the default or click Browse to specify a different directory and click Next.

10. The Enter Username and Password dialog appears. Accept the default db2admin user name, enter a password, and click Next. If the db2admin user name already existed from a previous DB2 installation, you must enter the existing db2admin password; otherwise you will be prompted to confirm that you want to create the new user name.

11. The Start Copying Files dialog appears. Click Next to continue.

12. The installation program installs DB2 on your hard disk. This may take several minutes.

13. The Install OLAP Start Kit dialog appears. Select Do Not Install The OLAP Starter Kit and click Continue.

14. When installation is complete, the Setup Complete dialog appears. Click Finish to exit the DB2 installation program.

15. The DB2 First Steps program executes automatically for you to begin working immediately with DB2.

Starting DB2 Enterprise Edition

After you install DB2 Enterprise Edition, you can use the DB2 First Steps program to begin working with DB2 immediately. After that, DB2 is started automatically each time you start your computer.

Uninstalling DB2 Enterprise Edition

Perform the following steps to uninstall DB2 Enterprise Edition:

1. Choose Start | Settings | Control Panel from the Windows taskbar
2. Double-click on the Add/Remove Programs application.
3. Select IBM DB2 from the list of currently installed programs and click Change/Remove.
4. The Confirm DB2 Deletion dialog appears. Click Yes to continue.
5. If DB2 is running, the INFORMATION dialog appears and asks you to confirm that you want to shut down the running DB2 processes. Click Yes to continue.
6. Windows removes all DB2 programs from your system.

MySQL

The following table lists details and facts about the product and the company:

Product name	MySQL 3.23.51
First shipment	1995
Platform	Windows 9x/Me, Windows NT4/2000/XP
Software limitations	None
Vendor	MySQL AB
Founded	1995
Annual sales	Privately held

Hardware and Software Requirements

MySQL 3.23 requires the following hardware and software:

Category	Requirements
Computer	Intel or compatible Pentium
Operating system	Windows 9x/Me, Windows NT4 SP3 or later, Windows 2000/Windows XP

Category	Requirements
Memory (RAM)	128MB or more recommended
Hard disk space	Approx. 50MB
Network software	TCP/IP

Installation Notes

If you have any further questions about MySQL installation, please refer to the MySQL Installation Instructions on the MySQL web site. At the time this book went to publication, the installation instructions were located at: http://www.mysql.com/doc/W/i/Windows_installation.html

If this MySQL-maintained web link becomes outdated or is no longer accurate in the future, you may want to check MySQL's main web site (www.mysql.com) to locate the installation instructions.

You can also go to the MySQL web site to download the most recent version of the MySQL DBMS.

MySQL Installation

Perform the following steps to install MySQL:

1. Log on to the system as a member of the Administrators group.

2. Insert the bonus CD-ROM into your CD-ROM drive.

3. Windows automatically launches the DBMS installation program on the CD-ROM. If the installation program does not launch automatically, double-click SQLINSTALL.EXE in the root directory of the CD-ROM to launch it manually.

4. The installation program displays a dialog prompting you to accept the McGraw-Hill/Osborne license agreement. Indicate your acceptance of the agreement and click Next.

5. The installation program displays the DBMS selection dialog. Select MySQL 3.23 from the list of DBMS choices and click Next.

6. The MySQL installation Welcome dialog appears. Click Next to continue.

7. The Information dialog appears. Click Next to continue.

8. The Choose Destination Location dialog appears and indicates the default directory into which the MySQL files will be copied. Accept the default or click Browse to specify a different directory and click Next.

9. The Setup Type dialog appears. Click Next to accept the Typical selection.

10. The installation program installs MySQL on your hard disk. This may take several minutes.

11. When installation is complete, the Setup Complete dialog appears. Click Finish to exit the MySQL installation program.

Starting MySQL

After you install MySQL, you can run the command lines client program mysql.exe (located in c:\mysql\bin) to begin working with MySQL immediately.

Uninstalling MySQL

Perform the following steps to uninstall MySQL:

1. Choose Start | Settings | Control Panel from the Windows taskbar.

2. Double-click on the Add/Remove Programs application.

3. Select MySQL Servers And Clients from the list of currently installed programs and click Change/Remove.

4. The Confirm File Deletion dialog appears. Click Yes to continue.

5. Windows removes all MySQL programs from your system.

Downloading the Oracle DBMS Software

The latest version of the Oracle DBMS takes up to three CD-ROMs, so in this second edition of *SQL: The Complete Reference*, we were not able to fit it onto the bonus CD-ROM along with the other brands of DBMS.

However, you can download the latest version of Oracle's DBMS directly from the Oracle web site. At the time this book went to publication, the latest version was available for download at http://otn.oracle.com/software/products/oracle9i/content.html.

McGraw-Hill/Osborne and the authors cannot be held responsible if this Oracle-maintained web link becomes outdated or is no longer accurate in the future, so if the link is not working, you may want to check Oracle's main web site (www.oracle.com) to download the most recent version of the Oracle DBMS.

Index

D

E

F

INTERNATIONAL CONTACT INFORMATION

AUSTRALIA
McGraw-Hill Book Company Australia Pty. Ltd.
TEL +61-2-9415-9899
FAX +61-2-9415-5687
http://www.mcgraw-hill.com.au
books-it_sydney@mcgraw-hill.com

CANADA
McGraw-Hill Ryerson Ltd.
TEL +905-430-5000
FAX +905-430-5020
http://www.mcgrawhill.ca

GREECE, MIDDLE EAST,
NORTHERN AFRICA
McGraw-Hill Hellas
TEL +30-1-656-0990-3-4
FAX +30-1-654-5525

MEXICO (Also serving Latin America)
McGraw-Hill Interamericana Editores S.A. de C.V.
TEL +525-117-1583
FAX +525-117-1589
http://www.mcgraw-hill.com.mx
fernando_castellanos@mcgraw-hill.com

SINGAPORE (Serving Asia)
McGraw-Hill Book Company
TEL +65-863-1580
FAX +65-862-3354
http://www.mcgraw-hill.com.sg
mghasia@mcgraw-hill.com

SOUTH AFRICA
McGraw-Hill South Africa
TEL +27-11-622-7512
FAX +27-11-622-9045
robyn_swanepoel@mcgraw-hill.com

UNITED KINGDOM & EUROPE
(Excluding Southern Europe)
McGraw-Hill Education Europe
TEL +44-1-628-502500
FAX +44-1-628-770224
http://www.mcgraw-hill.co.uk
computing_neurope@mcgraw-hill.com

ALL OTHER INQUIRIES Contact:
Osborne/McGraw-Hill
TEL +1-510-549-6600
FAX +1-510-883-7600
http://www.osborne.com
omg_international@mcgraw-hill.com

The GNU License

Linux is written and distributed under the GNU General Public License which means that its source code is freely-distributed and available to the general public.

GNU GENERAL PUBLIC LICENSE

Version 2, June 1991

Copyright (C) 1989, 1991 Free Software Foundation, Inc.

675 Mass Ave, Cambridge, MA 02139, USA

Everyone is permitted to copy and distribute verbatim copies of this license document, but changing it is not allowed.

Preamble

The licenses for most software are designed to take away your freedom to share and change it. By contrast, the GNU General Public License is intended to guarantee your freedom to share and change free software—to make sure the software is free for all its users. This General Public License applies to most of the Free Software Foundation's software and to any other program whose authors commit to using it. (Some other Free Software Foundation software is covered by the GNU Library General Public License instead.) You can apply it to your programs, too.

When we speak of free software, we are referring to freedom, not price. Our General Public Licenses are designed to make sure that you have the freedom to distribute copies of free software (and charge for this service if you wish), that you receive source code or can get it if you want it, that you can change the software or use pieces of it in new free programs; and that you know you can do these things.

To protect your rights, we need to make restrictions that forbid anyone to deny you these rights or to ask you to surrender the rights. These restrictions translate to certain responsibilities for you if you distribute copies of the software, or if you modify it.

For example, if you distribute copies of such a program, whether gratis or for a fee, you must give the recipients all the rights that you have. You must make sure that they, too, receive or can get the source code. And you must show them these terms so they know their rights.

We protect your rights with two steps: (1) copyright the software, and (2) offer you this license which gives you legal permission to copy, distribute and/or modify the software.

Also, for each author's protection and ours, we want to make certain that everyone understands that there is no warranty for this free software. If the software is modified by someone else and passed on, we want its recipients to know that what they have is not the original, so that any problems introduced by others will not reflect on the original authors' reputations.

Finally, any free program is threatened constantly by software patents. We wish to avoid the danger that redistributors of a free program will individually obtain patent licenses, in effect making the program proprietary. To prevent this, we have made it clear that any patent must be licensed for everyone's free use or not licensed at all.

The precise terms and conditions for copying, distribution and modification follow.

GNU GENERAL PUBLIC LICENSE TERMS AND CONDITIONS FOR COPYING, DISTRIBUTION AND MODIFICATION

0. This License applies to any program or other work which contains a notice placed by the copyright holder saying it may be distributed under the terms of this General Public License. The "Program", below, refers to any such program or work, and a "work based on the Program" means either the Program or any derivative work under copyright law: that is to say, a work containing the Program or a portion of it, either verbatim or with modifications and/or translated into another language. (Hereinafter, translation is included without limitation in the term "modification".) Each licenSee is addressed as "you".

Activities other than copying, distribution and modification are not covered by this License; they are outside its scope. The act of running the Program is not restricted, and the output from the Program is covered only if its contents constitute a work based on the Program (independent of having been made by running the Program). Whether that is true depends on what the Program does.

1. You may copy and distribute verbatim copies of the Program's source code as you receive it, in any medium, provided that you conspicuously and appropriately publish on each copy an appropriate copyright notice and disclaimer of warranty; keep intact all the notices that refer to this License and to the absence of any warranty; and give any other recipients of the Program a copy of this License along with the Program.

You may charge a fee for the physical act of transferring a copy, and you may at your option offer warranty protection in exchange for a fee.

2. You may modify your copy or copies of the Program or any portion of it, thus forming a work based on the Program, and copy and distribute such modifications or work under the terms of Section 1 above, provided that you also meet all of these conditions:

a) You must cause the modified files to carry prominent notices stating that you changed the files and the date of any change.

b) You must cause any work that you distribute or publish, that in whole or in part contains or is derived from the Program or any part thereof, to be licensed as a whole at no charge to all third parties under the terms of this License.

c) If the modified program normally reads commands interactively when run, you must cause it, when started running for such interactive use in the most ordinary way, to print or display an announcement including an appropriate copyright notice and a notice that there is no warranty (or else, saying that you provide a warranty) and that users may redistribute the program under these conditions, and telling the user how to view a copy of this License. (Exception: if the Program itself is interactive but does not normally print such an announcement, your work based on the Program is not required to print an announcement.)

These requirements apply to the modified work as a whole. If identifiable sections of that work are not derived from the Program, and can be reasonably considered independent and separate works in themselves, then this License, and its terms, do not apply to those sections when you distribute them as separate works. But when you distribute the same sections as part of a whole which is a work based on the Program, the distribution of the whole must be on the terms of this License, whose permissions for other licenSees extend to the entire whole, and thus to each and every part regardless of who wrote it. Thus, it is not the intent of this section to claim rights or contest your rights to work written entirely by you; rather, the intent is to exercise the right to control the distribution of derivative or collective works based on the Program.

In addition, mere aggregation of another work not based on the Program with the Program (or with a work based on the Program) on a volume of a storage or distribution medium does not bring the other work under the scope of this License.

3. You may copy and distribute the Program (or a work based on it, under Section 2) in object code or executable form under the terms of Sections 1 and 2 above provided that you also do one of the following:

a) Accompany it with the complete corresponding machine-readable source code, which must be distributed under the terms of Sections 1 and 2 above on a medium customarily used for software interchange; or,

b) Accompany it with a written offer, valid for at least three years, to give any third party, for a charge no more than your cost of physically performing source distribution, a complete machine-readable copy of the corresponding source code, to be distributed under the terms of Sections 1 and 2 above on a medium customarily used for software interchange; or,

c) Accompany it with the information you received as to the offer to distribute corresponding source code. (This alternative is allowed only for noncommercial distribution and only if you received the program in object code or executable form with such an offer, in accord with Subsection b above.)

The source code for a work means the preferred form of the work for making modifications to it. For an executable work, complete source code means all the source code for all modules it contains, plus any associated interface definition files, plus the scripts used to control compilation and installation of the executable. However, as a special exception, the source code distributed need not include anything that is normally distributed (in either source or binary form) with the major components (compiler, kernel, and so on) of the operating system on which the executable runs, unless that component itself accompanies the executable.

If distribution of executable or object code is made by offering access to copy from a designated place, then offering equivalent access to copy the source code from the same place counts as distribution of the source code, even though third parties are not compelled to copy the source along with the object code.

4. You may not copy, modify, sublicense, or distribute the Program except as expressly provided under this License. Any attempt otherwise to copy, modify, sublicense or distribute the Program is void, and will automatically terminate your rights under this License. However, parties who have received copies, or rights, from you under this License will not have their licenses terminated so long as such parties remain in full compliance.

5. You are not required to accept this License, since you have not signed it. However, nothing else grants you permission to modify or distribute the Program or its derivative works. These actions are prohibited by law if you do not accept this License. Therefore, by modifying or distributing the Program (or any work based on the Program), you indicate your acceptance of this License to do so, and all its terms and conditions for copying, distributing or modifying the Program or works based on it.

6. Each time you redistribute the Program (or any work based on the Program), the recipient automatically receives a license from the original licensor to copy, distribute or modify the Program subject to these terms and conditions. You may not impose any further restrictions on the recipients' exercise of the rights granted herein. You are not responsible for enforcing compliance by third parties to this License.

7. If, as a consequence of a court judgment or allegation of patent infringement or for any other reason (not limited to patent issues), conditions are imposed on you (whether by court order, agreement or otherwise) that contradict the conditions of this License, they do not excuse you from the conditions of this License. If you cannot distribute so as to satisfy simultaneously your obligations under this License and any other pertinent obligations, then as a consequence you may not distribute the Program at all. For example, if a patent license would not permit royalty-free redistribution of the Program by all those who receive copies directly or indirectly through you, then the only way you could satisfy both it and this License would be to refrain entirely from distribution of the Program.

If any portion of this section is held invalid or unenforceable under any particular circumstance, the balance of the section is intended to apply and the section as a whole is intended to apply in other circumstances.

It is not the purpose of this section to induce you to infringe any patents or other property right claims or to contest validity of any such claims; this section has the sole purpose of protecting the integrity of the free software distribution system, which is implemented by public license practices. Many people have made generous contributions to the wide range of software distributed through that system in reliance on consistent application of that system; it is up to the author/donor to decide if he or she is willing to distribute software through any other system and a licenSee cannot impose that choice.

This section is intended to make thoroughly clear what is believed to be a consequence of the rest of this License.

8. If the distribution and/or use of the Program is restricted in certain countries either by patents or by copyrighted interfaces, the original copyright holder who places the Program under this License may add an explicit geographical distribution limitation excluding those countries, so that distribution is permitted only in or among countries not thus excluded. In such case, this License incorporates the limitation as if written in the body of this License.

9. The Free Software Foundation may publish revised and/or new versions of the General Public License from time to time. Such new versions will be similar in spirit to the present version, but may differ in detail to address new problems or concerns.

Each version is given a distinguishing version number. If the Program specifies a version number of this License which applies to it and "any later version", you have the option of following the terms and conditions either of that version or of any later version published by the Free Software Foundation. If the Program does not specify a version number of this License, you may choose any version ever published by the Free Software Foundation.

10. If you wish to incorporate parts of the Program into other free programs whose distribution conditions are different, write to the author to ask for permission. For software which is copyrighted by the Free Software Foundation, write to the Free Software Foundation; we sometimes make exceptions for this. Our decision will be guided by the two goals of preserving the free status of all derivatives of our free software and of promoting the sharing and reuse of software generally.

NO WARRANTY

11. BECAUSE THE PROGRAM IS LICENSED FREE OF CHARGE, THERE IS NO WARRANTY FOR THE PROGRAM, TO THE EXTENT PERMITTED BY APPLICABLE LAW. EXCEPT WHEN OTHERWISE STATED IN WRITING THE COPYRIGHT HOLDERS AND/OR OTHER PARTIES PROVIDE THE PROGRAM "AS IS" WITHOUT WARRANTY OF ANY KIND, EITHER EXPRESSED OR IMPLIED, INCLUDING, BUT NOT LIMITED TO, THE IMPLIED WARRANTIES OF MERCHANTABILITY AND FITNESS FOR A PARTICULAR PURPOSE. THE ENTIRE RISK AS TO THE QUALITY AND PERFORMANCE OF THE PROGRAM IS WITH YOU. SHOULD THE PROGRAM PROVE DEFECTIVE, YOU ASSUME THE COST OF ALL NECESSARY SERVICING, REPAIR OR CORRECTION.

12. IN NO EVENT UNLESS REQUIRED BY APPLICABLE LAW OR AGREED TO IN WRITING WILL ANY COPYRIGHT HOLDER, OR ANY OTHER PARTY WHO MAY MODIFY AND/OR REDISTRIBUTE THE PROGRAM AS PERMITTED ABOVE, BE LIABLE TO YOU FOR DAMAGES, INCLUDING ANY GENERAL, SPECIAL, INCIDENTAL OR CONSEQUENTIAL DAMAGES ARISING OUT OF THE USE OR INABILITY TO USE THE PROGRAM (INCLUDING BUT NOT LIMITED TO LOSS OF DATA OR DATA BEING RENDERED INACCURATE OR LOSSES SUSTAINED BY YOU OR THIRD PARTIES OR A FAILURE OF THE PROGRAM TO OPERATE WITH ANY OTHER PROGRAMS), EVEN IF SUCH HOLDER OR OTHER PARTY HAS BEEN ADVISED OF THE POSSIBILITY OF SUCH DAMAGES.

END OF TERMS AND CONDITIONS

Appendix: How to Apply These Terms to Your New Programs

If you develop a new program, and you want it to be of the greatest possible use to the public, the best way to achieve this is to make it free software which everyone can redistribute and change under these terms.

To do so, attach the following notices to the program. It is safest to attach them to the start of each source file to most effectively convey the exclusion of warranty; and each file should have at least the "copyright" line and a pointer to where the full notice is found.

<one line to give the program's name and a brief idea of what it does.> Copyright (C) 19yy <name of author>

This program is free software; you can redistribute it and/or modify it under the terms of the GNU General Public License as published by the Free Software Foundation; either version 2 of the License, or (at your option) any later version.

This program is distributed in the hope that it will be useful, but WITHOUT ANY WARRANTY; without even the implied warranty of MERCHANTABILITY or FITNESS FOR A PARTICULAR PURPOSE. See the GNU General Public License for more details.

You should have received a copy of the GNU General Public License along with this program; if not, write to the Free Software Foundation, Inc., 675 Mass Ave, Cambridge, MA 02139, USA.

Also add information on how to contact you by electronic and paper mail.

If the program is interactive, make it output a short notice like this when it starts in an interactive mode:

Gnomovision version 69, Copyright (C) 19yy name of author Gnomovision comes with ABSOLUTELY NO WARRANTY; for details type `show w'. This is free software, and you are welcome to redistribute it under certain conditions; type `show c' for details.

The hypothetical commands `show w' and `show c' should show the appropriate parts of the General Public License. Of course, the commands you use may be called something other than `show w' and `show c'; they could even be mouse-clicks or menu items—whatever suits your program.

You should also get your employer (if you work as a programmer) or your school, if any, to sign a "copyright disclaimer" for the program, if necessary. Here is a sample; alter the names:

Yoyodyne, Inc., hereby disclaims all copyright interest in the program `Gnomovision' (which makes passes at compilers) written by James Hacker.

<signature of Ty Coon>, 1 April 1989
Ty Coon, President of Vice

This General Public License does not permit incorporating your program into proprietary programs. If your program is a subroutine library, you may consider it more useful to permit linking proprietary applications with the library. If this is what you want to do, use the GNU Library General Public License instead of this License.